VEDĀNTA WITHOUT MĀYĀ?

A Debate on Saptavidha-Anupapatti

मायाविरहितः वेदान्तः? सप्तविधानुपपत्तिविषये वादः

"When imagining with their intellects, they say, 'This is truth and this is truth' - all that indeed is truth. From you (O' God) there is nothing which is different. This disputation of the learned is only with reference to names."

Abhinavagupta

"The reason why philosophers trained in the Western traditions of philosophizing and located in the universities built on the Western model in this country do not know about these pandits lies primarily in the fact that these scholars carry on their intellectual activity in a language which is generally unknown to persons trained in the western traditions of knowledge. Few people know, in India or elsewhere, that Sanskrit is still the *living lingua-franca* of traditional scholarship in India, that the only language in which intellectual dialogue can be carried on between these persons from different parts of India, which may be as distant from each other as Kashmir and Kerala or Manipur and Gujurat, is Sanskrit and Sanskrit alone, as the only other language they know is their regional language which are as diverse as the regions they belong to."

Daya Krishna

"Though the polemics between Advaitins and Viśiṣṭādvaitins is unending, the conflicts which exist between the two systems does not seem to affect their value as particular approaches to Brahman. One may even go so far as to say that the two systems enrich and inspire each other with a mutual fecundity."

P.K Sundaram

VEDĀNTA WITHOUT MĀYĀ?

A Debate on Saptavidha-Anupapatti

मायाविरहितः वेदान्तः? सप्तविधानुपपत्तिविषये वादः

Edited by

GODABARISHA MISHRA

INDIAN COUNCIL OF PHILOSOPHICAL RESEARCH
and
MOTILAL BANARSIDASS PUBLISHERS
PRIVATE LIMITED • DELHI

First Edition : Delhi, 2015

In arrangement with
Indian Council of Philosophical Research
Darshan Bhawan, 36 Tughalakabad Institutional Area
New Delhi- 110 062

ISBN: 978-81-208-3979-3

MOTILAL BANARSIDASS
41 U.A. Bungalow Road, Jawahar Nagar, Delhi 110 007
8 Mahalaxmi Chamber, 22 Bhulabhai Desai Road, Mumbai 400 026
203 Royapettah High Road, Mylapore, Chennai 600 004
236, 9th Main III Block, Jayanagar, Bengaluru 560 011
8 Camac Street, Kolkata 700 017
Ashok Rajpath, Patna 800 004
Chowk, Varanasi 221 001

Laser Typeset by
R. MUKUNDAN, Sri Haygriva Computers, Chennai 600 061
Fonts - Hindi Sanskrit and Times3 and Times New Roman

Printed in India
by RP Jain at NAB Printing Unit,
A-44, Naraina Industrial Area, Phase I, New Delhi–110028
and published by JP Jain for Motilal Banarsidass Publishers (P) Ltd,
41 U.A. Bungalow Road, Jawahar Nagar, Delhi-110007

Dedicated to the Sacred and Immortal Memory of Professors

V. R. Kalyanasundara Sastri
R. Thangaswami
J. Venkatarama Sastri
K. Kunjunni Raja
S.M. Srinivasachari
Srinivasa Rao
M. Narasimhachary
S. Revathy

for their unfailing commitment to and enriching participation in creative contemporary debates on Vedānta in our times.

श्रीः

श्रीमन्तः सर्वशास्त्रेष्वविहतगतयः शिष्यसंक्रान्तविद्याः
वाग्देवीनृत्तरङ्गस्थलपरिणमितस्वीयजिह्वाग्रभागाः ।
युष्माकं सौमनस्यं निरवधिकरुणा वत्सलत्वं कथं वा
कार्तज्ञ्याविष्कृतेर्नः परिमितवचसां गोचरत्वं व्रजेयुः ॥ १

अस्याः गोष्ठ्याः प्रबन्धे समुचितधनमत्यादरेण प्रदाय
प्रोत्साहं दत्तवद्भ्यः वयमिह नितरां स्याम सर्वे कृतज्ञाः ।
संस्थाध्यक्षेभ्य एभ्यो स्थिरबहुलयशोभाजनेभ्यः महद्भ्यः
विद्वद्भ्यः भारतीयस्थितमतपरिषद् पण्डितेभ्यः गुरुभ्यः ॥ २

गोष्ठीयं विश्वविद्यालयभवनवरे सम्प्रचाल्येति पूर्वम्
सङ्कल्पो यः कृतोऽभूत् कथमपि समभूत् तस्य दैवात् विकल्पः ।
श्रीकुप्पुस्वामिशास्त्रिप्रविमलयशसा भासमानेऽसमाने
संस्थाने सा प्रवृत्ता निरवधिकृपया श्रीमतां माधवानाम् ॥ ३

श्रीमद्भ्यः माधवेभ्यः प्रथममिह वयं सर्वदा स्मः कृतज्ञाः
यद्येते नाङ्गीकार्षुः समुचितसमये नाभविष्यत् सभेयम् ।
सर्वं सङ्कल्पितं नस्समभवदनघं हन्त वाञ्छाधिकं तत्
पुण्याः पीयूषपूर्णाः उपकृतिनिरताः सन्ति सन्तः कियन्तः ॥ ४

सोढ्वा क्लेशान् पुनस्तान् गुरुतरकृपया भोजनावासरूपान्
युष्माभिः मद्रपुर्यामुषितमिह बुधाः वासरान् त्रीन् कथञ्चित् ।
तान् सर्वान् क्षामयेऽहं विनयविनमितेनोत्तमाङ्गेन दोषान्
अस्माकं शक्तिलोपात् कथमपि कलितान् दैवयोगोपजातान् ॥५

मायावादे यदुक्तं यतिपतिचरणैः दूषणं सप्तभेदं
सङ्गोष्ठी तद्विचारा समभवदतुला वासरान् त्रीन् अबाधम् ।
अस्माकं भागधेयं परिणतमधुना मानसं पूर्णतृप्तम्
कार्तज्ञ्याविष्कृतिस्सा कथमिव भवति प्रीतिभाजां सतां वः ॥ ६

सर्वे दिग्दन्तितुल्याः सुनिशितमतयः यूयमत्यन्तमान्याः
युष्माकं वादकाले पुनरपि पुरतः प्रादुरासन् महान्तः ।
श्रीमन्तः शङ्करार्याः यतिपतिचरणास्ते च रामानुजार्याः
एवं चानन्दतीर्थाः त्रिभुवनमहिताः स्वीयशिष्यप्रशिष्यैः ॥ ७

वादे वादे च नूनं भवति सुविशदः तत्वबोधो प्रमेयः
जिज्ञासूनां समेषां न खलु तदपरः कोऽप्युपायो निषेव्यः ।
ईर्ष्यासूयादिमुक्ता यदि भवति कथा युक्तियुक्ता मनोज्ञा
वैदुष्यं चारितार्थ्यं भजति च भवति श्रेयसे भूयसे नः ॥ ८

अस्माकं चाधमर्ण्यं कथमपि वचनैः नास्ति व्यङ्क्तुं हि शक्तिः
पौनःपुन्येन युष्मत्पदकमलयुगीवन्दने चाप्यशक्तिः ।
तस्मादस्माकमेषा निपततु पदयोः स्रग्धरा मुग्धमाला
सङ्गो भूयादभङ्गः पुनरपि भवतामल्प एवात्र काले ॥ ९

मुडुम्बै नरसिंहाचार्यः

CONTENTS

ABBREVIATIONS

BS	- Brahmasūtra
BU	- Bṛhadāraṇyaka Upaniṣad
CU	- Chāndogya Upaniṣad
KU	- Kaṭha Upaniṣad
MU	- Māṇḍūkya Upaniṣad
MVN	- Mūlāvidyānirāśaḥ
SBBD	- Śrībhāṣya-bhāṣyārtha-darpaṇa
SSBV	- Śrī Śaṅkarāśaṅkara-bhāṣya-vimarśaḥ
SSS	- Svāmī Saccidānandendra Sarasvatī
SU	- Śvetāśvatara Upaniṣad

क.	- कठोपनिषद्
गी.भा.	- गीताभाष्यम्
छा.	- छान्दोग्योपनिषद्
जै.सू.	- जैमिनीयसूत्रमाला
तै.	- तैत्तिरीयोपनिषद्
प.वि.	- पञ्चपादिकाविवरणम्
ब्र.सू	- ब्रह्मसूत्रम्
ब्र.सू.भा.	- ब्रह्मसूत्रभाष्यम्
बृ.	- बृहदारण्यकोपनिषद्
भ.गी.	- भगवद्गीता
वे.क.ल.	- वेदान्तकल्पलतिका
वे.सं.	- वेदार्थसंग्रहः
श.वि.	- शङ्कराशङ्करभाष्यविमर्शः
श्री.भा.	- श्रीभाष्यम्
श्वे.	- श्वेताश्वतरोपनिषद्

FOREWORD

Saptavidha-anupapatti: The seven objections against the notion of Māyā-avidyā of Advaita school have been the subject of intense debate between Advaitins and non-Advaitins for several centuries starting with Rāmānuja in the 11th century. The debate is so central - both philosophically and from the point of view of history of thought - that it deserves a thorough examination. This volume consists of essays which undertake, in their different ways, such an examination.

In Śaṅkara Vedānta, Māyā-avidyā is understood as the force or agency which creates the illusion of non-perception that manifests itself in the diversified forms of the objective world, which measures the immeasurable, creates forms in the formless, conceals the real and projects the unreal. Hence the only difference between man, the world and God is one of appearance and degree for ultimately they are non-different like the space inside a pot and space outside. Rāmānuja, however, differs from this nodal as well as basic proposition of Advaita and disagrees strongly with the Śaṅkarite concept of Māyā-avidyā. The Viśiṣṭādvaita school, in the post-Rāmānuja period, advances the debate which began with *Sapatavidha-anupapatti* of Rāmānuja. Counter-arguments of the Śaṅkara Advaitins in this debate and their rebuttals by the Viśiṣṭādvaitins form a continuity running into our own times.

This debate was the theme of a Seminar organized by the Indian Council of Philosophical Research, and the present volume is the edited version of the presentations made in this Seminar. Professor Godabarisha Mishra has shown his masterly touch in the editorial work. The volume serves the twin purpose of bringing alive a central debate in the Indian philosophical tradition and showing how it can impact our own thinking about issues which we take to be significant today. This book, I am sure, will prove to be a worthy successor to the Professor Daya Krishna edited *Saṁvāda*, published many years ago.

The philosophical community in the country will be grateful to Professor Godabarisha Mishra for his painstaking and extremely thoughtful editorial work in preparing this volume for publication. Researchers and scholars of philosophy will not only find the book useful, it is also quite likely to inspire works of similar nature in different areas of the Indian philsophical tradition.

Mrinal Miri
Chairman, ICPR, New Delhi

October 14, 2014

ACKNOWLEDGEMENT

This volume is an outcome of the proceedings of an ICPR National Seminar held during August 18-20, 1998 on "*Saptavidha-anupapatti*" a much debated topic in Vedānta. Since the seminar constituted the genesis of this book, it is appropriate to acknowledge those institutions and individuals whose help made it the success that it was. The principal source of funding for the seminar as well as the publication came from ICPR, New Delhi. To the authorities of Indian Council of Philosophical Research, past and present, I would like to express my thanks. I would also like to express my appreciations to the authorities of University of Madras and to my colleagues at the department of philosophy for their co-operation and those of Kuppuswamy Sastri Research Institute, where I worked earlier, for providing much needed logistics for conducting the sessions.

In organising a seminar involving a comtemporary debate on Māyā-avidyā, Professors Srinivasa Rao and M. Narashimhachary worked with me for about a year on the planning. To them, both of whom passed away during last academic year, (2012-13) I owe a special word of indebtedness.

Besides my gratitude to the authors who have come forward in revising their papers; my principal debt is to Dr. Mani Dravid who not only persuaded me to bring out this volume but went through all Sanskrit articles and offered suggestions for modification. To R. Mukundan, who did the typesetting and prepared the index, my special thanks are due. I wish to thank Dr. T.V. Vasudeva and Dr. K.S. Balasubramanian, my friends and former colleagues at the KSRI, for much needed editorial help.

I record my deep sense of gratitude to (Late) Professor Daya Krishna for being a constant inspiration not only to bring out this volume but also to work on such less-known areas of Indian philosophy. I am greatly beholden to Professor Mrinal Miri, Chairman, ICPR, for his kindness in writing the foreword.

University of Madras
October 2014 Godabarisha Mishra

INTRODUCTION

Godabarisha Mishra

The Indian philosophical scene has witnessed some of the most interesting, enduring and fierce debates among the three schools of Vedānta. The most prominent among the topics hotly debated for centuries is of māyā-avidyā. This concept is so central that the Advaita School which introduced this concept is frequently characterized as Māyāvāda. Rāmānuja who reacted to the school of Advaita by formulating his own system of Vedānta, i.e. Viśiṣṭādvaita, makes the concept of māyā-avidyā the prime target of his attack. He states his justly famous "Seven Objections" (*Saptavidha-anupapatti*) against the concept of māyā-avidyā in his *Śrībhāṣya*, almost exactly like Śaṅkara who sows the seed of this concept in his equally famous "*Adhyāsa-bhāṣya*" at the beginning of his commentary on the *Brahmasūtras*. This attack on the concept of māyā-avidyā initiated by Rāmānuja is vigorously continued by his followers and we have a detailed debate between the Advaitins and Viśiṣṭādvaitins on the question of māyā-avidyā that has spread over the centuries.

The question of māyā-avidyā is centrally connected to the very way of conceiving reality, i.e., Brahman in both Advaita and Viśiṣṭādvaita. For Advaita, it is axiomatic that Brahman is non-dual and absolutely featureless (nirguṇa) and therefore, the problem that naturally arises there is of explaining the multiplicity of entities and features encountered by us in the world of our experience. The concept of māyā-avidyā is invoked by Advaita as explanatory of this phenomenon. It is argued in Advaita that in view of the sole reality of nirguṇa Brahman, the universe of names and forms experienced by us is not ultimately real, and this unreality is variously referred to by the terms *mithyā*, *anirvacanīya* and *sadasad-vilakṣaṇa*. Thus, the concept of māyā-avidyā is used by Advaita to account for the experience of multiplicity and variety when, in fact, there is no entity except the sole nirguṇa Brahman.

Therefore, it can be easily seen that the concept of māyā-avidyā cannot be attacked if the notion of nirguṇa Brahman is allowed to remain as a constituent of Vedānta. Hence Rāmānuja starts by rejecting the notion of nirguṇa Brahman and substituting it by the notion of saguṇa Brahman. Since some of the Advaitins had held that the very notion of saguṇa Brahman was also due to māyā-avidyā, he is further compelled to defend the notion of saguṇa Brahman by attacking the concept of māyā-avidyā itself. This he does by formulating his seven famous objections, known as *Saptavidha-anupapatti*.

If Brahman is the only reality, Rāmānuja finds it hard to admit any entity like māyā-avidyā which has to be other than Brahman and therefore, begins his objections by asking where exactly this māyā-avidyā is located. Being insentient in nature, it cannot be located in Brahman who is sentient. It cannot also be located outside Brahman since there can be nothing "outside" Brahman. He also finds unacceptable the explanation offered by some Advaitins that māyā-avidyā is located in the beginningless jīva since the jīva itself has to be the product of māyā-avidyā according to the Advaitins themselves. Thus Rāmānuja finds māyā-avidyā without a legitimate locus (*āśraya*) and this is the first objection well known as (1) "*Āśraya-anupapatti*."

In the same way Rāmānuja raises six further objections about (2) the concealment of Brahman by māyā-avidyā and the projection of a false universe (*Tirodhāna-anupapatti*), (3) the nature of māyā-avidyā (*Svarūpa-anupapatti*), (4) the indescribable character of māyā-avidyā (*Anirvacanīya-anupapatti*), (5) the *Pramāṇa* by which this māyā-avidyā is known (*Pramāṇa-anupapatti*), (6) the means by which this māyā-avidyā is overcome (*Nivartaka-anupapatti*) and (7) whether this māyā-avidyā can be got rid of at all (*Nivṛttyanupapatti*). These objections are elaborated upon and are embellished by Viśiṣṭādvaita scholars like D.T. Tatacharya, Uttamur Viraraghavacharya and others and subsequently vigorously answered by contemporary Advaitins like Rāmarāya Kavi, Anantakrishna Sastri, to name a few.

This book contains substantially revised versions of the papers presented at the seminar held on *Saptavidha-anupapatti*. The seminar was structured around a number of topics, and some of those structures have survived the transition to book form. The book has been divided into four sections; first, "Background: Historical and Philosophical" has five papers. The first paper by R. Balasubramanian is a critical survey of the seven objections and answers to those objections as worked out in both the schools. The second paper by Kalyanasundara Sastri introduces the concept and explores the contribution made by Vidyāraṇya and Gaṅgādharendra Sarasvatī. Instead of getting into the debate proper, Kunjunni Raja takes a very neutral view and looks at the concept from pre-Śaṅkara period, mainly from the perspectives of Bhartṛhari and Buddhists. The next paper by Lakshmithathachar explores the views of Rāmānuja and tries to portray how the Rāmānuja's objections are still valid and cannot be so easily done away with as attempted by later Advaitins. The last paper of this section by M. Narasimhachary contends that the refutation of māyā-avidyā is not something that was started with Rāmānuja, but it was already there in pre-Rāmānuja period, in the writings of Nāthamuni and Yāmuna.

Titled as "Māyā-avidyā: The Concept and the Critique" the second section contains twelve essays by celebrated scholars debating on seven objections, since the last two objections are combined together. N.S. Rāmānuja Tatacharya has introduced the first objection, i.e. *Āśraya-anupapatti*, exactly the way Rāmānuja did in his *Śrībhāṣya* and this was contested by Vempati Kutumba Sastri from the view point of Advaita. Sastri adds many new ideas in his analysis to aid the already existing arguments found in the Advaita tradition. The next, i.e., *Tirodhāna-anupapatti* has been debated by two participants, V. Srivat-sankacharya and R. Krishnamurthi Sastri, both defending their own traditions and analyzing each point with new examples to establish their standpoints. The third objection, *viz. Svarūpa-anupapatti* was presented by S.M. Srinivasachari from Viśiṣṭā-dvaita standpoint and Muddulapalli Dattatreya Sastri made a case for Advaita view. *Anirvacanīya-anupapatti*, the fourth objection against māyā-avidyā was taken up by S.V. Rangaramanujacharyulu and was answered by Goda Venkateswara Sastri from Advaita perspective. V.S. Karunakaran and Sripada Subramanian examined the contentions of *Pramāṇānupapatti* raised by Rāmānuja from Viśiṣṭādvaita and Advaita angles respectively. The last two objections, *Nivartaka* and *Nivṛttyanupapatti* were combined and the participants were K.E. Devanathan and J. Venkatarama Sastri. The contents of the debates were so intense and the participation was so passionate that the participants could not find the time given during the sessions to be adequate to express their views. But one thing that was clearly felt was that everybody has something new to convey in addition to what has been already given in the earlier texts.

One of the glaring highlights of the seminar was the live-debate between two well-known scholars S.N.C. Raghunatha-charyulu and V. Swaminathan on the topic of māyā-avidyā and it was an involving debate ended in generating more heat than light between the protagonists of two schools; but still it was philosophically not only interesting, but quite rewarding. The debate was initiated by pointing out a text of a 20th century Advaita author, Rāmarāya Kavi, who in his *Śaṅkarāśaṅkara-bhāṣya-vimarśa* has threadbare criticized Rāmānuja for refuting the māyā-avidyā by his seven objections. The discussion on this debate was initiated by S.N.C. Raghunathacharyulu, who with his profound style and diction, and with very original arguments, refuted the views of Rāmarāya Kavi. The main thrust of this paper was that the tradition of Advaita can in no way defend the māyā-avidyā, unsuccessfully attempted by Rāmarāya. The answers to the objections came from V. Swaminathan who point by point answered the objections raised and vindicated the views of Advaitin with his impeccable arguments. This debate was quite interesting though fierce, but what is worth pointing out here is that the tradition of doing philosophy is not dead in India, as has been the pervasive view, but there are scholars, some known and quite many less-known, who are still busy doing philosophy as has been carried out since a millennia or more. This book briefly gives us an idea that the tradition of establishing a philosophical view and refuting it, what is said in Sanskrit as "*khaṇḍana-maṇḍana-paramparā*" has survived till date and I feel immensely grateful to these two living legends of both the Vedāntic traditions who have not only participated in the dialoge, but also contributed their papers to this volume.

"Māyā-Avidyā: Some Reflections" have been taken up in the fourth section. One of the major contributors to this debate in 19th century is Anantakrishna Sastri and it was he who wrote a text called *Śatabhūṣaṇī* answering all the (so-called) hundred objections raised in *Śatadūṣaṇī* of Vedāntadeśika. Mani Dravid gives a summary of the objections and the answers as presented in the writings of Anantakrishna Sastri. Śaṅkara's view on māyā-avidyā is taken up in the next essay by G.C. Nayak and he contends that Śaṅkara himself has placed the concept on such strong grounds that it hardly has any space for further dialogue or refutation.

The next essay by Haramohan Mishra is devoted to the concept of māyā-avidyā as available in the works of Madhusūdana Sarasvatī, the 16th century Advaitin, famous author of the *Advaitasiddhi*. A fresh debate on the concept of māyā-avidyā was attempted by Saccidānandendra Sarasvatī who in recent decades came up with the view that the post-Śaṅkara Advaitins have misunderstood the original tenets of Ācārya Śaṅkara. He upheld the view that there is nothing called the māyā-avidyā which is the cause of the world, subscribing to the view that cause and effect are not different (*ananyatva*). Srinivasa Rao's essay addresses to this theme. One of the champions in the Indian dialectics was Madhvācārya who stood as a pillar of opposition to the Advaita-views and he not only vehemently criticized Advaita but also pointed out the inadequacies of the Viśiṣṭādvaita school. His objections on the māyā-avidyā have been brought out by D. Prahladachar mainly pointing out how avidyā cannot be viewed as a positive entity as shown by Advaitins.

Dominic Goodall analyses the concept of māyā-avidyā from the Śaiva Siddhānta angle by criticizing the *Vivartavāda* of the Advaita school. S.M. Mishra attempts to bring out the concept on illusion as found in the non-Vedāntic schools of Indian Philosophy, mainly from the angle of Sāṅkhya and other early systems of Indian thought. Bijayananada Kar's essay on māyā in contemporary Indian philosophy harbors on the views of modern writers like Swami Vivekananda, K.C. Bhattacharya and the like.

The highlight of the essay of R. Thangaswami was to show the continuity of writing on the subject of māyā-avidyā from Rāmānuja till our times. He has given a bibliographic survey of the concept and shown how this has been a topic of live-debate for more than a millennium from Rāmānuja onwards.

The last essay again picks up the thread from the earlier essay, and links on to the first essay of R. Balasubramanian and makes a systematic survey of the concept from Rāmānuja through Rāmarāya up to our times. It was Rāmarāya Kavi who kick started the debate as a tirade against Viśiṣṭādvaita in his book *Śaṅkarā-śaṅkara-bhāṣyavimarśa*. An attempt has been made by G. Mishra, to reconstruct the history of the concept and its dialectical development as well as to show that the Indian tradition of debate is not a thing of the past, but is still alive which is testified in this paper. This essay also gives the hints and possibilities of further continuation of the debate along new lines and making evaluations on the basis of our contemporary knowledge as has been attempted by Paramananda Bharati.

The main objective of this book is to focus our attention on the significant issues arising out of this debate on māyā-avidyā and its development that has continued up to our times. The preparation of the final manuscript that resulted from the seminar was no less onerous a task than the organization of the seminar itself, partly because it was necessary to try to ensure that successive revisions of papers were not made totally in ignorance of revisions of related papers. Long years of work has gone into collecting and revising the papers and I wish that this book will generate fresh interest in the scholars and researchers to look into the less known areas of Indian philosophical tradition.

1

RĀMĀNUJA'S SAPTAVIDHĀNUPAPATTI: A REVIEW AND REAPPRAISAL

R. Balasubramanian

1. Rāmānuja as a Critic

The philosophy of Advaita has been the central target for criticism by both classical and contemporary Indian philosophers. Classical Indian philosophers like Yāmuna, Bhāskara, Rāmānuja, Madhva, and others have thoroughly examined the basic doctrines and the key concepts of Advaita from different perspectives—epistemological, metaphysical, linguistic, and soteriological. Contemporary Indian critics of Advaita belong to two categories—sophisticated and superficial. Sri Aurobindo, a notable critic of Advaita in our own times, belongs to the former category. Unlike classical Indian philosophers, he does not formulate his objections by getting into the details of the doctrines and arguments of Advaita. Instead, he objects in very general terms directing his criticisms against the *orientation* of Advaita system as a whole; and they are intelligible and significant only when viewed against the *ethos* or *geist* of the philosophy of Advaita. The objections raised by the other category of contemporary Indian philosophers are superficial and frivolous, dull and desultory revealing their ignorance of the system.

Of the classical Indian philosophers who examined and criticized the doctrines and concepts of Advaita, Rāmānuja is the foremost for two important reasons. First, he demolished the solid philosophical structure built by Śaṅkara, and this is no easy job. To use an expression which is in currency and has earned great respectability, he did 'deconstruction'—by questioning Śaṅkara's interpretation of scriptural texts and their supporting arguments, by redefining the concepts used in scripture and providing a different set of arguments in support of his hermeneutics vis-à-vis those of Advaita, and by demonstrating at every stage that he truly preserved the tradition of his illustrious preceptors. Second, he showed that his work was also creative and positive, not just "destructive" and negative; and for this he built a philosophical system founded on epistemology, metaphysics, linguistics, and hermeneutics, and also showed that harmony was the hallmark of his newly constructed system. If one carefully studies Rāmānuja's *Śrībhāṣya*, 1.1.1, one notices that he has successfully accomplished the twofold task of deconstruction and construction on the basis of his own premises.

Rāmānuja is at his best not only when he elucidates the Viśiṣṭādvaita position, but also when he examines and criticizes the views of others. I propose to consider in this paper the manner in which Rāmānuja in his *Śrībhāṣya* criticizes the Advaita doctrine of avidyā.

2. The Advaita Concept of Avidyā

Avidyā, otherwise called māyā, is the basic concept through which Advaita works out its metaphysics, epistemology, and ethics. The distinction between Brahman as *nirguṇa* and Brahman as *saguṇa*, the apparent difference between Brahman and the individual self, and the problem of the One appearing as many, which are important issues in the metaphysics of Advaita, presuppose the concept of avidyā. In the same way, the subject-object epistemology involving the distinctions of cogniser, cognitum, and cognition, and the theory of *vivarta* in terms of which the problem of error is sought to be explained, presuppose the concept of avidyā. Advaita insists that knowledge alone is the direct means to release because primal ignorance (avidyā), the root cause of the bondage of the individual self, can be removed only by the knowledge of the primal Being. So the concept of avidyā is also the rationale behind the code of conduct recommended for liberation. So, there is no wonder that avidyā is the corner-stone of Advaita Vedānta.

A brief explanation of this avidyā will help us follow Rāmānuja's criticism. Due to beginningless (*anādi*) avidyā, Brahman-Ātman which is pure, undifferentiated, non-relational, non-dual consciousness appears in the form of Īśvara and jīva. Avidyā is not mere absence of knowledge, but something positive (*bhāva-rūpa*) inasmuch as it is responsible for the appearance of the phenomenal world along with jīva and Īśvara. Ontologically, it cannot be determined to be real or even non-real. It is not non-real, because it is experienced; and it is not real since it ceases to exist when Brahman-Ātman is realized. Hence it is said to be *anirvacanīya*. Though beginningless, it has an end, because it can be terminated by Brahman-knowledge. It has two powers—the power of concealment (*āvaraṇa-śakti*) and the power of projection (*vikṣepa-śakti*). According to one explanation, Brahman alone is the locus (*āśraya*) of avidyā, for there is nothing else than Brahman to serve as the locus. According to another explanation, the jīva is the locus of avidyā. These two explanations are said to be from two perspectives within the framework of Advaita and hence they are held to be complementary and not contradictory.

The above doctrine of avidyā is unacceptable to Rāmānuja. Considering the important role of this concept of avidyā in Advaita, Rāmānuja examines it carefully and formulates his objections against it. He does this in the celebrated *Mahāsiddhānta* of the *Śrībhāṣya*, 1.1.1, raising seven major objections popularly referred to as *Saptavidha-anupapatti.* Apart from the difficulty in comprehending the long compounds which Rāmānuja is fond of using, the analysis which he works out through several alternatives for the purpose of criticizing the opponent's view cannot be easily understood. Consider, for example, the three alternatives which he introduces almost at the start of the third objection called *Svarūpānupapatti* for the purpose of the analysis of a point of view which is itself one of the two alternatives. The sentence begins with "*nāpi aparamārthaḥ, tathā sati hi-*"[1] One has to read and re-read passages of this type in Rāmānuja's *Śrībhāṣya* with the help of a commentary in order to understand him. The objections raised by modern scholars against the Advaita doctrine of avidyā pale into insignificance when compared with those raised by Rāmānuja. Further, it will be easier to follow the objections raised by the Viśiṣṭādvaitins like Vedānta Deśika of the post-Rāmānuja period if one is fully acquainted with the *saptavidha-anupapatti* of Rāmānuja.

3. On the Locus of Avidyā

According to Advaita, Brahman or the Self is the only reality. Since the appearance of the pluralistic universe is accounted for by avidyā, it is necessary to explain its locus (*āśraya*), i.e. the place from which it functions. Rāmānuja contends that it is impossible for the Advaitin to explain the locus of avidyā in the context of (i) his basic metaphysical position and (ii) his explanation of the nature of Brahman-Ātman. This objection is known as *Āśrayānupapatti*.[2] We may now go into the details of Rāmānuja's first objection.

Rāmānuja raises the basic question: what is the locus of avidyā? The Advaitins answer this question in two ways. According to the Bhāmatī school, the jīva is the locus; but according to the Vivaraṇa school, Brahman-Ātman is the locus. Rāmānuja considers and rejects these two answers as he finds both to be unsatisfactory. Though Rāmānuja here follows the lead given by Yāmuna, he throws new light on the issue under consideration through his elucidátion.

The answer of the Bhāmatī school does not engage the attention of Rāmānuja for long. He summarily rejects it in just one sentence by saying that since the jīva itself is the product of avidyā, it cannot also be claimed to be its locus without involving the fallacy of mutual dependence (*anyonyāśraya*). To avoid this fallacy, the Advaitin has to prove the jīva or avidyā independently of the other. Since he is not able to explain the jīva without recourse to avidyā, and avidyā without presupposing the jīva, his position is fallacious according to Rāmānuja and therefore to be rejected. The point of Rāmānuja's attack lies in the fact that the jīva is itself a fictitious entity whose appearance is due to avidyā; and so it makes no sense to claim that the jīva is the locus of avidyā.

According to Rāmānuja, the Vivaraṇa explanation that Brahman is the locus of avidyā fares no better. His main objection here is that Brahman which is of the nature of self-luminous knowledge (*svayam-prakāśa-jñānarūpa*) and avidyā which is its opposite, are mutually exclusive and that Brahman, therefore, cannot be the locus of avidyā. But by making a distinction between *vṛtti-jñāna* and *svarūpa-jñāna*, the Advaitin argues that while the former is opposed to avidyā, the latter is not. This distinction, Rāmānuja argues, is untenable. The *vṛtti-jñāna* or *viṣaya-jñāna* is the knowledge of Brahman. It is "knowledge that Brahman is of the nature of knowledge" (*jñāna-svarūpam brahma iti jñānam*).[3] Since both *vṛtti-jñāna* and *svarūpa-jñāna* are knowledge, what holds good for the one must also hold good for the other. For Rāmānuja, if *vṛtti-jñāna* is opposed to avidyā, then *svarūpa-jñāna* too must be.

There is yet another difficulty. When the Advaitin speaks about "knowledge that Brahman is of the nature of knowledge", it is a case of knowledge of Brahman, i.e. knowledge whose content is Brahman. This is inconsistent with the Advaita view that Brahman which is knowledge is not an object of another knowledge. So it is wrong on the part of the Advaitin to speak of "knowledge of Brahman".

Rāmānuja argues that the case of Brahman is entirely different from that of an insentient object like a shell. Consider the case of a shell which is mistaken for silver. The shell, itself being insentient (*jaḍa*), cannot remove the error by revealing its true nature. Knowledge is necessarily required for this. But Brahman itself is of the nature of knowledge. Being self-luminous, it can, without the aid of another knowledge, remove avidyā by revealing its nature. If so, where is the need, asks Rāmānuja, for "another knowledge" which is credited with the work of destroying avidyā?

What is the content of this "another knowledge" referred to earlier as *vṛtti-jñāna* or *viṣaya-jñāna*? Brahman, Rāmānuja argues, cannot be the content of this knowledge. The Advaitin may argue that this other knowledge is knowledge of the world, i.e. knowledge that the world is mithyā (*prapañca-mithyātva-viṣaya-jñānam*). Rāmānuja points out that this argument is not helpful to the Advaitin. Though this knowledge of the world removes our ignorance of it, it cannot remove our ignorance of Brahman, for it does not relate to Brahman, but only to the world. So, in spite of this knowledge of the world, ignorance of Brahman still persists and the Advaitin has to show how it can be removed. If Brahman by its very nature is non-dual and if it can on its own reveal its non-duality, there is no scope either for the perception of duality or for its sublation. Rāmānuja, therefore, concludes that Brahman which is *jñāna-svarūpa* cannot be the locus of avidyā.

However, Rāmānuja's argument does not invalidate the distinction between *svarūpa-jñāna* and *vṛtti-jñāna*. The knowledge which reveals the nature of an object and removes the ignorance about it has a content. Such knowledge, obtained through the mental mode (*antaḥ-karaṇa-vṛtti*), is called *svarūpa-viṣayā-jñāna* or *vṛtti-jñāna* which is pramāṇa-generated-knowledge. While the *vṛtti* corresponding to the cognition of an object like a pot or a tree has a form that is fragmented (*khaṇḍa*), in the case of the cognition of Brahman the *vṛtti* has no fragmented form, because Brahman has no form at all. So the modal cognition through which Brahman is apprehended is termed *akhaṇḍākāra-vṛtti-jñāna*. It is this knowledge obtained through *akhaṇḍākāra-vṛtti* that dispels ignorance which conceals the nature of Brahman. It is *vṛtti-jñāna* (otherwise called *svarūpa-viṣaya-jñāna*) that removes avidyā, and not *svarūpa-jñāna* which is Brahman-knowledge. The very fact that one is called *vṛtti-jñāna* and the other *svarūpa-viṣaya-jñāna* shows that there is an important difference between them, which can never be obliterated by just treating them both as knowledge. So Rāmānuja is wrong when he says that there is no difference between *svarūpa-jñāna* and *svarūpa-viṣaya-jñāna*.[4]

If knowledge which constitutes the nature of Brahman cannot remove avidyā, how can it remove avidyā through being reflected in the mental mode? The answer is that it is competent to do so in the same way as the light of the sun, when it passes through a lens, burns a heap of dry-grass though it cannot by itself do that. In the same way what is done by *vṛtti-jñāna* cannot be done by *svarūpa-jñāna*, i.e., it alone can destroy avidyā; *svarūpa-jñāna* cannot do that. Though the mental mode which removes avidyā is admitted to be valid (*pramā*), it is not real (*paramārtha*), because it also disappears when avidyā is destroyed. Only if it were to be real, there would be duality — Brahman which is real as well as *vṛtti-jñāna* which is real.

Rāmānuja now raises the objection against the very possibility of the knowledge of Brahman through *vṛtti-jñāna*. According to Advaita, Brahman being of the very nature of knowledge, cannot be the object of another knowledge. If so, Rāmānuja argues, there cannot be a knowledge which has Brahman as its object. It means that *svarūpa-viṣaya-jñāna*, i.e. knowledge of Brahman, admitted by the Advaitin is untenable.

This objection is also wrong. Though Brahman is knowledge by its very nature, so long as there is the empirical business of life (*vyava-hāra*) based on avidyā, the nature of Brahman remains concealed by avidyā; and so we speak of Brahman being apprehended through the modal cognition, consequent upon the removal of avidyā. It may be stated here that Brahman is not an object of knowledge in the sense in which an empirical thing, e.g. a tree is an object. Two conditions must be fulfilled if something is to be an object of knowledge. Both the mental mode (*vṛtti*) and the knowledge (*phala*) reflected therein are needed for cognizing an object. One of them alone will not do. But to cognize Brahman, we need only the mental mode referred to earlier as *akhaṇḍākāra-vṛtti*. Since Brahman itself is knowledge, the other condition is not required. Thus, though Brahman is not an object of knowledge like any empirical entity, it is nevertheless apprehended through the impermanent modal cognition.[5]

Rāmānuja's dialectics is intended to show that Advaita can never explain how ignorance of the true nature of Brahman (*brahma-svarūpa-ajñāna*) is removed. If Brahman which is knowledge is not opposed to ignorance as the Advaitin claims, what is it that is opposed to this ignorance such that it can remove it? Rāmānuja argues that it cannot be *vṛtti-jñāna* which is supposed to have Brahman as its content, for Brahman which is knowledge cannot *ex hypothesi* be an object of knowledge. Could it be said that the knowledge that the world, which is other than Brahman, is false (*brahma-vyatiriktasya mithyātva-jñānam*), destroys the ignorance of the true nature of Brahman? This alternative too, Rāmānuja contends, is not possible.

There are two alternatives here. Could it be said that the knowledge that the world which is other than Brahman is false is opposed to the ignorance of the true nature of Brahman? Or, is it opposed to the ignorance which makes one think that the world is real? Rāmānuja argues that the first alternative is not tenable. Knowledge and ignorance are, indeed, opposed to each other only if they refer to one and the same object. In this case, knowledge relates to "what is other than Brahman" (*brahma-vyatirikta*), whereas ignorance is about "the true nature of Brahman" (*brahma-yāthātmya*). Nor does the second alternative fare better. The knowledge that the world which is other than Brahman is false will undoubtedly remove the ignorance as a result of which one thinks that the world is real. But it cannot remove the ignorance about the true nature of Brahman, for its content is different from the content of the latter.

First of all, to say that the world which is other than Brahman is false, one must have the knowledge of the world. So long as a person does not have such a knowledge of the world, he cannot say that the world is false. Secondly, a person who does not know the real nature of Brahman cannot say that the world *which is other than Brahman* is false. To say that the world is something other than Brahman and that it is, therefore, false, one must know the real nature of Brahman. It follows that the knowledge that the world which is other than Brahman is false presupposes the knowledge of the true nature of Brahman. Thirdly, the knowledge of the true nature of Brahman cannot take place without removing the ignorance of the true nature of Brahman. It has already been stated that such a knowledge is obtained through *akhaṇḍākāra-vṛtti*. Consequently, when one knows that the world which is other than Brahman is false, one cannot be ignorant of the true nature of Brahman.[6] It is surprising that Rāmānuja should argue that the ignorance of the true nature of Brahman (*brahma-svarūpa-ajñānam*) persists even after attaining the knowledge of the falsity of the world. Since the Advaita position that Brahman-knowledge is not opposed to ignorance holds good, Brahman which is of the nature of knowledge is the locus of avidyā.

The position of Advaita, in the light of what has been said above, may be summarized as follows. (1) It is only *vṛtti-jñāna* that is opposed to avidyā, but not *svarūpa-jñāna*. (2) At the rise of the knowledge of Brahman through *akhaṇḍākāra-vṛtti*, ignorance of the true nature of Brahman gets removed. (3) Brahman which is *svarūpa-jñāna* reveals avidyā. (4) It is, therefore, not opposed to avidyā. (5) Since it is not opposed, it can be, and is, the locus of avidyā.

The Advaitin sometimes suggests a provisional explanation to overcome the alleged fallacy of mutual dependence between jīva and avidyā in the case of *jīva-ajñāna-vāda* of the Bhāmatī school by citing the example of the seed-sprout series. The two—seed and sprout—constitute a continuous series or stream (*pravāha*) which is beginningless (*anādi*). In the same way, the jīva arises because of avidyā, and avidyā because of the jīva; that jīva in its turn arises because of avidyā, and so on. Thus like the seed-sprout series, the jīva and avidyā constitute a continuous series which is beginningless (*pravāha-anādi*).

Strictly speaking, the analogy of the seed-sprout series does not hold good for the explanation of the relation between jīva and avidyā as there is a plurality of seeds and sprouts while there is no plurality of avidyā or of jīva. According to *jīva-ajñāna-vāda*, because of avidyā there is the jīva; and because of the jīva, there is avidyā. Both avidyā and jīva come into existence at the same time. Since a plurality of avidyā and of jīva is not admitted, the notion of series is not applicable. Since the mutual causal relation between avidyā and jīva does not take place more than once, the beginningless series (*pravāha-anāditva*) spoken of here by the *jīva-ājñāna-vādin* is only in the figurative sense.[7]

On the question of the relation between avidyā and jīva, the Advaitins of the Vivaraṇa tradition who subscribe to *brahma-ajñāna-vāda* maintain that while the status of the jīva is the result of avidyā, avidyā is not the result of the jīva. Thus they avoid the fallacy of mutual dependence (*anyonyāśraya-doṣa*). Though the jīva comes into existence because of avidyā, it is nevertheless said to be "beginningless" (*anādi*) because it is not possible to show that a particular jīva came into existence at a particular time due to avidyā. Since both jīva and avidyā are "beginningless" (*anādi*) according to Advaita, it is utterly irrelevant to raise the question of their chronological priority or posteriority.

Though the theory of the jīva being the locus of avidyā is not fallacious as shown above briefly, since the critics harp upon it being a fallacy, we will consider here its detailed defence by Madhusūdana Sarasvatī in his *Advaita-siddhi.* If it is fallacious, is it in respect of its origin (*utpatti*), knowledge (*jñapti*), or existence (*sthiti*)? It cannot be in respect of origin. There is, argues Madhusūdana Sarasvati, no mutual dependence between avidyā and jīva in respect of their origin, for both avidyā and jīva are beginningless. It cannot be in respect of knowledge because though avidyā is revealed by knowledge (*caitanya*) which constitutes the essential nature of the jīva, the *jīva-caitanya* does not require the help of avidyā for its revelation. If the charge of mutual dependence is made about their existence then the question is whether the two hang on each other (*parasparāśrita*), or the existence of one cannot be conceived apart from the existence of the other (*paraspara-sāpekṣa-sthiti*). Madhusūdana argues that neither of the alternatives is tenable. Though avidyā hangs on the *jīva-caitanya*, the reverse is not the case. Further, though the existence of avidyā cannot be thought of apart from the existence of *caitanya*, we cannot also say that the existence of *jīva-caitanya* cannot be thought of apart from the existence of avidyā. It is, therefore, wrong to say that the *jīva-ajñāna-vāda* of the Bhāmatī school is guilty of the fallacy of mutual dependence.[8]

4. On the Concealment of Avidyā

The second major objection of Rāmānuja is called *Tirodhāna-anupapatti*.[9] According to Advaita, avidyā has two powers, the power of concealment (*āvaraṇa-* or *tirodhāna-śakti*) and the power of projection (*vikṣepa-śakti*). Brahman is of the nature of homogeneous knowledge (*prakāśaika-svarūpam*), and avidyā by its power conceals or hides this nature. Rāmānuja asks: what does this concealment of knowledge mean? There are two possible replies. Concealment may mean either the obstruction of the origination of knowledge (*prakāśa-utpatti-pratibandha*), or the destruction of the knowledge that exists (*vidyamānasya vināśa*). The first alternative is untenable since knowledge which is Brahman is eternal and hence has no origination and the question of obstructing the origination of knowledge does not arise. The Advaitin is, therefore, left with the second alternative. The second alternative is even more unsatisfactory as it amounts to the destruction of Brahman whose essential nature is knowledge (*prakāśa-tirodhānam prakāśanāśa eva*). The alternatives are hence untenable.

Rāmānuja's query is that since Brahman is essentially of the nature of self-luminous consciousness, what is meant by saying that this nature is concealed or hidden by avidyā? He also says elsewhere that the concealment of the self-luminous consciousness cannot mean anything but its destruction. This concealment of consciousness may mean either obstructing the origination of consciousness, or destroying consciousness that exists. The first is ruled out because Advaita admits no origination for consciousness. According to Rāmānuja, there is every justification for the second alternative. *Svarūpa-tirodhāna*,

Rāmānuja says, is *svarūpa-aprakāśa.* Since it is the very nature of Brahman to be self-luminous, the concealment of this nature is possible only through the removal of that nature. Hence, this loss of the essential nature of Brahman through avidyā, an outside agency, is the loss of Brahman itself. It is possible to avoid this situation by making consciousness only an attribute of Brahman because while the loss of an attribute is not the loss of the thing of which it is an attribute, the loss of the essential nature of a thing is the loss of the thing itself. Since the Advaitin says that consciousness is the essential nature of Brahman, the concealment of this essential nature through avidyā can only mean, concludes Rāmānuja, the loss of Brahman itself.

Rāmānuja's argument is, indeed, ingenious. That he deliberately twists the meaning of the word "concealment" (*āvaraṇa*) in order to serve his own purpose is obvious. Consider the case of an object concealed from me. When some one asks me whether I know that object, I reply in the negative. Because of the concealment, I am not able to claim that it exists or that it is directly seen by me. But it does not follow from this that there is loss of that object. The same thing may be said of the concealment of Brahman.[10] Hence there is no loss of Brahman because of its concealment by avidyā. When the veil of avidyā is removed through knowledge, one may claim that Brahman exists or that it is directly seen. It must be borne in mind that this explanation of the work of avidyā is given from the relative standpoint of *vyavahāra.* From the absolute standpoint, there is no avidyā at all, and Brahman alone is; if so, Brahman is neither concealed nor destroyed by avidyā.

One may argue that there is a basic difference between the concealment of Brahman and the concealment of other objects. Everything other than Brahman is, according to Advaita, insentient. But Brahman is of the nature of self-luminous knowledge or consciousness. Therefore, the concealment of Brahman-knowledge by ignorance can only mean the loss or destruction of Brahman-knowledge because knowledge and ignorance, according to Advaita, are mutually exclusive like light and darkness.

This argument is not convincing. Firstly, the point at issue is not the difference between sentient Brahman and other insentient objects which is accepted by Advaita. Secondly, it is also true that knowledge (*jñāna*) and ignorance (*ajñāna*) are mutually opposed like light and darkness. A little clarification of this second point may be relevant here. When Advaita says that knowledge is opposed to ignorance, the knowledge so opposed is *vṛtti-jñāna* and not *svarūpa-jñāna.* Since the knowledge of these two types are different, it is possible to maintain that Brahman which is knowledge by nature (*svarūpa-jñāna*) is not opposed to avidyā. Hence, far from being opposed to avidyā, Brahman-knowledge is helpful to it not only in serving as its locus but also in its revelation. That is precisely why we can say that there is avidyā which conceals Brahman-knowledge. Brahman-knowledge and avidyā are related as the locus and the contained, and also as the revealer and the revealed.[11] When avidyā, though revealed by Brahman, conceals it, we say that Brahman is not known; and when avidyā is removed by the unitary cognition through the mental mode (*akhaṇḍākāra-vṛtti-jñāna*), we say that Brahman is known.

Further, our claim that Brahman is known or that it is not known, is based on the work of the internal organ. The cognition that one has in these cases is *vṛtti-jñāna*, which is different from Brahman which is *svarūpa-jñāna*. Hence, just because one has the cognition that Brahman does not exist or that Brahman is not seen, it does not follow that there is no Brahman. In other words, the concealment of Brahman as indicated by these cognitions does not imply the loss or destruction of Brahman because every such *vṛtti-jñāna* presupposes *svarūpa-jñāna.*

It is necessary at this stage to consider another objection of Rāmānuja that the concealment of Brahman-knowledge is not at all possible and that the Advaita explanation in this regard is fallacious. He says: "*Ajñāna* which is the cause of the concealment of Brahman's nature hides Brahman in so far as Brahman is conscious of it, and on the other hand that having hidden Brahman, it becomes the object of consciousness on the part of Brahman; and this evidently involves the fallacy of mutual dependence (*anyonyāśraya*)."[12] In short, Rāmānuja thinks that Advaita cannot give an intelligible explanation of the process of the concealment of Brahman.

This objection is wrong. First of all, Advaita does not hold that Brahman is conscious of *ajñāna*. When Rāmānuja asks whether avidyā first conceals Brahman and then becomes an object of Brahman's consciousness, or whether it first becomes an object of Brahman's consciousness and then hides it, he wrongly assumes that according to Advaita, Brahman is conscious of avidyā. Since Advaita denies *ajñānānubhava* to Brahman, the entire criticism of Rāmānuja is misconceived. Secondly, if one formulates the problem the way Rāmānuja does, the Advaita position cannot avoid the fallacy of mutual dependence (*anyonyāśraya*). But Advaita position is different. According to it, avidyā which conceals Brahman, is experienced by the jīva and not by Brahman.[13] So the Advaita view that Brahman-knowledge is concealed by avidyā becomes quite tenable. Brahman-in-itself is neither the witness to, nor has the experience of, avidyā. While Īśvara knows both avidyā and its manifestations, it is the jīva which is really the victim of avidyā. The redeeming feature here is that the jīva knows that it is ignorant.

5. On the Nature of Avidyā

The third objection called *svarūpa-anupapatti*[14] is focussed on the ontological status of avidyā and it forces the Advaitin into a dilemma of choosing between mutually exclusive and collectively exhaustive alternatives. Rāmānuja formulates the objections as follows:

> Your theory is that self-luminous consciousness, which is without object and without substrate, becomes, through the influence of a defect residing within itself, conscious of itself as connected with innumerable substrata and objects. Is then, we ask, that defect residing within consciousness something real or something unreal? The former alternative is excluded, as not being admitted by yourself. Nor can we accept the latter alternative; for if we did, we should have to view that defect as being either a knowing subject, or an object of knowledge, or knowing itself. Now it cannot be "knowing," as you deny that there is any distinction in the nature of knowing; and that "knowing," which is the substrate of the defect, cannot be held to be unreal, because that would involve the acceptance of the Mādhyamika doctrine, viz. of a general void. And if knowers, objects of knowledge, and knowing as determined by those two, are fictitious, i.e. unreal, we have to assume another fundamental defect, and are thus driven into a *regressus ad infinitum*. To avoid this difficulty, it might now be said that real consciousness itself, which constitutes Brahman's nature, is that

> defect. But if Brahman itself constitutes the defect, then Brahman is the basis of the appearance of the world, and it is gratuitous to assume an additional avidyā to account for the world. Moreover, as Brahman is eternal, it would follow from this hypothesis that no release could ever take place. Unless, therefore, you admit a real defect apart from Brahman, you are unable to account for the great world-error.

Let us consider one by one the several points raised by Rāmānuja in the course of his criticism.

The Advaitin does not say that the pure consciousness (*anubhūti*), due to avidyā, becomes conscious of itself, as the substrate of objects and also as connected with objects. He maintains, on the contrary, that the knower (*pramātā*), which is consciousness delimited by *ajñāna* or *antaḥkaraṇa*, by virtue of avidyā associated with it, understands the consciousness as the substrate of objects and also as what is connected with objects.[15] In other words, the distinction between *anubhūti* (consciousness) and *pramātā* (knower), which is important for the Advaitin, has been ignored by Rāmānuja. Consciousness-in-itself, which is Brahman-Ātman, has no imperfection whatsoever. It is, to use the words of Gauḍapāda, *anidram* and *asvapnam*.[16] *Nidrā*, which means sleep, is avidyā and that is responsible for the non-apprehension of reality. *Svapna*, which means dream, is mis-apprehension of reality. The ultimate reality which is pure consciousness and which is spoken of as *Turīya*, says Gauḍapāda, is *anidram* (i.e. free from avidyā) and *asvapnam* (i.e. free from mis-apprehension). While consciousness-in-itself is free from avidyā, the *pramātā* which is the jīva views consciousness *from its point of view* as not only the substrate of, but also as what is related to objects.

We now turn to the alleged defect of infinite regress (*anavasthā*) in the Advaita explanation. Rāmānuja wants to know whether avidyā is real or unreal. After pointing out that the Advaitin himself does not say that avidyā is real (*paramārtha*), Rāmānuja examines the other alternative. He asks: in what sense is avidyā unreal? Is it unreal as the knowing subject, or as the object of knowledge, or as "knowing" determined by the knower and the known? Whichever be the alternative, the Advaita position, according to Rāmānuja, is defective. His argument is as follows: since every one of these three alternatives is unreal (*kālpanika* or *aparamārtha*) from the Advaita point of view, the Advaitin has to account for their unreality. What is the cause of the defect called avidyā? The questioning does not and cannot stop here. We must ask: what is the cause of the cause of that defect? And the same question has to be repeated at every stage, leading to infinite regress (*anavasthā*). Thus, in whichever way the Advaitin tries to explain this unreality of avidyā, there is *anavasthā*.

But Rāmānuja's argument is untenable. Śruti says: "*māyā ca avidyā ca svayameva bhavati.*"[17] It means that māyā, which is avidyā, comes into existence of its own accord. While every object requires a cause for its coming into existence, avidyā does not require a cause. It is self-existent (*svatassiddha*), accounting for its own being and of other things. Thus, though avidyā is *aparamārtha*, the defect of *anavasthā* does not arise because avidyā is self-established.

Though avidyā is thus self-established (*svatassiddha*) it does not follow that it is eternal (*nitya*) like Brahman because it is removable by knowledge. There is another reason for its non-eternality. Avidyā is material or insentient (*jaḍa*), and whatever is material is not eternal. Only consciousness (*caitanya* or *jñāna*) which is without a beginning (*ajanya*) is eternal. Since avidyā is both *janya* and *jaḍa*, it is non-eternal and hence not real (*aparamārtha*) and its destruction is release. What is eternal can never be destroyed. Hence Rāmānuja's contention that a real defect (*pāramārthika-doṣa*) called avidyā which is different from Brahman has to be admitted for explaining the world-error, is wrong. Only if the defect is real, mokṣa can never be attained and it would also render scripture and its teaching futile. The utility of scripture can be justified only if it is admitted that avidyā is not *paramārtha*, and that scripture helps us to overcome it. Rāmānuja's contention that, if avidyā were to be unreal, it would not be possible to account for the falsity of the world, is equally untenable because the falsity or illusory character of the world is intelligible only if the world is a product of *aparamārtha* avidyā.

Another point raised by Rāmānuja may now be considered. Rāmānuja says that, with a view to avoid the fallacy of infinite regress, the Advaitin might argue that the real consciousness itself which is Brahman serves as the defect (*doṣa*), and that it accounts for the appearance of the world. Such a position, Rāmānuja remarks, would be detrimental to the Advaitin in two respects. For one, it would be gratuitous on the part of the Advaitin to assume avidyā which is said to be false or unreal like the world. For another, it would rule out the possibility of release because Brahman which is admitted to be the defect responsible for the world-show is eternal.

Rāmānuja's argument is unacceptable. We have already shown how the Advaita explanation of avidyā is free from the fallacy of infinite regress. Further, Brahman by itself cannot account for the world. Śruti says that Brahman in itself is neither the cause nor the effect.[18] Advaita holds the view that Brahman along with māyā-avidyā creates the world. It also speaks of the power of the supreme Self (*devātma-śakti*) as the cause of the world. This power is known as *ajñāna, māyā, avidyā, prakṛti*, and so on. To account for the world, there must be a cause that is capable of producing the world. Further, we infer the power inherent in the cause from the effect. The non-existence of the effect means the non-existence of the power. Being the *pratiyogin* of the non-existence of power, power cannot be eternal. In other words, the power (viz. *māyā-avidyā*) associated with Brahman is only *adhyasta*.[19] So, Brahman associated with māyā-avidyā which is superimposed on it is the cause of the world. That is why, the *Śvetāśvatara*, 4.9, speaks of Brahman as māyin. According to Advaita, while Brahman is the trans-figurative material cause (*vivartopādāna-kāraṇa*), avidyā-māyā is the trans-formative material cause (*pariṇāmy-upādāna-kāraṇa*) of the world. It is, therefore, wrong to say that the assumption of avidyā is gratuitous and that Brahman by itself can be the cause of the world.

6. On the Indeterminability of Avidyā

The Advaitin says that avidyā is not real (*sat*) because it is sublated. It is not non-real (*asat*) either because it is experienced. Ontologically it is something different from both real and non-real (*sadasad-vilakṣaṇa*) or "*anirvacanīya*" which means that it is indeterminable as real or as non-real. It means that the Advaitin accepts a third category in addition to, but different from, *sat* and *asat*; and avidyā and its products belong to this third category. Rāmānuja's fourth objection called *anirvacanīyatva-anupapatti* is a direct attack on this explanation of the Advaitin which, according to him, totally ignores the law of excluded middle.[20]

This explanation of the ontological status of avidyā is not acceptable to Rāmānuja. He argues along the following lines: It is well-known that we determine the nature of an object on the basis of our cognition[21] of it and therefore Rāmānuja asks: Is there any justification for the admission of an entity which is said to be neither real nor non-real? He holds that we have to answer this question by saying "no". Every cognition (*pratīti*) that we have presents itself in the form of *sat* or *asat*. When all our cognitions are thus restricted to the dual form of *sat* and *asat*, it is untenable to speak of an object which is different from both *sat* and *asat* as what is revealed by our cognition. The principle of "as the cognition, so the object" is to be accepted, and if it is not, then anything can be the content of any cognition. If that be the case, we can never be guided by our cognitions in our day-to-day life, and our life will come to a standstill. Since the Advaita explanation of the ontological status of avidyā in terms *sadasad-vilakṣaṇa* goes contrary to the evidence of our cognition, it has to be rejected. Rāmānuja has a dig at the Advaitin: he says that avidyā is, indeed, *anirvacanīya*, i.e. inexplicable, because there is no cognition in support of it (*pramāṇa-śūnyatvena anirvacanīyataiva syāt*).

The Advaitin accepts the principle that in our day-to-day life we are guided by our cognition with regard to the existence or non-existence of a thing. Also, he accepts the validity of the law of excluded middle which is based on the principle of exclusive disjunction. However, it is wrong to insist on the law of excluded middle where it does not hold good. If there is experiential evidence for the existence of a thing different from *sat* and *asat*, we cannot deny its existence on the basis of the law of excluded middle. Logic cannot legislate for experience; on the contrary, it is experience that decides the applicability or otherwise of a principle in a particular case. The nature of avidyā is such that it cannot be brought under the category of *sat* or of *asat*. Experience, which is another term for cognition, vouches for the existence of the third category of objects different from *sat* and *asat*. Consequently, it is wrong to argue by relying on the principle of exclusive disjunction that every object must be either *sat* or *asat* and that the existence of an object which is neither *sat* nor *asat* is inadmissible.

The critic argues that, instead of saying that avidyā is different from both real and non-real, it may be characterized as both real and non-real by formulating the criteria of real and non-real in a different way. The criteria as formulated by the critic are: (1) What is experienced is real (*pratīyamānatvāt sat*) and (2) what suffers contradiction is non-real (*bādhyamānatvāt asat*). Since avidyā is experienced, it is real; and since it is sublated, it is non-real. So in terms of these criteria, avidyā, the critic argues, may be characterized as of the nature of both real and non-real (*sad-asad-ākāram*).

This argument is untenable. First of all, there is no proving instance in support of the criterion that what is experienced or cognized is real.[22] This suggested criterion does not hold good in the case of Brahman because it is knowledge by its very nature, and is hence not what is cognized or experienced. Knowledge is different from the object of knowledge. What is knowledge by nature can never become an object of knowledge. Nor is it possible to apply the criterion to objects like pots. Far from accepting the reality of these objects, Advaita maintains that since these objects are cognized, they are *mithyā* or illusory. Secondly, the criterion that what is non-real (*asat*) suffers contradiction is wrong. There is no instance of negation of sky-flower as there is no prior cognition of it, which is necessary for its subsequent denial. Since the rope-snake is first cognized, it admits of subsequent denial. So it is wrong to say that what suffers contradiction is non-real; rather, one should say that what is never experienced or cognized is non-real, e.g. the sky-flower.

The critic joins issue with Advaita in a different way. He maintains that, though avidyā is different from the non-real, it is not so from the real (*asad-vailakṣaṇye satyapi na sadvailakṣaṇyam*). Just as we cognize the world and other objects as real, even so, the critic urges, we cognize avidyā as real. What is vouched for by our day-to-day experience can neither be ignored nor denied. Hence it is wrong to say that avidyā is different from both real and non-real.

In order to answer this objection it is necessary to invoke the distinction between the absolutely real (*pāramārthika-sat*) and the empirically real (*vyāvahārika-sat*). Brahman is absolutely real; it does not suffer contradiction at any time. On the contrary, any object which exists at one time and ceases to exist later on is not absolutely real. What is not absolutely real may nevertheless be empirically real. Avidyā is different from the real means it is different from the absolutely real. Advaita does admit that avidyā and the objects of the world which are experienced in our day-to-day experience are empirically real.[23] So the objection of the critic is beside the point as it does not touch the criterion of the real as formulated by Advaita.

The objection can be answered in another way. Being illusory, avidyā has no being or reality of its own. By erroneously ascribing reality to avidyā, we speak of it as if it is real in our day-to-day experience.[24] The Advaitin maintains that avidyā defies explanation in terms of the categories known to us. Avidyā cannot be different from Brahman, for in that case there would arise dualism which is flatly denied by scripture. Nor can it be identical with Brahman because no identity is possible between sentient Brahman and insentient avidyā. It cannot be both different and non-different from Brahman, because of contradiction. Further, since it is not caused by another object, it is not a composite entity made up of parts. But, as the cause of composite things, it cannot itself be devoid of parts.[25] This means that its nature cannot be determined in terms of the categories known to us, which is why it is said to be indeterminable (*anirvacanīya*) and also illusory (*mithyā*).

7. On the Evidence for the Positive Nature of Avidyā

According to Advaita, avidyā should not be viewed negatively as *jñāna-prāgabhāva*, i.e. antecedent non-existence of knowledge. It is positive (*bhāvarūpa*) since a negative entity cannot be the cause of anything. Avidyā not only conceals the real nature of Brahman, but projects the false universe as well. It is the material cause (*upādāna-kāraṇa*) of the pluralistic universe which we experience. Inasmuch as it does the work of concealment (*āvaraṇa*) and projection (*vikṣepa*), it must be positive. What is true of this primal ignorance (*mūlāvidyā*) is equally true of modal ignorance (*tūlāvidyā*) which conceals, for example, the real nature of a pot etc, which are empirical objects.

The Advaitin tries to establish the positive nature of avidyā by means of perception and inference, but not its existence. All of us, the Advaitin says, have direct perceptual experience of avidyā. For example, we say, "I am ignorant," "I don't know myself." Just as when I say, "I am happy," I have the direct experience of happiness, even so when I say, "I am ignorant" (*aham ajñaḥ*), I have the direct experience of avidyā. It is wrong to treat this as *jñānābhāva*. It is the general principle that knowledge of *abhāva* requires the prior knowledge of *pratiyogin* and *dharmin*. In the case of *jñānābhāva* relating to Brahman-Ātman, jñāna or knowledge is the *pratiyogin*; and the Self is the *dharmin*. If there is apprehension of jñāna as the *pratiyogin* and the Self as *dharmin*, there cannot be *jñānābhāva* and in the absence of such apprehension, one cannot at all speak of *jñānābhāva*. Such a difficulty, the Advaitin argues, will not arise if avidyā is treated as something positive.

By means of inference also it can be shown that avidyā is positive. The Advaitin gives the following inference:

> Pratijñā: *Pramāṇa-jñāna* is preceded by something else, which is different from its *prāgabhāva*, which hides the object of knowledge, which is terminated by knowledge, and which exists in the same place as knowledge.
>
> Hetu: Because knowledge possesses the property of illumining things not illumined before.
>
> *Dṛṣṭānta*: Just as the light of a lamp, which comes out first when lit in the dark, illumines things.

It may be noted that darkness (*tamas*) is not absence of light; but is something positive for the Advaitin. In the same way, avidyā also is something positive.

A brief explanation of the role of avidyā is necessary before answering the objections of Rāmānuja which come under *Pramāṇānupapatti*.[26] According to Advaita, one and the same avidyā is responsible for non-cognition in a few cases, for erroneous cognition in some cases, and for doubtful cognition in yet other cases. Non-cognition, erroneous cognition, and doubtful cognition—all these three are due to the work of avidyā. On superficial view, it may appear that only erroneous cognition (*anyathā-grahaṇa*, also called *viparyaya-jñāna*) is the result of ignorance but in fact even non-cognition (*agrahaṇa*) and doubtful cognition (*saṁśaya*) are due to ignorance. Precisely because one does not know exactly what is before oneself viz. whether it is a pillar or a man, that one has a doubtful cognition. Likewise, any failure to cognize is also due to ignorance exactly like wrong cognition. Advaita, therefore, maintains that the work of concealment, which is positive, cannot be done by a negative entity that is non-existent. If avidyā is explained negatively as absence or non-existence of knowledge, it cannot conceal the truth and project the false. Even the Logicians who are adepts in determining the nature of non-existence do not, as Sarvajñātman remarks,[27] assert that what is non-existent veils an object. In so far as avidyā does this work, it has to be viewed as something positive or existent.

We can drive home the point that avidyā is not mere absence of knowledge, but something positive, in yet another way. Advaita formulates the principle that concealment of the true nature of an object is the *sine qua non* for non-apprehension, mis-apprehension or doubt in respect of any object. An object which is not known at all is an object concealed totally by avidyā. If a little later it is known in a general way, but not in its specific nature or quality, we are still ignorant of its complete nature due to the veil of avidyā still not being fully lifted. If ignorance is nothing but absence of knowledge, when there is knowledge of an object in a general way, it should forthwith bring about the disappearance of ignorance. Ignorance, however, still persists even after knowing an object in a general way. And this proves, according to Sureśvara, that ignorance is something different from mere absence of knowledge, and it is this which is concealing the nature of an object, viz. it is the cause of non-cognition, or erroneous cognition, or doubt in respect of an object as the case may be.[28]

Rāmānuja maintains that the difficulty pointed out by the Advaitin with regard to interpreting avidyā as *jñāna-prāgabhāva* is present even if avidyā is explained as *bhāvarūpa*.[29] Rāmānuja asks: is Brahman-Ātman which is the locus as well as the content of avidyā (viewed as a positive entity) known or not known? If it is known, there is no room for avidyā also because the knowledge of Brahman-Ātman puts an end to avidyā. If it is not known, how can there be apprehension of avidyā because its apprehension requires the knowledge of its locus. Just as avidyā in the negative sense of "absence of knowledge" is not self-explanatory, even so avidyā in the positive sense is not self-explanatory. This point will become clear if we consider the different ways in which we can understand the meaning of *ajñāna*. The term "*ajñāna*", Rāmānuja says, can be understood in three ways. It may mean "absence of knowledge" (*jñānābhāva*), or "what is other than knowledge" (*tad-anyaḥ*), or "what is opposed to knowledge" (*tad-virodhī*).[30] In whatever way we construe the meaning, the term "*ajñāna*" presupposes "knowledge". It means that just as "*ajñāna*" in the sense of *jñānābhāva* presupposes something else, even so "*ajñāna*" viewed as a positive entity presupposes something else. The point which Rāmānuja wants to drive home is that the Advaitin should not make much fuss about the difficulty in the negative interpretation of avidyā. So Rāmānuja concludes that statements such as "I am ignorant", "I don't know myself", point to the absence of knowledge experienced by us.

Sureśvara's interpretation of the term "avidyā" is quite relevant in this connection. Sureśvara observes that the term "avidyā" must be explained in the same way as the word "*amitra*" is explained. When we speak of a person as *amitra*, we mean that he is other than, or opposed to, a friend. Similarly, the entity denoted by the word "avidyā" must be explained as something other than, or opposed to, knowledge. The word does not convey the sense of absence of knowledge.[31]

The experience of deep sleep also proves that avidyā is positive. A person recollects his experience of deep sleep by saying, "I did not know anything then." Recollection presupposes prior experience and in this case it can only be the recollection of the experience of ajñāna. The question now is whether *this ajñāna* experienced by him in deep sleep can be treated negatively as prior absence of knowledge (*jñānābhāva* or *jñāna-prāgabhāva*). The Advaitin's answer is in the negative. Generally speaking, knowledge of *abhāva* requires the knowledge of both the locus (*dharmin*) and the correlate (*pratiyogin*). One cannot speak of mere absence or non-existence with no reference to what is absent and where. Only with reference to both the pot (the correlate) and the ground (the locus), one can speak of the absence of the pot on the ground. Similarly, if one were to speak of "absence of knowledge" in deep sleep, it requires the knowledge of both the locus and the correlate at that time. Since the mind is wholly quiescent then, the person in the state of deep sleep cannot have the knowledge of both the locus and the correlate, which is necessary for the knowledge of "absence of knowledge". But yet one claims to know that he knew nothing. We have to therefore conclude, on the strength of the subsequent recollection in the waking state, that the person concerned had the knowledge or experience of avidyā which is quite different from absence or non-existence of knowledge.

If, according to Advaita, there is knowledge of avidyā in deep sleep, it amounts to saying that knowledge and ignorance co-exist at that time. But this, the critic argues, is untenable because the two are mutually opposed. This argument of the critic is without force. The word "knowledge" here may be understood in two senses. It may be understood either as knowledge which constitutes the essential nature of Brahman-Ātman (*svarūpa-jñāna*), or knowledge which arises through *avidyā-vṛtti*. We have already stated that *svarūpa-jñāna* which reveals avidyā is not opposed to it. In deep sleep there is avidyā as well as *avidyā-vṛtti*. Avidyā, which is the adjunct of the Self of deep sleep, is the causal condition of the mind. It is through *avidyā-vṛtti* that *prājña*, which is the name given to the Self of deep sleep, experiences both ignorance and happiness.[32] When deep sleep is followed by the waking state, the Self associated with the mind, which is only avidyā in the effect-form, recollects its previous experience of both ignorance and happiness. There is, therefore, no inconsistency in the co-existence of knowledge and ignorance in deep sleep.

There is yet another reason why avidyā is positive and is hence different from prior absence of knowledge. Knowledge destroys ignorance. If avidyā is nothing but the prior non-existence of knowledge, then knowledge can never destroy it because knowledge can arise only after the termination of its prior non-existence. When there is knowledge, there is no prior non-existence of knowledge; and when there is prior non-existence of knowledge, there is no knowledge. Hence the two cannot be related as the destroyer and the destroyed. However, since knowledge destroys ignorance, the latter should not be viewed negatively as prior non-existence of knowledge.[33]

Further, the prior absence of knowledge is never an object of direct perceptual experience. It is what we have to infer from the knowledge that arises subsequently.[34] If knowledge arises now, it implies that prior to its arising it was non-existent. Since the prior absence of knowledge has to be inferred from the subsequent rise of knowledge, it cannot be directly experienced. Inasmuch as avidyā is directly experienced, it must be different from the prior absence of knowledge. Let us consider this issue in another way to show why avidyā should not be understood as *jñāna-prāgabhāva*. What is the nature of the knowledge whose prior non-existence is meant here? Is it knowledge-in-general (*jñāna-sāmānya*)? Or, is it some specific knowledge (*jñāna-viśeṣa*)? Knowledge-in-general is knowledge which is undifferentiated, indeterminate, and non-relational, and so it is no other than Brahman which is eternal. What is eternal can never be absent at any time. Hence *jñāna-prāgabhāva* in the sense of the prior non-existence of knowledge-in-general is untenable.[35] The other alternative fares no better. When knowledge arises, it is specific and relational—specific because we are able to differentiate it as such-and-such from other cases of knowledge, and relational because it has a transcendent object to which it is related. But no one has direct access to prior non-existence of specific knowledge; that is, one does not directly experience it as such.[36] One does not, for instance, directly experience the prior non-existence of a pot or a table. Considering that avidyā is directly experienced while *jñāna-prāgabhāva* is not, it is wrong to treat avidyā negatively as prior absence of knowledge.

Since primal avidyā is removable by Brahman-knowledge, it has an end, and that which has an end must also have a beginning. Scripture speaks of the beginning of avidyā when it says that māyā-avidyā comes into existence without being caused by anything else.[37] What is positive or existent alone has a beginning and an end. It is absurd, says Sureśvara, to speak of either a beginning or an end of a negative entity. The Nyāya view that *prāgabhāva*, though without a beginning, has an end, and that *pradhvaṁsābhāva* which has a beginning has no end is not acceptable to the Advaitin who objects to associating these alleged negative entities with a certain act (*kriyā*) and a quality (*guṇa*)—the act of destruction and the quality of impermanence in the case of *prāgabhāva*, and the act of origination and the quality of permanence in the case of *pradhvaṁsābhāva*. One can speak not only of the origination or destruction, but also of a certain quality, of a pot which is positive or existent. But it is absurd to speak of origination or destruction of non-existence (*abhāva*). Nor can any quality be associated with it.[38] Since avidyā has both a beginning and an end and also is of the nature of the three guṇas (*triguṇātmaka*), it is not negative, but something positive or existent. Strictly speaking, there is no justification for accepting the existence of a negative entity. What is called *abhāva*, Sureśvara says, is only in imagination (*kalpanā-mātram*). "It is unreal like a stone-son."[39] It has no existence whatsoever. If so, it is wrong to treat avidyā which is directly experienced as a negative entity.

The ultimate position of Advaita is that avidyā cannot be characterized even as something positive or existent (*bhāvarūpa*). Strictly speaking, avidyā is illusory (*mithyā-rūpa*). If it is a truly positive or existent like Brahman, it cannot be negated; and if it is non-existent like a sky-flower, it cannot be cognized or experienced. But since it is both cognized and negated like a rope-serpent, it is an illusory appearance. If, from the relative standpoint of *vyavahāra*, we characterize it as *bhāvarūpa*, it is to suggest that what causes the appearance of the world of diversity cannot be negative. So long as our business of life continues, avidyā exists; consequently we speak of it as existent, though it is different from both the existent and the non-existent.[40]

Let us now consider the inference given by the Advaitin to prove that avidyā is positive. Rāmānuja says that the inference formulated by the Advaitin commits the fallacy of *viruddha* or contradictory middle.[41] The *hetu* given in the argument is a contradictory one because it proves what is not desired to be proved, but something else. The Advaitin holds that there is only one *ajñāna* which conceals Brahman-Ātman and which has, therefore, Brahman-Ātman as its content; and this *ajñāna* which he intends to prove may be called *brahma-viṣayaka-ajñāna*. But what he proves through the *hetu* is not this *ajñāna*, but a different *ajñāna*. Let us say: we are ignorant of *ajñāna* as something positive; and this ignorance whose content is *ajñāna* is now proved in this inference. So what is proved is *ajñāna-viṣayaka-ajñāna* which is different from *brahma-viṣayaka-ajñāna.*[42] So Rāmānuja says that the *hetu* is contradictory because, without proving what is desired to be proved, it proves some other *ajñāna.* The *hetu* is also *anaikāntika*, because it is not uniformly related to the *sādhya.*

These fallacies apart, there is another difficulty. What will happen when *ajñāna* is proved through inference? The moment *pramāṇa-jñāna* is obtained through inference, there will be no more *ajñāna* because *pramāṇa-jñāna* will destroy *ajñāna.* If so, Rāmānuja asks, how can the Self be the witness of *ajñāna*? Further, the example cited by the Advaitin in the inferential argument is defective because the example, i.e. the light of a lamp, has no proving power (*sādhana-vikala*). It is well-known that knowledge alone has the power of illumi-nation. But the light of a lamp does not by itself have the power of revealing things. It is no doubt useful, like a sense organ, for knowing things. Nevertheless, its role, like that of a sense organ, is an auxiliary one. Since knowledge alone reveals things not known before, the example of the light of a lamp adduced by the Advaitin is unsound. Therefore, the Advaitin has not proved by means of inference that avidyā is a positive entity.

It is necessary at this stage to clarify two points before dealing with the objection to the inference. The first is about the purpose of inference, and the second relates to the question whether avidyā is one or many. The question about the purpose of inference is whether it is to prove the existence of avidyā or anything else. It is not to prove existence because ignorance is a matter of common experience not requiring any proof. Avidyā is *prasiddha*, i.e. *anubhava-siddha.* Equally well known and not requiring proof are its products like the world. Śaṅkara says that whatever is apprehended by any pramāṇa like perception, etc. exists, and what is not so apprehended does not exist.[43] It therefore follows that what does not exist at all (*asat*) like the sky-flower is not grasped by anyone anywhere by any pramāṇa. Śaṅkara declares that this world of plurality, the realm of our daily business of life, is guaranteed by all the pramāṇas and it can never be denied without knowing another reality of a higher order, for a general principle holds good in the absence of a contrary instance.[44] The Advaitin denies the absolute reality of the world, but not its empirical reality which is vouchsafed by pramāṇas. What is *anubhava-siddha* does not require to be proved by inference and hence the inference stated earlier is for proving only the positive nature (*bhāva-rūpatva*) of avidyā and not for proving its existence. To attempt to prove the existence of universally experienced avidyā by inference is as absurd as it is unnecessary.

Let us now clarify the second point. Though avidyā is one it is distinguished as two for the purpose of analysis as *mūlāvidyā* and *tūlāvidyā*, i.e. primal ignorance and modal ignorance. The example of ether (*ākāśa*) will help us to understand this distinction. Even though ether is one, we still make a distinction between infinite ether (*mahākāśa*) and pot-enclosed-ether (*ghaṭākāśa*). The pot-enclosed-ether, is limited because the pots are finite and limited objects and hence such ether is manifold. According to Advaita, the scope of twofold ignorance is determined by the object to which it is related. While the function of primal ignorance centres round Brahman-Ātman, that of modal ignorance is related to empirical objects. Since empirical objects are many, modal ignorance is also viewed as many. The modal ignorance relating to a particular object gets removed by the pramāṇa-generated-knowledge of that object. This pramāṇa-generated-knowledge is *vṛtti-jñāna*, i.e. modal cognition. Empirical objects are manifold; modal ignorance concealing them is manifold and modal cognitions are also manifold. On the basis of the distinction between *mūlāvidyā* and *tūlāvidyā*, the Advaitin argues that the removal of the modal ignorance relating to any empirical object does not amount to the removal of the primal ignorance relating to Brahman-Ātman. Thus, while holding that avidyā is one, the Advaitin also maintains that avidyā is basically twofold as *mūlāvidya* and *tūlāvidya*.[45]

Ajñāna does the work of concealment, and the object concealed by it may be an empirical object like a rope, or the absolute reality, viz. Brahman-Ātman. Therefore, Rāmānuja's criticism of the inference that without establishing the positive nature of *brahma-viṣayaka-ajñāna*, it proves a different ajñāna, which is identified as *ajñāna-viṣayaka-ajñāna*, is untenable. In other words, it is not the case that the *hetu* is contradictory; nor is it *anaikāntika*.

Further, the concept of *ajñāna-viṣayaka-ajñāna* is not acceptable to the Advaitin, because it presupposes the concealment of *ajñāna,* which is absurd. Consider the case of a pot which I am not able to see in darkness. Here, I am not able to see the pot because it remains concealed by darkness; and when the darkness is removed by light, I see the pot. It, therefore, makes sense to speak about the concealment of the pot by ignorance and the removal of this concealment by knowledge. The case of *ajñāna* is quite different from that of the pot. If *ajñāna* does not show its presence, it is not because of its concealment by something else but because it is non-shinning, non-revealing, by its very nature (*svābhāvika eva tasya aprakāśaḥ*). In this respect, it is like darkness which does not shine and reveal its existence, even though it is not concealed by something else. Darkness conceals the existence of a pot; but darkness, we do not say, is concealed by another darkness.[46] So, the concept of *ajñāna-viṣayaka-ajñāna* presupposes the concealment of *ajñāna* by another *ajñāna*, which is absurd. This line of argument in which we bring in a second ajñāna as the concealer of the first will necessitate the postulation of a third ajñāna, and so on leading to infinite regress.

There is also another difficulty connected with the concept of *ajñāna-viṣayaka-ajñāna*. The critic could bring in the concept of *ajñāna-viṣayaka-ajñāna* only if the Advaitin were to say that *pramāṇa-jñāna* illumines *ajñāna* which remains concealed by another *ajñāna*; but he does not hold this view. On the contrary, he maintains that *pramāṇa-jñāna* destroys ignorance. Just as one perceives darkness through the functioning of the visual sense without requiring light, even so one experiences *ajñāna* through the Witness-self (*sākṣin*) without requiring *pramāṇa-jñāna*. It is necessary to emphasize that, according to Advaita, *ajñāna* is directly revealed by the Witness-self. Finally, the critic's objection against the example of the light of a lamp is puerile. It is common practice (*loka-prasiddhi*) to compare knowledge to light. Just as we say that the light of a lamp reveals objects, even so we say that knowledge generated by a pramāṇa reveals objects. The scriptural text too explains the work of light, taking note of what we say in our day-to-day experience. It is no doubt true that in the final analysis we know things through knowledge and that the senses, light, etc. are the necessary auxiliaries to the pramāṇa-generated-knowledge and there is no disagreement with Rāmānuja on this point.

8. On the Removability of Avidyā

In the sixth objection called *nivartaka-anupapatti*,[47] Rāmānuja maintains that the Advaita explanation of the removability of avidyā is untenable. According to Advaita, avidyā, though beginningless (*anādi*), has an end. But what removes avidyā? It is well-known that knowledge is the antidote to ignorance. What is required for the removal of avidyā is the knowledge of Brahman as *nirviśeṣa*. The Advaitin claims that śruti teaches the cessation of avidyā as taking place only from the knowledge of Nirviśeṣa-Brahman.

The argument of the Advaitin, according to Rāmānuja, proceeds on the assumption that Brahman is *nirviśeṣa* while that is not the truth because there is no pramāṇa in support of it. Rāmānuja maintains that perception, inference, and verbal testimony prove only a differentiated entity, and not one devoid of all difference.[48] For him even in *nirvikalpaka-pratyakṣa*, the object is perceived as such-and-such, i.e. as a differentiated entity. He shows that there is no justification for the claim that the object of *nirvikalpaka-pratyakṣa* is an undifferentiated one whereas that of *savikalpaka-pratyakṣa* is differentiated. In both, we perceive only a differentiated object. However, this does not mean that there is no distinction between the two kinds of perception for Rāmānuja. While the knowledge of the class feature is not possible at the stage of *nirvikalpaka-pratyakṣa*, it is possible in the other. Further, the object known through inference is bound to be a differentiated one. Then Rāmānuja moves on to show that even the object known through śabda is *saviśeṣa.* A sentence conveys a differentiated sense and this is true of both scriptural and secular sentences.

The above argument that perception, inference and verbal testimony do not prove the existence of an object free from distinctions is a general one. Rāmānuja cites several scriptural texts to show that they purport to teach that Brahman is *saviśeṣa*. Consider the *Śvetāśvatara* text, 3.8, which says: "I know the supreme Person of sun-like colour beyond darkness. Only by knowing him does one pass over death. There is no other path for going there." According to Rāmānuja, scriptural texts like this clearly show that Brahman is *saviśesa*. Negative texts which say that Brahman is *nirguṇa* convey the sense that Brahman is free from the qualities of *prakṛti* and not that it is devoid of all qualities. Again, the major text, "*tat tvam asi*," does not convey the sense of the oneness of a non-differentiated entity. The grammatical co-ordination (*sāmānādhikaraṇya*) between the two words "*tat*" and "*tvam*" is intended to convey the sense of one entity qualified by two aspects (*prakāradvaya-viśiṣṭa-ekavastu*). This text, says Rāmānuja, denotes Brahman which is not only the cause of the world, but which has also the individual souls as its body (*jīva-śarīraka-jagat-kāraṇa-brahman*). So all the scriptural texts teach that Brahman is *saviśeṣa*. Since Brahman as taught by scripture is *saviśeṣa*, it is wrong to say that avidyā can be removed by getting the knowledge of Brahman as *nirviśesa*.

It is not necessary for us to examine Rāmānuja's general argument. Our immediate concern is only with Brahman which is *nirguṇa* and defending it against Rāmānuja's contention that there is no pramāṇa which proves that Brahman is *nirguṇa*

First, let us consider the evidence of perception. The Advaitin does not deny that we get the knowledge of an object which is *saviśeṣa* through perception. What he claims is that perception also reveals the existence of *nirviśeṣa-vastu*. In support of his claim, the Advaitin cites the case of deep sleep as the evidence for Brahman-Ātman being *nirviśeṣa*. A person who recollects his deep sleep experience says that he was not aware of anything, subjective or objective, and that he was not aware of even himself as such-and-such at that time. Recollection presupposes the prior experience of what is recollected. What is experienced in deep sleep is the bare Self or consciousness devoid of distinctions. Though the Self or consciousness conditioned by the mind and the senses appears to be a differentiated entity in the waking and dream states, it is left alone untouched by the subject-object relation because of the absence of the functioning of the mind. By its very nature, Brahman-Ātman is *nirviśeṣa*, but it appears to be *saviśeṣa* because of the adjunct, i.e. mind and the senses, with which it is associated in the waking and dream states.[49] The *nirviśeṣa* nature of the Self is manifest in deep sleep, which is perceptual experience. The perceptual experience of deep sleep given to every one of us confirms the testimony of the scriptural text which says that the Self is "one only without a second" highlighting the absence of the three kinds of difference, *sajātīya-*, *vijātīya-*, and *svagata-bheda* in the Self.

The explanation of the distinction between *nirvikalpaka* and *savikalpaka* perception given by Rāmānuja is unacceptable. Rāmāmuja claims that the object of both indeterminate perception (*nirvikalpaka-pratyakṣa*) and determinate perception (*savikalpaka-pratyakṣa*) is *saviśeṣa*. What, then, is the difference between the two kinds of perception? While the generic feature of the object is apprehended in determinate perception, it is not perceived in indeterminate perception.[50] The Advaitin rejects Rāmānuja's explanation of the distinction between the two kinds of perception. The Advaitin maintains that perceptual knowledge is called *nirvikalpaka* on the basis of the object known through perception. If the object known involves distinctions (*vikalpa*), then the perceptual knowledge of which it is the content is termed *savikalpaka*. If the object known is free from distinction (*nirvikalpa*), then the resulting knowledge is called *nirvikalpaka*. So, if we consider the connotation of the terms "*vikalpa*" and "*nirvikalpa*", we will understand why we call one *nirvikalpaka* and the other *savikalpaka*. To say that the object apprehended for the first time by perception is *saviśeṣa* and then call this initial percep-tion *nirvikalpaka-pratyakṣa* is a contradiction in terms. If the object perceived is *saviśeṣa*, then the perception is necessarily *savikalpaka*; and if the perception is treated as *nirvikalpaka*, then its object cannot be *saviśeṣa*.[51]

The Advaitin claims that it is possible to establish the existence of *nirviśeṣa-vastu* by means of inference. Consider the following argument which proves that Brahman is *nirviśeṣa*:

> Brahman-Ātman is *nirviśeṣa*.
> Because it is experienced without qualities and distinctions in *suṣupti*.
> Whatever is experienced without qualities and distinctions is *nirviśeṣa*, pot being the negative example (*vyatireka-dṛṣṭānta*).

Rāmānuja argues that *śabda* by its very nature conveys only the knowledge of a differentiated entity. He employs two kinds of argument. There is first a general argument on the nature of *śabda* as a source of knowledge. This is followed by a specific argument in the form of a detailed examination of some of the scriptural texts in support of the view that Brahman, the highest reality, is *nirviśeṣa*. His general argument is as follows: A word which conveys some meaning consists of a stem (*prakṛti*) and a suffix (*pratyaya*). Since the meanings of the stem and the suffix are different, an individual word consisting of these two conveys a relational meaning (*viśiṣṭārtha*). It follows that a sentence which consists of a group of such words must necessarily convey a relational sense. If so, neither a word nor a sentence is capable of denoting an object which is *nirviśeṣa*.[52] This argument, the Advaitin maintains, does not have any force because it is an accepted principle that for ascertaining the meaning of a word or a sentence we have to take into consideration the intention (*tātparya*) of the speaker who utters the word or the sentence, or the context in which it occurs when the speaker is not known. It may be the case that sometimes a relational sense is conveyed, and at other times a non-relational sense. It all depends on what is intended to be conveyed. There is no rule that the purport of a word or a sentence must always be in a relational sense (*saṁsṛṣṭārtha* or *viśiṣṭārtha*). For example, when a father admonishes his son who eats all kinds of food provided by his friend of bad character saying, "You may as well eat poison," we have to construe the meaning of the sentence not literally, because it is not at all the intention of the father that his son should eat poison. He just means that his son should not eat junk food. Further, while the sentence "This flower is red" conveys a relational sense, the sentence "This is that Devadatta" conveys a non-relational sense, i.e. the sense of identity because that is the intended meaning.[53]

Rāmānuja's specific argument which is focused on the scriptural texts is not acceptable to the Advaitin. Extending the above principle of hermeneutics to the scriptural texts, the Advaitin argues that the sentence "*satyam jñānam anantam brahma*" conveys the idea that Brahman is *nirviśeṣa*[54] and the *mahāvākyas* of the Upaniṣads such as "That thou art", "I am Brahman", etc. convey the sense of non-difference between Brahman and the jīva i.e. the oneness or undifferentiated nature of Brahman-Ātman. To sum up: Brahman-Ātman is *nirviśeṣa*, and it is the knowledge of Brahman-Ātman that destroys *avidyā*, the root-cause of the bondage of the jīva.

9. On the Attainment of Liberation

Is the Advaita explanation of the attainment of *mukti* tenable? Rāmānuja's answer is "no". The last major objection called *nivṛttyanupapatti* brings out the difficulties as seen by Rāmānuja in the Advaita explanation of the attainment of *mukti*.[55]

He argues that the Advaitin develops his theory on the false assumption that bondage is unreal, something false (*mithyā*), avidyā being the cause of bondage. Since avidyā is mithyā, bondage cannot but be mithyā. So the Advaitin says that all that is required for the removal of bondage is knowledge of Brahman-Ātman. When this saving knowledge arises, avidyā is destroyed; and with its destruction bondage is also removed. This entire argument is fallacious according to Rāmānuja. He says that bondage which consists of the experience of pleasure and pain arising from the connection of the self with bodies of various kinds cannot be dismissed as unreal since it is real (*paramārtha*). This real thing cannot be removed by knowledge. Hence bondage is destroyed only through the grace of the Lord and it is obtained only by *bhakti* or *upāsanā*.

Secondly, the solution suggested by the Advaitin is like a remedy which aggravates the disease instead of curing it. The Advaitin says that the knowledge of the oneness of reality removes bondage. This is nothing but a pious wish because the alleged knowledge of the oneness of reality (*aikya-jñāna*) is itself false. When the supreme reality is *saviśeṣa*, to think of it as *nirviśeṣa* is false exactly like thinking of identity of jīva and Brahman which is not there. Such false knowledge will only strengthen the knot of bondage and not loosen it.

There is another difficulty. What is the ontological status of the "bondage-terminating" knowledge (*nivartaka-jñāna*)? Since everything other than Brahman is mithyā, the Advaitin holds this saving knowledge also to be mithyā. But, if it is mithyā, it must also be removed and this can be done only by searching for another knowledge which, again, also must be removed. Thus the search ends in infinite regress (*anavasthā*). We have, therefore, to tackle the problem of the removal of bondage in an entirely different way, and not in the way suggested by the Advaitin.

It is argued by the Advaitin that this "bondage-terminating" knowledge, after destroying all kinds of duality, destroys itself and disappears of its own accord. This argument, Rāmānuja says, is not convincing. Since the nature, origination and disappearance of this knowledge are all fictitious (*kālpanika*), caused by avidyā, it is only proper to find out some other agency capable of destroying avidyā. The Advaitin cannot solve the difficulty about the removal of "terminating knowledge" by invoking the nature of Brahman. Brahman which is of the nature of self-luminous knowledge is ever-existent. If so, Rāmānuja asks, how can a knowledge which is false originate at all when Brahman-knowledge which is real is ever-present?

The Advaita explanation is open to criticism from another point of view also. Rāmānuja asks the question: who has this "bondage-terminating" knowledge which negates everything other than Brahman? Does anyone other than Brahman, e.g. the jīva, possess this knowledge? Or does Brahman itself possess this knowledge? Rāmānuja observes that the first alternative is not possible. Since the Advaitin claims that everything other than Brahman is false, the one who has this knowledge, being different from Brahman, must be fictitious or false, and hence be negated. What is to be negated by the "terminating knowledge" cannot at the same time be the subject of that knowledge (*nivartaka-jñāna-karmatvāt-tatkartṛtva anupapatteḥ*). Further, the one who has this knowledge will not wish for one's own destruction by means of the knowledge of which he is the subject.

The second alternative fares no better. If it be said that Brahman itself is the knower, i.e. one who has this "bondage-terminating" knowledge, Rāmānuja suggests two possibilities for consideration in that connection. Is it the very nature (*svarūpa*) of Brahman to be the knower? Or is it something fictitious wrongly superimposed on Brahman (*adhyasta*)? The second possibility is not helpful to the Advaitin. While the "terminating knowledge" negates everything, it cannot negate the knower or the subject of that very knowledge. It means that the knower of this knowledge who is an instance of adhyāsa, and avidyā which is the cause of that adhyāsa, remain untouched by the "terminating knowledge". If it be said that they can be removed by another terminating knowledge (*nivartaka-jñānāntaram*), it will again lead to infinite regress. Nor can the Advaitin accept the second possibility. The Advaitin holds the view that Brahman by its very nature is knowledge and not the knower. Hence the question, "who has the bondage-terminating knowledge?" cannot be satisfactorily answered by the Advaitin.

To Advaita, the distinction between *vyāvahārika* and *pāramārthika* is important. In fact, the distinction between Nirguṇa-Brahman and Saguṇa-Brahman, the distinction between Brahman and jīva, the distinction between Īśvara and jīva—all these distinctions which are due to māyā-avidyā are meaningful only on the basis of the distinction between *vyāvahārika* and *pāramārthika*. The *vyāvahārika* state is empirically real; it is not an airy nothing. Though the jīva in its essential nature is non-different from Brahman, the empirical state in which it is caught is real, and so its bondage involving the triple characteristics of *jñātṛatva*, *kartṛtva*, and *bhoktṛtva* is also real. The Advaitin does not say that bondage is unreal, something false. If bondage were to be real, then it could not be removed because what is real is eternal and what is eternal can never be removed. So all the objections which Rāmānuja brings in under *nivṛttyanupapatti* need to be viewed in the context of the distinction between *vyāvahārika* and *pāramārthika*; and this distinction has been worked out on the basis of *adhyāsa*. A critic like Rāmānuja who refuses to accept the theory of *adhyāsya* with all the consequences arising therefrom functions in an entirely different framework; and so his criticisms of Advaita are intelligible only when viewed from the perspective of his framework.

The different objections which Rāmānuja has raised against the Advaita doctrine of avidyā must be considered in the context of the basic thesis of Advaita. The Advaitin says that Brahman-Ātman is knowledge by its very nature and that it is one and non-dual. If so, wherefrom does avidyā operate? How can it conceal the nature of Brahman which is ever-existent and ever-shining? How can its nature be explained? How can it be credited with a peculiar ontological status different from the real and the unreal? How can it be said to be something positive? How can it be removed? What removes it? According to Rāmānuja, the Advaitin has no satisfactory answer to any of these questions with reference to avidyā. We have seen in the preceding pages how best the Advaitins have tried to formulate answers to all these questions.

The issue here is not whether they can be answered or not. What is important for a student of philosophy is the question itself—the manner in which the question is raised and the substance of the question. The role of a critic is as important as the role of an expounder of a system. Rāmānuja plays both these roles with great distinction drawing his inspiration from *ubhaya-vedānta*. A critic who indulges in criticism just for the sake of criticism is not helpful to anyone. But a critic who helps others to develop an insight into the problem is, indeed, constructive. Rāmānuja is a constructive critic. He takes us to the root of the problem which is reviewed and examined, and helps us to look at it in the larger context of the system as a whole. A student of Advaita will gain an insight into his own system by a careful study of Rāmānuja's objections against Advaita as a whole.

NOTES

1. See Uttamur Viraraghavacharya, ed. *Śrībhāṣya* with the commentary, *Bhāṣyārtha-darpaṇa* (hereafter *ŚBBD*), Ubhaya Vedānta Granthamālā, Madras, 1963, Part I, p. 115.
2. *ŚBBD*, pp. 114 - 15.
3. *ŚBBD*, p. 114.
4. Rāmarāyakavi, *Śrī Śaṅkarāśaṅkara-bhāṣya-vimarśaḥ* (hereafter *ŚŚBV*), Guntur, 1953, p. 278.
5. *ŚŚBV*, p. 279: *nitya-jñānasya-brahmaṇaḥ anitya-vṛttijñāna-sadbhāvāt.*
6. Ibid.
7. Ibid., p. 282.
8. See Madhusūdana Sarasvatī, *Advaitasiddhi*, Nirnayasagar Press, Bombay, 1917, p. 585.
9. *ŚBBD*, p. 115.
10. *ŚŚBV*, p. 279: *brahmaṇas-tirodhānaṁ nāma asti bhāti iti vyavahāra aviṣayatvāpattiḥ.*
11. Ibid., p. 280: *yadajñānaṁ yena ajñānena viṣayīkṛtaṁ yadvṛttijñānaṁ yacca tena viṣayīkṛtaṁ tatsarvaṁ vastusāmānyena brahma abhāsyateva.*
12. *ŚBBD*, p. 123: *brahmasvarūpa-tirodhānahetubhūtam etad-ajñānaṁ svayam anubhūtaṁ sat brahma tiraskaroti, brahma tiraskṛtya svayaṁ tad-anubhava-viṣayo bhavati iti anyonyāśrayaṇam.*

13. *ŚŚBV*, p. 304: *brahmāvṛtya sthitameva tadajñānaṁ jīvena anubhūyata iti anyonyāśrayābhāvāt.*
14. *ŚBBD*, pp. 115-16.
15. See *ŚŚBV*, p. 281.
16. Gauḍapāda, *Māṇḍūkya-kārikā*, 1.16; also 4. 58: *sā ca māyā na vidyate.*
17. *Nṛsiṁhapūrvatāpinyupaniṣad*, 9.3.
18. *na tasya kāryaṁ karaṇaṁ ca vidyate.*
19. *ŚŚBV*, p. 283: "*tacca kāraṇaṁ vastu śaktameva bhavitumarhati, na aśaktikam; aśaktasya loke kāraṇatva adarśanāt. sā ca akāraṇaniṣṭhā śaktiḥ kāryagamyeti kṛtvā, kāryābhāve śaktyabhāva eva. evam abhāva pratiyogitvāt śaktiḥ anityaiva iti adhyastaiva.*"
20. *ŚBBD*, p. 116.
21. *sarvaṁ hi vastujātam pratīti-vyavasthāpyam.*
22. *ŚŚBV*, p. 287: *yat sat tat pratīyate ityatra dṛṣṭāntābhāvāt.*
23. Ibid., p. 288: *ajñānādeḥ pāramārthika-sattvābhāvāt asmābhiḥ sadvailakṣaṇyam ucyate, na tu vyāvhārika-sattvābhāva.*
24. Ibid., p. 288: *kāraṇa-brahma-sattāyāḥ kārye ajñānādau anugamādeva ajñānaṁ sadityādi-vyavahāraḥ, svatastu ajñānādeḥ sattvaṁ neti kṛttvā ajñānādeḥ sad-vailakṣaṇyam-uktam.*
25. See Sureśvara's *Mānasollāsa*, vv. 13-15.
26. *ŚBBD*, pp. 116-117.
27. See his *Saṅkṣepa-śārīraka*, 1.320: *na abhāvam-āvaraṇam āhuḥ abhāvaśauṇḍāḥ.*
28. See his *Naiṣkarmya-siddhi*, 3.7 and Jñānottama's commentary thereon.
29. *ŚBBD*, p.121: *yastu jñāna-prāgabhāva-viṣayatve virodhaḥ uktaḥ, sa hi bhāvarūpājñāne'pi tulyaḥ.*
30. Ibid., p. 122.
31. See R. Balasubramanian, ed. *Taittirīyopaniṣad-bhāṣya-vārtika of Sureśvara*, University of Madras, Madras, 1984, 2.179, p. 356.
32. *ŚŚBV*, p. 313: *suptau ca antaḥkaraṇa-vṛttir-nāstyeva. avidyā-vṛttireva asti, tasyāśca ajñāne satyeva sthitir-yukteti.*
33. See Sarvajñātman, *Saṅkṣepa-śārīraka*, 3.3. *na jñānāt prāgabhāva-kṣaya iti ghaṭate tatkṣaye tatprasūteḥ.*
34. *ŚŚBV*, p. 293: *jñānarūpa-kārya-kalpyasya jñānaprāgabhāvasya-anubhava-viṣayava ayogāt.*
35. Ibid., p. 293: *jñāna-sāmānyasya caitanya-rūpatvena tatprāgabhāva ayogāt.*
36. Ibid., p. 293: *jñāna-prāgabhāvānāṁ ca jñānaviśeṣa utpatteḥ prāg-vivicya anubhava ayogāt.*
37. See note (17).

38. Sureśvara, *Taittirīyopaniṣad-bhāṣya-vārtika*, op.cit., 1.31, p. 224.
39. Ibid., 1.32, p. 225.
40. *ŚŚBV*, p. 319.
41. *ŚBBD*, p. 126.
42. Viraraghavacharya in his commentary explains *anabhimata ajñānāntara* mentioned by Rāmānuja as *ajñāna-viṣayaka-ajñānāntara*.
43. See Śaṅkara's commenary on the *Brahma-sūtra*, 2.2.28.
44. Ibid., 2.2.31: *na hi ayaṁ sarva-pramāṇa-siddho loka-vyavahāraḥ anyattattvam anadhigamya śakyate apahnotum; apavādābhāve utsarga-prasiddheḥ.*
45. *ŚŚBV*, p. 296: *ajñānaṁ dvividhaṁ, mūlājñānam, tūlājñānam iti; tatra mūlājñānameva kāraṇabhūtam ekaṁ ca, tūlājñānaṁ tu anekavidham pratipuruṣam nidrādi bhedāt iti. tasmāt kāryabhūtaṁ kāraṇabhūtaṁ ca ajñānam bhāvarūpameva, na abhāvarūpam, abhāvasya nirupākhyasya kāryatva-kāraṇatva-rūpa-dharma ayogāt.*
46. Ibid., p. 315: *ajñānena āvṛtattvāt andhakāreṇeva ghaṭo na prakāśate. dīpena andhakārasyeva jñānena ajñānasya nāśe sati tu prakāśate. ajñānaṁ tu naivaṁ kenacid-āvṛtattvāt na prakāśate, kintu svābhāvika eva tasya aprakāśaḥ. yathā andhakāro anyena anāvṛto'pi svata eva na prakāśate; na hi ghaṭo'ndhakāreṇeva andhakāro' nyena āvṛta iti vaktuṁ śakyate.*
47. *ŚBBD*, pp. 145-49.
48. Ibid., p. 52: *ataḥ pratyakṣasya saviśeṣa-viṣayatvena pratyakṣādi-dṛṣṭasambandha-viśiṣṭaviṣayatvāt anumānamapi saviśeṣa-viṣayameva.*
49. *ŚŚBV*, pp. 30-40.
50. *ŚBBD*, p. 51.
51. *ŚŚBV*, p. 33.
52. *ŚBBD*, p. 50.
53. *ŚŚBV*, p.35.
54. Ibid., p. 157.
55. *ŚBBD*, pp. 159-60.

2

सप्तविधानुपपत्तिसमीक्षा

V.R. Kalyanasundara Sastri

अस्यां संगोष्ठ्यां सप्तविधानुपपत्तिसमीक्षेति विषयनिर्देशो मम कृतः। विषयस्यास्य श्रवणेनासञ्जातपुत्रनामकरणन्याय एव मम स्मृतिपथमारोहति। इयमनुपपत्तिरद्वैतिनामुपरि विशिष्टाद्वैतिभिः प्रदर्श्यते। परमार्थदशायां न काप्यनुपपत्तिः। अपरमार्थदशायां सर्वस्याप्युपपत्तिरिति पूर्वमेव समाहितत्वात् पूर्वाचार्यैः। विषयेऽस्मिन् विद्यारण्यस्वामिभिः पञ्चदश्यामेवमुक्तम् -

कूटस्थमनुपद्रुत्य करोति जगदादिकम् ।
दुर्घटैकविधायिन्यां मायायां किं नु दुष्करम् ॥ ६.१३४

प्रसरन्ति हि चोद्यानि जगद्वस्तुत्ववादिषु।
न चोदनीयं मायायां तस्याश्चोद्यैकरूपतः॥ ६.१३७

विस्मयैकशरीराया मायायाश्चोद्यरूपतः।
अन्वेष्यः परिहारोऽस्याः बुद्धिमद्भिः प्रयत्नतः॥ ६.१३९

अचिन्त्याः खलु ये भावाः न तांस्तर्केषु योजयेत्।
अचिन्त्यरचनारूपं मनसापि जगत्खलु॥ ६.१५०

स्वप्रकाशे कुतोऽविद्या तां विना कथमावृतिः।
इत्यादि तर्कजालानि स्वानुभूतिर्ग्रसत्यसौ॥ ६.१२७

स्वानुभूतावविश्वासे तर्कस्याप्यनवस्थितेः ।
कथं वा तार्किकम्मन्यः तत्त्वनिश्चयमाप्नुयात् ॥ ६.२९

अमुं विषयमधिकृत्य यद्यपि वक्तव्यं बहु वर्तते, तथापि सङ्गोष्ठीनियममपेक्ष्य यथाभानमधस्तात् किञ्चिल्लिख्यते।

श्रीशङ्कररामानुजमध्वाचार्या अवातरन्नत्र ।
ये किल सोपानततिं निरमासिषत मुक्तिसौधमधिरोढुम् ॥

इति काचनाभियुक्तोक्तिः श्रूयते। तत्र आद्यस्य मतमद्वैतम्। द्वितीयस्य मतं विशिष्टाद्वैतम्। तृतीयस्य मतं द्वैतम् इति भारते देशे सुप्रसिद्धम्। मतत्रयस्यास्य क्रमेण सङ्ग्रहश्लोकाः उदाह्रियन्ते। स्वाराज्यसिद्धौ -

१. कूटस्थं ब्रह्म विश्वं जनयति न विना मायया सा च मिथ्या
तस्मिन् शब्दप्रसिद्धेः परसमधिगमात्तन्निवृत्तिः श्रुतेश्च।
सैवाविद्या मृषार्था अपि समधिगताः कार्यदक्षाः प्रपञ्चः
तस्मान्मायूरपिञ्छच्छविरिव गगनो ब्रह्मसंविद्विवर्तः॥ २.२

अस्यैवार्थस्योपपादका अन्येऽपि केचित् श्लोकाः पञ्चदश्याः प्रदर्श्यन्ते -

अद्वितीयब्रह्मतत्त्वे स्वप्नोऽयमखिलं जगत् ।
ईशजीवादिरूपेण चेतनाचेतनात्मकम् ॥ ६.२११

भ्राम्यन्ते पण्डितम्मन्याः सर्वे लौकिकतैर्थिकाः।
अनादृत्य श्रुतिं मौर्ख्यात् केवलां युक्तिमाश्रिताः॥ ६.५८

पूर्वापरपरामर्शविकलास्तत्र केचन।
वाक्याभासान् स्वस्वपक्षे योजयन्त्यप्यलज्जया॥ ६.५९

अपेक्षते व्यवहृतिः न प्रपञ्चस्य सत्यताम्।
नाप्यात्मजाड्यं किन्त्वेषा साधनान्येव काङ्क्षति ॥ ९.८९ इति

विशिष्टाद्वैतद्वैतप्रतिपादकौ श्लोकौ क्रमेण एवं भवतः।

२. विष्णुः सर्वान्तरात्मा सकलगुणनिधिः सर्वशब्दाभिधेयः
भक्त्या लभ्यः प्रपत्त्या पुनरतिसुलभो भुक्तिमुक्तिप्रदाता ।
जीवाः सर्वेऽस्वतन्त्राः प्रकृतिरपि तथा किङ्कराः शङ्कराद्याः
इत्थं त्रय्यन्तसिद्धं निगमततिगतं ताड्यतां जैत्रभेरी ॥

३. श्रीमन्मध्वमते हरिः परतरः सत्यं जगत् तत्त्वतो
भिन्ना जीवगणाः हरेरनुचराः नीचोच्चभावङ्गताः।
मुक्तिर्नैजसुखानुभूतिरमला भक्तिश्च तत्साधनं
ह्यक्षादि त्रितयं प्रमाणमखिलाम्नायैकवेद्यो हरिः॥

तत्र मन्दवैराग्याणां तृतीयं मतं, मध्यमवैराग्याणां द्वितीयं मतम्, उत्तमवैराग्याणां प्रथमं मतमिति समरसभावनाः अभिप्रयन्ति। आचार्यत्रयानुसारिणः शिष्यास्तु

वृथैव कोलाहलं कुर्वन्ति। तत्रापि द्वैताद्वैतपदयोरेव श्रुतिदृष्टत्वात् द्वैतमद्वैतमिति पदद्वयमेव भवितुमर्हति। न तृतीयं विशिष्टाद्वैतम्। विशिष्टं चेन्नाद्वैतम्। अद्वैतं चेन्न विशिष्टम्। अतः पदयोः सामानाधिकरण्यमेवासङ्गतमिति विशिष्टाद्वैतमिति नामैव तावदसङ्गतम्। अतस्तन्नादरणीयम्।

अद्वैतभिन्नं सर्वमेव मतं द्वैतमेवेति केचन मन्यन्ते। अत एव शङ्करभगवत्पादैरपि पूर्वमेव "द्वैतिनो हि ते साङ्ख्याः योगाश्च नात्मैकत्वदर्शिन" (ब्र.सू.२.१.३) इत्युक्तं योगप्रत्युक्त्यधिकरणे। अत्रेदं विवेक्तव्यम्। अद्वैतज्ञानमेव दुःखासंवलितसुखाभिव्यक्तिरूपमोक्षसाधनम्। अभयप्राप्तिरेव मोक्षोऽत्र विवक्षितः। द्वैतविज्ञानं तु बन्धरूपदुःखसाधनम्। अयमर्थो "यदा ह्येव एष एतस्मिन्नदृश्येऽनात्म्ये" (तै.२.७) इत्यादिवाक्येन, "यदा ह्येवैष एतस्मिन्नुदरमन्तरं कुरुते अथ तस्य भयं भवति" (तै. २.७.१), इति वाक्येन च तैत्तिरीयके क्रमेण उक्तः। "द्वितीयाद्वै भयं भवति" (बृ. १.४.२), "मृत्योः स मृत्युमाप्नोति य इह नानेव पश्यति" (बृ. ४.४.१९), इत्यादि श्रुतिवाक्यैः द्वैतं दुःखात्मकमिति निर्णीतम्। सशरीरतैव द्वैतम्। अशरीरतैवाद्वैतम्। "अशरीरं वाव सन्तं" (छा. ८.१२.१), "अशरीरं शरीरेषु" (कठ. २.२२) इत्यादि श्रवणात्। किञ्च द्वैतं प्रेय इत्यद्वैतं श्रेय इति चोच्यते। तत्र द्वैतमविद्यामार्गः, अद्वैतं विद्यामार्गः इति ज्ञेयः। एते अधिकृत्यापि कठवल्ल्यामेवमुक्तम् -

श्रेयश्च प्रेयश्च मनुष्यमेतः तौ सम्परीत्य विविनक्ति धीरः।
श्रेयो हि धीरोऽभिप्रेयसो वृणीते प्रेयो मन्दो योगक्षेमाद्वृणीते॥ (२.२)

अन्यच्छ्रेयोऽन्यदुतैव प्रेयः ते उभे नानार्थे पुरुषं सिनीतः।
तयोः श्रेय आददानस्य साधु भवति हीयतेऽर्थाद्य उ प्रेयो वृणीते॥ (२.१) इति

भगवता श्रीकृष्णेनाप्येवमुक्तं गीतायाम् -

मामुपेत्य पुनर्जन्म दुःखालयमशाश्वतम्।
नाप्नुवन्ति महात्मानः संसिद्धिं परमां गताः॥ (८.१५)

तत्रापि द्वैतं यद्यपि "यत्र हि द्वैतमिव भवति तदितर इतरं पश्यति" (बृ.२.४.१४), इत्यादिना श्रुतिषु प्रतिपाद्यते तथाप्यधिगतत्त्वात् तन्न तात्पर्येण श्रुतिषु बोध्यते। किन्तु मायिकमनूद्यते। तदुक्तं -

प्रत्यक्षेणानुमित्या वा यस्तूपायो न बुध्यते।
एनं विदन्ति वेदेन तस्माद्वेदस्य वेदता॥

(तैत्तिरीयसंहिता-सायणभाष्यभूमिका)

इति उपदिश्यमानमपि मन्दमतीनामनवगाह्यमानत्वादनधिगतमद्वैतं ब्रह्मैव प्रमाणराजेन वेदेन तात्पर्येण प्रतिपाद्यते। तात्पर्यं चोपक्रमादिभिर्निर्णीयते। तदप्युक्तं-

उपक्रमोपसंहाराबभ्यासोऽपूर्वता फलम्।
अर्थवादोपपत्ती च लिङ्गं तात्पर्यनिर्णये॥ इति (विवरणतत्त्वदीपनम्)

श्रवणायापि बहुभिर्यो न लभ्यः शृण्वन्तोऽपि बहवो यं न विद्युः।
आश्चर्यो वक्ता कुशलोऽस्य लब्धा आश्चर्यो ज्ञाता कुशलानुशिष्टः॥ (कठ.२.७)

आश्चर्यवत् पश्यति कश्चिदेनमाश्चर्यवत् वदति तथैव चान्यः।
आश्चर्यवच्चैनमन्यः श्रृणोति श्रुत्वाप्येनं वेद न चैव कश्चित्॥ (गीता २.२९)

सर्वे वेदा यत्पदमामनन्ति तपांसि सर्वाणि च यद्वदन्ति।
यदिच्छन्तो ब्रह्मचर्यं चरन्ति तत्ते पदं सङ्ग्रहेण ब्रवीमि॥ (कठ.२.१५)

यदक्षरं वेदविदो वदन्ति विशन्ति यद्यतयो वीतरागाः।
यदिच्छन्तो ब्रह्मचर्यं चरन्ति तत्ते पदं सङ्ग्रहेण प्रवक्ष्ये॥ (गीता ७.२२)

इति कठवाक्येन गीतावाक्येन च निर्णीतः अयमर्थः। "पुरुषार्थोऽतः शब्दात् इति बादरायणः", (ब्र.सू. ३४.१) इति व्याससूत्रेण चायमर्थः स्फुटोऽवगम्यते। अत एव शङ्करभगवत्पादा अपि श्रुत्यादितात्पर्यविषयतयाऽमुमर्थं प्रतिपादयन्ति -

ब्रह्म सत्यं जगन्मिथ्या जीवो ब्रह्मैव नापरः।
मुक्तिरेकात्मविज्ञानादिति वेदान्तडिण्डिमः॥ इति। (वेदान्तडिण्डिमः ६१)

गौडपादैरप्युक्तं "मायामात्रमिदं द्वैतमद्वैतं परमार्थतः"(१.१७) इति।

अद्वैतं परमार्थो हि द्वैतं तद्भेद उच्यते।
तेषां उभयथा द्वैतं तेनायं न विरुध्यते ॥ (२.१८) इत्यादि च।

कथमेतदवगम्यते? किं वाऽत्र प्रमाणमिति न शङ्कनीयम्॥ श्रुतिः सूत्रं गीताशास्त्रं चेति त्रितयमपि प्रमाणमिति वक्ष्यते। अयमेवार्थः स्वाराज्यसिद्धौ भङ्ग्यन्तरेण उच्यते -

इत्थं यः कर्मबद्धः भ्रमति परवशः प्राणिभृज्जन्मसङ्घैः
दुःखस्यान्तं न वेत्ति स्मरति न च जनिव्रातमज्ञानयोगात्।
तं सर्वानर्थमूलप्रशमनविधिना स्वात्मराज्येऽभिषेक्तुम्
तात्पर्येण प्रवृत्ताः श्रुतिशिखरगिरः सूत्रभाष्यादयश्च॥ (१.५४) इति॥

तत्र श्रुतिषु तावत् ब्रह्म, "सदेव सौम्येदमग्र आसीदेकमेवाद्वितीयम्"(छा.६.२.१), "सत्यं ज्ञानमनन्तं ब्रह्म"(तै.२.१.१), "अस्थूलमनण्वह्रस्वमदीर्घम्"(बृ.३.८.८), "निष्कलं निष्क्रियं शान्तं" (श्वे.६.१९),"तदेतद्ब्रह्मापूर्वमनपरम्"(बृ.२.५.१९), इत्यादिभिरशेषैर्वाक्यैः सजातीयविजातीयस्वगतभेदरहिताद्वैतसत्यज्ञानानन्तस्थूलत्वादिधर्मरहितगुणक्रियादि-रहितापूर्वानपरत्वादिरूपेण प्रतिपादितम्। अन्यत्र चास्मादेव ब्रह्मणो जगदुत्पत्ति-प्रलयादिकं, "यतो वा इमानि भूतानि जायन्ते" (तै.३.१.१), "ततो वै सदजायत" (तै.३.२.७), "इदं सर्वमसृजत"(तै.३.२.६) इत्यादिभिः वाक्यैर्जगतो मिथ्यात्वप्रतिपादनार्थ-मुपन्यस्तम्। इदमप्युक्तं कैश्चित् -

व्यावहारिकवस्तुजातमिदं मृषेति विवक्षया।
प्रक्रियां रचयाम्बभूव विसृष्टिसंहृतिलक्षणाम्॥ इति

कथमेतावता जगतो मिथ्यात्वं सिद्धं भवतीति न शङ्कनीयम्। जगतो ब्रह्मकार्यत्वप्रति-पादनेन तत्सिद्धेः।कार्यं हि मिथ्या कारणमेव सत्यमिति च लोकसिद्धम् "वाचारम्भणं विकारो नामधेयं मृत्तिकेत्येव सत्यं" (छा. ६.१.४), इत्यादि श्रुत्यापि तत्सिद्धिः।

निरवयवात् निर्विशेषाच्च ब्रह्मणः सावयवस्य सविशेषस्य च जगतः कथमुत्पत्तिः स्यात्? सावयवमृदादित एव सावयवघटादेरुत्पत्तिदर्शनात् इति शङ्का न कर्तव्या। मायावशादेव रज्जुतः सर्पादिरिव स्वरूपानुपमर्देन ब्रह्मणो जगदुत्पत्तुमर्हति न मृदादेरिव घटः। अयमेव विवर्तवाद इत्युच्यते वेदान्तिभिः।"इन्द्रो मायाभिः पुरुरूप ईयते" (बृ.२.५.१९) इति, "अस्मान्मायी सृजते विश्वमेतत्" (श्वे. ४.९), इत्यादि श्रुतिस्मृति-वचनमप्यत्रानुसन्धेयम्। एतदप्युक्तं गौडपादैः -

अनिश्चिता यथा रज्जुः अन्धकारे विकल्पिता।
सर्पधारादिभिर्भावैः तद्वदात्मा विकल्पितः॥ (२.२७) इति

छान्दोग्यप्रतिपादितो मृद्घटादिदृष्टान्तोऽपि विवर्तवादस्यैव उदाहरणम्। यत्र प्रतीतस्य कार्यस्य पुनः कारणभावापत्तिः तत्र विवर्तः। यत्र तु तद्भावो नास्ति तत्रैव परिणामवादः, पयोदध्यादि तत्रोदाहरणमिति विवेकः। यत्र वस्तुस्वरूपानुपमर्देन वस्त्वन्तरं प्रतीयते यथा रज्वादितः सर्पादिः, स विवर्तवाद इत्यप्युच्यते। अघटनघटनापटीयसी माया। (मायापञ्चकम्) इति च। तदुक्तं पञ्चदश्यां -

निद्राशक्तिर्यथा जीवे दुर्घटस्वप्नकारिणी।
ब्रह्मण्येषा स्थिता माया सृष्टिस्थित्यन्तकारिणी॥ (१३.८६)

अयं भावः - निर्विशेषनित्यशुद्धबुद्धमुक्तस्वभावमपि ब्रह्म त्रिगुणात्मिका सदसद्भा-वादिरूपेण दुर्निरूपा महाद्भुताऽनिर्वचनीया च माया स्वस्वभावभूताऽऽवरणशक्त्या

वास्तवं ब्रह्मरूपमावृत्य विक्षेपशक्त्या सविशेषं सद्वैतमिव भासयति। रज्जुसर्पशुक्ति-रजतादिस्थलेषु प्रसिद्धोऽयमर्थः। अमुमेव प्रकारमाश्रित्य मन्दमतीनां बुद्ध्यवगाहनार्थं सविशेषमपि ब्रह्मावान्तरेण तात्पर्येण प्रतिपादितम्। तदप्युक्तमभियुक्तैः -

निर्विशेषं परं ब्रह्म साक्षात्कर्तुमनीश्वराः।
ये मन्दास्तेऽनुकम्प्यन्ते सविशेषनिरूपणैः॥ इति। (कल्पतरुव्याख्या- ब्र.सू. १.१.२०)

विकल्पतदभावाभ्यामसंसृष्टात्मवस्तुनि।
विकल्पितत्वलक्ष्यत्वसम्बन्धाद्यास्तु कल्पिताः॥ (पञ्चदशी १.५२)

एतदप्युक्तं गौडपादाचार्यैः-

आश्रमास्त्रिविधा हीनमध्यमोत्तमवृत्तयः।
उपासनोपदिष्टेयं तदर्थमनुकम्पया॥ (३.१६)

उपलम्भात् समाचारादस्तिवस्तुत्ववादिनाम्।
जातिस्तु देशिता बुद्धैरजातेस्त्रसतां सदा॥ (४.४२) इति

उपलम्भात् समाचारात्मायाहस्ती यथोच्यते।
उपलम्भात्समाचारादस्तिवस्तु तथोच्यते॥ (४.४४) इति च।

माया चेयं ज्ञानबाध्या। "भूयश्चान्ते विश्वमायानिवृत्तिः" (श्वे. १.१०),"निचाय्य तं मृत्युमुखात् प्रमुच्यते" (कठ.३.१५), "तमेव विदित्वाऽति मृत्युमेति" (श्वे. ३.८) इत्यादि श्रुतिवाक्यैः, "ज्ञानेन तु तदज्ञानं येषां नाशितमात्मनः" (गीता. ५.१६) इत्यादि गीतावाक्यैश्चावगम्यते। अत एव च भासमानत्वात् बाध्यमानत्वाच्च मायेयं मिथ्येत्युच्यते। मिथ्यालक्षणप्रसङ्गे विद्यारण्यस्वामिभिः पञ्चदश्यामेवमुक्तम् -

भातीति चेद्भातु नाम भूषणं मायिकस्य तत्।
यदसद्भासमानं तन्मिथ्या स्वप्नगजादिवत्॥(२.७०)

न निरूपयितुं शक्या विस्पष्टं भासते च या।
सा मायेतीन्द्रजालादौ लोकाः सम्प्रतिपेदिरे॥ (६.१४१)

एतावता "ब्रह्म सत्यं जगन्मिथ्या" इत्युपपादितम्। "जीवो ब्रह्मैव नापर" इत्यंशोऽपि नानाप्रकारैर्महावाक्यैरवगम्यते॥ वाक्यानां परपक्षीयैः कृतमपि कुव्याख्यानमस्मत् पूर्वाचार्यैरेव खण्डितमिति ज्ञेयम्। गीतायामपि "अहं सर्वस्य प्रभवः"(१०.८) "अहमादिर्हि भूतानाम्" (१०.२) इत्यादि भगवतो जगत्कारणत्वप्रतिपादकैः जगतः कार्यत्वप्रतिपादकैश्च वाक्यैः "ब्रह्म सत्यं जगन्मिथ्या" इत्ययमर्थोऽवगम्यते। "मया ततमिदं सर्वं जगदव्यक्तमूर्तिना" (गीता. ९.४) इत्यादि श्लोकद्वयेन च जगन्मिथ्यात्वं

स्फुटमुक्तम्। "क्षेत्रज्ञं चापि मां विद्धि" (गीता. १३.२) इत्यादिश्लोकेन "जीवो ब्रह्मैव नापरः" इत्ययमर्थोऽप्यवगम्यते।

ब्रह्मसूत्रेऽपि "जन्माद्यस्य यतः" (१.१.२) इति सूत्रेण जगद्ब्रह्मणोः कार्यकारणभाव-कथनेन "ब्रह्म सत्यं जगन्मिथ्या" इति "पुरुषार्थोऽतः शब्दात्" (३.४.९) इति सूत्रेण "जीवो ब्रह्मैव नापरः" इत्ययमर्थः प्रतिपादितः। तदेवं श्रुतिस्मृतिसूत्रैः "ब्रह्म सत्यं जगन्मिथ्या जीवो ब्रह्मैव नापरः"इत्ययमर्थः प्रतिपादितः। ब्रह्म च जगतो विवर्तोपादानम्। माया च परिणाम्यु-पादानमित्यभ्युपगमात् मायामिथ्यात्वमेव जगन्मिथ्यात्वे निबन्धनमिति ज्ञेयम्।

सत्यामेवं प्रामाणिक्यां विषयव्यवस्थायां ब्रह्मव्यतिरेकेण मायायास्तत्कार्यस्य वा कथमपि वास्तवस्वरूपस्यासिद्धेः आश्रयाश्रयिभावप्रमाणप्रमेयभावनिवर्त्यनिवर्तक-भावादीनामेवासम्भवात् तेषामनुपपत्तिकथनमभित्तिचित्रायमाणं भूषणमेवास्माकमद्वैतिनां न दूषणम्। अविद्यावस्थायां तु सर्वेषामेव तेषां कल्पितानां सम्भवात् न काप्यनुपपत्तिरिति मन्यामहे।

Summary: Professor Kalyanasundara Sastri expresses his happiness to participate in the seminar on a debate on māyā-avidyā. Being an eminent scholar in Advaita, he defends the position that māyā is central to the philosophy of Advaita. From the transcendental standpoint, there is no māyā and from the empirical standpoint, the concept of māyā does have an important place and the defects debated have been answered even by the earlier preceptors of Advaita.

Sastri quotes *Pañcadaśī* of Vidyāraṇya to defend the existence of māyā. He tries to show that: 1. māyā has the power to create the world and it is inconceivable. A wise person would do away with it by careful analysis. 2. The opponents may ask the question as to how would there be māyā-avidyā (nescience) in the self-luminous Brahman, i.e. the consciousness and without ignorance how would there be any concealment? Such arguments get rejected simply by the self-experience relating to knowledge and ignorance. Even the opponent has to trust his own experience as the first step to ascertain the knowledge of the reality.

Sastri cites an oft-quoted verse to show how Śaṅkara, Rāmānuja and Madhva have prepared the steps to climb on the pyramid of liberation. The essential tenet of all these schools are given as follows: In *Svārājya-siddhi* we find: "The universe is born out of the immovable Brahman, with the association of indeterminable māyā. As a result of *Śabda-pramāṇa*, there emerges the knowledge of Brahman which removes the māyā. That avidyā, though indeterminable, stimulates activity in the world. This can be substantiated by the example of the colourless ether, which appears with different colours like the feathers of a peacock. In a similar manner, the world is just a transfiguration of the Brahman." (*Svārājya-siddhi,* 1.2)

Sastri quotes a few verses from *Pañcadaśī* to substantiate the philosophical position of Advaita: "In the principle of non-dual Brahman, the appearance of the universe as God, soul and the like in the form of sentient and insentient beings, is like a dream." (6.211) "By resorting to this argument, and by disregarding Śruti, out of delusion, the so-called scholars think themselves as wise and roam around in the world of reason."(6.58) "There are some, who are obsessed with the chronology of occurrence of the Vedic passages, and shamelessly construe the Upaniṣadic statements to strengthen their own view points." (6.59) "Neither the reality of the world nor the insentience of the self is required for the performance of the action; it is only the right means that are required to do so." (9.89)

The Viśiṣṭādvaita and Dvaita views are presented as follows: - "Viṣṇu is the inner-self of all beings. Endowed with all auspicious virtues, he is the primary signification of all words. He, who is the bestower of enjoyment and liberation, can be attained by bhakti and *prapatti*. All the jīvas as well as prakṛti are dependent, and the other Godheads like Śiva are his attendants. Thus is the Lord (Viṣṇu) who is the direct import of all the Vedas and further understood by the series of scriptures. Let the drum of victory of Viśiṣṭādvaita be beaten to this effect."

"According to Madhva, Lord Hari is the Supreme, the world is absolutely real. The individual jīvas, the followers of Hari, are different from one another and are always graded as superior and inferior. The liberation, for which Bhakti is the only means, is the experience of one's own bliss. The perception etc., are the means of knowledge and God can be known through the Vedas."

The Dvaitins who proclaim the reality as marked by duality have less detachment. The second view belongs to Viśiṣṭādvaitins who have medium sense of detachment and the first view, viz., Advaita pertains to the persons having superior sense of detachment. The followers of these three views unnecessarily engage themselves in mutual oppositions. Since the two words like Dvaita and Advaita are used in the Śruti, there need not be a third view called Viśiṣṭādvaita. If it is *viśiṣṭa* (qualified) it is not Advaita. If it is Advaita, then it cannot be qualified (*viśiṣṭa*). Hence, there is no *sāmānādhikaraṇya*, appositional relationship between these two words, viz. *viśiṣṭa* and Advaita. Hence the views of the Viśiṣṭādvaita cannot be accepted.

It is usually understood that all the Indian philosophical traditions different from Advaita supposedly entertain Dvaita tenets. In his commentary to *Yogapratyukti-adhikaraṇa*, Śaṅkara refers to the fact that "dualists indeed are the followers of Sāṅkhya and Yoga and they do not see the non-duality in Ātman." This statement should be understood thus: "The knowledge of Advaita alone is the means to liberation, in which there is manifestation of bliss, and such a state is not associated with sorrow." What is intended to be conveyed here is that attainment of *abhaya* (fearlessness) is freedom from empirical bondage and such a state is liberation. Knowledge of duality, on the other hand, is in the form of bondage and it means suffering. From the Śruti passages like, 'From duality results fear', it is established that duality brings about suffering. Dvaita is a state of embodiment which leads a person to *preyas* and empirical happiness and Advaita is a state of disembodiment leading to that of liberation, *śreyas*. As such, Dvaita is the path of ignorance and Advaita is that of knowledge.

The subject matter of non-dualism is established by the Vedas. In spite of proper instruction, for a person with average intellect, it remains incomprehensible. This idea becomes evident in the passage: "After studying the Śruti, many do not comprehend this knowledge, many do not know even after repeated hearing. It is a matter of surprise that the teacher speaks of the unspeakable and competent is he who understands the incomprehensible."(KU, 2.7)

Bādarāyaṇa in his *Brahmasūtra,* (3.4.9) indicates the same idea of non-duality. Śaṅkara also establishes that the subject matter of

Śruti, etc. finally means: "Brahman is Real, the world is illusory, the jīva is Brahman alone and non-different from It." Liberation is attained by the knowledge of 'one-self' and this is proclaimed by Vedānta."

Gauḍapāda declares: "Dvaita is māyā alone and Advaita is the absolute." *Prasthānatraya* - Śruti, *Sūtra* and *Gītā* are the sources for such knowledge. In Śruti, the Brahman is described as: "it was before, is one and non-dual", "Existence-knowledge-bliss is Brahman", "not gross, not small, not long", "attributeless, non-doer, bliss," "that Brahman has neither a beginning nor an end," etc. - the implication of these Śruti statements is that Brahman is bereft of any type of difference: *sajātīya, vijātīya* or *svagata.* It does not have characteristics like gross, subtle, etc. It is free from qualities and actions, and does not have either a beginning or an end.

In another context, Brahman is described as the source of origination, destruction etc. which is evident from the passages like: "from whom these beings originated", "from that everything came into existence", "this created everything". By these statements the '*mithyātva*' i.e., falsity of the world is established.

The falsity of the world is also proved on the basis of an explanation of causality involving Brahman as the cause and world as an effect. This is established on the basis of *Chāndogya* statement-'pot etc, are mere names as modifications, but the cause - clay alone is real.'

Brahman is without any parts - *niravayava* and without any characteristics - *nirviśeṣa*, and the world is *sāvayava* - with parts and *saviśeṣa* and with many characteristics. How can such a world be produced by Brahman? One does not doubt the origin of *sāvayava* - pot etc, from a *sāvayava* - changeable clay. Similar is the case of a snake appearing on a rope due to māyā. By self-transfiguration it is possible for Brahman to create the world, not like the creation of pot from clay. This is called as *Vivartavāda* by Advaitins.

The *Chāndogya* example of clay and pot also is based on the principle of *Vivartavāda* alone. Where an effect resolves into its cause, it is spoken of as *vivarta.* In case of causality where such a modification is not found, it is said to be *Pariṇāmavāda*, which is different from examples like milk changing to curd etc. Where an entity without undergoing any transformation is revealed as an effect, like the rope seen as a snake, is spoken of as *vivarta,* transfiguration. Brahman is without any characteristics, is eternal, is pure, is knowledge. Māyā, in the form of *asat* and *sat*, with varied forms, is indescribable. By its very nature, māyā conceals *(āvaraṇa)* the true nature of Brahman, and projects (*vikṣepa*) Brahman with characteristics. Due to this projection, a person, lacking depth in thinking, understands the absolute Brahman to be associated with characteristics.

Māyā is said to be unreal as it is perceived and sublated subsequently. Thus it is established that "Brahman is real and the world is unreal." The other part of the verse, "jīva is Brahman alone and not different" is established by very many Upaniṣadic passages. Though these statements are wrongly interpreted by other schools, it is well known that such interpretations were refuted effectively by other earlier Advaita Ācāryas.

In the *Gītā*, the Lord by saying: 'I am the first of all', 'I am before all beings', etc., reveals himself as the cause of the world, and the world as the effect, and this proves the statement '*brahma satyam jagan mithyā*'.

In the *Brahmasūtra*, (1.1.2) "*janmādyasya yataḥ*" shows that the world and Brahman are related as cause and effect. The *sūtra* '*puruṣārtho'taḥ śabdāt*' also reveals that 'Jīva is Brahman not different from It." Thus, in *Śruti*, *Smṛti*, and *Brahmasūtras* '*brahma satyaṁ jagan mithyā jīvo brahmaiva nāparaḥ*' is established.

Professor Sastri concludes his speech by emphasising on the idea that Brahman is the transfigurative cause of the universe. Māyā is the transformative material cause. Since māyā is *mithyā*, the world being a product of māyā is also *mithyā*.

Māyā and its products can never be established in reality as presented in the form of seven objections. All such objections are untenable. It is like drawing a picture on the water or ether, not on a concrete surface. Finally, māyā-avidyā is like an ornament for us, the Advaitins, and not a defect. In the state of ignorance, there is the possibility of empirical existence and hence māyā-avidyā can never become untenable.

3

SAPTAVIDHĀNUPAPATTI : SOME REFLECTIONS

K. Kunjunni Raja

Saptavidhānupapatti, "the seven great untenables", are the seven main objections raised against the Advaita concept of avidyā or māyā by Rāmānuja, in the beginning of his *Śrībhāṣya.* Thus started the unending debate between Advaitins and Viśiṣṭādvaitins. Vedāntadeśika's *Śatadūṣaṇī* was ably met in the twentieth century by Anantakrishna Sastri's *Śatabhūṣaṇī.* A reply to this came by Uttamūr Vīrarāghavācārya in his *Paramārtha-dūṣaṇa* and by E.S. Varadācārya in his *Tattvasudhā.* The Sevenfold criticism against avidyā or māyā consists of the following.

1. Its *svarūpa* (nature) is riddled with contradictions.
2. Its description as *anirvacanīya* or inexplicable is untenable.
3. No valid means of knowledge (*pramāṇa*) supports such a theory.
4. What is the locus (*āśraya*) of avidyā? It can neither be Brahman nor jīva.
5. It is untenable to claim that avidyā obscures the nature of Brahman.
6. Its removal by knowledge (*jñāna-nirvartyatva*) is untenable.
7. *Avidyā-nivṛtti* is also untenable.

This seminar is organised to discuss these points in depth by competent scholars. The seven objections generally attributed to Rāmānuja against avidyā as interpreted by Śaṅkara and his followers have a history behind them. Some of these objections are much earlier than Śaṅkara himself. I shall illustrate with one example.

Kumārilabhaṭṭa in the *Ślokavārttika* (*Sambandha-ākṣepa-parihāra*, 85) says:

अन्येनोपप्लवेऽभीष्टे द्वैतवादः प्रसज्यते ।
स्वाभाविकमविद्यां तु नोच्छेतुं कश्चिदर्हति ॥

Avidyā must be either existent or non-existent; it must be either real or unreal. If it is real, Brahman and avidyā are both real and there is no scope for Advaita; since there are two existents. If avidyā is unreal, it cannot be destroyed. This objection is met by Śaṅkara, by saying that avidyā is indescribable (*anirvacanīya*) or (*sadasad-vilakṣaṇa*).

The author of the *Pañcadaśī* explains the position thus: from the point of view of Absolute Reality, avidyā and the universe (*prapañca*) projected by that do not exist. From the empirical point of view (*vyāvahārika* level of reality) it does exist, and is experienced by the soul; for those who want to investigate the problem, it is *sadasad-vilakṣaṇa*, indescribable.

The appearance of Brahman as the variegated world can be illustrated with an example. The same electricity appears as heat or cold, light or sound, and works as the inner soul of the fan and tube-light, fridge and heater, radio and television. This is what science teaches us. But in actual life they are all different. The variety and multiplicity at the empirical level are apparent manifestations due to the limitations of our sense organs and the mind. It may not be conceived mentally, but can be meaningfully used in calculation.

Many philosophers and seers consider that the earthly life is not an end in itself, but a road to our destination, which is better and happier. Their endeavour is deliverance from the present existence. Obviously, this is a pessimistic attitude. Buddhism, Sāṅkhya philosophy and the later Upaniṣadic thought take such a view. But in the *Ṛgveda*, and even in some of the early Upaniṣads, we do not find this attitude of pessimism. The aim of Vedic and early philosophical thinkers has been Brahman, which is *ānanda* or "bliss" in essence. Brahman is not alone having *ānanda*, but *ānanda* itself. The distinction between subject and object does not exist at this stage; which is something higher than the deep, dreamless sleep.

Bhartṛhari

Bhartṛhari who flourished in the beginning of the fifth century was an eminent Sanskrit grammarian and a great philosopher of language. He is famous for enunciating two theories of language *viz.* the *Sphoṭavāda* and the *Śabda-brahma-vāda*. I have been holding the view that these two theories, though interrelated, can also individually exist in isolation.

Bhartṛhari was an eminent pre-Śaṅkara Advaitin. He begins his *Vākyapadīya* with a clear statement that the Absolute Brahman is identical with the speech principle, and that the whole phenomenon of material existence is only a manifestation of this *Śabda-brahman*, of which *śabda* and *artha*, the symbol and the meaning are the only two aspects. This Speech essence which is identical with consciousness (*cit*) has no beginning or end, and appears in the form of various symbols or expressions on the one hand and the meanings in the form of ideas (*vikalpas*) on the other, and thus constitutes the entire phenomenal world.

अनादिनिधनं ब्रह्म शब्दतत्त्वं यदक्षरम् ।
विवर्ततेऽर्थभावेन प्रक्रिया जगतो यतः ॥ (*Vākyapadīya,* 1.1)

Symbols and meanings, *śabda* and *artha, nāma* and *rūpa* are only two aspects of the same principle. Though this Ultimate Reality, this speech essence, is one, it appears different on the basis of its *śaktis* like time and space, which are not different from itself; thus the world appears as evolutionary and pluralistic.

Though Bhartṛhari uses the term *"vivartate"*, for the manifestation of the world from the *śabdatattva*, in his theory, the phenomenal world never loses its direct ontological identity with Brahman. Śaṅkara's theory of *adhyāsa*; or the rope-snake identity; theory of superimposition does not explain Bhartṛhari's theory correctly. According to Bhartṛhari, the *śakti-s* like time and space are not different from Brahman; they have the capacity to bring out its potentiality into actuality. The question whether time and space are subjective or objective is solved by taking *śakti-s* as real, which bring forth from a real *śabda-brahman* a real world that is not māyā as in Śaṅkara's Advaita. Bhartṛhari has no necessity to have a *nirguṇa-brahman*, indescribable and transcendental. Revelation through intuitive power, an instantaneous flash of insight (*pratibhā*) can penetrate reality well beyond the empirical level.

Whether Bhartṛhari accepted only three stages in the manifestation of *vāk*, or *śabda*, or four has not yet been settled. He has stated that *śabda-tattva* has three stages in the course of its manifestation. *Paśyantī*, *Madhyamā* and *Vaikharī* -

वैखर्या मध्यमायाश्च पश्यन्त्याश्चैतदद्भुतम्।
अनेकतीर्थभेदायास्त्रय्या वाचः परं पदम्॥ (*Vākyapadīya,* 1.133)

Bhartṛhari's statement about the three levels of *vāk* does not preclude the acceptance of a higher level (*parā*) about which we cannot say anything. Utpaladeva says in his *Īśvara-pratyabhijñā-kārikā* (ISMeo, 1994, Rome, p.120) that "consciousness has, as its essential nature, reflective awareness (*pratyavamarśa*); it is the supreme word" (*parā-vāk*) that arises freely. It is freedom in the Absolute sense, the sovereignty of the supreme self.

चितिः प्रत्यवमर्शात्मा परा वाक् स्वरसोदिता।
स्वातन्त्र्यमेतन्मुख्यं तदैश्वर्यम् परमात्मना॥ (1.5.13)

According to Utpaladeva, *parā-vāk*, the highest level of *vāk* is so close to silence that the distinction between the supreme *vāk* and its power or energy is non-existent, and belongs only to theory. It is identified with Brahman by Bhartṛhari. Another pre-Śaṅkara Advaitin is Gauḍapāda. His view of Reality is akin to that of the Buddhist thinker Nāgārjuna, who spoke about two levels of reality *lokasaṁvṛtti-satya* and *paramārtha-satya.*[1]

द्वे सत्ये समुपाश्रित्य बुद्धानां धर्मदेशना।
लोकसंवृतिसत्यञ्च सत्यञ्च परमार्थतः॥ (*Mūlamadhyamika-kārikā*, 24.8)

Gauḍapāda also takes the same view of Absolute level and empirical level of truth. Śaṅkara added one more level of reality the *prātibhāsika*, as in the rope-snake, which has no essence. Even *svapna,* dream stage, as well as rope-snake error of perception, is given a lower level of reality that the empirical one. South Indian tradition of Sundarapāṇḍya also has this view. Śaṅkara did not reject empirical knowledge as mere illusion; it is a positive entity. A. G. Krishna Warrier has pointed out this special feature of Gauḍapāda.[2]

Another point in Gauḍapāda's philosophy is that he does not identify deep sleep as *mokṣa* as some other Upaniṣads seem to do. Even in deep-sleep *vṛttijñāna* exists; so on waking from sleep, he remains his original self (not a *jīvanmukta*). The references in many Upaniṣads giving deep sleep as an analogy for *mokṣa* need not necessarily be taken in their face value according to traditional scholars.

Bhavya who flourished between 490-570 C E, wrote *Madhyamaka-hṛdayakārikā,* together with his own commentary *Tarkajvālā*. Its Chapter 8 is on Vedānta. The presentation of Vedānta here as *Pūrvapakṣa* does not show any influence of Śaṅkara. Out of the 16 verses a few may be given here:

तमः परस्तात् पुरुषं महान्तं सूर्यवर्चसम् ।
मृत्युमत्येति मतिमान् मत्वात्मानं महेश्वरम् ॥ (8.2)

विश्वे भावास्ततो जाता ऊर्णनाभाविवांशवः ।
तस्मिन् प्रलीना विद्वांसो नाप्नुवन्ति पुनर्भवम् ॥ (8.5)

घटाकाशे यथैकस्मिन् रजोधूमादिभिर्वृते ।
तद्वत्ता न हि सर्वेषां सुखादेर्न तदात्मनः ॥ (8.13)

एकं सर्वगतं नित्यं परं ब्रह्माच्युतं पदम् ।
योगी युञ्जन् यदावेत्ति न तदैति पुनर्भवम् ॥ (8.16)

नित्यं तदविकल्पं च यत्र वाचामगोचरः ।
गिरस्तत्र प्रयुज्यन्ते भेदापहृतबुद्धिभिः ॥ (8.17)[3]

Of these verses यथैकस्मिन् घटाकाशे occurs also in *Gauḍapādakārikā*. We do not find any direct reference to Śaṅkara's Advaita in this summary. For attacking Bhartṛhari's *Śabdādvaitavāda*, Śāntarakṣita paraphrases the first *kārikā* of *Vākyapadīya* thus:

अथाविभागमेवेदं ब्रह्मतत्त्वं सदा स्थितम् ।
अविद्योपप्लवाल्लोको विचित्रं त्वभिमन्यते ॥ (*Tattvasaṅgraha*, 1.144)

The essence of linguistic expression is one and indivisible, while plurality of appearance is due to *avidyā*.

Maṇḍana Miśra

Maṇḍana Miśra, who is generally considered to have been an elder contemporary of Śaṅkara, and who was both a Mīmāṁsaka and an Advaitin, accepting both *Karma* and *Jñāna* as helping in the final release, advocated the view that *prasaṁkhyāna* meditation should be observed until *ātman* is realized, and that this *prasaṁkhyāna* is a kind of mental action. Śaṅkara rejects this kind of *prasaṁkhyāna* or *dhyāna* as the direct cause for release. In his *bhāṣya* of *Brahmasūtra* 1.1.4, Śaṅkara distinguishes between *dhyāna* or meditation and *jñāna* or knowledge. The knowledge of the meaning of identity statements or the *mahāvākyas* of the Upaniṣads is like perception which is automatic and which does not involve action. Action is involved only when there is a choice to do or not to do; *dhyāna* or meditation involves a choice and hence it is an action.

Śaṅkara

Śaṅkara, however, refers to and recommends *prasaṁkhyāna* in the *Upadeśasāhasrī,* (II.3. 112-116). He does not call it *dhyāna* or meditation; it is a kind of recapitulation and reflection, similar to *nididhyāsana.* Śaṅkara who rejects *prasaṁkhyāna* in the *Upadeśa-sāhasrī* (1.18. 9ff) does not explain the distinction between the two. *Prasaṁkhyāna* consists in recapitulating the conclusions reached through one's study and discussion with the teacher, and reflecting on them. (perhaps similar to *nididhyāsana.*)

This kind of reflection is described for seekers after final release, who are devoting themselves to destroying their acquired merit and demerit and do not wish to accumulate new ones. Mayeda calls it a kind of meditation; but it cannot be *dhyāna* which involves action; it must be a kind of reflection, based on awareness that the self is different from what I experienced through the senses.[4]

Śaṅkara makes it clear that the Absolute Brahman is beyond any definition in the ordinary sense of the word. Words can denote things only through one or the other of the following categories: name, form, action, distinction, genus and quality. Since Brahman is none of these, it is impossible to define or describe it. When Brahman is referred to as intelligence or bliss, it only means that a name, form and action is superimposed on it. If we want to describe its true nature free from the differences due to the limiting *upādhis*, it is impossible to refer to it. The only way to do so is by the negation of all possible means, 'not this, not this' (*neti neti*).

ननु कथमाभ्यां नेति नेति शब्दाभ्यां सत्यस्य सत्यं निर्दिदिक्षितमिति। उच्यते। सर्वोपाधिविशेषापोहेन। यस्मिन्न कश्चिद्विशेषोऽस्ति - नाम वा रूपं वा कर्म वा भेदो वा जातिर्वा गुणो वा तद्द्वारेण हि शब्दप्रवृत्तिर्भवति। न चैषां कश्चिद्विशेषो ब्रह्मणि अस्ति। अतो न निर्देष्टुं शक्यते इदं तदिति॥ (*BUB*. 2.3.6)

Bhartṛhari says that it is an experience, which cannot be communicated to others definitely; each has to experience it in his consciousness; even the person who has experienced does not know what it is.

इदं तदिति सान्येषामनाख्येया कथञ्चन।
प्रत्यात्मवृत्तिदृष्टा सा कर्त्राऽपि न निरूप्यते॥ (*Vākyapadīya,* 2.144)

Starting from the *Ṛgveda* up to the early classical literature in Sanskrit, we find many references to the Vedāntic ideal of oneness and *eka-puruṣa-vāda* though the modalities of understanding the concept of puruṣa has undergone substantial variations.

Conclusion

The above is a short elucidation of *Saptavidha-anupapatti* and the debate it has initiated in the Indian Philosophical tradition, mainly involving the Advaita concept of māyā-avidyā. But the way Advaita school has positioned its philosophy by highlighting a supra-empirical reality beyond human understanding through speech does not have much scope for debate since any debate is a transformation of speech and the reality that the Advaita points out is transverbal. It is here that the concept of *bhakti* may come to the rescue of all the schools of Vedānta since it is the realisation that matters and not a claim for one's superiority.

NOTES

1. David J. Kalupahana, *Mūlamadhyamika-kārikā of Nagarjuna The Philosophy of Middle Path,* SUNY, 1991, p. 331.
2. See A. G. Krishna Warrier, *God in Advaita,* Indian Institute of Advanced Study, Shimla, 1977, p. vii.
3. CHR Lindtner (Ed.), *Mādhyamikahṛdayam of Bhavya,* Adyar Library Series. 123, Chennai - 2001, pp. 79 - 81.
4. Sengaku Mayeda , (Ed.Tr.), *A Thousand Teachings: The Upadeśā-sahasrī of Śaṅkara*, SUNY, 1992, p. xxi.

4

SAPTAVIDHĀNUPAPATTI: A CRITICAL EXPOSITION

M. A. Lakshmithathachar

The philosophy of Vedānta is mainly based on the Upaniṣads and the *Brahmasūtras*. The Upaniṣads, by and large, assert that the individual soul (*jīvātmā*) and supreme soul are totally different and distinct entities, while there is possibility of interpreting certain Upaniṣadic passages to convey the identity between them. The philosophy of Advaita goes with the latter view and propounds the theory that in reality it is only the supreme soul that exists. However, one gets the feeling that the individual souls too have an existence of their own, independent of the supreme soul. According to Advaita, the existence of the individual soul being distinct from the supreme soul is due to an important factor which is known by the word '*upādhi*'. This *upādhi* is known as avidyā, generally translated as 'nescience'. The Advaita texts propound that this 'avidyā' which is the factor responsible for the supreme soul seemingly taking the form of individual soul is also unreal (*mithyā*). For the tradition of Śrī Rāmānuja, this is untenable, because, a factor, which by itself is unreal, cannot be instrumental in acting on a real object (the supreme soul in this case) transforming itself into a seemingly unreal object (the individual soul as deemed by Advaitins).

Advaitins cite an example to substantiate its view-point as follows: For example, it is well known that there exists only one moon. However, when we put a finger below our eye and push the eye up, an illusion is artificially created to perceive two moons. This perception of two moons while having the knowledge that there is only one moon is due to *upādhi* i.e., 'pushing up the portion below the eye by a finger'.

Similarly, though the supreme soul is one and only real object in this universe, due to the *upādhi* named avidyā there is the experience that the individual soul is different from the supreme soul.

At this point, Ācārya Rāmānuja argues and goes on to logically prove that avidyā, being by itself an unreal entity, as propounded by Advaitins, cannot be the cause of an illusion. Rāmānuja picks out what he sees as seven fundamental flaws in the Advaita philosophy for special attack; he sees them as so fundamental to the Advaita position that if he is right in identifying them as involving doctrinal contradictions, then Śaṅkara's entire system collapses.

As stated in *Mahāpūrvapakṣa,* Advaitins believe that the absolute reality, Brahman, is *nirviśeṣa* and self-illumined and the world is a superimposition on Brahman due to avidyā. This avidyā has two fold functions, namely, *āvaraṇa,* and *vikṣepa.* The first causes non-apprehension which leads to the second, namely misapprehension. As in the case of rope-snake illusion, when the ignorance conceals (*āvaraṇa*) the real object, rope, and projects (*vikṣepa*) a different object, snake to the view, the avidyā acts as an *āvaraṇa* to conceal Brahman and produces an illusion, *vikṣepa,* of the world of diversities. This avidyā is said to be beginningless. It also cannot be properly defined; it is neither a positive entity nor a negative entity and hence said to be as *sadasad-anirvacanīya,* which means that it cannot be termed as either '*sat*' or '*asat*' and hence inexplicable, *anirvacanīya.*

Rāmānuja proceeds to prove that this theory of māyā-avidyā is untenable on grounds of seven-fold charges called *Saptavidha-anupapatti* and those are: 1. *Āśraya-anupapatti* – Brahman cannot be the substratum of avidyā; 2. *Tirodhāna anupapatti*–concealment of Brahman is not possible; 3. *Svarūpa-anupapatti* – avidyā cannot be real; 4. *Anirvacanīya anupapatti* – avidyā is not inexplicable; 5. *Pramāṇa-anupapatti* – There is no *pramāṇa* to prove the existence of avidyā; 6. *Nivartaka-anupapatti* – *Śruti* texts cited in support of removing avidyā are not so; 7. *Nivṛttyanupapatti* – avidyā cannot be completely removed by mere knowledge.

1. Āśraya-anupapatti

It is said that avidyā creates illusion. Rāmānuja asks,

sā hi kimāśritya bhramaṁ janayati? na tāvat jīvamāśritya, avidyāparikalpitatvāt jīvabhāvasya; nāpi brahmāśritya; tasya svayamprakāśajñānasvarūpatvena avidyāvirodhitvāt; sā hi jñānabādhyā abhimatā.

"What is the substratum of avidyā? It cannot be the jīva, individual self which itself is the product of avidyā. Neither could it abide in Brahman which is *jñāna-svarūpa* and self-illumined; and hence contrary to avidyā which is said to be removed by *jñāna.*"

The Advaitins contend that it is the knowledge of Brahman as *jñāna-svarūpa* which removes avidyā. That is, avidyā exists in the absence of the *jñāna,* that is Brahman-knowledge. At the rise of this *jñāna*, avidyā is removed and hence the *jñāna* which is the *svarūpa* of Brahman can coexist with avidyā as it is not opposed to avidyā, not being the subject of knowledge. The subject of *jñāna* is Brahman as the *jñāna-svarūpa* and not the *jñāna*, which is His *svarūpa*. But Rāmānuja refutes this saying:

jñānasvarūpaṁ brahma ityanena jñānena brahmaṇi yaḥ svabhāvaḥ avagamyate sa brahmaṇaḥ svayamprakāśatvena svayameva prakāśata iti avidyāvirodhitvẹ na kaścit viśeṣaḥ svarūpatadviṣayajñānayoḥ iti.

As Brahman is *svayamprakāśa*, self-effulgent, it does not require another knowledge to reveal it like an inert pot. Hence the knowledge that is the nature of Brahman, *svabhāva* and the knowledge of Brahman are of the same nature and it cannot be said that while one is opposed to avidyā the other is not.

Further this knowledge of Brahman as *jñānasvarūpa* cannot be experienced as Brahman is *anubhūti* according to Advaita and does not need another *anubhūti*, perception, as in the case of shell-silver, to reveal itself. So the *jñāna* which is the *svarūpa* of Brahman is opposed to avidyā and hence avidyā cannot rest on Brahman.

2. Tirodhānānupapatti

The Advaitin next comes up with the argument that the knowledge which is opposed to avidyā does not have Brahman as its subject but the unreality of everything other than Brahman.

Rāmānuja asks whether the avidyā to which this knowledge is opposed is about the real knowledge of Brahman or about the reality of the universe. It cannot be the former, says Rāmānuja, *'na tāvat brahmayāthātmyajñāna-virodhi atadviṣayatvāt'* because it is said that Brahman is not the subject of the knowledge which removes avidyā. (*prapañcamithyātva-jñānaṁ tatsatyatva-rūpa ajñānena virudhyate*)

The Advaitins say that it obscures Brahman who is *svayamprakāśa* or of nature of light. *Tirodhāna*, obscuration must be of two kinds. Either it should prevent the light from appearing or it should destroy the light that appeared. The first is not possible because the light that is Brahman does not appear but is always present. So avidyā must destroy the light. But Brahman is not a substance with light as its attribute, in which case it can remain even after its light is destroyed.

As Brahman is Himself the *prakāśa*, the *tirodhāna* can only mean the destruction of Brahman.

3. Svarūpa-anupapatti

According to the Advaita, Brahman is pure perception, *anubhūti-mātra*, not connected with any perceiver or thing perceived. As such, if avidyā conceals Brahman, assuming that it rests in Brahman, that iś, *svāśrayadoṣa*, Rāmānuja asks whether it is real or unreal. It cannot be real as everything other than Brahman is unreal in Advaita. If it is unreal, it should be identified with seer, seen or another perception. It cannot be identical with *anubhūti*, perception, for Brahman alone is the perception unconnected with things, and as avidyā is unreal, Brahman will also be unreal which will land Advaita in the portals of Mādhyamika nihilism. If it is identified with seer or seen, both of which are unreal, avidyā itself being unreal, and another *doṣa* must be found for the appearance of the avidyā. That is, as the avidyā is said to be the cause of the unreal perception of things and the unreal seer, there should be a cause for the unreal avidyā which in its turn will require another and so on, resulting in the fallacy of *ad infinitum*, or *anavasthā*. If on the other hand avidyā is identified with Brahman it becomes real and there can be no removal of it.

4. Anirvacanīyatva-anupapatti

Avidyā can be proved as a positive entity by perception. *Anirvacanīyatva* is explained as being neither *sat* (existent), nor *asat* (non-existent), but different from both, *sadasadvilakṣaṇam*. This uniqueness, says Rāmānuja, is itself unique, because it cannot be proved by any *pramāṇa*. All cognitions are of things either existing or not existing.

But Advaitins contend that avidyā is perceptible as a positive entity and not as a mere absence of knowledge, or mere antecedent non-existence of knowledge. In the cognition 'I do not know' it is the perception of *ajñāna* whereas the cognition 'I do not know myself or another', as in deep sleep, denotes the function of avidyā.

Avidyā conceals the true nature of Brahman as being self-proved, undifferentiated, and unchanging entity with *jñāna* as his *svarūpa*. This is the *tirodhāna-śakti* of avidyā. The other function of avidyā is that it makes Brahman appear as the manifold universe by its *vikṣepa-śakti*. Hence this is sense perception only, though unreal because it is caused by avidyā which is also not real. But since it is a positive entity it cannot be unreal like the horn of a rabbit or a sky flower and hence it is classified as neither real nor unreal. Avidyā is not the antecedent non-existence of knowledge *jñāna-prāgabhāva-viṣayaḥ*, which can be cognized by *anupalabdhi*, non-perception, which is the sixth *pramāṇa* in Advaita.

The means of cognition are six in Advaita, namely, perception (*pratyakṣa*), inference (*anumāna*), aṇalogy (*upamāna*), verbal testimony (*śabda*), presumption (*arthāpatti*), and non-perception (*anupalabdhi*). The non-existence of a thing as in the knowledge that '*bhūtale ghaṭo nāsti*', there is no pot on the ground, is cognized by *anupalabdhi*. Other schools do not accept the last two *pramāṇas* of Advaita which are said to be included under inference and perception respectively.

The reason for saying that avidyā is not the absence of knowledge is that it is cognised while being experienced like that of '*aham sukhī*, I am happy'. In the cognition 'I do not know', there is a perception of *ajñāna* which requires the knowledge of 'myself' and the *jñāna* which is absent. So the cognition is that of *ajñāna* and therefore it is positive and not opposed to knowledge of 'myself' or its knowledge.

Rāmānuja here interrupts and says that avidyā may be a positive thing, that is, not a mere absence, but even then, it conflicts with Brahman who has *jñāna* as his nature, *bhāvarūpamapi ajñānaṁ vastu-yāthātmya-avabhāsa-rūpeṇa sākṣicaitanyena virudhyate.*

The Advaitin replies that avidyā is not opposed to Brahman but only to the knowledge of Brahman which removes it. In the case of shell perceived as silver, the *ajñāna* is not opposed to shell but, only to the knowledge of it. If *ajñāna* is perceived by sense perception then on its removal Brahman must be perceived by sense perception which is denied by the Advaitin. Reply to this is that all things, sentient and insentient are perceived by Brahman, the witness-self, *sākṣicaitanya*, as being existent or non-existent. So when the *ajñāna* is removed by *jñāna*, Brahman shines of its own accord but before that the witness-self manifests itself as the world, due to *ajñāna.*

Next the Advaitin shows that the positive nature of avidyā is known through inference. The knowledge that is valid is preceded by a substance. This substance is other than the previous non-existence of the knowledge and covers the subject of the knowledge. This substance which is in the same place as the knowledge is removable by the knowledge. This is the positive *ajñāna*. Hence avidyā is a positive substance removed by *jñāna* rising from *Vedāntavākyas* such as '*tat tvamasi*' like the darkness is removed when a brilliant light is brought in.

The Advaitin proceeds to show that darkness, *tamas*, is a positive substance to counter the objection – *ālokābhāvamātraṁ ca rūpādarśana abhāvamātraṁ vā tamaḥ; na dravyāntaraṁ, tat kathaṁ bhāvarūpa-ajñānasādhane nidarśanatayā upanyasyate.*

The darkness is the absence of light or non-perception of *rūpa* and how can that be cited as an example to prove the positive avidyā. *Tamas* is a substance which is sometimes thin and sometimes thick and it is perceived and lends itself to expressions like '*tamaḥ calati*,' (darkness moves) and '*nīlaṁ tamaḥ*,' (darkness is blue) etc. *Tamas*, therefore, cannot be included among other substances, like the five elements, time, soul, mind and direction; and this view also has been refuted by the Naiyāyikas.

Rāmānuja objects that positive *ajñāna* is not perceived by sense perception in the experience '*aham ajñaḥ, māṁ anyaṁ ca na jānāmi,*' nor it can be proved by argument. *Ajñāna* must be of someone or of something. If the 'I' is known then the knowledge of *svarūpa* of 'I' will remove the *ajñāna* 'I do not know myself and others.' If the 'I' is not known, then it cannot be perceived because it will not be known as to whom or of whom or what it is about. The Advaitin may reply that only the vivid knowledge is opposed to avidyā but the knowledge of the person to whom and of whom the avidyā exists is not vivid and hence it can co-exist with such knowledge.

This can be understood as follows: In the perception '*ahaṁ ajñaḥ, māṁ anyaṁ ca na jānāmi*' there is a knowledge of 'I' but it is not vivid. In the case of *rajju-sarpa*, the rope seen as a snake, the rope is vivid knowledge but it is seen as '*idaṁ*, this' which can coexist with ignorance of the rope. This ignorance projects an illusory perception of a snake. The knowledge of the serpent or 'this' is not opposed to ignorance, avidyā, of the knowledge of the rope.

Rāmānuja says that this explanation applies to *jñānaprāgabhāva*, prior non-existence of knowledge also. Before the knowledge arises there is the absence of knowledge. Only the vivid knowledge of the real nature is opposed to it and not the knowledge of that where it abides and the subject of the knowledge.

To explain this we can again resort to the rope-snake example. Before the rope is known there is the absence of the knowledge that it is rope, which is removed when the knowledge of the rope dawns. So the *prāgabhāva* of the *jñāna* that it is rope is opposed to the *jñāna* of the rope.

But the knowledge of the abode of *jñāna*, namely the rope, is not vivid but seen as 'this, which is the subject of the knowledge which has not yet arisen. So, says Rāmānuja, *ajñāna* is not a positive entity but only the absence of *jñāna*.

Ajñāna must mean either the absence of *jñāna* or other than *jñāna* or opposed to *jñāna*. In all these cases, it requires that the nature of *jñāna* should be known, says Rāmānuja. *ajñānamiti jñānābhāvaḥ; tadanyaḥ; tadvirodhi vā, trayāṇāṁ api tatsvarūpajñānāpekṣā avaśyāśrayaṇīyā.*

The Advaitin contends citing the example of darkness that it can be seen even without knowing about light at all. But Rāmānuja insists that when *tamas*, darkness is known as the absence of light, the knowledge of light is a pre-requisite. Moreover, *ajñāna* is acknowledged as the absence of knowledge by Advaitin also when it is said to be removed by *jñāna*. Hence avidyā is not a positive entity.

5. Pramāṇa-anupapatti - Scriptures do not prove Avidyā

The Advaitins usually quotes the text, '*anṛtena hi pratyūḍhāḥ*' (*CU*, 8-3-2) those which are true are covered by what is untrue, to prove the existence of avidyā. But Rāmānuja refutes the view that the word *anṛta* means what is unreal or undefinable, that is avidyā. He says that the word *anṛta* only denotes what is opposite of *ṛta,* which means such actions that are done to attain the Supreme, without a desire for fruit. This is made clear by the text '*ṛtaṁ pibantau sukṛtasya loke*, two enjoyers of the inevitable results of action', (*KU*, 1-3-1) and hence the bad karma which results in *saṁsāra* is *anṛtaṁ, ṛtaṁ - karmaphalābhisandhirahitaṁ paramapuruṣārādhanāveṣaṁ tatpraptiphalaṁ; atra tadvyatiriktaṁ sāṁsārikaphalaṁ anṛtaṁ, brahmaprāptivirodhi.* This is the meaning of the *Chāndogyopaniṣad* text quoted, says Rāmānuja, *viz. sarvāḥ prajāḥ aharahargacchantyaḥ itthaṁ brahmalokaṁ na vindanti anṛtena hi pratyūḍhāḥ.*

'All these beings here, though they go daily into the world of Brahman, (Brahman in the form of the world) yet do not find Him, for they are carried away by the untrue'. (*CU*, 8-3-1).

The next text is from *Yajurveda*, '*nāsadāsīt no sadāsīḥ*' (2-8-9). The text "*asat* did not exist; *sat* did not exist," goes on to say that *tamas* existed and by *tamas* it (Brahman) was concealed before and could not be known. The Advaitin takes the word *tamas* to mean avidyā which was neither *sat* nor *asat.* Rāmānuja questions it saying that if this were accepted then the word 'before' would be meaningless as Brahman is concealed even now. Moreover, the expression neither *sat* existed nor *asat* could very well refer to Brahman also. So, says Rāmānuja, the text actually describes the cosmic rest, *avyaya*. The word 'before' means 'before creation' when *tamas* is the state when the *sat* that is *jīva* and *asat*, the matter were in subtle condition and did not exist as such. This is proved by another text *avyaktaṁ akṣare līyate; akṣaraṁ tamasi līyate* (*Subālopaniṣad* - 2).

The unmanifest is dissolved in the immutable, *akṣara* and the *akṣara* dissolves in *tamas*. Hence the word *tamas* denotes *acit samaṣṭirūpāyāḥ prakṛteḥ sūkṣmāvasthā ucyate,* the subtle matter in the form of *prakṛti* from which the world evolves.

The text *"māyāṁ tu prakṛtiṁ vidyāt māyinaṁ tu maheśvaram,"* (*ŚU*, 4-10) does not refer to *anirvacanīyā-avidyā* but the *prakṛti* is referred to as *māyā* from which this wonderful world has come out. The owner of *māyā* is Īśvara who controls it but is not under its influence. This is evident from the previous sentence of the same text *asmānmāyī srjate viśvametat,* from this the owner of *māyā* creates this world. It is the *jīva* who is bound by *māyā* as proved by the text *anādimāyayā suptaḥ yadā jīvaḥ prabudhyate*, (*MU*, 11-29). When the *jīvā* who sleeps due to beginningless *māyā* wakes up. The Lord Himself says in the *Gītā* '*mama māyā duratyayā*', my *māyā* is difficult to transcend. Thus there is no support for the *anirvacanīya-avidyā* from the *śruti* texts nor for its being a positive entity.

The text '*tat tvamasī*' is explained by the Advaitin to mean the identity of the jīva with Brahman and due to the incongruity between the two, namely, the limited knowledge and power of a jīva, who is in bondage as compared with the infinite, omniscient and omnipresent and omnipotent Brahman, it is necessary to postulate the existence of avidyā which conceals Brahman so that the identity is not seen. Rāmānuja refutes this and says *aikya upadeśas tu tvaṁ-śabdenāpi jīvaśarīrakasya brahmaṇa eva abhidhānāt upapannataraḥ.*

The expression of identity between *jīva* and Brahman suffers no inconsistency because the word 'thou' also implies Brahman only who is the inner controller of the jīva being the inner self of the jīva who forms the *śarīra* of Brahman. This is denoted by the text *anena jīvena ātmanā anupraviśya nāmarūpe vyākaravāṇi* (CU, 6-3-2). I will enter this jīva as its *ātmā* and make name and form.

The Advaitins cite passages from *Viṣṇupurāṇa* which claim that Brahman alone is the reality and the world is only empirically real.

But Rāmānuja says that the real import of the passage is that in the world made up of sentient and insentient beings, the jīvas are not affected by the changes in the insentient and they are eternal and hence they are termed as existent while the insentient which is different and destructible are said to be non-existent. But both have Vāsudeva as their inner self. It is shown to be thus in the passage *tāni sarvāṇi tadvapuḥ; tatsarvaṁ vai harervapuḥ (Viṣṇupurāṇa,* 1-22-86-38*).* All that exists is His *śarīra*, and by the words *sa eva sarvabhūtātmā viśvarūpo yato avyayaḥ* (*Viṣṇupurāṇa*, 1-2-69). He alone is the Self of all beings, with cosmic form and immutable.

In all the passages in the *Viṣṇupurāṇa*, says Rāmānuja, there is no evidence of Brahman being *nirviśeṣa* or for the Avidyā which is neither *sat* nor *asat* abiding in Brahman. The terms *nāsti* and *asatya* indicate non-existence but not *anirvacanīya*. These two words denote insentient objects not because they are non-existent, *tuccha* or unreal, *mithyā* but only because they are perishable.

To sum up, ātman is *ādimadhyāntarahita*, without beginning, middle and end and always of the same nature and hence it is referred to as existent. The insentient, *acetana* is the object of enjoyment for the jīva and is transformed according to the karma of the jīva and perishable. Therefore it is termed as non-existent. The objects which are existent or non-existent with reference to time, place or action are *aparamārtha*, unreal and the ātman alone is fit to be cognised as *asti*, existent and hence *paramārtha*, real. The same view is expressed in *Viṣṇupurāṇa* by Maitreya, *"viṣṇvādhāraṁ yathā caitat trailokyaṁ samavasthitam, paramārthas ca me prokto yatha jñānapradhānataḥ."* You have taught me how these worlds are supported by Viṣṇu and how *ātman having jñāna* as his *svarūpa* is *paramārtha*, real, being important.

6. Nivartaka-anupapatti

Rāmānuja says *"tattvamasyādivākyeṣu samānādhikaraṇyam na nirviśeṣavastvaikyaparam."* The texts like 'that thou art' do not denote attributeless Brahman. As already pointed out by Rāmānuja in explaining the principle of *sāmānādhikaraṇya* referring to the purport of the Vedic text '*satyaṁ jñānaṁ anantaṁ brahma*' there is no need of dismissing the attributes in explaining the identity.

According to him the words 'that' and 'thou' both denote Brahman only that too as *saviśeṣa.* The contention that the removal of avidyā is effected by the knowledge of Brahman as *nirviśeṣa* is not tenable.

The Advaitins cite the statement '*so ayaṁ devadattaḥ*', this is that Devadatta, to prove his point that the primary meaning of the terms cannot be taken as the person qualified by different time and place is being spoken of as one. So the identity will be established only if the reference to time and place are given up. So too as 'that' denotes Brahman who is infinite and attributeless and 'thou' refers to jīva who is finite with limited knowledge and power, the identity can be established only by not considering the limitations of the jīva and the infinite nature etc. of Brahman in which case both will be identical in essence. This can be accomplished only by the removal of avidyā through the real knowledge of the Brahman as attributeless which serves as the *nivartaka* of avidyā.

Rāmānuja refutes this, saying, "*tatpadaṁ hi sarvajñaṁ satyasaṅkalpaṁ jagatkāraṇaṁ brahma parāmṛśati; tadaikṣata bahusyāṁ iti tasyaiva prakṛtatvāt.*" The word 'that' in 'that thou art' refers only to Brahman omniscient and omnipotent, who is the cause of the world as denoted by the sentence 'it will become many'.

Even in the example '*so'yaṁ devadattaḥ*' there is no necessity for adopting secondary meaning, *lakṣaṇā* of the words because the person connected with the past and the present times is one only. If the word 'that' is taken to mean pure attributeless Brahman then it will conflict with the sentence 'it willed to become many and the promissory statement '*ekavijñānena sarvavijñānam*', by knowing the one, everything becomes known. Hence the word 'that' denotes Brahman who is *saviśeṣa* and the word 'thou' refers to the Brahman who is the real self of the jīva which alone is meant by 'that thou art'.

Rāmānuja further proceeds to show that there is no sublation here as in the case of shell-silver. The word 'that' does not bring up any attribute that sublates the first perception of 'thou' as in the case of shell-silver as according to Advaita as Brahman is attributeless. What is meant here is this: When the shell is seen as silver, the attribute of silver, that is silverness, is seen in the shell which is sublated when the shell becomes known as such due to the perception of the attribute shellness. In the explanation of '*tat tvamasī*' by the Advaitin there can be no attribute of Brahman which becomes known to cause the sublation of the perception of the jīva as such, because Brahman is said to be attributeless.

The Advaitins may contend that it is not necessary to perceive some attribute in the substantive entity in order to remove the first erroneous impression. It is enough to show that *svarūpa*, the real nature of the substance is hidden from one's sight by some defect, becomes visible when the defect is removed.

Rāmānuja says that if *svarūpa* of Brahman is concealed, there can be no misapprehension and if not concealed there is no need for removal of misconception. Unless an attribute which is real and hidden is admitted, there can be no sublation. Rāmānuja explains this by the analogy of a prince, getting lost while very young; did not know his identity on account of being brought up by hunters. His misconception will not be removed by merely stating that he is not a hunter but only by the knowledge that he is a prince.

Rāmānuja interprets the text '*tat tvamasi*' in such a manner that both the words '*tat*' and '*tvam*' retain their primary meaning and need no recourse to *lakṣaṇā*, secondary meaning, as the Advaitin claims. The *samānādhikaraṇya*, apposition, is achieved by the two words meaning the same Brahman, qualified with two attributes, namely, possessing infinite number of auspicious attributes and being the cause of the world on one hand and being the indwelling Self of all on the other. This explanation is consistent with the beginning of the passage 'it willed to become many,' and also the promissory statement of '*ekavijñānena sarvavijñānam*' as the gross world consisting of sentient and insentient beings, which form His body in their subtle state, is the effect of Brahman, being ensouled by Him. This is brought up by the previous sentence to '*tat tvamasi*' that all this is ensouled by Brahman. '*aitadātmyaṁ idaṁ sarvam*'. The reason for this is stated in *sanmūlāḥ saumya imāḥ sarvāḥ prajāḥ ṣadāyatanāḥ satpratiṣṭhāḥ*, all these beings have their root in *sat*, rest in *sat* and dissolved in *sat* (*CU*, 6-8-4).

Rāmānuja quotes other texts also to show that Brahman is the Self of all the sentient and the insentient and the identity of Brahman with jīva is established through the *śarīrātmabhāva*, the body-soul relationship.

1. *antaḥ-praviṣtaḥ śāstā janānām sarvātmā* (*Taitirīyāraṇyaka*, 3-11-21). The inner Self is the controller of all.
2. *yaḥ ātmani tiṣthan ātmanaḥ antaraḥ yaṁ ātmā na veda yasya ātmā śarīraṁ ya ātmānaṁ antaro yamayati sa ta ātmā antaryāmyamṛtaḥ* (*BU*, 5-7-4). He, the immortal, inner ruler, is the inner Self, situated inside the *ātmā* whom *ātmā* did not know and who controls the *ātmā* from within to whom the *ātmā* is the *śarīra*.
3. *anena jīvena ātmanānupraviṣya nāmarupe vyākaravāṇi*, (*CU*, 6-3-2). I will enter into the *jīva* as its inner self and will make *nāma* and *rūpa*.

Therefore, says Rāmānuja, the identity of all beings, sentient and insentient with Brahman can be established only through the *śarīra-śārīri-bhāva*. And as all that is other than Brahman is His *śarīra* the denotation of everything terminates only in Brahman.

> *ataḥ cidacidātmakasya sarvasya vastujātasya brahma-tādātmyaṁ ātmaśarīrabhāvādeva iti avagamyate; tasmāt brahmavyatiriktasya kṛtṣnasya taccharīratvenaiva vastutvāt tasya pratipādako'pi śabdaḥ tatparyantameva svārtham abhidadhati.*

7. Nivṛttyanupapatti

The view of the Advaitin that the Avidyā can be removed only through the knowledge of identity is refuted by Rāmānuja, who says, '*brahmātmaikatvavijñānena avidyānivṛttiḥ yuktā iti tadayuktam, bandhasya pāramārthikatvena jñāna-nivartyatva abhāvāt.* That is, the bondage being not illusory but real it cannot be removed by mere knowledge. Rāmānuja explains bondage as: *puṇyāpuṇya-rūpa-karmanimittadevādi-śarīrapraveśa-tatprayukta-sukhaduḥkh-ānubhava-rūpaḥ bandhaḥ*.

The experience of pleasure and pain by entering into the bodies of Deva etc., according to the result of meritorious and sinful actions. This cannot be illusory and can be removed only through the grace of the Lord by means of devotional worship. This can be destroyed only by the knowledge of Brahman as the inner self and controller and not of identity with Brahman. Moreover, says Rāmānuja, the knowledge that is said to remove avidyā is also unreal as everything except Brahman is *mithyā* for Advaitin and hence another knowledge that removes this one should be sought. This second knowledge also being *mithyā,* it will lead to ad-infinitum, *anavasthā*. If the removing knowledge is said to perish after removing avidyā, such an argument cannot be accepted. This knowledge which removes everything that is not Brahman is said to be mere *cit*, consciousness. If so, Rāmānuja asks, who is the knower? It cannot be the 'I' the object of avidyā which is removed with the avidyā. It cannot be Brahman either, since Brahman is not a knower but pure consciousness according to Advaita. If the knower and the knowledge are said to disappear along with the rest, being other than Brahman, it is absurd, says Rāmānuja, like one cutting down everything other than the ground, which includes cutting down himself and the act of cutting down itself, '*bhūtalavyatiriktaṁ kṛtsnaṁ devadattena chinnaṁ ityasyāmeva chedanakriyāyāṁ chettuḥ asyāḥ chedanakriyāyāśca chedyanupraveśana-vacanavat upahāsyam.*'

Rāmānuja concludes the *Mahāsiddhānta* by saying: "*tasmāt anādikarmapravāha-rūpājñānamūlatvāt bandhasya tannibarhaṇaṁ uktalakṣaṇajñānādeva.*" That is, as bondage is due to the result of beginningless flow of karma, its removal can be only through the knowledge that Brahman is the inner-self and ruler different from souls and matter. This knowledge can arise only through the grace of the Lord, by following the *varṇāśrama-dharma* and duties enjoined in the Vedas, not desiring result but as an offering to the Lord which culminates in intense devotion and meditation leading to *mokṣa*. As this requires the knowledge of Vedas the study of the Pūrvamīmāṁsā is the pre-requisite to the study of Vedānta.

Note

1. All the Sanskrit quotations in this article are taken from: *Śrībhāṣyam: Śārīrakamīmāṁsābhāṣyam* (Critical Edition), Chief Editor: M.A. Lakshmithathachar, The Academy of Sanskrit Research Series - 4, Melkote, 1985.

5

THE PRE-RĀMĀNUJA VIŚIṢṬĀDVAITINS AND THEIR CRITICISM OF THE MĀYĀVĀDA

M. Narasimhachary

The pre-Rāmānuja Vaiṣṇava thinkers who criticized the Advaitins' concept of māyā-avidyā are Nāthamuni and Yāmuna. Nāthamuni's two works *viz.*, the *Nyāyatattva* and the *Yogarahasya* are mere names to us, but for the fact that a few quotations from the *Nyāyatattva* are available to us. Rāmānuja, in his *Śrībhāṣya* (under 1.1.1), at the beginning of the *Mahāsiddhānta* quotes three verses. They are:

jñānarūpaṁ paraṁ brahma tannivartyaṁ mṛṣātmakam
ajñānaṁ cet tiraskuryāt, kaḥ prabhus tannivartane?

jñānaṁ brahmeti cet jñānaṁ ajñānasya nivartakam
brahmavat tatprakāśatvāt, tadapi hyanivartakam.

jñānaṁ brahmeti vijñānaṁ asti cet, syāt prameyatā
brahmaṇo'nanubhūtitvaṁ tvaduktyaiva prasajyate.[1]

Sudarśana Sūri, in his *Śrutaprakāśikā*, identifies these verses as those of Nāthamuni (*atra nāthamunibhir uktān ślokānāha*).[2] It is presumed that these formed part of the *Nyāyatattva*.

Rāmānuja quoted the first of these verses under "*āśrayānupapatti*". Roughly translated, it means: "If ignorance, which is of the nature of unreality and is removable by knowledge can conceal the highest Brahman, then who else will be capable of removing that ignorance?" Rāmānuja quoted this to point out that according to

Advaitins, avidyā (called ajñāna by Nāthamuni) can be sublated by knowledge. Incidentally, this verse of Nāthamuni also spells out the "*Tirodhāna-anupapatti.*"

The second verse of Nāthamuni means: "If you contend that the knowledge to the effect, 'Brahman is knowledge' (Consciousness) can remove avidyā, that knowledge being not something different from the essential nature of Brahman, it cannot constitute an effective remover of Ignorance." One may note here the germ of "*Nivartaka-anupapatti*". The third verse quoted here means: "If one has the knowledge that Brahman Itself is knowledge, then Brahman becomes cognisable. But according to your own statement, Brahman cannot become an object of experience." Commenting on this, Sudarśana Sūri says:

> *kiṁ svarūpabhūtajñānāt nivartakajñānasya viṣayavaiṣamyam asti vā na vā? asti cet - saviśeṣatvaṁ, no cet, svarūpameva nivartakaṁ syāt; pramāṇajanyajñānam anivartakaṁ vā syāt; puro'vasthitabhāsvaravastuviṣayajñānavat; pramāṇajanyajñānatvam na nivartakatve prayojakam; idaṁ śuklabhāsvaradravyamiti vākyajanyasya jñānasya nivartakatvābhāvāt; tasmāt bhramasahakārāt atiriktākāraviṣayatvaṁ nivartakatve prayojakam.*"[3]

It is clear from the above, that Rāmānuja is not the first critic to point out "*anupapattis*" in the Advaitins' concept of māyā-avidyā. Nāthamuni, as the verses cited from him show, was perhaps the first Vaiṣṇava theologian to have criticised avidyā.

The next writer and the immediate predecessor and Paramācārya of Rāmānuja who subjected avidyā to a systematic criticism was Yāmuna (Āḷavandār). His *Saṁvitsiddhi*, which is unfortunately full of gaps, provides an insight into his analysis of the concept of māyā/avidyā.

The term "avidyā" may be explained as the "absence of vidyā." But according to this interpretation, Avidyā would become an absolute non-entity like hare's horn, and so it cannot have any hand in the world-manifestation. The other alternative is that avidyā is different from vidyā which would only undermine the Advaitic declaration that avidyā is "*anirvacanīya*". Yāmuna observes:

> *athārthāntarabhāvo'pi tasyāste bhrāntikalpitaḥ*
> *hantaivaṁ satyavidya iva vidyā syāt paramārthataḥ*

kiñca śuddhājaḍā saṁvit, avidyeyaṁ tu nedṛśī
tatkena hetunā seyam anyaiva na nirūpyate?[4]

Yāmuna feels that avidyā has got to be an entity different from vidyā which is unalloyed and self-manifest, since the former is diametrically opposed to it. Even on the view that avidyā is that which is opposed (*viruddha*) to vidyā, avidyā can find no place at all since according to Advaita, the entire universe is pervaded by a single unqualified *Saṁvit*, thus leaving no room for avidyā.

Speaking about the question of "*āśraya*" (locus) for avidyā, Yāmuna says it cannot be proved at all. Jīva cannot be the locus since it is not possible to specify who the jīva is. If jīva is said to be the substrate of avidyā, then there will be the fallacy of *anyonyāśraya* since *jīvatva* and avidyā are interdependent.

kiñcāsau kasya? jīvasya; ko jīvaḥ? yasya seti cet nanvevam -asamādhānam
anyonyāśrayaṇaṁ bhavet narte jīvād avidyā syāt, na ca jīvaḥ tayā vinā.[5]

This cannot be explained away on the analogy of "*bījāṅkuranyāya*", as contended in the *Brahmasiddhi* ("*anāditvād ubhayoravidyā-jīvayoḥ bījāṅkurasantānayoriva netaretarāśrayatvaṁ*").[6] Yāmuna points out that unlike the *bīja* and *aṅkura*, the jīva is unborn. The only other way is to admit that Brahman Itself is the *āśraya* which is absolutely non-admissible. Brahman is omniscient. It should not be contended that omniscience is just an outcome of avidyā and thus illusory since texts like "*parāsya śaktir vividhaiva śrūyate, svābhāvikī jñāna-balakriyā ca*" (*Śvetāsvatara Upaniṣad*, VI.8) declare the perfections of Brahman to be natural and positive. The Advaitins may try to prove that omniscience is illusory through inference on the ground that omniscience consists in the cognition of difference (*bheda*).

In reply Yāmuna would say that the same reason, viz., "cognition of differences" would itself establish the reality of Omniscience, as in the case of the Mīmāṁsā principles of *śabdāntara, abhyāsa, saṅkhyā, guṇa, prakriyā* (content) and *nāmadheya* (name).[7]

bhedāvabhāsagarbhatvāt atha sarvajñatā mṛṣā
tata evāmṛṣā kasmāt na syāt śabdāntarādivat?

In the Pūrva-mīmāṁsā system, the above principles are employed to distinguish one rite from another on the basis of the distinction of one *apūrva* from another, resulting from the performance of those rites. These principles involve the cognition of difference, and are also held valid and real. Likewise, since Omniscience involves the cognition of differences, it should also be admitted to be valid and real. Further, if the Omniscient Brahman Which is ever free from bondage Himself forms the *āśraya* of ignorance, there could be nothing in the world to dispel it.

sarvajñe nityamukte'pi yadyajñānasya sambhavaḥ
tejasīva tamaḥ tasmāt na nivarteta kenacit. [8]

It may be noted that this idea of Yāmuna is an echo of the verse "*jñānarūpam paraṁ brahma*" of Nāthamuni quoted above. In other words, this spells out the "*Nivartaka-anupapatti*". The Advaitins cannot state that the validity of scriptures which speak of Omniscience of the Lord is merely conventional and that absolute validity is open only to texts which speak of the Oneness of Brahman, for, there is no proof for such a claim, observes Yāmuna.

sarvajñatvādivacana - prāmāṇyam vyāvahārikam
tāttvikam tu pramāṇatvam advaitavacasāmiti
niyāmakam na paśyāmo nirbandhāt tāvakādṛte. [9]

A further defect in this theory of the Advaitins is that one and the same Brahman cannot simultaneously be the *āśraya* and the *viṣaya* of avidyā.

āśrayapratiyogitve parāparavirodhinī
kathaṁ vaikarasam brahma saditi pratipadyate? [10]

Yāmuna then turns his attention to the claim of the Advaitins that Māyā is indefinable (*anivarcanīya*). For the Advaitins, avidyā is not an entity (*na vastu*). If that be true, how can it form an object of thought and discussion? asks Yāmuna. Further, they say that avidyā cannot be an absolute non-entity like a sky-lotus. When they say that it is not an *avastu*, the double negative would yield a positive sense, in which case it would mean that avidyā is a real entity. When such a definition is possible, how can avidyā be "*anirvacanīya*"?

kiñcāvidyā na ced vastu, vyavahāryaṁ katham bhavet?
nāpyavastviticoktau tu vastutvaṁ siddhyati dhruvam.
niṣidhyate samastena nañā vastviti cet matam

samastena naňā vastu prathamam yanniṣiddhyate
pratiprasūtaṁ vyastena punastaditi vastutā.[11]

On the basis of these statements of Yāmuna we can presume that the refutation of the concept of māyā-avidyā found in the *Śrībhāṣya* of Rāmānuja pointing out several *anupapattis* has its precursor in the works of Yāmuna, who himself was inspired by his grandfather Nāthamuni.

The excellence of Rāmānuja system, as observed by K. Seshadri, however, lies not in the refutation of the avidyā-māyā of the Advaitins, but in the mysticism of the Āḷvārs and the mystic implications found in the works of Ācāryas like Yāmuna and Rāmānuja.[12] But a discussion on the sevenfold inconsistencies in avidyā-māyā as formulated by Rāmānuja and expounded by writers like Vedāntadeśika (*Śatadūṣaṇī*) has its own charm and utility. Conclusions may perhaps be never made; but the exchange of views by erudite scholars representing different systems like Advaita, Viśiṣṭādvaita and Dvaita on the single theme "*Saptavidhānupapattis*" keeps the door of debate still open, enthusing young and promising scholars in their specialised studies.

NOTES

1. Uttamur Viraraghavacharya, (ed.) *Śrībhāṣya* with the commentary *Śrutaprakāśikā* of Sudarśanasūri, Śrī Viśiṣṭādvaita-pracāriṇī-sabhā, Madras, 1989. Part I, p. 257.
2. Ibid., p. 257.
3. Ibid., p. 258.
4. Uttamur Viraraghavacharya,(ed.) *Siddhitraya of Yāmuna*, (with an English commentary by R. Ramanujacharya) Ubhaya Vedanta Grantha-mala Book Trust, Nathamuni St., Madras - 17, 1972, p.106.
5. Ibid., p.107.
6. See *Brahmasiddhi* with Śaṅkhapāṇi's commentary ed. by. S. Kuppuswami Sastri, Madras Government Manuscripts Series No. 4, 1937, p.10.
7. Cf. *Saṁvit-siddhi* in *Siddhitraya*, op. cit. p.107.
8. SS. p. 305.
9. Ibid., p. 306.
10. Ibid., p. 306.
11. Ibid., p. 307.
12. See K. Seshadri, "Viśiṣṭādvaita - Its Mystical and Metaphysical Undertones", *Journal of Madras University*, 32.1.2, 1971, pp-22-46.

6

आश्रयानुपपत्तिः

N. S. Ramanuja Tatacharya

अविद्याया आश्रयानुपपत्तिः आदौ श्रीभाष्यानुसारेण निरूप्यते। जिज्ञासाधिकरणे तावत् अविद्या किमाश्रित्य भ्रमं जनयतीत्याक्षेपं कृत्वा न तावज्जीवमाश्रित्य जीवभावस्याविद्याकल्पितत्वेन सत्यामविद्यायां तदधीनकल्पनविषयः जीवभावः, सति च जीवभावे तदाश्रिताविद्यासिद्धिरित्येवमन्योन्याश्रयदोष इति भाष्ये उक्तम्। आरम्भणाधिकरणे चाविद्याया जीव आश्रय इति पक्षो विस्तरेण दूषितः। तथा हि -

एकमेव ब्रह्म सर्वशरीरेषु जीवभावमनुभवति चेत् यथा पादे मे वेदना शिरसि मे वेदनेत्यनेकवेदनास्वेकस्यैवानुसन्धानं, तथाऽनेकशरीरोपाधिव्यवस्थितानेकवेदनास्वेकस्यैवानुसन्धानप्रसङ्गात्। न चैतदस्ति। अन्यथा चरणतललग्नकण्टकोद्धरणाय पाणितलव्यापारवत् मैत्रशरीरलग्नकण्टकोद्धरणाय चैत्रशरीरव्यापारप्रसङ्गात्। जीवेश्वरबद्धमुक्तशिष्याचार्यज्ञत्वज्ञत्वादिव्यवस्था च न स्यादिति चेत् - अत्राहुः जीवाज्ञानवादिनः-

एकस्यैव ब्रह्मणः प्रतिबिम्बभूतानां जीवानां सुखित्वदुःखित्वादयः एकस्यैव मुखस्य प्रतिबिम्बानां मणिकृपाणदर्पणादिषु दृश्यमानानामल्पत्वमलिनत्वमहत्त्वविमलत्वादिवत् तत्तदुपाधिवशाद्व्यवस्थाप्यन्ते॥

ननु "अनेन जीवेनात्मनानुप्रविश्य" इत्यादिश्रुतेः न जीवाः ब्रह्मणो भिद्यन्त इति चेत्- सत्यं परमार्थतो न भिद्यन्त इति। वयं तूपाधिकल्पितं भेदमाश्रित्येमां व्यवस्थां ब्रूमः॥

ननु कस्येयं कल्पना? न तावत् ब्रह्मणः, तस्य परिशुद्धज्ञानस्वरूपस्य कल्पनाशून्यत्वात्। नापि जीवानाम् - इतरेतराश्रयप्रसङ्गात् - कल्पनाधीनो जीवभावः, जीवाश्रया च कल्पनेति। नैतदेवम् - अविद्याजीवभावयोर्बीजाङ्कुरन्यायेनानादित्वात्॥

किञ्च प्रासादनिगरणादिवदनुपपन्नतैकवेषायामवस्तुभूतायामविद्यायां नेतरेतराश्रयादयो वस्तुदोषाः अनवक्लृप्तिम् (असिद्धिम्) आवहन्ति॥

वस्तुतो ब्रह्मव्यतिरिक्तानां जीवानां स्वतःशुद्धत्वेऽप्यौपाधिकाशुद्धिसम्भवादविद्याश्रयत्वोपपत्तेः जन्मजरामरणादेः काल्पनिकत्वोपपत्तिः। यथा वस्तुतो मुखव्यतिरिक्तेऽपि मुखप्रतिबिम्बे मणिकृपाणाद्युपाधिवशात् श्यामतादिरूपाऽशुद्धिः तद्वत्। प्रतिबिम्बगतश्यामतादिवत् जीवगताशुद्धिरपि भ्रान्तिरेव। अन्यथाऽनिर्मोक्षप्रसङ्गात्। अशुद्धिविषयभ्रमेणोत्तरोत्तराविद्याश्रयत्वम्, अविद्याश्रयत्वेनोत्तरोत्तराशुद्धिविषयभ्रम इत्यन्योन्याश्रय इति नाशङ्कनीयम्। जीवानां तादृशभ्रमस्य प्रवाहानादित्वेन तद्धेत्वपेक्षाविरहात्।

अयं जीवाश्रयाज्ञानपक्षः श्रीभाष्येऽनूदितो भामत्यां तत्र तत्र दृश्यते। "तदधीनत्वादर्थवत्" (ब्र. सू. १.४.३) इति सूत्रे "अविद्यात्मिका हि बीजशक्तिरव्यक्तशब्दनिर्देश्या परमेश्वराश्रया मायामयी महासुप्तिः" इति शाङ्करभाष्यव्याख्यानभामत्याम् "जीवाधिकरणाप्यविद्या निमित्ततया विषयतया वा ईश्वरमाश्रयत इति ईश्वराश्रयेत्युच्यते, न त्वाधारतया, विद्यास्वभावे ब्रह्मणि तदनुपपत्तेः" इत्युक्तम्। तत्रैव -

> न वयं प्रधानवदविद्यां सर्वजीवेष्वेकामाचक्ष्महे, येनैवमुपालभ्येमहि। किन्त्वयं प्रतिजीवं भिद्यते। तेन यस्यैव जीवस्य विद्योत्पद्यते, तस्यैव साऽविद्याऽपनीयते, न जीवान्तरस्य। भिन्नाधिकरणयोर्विद्याविद्ययोरविरोधात्। तत् कुतः समस्तसंसारोच्छेदप्रसङ्गः। न चाविद्योपाधिभेदाधीनः जीवभेदः, जीवभेदाधीनोऽविद्याभेद इति परस्पराश्रयादुभयासिद्धिरिति वाच्यम्। अनादित्वाद्बीजाङ्कुरवदुभयसिद्धेः। अविद्यात्वमात्रेणैकत्वव्यवहारः अव्यक्तमिति अव्याकृतमिति च। इति प्रतिपादितम्॥

जीवस्याविद्याश्रयत्वानुपपत्तिः

जीवस्याकल्पितस्वाभाविकरूपेणाविद्याश्रयत्वं वा कल्पिताकारेणाविद्याश्रयत्वं वा। नाद्यः, ब्रह्मणोऽविद्याश्रयत्वमिति पक्ष एव पर्यवसानात्। न द्वितीयः, जडस्यैवाविद्याश्रयत्वमिति पर्यवसानात्। ब्रह्म चिद्रूपम्। कल्पितं तु जडम्। तदुभयातिरिक्तानभ्युपगमात् कल्पिताकारेणाविद्याश्रयत्वे, जडस्यैव ह्यविद्याश्रयत्वमुक्तं भवति। स्वरूपस्याखण्डैकरसस्याविद्यामन्तरेण विशिष्टरूपत्वासिद्धेः। तथा चाविद्याश्रयत्वे सति विशिष्टरूपत्वं, विशिष्टाकार एवाविद्याश्रय इत्यन्योन्याश्रयो दोषः॥

किञ्च बन्धमोक्षव्यवस्थासिद्ध्यर्थं हि जीवाज्ञानवादाश्रयणम्। सा तु व्यवस्था जीवाज्ञानपक्षेऽपि न सिद्ध्यति। अविद्यानाश एव हि मोक्षः। तत्रैकस्मिन्मुक्तेऽविद्याया विनाशादितरेऽपि मुच्येरन्। इतरेषाममुक्तत्वादविद्या तिष्ठतीति चेत्तर्ह्येकस्याप्यमुक्तिः स्यात्, अविद्याया अविनष्टत्वात्॥

प्रतिजीवमविद्याभेदः कल्प्यते। तत्र यस्याविद्या विनष्टा स मोक्ष्यते, यस्य त्वविनष्टा स भन्त्स्यत इति चेन्न। प्रतिजीवमिति जीवभेदमाश्रित्य ब्रूषे। स जीवभेदः किं स्वाभाविक

उताविद्याकल्पितः? नाद्यः, अद्वैतहानिप्रसङ्गेनानभ्युपगमात्। जीवभेदसिद्ध्यर्थस्य चाविद्याकल्पनस्य व्यर्थत्वात्। न द्वितीयः, तत्रेयं जीवभेदकल्पिकाऽविद्या किं ब्रह्मण उत जीवानाम्। ब्रह्मण इति चेत् - ब्रह्माज्ञानवादप्रसङ्गः। अथ जीवानां, किमस्या जीवभेदक्लृप्ति-सिद्ध्यर्थतां विस्मरसि। तथा च जीवभेदकल्पकाविद्या जीवभेदकल्पनात् प्रागेव न जीवानाश्रयितुं क्षमा, जीवासिद्धेः ॥

न च बीजाङ्कुरन्यायः सम्भवति। बीजाङ्कुरेषु ह्यन्यदन्यद्बीजमन्यस्यान्यस्याङ्कुरस्योत्पादकम्। इह तु याभिरविद्याभिर्ये जीवाः कल्प्यन्ते तानेवाश्रित्य तासां सिद्धिरिति वैषम्यात्। एतदुक्तं भवति - बीजाङ्कुरेषूत्पादकबीजस्योत्पाद्याङ्कुरापेक्षा नास्ति। उत्पादकमङ्कुरमन्यत्, उत्पाद्यं चान्यत्। अत्र तु जीवभेदकल्पकाऽविद्यायाः कल्पनीयजीवाश्रयापेक्षाऽस्ति। कल्पकाऽविद्याश्रयो जीवः, स एव कल्प्यश्चेति वैषम्यमिति ॥

अथ बीजाङ्कुरन्यायेन पूर्वपूर्वजीवाश्रयाभिरविद्याभिरुत्तरोत्तरजीवकल्पनं ब्रूमः। जीवाना-मविद्यानां प्रवाहतोऽनादित्वं स्वीक्रियते। उत्पाद्योत्पादकाङ्कुरव्यक्तिभेदवत् कल्पकाविद्याश्रय-कल्प्यजीवव्यक्तिभेदान्न पूर्वोक्तदोष इति चेत्, तथा सति जीवानां भङ्गुरत्वम् अकृताभ्यागमः कृतविप्रणाश इत्यादिदोषप्रसङ्गः। जीवस्वरूपनित्यत्व-प्रतिपादकश्रुतिविरोधश्च ॥

एवं जीवाख्यधर्मिणः प्रवाहानादित्वकल्पने दूषणमुक्तम्। अथ जीवत्वधर्म-तत्कल्पकाविद्ययोः प्रवाहानादित्वेऽपि तदेव दूषणमतिदिशति - अत एव ब्रह्मणः पूर्वपूर्वजीवाश्रयाभि-रविद्याभिरुत्तरोत्तरजीवभावकल्पनमपि निरस्तमिति। निरासप्रकारश्चैवं - अविद्या-प्रवाहेऽभ्युपगम्यमाने तत्तत्कल्पितजीवभावस्यापि तद्वत्प्रवाहानादिता स्यान्न ध्रुवरूपता। आमोक्षां जीवभावविशिष्टस्य ध्रुवरूपत्वमिष्टं न सिद्ध्येत् ॥

यच्चोक्तम् - अविद्याया अवस्तुरूपत्वेनानुपपन्नतैकवेषायां तस्यां नेतरेतराश्रयादयो वस्तुदोषाः अनवक्लृप्तिमावहन्तीति, तथा सति मुक्तान् परं च ब्रह्माश्रयेदविद्या। शुद्धविद्या-स्वरूपत्वादशुद्धिरूपाविद्या न तत्र प्रसजतीति चेत् - किमुपपत्त्यनुवर्तिनी अविद्या? एवं तर्ह्यन्योन्याश्रयादिभिरुक्ताभिरुपपत्तिभिर्जीवानपि नाश्रयेत् ॥

अविद्याया जीवाश्रितत्वे मोक्षानुपपत्तिः

किञ्च जीवाश्रयाया अविद्यायास्तत्त्वज्ञानोदयान्नाशे सति जीवो नश्येद्वा न वा? यदि नश्येत्, स्वरूपोच्छित्तिलक्षणो मोक्षः स्यात्। नो चेदविद्यानाशेऽप्यनिर्मोक्षः। ब्रह्मस्वरूपातिरिक्तजीवत्वस्याभावात् ॥

यच्चोक्तं मणिकृपाणदर्पणादिषूपलभ्यमानमुखमलिनत्वविमलत्वादिवत् शुद्ध्यादि-व्यवस्थोपपत्तिरिति। तत्रेदं विमर्शनीयम् - अल्पत्वमलिनत्वादयः औपाधिका दोषाः

कदा नश्येयुरिति। कृपाणाद्युपाध्यपगम इति चेत् - किं तदा अल्पत्वाद्याश्रयः प्रतिबिम्बं तिष्ठति वा न वा? तिष्ठति चेत् तत्स्थानीयस्य जीवस्यापि स्थितत्वात् अनिर्मोक्षप्रसङ्गः। नश्यति चेत् तद्वदेव जीवनाशात् स्वरूपोच्छित्तिलक्षणो मोक्षः स्यात्।

किञ्च यस्य ह्यपुरुषार्थरूपदोषप्रतिभासः तस्य तु तदुच्छेदः पुरुषार्थः। तत्र किमौपाधिकदोषप्रतिभासः बिम्बस्थानीयस्य ब्रह्मण उत प्रतिबिम्बस्थानीयस्य जीवस्य उतान्यस्य कस्यचित्। आद्ययोः कल्पयोर्दृष्टान्तोऽयं न सङ्गच्छते। मुखस्य मुखप्रतिबिम्बस्य चाल्पत्वादिदोषप्रतिभासशून्यत्वात्। न हि मुखं तत्प्रतिबिम्बं वा चेतयते। ब्रह्मणो दोषप्रतिभासे ब्रह्माविद्याप्रसङ्गश्च। तृतीयोऽपि कल्पो न कल्पते, जीवब्रह्मव्यतिरिक्तस्य द्रष्टुरभावात्।

किञ्चाविद्याकल्प्यस्य जीवस्य कल्पकः (भ्रमाश्रयः) कः? न तावदविद्या, अचेतनत्वात्। नापि जीवः, आत्माश्रयदोषप्रसङ्गात्। शुक्तिकारजतादिवदविद्या-कल्प्यत्वात् जीवभावस्य। अयं भावः - कल्पकत्वात् सिद्धिः कल्प्यत्वादसिद्धिश्चेति स्वसिद्धेः स्वापेक्षा। जीवविषयभ्रमाश्रये सिद्धे हि जीवक्लृप्तिः। जीवसिद्धेः स्वविषयभ्रमा-श्रयभूतेन स्वेनैव सापेक्षत्वादात्माश्रयत्वमिति। शुक्तिकारजतादिवदित्यादिना अनुपपत्त्यन्तरमुच्यते। कल्प्यत्वात् च भ्रमाश्रयत्वमनुपपन्नम्। न हि दोषकल्प्यश्च रजतमर्थाश्रय इति। ब्रह्मैव कल्पकमिति चेत् ब्रह्माज्ञानमेवायातम्।

अविद्याया ब्रह्माश्रितत्वानुपपत्तिः

यद्यसौ परमात्मा त्वदुक्तप्रकारेण संविन्मात्रस्वरूपः यदि वा यथाश्रुति सर्वज्ञः नोभयथाऽपि तस्याज्ञानाश्रयत्वं सम्भवति। तथा हि - न तावत् घटादिवत् ज्ञातृत्वात्यन्ताभावलक्षणमज्ञानमिह विवक्षितम्। तस्य ब्रह्मण्यपि घटादाविव यावत्स्वरूपभावित्वेन स्वरूपे सति निवर्तयितुमशक्यत्वात्। नापि ज्ञानप्रागभावप्रध्वंसौ। ब्रह्मणि धर्मभूतस्य ज्ञानस्य कदाचिदप्यनभ्युपगमात्। नापि ज्ञानान्योन्याभावः, ज्ञानान्तरानङ्गीकारात्, स्वप्रतियोगिकभेदायोगाच्च। वृत्तिज्ञानात् अध्यस्तज्ञानाद्वा भेदस्य नित्यत्वेन निवर्त्यतयाऽभिमताज्ञानत्वायोगात्। भावरूपाज्ञानानभ्युपगमादेव नाभावान्तरमपि।

अतो यत्तदज्ञानं ज्ञाननिवर्त्यमभिमतं, तदज्ञानं ज्ञातर्येव भवितुमर्हति। ज्ञानस्य स्वाश्रय एवाज्ञाननिवर्तकत्वव्याप्तेः। न हि देवदत्तगतेन ज्ञानेन यज्ञदत्तगतमज्ञानं निवर्तते।

नन्वीश्वरादिगतेन ज्ञानेन कथं तदनुग्रहविषयजीवगताज्ञाननिवृत्तिस्तवेति चेन्न। तत्र शक्तिविशेषोपबृंहितत्वेन तदुपपत्तेः। न हि प्रकाशाकारतामात्रेण तत्र परगताज्ञाननिवर्तकत्वं, तथा सति नित्यं तन्निवृत्तिप्रसङ्गात्। अतो जीवगतेनान्तःकरणगतेन वा तत्त्वज्ञानेन ब्रह्माज्ञाननिवृत्तिरिति प्रत्युक्तम्। तदज्ञानं तज्ज्ञाननिवर्त्यमज्ञानं न तत् ज्ञातृत्वप्रसक्तिशून्ये ब्रह्मणि भवितुमर्हति। तथा च भाष्यं - "विवादाध्यासितमज्ञानं न ज्ञानमात्रब्रह्माश्रयम्,

अज्ञानत्वात्, शुक्तिकाद्यज्ञानवत्, ज्ञात्राश्रयं हि तत्"- इति। ब्रह्म नाज्ञानास्पदं ज्ञातृत्वविरहात् घटवदिति च।

ननु कल्पितं ज्ञातृत्वं ब्रह्मणोऽप्यस्तीति तस्याज्ञानाश्रयत्वोपपत्तिरिति चेन्न। अहङ्कारोपहितवेषेणैव तस्य ज्ञातृत्वकल्पनाङ्गीकारात् सुषुप्तिमरणादिष्वहङ्कार-प्रलयेऽपि संविदात्मनोऽज्ञानाश्रयत्वाभ्युपगमाच्च। ततश्च शुक्तिकाज्ञानवत् ब्रह्माज्ञानमप्यहमर्थ-निष्ठमिति वा कल्पनीयम्, सर्वत्र ब्रह्माज्ञानं वा त्यक्तव्यम्। यश्च वस्तुतो ज्ञातृत्वं परिगृह्याज्ञानमपि ब्रह्मणि स्थापयेत्, सोऽपि नित्यसर्वज्ञत्वानुपपत्त्या निरसनीयः।

किञ्च ब्रह्मप्रकाशबाध्यं ब्रह्माज्ञानमभिमतम्। ब्रह्म च नित्यस्वप्रकाशरूपम्। ततस्तेजसीव तिमिरं कथं तत्राज्ञानं स्यात्। तच्चेत् स्वस्मिन्नज्ञानं सहेत, कस्तस्य निवर्तकः।ब्रह्मविषयकं वृत्तिज्ञानमज्ञाननिवर्तकमिति चेत् - अनुभाव्यत्वे ब्रह्मण्यभ्युपगम्यमाने ब्रह्मणोऽननुभूतित्वप्रसङ्ग इति भवद्भिरेवोक्तत्वात् तद्विरोधः।

ननु भवन्मतेऽपि जीवस्वरूपं स्वप्रकाशं, तदेव चाज्ञानाश्रयतयाऽभिमतमिति चेत् सत्यम्। तथापि न तत्र विरोधः। न हि स्वप्रकाशांशप्रत्यनीकमप्रकाशांशं प्रत्यगात्मनो ब्रूमः। अपि तु तस्यैव देहेन्द्रियादिविलक्षणस्य स्वप्रकाशत्वनित्यत्व-स्वादुतमत्वादि धर्मविषयकमज्ञानम्। तच्च तदात्मगतेन विशिष्टविषयकेण ज्ञानेन निवर्तते। यथा च शबरसंवर्धितस्य राजकुमारस्य शबरतयाऽऽत्मानमभिमन्यमानस्य प्रकाशमान एव स्वात्मनि क्षत्रियत्वाज्ञानं, तच्चोपदेशादिजन्यराजत्वज्ञानेन निवर्तते। तद्वदत्रापि।

किञ्च ब्रह्मणो नित्यमुक्तत्वमज्ञानाश्रयत्वे कथं घटेत? अज्ञानाश्रयत्वं हि बन्धः। न ह्यज्ञानाश्रयत्वमनन्तर्भाव्य कश्चिद्बन्धो नाम। न च बन्धाभावादन्या मुक्तिः। ये च मुक्तिदशायां पाषाणवदज्ञानमिच्छन्ति तेऽपि न तदानीं संसारबीजभूतमज्ञानमनुमन्यन्ते।

अस्मन्मते तु यद्यपि सार्वज्ञमात्मनां स्वरूपप्रयुक्तं, तत् उपाधिवशात् निरुद्धमिदानीं न विद्यत इति बन्धमोक्षयोः कालभेदान्न विरोधः। अस्माकमप्यविद्यातन्निवृत्त्योः पौर्वापर्यान्न विरोध इति चेत्तर्हि नित्यमुक्तत्वव्याघातः।

अपि च ब्रह्मणः सर्वज्ञत्वादज्ञानाश्रयत्वं न सम्भवति। न हि सर्वः सर्वं जानाति यत्किञ्चित् सर्वमेव वा न जानातीति सम्भवति। श्रूयते हि "यः सर्वज्ञः सर्ववित्" इति। स्वयश्च ब्रवीति -

वेदाहं समतीतानि वर्तमानानि चार्जुन।

भविष्याणि च भूतानि मां तु वेद न कश्चन॥ इति। स्मरन्ति च -

"सर्वज्ञः सर्ववित् सर्वशक्तिज्ञानबलर्द्धिमान्" इत्यादि। श्रीभाष्ये ब्रह्मणः स्वयम्प्रकाशज्ञान-रूपत्वेनाविद्याविरोधित्वादविद्याश्रयत्वं न सम्भवतीत्युक्तम्। तदनन्तरं ज्ञानस्वरूपं

ब्रह्मेत्याकारकं वृत्तिज्ञानमज्ञानस्य निवर्तकं, न तु ब्रह्मस्वरूपभूतं ज्ञानमित्याशङ्क्य उभयोरपि ब्रह्मस्वरूपप्रकाशत्वे सत्यन्यतरस्याविद्याविरोधित्वमन्यतरस्य नेति विशेषानवगमात् - ज्ञानविषयत्वे ब्रह्मणोऽननुभूतित्वप्रसङ्गाच्चेति समाहितम् ॥

तदुपरि अधिष्ठानत्वात् शुक्त्यादिवत् ब्रह्मस्वरूपं न भ्रमविरोधीत्याशङ्क्य "शुक्त्यादयस्तु स्वयाथात्म्यप्रकाशे स्वयमसमर्थाः स्वाज्ञानाविरोधिनः तन्निवर्तने ज्ञानान्तरमपेक्षन्ते, ब्रह्म तु स्वानुभवसिद्धस्वयाथात्म्यमिति स्वाज्ञानविरोध्येव" इति ग्रन्थेन उक्तानुमाने जडत्वमुपाधिरित्युक्तम् ॥

द्वयी ह्यद्वैतिनां गतिः। ब्रह्मविषयकप्रमाणज्ञानं भ्रमनिवर्तकं प्रपञ्चमिथ्यात्व-विषयकज्ञानं भ्रमनिवर्तकमिति च। तत्र प्रथमपक्षो दूषितः। अथ द्वितीयपक्षः पर्यालोच्यते। किमिदं ब्रह्मव्यतिरिक्तमिथ्यात्वज्ञानं ब्रह्मयाथात्म्यज्ञानविरोधि उत प्रपञ्चसत्यत्व-रूपाज्ञानविरोधि? नाद्य, ब्रह्मयाथात्म्याविषयकत्वात्। ज्ञानाज्ञानयोरेकविषयकत्वेन हि विरोधः। प्रपञ्चमिथ्यात्वज्ञानं तत्सत्यत्वरूपाज्ञानेन विरुध्यते, तेन प्रपञ्चसत्यत्व-रूपाज्ञानमेव बाधितमिति ब्रह्मस्वरूपाज्ञानं तिष्ठत्येव ॥

ननु ब्रह्मस्वरूपाज्ञानं नाम तस्य सद्वितीयत्वज्ञानमेव। तत्तु ब्रह्मव्यतिरिक्त-मिथ्यात्वज्ञानेन निवृत्तम्। स्वरूपं तु स्वानुभवसिद्धमिति चेन्न। ब्रह्मणोऽद्वितीयत्वं स्वरूपं धर्मो वा। आद्ये तत्स्वानुभवसिद्धमिति तद्विरोधिसद्वितीयत्वरूपाज्ञानं तद्बाधं न स्याताम्। द्वितीये अनुभवरूपस्य ब्रह्मणोऽनुभाव्यधर्मविरहस्य भवतैव प्रतिपादितत्त्वात् तद्विरोधः। अतो ज्ञानरूपस्य ब्रह्मणो विरोधादेव नाज्ञानाश्रयत्वम् - इति निगमितम् ॥

Summary: Professor Ramanuja Tatacharya has taken up Rāmānuja's refutation of the māyā-avidyā, defending the untenability of the locus (*āśraya*) of avidyā, i.e., *Āśrayānupapatti,* as portrayed in the *Śrībhāṣya*. In the *Jijñāsādhikaraṇa* of *Śrībhāṣya,* a question was raised as to what is the locus of avidyā? It cannot be the jīva, the individual soul, since the very existence of the jīva pre-supposes avidyā. Since avidyā is imagined, the state of jīva is also imagined. If it is said that jīva is the locus of avidyā, then there will be mutual dependency. Rāmānuja, in the *Ārambhaṇādhikaraṇa* too, refuted the view that the jīva is the locus of avidyā.

The jīvas, according to Advaita, though possess intrinsic purity, are different from Brahman because of their association with limiting adjuncts. They are the locus of avidyā and the states of birth, old age, death are the imaginary states. It is like the face of a person which is different from the reflection of the face inside a mirror since the defects associated with the medium of reflection, i.e., mirror, also gets associated with the reflection. Similarly, the impurities in the individual soul are due to delusion. If such a view is not accepted, then Advaitin cannot justify his concept of liberation.

In his commentary to the *Brahmasūtra* (1.4.3.), "*tadadhīnatvādarthavat*", (being dependent on that, it serves some purpose) Śaṅkara states that the potential power, constituted by avidyā, which is mentioned by the word unmanifest, rests on God and is comparable to magic and it is a kind of deep-slumber in which the transmigrating souls sleep without any consciousness of their real nature. Vācaspati, on the basis of this passage, states that the ignorance is located in the jīva.

Now a question may be raised; Is it by very nature that the jīva is the locus of avidyā or in its imaginary form? The first view is not right because it is accepted that Brahman is the locus of avidyā. The second view is also not correct since jīva is accepted to be the locus of avidyā. Moreover, the view that jīva is ignorant is resorted to in order to establish the scheme of bondage and liberation.

The jīva, according to Rāmānuja, cannot be the locus of avidyā. In Advaita, liberation is removal of ignorance. If such a view is accepted, then the destruction of avidyā by one jīva should result in the liberation of all others. Since all others are not liberated, avidyā continues. If this is accepted, even if one non-liberated person is present, it is due to the non-destruction of avidyā.

According to Advaita, there is difference of avidyā in each jīva. It cannot be said that whose avidyā is destroyed, he is liberated and whosesoever avidyā is not destroyed he is bound. The question will arise: is such a difference in the jīvas natural or a product of ignorance? We cannot accept that the difference in the jīvas is natural because according to Advaita, such a difference is only imagined. The second view, viz., difference is a product of ignorance is also not right, because there would arise the question as to whether this ignorance which assumes the difference in the jīva, belongs to jīvas or to Brahman. If it belongs to Brahman, then the Brahman would have ignorance. If it belongs to jīva, we should not forget that avidyā is the criteria for assuming differences between the jīvas. Then the avidyā which is responsible for bringing about the difference between jīvas, exists before assuming the difference in the jīvas. Hence avidyā is not capable of being the locus of jīvas and the existence of the jīva cannot be established.

There is another problem as far as avidyā is concerned because it is of a particular make and a non-entity. In that case, how would the avidyā be the locus of the liberated souls and the supreme Brahman. Since Brahman is pure-knowledge, the impure avidyā cannot be located in It. In our empirical world situation, we see that the ignorance continues and therefore, avidyā cannot be the locus of jīva.

However, avidyā, which is said to be located in jīva, gets destroyed by the attainment of the knowledge of the reality, i.e. Brahman. In that case, will the jīva get destroyed or not? If jīva is destroyed, then liberation would mean the destruction of one's own form. If it is not so, then it would mean that even after the destruction of ignorance liberation is not attained, since there is the absence of the jīva other than that of Brahman.

That ignorance which is to be removed by knowledge, could only remain in a knower. Never indeed by the knowledge attained by Devadatta, the ignorance in Yajñadatta can be removed. The illumination pertaining to a particular person cannot remove ignorance in another person and if that is the case there will be the removal of ignorance eternally.

We may say that the state of being the knower is assumed in Brahman and that accounts for its being the locus of ignorance. It is not so. Brahman cannot be assumed to be the knower since it exists transcending the ego. In the state of deep-sleep and death there is no ego. In a similar manner, we cannot accept the Brahman to be the locus of ignorance. Brahman is eternally self-luminous. Hence as darkness cannot exist in the light, the ignorance cannot remain in Brahman. If Advaitns say that Brahman is the locus of ignorance, then who will remove it? On the other hand, if you say the modal knowledge (*akhaṇḍākāra-vṛtti-jñāna*) pertaining to Brahman is the remover of ignorance then Brahman would be an object of experience, whereas Brahman cannot be an object of experience according to Advaita.

How would the Advaitin say that Brahman is eternally liberated if it is the locus of ignorance? Without being located in ignorance there is no bondage. There is no liberation which is in the form of absence of knowledge. Those who expect to remain in ignorance in the state of liberation, they do not understand that ignorance is the cause of the world.

The Advaitins will have two-fold explanation. The knowledge "about Brahman" is dispeller of ignorance and the "knowledge of illusoriness of the world" is also the dispeller of ignorance. The first view is defective as shown above. On the second view, the question arises: whether the knowledge of falsity of the world which is different from Brahman is opposed to the knowledge of Brahman itself or it is opposed to the ignorance in the form of the reality of the world? The first is not correct, since Brahman is of the nature of its own objectivity. We cannot say the same object can be known and at the same time there is ignorance of that object. The knowledge of falsity of the world is opposed to the ignorance in the form of the reality of the world. Therefore, what is sublated is the ignorance about the reality of the world. Hence, ignorance relating to the essential nature of Brahman remains.

Then again, the ignorance of the essential nature of Brahman is in the form of its being associated with duality that is dispelled by the knowledge of falsity which is different from Brahman. If Advaitins say that the essential nature of Brahman is consciousness, it is not so. They have to specify whether the state of non-duality in case of Brahman is its essential characteristics or attributes. If the first is accepted, that is given to one's own experience i.e., the ignorance which is in the form of duality and the sublation of duality are opposed to the self-illumination of Brahman and therefore, self-illumination in case of Brahman cannot be proved.

If the second, since Brahman is of the nature of consciousness, it cannot be an object to be experienced. Hence the conclusive view is that since Brahman is of the form of knowledge, it cannot be the locus of ignorance.

7

ADVAITIN'S CRITIQUE OF ĀŚRAYĀNUPAPATTI

Vempaty Kutumba Sastry

"Avidyā" sometimes also referred to as "māyā" is the foundational concept of Advaita doctrine. Unlike the Viśiṣṭādvaitins, who accept three realities, namely Brahman, jīva and jagat, Advaitins accept only one ultimate reality, the Brahman, which according to them is self-luminous consciousness, without any attribute what-so-ever. For them, every other entity is only *asvaprakāśa* and *paricchinna*. Indeed, things other than the Brahman derive their existence on account of their superimposition on the Brahman, which is of the nature of existence. They get cognized only on account of the reflection of the Brahman, the consciousness. However, we should not lose sight of the fact that the jīva, the soul and the *jagat*, the world with all their countless divisions and varieties, are as real for the Advaitins as they are for any other school of philosophy prior to one's own liberation. They appear to be unreal and superimposed only from the point of view of the liberated. Thus to resolve the problem of one and many, the mediation of avidyā has become unavoidable for the Advaitin.

The genius of Rāmānuja has rightly assessed the importance of the concept of avidyā in the Advaitavedānta and spared no effort to strike it down. Thus came his famous theory of seven untenables of which the first one is the *Āśrayānupapatti* with which we are concerned in this paper. Rāmānuja asks whether the avidyā is located in the individual self i.e., jīva, or in the Brahman. Both ways, there are problems as follows:

1. If avidyā is located in jīva , the individual self, then the mutual interdependence is unavoidable, as jīva presupposes the notion of avidyā .
2. The second alternative is also not possible because Brahman, the self-luminous consciousness and the avidyā are mutually exclusive and thus cannot have the locus-loci relation. The Advaitin contends that there is no opposition between the consciousness, the Brahman and the avidyā for the simple reason that Brahman reveals avidyā and that which terminates avidya is *vṛttijñāna.*
3. Rāmānuja sees no distinction between what is called by the Advaitin as *svarūpajñāna* of the Brahman and the *vṛttijñāna* in the form that, "Brahman is self-luminous consciousness" for the simple reason that Brahman is self-luminous as it stands always self revealed. Hence, the *vṛttijñāna* reveals the same fact what on its own accord, stands revealed. Therefore, if *vṛttijñāna* is held to be in opposition to the avidyā and hence its destroyer, the *svarūpajñana* must also be held the same way. Therefore, avidyā cannot have the Brahman as its locus.
4. Rāmānuja is of the view that there is no possibility of any *vṛttijñāna* with Brahman as its content. For, if such *vṛttijñāna* is held to be possible then a contingency arises that Brahman too becomes an object of another cognition. This is not possible because it is self contradictory to accept something as self-luminous and yet to be an object of another cognition. Therefore, if knowledge is held to be the destroyer of avidyā, it must be the *svarūpajñāna* of the Brahman, for *vṛttijñāna* with Brahman as its content is not a possibility. Since, *svarūpajñāna* of the Brahman is eternal, acceptance of avidyā as located in Brahman becomes untenable.

5.a) Rāmānuja holds that it is futile to argue that the destroyer of avidyā is not the *brahmajñāna*, but the knowledge that everything other than the Brahman is non-real. For such knowledge is efficacious to remove the ignorance that the objects other than Brahman are real. For, it is a well established norm that knowledge removes ignorance only when the content and locus happen to be one and the same with regard to the knowledge and the ignorance. In this case, the content of the ignorance is the Brahman; whereas the content of knowledge is the world.

Vedāntadeśika devoted two chapters to examine the defence of the Advaitins to the two alternatives raised by Rāmānuja, namely, 1) Jīva as the locus of avidyā, (chapter 40), 2) Brahman as the locus of avidyā (chapter 19). In chapter forty, he examines the alternative that jīva is the locus of avidyā, and herein one may find that he is completely indifferent to the Advaitin's argument. When we closely read him, it becomes clear that he has only one question against Advaitin and that is about mutual inter-dependency raised by Rāmānuja, except making few more alternatives and using jargon of philosophical Sanskrit writing. Further, while restating the position of Advaitins he combines the theories of Bhāmatī as well as Vivaraṇa schools which causes greater confusion. He examines the *bimba-pratibimba* relation in between the Brahman and the jīva which was held by the Vivaraṇa school at length in a section which is devoted to examine the position that avidyā is located in the jīva which position was held by the Bhāmatī school.

5.b) Sudarśanasūri points at the possibility of infinite regress. He claims that if the world is held to be non-real and super-imposed on Brahman caused by avidyā, then avidyā, being a non-real and a superimposed entity should have a cause for its superimposition on Brahman. Similarly, such cause should have another cause for its superimposition. On the other hand, if it is held to be real then the theory of Advaita gets affected.

6. Vedāntadeśika shows three possible alternatives to hold that jīva is the locus of avidyā. 1) Whether jīvas are held to be the locus of avidyā, in their natural and essential form, i.e., in the form of Brahman or, 2) whether in the form which is other than their natural and essential form, and which is superimposed on their natural and essential form i.e., in the form of *antaḥkaraṇa* or 3) whether in their natural and essential form as qualified (*viśiṣṭa*) by the superimposed form.

The basis for these three alternatives is the position held by the Advaitins with regard to the nature of jīva. For Advaitins the jīva is a complex entity of which pure-consciousness i.e., Brahman is its true nature as well as the substratum and the physical adjunct i.e., *antaḥkaraṇa* which is superimposed on it. The above three alternatives are understood on the basis of the substratum, of the limiting adjunct and both put together.

Here, the first two alternatives are not required to be examined because Vedāntadeśika has devoted one full chapter to examine the issue whether the Brahman can be the locus of avidyā (chapter 19) and Advaitins themselves ruled out the possibility of *antaḥkaraṇa* or any other inert object as locus of avidyā. It has been argued by them that there is no necessity to accept a cover of avidyā for an object which is *asvaprakāśa* or insentient by its nature. Therefore, only the third alternative is relevant to the context and under that Vedāntadeśika poses the same old question of mutual interdependency which was raised by Rāmānuja.

Vedāntadeśika, under chapter 19, examines the issue whether pure consciousness can be the locus of avidyā. Here too, he devotes considerable space to examine various alternatives from the point of view of treating avidyā to be one or the other form of negation, which according to Advaita is totally uncalled for. He criticizes the theory that avidyā which is held to be a positive entity is located in the pure consciousness i.e., Brahman mainly through four more arguments as follows:-

7. Brahman cannot be held as locus of avidyā because it is not held to be the knower (*jñātā*) by the Advaitins. He maintains that knowledge dispels only such ignorance which collocates with the knowledge. It means that the knowledge of Devadatta cannot dispel the ignorance of Yajñadatta. Since Advaitins do not hold the Brahman as knower, the avidyā cannot locate itself in it. For the same reason it is not possible to hold that by the *samyagjñāna* which exists in the individual soul the avidyā which is located in the Brahman can be removed.
8. Secondly, Vedāntadeśika's second objection is the same as that of Rāmānuja. It has been discussed earlier that Brahman cannot be the locus of avidyā for it is held to be self-luminous and hence in opposition to avidyā .
9. Thirdly, Advaitins hold that the Brahman is eternally liberated, *nityamukta*. This will not be possible if avidyā is located in the Brahman. For, bondage is nothing but the association with avidyā and it's removal is spoken of as liberation. Therefore, it is a contradiction in terms that Brahman, who is eternally liberated is the locus of avidyā .
10. Fourthly, Brahman is said to be omniscient. Omniscience means knowing everything. If anything remains unknown by it, it cannot be held omniscient.

Thus, by looking into the prominent texts of Viśiṣṭādvaita, we can identify around ten objections to the theory related with the location of avidyā. When we carefully study them, it will be clear to us that the two prominent objections raised by Rāmānuja do really pose greater challenge to the Advaitins than the others. They are 1) the problem of mutual interdependency if jīva is held to be locus of avidyā and 2) or the problem of mutual opposition of the pure conciousness and avidyā if Brahman is held to be the locus of avidyā. Though both the Brahman and the jīva are held to be the locus of avidyā according to two prominent schools of Advaita, it may be noticed that majority of Advaitins hold the view that Brahman is locus of avidyā.

Hence, let us now look into the defense provided by the Advaitins to hold that the Brahman, is the locus of avidyā. Two basic philosophical issues to be examined in this connection are: 1) Whether an entity held to be self-ḷuminous can accept and tolerate a cover of avidyā, 2) Whether the self luminous pure consciousness and avidyā are mutually opposed.

According to Advaita, Brahman which is attributeless, self-luminous and without a second is the only reality. Everything else other than Brahman is avidyā and its effects. Avidyā and its effects are held to be inert and non-self luminous objects. They require contact with the Brahman in the form of *sākṣin* to be illumined and to be cognised. This position is maintained on the strength of the Upaniṣadic statement, "*tasya bhāsā sarvamidaṁ vibhāti.*" This Upaniṣadic statement is quite clear as it enumerates all the known sources of light and states that they are not, indeed, luminous, but they appear to be luminous only on account of their contact with the lone luminous object, Brahman. This particular Upaniṣadic statement, unlike many other statements, does not give room for any sort of twisting, however skilled the manipulator may be. Now, every one who agrees upon the Upaniṣadic authority is bound to construct a theory by which the above statement may be upheld. Every object in this world is in contact with the *sākṣin* either directly or indirectly, in a known way or in an unknown way. "*sarvaṁ vastu jñātatayā vā ajñātatayā vā sākṣicaitanyasya viṣaya eva*". Avidyā is also an object like any other object. Hence, it should also be in contact with the self-luminous Brahman to be cognised. It is like the cloud which is not luminous, covers the self-luminous sun and in turn gets illuminated by the light of the sun. Similarly, avidyā conceals the Brahman and gets cognised by the consciousness which results in our having experience such as "*ahaṁ ajñaḥ*" (I am ignorant.) Therefore, one is compelled to accept that avidyā too is cognised by the *sākṣin* i.e. Brahman. This is not possible if we maintain that Brahman and avidyā are locked in opposition. Hence, there is no opposition among them and, therefore, avidyā can be located in the Brahman just as the avidyā which conceals the true nature of shell locates itself in the shell only. One may say that in the example the shell is an inert object while in the present case Brahman is self-luminous. Yes, but there is awareness of avidyā in everyone's experience. How to account for our experience if self-luminous Brahman is in opposition with it and dispels it? Therefore, one is compelled to deny opposition between the Brahman and avidyā. Hence avidyā locates itself in the Brahman. This is clearly stated by Sureśvara:-

āśrayatvaviṣayatvabhāginī nirvibhāgacitireva kevalā
pūrvasiddhatamaso hi paścimo nāśrayo bhavati nāpi gocarah.

Another argument to substantiate the above position is that avidyā by its very nature conceals the object in which it is located. Since the objects other than the Brahman are non self-luminous there is no necessity to conceal them further. Brahman who is self-luminous is fit to be concealed and hence avidyā is located in it.

One of the major objections raised against this position is that the avidyā and its dispeller *vṛttijñāna* are located in two different locations as avidyā remains in the pure-consciousness i.e., Brahman and *vṛttijñāna* will remain in the person, say, Devadatta. It is held by all that both the objects - that which is dispelled and that which is its dispeller - need to be located in one and the same location. It is not very difficult to answer the above objection if we understand clearly the Advaitin's stand on it. During the stage of *akhaṇḍā-kāravṛttijñāna* which alone is held to be the dispeller of avidyā, the jīvas are not viewed as different persons like Devadatta and Yajña-datta and the like for these distinctions are based on the distinction of body-mind complex and as *akhaṇḍākāravṛtti* takes place only after sublating the said body-mind complex. Therefore, the *akhaṇḍākāra-vṛttijñāna* locates itself in the pure-consciousness of Devadatta which is identical with the Brahman. In this way both avidyā and the said *vṛttijñāna* stand to have been located in one and the same location. Therefore, no violation of the said principle. Further, there is no contingency that by the removal of avidyā of Devadatta, Yajñadatta should also be liberated. For, even though pure-consciousness is one and the same in every person and though avidyā also is only one, yet to avoid the above said contingency individual avidyās are also accepted. Therefore, when *akhaṇḍā-kāravṛtti* takes place in one particular jīva, say in Devadatta, it locates in the pure-consciousness only from the point of view of Devadatta, and hence he only is liberated, not Yajñadatta.

Further, it may be noted that by the knowledge of pot in Devadatta the ignorance of cloth in Devadatta is not removed. This establishes that knowledge removes ignorance not only when both of them are located in one and the same locus, but also when both of them happen to have one and the same entity as their content. At the stage of *akhaṇḍākāravṛtti*, the pure consciousness pertaining to the individual jīva is the content of avidyā and the same is content of the *akhaṇḍākāravṛtti* too. Therefore, the above said contingency does not arise.

Also, the rule that the dispeller and dispelled should be located in one and the same location does not seem to hold good either in worldly instances or in the doctrine of Viśiṣṭādvaita. For example: a lamp switched on in the adjoining room dispels the darkness in the next room. If you say that collocation takes place on account of travel of light, we can say that in the present case too, the expansion of *vṛtti* in the form of pure consciousness accounts for the collocation. The Viśiṣṭādvaitins accept that on account of the desire of God, the actions of the jīvas are terminated. In this case, it is clear that the terminating-desire is located in God and terminated-actions are located in the jīva, thus violating the said rule. Also, the Viśiṣṭādvaitins hold that on account of the actions of the jīvas pleasure of God is obtained. Here, the result, namely, pleasure is in God and the cause action is in the jīva. Hence, here also the said rule of collocation is clearly violated. Whatever way they find to explain this to make the *śruti* meaningful will be applicable for Advaitins too.

Therefore, those who uphold the supreme validity of the Upaniṣadic statements should always attempt to construct such theories because of which the teachings of the Upaniṣads will stand vindicated. There is no room for pure reason in the Vedānta. Reason should be exercised only to vindicate the Upaniṣadic stand. If any Vedāntin deviates from this path somewhere or other he will also fall in the pit dug by him. This is the spirit behind the replies given by the Advaitins that māyā is indescribable and cannot be probed into with reason and so on. This does not mean that they cannot formulate arguments to ward-off various contingencies in *māyāvāda*. It only means that when māyā is brought into the picture to explain the inexplicable, some uncommon and inexplicable aspects are allowed to govern it. Advaitins argue that when the Upaniṣads speak in clear terms that māyā is located in the self-luminous Brahman, we need to find out some way or the other to resolve mutual opposition between them. The following Upaniṣadic passages may be cited for this:

māyāṁ tu prakṛtim vidyāt māyinaṁ tu maheśvaram (ŚU, 4.10)

taratyavidyāṁ vitatāṁ hṛdi yasminniveśete
yogī māyā mameyāya tasmai vidyātmane namaḥ. (*Viṣṇupurāṇa*, 5.17.15)

ajñānenāvṛtaṁ jñānam tena muhyanti jantavaḥ (*Gītā*, 5. 15)

anṛtena hi pratyūḍhāḥ. (CU. 8-3-2)

When such authoritative texts clearly speak about avidyā or māyā covering the self-luminous consciousness they should be held not in opposition. Therefore, what is referred to by the term *svarūpajñāna* to distinguish it from the *vṛttijñāna* is not in opposition with avidyā .

The above fact is born out by the experience of every person during deep sleep state. It is well accepted by all that during deep sleep the *antaḥkaraṇa* which is the adjunct of jīva also merges into its cause, avidyā. After waking up the person recollects avidyā and expresses "*gāḍhaṁ mūḍhohamāsaṁ, na kiñcit avediṣam.*" This recollection presupposes experience and since during deep-sleep there is none other than the pure-consciousness to reveal and experience the avidyā and since this experience is not possible if pure-consciousness and avidyā are held to be in opposition, one is compelled to accept that they are not in opposition.

Thus, there are enough number of arguments in favour of Advaitic standpoint apart from the *śrutis*. But, to highlight the indescribability of avidyā is to give proper recognition to the authority of the *śrutis*. The *Pañcadaśī* makes the position clearer:-

svaprakāśe kuto'vidyā tāṁ vinā kathamāvṛtiḥ
ityādi tarkajālāni svānubhūtirgrasatyasau.

svānubhūtavaviśvāse tarkasyāpyanavasthiteḥ
kathaṁ vā tārkikaṁmanyaḥ tattvaniścayamāpnuyāt

budhyārohāya tarkaścedapekṣeta tathā sati
svānubhūtyanusāreṇa tarkyatāṁ mā kutarkyatām. (*Pañcadaśī* - 6,28-33)

Another important point to be clarified in respect of the present topic is how the *akhaṇḍākāravṛttijñāna* removes avidyā when *svarūpajñāna* which is of the same form was unable to do so. It is rather very simple. Whenever we know any object, pot or cloth, the ignorance pertaining to that object gets removed. It means that for the removal of *ajñāna* pertaining to anything, it is a precondition that such a thing should become object of epistemic activity of the knower. Obviously, knowing some thing is an epistemic activity. Thus when pot becomes an object of epistemic activity of the knower it becomes known and the ignorance of it stands removed. Similarly, to remove avidyā which is located in the Brahman, Brahman has to become an object of epistemic activity of knower. It is possible only when the *antaḥkaraṇa* of the knower takes the form of the Brahman, Brahman becomes object of epistemic activity. Such an epistemic cognition in the form of "I am the Brahman" which is technically called as *akhaṇḍākāra-vṛttijñāna* only is capable of removing the avidyā of the Brahman. To put it in simple way, it is not the *Brahmajñāna* which removes avidyā but *Brahmaviṣaya-jñāna*. Rāmānuja says that there is no distinction among the two *jñānas*, but distinction is very clear that in the former Brahman is cognised not as a "*viṣaya*" (object) whereas in the later it is cognised as "*viṣaya*". No one can deny the fact that anything in the world will not be known unless it becomes object (*viṣaya*) of the epistemic activity. The same should hold good with regard to the Brahman too. The *svarūpajñāna* does not make Brahman *viṣaya* into any epistemic activity. Hence it cannot remove avidyā. We can put it in another way. Association of avidyā and Brahman as made out by the *svarūpajñāna* is ontological in its nature (if the term ontological be used with reference to both real and non-real entities). Whereas it is epistemic in its nature when it is made out by the *akhaṇḍākāra-vṛttijñāna*.

Rāmānuja has rightly pointed it out as to how can Brahman be regarded as an object of another cognition. Would it not end in accepting the objectivity of the Brahman which is contradictory to *svaprakāśatva* or self-luminosity? Advaitin says no. For this purpose he makes a distinction between *vṛttivyāpyatva* and *phalavyāpyatva* and holds that things that are *vṛttivyāpyas* do not carry objectivity whereas things which are *phalavyāpyas* carry objectivity. Therefore, there is no difficulty in accepting objectivity to the Brahman which is equally undesirable for the Advaitin, because Brahman did not become *phalavyāpya*.

The above analysis provides the necessary replies to the objections raised by Vedāntadeśika too. The last objection that Brahman may cease to be omniscient if it is agreed to be the locus of avidyā needs a little more clarification. Strictly speaking, Brahman is not held to be omniscient. It is Īśvara who is omniscient according to Advaita.

Turning our attention towards the theory that avidyā is located in the jīva, we may say that Rāmānuja did not take this position very seriously. He strikes it down with one crisp comment that such position will result in the mutual interdependency. But, according to Advaita, both avidyā and jīva are beginningless and hence their chronological priority cannot be looked into. In fact it is very simple to prove that avidyā is *anādi* as ignorance of any object cannot have a cut-off date whereas *avidyā-nivṛtti* can have such a date. Pot is known today. Its knowledge has a beginning. But, if we ask when from were you having its ignorance, it does not carry any sense. Mutual interdependency cannot have any relevance with regard to the objects that do not have origination at any given date.

8

तिरोधानानुपपत्तिः

V. Srivatsankacharya

सन्मात्रब्रह्मणः भावरूपेणाज्ञानेन तिरोधानं इत्यभ्युपगमे, "आश्रयोऽस्यास्तिरोधिः स्वरूपं सदसदन्यता। मानं निवर्त्तकं चैव निवृत्तिर्नोपपद्यते॥" इत्यस्मदाचार्यसङ्गृहीतया रीत्या सप्तविधा अनुपपत्तयः पूर्वाचार्यैरुद्धाटिताः। तास्वद्य तिरोधानानुपपत्तिमधिकृत्य यथोपदेशं यथाग्रन्थं किञ्चिदिव विवृणुमः।

"अविद्यया प्रकाशैकस्वरूपं ब्रह्म तिरोहितम् - इति वदता स्वरूपनाश एवोक्तः स्यात्। प्रकाशतिरोधानं नाम - प्रकाशोत्पत्तिप्रतिबन्धः, विद्यमानस्य विनाशो वा। प्रकाशस्य अनुत्पाद्यत्वाभ्युपगमेन प्रकाशतिरोधानम् - प्रकाशनाश एव।" इत्यस्मद्भाष्यकारा अभ्यधुः। अत्र वस्तुतिरोधानं नाम - वस्तुना इन्द्रियसन्निकर्षप्रतिबन्धः, वस्तुविषयकज्ञानप्रतिबन्ध एव वा। परेषां मते ब्रह्मणो ज्ञानाविषयत्वात् प्रकाशतिरोधानमेव ब्रह्मतिरोधानम् इत्यापद्येत। तत्र विद्यमानस्य वस्तुनः सत्यभूतेन आवारकेण च्छादनमेव तिरोधानमिति प्रतीमः। अवस्तुभूतया मिथ्यारूपयाऽविद्यया प्रकाशस्वरूपस्य ब्रह्मणः कथं तिरोधिः स्यात्? "अविद्या तच्चितोर्योगः षडस्माकमनादयः" इति अनादित्वाङ्गीकारेणापि न निस्तारः; आदौ अन्तःकरणादिरूपवृत्तिज्ञानरूपकारणाभावादेव तदनुदयात् कथं तयाविद्यया तिरोधिः स्यात्?

किञ्च, अविद्याया अनादित्वं किं स्वरूपतः? उत प्रवाहानादित्वम्? आद्ये - स्वरूपानादेर्नाशासम्भवात्, सर्वदा भानप्रसङ्गः। प्रवाहानादित्वे पुण्यपापरूपकर्मादिवत् विद्यानाश्यत्वेऽपि, ब्रह्मण औत्पत्तिकोऽविद्यासम्बन्धोऽभ्युपेयः स्यात्। तथा च ब्रह्मवत् वस्त्वन्तरसद्भावोऽवश्यमङ्गीकरणीयः स्यात्।

एतादृशाज्ञानानुभवः कस्य? यदि ब्रह्मणः, तर्हि नित्यमुक्तस्वप्रकाशचैतन्यैकस्वरूपस्य तस्य कथमज्ञानानुभवः? स्वानुभवस्वरूपत्वेन ब्रह्मणः तदसम्भवात्। स्वानुभवस्वरूपमपि ब्रह्म तिरोहितस्वरूपम् अज्ञानमनुभवति इति न वक्तुं शक्यते। तत्र तिरोहितस्वरूपत्वं

नाम किम्? यदि अप्रकाशितस्वरूपत्वम्? तर्हि स्वानुभवस्वरूपस्यापि ब्रह्मणः क्वचिद्देशेऽप्रकाशितस्वरूपत्वमिति आयातम्; अतश्च व्याघातः। स्वानुभवस्वरूपस्यापि अन्यस्माद् अप्रकाशितस्वरूपत्वं सङ्गच्छते इति चेत् - तदेव न सङ्गच्छते इति ब्रूमः। प्रकाशान्तरेण ब्रह्मण्येवाप्रकाशरूपधर्माङ्गीकारेण प्रकाशनाश एव पर्यायोक्तः स्यात्। अयं भावः - इदं तिरोधानं सर्वप्रकाशनिवर्तनम् इत्यभ्युपगमे, अनुभवस्य आद्यन्तरहितत्वात् स्वानुभवस्वरूपस्य अप्रकाशितस्वरूपत्वं न सङ्गच्छते॥ कतिपयप्रकाशनिवर्तनं तिरोधानम्, इत्यभ्युपगमे - ब्रह्मणः सांशत्वापत्तिः, इति।

"विशदस्वरूपस्यापि अविशदस्वरूपत्वापादानं तिरोधानम्" इति यद्युच्येत - तदाऽपि प्रत्यक्षैकस्वरूपे स्वात्मनि पारोक्ष्यलक्षणावैशद्यस्य आपादयितुमशक्यत्वात् नेदं युक्तम्। नो चेत् - ब्रह्मस्वरूपनाश एव स्यात्। किञ्च, निर्विकारे निर्विशेषे स्वप्रकाशात्मनि वस्तुनि विषयातिरेकलक्षणवैशद्यस्य दुर्निरूपत्वात् कथमिदमुपपद्यताम्? वेदान्तश्रवणजन्यवृत्तिविशेषविषयत्वमेव वैशद्यम्, तच्च पूर्वं न विद्यते, इति चेत् - तस्य वैशद्यस्य प्रकाश्यातिरेके ब्रह्मणः सविशेषत्वमभ्युपेयं स्यात्। प्रकाश्यानतिरेके तु स्थितमपि वैशद्यं नोपकारकम्। अतश्च विशदस्वरूपत्वं ब्रह्मणो भज्येत॥ वस्तुतस्तिरोधानाभावेऽपि सच्चिदानन्दैकरसं ब्रह्म अविद्यया तिरोहितस्वरूपम् अविशदमिव लक्ष्यते - इत्यपि वक्तुं न शक्यते। पूर्वोक्तरीत्या सांशे एव विशदाविशदावभासो लोके दृष्टचरः। दूरस्थः पर्वतः चक्षुषा गृह्यमाणोऽविशदः; समीपगमने स एव पूर्वापेक्षया विशद इत्यानुभविकम्। सर्वदा स्वयम्प्रकाशे ज्ञानागोचरे ज्ञानस्वरूपे ब्रह्मणि अवेद्ये वैशद्यावैशद्यसम्भावना कथमुपपद्यते?

एवम्, "अस्ति प्रकाशते इति व्यवहारयोग्यताविरहः आवरणम्" इति पक्षेऽपि एतादृशज्ञानस्य सहकारि किम्? इति वक्तव्यम्। अस्ति प्रकाशते इति व्यवहारस्य, नास्ति न प्रकाशते इति व्यवहारस्य वा सहकारिवैकल्यादेव असिद्धिः सुगमा। अतश्च, ब्रह्म प्रति इदमावरणं कल्प्यते - इतीदं न सङ्गच्छते॥ अस्यावरणस्य अनादित्वात् नान्यापेक्षा - इत्यपि वक्तुं न शक्यते। ब्रह्मणः स्वप्रकाशत्वादेव सर्वदा अस्ति प्रकाशते इति व्यवहारयोग्यतायाः विद्यमानत्वेन, एतादृशव्यवहाराभावः कथं भवेत्। प्रसिद्धं किल काव्यादिष्वपि "सामानाधिकरण्यं हि तेजस्तिमिरयोः कुतः?" इति। किञ्च ब्रह्मणः कथञ्चिदावरणेऽङ्गीकृतेऽपि, साक्षिणोऽप्यावृतत्वात् जगदान्ध्यप्रसङ्गः। ततश्च प्रपञ्चभेदतत्सत्यत्वादिति वृत्त्यर्थः प्रयत्नः कस्य? कल्पितो जीवोऽनादिरपि, जीवरूपताऽविद्यया इत्येव वक्तव्यम्। तथा च ब्रह्मेतरद् वस्तु स्वरूपतोऽनादीत्येवागतम्॥

किञ्च, "दृश्यत्वात् जडत्वाद् विनाशित्वाच्च परिच्छिन्नाऽप्यविद्या, अनिर्वचनीयत्वेन विचारासहा आवरणविक्षेपशक्तिद्वयवती सर्वगतं चिदात्मानं आवृणोति - अङ्गुलिरिव

नयनसन्निहिता सूर्यमण्डलम्। तत्र चक्षुष एव आवरणे - अङ्गुलेरप्यभानप्रसङ्गात्, अधिष्ठानावरणमन्तरेण विक्षेपानुपपत्तेश्च" (सिद्धान्तबिन्दुः) इति युष्माभिः प्रदर्शितायां गत्यामपि, आवरणविक्षेपयोः पूर्वापरकालभावित्ववत्, तिरोधानतज्जन्यव्यावहारिकप्रपञ्चयोः कार्यकारणभावेन पौर्वापर्यम् अवश्यम् अभ्युपेयम्। ततश्च उभयोरनादित्वेन प्रतिपादनं कथं सङ्गच्छते? अपि च, एवं रीत्या समर्थनेऽपि, आवरणविक्षेपयोः कमधिकृत्य प्रवृत्तिः? अपि च, एवं रीत्या समर्थनेऽपि, आवरणविक्षेपयोः कमधिकृत्य प्रवृत्तिः? इति विचारे - जीवोऽप्यनादिरिति स्वीक्रियते युष्माभिः। एवं अगत्या - जीवादीनाम् अनादित्वे अद्वितीयवादः कथं घटेत। साङ्ख्यवत् अन्तःकरणस्य त्रैविध्यमाश्रित्य, "कर्तृभागावच्छिन्नश्चिदंशः प्रमाता। क्रियाभागावच्छिन्नचिदंशः प्रमाणम्। विषयगतोऽभिव्यक्तियोग्यत्वभावा-वच्छिन्नचिदंशः प्रमितिः "इत्येवंरीत्या निरंशे अंशभेदप्रदर्शनपुरस्सरं तेषां स्वरूपविवेचनं यत्कृतम् - तदपि किमर्थम्? "निर्विभागचितः कथमेवं घटते?" इति प्रश्नमुपक्षिप्य, "आवरणमहिम्नैव" इति यत् समाधानम् - तदत्र समाधिर्दुर्वच इत्यभिप्रायेणैवेति मन्यामहे। "अनुभवबलेन एवं स्वीकृतम्" इति व्याख्यानमपि सुदुर्विवेचमित्याशयेनैव स्यात्। अतश्च, एतादृशसरण्या-श्रयणापेक्षया "न कर्माविभागादिति चेन्न अनादित्वात्..." इति सूत्रोक्तरीत्या सर्वसिद्धान्तसिद्धस्य पुण्यपापरूपकर्मणोऽनादित्वेन स्वीकृत्य महर्ष्यादृतः पन्था आश्रयितुं वरम्।

भ्रमस्थलेषु अधिष्ठानस्य सत्यत्वं सर्वैरभ्युपगतम्। अत्र, अविद्यायाः अधिष्ठानभूतं ब्रह्म अविद्ययैव तिरोहितम् - इत्यङ्गीकारात्, ब्रह्म प्रकाशप्रतिपक्षभूतम् इत्येवायातमिति पूर्वोक्तास्ते एव दोषाः। तेजस्तिमिरयोरिव प्रकाश - तत्प्रतिपक्षयोः सामानाधिकरण्यासम्भवात्। प्रकाशप्रतिपक्षानुगुणं ब्रह्म इत्यभ्युपगमेऽपि - तदानुगुण्येन किं प्रयोजनम्? इति वक्तव्यम्। स्वप्रकाशस्य ब्रह्मणः स्वप्रकाशप्रतिपक्षानुगुण्येन किं साधितं स्यात्? न हि परव्यामोहकैन्द्रजालिकवत् केनचिद्धेतुना ब्रह्म प्रवर्तते। प्रकाशप्रतिपक्षानुगुण्यस्य अनादित्वसम्पादनेऽपि स एव दोषः। "परं ब्रह्मैवाज्ञं भ्रमपरिगतं संसरति यत् परोपाध्यालीढं विवशमशुभस्यास्पदमिति।" (वेदार्थसंग्रहः:२) इति पूर्वाचार्योक्तरीत्या अनादिभ्रान्त्या साध्यस्य कस्याप्यभावात् नैतदुपपद्यते। यदि प्रकाशानुगुणमेव ब्रह्म स्वतो भातीत्यभ्युपेयते, तर्हि तिरोधानवाचोयुक्तिः कथम्?

स्वयम्प्रकाशे ब्रह्मणि कथम् अध्यासादिकम्? अधिष्ठाने प्रकाशमाने एव अध्यासोऽपि तत्र भवति, इति चेत् - तर्हि तिरोधानं कथम्? किमर्थं च तिरोधानापगमाय वेदान्तवाक्यश्रवणादिकम्? यथावत् प्रकाशमानेऽपि अध्यासायोगात् अप्रकाशमानत्वमपि स्वीकुर्म इति चेत् - स्वप्रकाशस्य वस्तुनो निर्विशेषस्य एतादृशाविद्याशतकल्पनेनापि स्वरूपाप्रकाशो न कथञ्चिदपि कर्तुं शक्यत इति प्रयासवैयर्थ्यमेव॥

किञ्च, ईदृशम् अविद्याकार्यम् अवैशद्यं तत्त्वज्ञानोदयात् निवर्तते वा न वा? न निवर्तति चेत् - कदाऽप्यनिर्मोक्षप्रसङ्गः। तदर्थं तत्त्वमस्यादिवाक्यार्थश्रवणादीनां नैरर्थक्यं च। निवृत्तौ तु - वस्तु किं रूपम्? कथम्भूतमिति विवेचनीयम्॥ ननु विशदस्वरूपमेव, इति चेत् - तच्च विशदस्वरूपं तत्त्वज्ञानोदयात् प्राक् अस्ति न वा? पूर्वमेव वैशद्यमस्ति चेत् - नित्यमुक्तस्वभावस्य ब्रह्मणः कथं प्रतीतिः? मोक्षस्य कार्यत्वात्। "कार्यं सर्वमनित्यम्" इत्यभ्युपगच्छतां भवतां मते, अनित्यता च स्यात्। "न जातु कश्चित् नाहमिति विपर्येति, न वा 'अहमस्मि न वा?' इति सन्देधि " इति हि भवद्भाष्यसूक्तिः।

किञ्च, ऽयमविद्यावादः "अविद्यया प्रकाशस्वरूपस्य तिरोधानम्" इति वादश्च भट्टकुमारिलैरेवं निरीक्षितः, परीक्षितश्च सम्बन्धाक्षेपपरिहारप्रकरणे-

स्वयं च शुद्धरूपत्वाद् असत्त्वाच्चान्यवस्तुनः।
स्वप्नादिवद् अविद्यायाः प्रवृत्तिस्तत्र किंकृता?
अन्येनोपप्लवेऽभीष्टे द्वैतवादः प्रसज्यते। इति। (श्लोकवार्तिकम् - ८४)

अनादिरियमविद्या इत्यत्रापि "स्वाभाविकीम् अविद्यां च नोच्छेत्तुं कश्चिदर्हति" इति प्रतिविहितम्। अयं भावः-"पराऽस्य शक्तिः विविधैव श्रूयते स्वाभाविकी ज्ञानबलक्रिया च", "न ते विष्णो जायमानो न जातः देव महिम्नः परमन्तं वेद " इत्याद्याः श्रुतयः ब्रह्मणो ज्ञानबलक्रियाशक्त्याद्याः स्वाभाविकाः, विविधाः, पराः इत्याम्रेडयन्ति। एवं स्थिते अविद्यासम्बन्धस्य स्वाभाविकत्वं औत्पत्तिकत्वं च यदि ब्रह्मणोऽङ्गीक्रियते - तर्हि एताः श्रुतयो व्याकुप्येयुरिति।

अपि च, आत्मनः कर्तृत्वं नेति परेषां मतस्थितिः। स्पष्टमिदं बृहदारण्यकभाष्ये। बृहदारण्यकवार्त्तिकेऽपि -

आत्मा कर्त्रादिरूपश्चेद् मा काङ्क्षीस्तर्हि मुक्तताम्।
न हि स्वभावो भावानां व्यादर्तेतौष्ण्यवद् रवेः॥ (सम्बन्धवार्तिकम् - ५५)

इति सदृष्टान्तमयं पक्षः समर्थितः। ज्ञानकर्मत्वम् , ज्ञातृत्वम्, कर्तृत्वमित्यादिकं ब्रह्मणो न, तस्य शुद्धचैतन्यस्वरूपत्वात् - इति वादिनां मते - ईदृशज्ञाननिवृत्त्यर्था प्रवृत्तिः, कस्य? कथम्?- 1."अज्ञानानुपहितं शुद्धचैतन्यम् - ईश्वरः। अज्ञानोपहितं जीवः" इति वा, 2. अज्ञानोपहितं बिम्बचैतन्यम् - ईश्वरः। अज्ञानप्रतिबिम्बचैतन्यम् जीवः" (सिद्धान्तबिन्दुः) इत्यभ्युपगन्तॄणां मते - एकजीववाद एवान्ततो गत्वा पर्यवसानात्, तस्यैव च "मुख्यो वेदान्तसिद्धान्तः" इति युष्माभिः स्वीकारात् एकजीववादे ये दोषाः - ते सर्वे तत्रैवात्रापि सम्भवेयुः।

"सच्चिदानन्दस्वरूपे ब्रह्मणि सदंशे चिदंशे आनन्दांशे च नावरणम्; अपि तु पूर्णानन्दांशे एव" इति विवरणसिद्धान्तः। अत्रापि "अस्ति प्रकाशते इति व्यवहारः प्रतिबन्धकनिबन्धनः" इत्युपपादनं कथं घटताम्? किञ्च, निरंशे ब्रह्मणि अंशत्रयसद्भावे किं प्रमाणम्? यदि "सत्यं ज्ञानम् अनन्तं ब्रह्म," "विज्ञानमानन्दं ब्रह्म" इति तत्प्रतिपादकश्रुतिसमुदायः प्रमाणम्, तर्हि श्रुत्युक्तरीत्या सत्त्वचित्त्वानन्दवत्त्वादीनां ध र्मत्वेनैव भासमानत्वात् सधर्मकत्वमेव ब्रह्मणः स्यात्। "अद्वितीयत्व श्रुतिः गुणतोऽपि सद्वितीयतां न सहते" इति युष्मत्सिद्धान्तभङ्गः स्यात्।

किञ्च, अविद्यया ब्रह्मणस्तिरोधिमभिदधद्भिरिदमत्र विवेचनीयम् - किं ब्रह्मणस्तिरोधानं सर्वदैव? अथ वा अतिरोहिताऽपि दशा कदाचिद् वर्तते? इति। यदि सर्वदैव तिरोहितत्वम्, तर्हि "शुको मुक्तः, वामदेवो मुक्तः" इत्याद्याः सङ्कथाः कथम्? शुकादिमुक्तिः कल्पनयेति न वक्तुं शक्यम्,

वीतरागभयक्रोधा मन्मया मामुपाश्रिताः।
बहवो ज्ञानतपसा पूता मद्भावमागताः॥ (गीता, 4-10)

इत्यादिप्रमाणानाम् अप्रमाणकोटिनिक्षेपप्रसङ्गात्। न च ते शुकादयोऽद्यापि ब्रह्मणैक्यं न गता इति वक्तुं शक्यते॥ अतिरोहितदशाऽपि कदाचिद् यद्यङ्गीक्रियेत - तर्हि सा कदा? कस्य? ननु सर्वदा - इति वक्तुं न शक्यम्। व्यावहारिकस्य तिरोधानस्य अपनोद्यत्वसाधनार्थम् एतावत्प्रयासानां वैयर्थ्यापत्तेः॥ वस्तुतः तिरोधानस्याप्यसत्यत्वात् न दोषोऽयम् - इति न वक्तुं न शक्यम्। ब्रह्मणस्तिरोधायकत्वे प्रमाणत्वेनोदाहृतानां वचानानां निर्विषयत्वप्रसङ्गात्। अनिर्वचनीयत्वेन अविद्यास्थापनप्रयासानां वैयर्थ्यापाताच्च। नित्यतिरोधानं तु न भवदभीष्टम्; ब्रह्मणो नित्यतिरोहितत्वप्रसङ्गात्॥

किञ्च, तिरोधानत्वेन विवक्षितस्य भावरूपस्याज्ञानस्य प्रकाशविरोधित्वे- अध्यासानुपपत्तिः। अधिष्ठानप्रकाशं विना अध्यासस्यैव असम्भवात्। प्रकाशविरोधित्वे तु तिरोधानमेव न स्यात्। तिरोधानकल्पने प्रयोजनाभावश्च॥

"वैशद्यविघटनं तिरोधानम्" इत्यपि न युक्तम्। पूर्वोक्तसर्वदोषतादवस्थ्यादेव॥ एवम्, "अनवधारणत्वापादनं तिरोधानम्" इति निर्वचनमपि न युज्यते। तस्य स्वरूपानतिरेके अविद्याधीनत्वं न स्यात्, अनवधारणत्वापादनस्वरूपमेव हि तिरोध नम्। स्वरूपातिरेके तु - तादृशस्य स्वरूपस्य अध्यासविरोधित्वाभावे तत्कल्पनं व्यर्थमेव॥

इत्थम् - "अवधारणत्वनिवर्तकं तिरोधानम्" इत्यपि न युज्यते। अवधारणनिवृत्तेः सत्यत्वे - अद्वैतहानिः। मिथ्यात्वे - स्वरूपस्यैव अवधारणात्मकत्वेन निवृत्तिकल्पनं व्यर्थम्; स्वरूपस्य कदाऽप्यनपायात्। ततश्च -

பிரிவில்லா இருள் ஒன்று பிணக் கொன்றில்லா பெருவெயிலை மறைத்துலகம் காட்டும் என்ன அறிவில்லா அறிவொன்றை, அவித்தைமுடி அகம் புறம் என்றிவையனைத்தும் அமைக்கும் என்பார்.[1]

इति आचार्यसार्वभौमैः परमतभङ्गे प्रतिपादितया रीत्या वर्णनं कथं धियमधिरोहेत्? इति आस्माको वादः।

आवरणेनाभिभवः कथं भवति? इत्यत्र "चैतन्यमात्रावरकस्य अज्ञानस्य विषयावच्छिन्ने प्रदेशे खद्योतादिप्रकाशेन महान्धकारस्येव, ज्ञानेन एकदेशेन नाशः" इति कश्चन पक्षः परैः प्रस्तुतः। एवम्। "कटवत् संवेष्टनं वा", "भीतभटवदपसरणं वा अभिभवः" इत्यपि पक्षद्वयं प्रदर्शितम्। अत्र सर्वत्र कल्पितयाऽविद्यया, कल्पितस्य जीवस्य, कल्पितेन शास्त्रेण - शास्त्रजन्यात्मैक्यप्रपञ्चमिथ्यात्वज्ञानेन निर्वाह आश्रितः। अविद्यया जीवक्लृप्तिः, कल्पितो जीवोऽविद्याश्रयः इति परस्पराश्रयदोषस्य अत्र सर्वत्र तुल्यत्वात्, उभयोरनादित्वेऽपि न निस्तार इत्यास्माकः पक्षः। एतद्दोषपरिजिहीर्षया यदि स्वपरनिर्वाहकपक्ष आश्रीयते, तदाऽपि न निस्तारः; अवस्तुभूते स्वपरनिर्वाहकत्वानङ्गीकारात्। वस्तुभूतो दीपप्रकाशः स्वपरनिर्वाहकः सन् स्वं, स्वप्रकाश्यं वस्तुजातं च अवगमयति इति पश्यामः। न हि अवस्तुभूतो वन्ध्यासुतः स्वपरनिर्वाहको दृष्टः। "कटवत् संवेष्टनं वा अभिभवः" इत्युदाहरणेऽपि कटो वस्तुभूतः, तेन वस्त्वन्तरस्य वेष्टनं युज्यते। भीतभटापसरणस्थलेऽपि - भीतो भटः राज्ञः पुरतो न तिष्ठति, अपसृतोऽन्यत्र गच्छति। कुतः? वस्तुतः स वर्तते। एवमत्र वक्तुं न शक्यते। सूर्यो मेघेन च्छन्नः इत्यत्रापि आवारको मेघः, तद्द्रष्टा देवदत्तः, सूर्यश्चेति त्रितयमपि सत्यभूतम्। अविद्याऽप्यसत्यभूता, जीवोऽप्यसत्यः, अन्ततो गत्वा ब्रह्मतिरोधिरपि असत्यः, असत्यभूताविद्यादौ प्रमाणत्वेन प्रदर्शिताः श्रुत्यादयोऽप्यसत्यभूताः, परं तु असत्यादपि सत्यसिद्धिर्भवति इति लौकिकदृष्टान्ताद्याश्रयणेन निर्वहणक्लेशः किमर्थः? "मम माया" इति व्यधिकरणविभक्त्या अविद्या ब्रह्माश्रिता नेति स्पष्टम्। मायाशब्दोऽपि न मिथ्यार्थक इति पूर्वैः सप्रमाणं बहुधा निरूपितम्।

अतश्च सत्यभूतायाः प्रकृतेः ब्रह्मणोऽन्यस्याः शास्त्रानुसारं यावदनभ्युपगमः तावदित्थम्भूता अनुपपत्तय उद्यन्त्येव।

त्रिभिर्गुणमयैर्भावैरेभिः सर्वमिदं जगत्।
मोहितं नाभिजानाति माम् एभ्यः परमव्ययम्॥ (गीता, 7-13)

इत्युक्तरीत्या "प्रकृत्याऽस्य तिरोधिः" इति पूर्वाचार्यवाक्यानुसारं प्रकृत्या जीवानां ब्रह्मविषयकतिरोधानम्, न तु अखण्डैकरसब्रह्माश्रित्यैवाविद्या विलसति, इत्यभ्युपेयम्। "अस्मान्मायी सृजते विश्वमेतत् तस्मिंश्चान्यो मायया सन्निरुद्धः" इति श्रुत्या जीवस्यैव मायया ब्रह्मविषयकतिरोधानतदुत्थविक्षेपादिकमिति स्पष्टम्। अविद्याया जीवमावृत्य विक्षेपः इति अविद्याजीवयोरुभयोरप्यनादित्वाङ्गीकारेणापि भवत्पक्षे अन्ततो गत्वा जीवस्य ब्रह्मभावः, ब्रह्मणो वा जीवभाव इत्युभयथाऽपि ऐक्याङ्गीकारात्, ब्रह्मण एव दोषा भवेयुः। "मायां तु प्रकृतिं विद्यात्" इति वचनव्यक्त्या च माया इति प्रकृतेर्नामान्तरम् इत्येव ज्ञाप्यते। भवदभिमतरीत्या मायाशब्दो मिथ्यावचनो यद्यभविष्यत् "प्रकृतिं तु मायां विद्यात्" इति निरदेक्ष्यत्। नैवं दृश्यते। अतश्च मायाशब्द आश्चर्यवचन एव।

नाहं प्रकाशः सर्वस्य योगमायासमावृतः।
मूढोऽयं नाभिजानाति लोको मामजम् अव्ययम्॥ (गीता, 7-25)

इत्यत्रापि, एतावन्तं कालं न कोऽपि तिरोहितं ब्रह्म ज्ञातवान् - इत्यर्थो न विवक्षितः। "यान्ति मद्याजिनोऽपि माम्", "बहवो ज्ञानतपसा पूता मद्भावमागताः" इत्यादिभिः विरोधात्।

अस्मन्मतरीत्या बद्धदशायां ज्ञानसङ्कोचेन ब्रह्मणोऽज्ञातत्वम्। मुक्तौ स्वाभाविकेन आविर्भूतस्वरूपेण ज्ञातत्वं च सङ्गच्छते। "उत्तराच्चेत् आविर्भूतस्वरूपस्तु" "सम्पद्या-विर्भावः स्वेन शब्दात्" इत्यादीनि मुक्तदशायां स्वाभाविकज्ञानप्रादुर्भावे प्रमाणानि।

यथा न क्रियते ज्योत्स्ना मलप्रक्षालनान्मणेः।
यथोदपानकरणात् क्रियते न जलाम्बरम्।
सदेव नीयते व्यक्तिम्, असतः सम्भवः कुतः॥

इति शौनकवाक्यमुदाहृत्य भाष्ये ज्ञानस्य स्वाभाविकस्य बद्धदशायां सङ्कोचः, परं ज्योति-रूपसन्नस्य परसङ्कल्पात् प्रकाशश्च प्रदर्शितः। "अनृतेन हि प्रत्यूढाः" "नीहारेण प्रावृताः" इत्यादिश्रुतीनामुपबृंहणरूपेण -

विष्णुशक्तिः परा प्रोक्ता क्षेत्रज्ञाख्या तथाऽपरा।
अविद्या कर्मसंज्ञाऽन्या तृतीया शक्तिरिष्यते॥
यया क्षेत्रज्ञशक्तिः सा वेष्टिता नृप सर्वगा।
संसारतापान् अखिलान् अवाप्नोत्यतिसन्ततान्॥ इति

श्रीविष्णुपुराणवाक्यानि पूर्वैः प्रदर्शितानि। एतेन अविद्या इति कर्मण एव नामान्तरम् इति, तच्च कर्म अनादि इति सूत्राद्यारूढम् इति च बोधितमवधेयम्। चार्वाकेतरसर्व-सिद्धान्तेष्वपि पुण्यपापरूपकर्मणामनादित्वम्। व्यवस्थितरूपेण तत्तज्जीवविषये

सुखदुःखोपलम्भात् जीवबहुत्वमित्यादिकं तु "व्यवस्थातो नाना" "नानात्मानो व्यवस्थातः" इति न्यायवैशेषिकादिभिरपि सम्मतमिति न विवादलेशः। किञ्च विद्यया मोक्षः इतिवत् विद्येतरया अविद्यया बन्ध इति वक्तव्ये ईशोपनिषत् -

विद्यां चाविद्यां च यस्तद् वेदोभयँ सह।
अविद्यया मृत्युं तीर्त्वा विद्ययाऽमृतमश्नुते॥ इत्याह।

"सुकृतं दुष्कृतं सर्वे पाप्मानः" इति श्रुतौ सुकृतस्यापि पाप्मत्वेन व्यवहारवत्। अत्र सहोपात्तत्वात् विद्येतरत् अविद्या कर्म, तच्च सुकृतदुष्कृतात्मकत्वेनोभयविधमपि दुष्कृतस्य हानद्वारा, सुकृतस्योपादानद्वारा च विद्योपकारकं भवति - अस्यां श्रुतौ अविद्येति कर्मैवानुसंहितम्। इयं च श्रुतिः-

इयाज सोऽपि सुबहून् यज्ञान् ज्ञानव्यपाश्रयः।
ब्रह्मविद्यामधिष्ठाय तर्तुं मृत्युमविद्यया॥ इति

विष्णुपुराणेनोपबृंहिता। अतश्च अविद्याशब्दस्याज्ञानार्थकत्वेऽपि न सर्वत्रेदृशार्थकत्वम्। तेन कर्मणा बन्धः, विद्यया मोक्षः, मोक्षे ज्ञानविकासः, बन्धे सङ्कोच इत्यास्माकः सिद्धान्तः श्रुतिमूलः। अतश्च वेदनोपासनादिप्रसन्नपरमपुरुषसङ्कल्पवशादेव मुक्तिरिति सर्वमनवद्यम्।

स्वयं सर्वं पूर्णं स्फुटमनुभवन् ब्रह्म परमं
स्वमायासम्बन्धस्थगितनिजबुद्धिप्रसरणात्।
अवेक्ष्यैतान् जीवान् विविधसुकृतव्याजघटनात्
स्वरूपाविर्भावप्रभृति वितरत् स्वं विवृणुते॥

Summary: The above essay deals with *Tirodhānānupapatti* (objection to the idea that māyā-avidyā conceals Brahman). Professor V. Srivatsankacharya presents the views of Viśiṣṭādvaita highlighting the *Śrībhāṣya* position that māyā-avidyā canot conceal Brahman. According to Advaita, avidyā has two powers, the power of concealment (*āvaraṇa-* or *tirodhāna-śakti*) and the power of projection (*vikṣepa-śakti*). Brahman is of the nature of homogeneous knowledge (*prakāśaika-svarūpam*), and avidyā by its power conceals this nature. Rāmānuja asks: what does this concealment of knowledge mean? There are two possible replies. Concealment may mean either the obstruction of the origination of knowledge (*prakāśa-utpatti-pratibandha*), or the destruction of the knowledge that exists (*vidyamānasya vināśaḥ*). The first alternative is untenable since knowledge which is Brahman is eternal and hence has no origination and the question of obstructing the origination of knowledge does not arise. The Advaitin is, therefore, left with the second alternative. The second alternative is even more unsatisfactory as it amounts to the destruction of Brahman whose essential nature is knowledge.

The Advaitins may possibly answer the above objection by saying that the term "concealment" means that the Brahman becomes capable of being spoken of as "It does not exist" (*nāsti*), "It does not manifest" (*na prakāśate*), even when all the causal apparatus (*sāmagrī*) is available to make known that "It does exist" and that "It does manifest".

The first objection against this reply is that meanings cannot be assigned to words that are not found in accordance with worldly usage. In common parlance, when entities like *tamas* etc., conceal light, the term concealment is not understood in the Advaitic sense. To say that there arises the usage (*vyavahāra*) as "*nāsti, na prakāśate*" even when all the causal apparatus (*sāmagri-s*) are present, is also not sound. This is because; "absence of obstruction" (*āvaraṇa-abhāva*) is included in the *sāmagrī*, the causal apparatus. In the present case, avidyā is accepted by the Advaitins to be an obstructing entity which conceals the *prakāśa* of Brahman. That being the case it is not proper to say that when there is causal-apparatus operative there is no manifestation. Hence the defect of *Tirodhāna-anupapatti* could not be refuted by the Advaitins.

NOTES

1. In the *Paramatabhaṅga* (*Pracchanna-baudhha-bhaṅgādhikara*), Vedāntadeśika points out the view of the Advaitins in a nutshell as: the darkness - free from distinctions - after concealing the sun's brightness [which never gets diminished] enlightens the world; as though using the above phenomenon as the example, "avidyā" could conceal Brahman - which is itself knowledge, but which does not have knowledge as attribute and then "avidyā" could project all things consisting of all five elements (*pañcabhūtas*).

   See V.N. Srirama Desikacarya, (Ed. and commented) Śrī Vedāntadeśika's *Paramatabhaṅga* (*Pracchanna-baudhha-bhaṅgādhikara*) in *Sri Desika Prabandha*, LIFCO, Chennai - 600017, 1995, p. 165.

9

तिरोधानानुपपत्तिपरिहारः

R. Krishnamurthi Sastri

अद्वैतसिद्धान्ते स्वयम्प्रकाशसत्तामात्रे निर्विशेषब्रह्मात्मनि स्वरूपतिरोधानेन ईशित्रीशितव्याद्यनेकविकल्पनानां मूलमविद्या अनिर्वचनीयेत्यद्वैतिभिः स्वीक्रियते। इयमेवाविद्या माया, अक्षरम्, अव्यक्तं, शक्तिः, इत्यादि शब्दैरभिधीयते तत्र तत्र। कुत्रचिद्वेदे "नीहारेण प्रावृता" (तै. संहिता - ६.२) इत्यत्र नीहारशब्देन, "अनृतेन हि प्रत्यूढाः"-इत्यत्रानृतशब्देन च व्यपदिश्यते। मायाविद्ययोः स्वरूपस्यैकत्वेऽपि शक्तिभेदाद्भेदव्यपदेशः कुत्रचित्। अत एव तयोर्भेदस्य वास्तविकत्वमादाय एवं श्रूयते।

तरत्यविद्यां विततां हृदि यस्मिन्निवेशिते।
योगी मायाममेयाय तस्मै सत्यात्मने नमः॥ इति।

श्रीमद्भगवद्गीतायामपि-

अज्ञानेनावृतं ज्ञानं तेन मुह्यन्ति जन्तवः।
ज्ञानेन तु तदज्ञानं येषां नाशितमात्मनः॥

तेषामादित्यवज्ज्ञानं प्रकाशयति तत्परम्॥ इति
नाहं प्रकाशः सर्वस्य योगमाया समावृतः॥ इति च।

अस्याश्चाविद्याया आश्रयो विषयश्च शुद्धं ब्रह्मचैतन्यमेव। अत एवोक्तं संक्षेपशारीरकाचार्यैः-

आश्रयत्वविषयत्वभागिनी निर्विभागचितिरेव केवला।
पूर्वसिद्धतमसो हि पश्चिमो नाश्रयो भवति नापि गोचरः॥ इति।

कथमियमविद्या ज्ञानस्वरूपं चैतन्यं तिरोधत्त इत्यज्ञानकर्तृकचैतन्यतिरोधानानुपपत्तिः विशिष्टाद्वैतिभिरुद्भाव्यते। उक्तं हि नाथमुनिना-

आक्षेपः- ज्ञानरूपं परंब्रह्म तन्निवर्त्यं मृषात्मकम्।

अज्ञानं चेत्तिरस्कुर्यात् कः प्रभुस्तन्निवर्तने॥ इति

न हि तमः सूर्यं तिरोहितुं प्रभवति। यदि तमसा तिरोधानमनुपपद्यमानमपि स्वीक्रियेत तर्हि को वाऽन्यः सूर्यात् तं निवारयेत्। उक्तं हि माघेन-

"ऋते रवेः क्षालयितुं क्षमेत कः क्षपातमस्काण्डमलीमसं नभः।" इति।

किञ्च, ब्रह्मस्वरूपप्रकाशस्याऽऽवरणं नाम किमिति विवेक्तव्यं - १. किमुदयप्रतिबन्धः प्रकाशस्य उत २. नाशो वा? उभयमपि नैव सम्भवति, अनाद्यनन्तप्रकाशरूपत्वादात्मनः। अपि च प्रकाशमाने आत्मन्यावरणं नैव सम्भवति, स्वरूपावभासस्याज्ञानविरोधित्वात्। अप्रकाशमानेऽपि सा न स्वीकार्या, निर्विषयाविद्याया अनवभासात्। तस्मात् स्वप्रकाशे निरंशे ब्रह्मण्यविद्यया तिरोधानं कथमपि न सङ्गतम् - इत्याक्षेपस्य सारः।

समाधानम् - स्वरूपप्रकाशस्योदयनाशौ नास्माभिरावरणमित्यस्मदनुक्तेः आक्षेप्तुः इदमनुक्तोपालम्भनमेव। परन्तु अस्माभिः आवरणकृत्यं नाम - "नास्ति न प्रकाशते" इति व्यवहारः, 'अस्ति प्रकाशते' इति व्यवहाराभावो वा। आवरणस्वरूपं तु तद्योग्यता। सा अज्ञानसम्बन्धरूपा सुषुप्त्यादिसाधारणी आब्रह्मसाक्षात्कारमनुवर्तते। तेन सुषुप्तावनावरणं न भवति। मोक्षकाले त्वखण्डाकारवृत्तिप्रतिबिम्बितचैतन्येन अज्ञानस्य विप्लुष्टत्वादज्ञानसम्बन्धस्याभावान्नैवावरणम्। इदं चाऽऽवरणमनादीति हेतोः न तस्याप्यावरणान्तरापेक्षा। उक्तं हि -

जीव ईशो विशुद्धा चित् तथा जीवेशयोर्भिदा।

अविद्या तच्चितोर्योगः षडस्माकमनादयः॥ इति॥

एवं स्वीकारेण चण्डमारुतोक्तं - "नास्ति न प्रकाशते" इति भ्रान्तिरपि आवरणसाध्यत्वेन आवरणत्वायोगः' इति वाक्यं परास्तम्।

इदं चावरणं शुद्धचैतन्यमात्रविषयं; तस्यैव केनचिद्रूपेण प्रकाशमानस्यापि अपरेण रूपेण अप्रकाशमानताया निर्वाहार्थमावरणस्य कल्पनात्। निर्विभागमपीदं चैतन्यमावरणमहिम्नैव "पूर्णानन्दात्मना नास्ति न प्रकाशते" इति व्यवहारगोचरो भवति, तदेव सत्वचित्वाभ्यामतिरोहितं च भवति। अत एव भामत्यां स्पष्टमुक्तं -

"सत्यं प्रत्यगात्मा स्वयम्प्रकाशत्वादविषयोऽनंशश्च, तथाप्यनाद्यनिर्वचनीयाविद्यापरिकल्पितबुद्धि ... अवच्छेदेन अनवच्छिन्नोऽपि अवच्छिन्न इव..." इति। पञ्चपाद्यामप्युक्तम् "सत्वचित्त्वादयो धर्माः अपृथक्त्वेऽपि चैतन्यात् पृथगिव अवभासन्ते"। इति॥

किञ्च, इदमावरणमवश्यं शुद्धचैतन्ये स्वीकार्यम्। अन्यथा अस्ति प्रकाशते इति व्यवहारसामग्र्यां सत्यां नास्ति न प्रकाशते इति व्यवहारः कथमुपपद्येत। घटादावपि अस्तीत्यादिव्यवहारसामग्र्यां निर्दुष्टेन्द्रियघटादिसन्निकर्षरूपायां सत्यां 'नास्ति न प्रकाशत इति व्यवहारः खलु तमोजन्यावरणप्रयुक्तो लोकेऽनुभूयते। आलोकोऽपि घटास्तित्व-व्यवहारसामग्र्यामन्तर्भूतः इति तु न शङ्क्यं; तमो निवृत्त्या तस्यान्यथासिद्धत्वात्। एवञ्च घटादिस्थले यथा सामग्र्यां सत्यामावरणं तमसा भवति एवमत्र चिदात्मस्वरूपस्यैव सामग्रीरूपत्वेन तत्सत्तायामपि नास्तीत्यादिव्यवहारयोग्यतापत्तिः अज्ञानेनैव वक्तव्यम्। स्थिते चैवं घटादावस्तित्वव्यवहारार्थमालोकेन तमसोऽपगम इव प्रकृते आगमिकेना-खण्डाकारवृत्तिरूपेण प्रमाणजन्यज्ञानेन, अज्ञानस्य बाधे सति यथावस्तुस्वरूपमवभासते।

शङ्का - अखण्डाकारवृत्तिरूपमागमिकं ज्ञानमप्यज्ञानोपादानकमिष्यते। एवञ्च कथं अनेन स्वोपादानस्य बाधो भवेत् - इति।

समाधानम् - वृश्चिकादौ, कदलीगर्भादौ लोके सोपादाननाशकत्वस्य दृष्टत्वात्, "न हि दृष्टेऽनुपपन्नं नाम" इति न्यायात्, "ज्ञानेन तु तदज्ञानं येषां नाशितमात्मनः" इति शास्त्राच्च वृत्तेः सोपादाननाशकत्वमुपपद्यते ॥

अथवा नैव वृत्तिरूपं अविद्योपादानकं ज्ञानं अज्ञानबाधकम्। परन्तु तत्र प्रतिबिम्बितं चैतन्यमेव तस्य बाधकम्। तस्य चैतन्यस्य स्वतोऽज्ञानभासकत्वेऽपि वृत्त्युपारूढस्य तन्नाशकत्वं सूर्यकान्तमण्युपारूढभानोरिवोपपद्यते। तथा चोक्तं सिद्धाञ्जने - "तृणाद्यवभासकसूर्यकरनिकरस्यैव पतङ्गकान्ताभिव्यक्तस्य तद्दाहकत्वदर्शनात्, अरण्य-नुगताग्नेः अतद्दाहकस्यापि निर्मथनाभिव्यक्तस्य तद्दाहकत्वदर्शनाच्च" - इति। आत्मनः प्रकाशरूपत्वेनाविद्यावरणासम्भवः तु नैव शक्यः, अपवरकालोकादौ अन्धकारारोपः इव अज्ञानारोपसम्भवात्।

किञ्च मेघैः सूर्यस्यावरणं, अथापि तेनैव सूर्येण तेषां मेघानामपि भानं यथा दृष्टत्वात् स्वीक्रियते, एवं तदुदाहारणेनापि अत्रात्मनि अज्ञानेनावरणं तेनैव च तस्य भानं चोपपद्यते इति द्रष्टव्यम्।

आक्षेपः - विषमो दृष्टान्तः उक्तः। सूर्यप्रकाशस्य ज्ञानरूपत्वं नास्ति, मेघैश्च प्रकाशप्रसरस्य प्रतिबन्धश्च भवति इति तत्र युज्यते आवरणम्। ब्रह्मप्रकाशस्य तु ज्ञानरूपत्वात्, तन्नाशाभावे ब्रह्मग्रहणमस्त्येवेति कथं तिरोधानं अज्ञानेन भवेत्?

समाधानम् - यदि सूर्यब्रह्मप्रकाशयोर्वैलक्षण्यं, तथा अन्धकाराज्ञानयोश्च वैलक्षण्यं स्वीक्रियेत, तर्हि कथं तेजस्तिमिरयोः इव ज्ञानाज्ञानयोः विरोधोऽभिसंहितो भवद्भिः? यदि प्रकाशाप्रकाशाभ्यां अप्रकाशतिरोधानाभ्यां च साम्यं उच्येत तर्हि प्रकृतेऽपि

मेघैस्तिरोधानं प्रकाशस्य कथं न दृष्टान्ततामर्हति? स्वरूपज्ञानाज्ञानयोस्तु विरोध-कथापि नैव वर्तते। अन्यथा भवन्मतेऽपि कर्मरूपाविद्यासम्बन्धः जीवस्य स्वरूप-ज्ञानस्य कथं स्यात्? तस्मात् ब्रह्मरूपं ज्ञानं नाज्ञाननाशकम्। अत एव यावदखण्डाकारवृत्ति ब्रह्मणो नैव ग्रहणमपि, इति हेतोः अज्ञानेन ब्रह्मणस्तिरोधानं नानुपपन्नम्।

इदं च शुद्धचिन्मात्रविषयं अज्ञानं शुद्धाकारवृत्त्यैव नाश्यं, न त्ववच्छिन्नविषय-वृत्त्या इति, घटादिविज्ञानादपि मोक्षापत्तिर्निशङ्क्या। एवमेव अहन्त्वेन भासमानेऽप्या-त्मनि अनवच्छिन्नानन्दात्मनाऽप्रकाशात्, 'नास्ति न प्रकाशते इति व्यवहारयोग्यताख्यम् आवरणं निराबाधमेव अनवच्छिन्नब्रह्मानन्दोऽपि अनवच्छिन्नं शुद्धं ब्रह्मैव न तु अहमर्थः इति हेतोः। अहन्त्वेन आत्मनो यद्भानं तत् न अनवच्छिन्नानन्दात्मभानम्। तस्मात् अहमो ज्ञानान्नैव मोक्षः। एवं स्वीकारेण चण्डमारुतोक्तं - "इदानीमप्यहमाकारवृत्तेः अज्ञानविरोधित्वपक्षेऽपि आवरणासम्भवः", इति वाक्यं पराहतम्॥ इतः परं विशिष्टाद्वैतसिद्धान्तिनां पक्षमुक्त्वा विमृश्यते। तेषां श्रीभाष्याभिमतं मतमिदम् -

> जीवचैतन्यं ब्रह्मस्वरूपं च स्वस्मै प्रकाशते, परस्मै न प्रकाशते; परस्मै प्रकाशो हि धर्म-भूतज्ञानाधीनः, धर्मभूतज्ञानस्य स्वयं प्रकाशत्वेऽपि सातिशयतत्सङ्कोचविकासाभ्यां परस्मै अप्रकाशः; निरतिशयविकासमात्रेण तु नित्यसिद्धेन, निरतिशयभक्त्याराधित-भगवत्सङ्कल्पसिद्धेन वा धर्मभूतज्ञानेन मुक्तात्मनां भगवतश्च सर्वज्ञत्वादि स्वीक्रियते। तत्र धर्मभूतज्ञानसङ्कोचविकासौ किञ्चिज्ज्ञत्वप्रयोजकौ कर्माधीनौ एव कर्मरूपाविद्या-कृत्यमावरणं नाम। तत्रापि सङ्कोचः सर्वथाऽज्ञानं विषयाणां यथा सुषुप्त्यादौ, जाग्रदादौ तु केषाञ्चन कदाचन ज्ञानं; केषाञ्चन कदाचनाज्ञानम्। यत्र तु विकासः तत्रानावरणं यत्र संकोचः तत्रावरणमिति विवेक इति।

एवं च सति तेषां मते धर्मभूतज्ञानसङ्कोचः कर्मकृतमावरणमिति फलति। अत्रायं विमर्शः- इयं कर्मरूपाविद्या जीवगता उत ईश्वरगता? जन्मान्तरानुष्ठित-कर्मणां आफलोत्पत्ति भगवत्सङ्कल्परूपत्वात्, तस्य च भगवन्निष्ठत्वात् अविद्यायाः जीवाश्रयत्वमनुपपन्नम्।एवं, जन्मान्तरानुष्ठितकर्माधीनस्य भगवत्सङ्कल्पस्य फलोत्पत्त्यनन्तरं क्षयस्यावश्यकत्वात्, प्रतिक्षणं घटपटादिज्ञानसङ्कोचविकासोदयात्, तावन्मात्रेण च प्रारब्धतदितरकर्मणां साफल्यात् सुखदुःखादिसाधनत्वानुपपत्तिः। तावत्पर्यन्तं संकल्पावस्थाने तु तत्तदवान्तरफलजननशक्त्यः भगवत्सङ्कल्पेषु स्वीकार्याः। ततश्च शक्तिविशेषनाशेऽपि शक्त्यन्तरेण मुख्यफलोदयपर्यन्तं कर्म अनुवर्तते इति वक्तव्यम्। ततश्च सकृत् घटज्ञानेऽपि पौनःपुन्येन घटाज्ञानतज्ज्ञानादयः उपपद्येरन्

इति या रीतिः तेषां मते अङ्गीकार्या सैव रीतिः - अद्वैतमतेऽपि घटादिज्ञानेषु तत्तदवच्छिन्न-चैतन्याश्रितानामविद्याशक्तिमात्राणां कटवद्वेष्टनं, भीतभटवदपसरणं, घटादिज्ञानेषु नष्टेषु पुनरावरणं नोपपद्यते इत्येवं वक्तुं सुकरा। एवं च सति घटादिज्ञान-मात्रात् न मुक्त्यापत्तिः। एवमेव तत्तज्जीवभेदेन कर्मणां भेदात् यथा एकमुक्तौ न सर्वमुक्तेरापत्तिः श्रीभाष्यमते, तथाऽस्माकमपि मते जीवभेदेनावस्थाज्ञानानां अज्ञानानां वा नानात्वस्य स्वीकारेण एकमुक्तौ न सर्वमुक्तिः।

परन्तु इदमत्रालोचनार्हं यत् - इयं कर्मरूपाविद्या यदि सादिः ईश्वराधीना स्वीक्रियेत तर्हि अन्योन्याश्रयः - ईश्वरसङ्कल्पाधीनं कर्म, कर्माधीनश्च ईश्वरसङ्कल्पः इति। यदि सा सादिः जीवाधीना उच्येत, तदापि पूर्वोक्तदोषात् न निवृत्तिः - कर्माधीनं स्थूलचिद्रूपत्वं जीवत्वं वा, जीवत्वाधीनं च कर्म इति। अपि च कर्मणो भगवत्सङ्कल्परूपस्य जीवाश्रयत्वानुपपत्तिश्च स्यात्। एतद्दोषपरिहारार्थं कर्मरूपा-विद्यायाः अनादित्वं यदि उच्येत तत्तु तत्त्वत्रयसिद्धान्तभङ्गापत्त्या न सम्भवति। प्रवाहतोऽनादित्वं स्वीकृत्यापि न निर्वोढुं शक्यते, यतः उपादानोपादेयभावस्थले एव बीजाङ्कुरादौ तत् स्वीक्रियते। पकृते तु ईश्वरसङ्कल्पस्य धर्मभूतज्ञानसङ्कोचविकासयोश्च नास्त्युपादानोपादेयभावः। अतः कर्मरूपाविद्यया तिरोधानं किंरूपं इति तन्मते दुष्करं वक्तुम्। किञ्च, धर्मभूतज्ञानसङ्कोचः तत्तिरोभावः न भावरूपः पदार्थः, आवरणं तु भावरूपम् इत्यतः तस्य नावरणत्वं सम्भवति।

अन्यच्च अविद्यया आवरणं नाम तस्या एव धर्मविशेषो भवितुमर्हति, तमसः आवरकत्वं हि तमोगतमेव। आवरणकृत्यं तु आवृतस्य प्रकाशाभावः। तत्रैवं सति अविद्यावृते धर्मभूतज्ञानसङ्कोचात् प्रकाशाभावः आवरणकृत्यमिति वक्तव्यम्। तत्र किमविद्यावृतं - घटादयो वा? धर्मिज्ञानं वा? नाद्यः घटादीनां कर्मभिरसम्बन्धात् तैः घटादीनामनावृतत्वाच्च। न द्वितीयः जीवाश्रितायाः ईश्वराश्रितसङ्कल्परूपायाः वा अविद्यायाः स्वप्रकाशत्वरूपाप्रकाशकत्वायोगात्, अन्यथा स्वप्रकाशत्वभङ्गापत्तेः। तस्मात् स्थूलोऽहं इत्यादिप्रतीतिनिर्वाहोऽपि कर्माविद्यत्वपक्षे नोपपद्यते, अन्योन्याश्रयात् - कर्मापेक्षः स्थूलोऽहमिति प्रत्ययः तदपेक्षश्च कर्म इति। तथाहि भगवत्पादीयं भाष्यम् - "नित्यं अशरीरत्वं अकर्मनिमित्तत्वादित्यवोचाम। तत्कृतधर्माधर्मनिमित्तं सशरीरत्व-मिति चेत्, न, शरीरसम्बन्धस्यासिद्धत्वेन धर्माधर्मयोः आत्मकृतत्वासिद्धेः। शरीर-सम्बन्धस्य धर्माधर्मयोः तत्कृतत्वस्य च इतरेतराश्रयत्वप्रसङ्गात्, अन्धपरम्परैषा अनादित्वकल्पना" (ब्र.सू. 1.1.4.) इति। बीजाङ्कुरस्थले तु नान्धत्वं यतः बीजादङ्कुरोत्पत्तेः प्रत्यक्षतो दर्शनात्। प्रकृते तु शरीरस्य कर्मजन्यत्वस्याप्रत्यक्षत्वम् इति भेदः। एवं परमतेऽपि आवरणासम्भव आपाद्यः।

उपसंहारः - तस्मात् स्वप्रकाशे आत्मनि भासमानेऽपि "पूर्णानन्दात्मना न भाति" इति विपरीतव्यवहारयोग्यत्वमेव आवरणं, निर्विभागेऽपि चैतन्ये अविद्यासामर्थ्यात् अनुभवबलाच्च कल्पिताः अंशाः स्वीक्रियन्ते। सा चाविद्या अनादिरिति न कल्पकान्तरापेक्षाद्वारा अनवस्थादोषः।

भासमाने कथमभानम् इति मुख्यं चोद्यं तावत्, दशमूढकथया निर्मूलीकार्यम् इति सर्वमनवद्यम्।

यदज्ञातं जीवैर्बहुविधजगद्विभ्रमधरं
वियद्यद्वद्बालैः तलमलिनतायोगिकलितम्।
तदुन्मुद्रज्ञानप्रततसुखसद्ब्रह्म परमं
नमस्यामः प्रत्यक्श्रुतिशतशिरोभिः प्रकटितम्॥

Summary: In attempting to refute the claims of Viśiṣṭādvaita school in their elucidation of *Tirodhāna-anupapatti,* Professor R. Krishnamurthi Sastri presents here the Advaita view in support of māyā-avidyā. To the Advaitin's claim that avidyā conceals the self-luminous nature of Brahman and projects the world, Rāmānuja says that such an idea is fallacious. Concealment can happen in two ways: (1) either the rise of luminosity (i.e. *prakāśa*) is obstructed or (2) luminosity which already there is destroyed. In the case of Brahman, which is eternally self-luminous, both these types of concealments are not possible.

Advaitins retort saying that the first of the above alternatives is ruled out because Advaita admits no origination for consciousness. *Svarūpa-tirodhāna*, Rāmānuja says, is *svarūpa-aprakāśa*. Since it is the very nature of Brahman to be self-luminous, the concealment of this nature is possible only through the removal of that nature. Hence, this loss of the essential nature of Brahman through avidyā, an outside agency, is the loss of Brahman itself. It is possible to avoid this situation by making consciousness only an attribute of Brahman because while the loss of an attribute is not the loss of the thing of which it is an attribute, the loss of the essential nature of a thing is the loss of the thing itself. Since the Advaitin says that consciousness is the essential nature of Brahman, the concealment of this essential nature through avidyā can only mean, as Rāmānuja says, the loss of Brahman itself.

Advaitin emphatically says that Rāmānuja deliberately twists the meaning of the word "concealment" (*āvaraṇa*) in order to prove his standpoint. Consider the case of an object concealed from me, when some one asks me whether I know that object, I reply in the negative. Because of the concealment, I am not able to claim that it exists or that it is directly seen by me. But it does not follow from this that there is loss of that object. The same thing may be said of the concealment of Brahman. When the veil of avidyā is removed through knowledge, one may claim that Brahman exists or that it is directly seen. It must be borne in mind that this explanation of the work of avidyā is given from the relative standpoint of *vyavahāra*. From the absolute standpoint, there is no avidyā at all, and Brahman alone is; therefore, Brahman is neither concealed nor destroyed by avidyā.

One may argue that there is a basic difference between the concealment of Brahman and the concealment of other objects. Everything other than Brahman is insentient according to Advaita. But Brahman is of the nature of self-luminous knowledge or consciousness. Therefore, the concealment of Brahman-knowledge by ignorance can only mean the loss or destruction of Brahman-knowledge because knowledge and ignorance, according to Advaita, are mutually exclusive like light and darkness.

Firstly, the point at issue is not the difference between sentient Brahman and other insentient objects which is accepted by Advaita. Secondly, it is also true that knowledge (*jñāna*) and ignorance (*ajñāna*) are mutually opposed like light and darkness. A little clarification of this second point may be relevant here. When Advaita says that knowledge is opposed to ignorance, the knowledge so opposed is *vṛtti-jñāna* and not *svarūpa-jñāna*. Since the knowledge of these two types are different, it is possible to maintain that Brahman which is knowledge by nature (*svarūpa-jñāna*) is not opposed to avidyā. Hence, far from being opposed to avidyā, Brahman-knowledge is helpful to it not only in serving as its locus but also in its revelation. That is precisely why we can say that there is avidyā which conceals Brahman-knowledge. Brahman-knowledge and avidyā are related as the locus and the contained, and also as the revealer and the revealed. When avidyā, though revealed by Brahman, conceals it, we say that Brahman is not known; and when avidyā is removed by the unitary cognition through the mental mode (*akhaṇḍākāra-vṛtti-jñāna*), we say that Brahman is known.

Further, our claim that Brahman is known or that it is not known, is based on the work of the mind. The cognition that one has in these cases is *vṛtti-jñāna*, which is different from Brahman which is *svarūpa-jñāna*. Hence, just because one has the cognition that Brahman does not exist or that Brahman is not seen, it does not follow that there is no Brahman. In other words, the concealment of Brahman as indicated by these cognitions does not imply the loss or destruction of Brahman because every such *vṛtti-jñāna* presupposes *svarūpa-jñāna*.

It is necessary at this stage to consider another objection of Rāmānuja that the concealment of Brahman-knowledge is not at all possible and that the Advaita explanation in this regard is fallacious.

This objection is wrong. First of all, Advaita does not hold that Brahman is conscious of *ajñāna*. When Rāmānuja asks whether avidyā first conceals Brahman and then becomes an object of Brahman's consciousness, or whether it first becomes an object of Brahman's consciousness and then hides it, he wrongly assumes that according to Advaita Brahman is conscious of avidyā. Since Advaita denies *ajñānānubhava* to Brahman, the entire criticism of Rāmānuja is misconceived. Secondly, if one formulates the problem the way Rāmānuja does, the Advaita position cannot avoid the fallacy of mutual dependence (*anyonyāśraya*). But according to Advaita, avidyā which conceals Brahman, is experienced by the jīva and not by Brahman. So the Advaita view that Brahman-knowledge is concealed by avidyā becomes quite tenable. Brahman-in-itself is neither the witness to, nor has the experience of, avidyā. While Īśvara knows both avidyā and its manifestations, it is the jīva which is really the victim of avidyā. The redeeming feature here is that the jīva knows that he is ignorant. Hence Rāmānuja's view that avidyā cannot conceal Brahman is ill-conceived.

10

SVARŪPĀNUPAPATTI IN VIŚIṢṬĀDVAITA

S.M. Srinivasachari

Of the seven *Anupapattis* pointed out by Rāmānuja in his classic *Śrībhāṣya* against the doctrine of Avidyā, the *Svarūpā-nupapatti* assumes special significance. The concept of avidyā is admitted by the Advaita Vedānta as the cosmic principle to account for the illusory appearance of the manifold universe. One should know its nature (*svarūpa*). What is its *svarūpa*? This is the basic question that the critic of Advaita raises. Rāmānuja therefore, subjects it to a critical analysis and in the absence of a satisfactory answer forthcoming, he regards the theory as untenable.

The first important question that is raised regarding the nature of avidyā is whether it is real (*pāramārthika*) or unreal (*apāramārthika*), the two possible alternatives which are generally accepted by the critics. If avidyā were a non-existent entity like the sky-flower, this question would become irrelevant. But it is admitted by the Advaitin as a positive entity capable of concealing the true nature of the Brahman and projecting the illusion of the universe. It is therefore, to be regarded either as real or unreal. If it is taken as real, it is further asked whether it is different from Brahman or non-different from it. If it is admitted as different it would amount to the admission of two reals which mitigate against the basic tenet of Advaita. If on the contrary avidyā is regarded as non-different from Brahman being eternal, the world-illusion would also be eternal.

In order to avoid this situation avidyā may be admitted as unreal, but even then the difficulties pointed out earlier would be unavoidable.

Is this avidyā which is illusory in character different or non-different from Brahman? Obviously, it is different from Brahman. The appearance of what is illusory is generally due to some defect (*doṣa*). Now, what is that defect on which avidyā depends? If a defect be admitted as the source of manifestation of avidyā then that defect being illusory in character would require another defect for its manifestation and so on *ad-infinitum* (*anavasthā*). Just to overcome this difficulty, if it be held that Brahman itself causes the manifestation of avidyā, then Brahman being the eternal, the appearance of avidyā too would be eternal. This objection is met by regarding avidyā as beginningless (*anādi*) and there is no need to postulate another defect to account for the manifestation of avidyā. The critic does not accept this argument as satisfactory. If avidyā is *anādi*, it would mean that it is not dependent on a defect for its appearance. Avidyā insofar as it is illusory in character must necessarily depend on a defect for its appearance, even though it may be beginningless. If it could manifest itself without an extraneous cause, it would become real like Brahman which is self-manifest.

The next question which is raised against the nature of avidyā is whether or not avidyā manifests at all? If it does not, it would amount to a non-entity, like the sky-flower which never exists. If it manifests then in what form does it manifest? Does it manifest as the very nature of avidyā or that of Brahman or as the characteristic (*dharma*) of either avidyā or Brahman? These are the four possible ways in which the manifestation of avidyā can be conceived but none is logically tenable. It cannot be the nature of avidyā since in that case avidyā as a self-manifest entity would become real like Brahman. As Brahman is eternal, the manifestation of avidyā too would be eternal, and consequently there would be no release as long as avidyā persists. Nor does it manifest as the dharma of either avidyā or Brahman since neither of them is admitted by the Advaitin as the knower (*jñātā*) in the real sense of the term in which it can inhere as the dharma.

Another important question that is raised against the nature of avidyā is whether or not it has a locus (*āśraya*)? Avidyā like *jñāna* implies some person to whom it belongs and some object to which it refers. Now what is the content of avidyā? Brahman itself is both the locus and content of avidyā as there is nothing else beside it. But

Brahman, according to Advaita is self-luminous knowledge; it is opposed to avidyā like light is to darkness. To overcome this difficulty, some Advaitins maintain that jīva is the locus of avidyā. The soundness of these arguments in defence of Advaitins would have been discussed under the topic of *āśrayānupapatti.* However, more important than the *āśraya* is the discussion on the very concealment of the true nature of Brahman (*tirodhāna*) as a result of which the illusion of universe arises, and that is seriously questioned by Rāmānuja. *Tirodhāna,* according to Viśiṣṭādvaita, amounts to the destruction of the very *svarūpa* of Brahman which is essentially of the nature of knowledge (*jñāna-svarūpa*).

The details of the criticism of the theory would be covered under the topic of *tirodhāna-anupapatti.*

The most crucial criticism levelled by Rāmānuja against the nature of avidyā is that it is not a positive entity (*bhāvarūpa*) on the basis of which the Adavitin defends the possibility of subsistence of avidyā in Brahman and also its concealment. The Advaitin contends that avidyā as a positive entity is totally opposed to the self-luminous, Brahman. It can, therefore, subsist in Brahman and also conceals its true nature as a result of which the world-illusion arises. That avidyā is a positive entity is sought to be established by means of perception, inference and scriptural texts. This theory is critically examined in great detail by Rāmānuja and it is shown that none of the pramāṇas prove it. The inference in particular advanced by Citsukha in defence of the theory is fallacious. The scriptural text quoted by the Advatins in support of it are shown to convey an import other than what is claimed by the Advaitins.

According to the Advaitin, avidyā is removed by true knowledge of the Brahman. The theory of *Avidyā-nivartaka* and also the very cessation of it (*nivṛtti*) after the dawn of Brahman knowledge are considered by Rāmānuja as untenable. The details of these criticisms are dealt separately. The critical examination of the doctrine of avidyā by Rāmānuja in a methodical way from different standpoints are intended to show that the whole idea of māyā-avidyā is riddled with contradictions and is not sustainable both logically and philosophically.

Against all these criticisms, the Advaitins may contend that these are only applicable to what is real and an existent entity but not to avidyā or māyā on the ground that unintelligibility itself is the characteristic feature of avidyā. Thus it is stated that unintelligibility is the ornament and not a blemish (*durghaṭatvam avidyāyāḥ bhūṣaṇaṁ na tu dūṣaṇam*). The author of *Brahmasiddhi* says: *"na hi māyāyāṁ kācidanupapttiḥ anupapadyā anarthaiva hi māyā."* Vedāntadeśika, in his *Śatadūṣaṇī* mainly devoted to the criticism of the Advaita doctrines, has set aside this argument as a mere dogmatic statement of the Mādhyamikas to defend the Śūnyavāda. The criticism levelled by Rāmānuja are to be accepted as valid and these cannot therefore be easily set aside.

11

स्वरूपानुपपत्तिखण्डनम्

Muddulapalli Dattatreya Sastri

भगवद्रामानुजैः श्रीभाष्ये प्रथमाध्याये प्रथमपादे जिज्ञासाधिकरणे पूर्वपक्षनिरूपणे अद्वैतवादे अविद्याया अथ वा मायायाः स्वीकारे सप्तविधानुपपत्तयः सम्भवन्ति इत्यभ्यधायि। ताश्चानुपपत्तयः- आश्रयानुपपत्ति-स्वरूपानुपत्ति-तिरोधानानुपपत्ति-अनिर्वचनीयत्वानुपपत्ति-प्रमाणानुपपत्ति-निवर्तकानुपपत्ति-निवृत्त्यनुपपत्तिरूपाः - यासु अन्यतमाऽनुपपत्तिः स्वरूपानुपत्तिः। एतदनुपपत्तिनिरूपणे श्रीभाष्योक्तार्थः सङ्गृह्योच्यते॥

अनुभूतिस्वरूपं ब्रह्म निराश्रयं निर्विषयकञ्च, तथापि स्वप्रकाशस्वरूपं स्वाश्रयदोषवशाद् अनन्ताश्रयमनन्तविषयमात्मानमनुभवति इति। अत्राऽविद्या पारमार्थिकी चेत् ब्रह्मणः सद्वितीयत्वप्रसङ्गः। अतोऽविद्याऽपारमार्थिकी मिथ्यारूपा अङ्गीकार्या। तर्हि तदा अविद्यायाः स्वरूपं किम्? दृक्-द्रष्टृ-दृश्येषु किं स्वरूपमिति, अविद्यायाः दृग्रूपत्वे ज्ञानद्वयस्याऽऽवश्यकता स्यात् - ब्रह्मस्वरूपमेकं ज्ञानं अविद्यास्वरूपं दृग्रूपं द्वितीयं ज्ञानमिति। अद्वैतमते ब्रह्मात्मकदृग्रूपज्ञानभिन्नज्ञानस्य अभावात्। अविद्यात्मक-ज्ञानस्वीकारे, ब्रह्मात्मकज्ञानस्य तिरोधानं स्यात्। निर्गुणब्रह्मस्वरूपतिरोधानं नाम ब्रह्मस्वरूपनाश एव। एतद्दोषाभावाय अविद्यारूपज्ञानस्वीकारे एकं ब्रह्मरूपज्ञानमेव अविद्या इत्युच्येत। अविद्यानाशे आत्मन एव नाशः स्यात्। एवञ्चेत् माध्यमिकपद्धत्या नाशो भवति। वस्तुतः अद्वैतमते ज्ञानस्वरूपं ब्रह्म नित्यमद्वितीयं परमार्थरूपञ्च इति सिद्धान्तहानिः। अतः ज्ञानस्वरूपा न भवत्यविद्या इति दृशिस्वरूपानुपपत्तिः।

अविद्या ज्ञातृरूपा ज्ञेयरूपा च न भवति। यतः ज्ञातुर्ज्ञेयस्य वा आविद्यकत्वात् अविद्याजन्यत्वात्। अतः अविद्यायाः ज्ञातृज्ञेयादि (निरूपणे) कारणभूतायाः कार्यरूपत्वं न सम्भवति। यदि ज्ञातृज्ञेयसम्भवाय द्वितीयामविद्यामङ्गीकुर्यात् तदा तस्याः अविद्यायाः स्वरूपमपि आश्रयरूपं वा विषयरूपं वा इति, प्रकाशरूपत्वे पुनस्तद्ग्राहिका अन्याऽविद्या स्वीकार्या, पुनस्तथैवेत्यविद्याया अनवस्थापत्तिः इति ज्ञातृज्ञेयस्वरूपानुपपत्तिः।

अनवस्थापरिहारार्थं परमार्थरूपा अविद्या ग्राह्या, अनुभूतिस्वरूपायाः दोषत्वे तदुत्पन्नस्य प्रपञ्चस्यापि दोषत्वापत्तिः। प्रपञ्चकारणभूतब्रह्मज्ञानरूपा चेत् तदुत्पन्न प्रपञ्चोऽपि नित्यः (स्यात्) भवति इति अविद्यायाः पारमार्थिकत्वम् स्वीकार्यमिति श्रीभाष्याशयः फलति ॥

उपर्युक्तार्थे अद्वैतिनः एवं स्वाभिप्रायं निरूपयन्ति - भावरूपा ज्ञाननिवर्त्यस्वरूपा एषाऽविद्या न पारमार्थिकी ब्रह्मज्ञानबाध्यत्वात् अपारमार्थिकी। दृग्रूपा द्रष्टृरूपा वा न भवत्यविद्या, किन्तु दृश्यरूपा। दृश्यत्वञ्च फलव्याप्यत्वं (चिद्भास्यत्वम्) साक्षिभास्यत्वं वा। अतः ज्ञेयस्वरूपस्वीकारेऽपि अनवस्थापत्तिर्नास्ति। घटादिदृश्यप्रपञ्चस्य मूलदोषान्तरापेक्षास्ति। अनादिरपि जीवः अविद्यापेक्ष एव भवति। अविद्या तु न दोषान्तरापेक्षा भवति। एवं स्वप्रकाशचैतन्यरूपस्य ब्रह्मणोऽपि अनादेः नाविद्यापेक्षा अन्यापेक्षा वा। "जीव ईशो विशुद्धा चित् तथा जीवेशयोर्भिदा। अविद्या तच्चितोर्योगः षडस्माकमनादयः॥" इत्युक्तेः जीवादि अनादिषट्(क)पदार्थमध्ये अविद्याब्रह्मणोरेव इतरानपेक्षानादिस्वरूपं स्वत एवास्ति। अविद्यायाः ब्रह्मण इव अविद्यान्तरापेक्षा नास्ति चेत् ब्रह्मवदविद्यायाः पारमार्थिकत्वं कुतो नास्तीति प्रश्ने, श्रुतिभिः ब्रह्मण एव सत्यत्वबोधनात् (सत्यं ज्ञानमनन्तं ब्रह्म)। एवमविद्यायाः बाध्यत्वमपि बोध्यते - "नेह नानास्ति किञ्चन"। "सत्यमबाध्यं बाध्यं मिथ्या," "ज्ञानं अज्ञानस्यैव निवर्तकम्" इति वचोभिः॥

बाध्यत्वं तु बाध्याधिकसत्ताकार्थविषयकज्ञानेन भवति। न समानसत्ताकार्थविषयकज्ञानेन। यथा शुक्तिरजतस्थले। शुक्तिसाक्षात्कारेण व्यावहारिकेण ततो निकृष्टं प्रातिभासिकं रजतज्ञानं बाध्यते। एवं प्रपञ्चसत्यत्वज्ञानं व्यावहारिकं प्रति प्रपञ्चाभावत्वोपलक्षिताभावरूपब्रह्मरूपत्वेनैव प्रपञ्चाभावज्ञानं बाधकं नाभावविशिष्टेन व्यावहारिकरूपेण इति मते अपरमार्थस्य अधिष्ठानत्वशङ्कापि न भवति। अद्वैतमते अधिष्ठानस्य अपारमार्थिकत्वे अनवस्थादोषो न भवति परन्तु पारमार्थिकाधिष्ठाने आरोपितस्य प्रपञ्चस्य अधिष्ठानज्ञानेन बाध्यत्वं न सिध्यतीति अतः माध्यमिकानुप्रवेशः नास्ति॥

अनवस्थानिरासः

अविद्या दृश्या इति अपरमार्थत्वमागतम्। एवं कल्पनामूल अज्ञानरूपदोषसापेक्षत्वेनानवस्था भवतीति, केयमनवस्था? सजातीयाप्रमाणिकानन्तपदार्थकल्पनाविश्रान्त्यभावः अनवस्था चेदस्तु तावदनवस्था। आत्मज्ञानातिरिक्ता सर्वापि कल्पना भ्रमः इत्यभ्युपगम्यते। अतः विशिष्टाद्वैतिभिः किमापाद्यते अप्रामाणिकी कल्पना इति। अपि च अविद्याकल्पनायाः अनादित्वेन तन्मूलदोषान्तरानपेक्षायाम् अनवस्था नास्त्येव।

सुदर्शनाचार्यैः प्रपञ्चस्याविद्याकल्पिततत्वपक्षे प्रकारान्तरेण दोषा उक्ताः। तेऽपि दोषाः न सम्भवन्ति अद्वैतमते। तथा हि - पूर्वपक्षस्तावदित्थम् - ब्रह्मण्यविद्यया प्रपञ्चः कल्पितः,

साऽविद्यापि केनचिदन्येन कल्पितैव। अविद्याया अकल्पितत्वे पारमार्थ्यप्रसङ्गः, अविद्याकल्पकः पदार्थः केनचिदन्येन कल्पितः सोऽप्यन्येन इत्यनवस्था - भामतीप्रस्थानानुयायिनस्तु बीजाङ्कुरन्यायवदविद्यया जीवः जीवादविद्या इति प्रवाहानादित्वेनानवस्था नास्तीति पर्यहरन्। अस्मिन्पक्षे जीवनित्यत्वबोधक श्रुतयः विरुध्येरन्, कृतहानाकृताभ्यागमप्रसङ्गः, आमोक्षाज्जीवस्य स्थायित्वमपि भज्येतेत्यभिप्रेत्य भामतीपक्षमपहाय विवरणपक्षमाश्रित्याविद्यायाः स्वरूपानादित्वं स्वीकृत्यानवस्था परिहृता।

एतत्पक्षद्वयमपि न युक्तिमदिति श्रुतप्रकाशिकाकारा अभिप्रयन्ति - अविद्यायाः स्वरूपानादित्वेऽपि मूलदोषापेक्षाऽस्त्येव। यथा जीवस्यानादित्वेऽप्यविद्यापरिकल्पितत्वं स्वीक्रियते तथा अविद्यायाः स्वरूपानादित्वेऽपि मूलदोषापेक्षा इति। यद्यद्वैतिनः अविद्यायाः दुर्घटत्वेनानवस्था नास्तीति वदेयुस्तर्हि दुर्घटत्वं नाम उपपत्तिनिरपेक्षत्वं तदेवाविद्याया अपारमार्थ्यसाधकं चेत् प्रपञ्चस्योपपत्तिनिरपेक्षत्वेन मूलदोषापेक्षा न स्यात्। निवर्तकज्ञाने सत्यपि अविद्या अवतिष्ठेत। ज्ञानाज्ञानयोः समानविषयकयोः निवर्त्यनिवर्तकभावस्य भङ्गः प्रसज्येत। यद्युपपत्तिसापेक्षत्वमविद्यायाः स्वीकृत्य ज्ञानविरोधित्वादविद्या न तिष्ठतीति चेत् तर्हि उपपत्त्यनुवर्तित्वेन अनवस्था तदवस्थैव। किञ्च अविद्यायाः दुर्घटत्वे मुक्तान् परब्रह्म च अविद्या आश्रयेत्। शुद्धस्वरूपं ब्रह्म अशुद्धस्वरूपा अविद्या नाश्रयति चेत् तदा अविद्या उपपत्तिमती स्यात्। मोक्षेऽपि ब्रह्म आश्रयेदविद्या इत्युक्तौ बाधकज्ञाने सति अपरमार्थभूता अविद्या न तिष्ठतीति प्रतिवक्तव्यमद्वैतिना, तदा पुनरायातमुपपत्तिसापेक्षत्वं बाधकसन्निधौ न बाध्यसिद्धिरिति। अतः अनवस्था दुष्परिहरा इति पूर्वपक्षोक्तिसंक्षेपः॥

अत्रोच्येत - अविद्या कर्मेति विशिष्टाद्वैतमतेऽपि जीवाश्रययोः कर्मदेहादिप्रपञ्चयोः बीजाङ्कुरयोरिवान्योन्यकार्यकारणभावादनवस्थापरिहारार्थं प्रवाहानादित्वमभ्युपेयं, यतः कर्माभावे देहादिसम्भवो नास्ति, देहाद्यभावे वा कर्मसम्भवः। जीवो हि देहादिमान् सन् सुकृतं दुष्कृतं वा करोति, सुकृतदुष्कृतवशात् देहवान् भवति, अतः देहकर्मणोरन्यतरस्य अनादित्वं वक्तुं न शक्यते, यथा बीजाङ्कुरयोः। यद्ययं कर्मविषयकः अन्योन्याश्रयदोषः (स्वज्ञानाधीनज्ञानाधीनज्ञानाविषयत्वरूपः) देहकर्मविषयकः प्रवाहानादित्वेन निवर्तते इत्युच्येत तर्हि जीवाज्ञानवादिमतेऽपि (अद्वैते) जीवादविद्याऽविद्यातो वा जीवः इत्यन्योन्याश्रयः कुतः प्रवाहानादित्वस्वीकारे न निवर्तते? निवर्तत एव॥

जीवस्य अनित्यत्वं श्रुत्यादिविरुद्धं - "न जायते म्रियते वा विपश्चित्, जीवो ब्रह्मैव" इत्यादि श्रुतिभिः नित्यत्वनिरूपणात् इति न वक्तव्यम्। अविद्याजन्यस्य जीवस्य अनित्यत्वं श्रुत्याद्यभिमतमेव, यत् जीवस्य पारमार्थिकं तत्त्वं चैतन्यं तत् नित्यमुच्यते॥

अयमत्र विशेषः - कर्माणि देहाश्च नाना भवन्ति, अविद्याजीवौ तु द्वावेव। अविद्याजीवौ युगपदेव अभूताम्। यथा कर्मदेहयोः बीजाङ्कुरयोः - सम्प्रदायाविच्छेदः तथा अविद्याजीवयोः नास्ति। अतः प्रवाहानादिकल्पनापि न प्रधाना किन्त्वौपचारिक्येव। वस्तुतस्तु बीजाङ्कुर-स्थले कर्मदेहस्थले जीवाविद्याविषये च पौर्वापर्यस्य वक्तुमशक्यत्वात् अविद्यातो जीवो वा जीवादविद्या वा, देहात् कर्म वा कर्मणो देहो वा इत्यादि प्रश्नाः निरुत्तराः भवन्ति।

यस्तूभयोः समो दोषः परिहारोऽपि वा समः।
नैकः पर्यनुयोक्तव्यः तादृगर्थविचारणे॥ (श्लोकवार्तिकम्, शून्यवादः - २५२)

इत्युक्त्या प्रवाहानादित्वेन अनवस्थानिरासः। अविद्याजीवयोरनादित्वे श्रुतिरपि प्रमाणं भवति - "अजो ह्येको जुषमाणोऽनुशेते इति जीवानादित्वे, "अजामेकां लोहितशुक्लकृष्णाम्" इत्यविद्याया अनादित्वे। अत्र अजत्वमनादित्वमेव न तु जन्माभावः तथा सति अनन्तत्वापत्तिः "यस्यादिरस्ति तस्यैव अन्तः"। अतः कार्यकारणभूतावपि अविद्याजीवौ आमोक्षं स्थायिनावेव इति जीवाज्ञानवादिमते न कश्चिद्दोषः। प्रकाशात्मश्रीचरणानां विवरणाचार्या-णामभिप्रायानुसारेण ब्रह्माश्रिताऽविद्या। तन्मतमपि निर्दुष्टमेव। जीवस्य अविद्याकार्यत्वेऽपि अविद्यायाः जीवकार्यत्वं नास्ति अनुक्तत्वात्। जीवस्य अविद्याकार्यत्वं तु "जीवेशावाभासेन करोति" इति श्रुत्या -

स्वाज्ञानकल्पितजगत्परमेश्वरत्वजीवत्वभेदकलुषीकृतभूमभाव
स्वाभाविकस्वमहिमस्थितिरस्तमोहा प्रत्यक्चितिर्विजयते भुवनैकयोनिः॥ इति

सङ्क्षेपशारीरकाचार्याद्युक्त्या च सिद्धम्। एवमविद्याजन्योऽपि जीवः अनादिरेव जन्मकाल-निर्वचनासम्भवात्। अस्मिन्काले अविद्यावशात् अयं जीव आसीदिति निरूपयितुं न शक्यते। अविद्या ब्रह्मणि स्वत एवास्तीति न मूलदोषापेक्षा। अन्यच्च अतीन्द्रियार्थे अनुभवाद्यतिरस्कार्ये अस्माकमास्तिकानां श्रुतिरेव प्रमाणं भवति। सा च श्रुतिः "माया चाविद्या च स्वयमेव भवति" इति। अतोऽनवस्था नास्ति।

अज्ञानं विना ब्रह्मैव प्रपञ्चहेतुरिति शङ्कानिरासः

अविद्या न परिकल्पिता किन्तु श्रुत्यैवोक्ता। तस्याश्च जगद्भ्रमकारणत्वं विद्यते इति। एवं सति मोक्षेऽपि ब्रह्मणि अविद्या स्यात् इत्यापत्तिस्तु ज्ञानेन तन्नाश इत्युक्त्या परिहार्या। एवं स्वप्रकाशस्य ब्रह्मणः सर्वथा अनावृतस्य अधिष्ठानत्वे भ्रमनिवृत्तिर्न स्यात्। अज्ञानाङ्गीकारे भ्रमनाशस्सम्भवति। असाधारणरूपेण अज्ञातस्य साधारणरूपेण ज्ञातस्य ब्रह्मणः भ्रमोपादानत्वम् असाधारणाकारस्य ज्ञाने च भ्रमनिवृत्तिः। तथा इदं

रजतमिति अधिष्ठानसामान्यविशेष्याकारोपविशेषप्रकारकज्ञानभ्रमः। तत्राधिष्ठानस्य इदमः इदन्त्वेन ज्ञातत्वेऽपि शुक्तित्वेनाज्ञातत्वात् अधिष्ठानविशेषरूपेण इयं शुक्तिः इति यदा ज्ञानं भवति तदा रजतभ्रान्तिर्निवर्तते। एवं ब्रह्मज्ञानात् अज्ञानतत्कार्यसंसारयोरुभयोरपि निवृत्तिर्भवति॥

ब्रह्मण्येव अन्यनिरपेक्ष अनाद्यध्यासप्रवाहवैचित्र्येण सर्वाध्याससिद्धेः अविद्या-कल्पना निर्मूला" इति शतदूषणीभाषणमपि न मर्षणीयम्। किमनावृतं ब्रह्म सर्वाध्यासहेतुः उत आवृतम्? यद्यनावृतं ब्रह्म अध्यासहेतुः तर्हि अध्यासनिवर्तकः कः? किं ब्रह्मप्रकाशः अथवा यत्किञ्चिदन्यत्? अनावृतब्रह्मणः प्रकाशत्वे तर्हि अध्यासः न स्यात्। यदि न प्रकाशते तर्हि ब्रह्मणः स्वप्रकाशत्वहानिः। अप्रकाशस्य सत्त्वे प्रमाणाभावात् तुच्छाधिष्ठानक अध्यासः इत्युक्तः स्यात्॥

उत्पन्नस्याध्यासस्य निवर्तकाभावात् मुक्त्यभावप्रसङ्गः। आवृतस्याधिष्ठानत्वे अज्ञानेनावरणमुतान्येन। यदि अज्ञानम् आवारकं तर्हि घट्टकुटीप्रभातवृत्तान्तमनुसरति। यदि ज्ञानप्रागभावः दग्धमूलः अनभ्युपगमपराहतः सः अकिञ्चित्करः। अतः अनायत्या अज्ञानमङ्गीकरणीयम्॥

नित्यशुद्धचित्स्वरूपस्य ब्रह्मणः सदा प्रकाशरूपत्वेऽपि न प्रकाशते अज्ञानेन आवृतत्वात्। प्रमाणाजन्यं शुद्धचैतन्यं नावरणविरोधि भवति। तदुक्तं पञ्चपादिकादिषु - "तद्भासकस्य तदनिवर्तकत्वात्" इति। अविद्यादि सर्वावभासकस्य शुद्धचैतन्यस्य अविद्यानिवर्तकत्वं नास्ति। स्वप्रकाशचैतन्येन गृहीता अविद्या स्वग्राहकं भासकं वा चैतन्यं कथमावृणुयात् इति तु शङ्का न कार्या। अज्ञानस्य असाध्यं किमपि नास्ति। तदुक्तं प्राचीनैः -

यत्प्रकाशादविद्यादि सिद्ध्यतीव दिवानिशम्।
तमप्यपह्नुतेऽविद्या नाज्ञानस्यास्ति दुष्करम्॥

इति। एतादृशब्रह्मावारकाविद्याया निवृत्तिर्महावाक्याद्यखण्डाकारसाक्षात्काराधीना। साक्षात्कारात्प्राक् अनिवृत्तत्वात् अज्ञानं भासत एव। ब्रह्माज्ञाने अज्ञानेन ब्रह्मणः आवरणमेव हेतुः, न तत्त्वज्ञानप्रागभावः अज्ञानकार्यं सर्वं तत्त्वज्ञानप्रागभावेन न सम्भवति भ्रमे प्रागभावस्य अहेतुत्वात्। शुक्तिरजतादिज्ञाने (भ्रमे) शुक्त्याद्यभावो वा तद्विषयकवृत्तिप्रागभावो वा कारणं न भवति। तत्र पल्लवाज्ञानमेव कारणं तत्र रजततदाकारवृत्त्योरुभयोरपि यौगपद्यात्। अतः ज्ञानप्रागभावेनैव सर्वनिर्वाहे किं भावरूपाज्ञानेन इति शङ्का निरस्ता॥

इदन्तु तत्त्वम् - अध्यासः सत्यमधिष्ठानमपेक्षते। अधिष्ठानत्वं तु केनचन रूपेण आवरणं विना नोपपद्यते इति कथमावरणरूपाविद्यां विनाऽधिष्ठानम्? अधिष्ठानं विना

कथमध्यासः? आत्माधिष्ठानकभ्रमे आरोपाधिष्ठानयोः विषमसत्ताकयोः सम्बन्धः तादात्म्यरूपोऽध्यस्तः। भूतलादौ घटादिसंसर्गस्तु नाध्यस्तः, समसत्ताकयोराधाराधेयभावमात्रमेव नाधिष्ठानारोप्यभावः। अतोऽज्ञानविषयत्वं विनाऽधिष्ठानत्वं न सिध्यति। अज्ञानाविषयत्वस्य अधिष्ठानत्वे शशशृङ्गेऽपि घटादिभानापत्तिः। एवञ्च साक्षिभास्यत्वेन दृश्यस्वरूपा, ज्ञाननिवर्त्यत्वरूपेण मिथ्याभूता, भ्रमं प्रति परिणाम्युपादानकारणरूपा भावरूपा अविद्या अभ्युपगन्तव्या इति अद्वैतिनामाशयः॥

Summary: Professor Muddulapalli Dattatreya Sastri deals with the refutation of the Viśiṣṭādvaitin's objection against māyā-avidyā called *svarūpa-anupapatti.* Rāmānuja formulates the objection saying that avidyā, according to Advaita, should be accepted to be either real or illusory. If it is accepted to be real, then the spirit of Advaita will be lost, for there will then be two reals - Brahman and Avidyā, if it is accepted to be illusory, then there should be another factor in order to account for its illusory character. This is because the illusory factor avidyā itself is accepted only in order to account for the illusoriness of the world. If that again is accepted to be illusory, another factor will be required by the same logic in order to account for its illusoriness. And the same questions will be repeated in the case of that factor, due to which another will have to be accepted, which process will go on *ad infinitum.*

The Advaitin does not say that the pure-consciousness (*anubhūti*), becomes conscious of itself due to avidyā as the substrate of objects. He maintains, on the contrary, that the knower (*pramātā*), which is consciousness delimited by *ajñāna* or *antaḥkaraṇa*, by virtue of avidyā associated with it, understands the consciousness as the substrate of objects and also as what is connected with objects. In other words, the distinction between *anubhūti* (consciousness) and *pramātā* (knower), which is important for the Advaitin, has been ignored by Rāmānuja. Consciousness-in-itself, which is Brahman-Ātman, has no imperfection whatsoever. The ultimate reality is pure consciousness and is free from avidyā, the *pramātā* which is the jīva views consciousness from its point of view as not only the substrate of, but also as what is related to, objects.

We now turn to the alleged defect of infinite regress (*anavasthā*) in the Advaita explanation. Rāmānuja wants to know whether avidyā is real or unreal. After pointing out that the Advaitin himself does not say that avidyā is real (*paramārtha*), Rāmānuja examines the other alternative. He asks: in what sense is avidyā unreal? Is it unreal as the knowing subject, or as the object of knowledge, or as "knowing" determined by the knower and the known? Whichever be the alternative, the Advaita position, according to Rāmānuja, is defective. His argument is as follows. Since each of these three alternatives is unreal (*kālpanika* or *aparamārtha*) from the Advaita point of view, the Advaitin has to account for their unreality. What is the cause of the defect called avidyā? The questioning does not and cannot stop here. We must ask: what is the cause of the cause of that defect? And the same question has to be repeated at every stage, leading to infinite regress (*anavasthā*). Thus, in whichever way the Advaitin tries to explain this unreality of avidyā, there is *anavasthā*.

In support of his argument, Advaitin quotes Śruti statement, "*māyā ca avidyā ca svayameva bhavati*" to prove that avidyā comes into existence of its own accord. While every object requires a cause for its coming into existence, avidyā does not require a cause. It is self-existent (*svatassiddha*), accounting for its own being and of other things. Thus, though avidyā is *aparamārtha*, the defect of *anavasthā* does not arise because avidyā is self-established. However, avidyā is not eternal and is removable by knowledge. The other reason for its non-eternality is that avidyā is material or insentient (*jaḍa*), and whatever is material is not eternal. Only consciousness (*caitanya* or *jñāna*) which is without a beginning (*ajanya*) is eternal. Since avidyā is both *janya* and *jaḍa*, it is non-eternal and hence not real (*aparamārtha*) and its destruction is liberation. Hence Rāmānuja's contention that a real defect (*pāramārthika-doṣa*) called avidyā which is different from Brahman has to be admitted for explaining the world-error, is wrong. Only if the defect is real, liberation can never be attained and it would also render Upaniṣadic teaching futile. The utility of Upaniṣads can be justified only if it is admitted that avidyā is not *paramārtha*, and that Śruti helps us to overcome it. Rāmānuja's contention that, if avidyā were to be unreal, it would not be possible to account for the falsity of the world, is equally untenable because the falsity or illusory character of the world is intelligible only if the world is a product of *aparamārtha* avidyā.

Rāmānuja says that, with a view to avoid the fallacy of infinite regress, the Advaitin might argue that the real consciousness itself which is Brahman serves as the defect (*doṣa*), and that it accounts for the appearance of the world. Such a position, Rāmānuja remarks, would be detrimental to the Advaitin in two respects. For one, it would be gratuitous on the part of the Advaitin to assume avidyā which is said to be false or unreal like the world. For another, it would rule out the possibility of liberation because Brahman which is admitted to be the defect responsible for the world-show is eternal.

Rāmānuja's contention is wrong because Brahman by itself cannot account for the world. Śruti says that Brahman in itself is neither the cause nor the effect. Advaita holds the view that Brahman along with māyā-avidyā creates the world. It also speaks of the power of the supreme Self (*devātma-śakti*) as the cause of the world. This power is known as *ajñāna, māyā*, *avidyā*, *prakṛti*, and so on. To account for the world, there must be a cause that is capable of producing the world. Further, we infer the power inherent in the cause from the effect. The non-existence of the effect means the non-existence of the power. Being the *pratiyogin* of the non-existence of power, power cannot be eternal. In other words, the power (viz. *māyā-avidyā*) associated with Brahman is only *adhyasta.* So, Brahman associated with māyā-avidyā which is superimposed on it is the cause of the world. According to Advaita, while Brahman is the trans-figurative material cause (*vivartopādāna-kāraṇa*), avidyā-māyā is the trans-formative material cause (*pariṇāmy-upādāna-kāraṇa*) of the world. It is, therefore, wrong to say that the assumption of avidyā is gratuitous and that Brahman by itself can be the cause of the world.

12

अनिर्वचनीयत्वानुपपत्तिविचारः

S.V. Rangaramanujacharyulu

भगवद्रामानुजास्तावदविद्याया अनिर्वचनीयत्वमभ्युपगच्छतामभिप्रायाननूद्याश्रयतिरोधानस्वरूपाद्यनुपपत्तिनिरूपणपुरस्सरं तस्या अनिर्वचनीयत्वस्याप्यनुपपत्तिं सयुक्तिकमुपापादयन्। तत्र तावत् पूर्वपक्षिसम्मतमविद्याया मिथ्याभूतजगदुपादानतया मिथ्यात्वं कार्यकारणसालक्षण्यावश्यंभावनियमपरिकल्पितमुपपादयितुं स्वरूपमित्थमुपदर्शितं तैः "एवं चिन्मात्रवपुषि परे ब्रह्मणि दोषपरिकल्पितमिदं देवतिर्यङ्मनुष्यस्थावरादिभेदं सर्वं जगत् यथावस्थितब्रह्मस्वरूपावबोधबाध्यं मिथ्यारूपम्। दोषश्च स्वरूपतिरोधानविविधविचित्रविक्षेपकरी सदसदनिर्वचनीयाऽविद्या" इति; "वस्तुस्वरूपतिरोधानकरमान्तरबाह्यरूपविविधाध्यासोपादानं सदसदनिर्वचनीयम्, अविद्याऽज्ञानादिपदवाच्यं वस्तुयाथात्म्यज्ञाननिवर्त्यं ज्ञानप्रागभावव्यतिरेकेण भावरूपमेव किञ्चिद्वस्तु प्रत्यक्षानुमानाभ्यां प्रतीयते" इति च श्रीभाष्ये पूर्वपक्ष्यभिप्रायानुवादेनावगम्यते। एवं निरुक्ताया अविद्याया अनिर्वचनीयत्वेन मिथ्यात्वमपि मिथ्यात्वलक्षणदर्शनेनैव स्पष्टीभवति, यथा "मिथ्यात्वं नाम प्रतीयमानत्वपूर्वकयथावस्थितवस्तुज्ञाननिवर्त्यत्वम्" इति। अत्र प्रतीयमानत्वपूर्वकत्वविशेषणेनासद्व्यावृत्तिः, असतोऽप्रतीयमानत्वात्, यथावस्थितवस्तुज्ञाननिवर्त्यत्वमिति विशेषणेन सद्व्यावृत्तिः, सतो यथावस्थितवस्तुज्ञाननिवर्त्यत्वाभावात्।

अतः सदसद्विलक्षणत्वमेव मिथ्यात्वस्वरूपमत्र पर्यवस्यति। इदमेव मिथ्यात्वलक्षणमविद्याया अपि सदसदनिर्वचनीयत्वमवस्थापयति। अविद्यायाः सत्त्वाभ्युपगमेऽद्वैतहानेः; असत्त्वाभ्युपगमे कार्यकरत्वव्याहतेश्चेति सदसद्वैलक्षण्यमेव, शुक्तिरजतादिवत्। शुक्तौ नेत्रदोषवशात् प्रतीतं हि रजतं प्रतीतिबाधाभ्यां सदसदनिर्वचनीयमेवापूर्वं किञ्चिदित्यवश्याभ्युपेयत्वात् ब्रह्मण्यविद्यात्मकानिर्वचनीयमिथ्याभूतदोषविशेषपरिकल्पितं विविधविचित्रप्रपञ्चवस्तुजातमपि मिथ्याभूतमनिर्वचनीयमेवेति पूर्वपक्षाशयः।

ब्रह्माध्यस्ताविद्यिकमिथ्याभूतानिर्वचनीयप्रपञ्चप्रतीतिमुपपादयितुं तथाविधत्वेनाभिमतान् दृष्टान्तान् ददति पूर्वपक्षिणो यथा- (१) शुक्तिकाप्रतीतरजतम् (२) स्वप्नदृष्टतुरगादि (३) मृगमरीचिका (४) शङ्खपीतिमा (५) द्विचन्द्रप्रतीतिः (६) अलातचक्रप्रतीतिः इत्यादीन्। एतेषु सर्वेष्वपि दृष्टान्तभूतेषु वस्तुषु प्रतीतेः केवलं तत्क्षणभ्रान्तिपरिकल्पितत्वेन प्रातिभासिकत्वमास्थीयते भ्रान्तपुरुषमात्रप्रतिभासात्। यद्यपि जागतिकवस्तु-विषये प्रतीतिः अविद्याकल्पिता तथापि, प्रातिभासिकवस्तुवत् तात्कालिकदोषपरिकल्पना नास्तीति, सार्वजनीनव्यावहारिकानुभवगोचरत्वमस्तीति च भेदं पुरस्कृत्य व्यावहारिकत्वमात्रं स्वीक्रियते। दोषकल्पितत्वं, तत्त्वज्ञानबाधितत्वं च शुक्तिरजता-दितुल्यमेव जागतिकवस्तु-प्रतीतेरपीति मिथ्यात्वमनिर्वचनीयत्वं च तुल्यमेवेति तदाशयः। नेमं पक्षमूरीकुर्वन्ति स्म भगवद्रामानुजाः।

अत्र च भगवद्रामानुजैः अविद्याया अनिर्वचनीयत्वनिराकरणाय बहवो युक्तयो निदर्शिताः श्रीभाष्ये। अविद्याया मिथ्याभूतोपादानकारणत्वनिदर्शनाय मिथ्याभूतकार्यानुकूलतयाऽनिर्वचनीयत्वं पूर्वपक्षिभिः साधितमिति मिथ्यात्वलक्षणपरिशीलनेनैव स्पष्टं भवति। मिथ्याभूतकार्यस्य मिथ्याभूतमेवोपादानं कारणं भवेदिति पूर्वपक्षिणां युक्तिः। एतन्न युज्यते। "न विलक्षणत्वात्" इत्यधिकरणोक्तन्यायेन तत्परिहारात्। तत्र ह्यधिकरणे यथा मक्षिकादेः सकाशात् तद्विलक्षणस्य कृम्यादेरुत्पत्तिः, तथा ब्रह्मणः सकाशादचेतन-त्वादिविशिष्टस्य विलक्षणस्यापि जगत उत्पत्तिर्भवितुमर्हतीति साधितम्। अतो मिथ्याभूतस्य कार्यस्य मिथ्याभूतमेव कारणं भवेदिति नास्ति नियमः।

न खल्वनिर्वचनीयाज्ञानविषया काचिदपि प्रतीतिर्विद्यते। ननु प्रतीतिबाधाभ्यामेव तदन्यथानुपपत्त्याऽनिर्वचनीयत्वसिद्धिरिति चेत्तदपि न। यदि भावरूपाज्ञानस्य प्रतीत्यादिविषयत्वं तर्हि तस्य प्रतीयमानत्वमेव स्यान्नानिर्वचनीयत्वम्। अथ यद्यनिर्वचनीयत्वं तर्हि तस्य केनापि प्रमाणेन उपलम्भाभावेन प्रतीत्यादिविषयत्वं न स्यात्। ननु भ्रान्तदृष्ट्या शुक्तिकायां रजतं प्रतीयत इति न सर्वात्मना तदसत्। सर्वात्मनाऽसतः प्रतीत्यसम्भवात्। प्रतीतं च तत् पश्चादधिष्ठानशुक्तियाथात्म्यज्ञानेन बाध्यते। अतो न सत्; सतो बाध्यत्वाभावात्। न वा ह्यरजतं रजतत्वेन भासत इति वक्तुं शक्यम्, अन्यस्यान्यत्वेनावभासायोगात्। अतोऽगत्या सत्त्वेनासत्त्वेन वा निर्वक्तुमशक्यं रजतं तत्रोत्पद्यत इत्यवश्यमेव वक्तव्यमिति चेन्न। तादृशानिर्वचनीयापूर्वरजतकल्पनायां सत्यामपि तस्यानिर्वचनीयवस्तुनो निर्वचनीयत्वेनावभासोऽवश्याश्रयणीय एव। इतरथा हि तस्य कथमपि निर्वक्तुमशक्यत्वेन प्रतीतिविषयत्वं, प्रवृत्तिविषयत्वं, बाधविषयत्वं, भ्रमविषयत्वं च न स्यात्। न हि कारणेन विनैव

प्रतीत्यादयः कल्प्यन्तामिति वक्तुं युक्तं, नितान्तमपरिदृष्टस्याकारणकस्य वस्तुनः कल्पनायोगात्।

अत्रेदं प्रष्टव्यम्। किं तत्र शुक्तिकायामुत्पन्नं रजतमनिर्वचनीयमित्येव, अर्थात् अनिर्वचनीयत्वाकारेणैव प्रतीयते, उत परमार्थरजतत्वेन। न तावदनिर्वचनीयत्वाकारेण, तथा चेत् भ्रान्तिबाधयोः प्रवृत्तेरप्यसम्भवात्। अनिर्वचनीयमिदं रजतमिति जानन्तं न कञ्चन भ्रान्तं वक्तुं शक्नुमः, नापि तत्र बाधस्य प्रसक्तिरस्ति, तादृशानिर्वचनीयत्वेन परिज्ञातरजतं प्रति पुरुषप्रवृत्तेरसम्भवात्। अनिर्वचनीयरजतस्यानुपयोगादेव हि पुरुषाप्रवृत्तिः। अतः शुक्तिकायां ज्ञायमानं रजतं यथार्थरजतत्वेनैव ज्ञायते, तेनैव तदुपयोगित्वबुद्ध्या पुरुषप्रवृत्तिः, रजतांशानामल्पत्वादनुपयोगित्वज्ञानेन तद्रजतबाधश्चेति युज्यते। तथा चात्र शुक्तिकैवाल्पाल्परजतांशसम्मिश्रिता रजतत्वेन प्रतीयते शुक्त्यंशापरिग्रहात्, पश्चात् बाध्यते शुक्त्यंशभूयस्त्वपरिग्रहणादित्यवश्यास्थेयम्। तथा चान्यस्यान्यथाप्रतीतिरवश्य-मङ्गीकर्तव्या, तथैव प्रतीतिप्रवृत्तिबाधभ्रमत्वादीनामुपपत्तेः। इदमप्यत्र प्रष्टव्यम्, यदनिर्वचनीयं रजतमुत्पद्यत इत्युच्यते, तत्रैतादृशानिर्वचनीयवस्तूत्पत्तौ किं कारणमिति। तथाप्रतीतिरेव कारणमिति समाधानं तु न युज्यते। कारणस्य कार्यपूर्ववर्तित्वनियमात्, प्रथमतोऽनिर्वचनीय-वस्तूत्पत्तिः, तदनन्तरं तद्विषयिणी प्रतीतिरित्येव वक्तव्यत्वात्। तथा चाऽनिर्वचनीय-वस्तूत्पत्तेः प्राक् प्रतीतेः निर्विषयत्वापत्तिरेव। न चेयं प्रतीतिरेवानिर्वचनीयं वस्तूत्पाद्य स्वयं विषयीकरोति तद्वस्तु इति कथनं युज्यते। न हीन्द्रियगतो दोष एतादृशं वस्तूत्पादयति, दोषस्य पुरुषाश्रितत्वेन शुक्तिकायामनिर्वचनीयवस्तूत्पादनेऽसमर्थत्वात्; न वा इन्द्रियाण्येव तथाविधवस्तूत्पादनसमर्थानि, तेषां ज्ञानकारणत्वेन वस्तूत्पादकत्वाभावात्। एवं दोषग्रस्तानीन्द्रियाण्यपि स्वजन्यज्ञान एव विशेषमापादयन्ति न तु वस्तुनि। अनादिसिद्धं मिथ्याज्ञानमेव तथाविधानिर्वचनीयवस्तूत्पादनसमर्थमित्यपि न मनोरमम्। मिथ्याभूतस्या-ज्ञानस्यार्थक्रियाकारित्वायोगात्। किञ्चैतादृशभावरूपाज्ञानस्य मिथ्याभूतस्य प्रमाणानुपपत्ति-निदर्शनेनैवासिद्धेः भगवद्रामानुजैरुपपादितत्वादविद्यमानतादृशाविद्योपादानत्वेना-निर्वचनीयवस्तूत्पत्तिकथनमन्धस्य जात्यन्धेन मार्गदर्शनमिव उपहासास्पदमेव।

इदमप्यत्र प्रष्टव्यं यदिदमनिर्वचनीयमपूर्वं शुक्तिकायामुत्पद्यमानं रजतं कथं वा सत्यरजतबोधकेन रजतशब्देन तद्बुद्ध्या च विषयीक्रियते। कथं वा न घटादिबुद्धि-शब्दाभ्याम्? तत्र सादृश्यमेव तथाविषयीकरणे हेतुरिति चेत् रजतसदृशमित्येव प्रतीतिः स्यान्न तु रजतमिति। न च तत्र रजतादिजातिरस्ति, जातेः सत्त्वे किं तस्याः परमार्थत्वं मिथ्यात्वमिति विकल्पे परमार्थत्वेऽपरमार्थान्वयस्य, अपरमार्थत्वे परमार्थान्वयस्य चायोगात्। अनिर्वचनीयस्य तस्य रजतादेः भवन्मतेऽपरमार्थत्वेन, परमार्थबुद्धिशब्दयोर्निर्वाहकत्वस्या-

सङ्गतत्वाच्च। किञ्च जगतोऽनिर्वचनीयत्वसाधनाय दृष्टान्ततया निदर्शितेषु शुक्तिरजतादि-सकलदृष्टान्तेष्वनिर्वचनीयत्वेन स्थाप्यमानं वस्तु नानिर्वचनीयं, किन्तु यथार्थमेव। त्रिवृत्करणप्रक्रियया तत्तद्वस्त्ववयवानां तत्र तत्रांशतः सत्त्वेनैव तस्य तस्य तथा तथा व्यवहारो वास्तविक एव। अत एव शुक्तिकायामुपलभ्यमानं रजतं, रज्जावुपलभ्यमानः सर्पः, स्वप्नेषु परिदृश्यमानाः पदार्था इत्येवमेते सर्वेऽपि नानिर्वचनीयाः। तदेतदुक्तम्।

तदेव सदृशं तस्य यत्तद्द्रव्यैकदेशभाक्।
शुक्त्यादौ रजतादेश्च भावः श्रुत्यैव चोदितः॥

रूप्यशुक्त्यादिनिर्देशभेदो भूयस्त्वहेतुकः।
रूप्यादिसदृशश्चायं शुक्त्यादिरुपलभ्यते॥

अतस्तत्रास्य सद्भावः प्रतीतेरपि निश्चितः
कदाचिच्चक्षुरादेस्तु दोषाच्छुक्त्यंशवर्जितः॥

रजतांशो गृहीतोऽपि रजतार्थी प्रवर्तते।
दोषहानौ तु शुक्त्यंशे गृहीते तन्निवर्तते॥
अतो यथार्थं रूप्यादिविज्ञानं शुक्तिकादिषु॥" इति।

तथाच शुक्तिप्रतीतरजतस्य सत्यत्वमेव, न त्वनिर्वचनीयत्वम्। एवं स्वाप्निकपदार्था अपि तत्तज्जनमात्रानुभाव्यतया भगवतैव तत्तददृष्टानुसारेण निर्मिता इति सत्या एव। शङ्खगतपीतादिग्रहणमपि यथार्थमेव। नयनगतपीतिमगुणस्य नायनकिरणद्वारा शङ्खे प्रसृतत्वान्न तत्र पीतिम्नोऽनिर्वचनीयत्वम्। मृगमरीचिकायामपि त्रिवृत्करणप्रक्रियया पृथ्वीजलतेजसां सत्त्वेऽपि नयनगतदोषवशात् तेजःपृथिव्यंशविवर्जितकेवलजलांश-परिग्रहणात् यथार्थत्वमेव तत्र प्रतीतस्य जलस्य। एवमेवालातचक्रे दर्पणादौ चालातमुखादि-ग्रहणमपि यथार्थमेव। द्विचन्द्रग्रहणेऽपि, अङ्गुल्यवष्टम्भेन तिमिरेण वा नयनकिरणप्रसारगति-भेदात् सामग्रीभेदः। अतस्तत्र द्विचन्द्रग्रहणमपि यथार्थमेव, तत्र सामग्रीभेदः पारमार्थिक इति तत्कृतद्विचन्द्रग्रहणमपि परमार्थमेव। इदमत्र न विस्मर्तव्यं यत् सर्वज्ञः सर्वशक्तिः परमात्मैव कांश्चन सर्वानुभवयोग्यान् कांश्चन तत्तत्पुरुषमात्रानुभवयोग्यांश्च सुखदुःखापेक्षा फलानुभवा-नुभाव्यान्, तत्तत्कालावसानान् सृजतीति, न तत्र किञ्चिदपि वस्तु अनिर्वचनीयमिति वक्तुं शक्यम्। नह्येकपुरुषानुभाव्यत्वमात्रेण परिमितकालवर्तित्वमात्रेण वा मिथ्यात्वं कस्यापि प्रतीयमानस्य वस्तुनः कल्पयितुं शक्यं, सर्वस्यापि प्रतीतेः परमार्थत्वात्।

न चेदमनिर्वचनीयं वस्तु नासदीयसूक्तसिद्धमित्यपि कथनं युज्यते, तत्र सदसच्छब्दाभ्यां चेतनाचेतनयोः परामृष्टत्वात्। तमश्शब्देन च चिदचित्प्रलयस्थानम्

अचित्समष्टिरूपमेव परामृश्यत इति सुवचत्वात्, अविभक्तनामरूपविभागतया चिदचितोः प्रलयावस्थायामवस्थानस्यैव तत्र विवक्षितत्वेन तमश्शब्देन सूक्ष्मदशामात्रप्रतिपादनाच्च। तथा च श्रुत्यन्तरमेतद्विषयकं यथा "अव्यक्तमक्षरे लीयते, अक्षरं तमसि लीयते, तमः परे देव एकी भवति" इति।

तथा च प्रकृतेः सूक्ष्मदशैवात्र तम इति व्यवह्रियत इति, तस्या अवस्थाया मायाशब्देन प्रतिपादनान्नानिर्वचनीयत्वं मिथ्यात्वं वा। मायाशब्दस्य मिथ्यार्थकत्वाभावात्। असुरराक्षस-शस्त्रादिषु मायाशब्दप्रयोगदर्शनात्, आश्चर्यकरशक्तिपरत्वेनैव मायाशब्दस्य बहुलप्रयोगात्।

अत्रैव सन्दर्भे कतिचनाऽऽधुनिकविद्वांसोऽनिर्वचनीयत्वानुपपत्तिनिरूपणप्रक्रियायां भगवद्रामानुजनिदर्शितायां कांश्चन दोषाभासानुद्भावितवन्त इति सङ्ग्रहेण तत्प्रतिविधानमप्यत्र क्रियते।

(१) त्वन्मते (रामानुजमते) रूप्यज्ञानस्यापि सत्यत्वात् बाधकत्वापातात् इति। तन्न। रूप्यज्ञानस्य सत्यत्वेऽपि ज्ञानविषयीभूतरूप्यांशानामत्यन्ताल्पत्वेनाऽऽपणे विनियोक्तु-मनर्हत्वेनैव पुरुषप्रवृत्तेर्बाधितत्वात् भ्रमत्वाभ्युपगमः, न तु सर्वात्मना रजतज्ञानस्यासत्यत्वा-भ्युपगमेनेति भवन्मतापेक्षया भेदात्। भवन्मते तु बाध्यत्वं नाम सर्वात्मना मिथ्यात्वनिश्चय एव रजतांशानाम्।

अत एव चाकचिक्यरूपदोषहेतौ सति शुक्तिभूयस्त्ववैकल्येन जायमानं रजतज्ञानं यथार्थरजतांशविषयकत्वेन यथार्थमपि अनुपयोगिन्युपयोगित्वबुद्धिजननरूपचाक-चिक्यदोषमूलत्वेन भ्रान्तिरित्यभ्युपगमेऽदोषात्। न च रजतज्ञानस्य त्वन्मते सद्विषयत्वेन, दोषस्य तत्र हेतुत्वकल्पनं विफलमिति वाच्यम्। दोषस्यापि सत्यत्वेन तत्कार्यस्यापि सत्यत्वस्यावश्यास्थेयत्वात्। न च घटादिज्ञानमपि दोषहेतुकमापद्येतेति वाच्यम्, घटादि-ज्ञानस्य यथार्थत्वे (अदुष्टेन्द्रियजन्यत्वे) दोषहेतुकत्वकल्पनासङ्गतेश्च। जगतोऽविद्या-कल्पितत्वनिरासाच्च। शुक्तिरजतादिजन्यानुभवस्य घटाद्यनुभवस्य च सर्वात्मना भेदस्यैव सर्वानुभवगोचरत्वात्।

अत एव श्रुतिप्रतिबोधितयाथार्थ्यस्य सर्वानुभवगोचरस्य जगतोऽपि शुक्तिरजतादि-दोषजन्यज्ञानसाम्यं नास्माभिरभ्युपेयते। इयमेव गतिः तदितरदृष्टान्तेष्वपीति ज्ञेयम्। "नीरप्राये क्षीरज्ञानमिव शुक्तिप्रायेऽपि रूप्यज्ञानं न भ्रमः, उभयत्रेदं क्षीरमिदं रजतमित्यनुभव-सत्वात्", इति यदुक्तं तन्न, शुक्तिकायां चाकचिक्यवशात् शुक्तिभूयस्त्ववैकल्येन गृहीतस्य रजतस्य पश्चाद्बाधितत्वेन यथा भ्रमत्वोपगमः, तथैव नीरभूयस्त्वज्ञानवैकल्येन धावल्यादि-रूपसाम्यात् झटिति गृहीतं क्षीरं पुरुषप्रवृत्तिजनकमपि पश्चान्नीरभूयस्त्वग्रहणबाधितत्वेन नेदं क्षीरमिति निश्चीयत इति भ्रमत्वेन निश्चयस्यापि तुल्यत्वात्। एतेन "एवं च परमते

रूप्यज्ञानस्य भ्रमत्वं दुःसम्पादम्" इति यदुक्तं तत्प्रतिविहितमेव। भ्रमत्वव्यवहारस्य पूर्वोक्तरीत्योपपादितत्वात्।

किञ्च यदुक्तम् - सत्ख्यातिमते शुक्तिरजतादेरकार्यकरत्वं दुःसम्पादं, शुक्तिशकलसम्भिन्नात्यल्परजतस्यापि विपणिगतरजतवदर्थक्रियाकारित्वावश्यम्भावात्। यद्युपलभ्यमानं रजतमकार्यकरमित्येवोपलभ्येत तदा प्रवृत्तिरेव न स्यात्। या विसंवदेत, यदि च कार्यकरं तर्हि न स भ्रमः। यदि तथापि भ्रम इत्युच्यते तर्हि अन्यथाख्यात्यापत्तिः, अतः रजतस्याकार्यकरत्वोक्तिः परेषां मुधैव" इति, तदेतत् सर्वं मूलग्रन्थकर्तुरभिप्रायस्थगनतात्पर्यमूलकमेव, न वस्तुतत्त्वम्। शुक्तिरजतादेरकार्यकरत्वमिति सर्ववादिसम्प्रतिपन्नमेव। अत एव तज्ज्ञानस्य भ्रमत्वव्यवहारोऽपि मतभेदेन सम्मत एव। अत्राकार्यकरत्वं नाम कीदृशमिति विवेचनीयम्। आपणे शुद्धरजतवत् वस्तुनिर्माणोपयोगित्वराहित्यमेव न त्वन्यत्।

सर्वात्मना कार्यकरत्वं नास्तीति को वा वक्तुमुत्सहते। पुरुषप्रवृत्तिसम्पादनरूपस्य कार्यस्य शुक्तिरजतेनैव सम्पादनीयत्वात्। पुरुषप्रवृत्तिस्तावत् द्विप्रकारा - प्राथमिकप्रवृत्तिः पार्यन्तिकप्रवृत्तिरिति। द्विविधाऽपि प्रवृत्तिः कार्यरूपैव। तत्र शुक्तिस्थं रजतं प्रथमप्रवृत्तिरूपं कार्यं जनयत्येव, द्वितीयपार्यन्तिकप्रवृत्तिरूपं कार्यं तु न साधयति, शुक्तिरजतस्य आपणेऽनुपयोगित्वात्, यद्युपलब्धिवेलायामेवेदं न कार्यकरमिति जानीयात् पुरुषः, तर्हि न प्रवर्तेतैव। अतः प्रथमदर्शने चाकचिक्यवशात् शुक्तिकांशस्थगनेन प्रतिभातं रजतं यथार्थमिति गृह्णन्नेव पुरुषः प्रवर्तत इति तद्रजतस्य कार्यकरत्वम्। शुक्त्यंशभूयस्त्वसाकल्यग्रहणेन स्वोपलब्धस्य रजतस्य ज्ञानविषयीभूतस्याऽऽपणानुपयोगित्वावबोधेन पुरुषपार्यन्तिकप्रवृत्तेः प्रतिबन्धादकार्यकरत्वं चोपपद्यत एव, यत्कृतो भ्रमत्वव्यवहारः, न तु सर्वात्मनाऽसत्यत्वकृत इति सूक्ष्मदृशानुशीलने विस्पष्टं प्रतीयते। तथा च शुक्तिरजतस्य सत्यत्वादेव प्रथमकार्यकरत्वम्, अल्पत्वादेव पार्यन्तिककार्याकरत्वं भ्रमत्वव्यवहारास्पदत्वश्चेति नात्रान्यथाख्यात्यापत्तिः; सत्यरजतस्यैव शुक्तिकास्थस्य तद्विविक्तत्वेन ग्रहणात् इत्यलं पल्लवितेन।

यत्तावत् 'ब्रह्मास्ति', 'घटोऽस्ति', इत्युभयत्राप्यस्तित्वस्यासत्यपि भेदे भेदकल्पनाय यः प्रयासः सोऽपि व्यर्थ एव। न च त्रैकालिकाबाध्यत्वरूपं १सत्यत्वं ब्रह्मण्येव न तु घटादिजागतिकवस्तुष्विति वाच्यम्। घटादिवस्तुष्वपि स्वरूपपरिणामसत्वेऽपि मूलवस्तुनोऽविनश्यत्वेन त्रैकालिकबाधरहितसत्यत्वस्याव्याहतत्वाच्चेति विरम्यते॥

Summary: Sri S.V. Rangaramanujacharya presents the fourth objection of Rāmānuja on the untenability of avidyā, as portrayed by

Advaitin as *anirvacanīya or sadasad-vilakṣaṇa.* For Advaitins, avidyā is neither *sat* (existent) nor *asat* (non-existent), but which eludes being defined either as *sat* or *asat.* To Rāmānuja, this position, however, is not acceptable. Those who know the objects of the world through *pramāṇa-s*, know them either as *sat* or as *asat.* Never indeed it is observed in common parlance that something is neither *sat* nor *asat.* Hence the acceptance of avidyā as indescribable either as *sat* or *asat* could not be maintained. It means that the Advaitin accepts a third category in addition to, but different from, *sat* and *asat.* Avidyā and its products belong to this third category. Rāmānuja's objection called *anirvacanīyatva-anupapatti* is a direct attack on this explanation of the māyā-avidyā, which, according to him, totally ignores the law of excluded middle.

Since the Advaita explanation of the ontological status of avidyā in terms *sadasad-vilakṣaṇa* goes contrary to the evidence of our cognition and it has to be rejected. Rāmānuja has a dig at the Advaitin: he says that avidyā is, indeed, *anirvacanīya*, i.e. inexplicable, because there is no cognition in support of it (*pramāṇa-śūnyatvena anirvacanīyataiva syāt*).

Advaitins answer the above saying that *sat* is defined as that which could not be sublated in the three divisions of time and *asat* as that which is simply a non-entity (*nissvarūpa*). And *anirvacanīya* is something which is different from both. In the case of avidya, it becomes sublated by *brahmajñāna* due to which it cannot be held to *asat*, since it is perceived. Something which is *nissvarūpa* cannot be perceived. Hence, *ajñāna* could very much be said to be *anirvacanīya.*

In refuting the above assertion, Rāmānuja says that in our ordinary experience, that which is existent is said to be *sat* and that which is non-existent is *asat.* But the Advaitins, discard such a universal experience and definition, and fabricate some other definition, which goes against experience. Further, even acceptance of the definitions of the Advaitins does not liberate *ajñāna* from defects. That is, if *sat* is accepted to be "unsublatable", then such a characteristic cannot be there in Brahman, for it is accepted to be without characteristics. Further, it is known from *śāstras* that even prakṛti, etc., are endowed with such a character, and hence according to *śāstras*, prakṛti etc., have *sattva* due to which they cannot be different from *sadasat.*

Furthermore, defining *asattva* as *nissvarūpa* also cannot be established. It may be asked if such an *asattva* (i.e. *nissvarūpa*) is known at any place or not. If it is known, then it amounts to saying that *asattva* is known in that form (*svarūpa*) and hence it cannot be said to be *nissvarūpa*. If it is not known anywhere, then it will only result in the non-existence of anything known as *asattva*. Hence as *asattva* itself could not be esteablished, it is not possible to prove something different from *asat*. Therefore, *anirvacanīyatva*, as a feature of avidyā, cannot be established.

13

ADVAITIN'S CRITIQUE OF ANIRVACANĪYĀNUPAPATTI

Goda Venkateswara Sastri

The philosophy of the Upaniṣads, as envisaged by Śaṅkara, comes with the view that the ultimate reality is *nirākāra* – formless, *nirguṇa*–devoid of qualities and *adṛṣya* – beyond the world of empirical perception. At the same time, the ultimate reality, the Brahman, is also the cause, sustainer and destroyer of all the worlds. All beings, sentient and insentient have their origin in Brahman. The Brahman as the material and ostensible cause of these worlds, full of myriad names and forms can be explained only with the help of māyā-avidyā. As Vidyāraṇya puts it, "the māyā is in the form of *śakti*, energy inherent in the Brahman, (*nistattvā kāryagamyāsyā śaktir māyāgniśaktivat*, *Pañcadaśī,* 2.47). This potency, i.e., māyā, has no substantiality of its own and can be known only from its effects, just like the potency of fire.

All the material causes in the world are subject to transformation and therefore, they cease to be eternal. Transformation (*vipariṇāma*) is the addition or subtraction of a property to an object and the process of transformation ends with the destruction of the object. Therefore, Brahman cannot be accepted as transforming itself into the world as clay transforms into a pot, or gold transforms into an ornament, since in that case Brahman would be like any empirical object subject to destruction. To overcome this difficulty of simultaneously accepting Brahman as *Nirākāra*–formless, *Nirguṇa*–devoid of qualities and *vyāpaka*–all pervasive and at the same time as the sole material cause of all these worlds, both being the principal teachings of the Upaniṣads; māyā has to be drawn in Brahman as the material cause of the world not like the clay to a pot or gold for an ornament, but like the rope to a rope-snake or a shell towards the shell-silver. Such a transformation is known as *vivarta-upādāna* in contrast to the former as *pariṇāmi-upādāna*. Thus we find that Brahman, though called as the material cause of the world, actually does not transform itself into the world. This transformation is possible only with the help of māyā-avidyā. If this special kind of material causality is not accepted, then either we will have to compromise with the *nirākāra*–formless state of Brahman or accept a state of the absence of Brahman itself. This is because we find only objects having a form get transformed into effects like clay into a pot or gold into an ornament. Brahman being *nirākāra*–formless cannot get itself transformed into the worlds. If so we shall have to face the wrath of Śruti, since they teach Brahman as *niravayava*–devoid of limbs etc. Also a limbless (*niravayava*) object when transformed has to do so in toto and not in parts; as milk in a vessel totally transforms itself into curds. One cannot conceive a part of *niravayava* object transforming into an effect and at the same time another part of the same remaining in its own state. Now by the same argument if Brahman has to transform itself into the worlds, being *niravayava* Brahman has to totally get itself transformed into world. If one accepts such a proposition, then the difficulty arises: what will happen to a person who gets liberated? As per the Upaniṣads he has to become one with Brahman – *sa yo ha vai tat paramam brahma veda brahmaiva bhavati* – "He who knows the supreme Brahman becomes one with Brahman." As the Brahman, entirely has got transformed into the worlds, we do not have the Brahman in its own state now with which the liberated soul will get united. Thus the *vivarta-kāraṇatva* – a special kind of causality has to be accepted. This has been clearly enunciated by the sage Vyāsa in his aphorism "*kṛtsna prasakti hi niravayava śabda kopo vā*" (BS. 2.1.26). Thus we find that māyā-avidyā is a prime concept in the interpretation of the Upaniṣads without compromising the principal teaching that the Brahman is devoid of any characteristics. Śaṅkara had taken full advantage of this māyā-avidyā concept in his *Prasthāna-traya-bhāṣya*. For

Śaṅkara, māyā-avidyā, the very basis of superimposition, the prime cause for all the miseries of living beings had to be understood and distinguished from the Brahman, which is spoken of as the goal. When one inquires into the nature of Brahman, māyā-avidyā slowly gets loosened; its shackles get removed and totally annihilated by the direct experience of Brahman.

Rāmānuja strongly proclaimed that the only way to attain liberation is the grace of God which can be attained by devotion. Since everything is real, including rope-snake, there is no place for māyā-avidyā. Having taken up such a position, he started refuting the Advaita method of interpretation of the reality, especially the māyā-avidyā. This has to be done to make his position rooted in his philosophy of realism. This he has done in his *bhāṣya* by presenting seven fallacies against māyā-avidyā. These arguments were ably countered by Advaitins comprehensively in their works. With this background, let us now move to the topic *Anirvacanīya-anupapatti*, fallacy regarding the unexplainable nature of māyā-avidyā. The main objections raised in the *Śrībhāṣya* are as follows:

1. Since all the objects are perceived as either *sat* or *asat,* there can never be a *sadasad-vilakṣaṇa* object as stated by the Advaitin.

2. *Sat* and *asat* objects are comprehended by their corresponding knowledge only. If such a condition is not accepted, then anything could become the object of any knowledge and there will only be chaos.

3. *Sat* and *asat* are mutually exclusive. If an object is *sat* it cannot be *asat* and vice-versa. There cannot thus be an object which is neither *sat* nor *asat*. Hence neither the silver on nacre or māyā can be *anirvacanīya* – i.e. neither *sat* nor *asat*.

4. Even if an object is perceived as non-*sat* or non-*asat*, one cannot take the object as different from *sat* and *asat*. This will lead only to indecision as in the case of a doubt as to whether Brahman is Saguṇa or Nirguṇa. If the Pūrvapakṣa is put forth as only Saguṇa and Siddhānta as Nirguṇa, then one may have to conclude (as per Advaitin's argument) that Brahman is neither Saguṇa nor Nirguṇa as both views are perceived and thus comprehended. Hence māyā-

avidyā cannot be *anirvacanīya*. Before actually going to the answers given by the Advaitins let us consider certain basic facts for a proper understanding of the issue.

Advaitins accept four major classes or sets in which the various objects could be classified as far as reality is concerned. They are: 1. *Pāramārthika* – Here Brahman alone is the member. 2. *Vyāvahārika* – māyā-avidya and its effects – all objects in the world perceived by us except the snake on the rope etc. 3. *Prātibhāsika* – objects of wrong knowledge like, the snake on the rope, silver on the shell etc. 4. *Asat* - non-existent entities. They can never be perceived by our senses at any point of time.

Barring the members of last class, the objects in the first three classes have to be perceived. But the Brahman belonging to the first set too cannot be perceived as by definition. It is *aprameya* – beyond our sensory perception. It is known only by *Śāstra* and that too indirectly. The objects in the *vyāvavahārika* or *prātibhāsika* classes alone are perceived. The difference between them is that the objects in the third set are negated quickly whereas those of second variety are more or less permanent in the ordinary sense, i.e. they do not get negated as quickly as that of the *prātibhāsika* objects. All objects belonging to the sets two and three i.e. both *vyāvahārika* and *prātibhāsika* are either māyā or the effects of māyā-avidyā. They are perceived as *sat* i.e. as existing. They will be negated later by the *bādhaka-jñāna* – i.e. the sublating knowledge.

Advaitins hold the view that all such objects are neither *sat* nor *asat* but *sadasad-vilakṣaṇa*, i.e. different from both *sat* and *Asat*. They are not *sat* because, if they were to be *sat* they would not have been negated at all, in all the three periods of time viz., past, present and future and in such a case they would naturally have been classified in the first set as *Pāramārthika*. They are not *asat* too, for if they were *asat* they would not have been perceived at all like the son of a barren woman, the horn of a hare etc. In such a case they would have naturally been allotted their due place in the fourth set. Since they are perceived by our senses and at the same time negated, they are classified differently from both *sat*, which is *trikālābādhya*, i.e. never negated and *asat*, i.e., *niḥsvarūpa* or *pratityanarha*, that is never perceived. The sub-classification among *vyāvahārika* and *prātibhāsika* is only due to their span of time before negation and the knowledge with which it is negated. The *vyāvahārika* objects do generally exist for a fairly long time, sometimes certain objects like the *ākāśa* – ether etc. exist till the knowledge of the ultimate dawns on us i.e. they are negated by the *Brahmajñāna* only. In the meantime they may change their shape like a pot breaking into tiny particles, cloth torn into small pieces etc. But they are negated totally only by the knowledge of the Brahman. The *prātibhāsika* objects however are negated by the knowledge of the substratum which may apparently be other than the Brahman, as the knowledge of the shell negating the superimposed silver, the knowledge of the rope negating the superimposed snake.

Further if *sat* is negated then the object need not necessarily be *asat*, it may also be *vyāvahārika* or *prātibhāsika*. Similarly an object stated as not belonging to the *asat*, need not necessarily belong to the first set *i.e. sat*. It may also belong to either *vyāvahārika* or *prātibhāsika*. That is to say that *sat* and *asat* are not antonyms. In fact the objects of second and third sets viz., *vyāvahārika* and *prātibhāsika* do not belong either to *sat* or *asat*. That is why they are classified differently from both of them. They are neither *sat* – as they are being negated, nor *asat* as they are perceived. With this background let us review the *Śrībhāṣya* position.

1. The first objection is that all objects are perceived either as *sat* or as *asat* and hence there cannot be an object which is *sad-asad-vilakṣaṇa*. Now both Brahman and *asat*-objects are never perceived. Brahman is not perceived as it is beyond the field of sense organs and mind. It is known only by the *śāstric* inquiry. All *asat* objects are never perceived. This being the case, the objects perceived are only the objects belonging to *vyāvahārika* or *prātibhāsika* class. They are *māyika*, i.e. effects of māyā. As stated earlier, since they are negated either by the knowledge of their substratum or by the Brahman knowledge, they cannot belong to the *sat* class - if they are *sat* they can never be negated. Hence necessarily they must not belong to either *sat* or *asat* and rightly they are called *sadasad-vilakṣaṇa* or *anirvacanīya*. The statement that all objects are perceived as *sat* and *asat* itself is wrong, as *sat* and *asat* cannot be perceived. In reality,

the objects of *vyāvahārika* and *prātibhāsika* classes are perceived as *sat* because they are connected by a relation called *tādātmya* with the *sat* i.e. Brahman, as they are superimposed on Brahman which alone is the *sat*. The *asat* objects too cannot be perceived. But when silver appearing on a shell, snake appearing on a rope etc, are negated, they are conceived as *asat* – since we then experience as though we have perceived a non-existing object. i.e. silver or snake did not really exist where they were perceived. This leads us to think that they are asat. Really at the time of conceiving them, they were superimposed on the Caitanya, i.e. consciousness, conditioned by the objects on which they are located, and that made us perceive them as existing. Hence the wrong knowledge. We have thus arrived at the conclusion that both *sat* (Brahman) and *asat* (son of barren women, horn of a hare etc.) cannot be perceived. What is supposed to be perceived as *sat* and *asat* are really the objects belonging to *vyāvahārika* or *prātibhāsika* class which are *māyika* i.e. effects of māyā – which thus are different from both *sat* and *asat* or *sadasad-vilakṣaṇa*, i.e. *anirvacanīya*. In fact this leads the Advaitin to postulate as *vimatam mithyā dṛṣyatvāt suktirūpyavat.* (That which is perceived is illusory like silver perceived on the shell.)

2. The second objection is that if objects perceived as *sat* and objects perceived as *asat* are not accepted as *sat* and *asat* respectively then anything can become the object of any knowledge and there will only be chaos. This has already been answered above. What is perceived are only the *vyāvahārika* or *prātibhāsika* objects and not objects belonging to *sat* or *asat* classes. The reason for their perception as existing objects at the time of perception is due to their superimposition on the Brahman. This being the case, there is no question of anything becoming the object of any knowledge.

3. For the third objection – if one is not *sat* it becomes *asat* and *vice versa*. Thus there can never be an object simultaneously belonging to *sat* and *asat* as that will mean that the object is *sad-asat*, which is contradictory. The answer for this had already been discussed earlier. Negation of *sat* does not necessarily mean *asat*, it may also be *anirvacanīya* i.e. either *vyāvahārika or prātibhāsika*. Similarly negation of *asat* does not necessarily mean *sat* as it may also be

anirvacanīya. Hence the middle set belongs only to *anirvacanīya* and not for *sad-asat*. *Sat* and *asat* being contradictory cannot co-exist in an object. i.e. the same object can never simultaneously be *sat* as well as *asat*. But an object can at the same time be different from both *sat* and *asat* as we have the examples like the silver on the nacre, or snake on the rope etc. They are not *sat* as they are negated at a later time by the knowledge of their substratum, nor are they *asat* as they are perceived.

4. The forth objection that acceptance of *sadasad-vilakṣaṇa* will lead only to indecision is also not tenable. The reason being that we are not negating the *sadasad* after having accepted it. An object can never be *sad-asad* simultaneously, but it can be *sadasad-vilakṣaṇa*. This has been established by our foregoing argument. Hence there is no question of any doubt or indecision.

Conclusion

Thus the objections raised against māyā-avidyā, having been answered, the *anivacanīya* nature of māyā-avidyā is established. Further the definition of *sat* and *asat* have been coined in such a manner that they do not contradict each other. Even if they seem to be mutually exclusive, we can still have a *sadasad-vilakṣaṇa* as we come across the example of *saṁyoga* and *saṁyogābhāva* simultaneously existing in a tree. Thus there is no contradiction in the absence of *sat* as well as *asat* existing simultaneously in the *vyāvahārika* or *prātibhāsika* objects leading to their *anivarcanīya* nature. All the objections raised by the author as well as the followers of the *Śrībhāṣya* could thus be answered by the arguments already presented by the post-Śaṅkara Advaitins. Finally, it appears as viewing a crystal from different angles. If perceived directly it is pure, clear and when viewed at an angle, it appears as having some other shape or colour. All other colours and shapes appearing due to the position of the viewer and the angle of vision as happens in the perception of the empirical world objects will one day merge to give way for a clear and pure blissful vision of non-dual Brahman.

14

PRAMĀṆĀNUPAPATTI IN VIŚIṢṬĀDVAITA

V.S. Karunakaran

Śrī Rāmānuja has raised seven objections against the concept of māyā-avidyā in Advaita, known as *Saptavidha-anupapatti*. Of these, the fifth objection, i.e., *Pramāṇānupapatti* will be the theme of discussion in this paper. As in the *Āśrayānupapatti,* it is discussed whether Brahman or jīva should be the locus of avidyā, similarly, in the *Pramāṇānupapatti* there are three difficulties raised in accepting māyā-avidyā:

1. Difficulty on the basis of perception
2. Difficulty on the basis of inference &
3. Difficulty on the basis of verbal authority

Taking the above three into consideration, we may be able to speak of ten untenabilities, instead of seven, as currently accepted by Viśiṣṭādvaitins against the concept of māyā-avidyā in Advaita Vedānta.

Advaitin's Contention

The Advaitins contend that avidyā (ignorance) is a positive entity. It is positive because it obscures Brahman and projects the illusory world of duality. The Viśiṣṭādvaitins contend that the theory of such an avidyā does not have the support of any valid means of knowledge. In one way, the Advaitins also accept this. Sureśvara says: "He who desires to see avidyā through the knowledge generated by a *pramāṇa* could certainly see the darkness in the interior of a cave by means of a lamp."

Yet, the Advaitins put forth several points of *pramāṇa* hoping to render the doctrine of a positive avidyā meaningful. They declare that all the three valid means of knowledge, i.e., 1. direct experience (*pratyakṣa*), 2. inference (*anumāna*) and, 3. verbal testimony (*Śabda*) support their theory. Let us examine their claim.

Direct Experience: A Means of Knowledge for Positive Ignorance

The direct experience referred to is the experience of everyone as "I am ignorant (*aham ajñaḥ*)". Here, ignorance does not mean absence of any knowledge in general. Because, there is the knowledge of the entity and also its location. The perception that there is no pot, requires knowledge of two basic facts, i.e. knowledge of the pot and that of its location, There are three factors involved in the experience of "I am ignorant." 1. The person having the experience, 2. the experience of the reciprocal entity (called *pratiyogi-jñānam*) and 3. the location. When there are three such knowledges, how can one say that ignorance is absence of knowledge? The Advaitins, therefore, conceive of ignorance as a positive entity, because a positive entity does not need the knowledge of the location and of the *pratiyogi*. Thus, the direct experience that "I am ignorant" itself is an authentic means of knowledge to prove that ignorance is a positive entity.

This argument of Advaitins does not help because even if it is accepted that ignorance is positive, all the defects pointed out in the perception "I am ignorant", - the experience of self and self as the locus of ignorance - are understood, i.e., a person thus has the knowledge of the self and himself as the locus for ignorance. Then, how can he be ignorant?

Normally, such experiences of ignorance like "I am ignorant" refer to the deep-sleep state. The phrase "I am ignorant (*aham ajñaḥ*)" refers to a post-sleep inference of the situation during sleep. This means that during one's deep-sleep one's mind was not active.

As per the Vedas, the soul is of the form of knowledge and also has got the capacity to know a thing. This capacity to know a thing can be called proprietary knowledge (*dharmabhūta-jñāna*). This *dharmabhūta-jñāna* does not function fully during sleep but functions to a very limited extent, depending on the soul's *pūrva-janma-*

karma. It (the soul), by itself, does not need the support of the *dharmabhūta-jñāna* . But other activities of the self, as, I see, I understand, I read, I walk, etc., are realised by the soul only through the proprietary knowledge. Hence, the statement "I am ignorant" means my *dharmabhūta-jñāna* was not functioning at that time. This is the inference made using the *dharmabhūta-jñāna*, when it becomes functional. Hence, it is not correct to say that the experience "I am ignorant" goes to prove ignorance as a positive entity.

Viśiṣṭādvaitins do accept *abhāva* as positive (*abhāvo bhāva-rupaḥ*). But still, according to them, ignorance (absence of know-ledge), cannot be positive.

It is because the experience "I am ignorant (*aham ajñaḥ*)" means that the *dharmabhūta-jñāna* has limited or no operation at that time. In Advaita however, there is no such thing called proprietary knowledge (*dharmabhūta-jñāna*). That the soul is made of knowledge and also has *dharmabhūta-jñāna* is based on the Vedas. Whereas the Advaitins do not have such a clear textual sanction to hold that the soul does not have *dharmabhūta-jñāna*. Their concept of ignorance as a separate positive entity is only their own fabrication which has no textual authority.

Inference as a Means of Knowledge

Advaitins also adduce inferences to substantiate the positive nature of ignorance. It runs thus:

Knowledge established by a *pramāṇa* is preceded by some-thing else which is different from the prior non-existence of knowledge, which obscures the object of knowledge and which exists in the same place as knowledge; because knowledge possesses the property of manifesting things not illumined before, just as the first spark of light of a lamp lit in the dark place manifests things.

According to this syllogism, the valid means of knowledge like "*tatvamasi*" are preceded by a positive entity. That positive entity:

1. is different from absence of the valid knowledge,
2. has the power of concealing the target of this knowledge,
3. is annihilated by this knowledge and
4. occupies the same location to be occupied by the knowledge.

The reason for this postulation is, "valid means of knowledge always shows an item not known earlier". An example for this is the first spark of a lantern in a dark room.

1. The darkness in the room is an entity different from absence of light.
2. The darkness has concealed the items in the room.
3. Light expels the darkness.
4. Darkness had been present in the same location where light has now come.
5. Darkness is a positive entity.

So, ignorance should also be a positive entity.

Let us examine this: Even this knowledge of inference is a valid source of knowledge. If this inference can establish positive ignorance, then this should lead us to another positive ignorance which had concealed the target of this ignorance and which is to be repelled by this ignorance and which is also present in the same location of this ignorance. That means avidyā, being established as a positive entity had been concealed by another positive entity. That means Brahman does not have direct experience of ignorance.

The whole attempt of Advaitins is to establish that Brahman is being influenced by ignorance - a positive entity. But by this syllogism, they themselves have proved that Brahman has no direct experience of the positive ignorance. Then, how would they explain its creation?

It may be argued that ignorance can be a positive entity and can influence Brahman by its mere presence even without being experienced by Brahman. This argument is not tenable because any unreal entity has to be directly experienced by one to be influenced by it. Only real entities can influence by their mere presence without being directly experienced. And real entities like darkness can be removed only by a repelling force and not by a mere knowledge of it. (Example: Somebody is in a dark room. He is not able to visualise things. The knowledge that he is in a dark room does not help him to visualise things, unless, darkness is repelled by a suitable light. Mere knowledge of light or darkness alone does not help him).

One thing is to be noted here: , darkness, of course, is a positive entity. It is also real. But it is not repelled by the knowledge that it is dark. It needs light.

Now by this syllogism, positive ignorance, which cannot be repelled by knowledge, is being established by the reason that it is able to manifest things concealed. This is a defect in logic because reason exists in things, which cannot be proved using that reason. This is called *vyabhicāra*.

The analogy given is defective because, the identification of entities in a dark room is not by the first spark of light. A blind man in the dark room cannot identify the items by any spark of light. This means identification of entities requires light and other things. Thus the syllogism of Advaitins suffers many logical defects because the analogy suffers the defects of *vyāpti-bhaṅga*.

There can be counter syllogisms also, like, valid means of knowledge is not preceded by any positive ignorance, because it is valid means of knowledge put forth by the Advaitins to establish positive ignorance.

Textual Authority

Advaitins hold that the Śruti establishes ignorance as a positive entity. In the text quoted by them, accepting the meaning for the word "*anṛta*" as the activities done with the desire of enjoying the fruits will be more appropriate and in conformity with many corresponding authentic texts.

Similarly, the "*nāsadāsīt*" text also does not help the Advaitins because the word "*tamas*" used in the Śruti denotes only the minute stage of a mixture of the *cit* and *acit*.

The term māyā also does not refer to avidyā. Māyā means wonderful and in literature there are instances of such usage in *Rāmāyaṇa* and other texts. In fact the conclusion in *tatvamasi* should not be tried to be solved by making You = Tat + avidyā. Instead, it should be, You = He. (Because, He resides in you as your inner-self.)

Thus, there is no need for bringing the concept of positive ignorance having no sanction in the Śruti texts. When confronted with all these attacks, Advaitins ultimately comes out with the reply that, avidyā could not be defined with the hope that this undefinability of avidyā itself will counter all logical assaults.

15

प्रमाणानुपपत्तिखण्डनम्

Sripada Subramanian

जीव ईशो विशुद्धा चित् विभागश्च तयोर्द्वयोः।
अविद्या तच्चितोर्योगष्षडस्माकमनादयः॥

इति षट्सु अनादिपदार्थेषु अविद्या एका। संक्षेपतः अविद्यालक्षणान्युच्यन्ते। (1) अनादित्वे सति, भावरूपत्वे सति ज्ञाननिवर्त्यत्वम् अविद्यायाः लक्षणम्। उत्तरज्ञान-निवर्त्य पूर्वज्ञाने अतिव्याप्तिवारणाय अनादित्वविशेषणम्। ज्ञानप्रागभावे अतिव्याप्तिवारणाय भावरूपत्वविशेषणम्। अनादिभावरूपे आत्मन्यतिव्याप्तिवारणाय ज्ञाननिवर्त्यत्वविशेषणम्। शुक्तिरूप्योपादानमप्यज्ञानं अनादिचैतन्याश्रितत्वात् अनाद्येव। अतः शुक्त्याद्यज्ञाने नाव्याप्तिः। भावत्वं चात्र अभावविलक्षणत्वमात्रंविवक्षितम्। अतः आरोपिताभावोपादानाज्ञाने नाव्याप्तिः। (2) भ्रमोपादानत्वं द्वितीयं अज्ञानलक्षणम्। अज्ञानस्य विश्वभ्रमोपादानत्वात् तत्र लक्षणसङ्गतिः। इदञ्च लक्षणं विश्वभ्रमस्योपादानमज्ञानं, तादृशाज्ञानस्याधिष्ठानं ब्रह्मेति पक्षे। न तु विश्वभ्रमोपादानं ब्रह्म, ब्रह्मसहिताज्ञानं वा इति पक्षे। अतो ब्रह्मणि नातिव्याप्तिः। अभावभ्रमस्यापि भावात्मकमेव अज्ञानमुपादान-कारणमिति न दोषः। (3) ज्ञानत्वेन रूपेण साक्षाज्ज्ञाननिवर्त्यत्वं तृतीयमविद्यालक्षणम्। ज्ञानत्वावच्छिन्ननिवर्तकतानिरूपित साक्षान्निवर्त्यत्वमित्यर्थः। उत्तरज्ञाननिवर्त्ये पूर्वज्ञाने ज्ञानत्वेन ज्ञाननिवर्त्यत्वं नास्ति। किन्तु उत्तरभाविविशेषगुणत्वेनैवेति न तत्रातिव्याप्तिः। अज्ञानं तु ज्ञानत्वेन साक्षाज्ज्ञाननिवर्त्यमिति तत्र लक्षणसङ्गतिः।

आश्रयत्वविषयत्वभागिनी निर्विभागचितिरेव केवला।
पूर्वसिद्धतमसो हि पश्चिमो नाश्रयो भवति नापि गोचरः॥

अज्ञानस्य आश्रयः शुद्धचैतन्यं ब्रह्मैव। अज्ञानकार्यः पश्चाद्भावी जीवः पूर्वसिद्धाज्ञानस्य आश्रयः विषयो वा न भवति। एवं शुद्धचैतन्यमेव अज्ञानविषयः। तस्य अकल्पितत्वेन

अन्योन्याश्रयादिदोषाप्रसक्तेः। एवं शुद्धचैतन्यस्य स्वयंप्रकाशत्वेन प्रसक्तप्रकाशे तस्मिन् आवरणकृत्यसम्भवाच्च। जीवादेः जडस्य च अविद्याविषयत्वं नास्ति। तस्याज्ञान-कल्पितत्वात् स्वकल्पितस्य जीवादेः स्वविषयत्वे अन्योन्याश्रयात्। एवं जडस्य अप्रसक्तप्रकाशत्वेन तस्मिन् आवरणकृत्यासम्भवाच्च।

घटादिव्यावहारिकप्रपञ्चस्य शुक्तिरूप्यादि प्रतिभासिकस्य च अज्ञानमुपादान-कारणम्। तच्च परिणाम्युपादानम्। ब्रह्म तु विवर्तोपादानम्। तत्त्वमसीत्यादिमहावाक्य-जन्याखण्डतत्त्वसाक्षात्कारेण शुद्धचैतन्यस्यावरणभूताविद्यायाः अविद्याप्रयुक्तकार्याणाञ्च निवृत्तिर्भवतीत्यद्वैतवेदान्तसिद्धान्तः।

अत्र श्रीभाष्यकाराणां श्रीमद्रामानुजाचार्याणामयं सिद्धान्तः श्रीभाष्ये एवमुपपादितः। "यदप्युच्यते, निर्विशेषे स्वयंप्रकाशे वस्तुनि दोषपरिकल्पितम् ईशेशितव्याद्यनन्तविकल्पं सर्वं जगत्। दोषश्च स्वरूपतिरोधानविविधविचित्रविक्षेपकरी, सदसदनिर्वचनीया अनाद्यविद्या। सा चावश्यमभ्युपगमनीया। "अनृतेन हि प्रत्यूढाः", इत्यादिश्रुतिभिः। ब्रह्मणः तत्त्वमस्यादिवाक्यसामानाधिकरण्यावगत जीवैक्यानुपपत्त्या च। सा तु न सती। भ्रान्तिबाधयोरयोगात्। नाप्यसती। ख्यातिबाधयोश्चायोगात्। अतः कोटिद्वय-विनिर्मुक्ता इयमविद्येति तत्त्वविदः इति। "इत्येवं प्रकारेण पूर्वपक्षमुपपाद्य" तदयुक्तमित्यादिना (1) आश्रयानुपपत्तिः (2) तिरोधानानुपपत्तिः (3) स्वरूपानुपपत्तिः (4) अनिर्वचनीयत्वानुपपत्तिः (5) प्रमाणानुपपत्तिः (6) निवर्तकानुपपत्तिः (7) निवृत्त्यनुपपत्तिः इति सप्तविधानुपपत्तिभिः भावरूपमज्ञानं निराकृतवन्तः श्रीभाष्यकाराः।

तत्र अद्वैतवेदान्ताभिमताज्ञाननिराकरणे प्रमाणानुपपत्तिरेका। अस्मिन् निबन्धे अद्वैतमतरीत्या अज्ञाने प्रमाणं प्रथमतः निरूप्यते। अनन्तरं तत्र श्रीभाष्यकाराणा-मनुपपत्तिं प्रदर्श्य तस्याः समाधानं च वदामि।

अज्ञानसद्भावे प्रत्यक्षं प्रमाणं निरूप्यते। तथाहि- "अहमज्ञः, मामन्यं च न जानामि" इति सामान्यतः प्रत्यक्षं, त्वदुक्तमर्थं न जानामीति विशेषतः प्रत्यक्षं, "एतावन्तं कालं सुखमहमस्वाप्सं, न किञ्चिदवेदिषम्" इति जाग्रत्कालीनस्मरणसिद्धं सौषुप्तञ्च प्रत्यक्षं अज्ञाने प्रमाणम्। एतादृशसाक्षिप्रत्यक्षेषु भावरूपमज्ञानमेव विषय इति अज्ञाने प्रत्यक्षं प्रमाणं वर्तते।

(1) अत्रेयमाशङ्का वर्तते। शुद्धचैतन्यस्यैव अज्ञानाश्रयत्वेन अहमर्थस्य जीवस्य अज्ञानानाश्रयत्वेन कथमिदं साक्षिप्रत्यक्षं भावरूपज्ञाने प्रमाणं भवितुमर्हति? अतः उक्तप्रत्यक्षस्य ज्ञानाभावविषयकत्वमेव वक्तव्यमिति शङ्का। तस्याः समाधानं तु अज्ञानाश्रयीभूत चैतन्ये अन्तः करणतादात्म्याध्यासेन एकाश्रयत्वसम्बन्धेन अहमज्ञ

इत्यादिप्रतीतेरुपपत्तेः। एकाश्रयत्वसम्बन्धः सामानाधिकरण्यसम्बन्धः। यथा "एकं रूपमिति प्रतीतेः एकत्ववद्रूपमिति नार्थः। गुणे गुणानङ्गीकारात् रूपे एकत्वस्याभावात् तादृशप्रतीतेः भ्रमत्वापातात्। किन्तु सामानाधिकरण्यसम्बन्धेन एकत्वविशिष्टं रूपमित्यर्थः। एकत्वरूपयोः सामानाधिकरण्यं घटादौ वर्तते। तद्वत् "अहमज्ञः" इति प्रतीतेः अज्ञानवत् अन्तःकरणमिति नार्थः। किन्तु सामानाधिकरण्यसम्बन्धेन अज्ञानविशिष्टमन्तःकरणमित्यर्थः। अज्ञानान्तःकरणयोरुभयोरपि शुद्धचैतन्येऽध्यासात् तयोः सामानाधिकरण्यं शुद्धचैतन्ये वर्तते।

(2) अन्या आशङ्का। जडे घटादौ आवरणकृत्यस्याभावात् घटं न जानामीत्यादिप्रतीतौ घटाविषयकाज्ञानं न विषयः। किन्तु घटविषयकज्ञानाभाव एव विषयः। तद्वदेव "अहमज्ञ" इत्यादिप्रतीतावपि अज्ञानाश्रयान्तःकरणं न विषयः। किन्तु अन्तःकरणे ज्ञानाभाव एवावगाहते इति शङ्का। समाधानन्तु घटं नं जानामीत्यादावपि घटादेः नाज्ञानाश्रयत्वं, किन्तु घटाद्यवच्छिन्नचैतन्यस्यैव अज्ञानावृतत्वं, अज्ञानाश्रयत्वञ्च उच्यते। तथा च "अहमज्ञ" इत्यादिप्रतीतेरपि अज्ञानविषयकत्वमेव, न तु ज्ञानाभावविषयकत्वम्।

(3) अन्या आशङ्का। साक्षिवेद्ये सुखदुःखज्ञानादौ प्रातिभासिके च शुक्तिरूप्यादौ भावरूपाज्ञानाभावेन तत्र "न जानामीति प्रतीतिः कथमुपपद्यत इति शङ्का। समाधानन्तु स्वस्मिन् विद्यमाने साक्षिवेद्ये सुखादौ, स्वभ्रमसिद्धे रूप्यादौ च "सुखं न जानामि," "दुःखं न जानामि", "शुक्तिरजतं न जानामीत्यादि व्यवहारासम्भवात्। परसुखादौ "न जानामीति" व्यवहारस्य प्रमातृगताज्ञानेनैव उपपत्तेः। अज्ञानं द्विविधम्। प्रमातृगतं, विषयगतञ्च। प्रकृते प्रमातृगताज्ञानेन परकीयसुखादौ "न जानामीति" व्यवहारः। तादृशप्रमातृगताज्ञानञ्च परोक्षज्ञानेन निवर्त्यते। एवञ्च परोक्षज्ञानेन प्रमातृगताज्ञाने नाशितेऽपि, विषयगताज्ञानसत्वेन "न जानामीति" व्यवहारापत्तिरिति वक्तुं न शक्यते। प्रमातृगताज्ञानप्रयुक्तकार्यस्य "न जानामीति" व्यवहारस्य विषयगताज्ञानेनापादयितुमशक्यत्वात्। विषयगताज्ञानेन "विषयो न भातीत्येव" व्यवहारो जायते, न तु "न जानामीति" व्यवहारः।

(4) अन्या आशङ्का। "मयि ज्ञानं नास्तीति" प्रतीतिः यथा ज्ञानाभावमवगाहते, तथा "अहमज्ञ" इति प्रतीतिरपि ज्ञानाभावमेव अवगाहताम्। प्रथमज्ञाने ज्ञानाभावः विशेष्यतया, द्वितीयज्ञाने विशेषणतया च भासते । यथा अघटं भूतलमिति प्रतीतौ घटाभावः विशेषणतया, "भूतले घटो नास्तीति" प्रतीतौ च विशेष्यतया भासते। तादृशप्रतीत्योः विषयभेदो नास्ति। तद्वदेवात्रापि विशेषणविशेष्यभावव्यत्यासं विना विषयभेदप्रतीतिर्नास्ति "मयि ज्ञानं नास्ति", "अहमज्ञ" इति प्रतीत्योः विषयकृतभेदस्यासत्त्वात् ज्ञानाभावेन अज्ञानस्य गतार्थत्वैवेति "अहमज्ञ" इति प्रत्यक्षप्रतीतिः न भावरूपज्ञानसाधिका

इति शङ्का। समाधानन्तु "मयि ज्ञानं नास्ति", "अहमज्ञ" इति प्रतीत्योः विषयकृतं वैलक्षण्यं नास्ति। उभयोरपि प्रतीत्योः अज्ञानरूपभावविषयकत्वमेव, न तु ज्ञानाभाव-विषयकत्वम्। धर्मि-प्रतियोगिज्ञानाज्ञानाभ्यां ज्ञानसामान्याभावस्य आत्मनि व्याहतत्वेन "मयि ज्ञानं नास्तीति" प्रतीतेः ज्ञानाभावविषयकत्वासम्भवात्। "मयि ज्ञानं नास्तीति प्रतीतौ आत्मा धर्मी, ज्ञानं प्रतियोगि। तदुभयज्ञानसत्त्वे ज्ञानसामान्याभावः व्याहतः। तदुभयज्ञानाभावे धर्मिप्रतियोगिज्ञानाभावेन ज्ञानाभावप्रतीतिः व्याहता। अतो "मयि ज्ञानं नास्तीति" प्रतीतेरपि भावरूपाज्ञानविषयकत्वमेव वक्तव्यम्। प्रतियोगितावच्छेदकावच्छिन्नप्रतियोगिज्ञानमेव अभावबुद्धौ हेतुः। यथा घटाभाववद्भूतलमिति भूतले घटाभावबुद्धौ प्रतियोगितावच्छेदक घटत्वावच्छिन्न घटरूपप्रतियोगिज्ञानं तथा "मयि ज्ञानं नास्तीति" प्रतीतौ आत्मनि ज्ञानाभाव बुद्धौ प्रतियोगितावच्छेदकं ज्ञानत्वं, तदवच्छिन्न ज्ञान रूप प्रतियोगि ज्ञानं हेतुः। तादृशप्रतियोगि ज्ञानाज्ञानाभ्यां व्याहत्या न ज्ञानाभावविषयं तादृशं प्रत्यक्षम्।

"मयि ज्ञानं नास्तीति" प्रतीतिः वायौ रूपं नास्तीति प्रतीतिवत् यावद्विशेषा-भावान्य-सामान्याभावविषया, सामान्यावच्छिन्नप्रतियोगिताकयावद्विशेषाभावविषया वा अभ्युपेया। तथा च तत्कारणीभूत धर्मिप्रतियोगि-ज्ञानाज्ञानाभ्यां व्याघातो दोषः। यत्किञ्चिद्विशेषाभावस्य "सामान्यावच्छिन्नप्रतियोगिताकत्वाभावात्।" अभावज्ञाने प्रतियोग्यंशे प्रकारीभूतधर्मस्यैव प्रतियोगितावच्छेदकत्वात्। अन्यथा घटो नास्तीत्यादौ पटत्वाद्यवच्छिन्न-प्रतियोगित्वभानापत्तेः। सामान्यावच्छिन्न-प्रतियोगिताकत्वेन विशेषाभावस्यापि भाने सामान्यभावसिद्धिर्न स्यात्। अभावधीमात्रे तथा सम्भवात्। यावद्विशेषाभावान्य सामान्याभावानभ्युपगमेऽप्ययं दोषः। यत्किंचिद्विशेषाभावस्य सामान्यावच्छिन्नप्रतियोगिताकत्वे घटवत्यपि भूतले "निर्घटं भूतलम्" इति प्रतीतिः स्यात्। वायौ रूपं नास्ति, पुरोदेशे रजतं नास्तीत्याद्याप्तवाक्यजन्यप्रतीत्यनन्तरमपि तत्तत्संशयनिवृत्तिर्न स्यात्। एकविशेषाभावबोधनेऽपि विशेषान्तरमादाय संशयोपपत्तेः।

(5) अन्या आशङ्का - "मयि ज्ञानं नास्तीति" प्रतीतेः ज्ञानाभावविषयकत्वे व्याघातो दोषो दत्तः, तथा अज्ञानविषयकत्वेऽपि व्याघातो दोषः प्रसज्यते। तथा हि - अज्ञानपदेन ज्ञानविरोधित्वेनैव अज्ञानं प्रतीयते। उक्तञ्च विवरणे - "अज्ञानमिति द्वयसापेक्ष ज्ञानपर्युदासेनाभिधानात्" इति। द्वयञ्च धर्मी प्रतियोगी च। तथा च विरोध निरूपकज्ञानस्य ज्ञानाज्ञानाभ्यां अद्वैतमतेऽपि कुतो न व्याघातः। एवं निर्विषयाज्ञाना-प्रतीतेः सविषयकस्यैव अज्ञानस्य प्रतीतेः विषयज्ञानाज्ञानयोरपि व्याघातः आपादनीयः।

यत्रोभयोः समो दोषः परिहारोऽपि वा समः।
नैकः पर्यनुयोक्तव्यस्तादृगर्थविचारणे॥

इति न्यायेन उभयपरिहरणीयस्य व्याघातस्य ज्ञानाभावपक्ष एवापादनमनुचितमिति शङ्का। समाधानन्तु ज्ञानविरोध्यज्ञानमित्यत्र न विप्रतिपत्तिः। किन्तु विरोधनिरूपकज्ञानं तद्विषयश्च साक्षिवेद्यौ भवतः। साक्षिज्ञानञ्च साक्षिवेद्यस्याज्ञानस्य निवर्तकं न। किन्तु अज्ञानसाधकमेव। प्रमाणजन्यान्तःकरणवृत्तेरेव अज्ञाननिवर्तकत्वमिति न व्याघातो दोषः। अज्ञानग्रहे विषयगोचरप्रमापेक्षायां व्याहतिः स्यादेव। सा च नास्ति। तदुक्तं विवरणे - "सर्वं वस्तु" ज्ञाततया अज्ञाततया वा (ज्ञानान्तरसापेक्षं, तन्निरपेक्षं वा) साक्षिचैतन्यस्य विषय एवेति"। ज्ञानाभावपक्षे तु नैवं वक्तुं शक्यते। भावरूपाज्ञानस्य साक्षात् साक्षिवेद्यत्वेन तदवच्छेदक विषयादेः अज्ञानद्वारा साक्षिवेद्यत्वसम्भवेऽपि ज्ञानाभावस्य अनुपलब्धि-गम्यत्वेन साक्षात् साक्षिवेद्यत्वाभावात् न ज्ञानाभावद्वारा ज्ञानाभावावच्छेदक-विषयादेः साक्षिवेद्यत्वमिति वैषम्यात्। अपि च उत्पन्नं ज्ञानं साक्षात् साक्षिवेद्यम्। तस्मिंश्चोत्पन्ने तद्विषयोऽपि स्फुरतीति कुतो ज्ञानाभावेऽपि। अज्ञान-विशेषणतया तु अनुत्पन्नमपि ज्ञानं साक्षिवेद्यमिति न दोषसाम्यम्।

एवं स्थिते श्रीभाष्यकाराणां भावरूपाज्ञाननिराकरणं श्रीभाष्ये "अत्रोच्यते" इत्यादिना एवं वर्तते। "अहमज्ञः", "मामन्यं च न जानामि" इत्यत्रोपपत्तिसहितेन केवलेन च प्रत्यक्षेण न भावरूपमज्ञानं प्रतीयते। यस्तु ज्ञानप्रागभावविषयत्वे विरोधः उक्तः, स हि भावरूपाज्ञानेऽपि तुल्यः। विषयत्वेनाश्रयत्वेन च अज्ञानस्य व्यावर्तकतया प्रत्यगर्थः प्रतिपन्नो वा अप्रतिपन्नो वा। प्रतिपन्नश्चेत् तत्स्वरूपज्ञाननिवर्त्यं तदज्ञानं तस्मिन् प्रतिपन्ने कथमिव तिष्ठति। अप्रतिपन्नश्चेत् व्यावर्तकाश्रयविषयज्ञानशून्यमज्ञानं कथमनुभूयेत" इति श्रीभाष्यग्रन्थः।

अस्य श्रीभाष्यग्रन्थस्य व्याख्यानं श्रुतप्रकाशिकाग्रन्थः एवं वर्तते। स्वरूपज्ञानं स्वरूपावभासः। स्वतो वा प्रमाणान्तरेण वा स्वरूपावभासनिवर्त्यमित्यर्थः। "इदं रजतम्" इत्यत्र इदं शुक्लभास्वरम्" इत्येवंरूप प्रमाणज्ञानशते जातेऽपि भ्रमानिवृत्तिदर्शनात् प्रमाणज्ञानत्वं अप्रयोजकमिति सिद्धवत्कारेण तत्स्वरूपज्ञाननिवर्त्यमित्युक्तम्। व्यावर्तकाश्रय-विषय-ज्ञानशून्यम् - आश्रयतया विषयतया च व्यावर्तकः प्रत्यगर्थः, तदवभासशून्यम्। विषयत्वेनेत्यादिना भाष्येण स्वात्मविषयाज्ञानप्रतिपत्तौ विरोधतुल्यत्वं दर्शितम्। घटादि-विषयाज्ञान-प्रतीतावपि अज्ञानस्य विषयत्वेन व्यावर्तकतया घटः प्रतिपन्नो वा न वा। प्रतिपन्नश्चेत् घटस्वरूपज्ञाननिवर्त्यं घटाज्ञानं तस्मिन् घटे प्रतिपन्ने कथमिव तिष्ठति। घटोऽप्रतिपन्नश्चेत् व्यावर्तकविषयज्ञानशून्यमज्ञानं कथमनुभूयेत इत्यर्थसिद्धो विरोधो द्रष्टव्यः।" इति॥

अस्य प्रश्नस्य समाधानमुक्तप्रायमेव। सर्वं वस्तु ज्ञाततया अज्ञाततया वा साक्षिगोचर इति विवरणोक्त्या अज्ञानग्रहे साक्षिचैतन्यापेक्षायामपि विषयगोचरप्रमानपेक्षणात्

भावरूपाज्ञानपक्षे न व्याहतिः। वृत्तिज्ञानस्य साक्षिवेद्यत्वेऽपि तदभावस्य साक्षिवेद्यत्वाभावेन न ज्ञानाभावस्यापि साक्षिमात्रापेक्षत्वेन व्याहत्यभावः। एवञ्च "अहमज्ञ" इति प्रत्यक्षं भावरूपाज्ञानविषयमेवेति सिद्धम्।

भावरूपाज्ञानस्वीकारे अन्योऽपि दोषः उक्तः श्रीभाष्ये। तत्रैवमुक्तम्। "नित्यमुक्त-स्वप्रकाश-चैतन्यैकस्वरूपस्य ब्रह्मणः अज्ञानानुभवश्च न सम्भवति। स्वानुभवस्वरूपत्वात्। स्वानुभवस्वरूपमपि तिरोहितस्वस्वरूपमज्ञानमनुभवतीति चेत् - किमिदं तिरोहित स्वस्व-रूपत्वम्। अप्रकाशितस्वरूपत्वमिति चेत्। स्वानुभवरूपस्य कथमप्रका-शितस्वरूपत्वम्। स्वानुभवस्वरूपस्यापि अन्यतः अप्रकाशितस्वरूपत्वमुपपद्यत इति चेत्, एवं तर्हि प्रकाशाख्यध र्मानभ्युपगमेन प्रकाशस्यैव स्वरूपत्वात् अन्यतस्स्वरूपनाश एव स्यादिति पूर्वमेवोक्तम्।" इति।

तन्न। "नास्ति, न प्रकाशते" इत्यादिव्यवहारार्हतापादनरूपं तिरोधानं स्वप्रकाशेऽपि ब्रह्मणि सम्भवति। तच्च आब्रह्मज्ञानं अवतिष्ठते। अतस्तावत् आत्मनः अज्ञानोपसृष्ट-स्वरूपत्वमेवेति न स्वरूपनाशप्रसक्तिः।

विवरणकारोक्तमनुमानमपि अज्ञाने प्रमाणम्। तथाहि - विवादपदं प्रमाणज्ञानं स्वप्रागभावव्यतिरिक्तस्वविषयावरणस्वनिवर्त्यस्वदेशगतवस्त्वन्तरपूर्वकम् अप्रकाशितार्थ-प्रकाशकत्वात्, अन्धकारे प्रथमोत्पन्न प्रदीपप्रभावत् इति।

प्रथमतः पक्षविषये विचारः। पक्षांशे प्रमाणपदमनुक्त्वा प्रमामात्रस्य पक्षत्वेन निवेशे सुखादिप्रमायां साक्षिचैतन्यरूपायां अज्ञानानिवर्तिकायां बाधः। अतस्तद्वारणाय प्रमाणपदम्। एवञ्च प्रमाणजन्य प्रमावृत्तेरेव पक्षत्वेन सुखादिप्रमायाः तादृशत्वाभावेन तस्याः पक्षबहिर्भावेन न तत्र बाधः। विवादपदमिति विशेषणाभावे "इदं रजत" मित्यादि भ्रमस्थलीय इदमाकार धर्म्यंश प्रमाणवृत्तौ अज्ञानानिवर्तिकायां बाधः। अतस्तस्याः पक्षबहिर्भावार्थं विवादपदमिति विशेषणम्। विशेषाकार प्रमाणवृत्तिरित्यर्थः। इदमाकारायाः प्रमाणवृत्तेः सामान्याकारत्वेन तस्याः पक्षबहिर्भावेण न तत्र बाधः।

साध्यविषये विचारः। स्वप्रागभावव्यतिरिक्त-स्वविषयावरण स्वनिवर्त्यस्वदेशगत वस्त्वन्तरपूर्वकत्वं साध्यम्। स्वपदेन सर्वत्र प्रमाणज्ञानं ग्राह्यम्। अत्र स्वप्रागभाव-व्यतिरिक्तत्वविशेषणानुपादाने स्वप्रागभावेनार्थान्तरं स्यात्। न च "ज्ञानमज्ञानस्यैव निवर्तकमिति नियमात् स्वनिवर्त्यपदेनैव प्रागभावव्युदासे" आद्यविशेषणं व्यर्थमिति वाच्यम्। प्रमा प्रमात्वेन अज्ञानस्यैव निवर्तिका, अन्येषां प्रमाप्रागभावादीनां तु प्रतियोगित्वादिनैव निवर्तिका, न तु प्रमात्वेन इत्यर्थे उक्तनियमस्य तात्पर्यात्। एवञ्च प्रमाणज्ञाननिवर्त्यत्वस्य प्रमाणज्ञानप्रागभावेऽपि सत्त्वेन प्रागभावादिना अर्थान्तरवारणाय आद्यविशेषणं सार्थकमेव।

न च स्वविषयावरणपदेनैव प्रागभावव्युदासः, प्रमाविषयं प्रति प्रागभावस्य आवरणत्वाभावादिति वाच्यम् "अस्ति प्रकाशते" इति व्यवहारविरोधित्वरूपस्यावरणत्वस्य भावाभावसाधारणत्वात्।

एवं साध्ये स्वविषयावरणत्वरूपद्वितीयदलस्यानिवेशे वृत्ति (प्रमाणज्ञान) जनकेनादृष्टेन अर्थान्तरं स्यात्। वृत्तिजनकादृष्टेऽपि वृत्तिप्रागभावव्यतिरिक्तत्वस्य, वृत्तिनिवर्त्यत्वस्य, स्वदेशगतत्वस्य वस्त्वन्तरत्वस्य च सत्त्वात्। द्वितीयदलनिवेशे तु अदृष्टस्य वृत्तिजनकत्वेन वृत्तिविषयावरणत्वाभावेन नादृष्टेन अर्थान्तरम्। न च स्वविषयावरणत्वविशेषणं व्यर्थम्। स्वविषयत्वं जडे चैतन्ये च वर्तते। तत्र जडरूपविषयस्य अप्रकाशत्वात् तत्र अज्ञानावरणमेव नास्ति। चैतन्यरूपविषयस्य च अज्ञानादि साक्षितया भासमानत्वात् चैतन्यस्य अज्ञानभासकत्वमेव, न तु तत्र अज्ञानमावरणमिति वाच्यम्। अज्ञानादिसाक्षितया चितः प्रकाशमानत्वेऽपि, "साक्षिचैतन्यमस्ति", "साक्षिचैतन्यं भाति" इति, व्यवहाराभावेन चैतन्यांशे आवरणस्यावश्यकत्वात्।

एवं साध्ये स्वनिवर्त्यत्वरूप-विशेषणस्याभावे वृत्तिप्रतिबन्धकेनादृष्टेन अर्थान्तरं स्यात्। तन्निवेशे तु वृत्तिप्रतिबन्धकस्यादृष्टस्य वृत्तिनिवर्त्यत्वाभावेन नार्थान्तरम्। न च चरमसाक्षात्कारोत्पत्ति प्रतिबन्धकादृष्टस्य चरमसाक्षात्कारानिवर्त्यत्वे न मिथ्यात्वासिद्धिः, तन्निवर्त्यत्वे तु तेनार्थान्तरवारणमशक्यमिति वाच्यम्। चरमसाक्षात्कारोत्पत्ति प्रतिबन्धकादृष्टे विद्यमाने न चरमसाक्षात्कारोत्पत्तिरिति मननिदिध्यासनादिना प्रथममदृष्टनिवृत्तेः, कारणात्मना स्थितस्य तस्यादृष्टस्य चरमसाक्षात्कारनिवर्त्यत्वाच्च मिथ्यात्वम्। न चैवमपि स्वनिवर्त्यत्वं तत्र व्याहतमिति तेनार्थान्तरमिति वाच्यम्। स्वनिवर्त्यत्वविशेषणस्य स्वनिवर्त्यस्वरूपत्वे तात्पर्यात्। अदृष्टस्य कारणात्मना स्थितत्वेऽपि स्वरूपतोऽवर्तमानत्वेन स्वनिवर्त्यस्वरूपत्वस्य तत्रासत्त्वेन न तेनाथान्तरम्। एवं साध्ये स्वदेशगतत्वरूप चतुर्थदलस्यानिवेशे विषयगताज्ञातत्वेन अर्थान्तरं स्यात्। तन्निवेशे तु प्रमावृत्तिदेशे अन्तःकरणे अज्ञातत्वं नास्तीति नार्थान्तरम्। अज्ञातत्वस्य विषय एव सत्त्वात्।

एवं वस्त्वन्तरपदं प्रमामात्रस्य भ्रमपूर्वकत्वसिद्धिमादाय भ्रमेणार्थान्तरवारणाय निविष्टम्। तन्निवेशे च वस्त्वन्तरपदं स्वनिवर्त्यजन्यभ्रमान्यार्थकम्।. एवञ्च जन्यभ्रमेण नार्थान्तरम्। तच्च वस्त्वन्तरं अनाद्यज्ञानमेव भवति।

हेतुविषये विचारः। उक्ताज्ञानसाधकानुमाने अप्रकाशितार्थप्रकाशकत्वं हेतुः। अत्र च हेतौ प्रकाशकत्वं प्रकाशकपदवाच्यत्वं, अप्रकाशविरोधित्वं वा ज्ञानालोकयोः पक्षदृष्टान्तयोः साधारणम्। प्रदीपप्रभायाः प्रकाशकपदवाच्यत्वं, अप्रकाशविरोधित्वं वा प्रकाशकत्वं वर्तते। एवं प्रमाणज्ञानस्यापि प्रकाशकपदवाच्यत्वं अप्रकाशविरोधित्वं वा अप्रकाशकत्वं वर्तते।

दृष्टान्तविषये विचारः। "अन्धकारे प्रथमोत्पन्नप्रदीपप्रभावत्" इति दृष्टान्ते अन्धकारे प्रथमोत्पन्नत्वविशेषणं अन्धकाराव्यवहितोत्पत्तिकत्वार्थकम्। तेन न प्रथमपदवैयर्थ्यम्। न वा अन्धकारव्यवहितोत्पत्तिक-द्वितीयादिप्रभायां न साध्यसाधनवैकल्यं दोषः।

भावरूपाज्ञाने अनुमानप्रमाणनिराकरणपरः श्रीभाष्यग्रन्थः एवं वर्तते। "यदुक्तं अनुमानेनापि भावरूपमज्ञानं सिद्ध्यतीति, तदयुक्तम्। अनुमानासम्भवात्। ननूक्तमनुमानम्। सत्यमुक्तं, दुरुक्तं तु तत्। अज्ञानेऽप्यनभिमताज्ञानान्तरसाधनेन विरुद्धत्वात् हेतोः। तत्राज्ञानान्तरासाधने हेतोरनैकान्त्यम्। साधने च तदज्ञानमज्ञानसाक्षित्वं निवारयति। ततश्चाज्ञानकल्पना निष्फला स्यात्। दृष्टान्तश्च साधनविकलः। दीपप्रभाया अप्रकाशितार्थप्रकाशकत्वाभावात्। सर्वत्र ज्ञानस्यैव हि प्रकाशकत्वम्। सत्यपि दीपे ज्ञानेन विना विषयप्रकाशाभावात्। ...प्रतिप्रयोगाच्च। (अस्यानुमानस्य प्रतिकूलतर्कपराहतिरुच्यते। स्वदेशगतत्व-स्वविषयावरणत्व-स्वनिवर्त्यत्वानां प्रतिकूलं यथाक्रममनुमानत्रयं अज्ञानं पक्षीकृत्य उच्यते।) (1) विवादाध्यासितमज्ञानं न ज्ञानमात्रब्रह्माश्रयं अज्ञानत्वात् शुक्तिकाद्यज्ञानवत् ज्ञात्राश्रयं हि तत् (2) विवादाध्यासितमज्ञानं न ज्ञानमात्रब्रह्मावरणं अज्ञानत्वात् शुक्तिकाद्यज्ञानवत् विषयावरणं हि तत्। (3) विवादाध्यासितमज्ञानं न ज्ञाननिवर्त्यं ज्ञानविषयानावरणत्वात् - यत् ज्ञाननिवर्त्यमज्ञानं तत् ज्ञानविषयावरणं यथा शुक्तिकाद्यज्ञानम्।" इति।

अत्र श्रुतप्रकाशिकायां एवमुक्तम्। "अस्य प्रमाणज्ञानस्य (निरुक्तानुमानस्यापि प्रमाणज्ञानसामान्यान्तर्गतत्वेन) अप्रकाशितार्थप्रकाशकत्वात् स्वविषयावरणाज्ञानान्तरसाधकत्वे सति, तदज्ञानं ब्रह्मस्वरूपाच्छादकं सिषाधयिषितमज्ञानमावृणोति। तेनावृतत्वात् तदज्ञानं ब्रह्मणा न साक्षात्क्रियते। अपरमार्थस्य अप्रतीयमानस्य कार्यकरत्वायोगात् अज्ञानकल्पना निष्फला। तिरोधानरूपकार्यार्थं हि तत्कल्पना। यद्यसाक्षात्कृतमेव कार्यकरं, तदा सत्तया कार्यकरमिति काचादिवत् सत्यत्वात् ज्ञाननिवर्त्यं न स्यात्। एवमज्ञानस्य ज्ञानानिवर्त्यत्वे। निष्फलत्वे।, कारणतयानभिमताज्ञानान्तरसाधकत्वम्। तदसाधने च अनैकान्त्यमुक्तम्" इति। अपि च श्रीभाष्यग्रन्थः एवं वर्तते। स्वप्रागभावव्यतिरिक्त वस्त्वन्तरपूर्वकमिति व्यर्थविशेषणोपादानेन प्रयोगकुशलता चाविष्कृता। अतोऽनुमानेनापि न भावरूपाज्ञानसिद्धिः। इति।

विशिष्टाद्वैतिनामयमाशयः- निरुक्तानुमानेन अज्ञानं भावरूपं साधयितुं न शक्यते। तथाहि- निरुक्तानुमानस्यापि प्रमाणज्ञानसामान्यान्तर्गतत्वेन अप्रकाशितार्थप्रकाशकत्वमङ्गीकार्यम्। एवञ्च उक्तानुमानविषयाज्ञानेऽपि अनभिमताज्ञानान्तरसिद्धौ

तादृशमज्ञानं ब्रह्मस्वरूपाच्छादकमज्ञानमावृणोतीति तदावृतत्वात् स्वाज्ञानं स्वात्मना नानुभूयेत। ततश्चापरमार्थस्य अप्रतीयमानस्य अकार्यकरत्वेन तत्कल्पना निरर्थिका स्यात्। तत्राज्ञानन्तरासिद्धौ तत्रैव बाधः। अपक्षत्वे वा व्यभिचारो दोषः। इति श्रीभाष्यकाराणामाशयः।

अत्र अद्वैतिनामयमाशयः। अज्ञाने अनभिमताज्ञानान्तरसिद्धावपि ब्रह्मस्वरूपतिरोधायकाज्ञानावरकाज्ञानान्तरसाक्षित्वं आत्मनो न व्याहन्यते। यादृशमज्ञानावच्छिन्नचैतन्यं इदमज्ञानमावृणोतीत्युच्यते तादृशचैतन्येन अज्ञानान्तरानुभवे दोषाभावात्। स्वावृतप्रकाशप्रकाश्यत्वादज्ञानस्य। अज्ञानान्तरस्यापि ब्रह्मस्वरूपतिरोधायकत्वाभ्युपगमे बाधकाभावाच्च। अथवा सत्तया अज्ञानस्य तिरोधायकत्वपक्षाभ्युपगमेऽपि न दोषः। काचादेरपि मिथ्यात्वात्। इति।

साध्यें च व्यर्थविशेषणानि इति यत् श्रीभाष्ये उक्तं तन्न। साध्यगतविशेषणानां सार्थक्यं प्रतिपादितम्। एवं दृष्टान्ते साधनवैकल्यदोषोऽपि परिहृतः। एवं त्रयः प्रतिकूलतर्का अपि न युज्यन्ते। आद्ये शुक्तिकाद्यज्ञानं दृष्टान्तीकृत्य तत्र ज्ञात्राश्रयत्वमेव वर्तते, न तु ज्ञानाश्रयत्वमित्युक्तम् तन्न। दृष्टान्ते शुक्तिकाद्यज्ञाने ज्ञानान्तरत्वाभावो न विज्ञाने इत्यस्ति साध्यवैकल्यं दोषः। अपि च हेतुरस्तु, साध्यं मास्तु इति व्यभिचारशङ्कायां तन्निवर्तयितुं अनुकुलतर्को नास्ति। द्वितीयप्रतिकूलतर्के शुक्तिकाद्यज्ञानं विषयावरणमेव न तु ब्रह्मावरणमित्युक्तम्। तन्न, विषयावरणमित्यस्य विषयावच्छिन्नचैतन्यावरणमित्येवार्थ - इति न दोषः। अपि च द्वितीयप्रतिकूलतर्के अज्ञानं विषयमावृणोतीति, प्रथमप्रतिकूलतर्के अज्ञानं ज्ञात्राश्रयमिति चोक्तम्। तत्तु युक्तिसहं न भवति। यमावृणोति तदाश्रयमेवाज्ञानमिति वक्तव्यम्। न तु अन्याश्रयम्। तृतीयप्रतिकूलतर्कानुमानेन अज्ञाने ज्ञाननिवर्त्यत्वाभावः साध्यते। तन्न। "तरति शोकमात्मवित्" इत्यादिश्रुत्या अज्ञाने ज्ञाननिवर्त्यत्वसिद्धेः उक्तानुमाने बाधदोषसद्भावात्।

भावरूपाज्ञाने श्रुतिप्रमाणं निराकरिष्यमाणः श्रीभाष्यग्रन्थः एवं वर्तते। "यत्पुनः सदसदनिर्वचनीयमज्ञानं श्रुतिसिद्धमिति, तदसत्। "अनृतेन हि प्रत्यूढा" इत्यादिषु अनृतशब्दस्यानिर्वचनीयानभिधायित्वात्। ऋतेतरविषयो हि अनृतशब्दः। ऋतमिति कर्मवाचि। "ऋतं पिबन्ताविति वचनात्" इत्येवं रीत्या श्रीभाष्यग्रन्थो वर्तते।

अत्रेदमद्वैतिनां समाधानम्। अज्ञाने श्रुतिः प्रमाणं वर्तते। छान्दोग्ये अष्टमाध्याये "तद्यथापि हिरण्यं निधिनिहितमक्षेत्रज्ञा उपर्युपरि सञ्चरन्तो न विन्देयुः एवमेवेमाः सर्वाः प्रजाः अहरहर्गच्छन्त्य एतं ब्रह्मलोकं न विन्दन्त्यनृतेन प्रत्यूढाः" इति श्रुतिः ब्रह्मज्ञानप्रतिबन्धकत्वेनानृतं ब्रुवाणा अज्ञाने प्रमाणम्। न च ऋत शब्दस्य "ऋतं पिबन्तौ" इति श्रुतौ, "ऋतं

सत्यं तथा धर्मः" इति स्मृतौ च सत्कर्मणि प्रयोगदर्शनात् अनृतशब्दस्य दुष्कर्मपरत्वम्। तथा च " अनृतेन प्रत्यूढाः" इत्यस्य दुष्कर्मप्रतिबद्धाः इत्यर्थ इति वाच्यम्। (1) उत्तरत्र "य आत्मा अपहतपाप्मा" इत्यादिना आत्मनः अपहतपाप्मत्व-प्रतिपादनेन पापकर्मणामभावप्रतिपादनेन दुष्कर्मप्रत्यूढत्वविरोधात् (2) सुषुप्तौ कर्ममात्रनाशे दुष्कर्मणोऽप्यभावात्। (3) कारणात्मनावस्थाने च अज्ञानस्यावश्यकत्वात्। (4) कर्मण आवरणत्वानुपपत्तेश्च। ब्रह्मज्ञानप्रतिबन्धकतया हि अनादिब्रह्मावरकं ज्ञाननिवर्त्यं वाच्यम्। तच्चाज्ञानमेव। तथा च कर्मैव प्रधानमपि नानृतपदाभिधेयम्। तयोः ज्ञाननिवर्त्यत्वाभावात्। अज्ञानस्य ज्ञाननिवर्त्यत्वे च "भूयश्चान्ते विश्वमायानिवृत्तिः" इति श्रुतिः प्रमाणम्। न चात्र निवृत्तिः तरणमात्रम्। "मायामेतां तरन्ति ते" इति स्मृतेरिति वाच्यम्। ज्ञानहेतुकतरणस्य निवृत्त्यतिरिक्तस्यासम्भवेन निवृत्ति-तरति पदयोरुभयोरपि नाशमात्रार्थत्वात्। न च मायाशब्दार्थः नाज्ञानम्। मायिनो ब्रह्मणोऽज्ञानित्वे "यः सर्वज्ञः सर्ववित्" इत्यादि सर्वज्ञत्वनिरवद्यत्वादि-श्रुतिविरोध इति वाच्यम्। मायात्मकोपाधेः प्रतिबिम्बपक्षपातित्वेन प्रतिबिम्बे जीवे एव मायागतधर्माः असर्वज्ञत्वादयो भासन्ते, न तु बिम्बभूतेश्वरे। अत ईश्वरे असर्वज्ञत्वाद्यापादनायोगात्। सर्वज्ञत्वाद्यैश्वर्यस्य मायानिबन्धनत्वाच्च।

तस्मात् "अनृतेन प्रत्यूढाः", "नीहारेण प्रावृताः", "तम आसीत्", "मायां तु प्रकृतिं विद्यात्", "अविद्यायामन्तरे वर्तमानाः", "भूयश्चान्ते विश्वमायानिवृत्तिः" इत्याद्याः श्रुतयः अज्ञाने प्रमाणमिति स्थितम्।

जीवस्यानवच्छिन्नब्रह्मानन्दाप्रकाशान्यथानुपपत्तिरपि अज्ञाने प्रमाणम्। न च जीवस्य ब्रह्मभेदेनैव तादृशाप्रकाशोपपत्तिरिति वाच्यम्। जीवब्रह्मभेदस्यानङ्गीकारात्। न चानवच्छिन्नानन्दस्य प्रकाशमानप्रत्यङ्मात्रत्वेन अप्रकाशमानत्वानुपपत्तिरिति वाच्यम्। द्वैतमते यथा आत्मनि शरीरभेदस्य आत्मत्वेन प्रकाशमानत्वेऽपि शरीरभेदत्वेन अप्रकाशमानत्वं तथा आत्मनः चैतन्यस्वरूपेण प्रकाशमानत्वेऽपि अनवच्छिन्नानन्दस्वरूपेण अप्रकाशमानत्वमुपपद्यते इत्यदोषात्।

एवं भ्रमस्य सोपादानत्वान्यथानुपपत्तिरपि अज्ञाने प्रमाणम्। न चान्तःकरणमुपादानमस्तु इति वाच्यम्। अन्तःकरणस्य ज्ञानजनने प्रमाणव्यापारसापेक्षत्वेन, प्रमाणाविषये शुक्तिरूप्यादौ अन्तःकरणस्य ज्ञानाजनकत्वात्। अन्तःकरणस्य सादित्वेन अनादिभ्रम-परम्परानुपादानत्वाच्च। न च ब्रह्मैव उपादानमस्तु इति वाच्यम्। तस्य अपरिणामित्वात्। न च शुक्त्यादेः यथा विवर्ताधिष्ठानत्वेन उपादानत्वं, तथा ब्रह्मणोऽपि विवर्ताधिष्ठानत्वेन उपादानत्वमस्तु इति वाच्यम्। अविद्यामन्तरेण अतात्त्विकान्यथाभावलक्षणस्य विवर्तस्यैवासम्भवात्। शुक्त्यादेरपि अधिष्ठानचैतन्यावच्छेदकतया विवर्ताधिष्ठानत्वाभावात्।

तस्मादर्थापत्तिरविद्यायां प्रमाणम्। एवं अद्वैतमतरीत्या अविद्यायां प्रत्यक्षस्य, अनुमानस्य, श्रुतेः, अर्थापत्तेश्च प्रमाणस्य प्रदर्शितत्वेन अविद्यायां प्रमाणानुपपत्तिः वक्तुमशक्या इति अद्वैतवेदान्तसिद्धान्तः।

Summary: Dr. Sripada Subramanian critically examines Rāmānuja's *Pramāṇa-anupapatti.* According to Advaita, non-cognition, erroneous cognition, and doubtful cognition—all these three are due to avidyā. Advaita, therefore, maintains that the work of concealment, which is positive, cannot be done by a negative entity that is non-existent. If avidyā is explained negatively as absence or non-existence of knowledge, it cannot conceal the truth and project the false.

If ignorance is nothing but absence of knowledge, when there is knowledge of an object in a general way, it should forthwith bring about the disappearance of ignorance. Ignorance, however, still persists even after knowing an object in a general way.

Rāmānuja maintains that the difficulty pointed out by the Advaitin with regard to interpreting avidyā as *jñāna-prāgabhāva* is present even if avidyā is explained as *bhāvarūpa.* Rāmānuja asks: is Brahman-Ātman which is the locus as well as the content of avidyā known or not known? If it is known, there is no room for avidyā also because the knowledge of Brahman-Ātman puts an end to avidyā. If it is not known, how can there be apprehension of avidyā because its apprehension requires the knowledge of its locus. Just as avidyā in the negative sense of "absence of knowledge" is not self-explanatory, even so avidyā in the positive sense is not self-explanatory. The term "*ajñāna*", Rāmānuja says, can be understood in three ways. It may mean "absence of knowledge" (*jñānābhāva*), or "what is other than knowledge" (*tad-anyaḥ*), or "what is opposed to knowledge" (*tad-virodhī*). In whatever way we construe the meaning, the term "*ajñāna*" presupposes "knowledge". It means that just as *ajñāna*" in the sense of *jñānābhāva* presupposes something else, even so *ajñāna* viewed as a positive entity presupposes something else. So Rāmānuja concludes that statements such as "I am ignorant", "I don't know myself", point to the absence of knowledge experienced by us.

To answer the above, Advaitins reply saying that the experience of deep sleep also proves that avidyā is positive. A person recollects his experience of deep-sleep by saying, "I did not know anything then." Recollection presupposes prior experience and in this case it can only be the recollection of the experience of *ajñāna*. The question now is whether this *ajñāna* experienced by him in deep-sleep can be treated negatively as prior absence of knowledge (*jñānābhāva* or *jñāna-prāgabhāva*). Generally speaking, knowledge of *abhāva* requires the knowledge of both the locus (*dharmin*) and the correlate (*pratiyogin*). One cannot speak of mere absence or non-existence with no reference to what is and where it is absent. Only with reference to both the pot (the correlate) and the ground (the locus), one can speak of the absence of the pot on the ground. Similarly, if one were to speak of "absence of knowledge" in deep-sleep, it requires the knowledge of both the locus and the correlate at that time. Since the mind is wholly quiescent then, the person in deep sleep cannot have the knowledge of both the locus and the correlate, which is necessary for the knowledge of "absence of knowledge". But yet one claims to know that he knew nothing. We have to therefore conclude, on the strength of the subsequent recollection in the waking state, that the person concerned had the knowledge or experience of avidyā which is quite different from absence or non-existence of knowledge.

If, according to Advaita, there is knowledge of avidyā in deep sleep, it amounts to saying that knowledge and ignorance co-exist at that time. But this, Ramanuja argues, is untenable because the two are mutually opposed. Advaitins answer this saying that the word "knowledge" here may be understood in two senses. It may be understood either as knowledge which constitutes the essential nature of Brahman-Ātman (*svarūpa-jñāna*), or knowledge which arises through *avidyā-vṛtti*. We have already stated that *svarūpa-jñāna* which reveals avidyā is not opposed to it. In deep-sleep there is avidyā as well as *avidyā-vṛtti*. Avidyā, which is the adjunct of the Self of deep sleep, is the causal condition of the mind. It is through *avidyā-vṛtti* that *prājña*, which is the name given to the Self of deep-sleep, experiences both ignorance and happiness. When deep sleep is followed by the waking state, the Self associated with the mind, which is only avidyā in the effect-form, recollects its previous experience of both ignorance and happiness. There is, therefore, no inconsistency in the co-existence of knowledge and ignorance in deep-sleep.

There is yet another reason why avidyā is positive and is hence different from prior absence of knowledge. Knowledge destroys ignorance. If avidyā is nothing but the prior non-existence of knowledge, then knowledge can never destroy it because knowledge can arise only after the termination of its prior non-existence. When there is knowledge, there is no prior non-existence of knowledge; and when there is prior non-existence of knowledge, there is no knowledge. Hence the two cannot be related as the destroyer and the destroyed. However, since knowledge destroys ignorance, the latter should not be viewed negatively as prior non-existence of knowledge.

Further, the prior absence of knowledge is never an object of direct perceptual experience. It is what we have to infer from the knowledge that arises subsequently. If knowledge arises now, it implies that prior to its arising it was non-existent. Since the prior absence of knowledge has to be inferred from the subsequent rise of knowledge, it cannot be directly experienced. Inasmuch as avidyā is directly experienced, it must be different from the prior absence of knowledge. Let us consider this issue in another way to show why avidyā should not be understood as *jñāna-prāgabhāva*. What is the nature of the knowledge whose prior non-existence is meant here? Is it knowledge-in-general (*jñāna-sāmānya*) or, is it some specific knowledge (*jñāna-viśeṣa*)? Knowledge-in-general is knowledge which is undifferentiated, indeterminate, and non-relational, and so it is none other than Brahman which is eternal. What is eternal can never be absent at any time. Hence *jñāna-prāgabhāva* in the sense of the prior non-existence of knowledge-in-general is untenable. The other alternative fares no better. When knowledge arises, it is specific and relational—specific because we are able to differentiate it as such-and-such from other cases of knowledge, and relational because it has a transcendent object to which it is related. But no one has direct access to prior non-existence of specific knowledge; that is, one does not directly experience it as such. One does not, for instance, directly experience the prior non-existence of a pot or a table. Considering that avidyā is directly experienced while *jñāna-prāgabhāva* is not, it is wrong to treat avidyā negatively as prior absence of knowledge.

16

निवर्तकानुपपत्तिः निवृत्त्यनुपपत्तिश्च

K.E. Devanathan

निवर्तकानुपपत्तिः - श्रीभाष्यकाराशयः

निर्विशेषब्रह्मज्ञानादविद्यानिवृत्तिर्भवतीत्यद्वैतिनः। तत्र युक्तम्। सर्वाण्यपि वेदान्तवाक्यानि "वेदाहमेतं पुरुषं महान्तमादित्यवर्णं तमसः परस्तात्। तमेवं विद्वानमृत इह भवति" इत्यादीनि सविशेषब्रह्मज्ञानादेव मोक्षं प्रतिपादयन्ति। न च "तत्त्वमसि" इत्यादि महावाक्यमखण्डार्थपरं, तद्वाक्यजन्यात् स्वरूपमात्रविषयकज्ञानादविद्यानिवृत्तिर्भवतीति वाच्यम्। तत्र हि तत्पदं जगत्कारणत्वादिगुणविशिष्टमभिधत्ते। पूर्वं "सदेव सोम्येदमग्र आसीत्, तदैक्षत बहु स्यां प्रजायेये"ति प्रभृतिभिः वाक्यैः सर्वकारणत्वसर्वज्ञत्वसत्यसङ्कल्पत्वादिविशिष्टस्यैव ब्रह्मणः प्रतिपादनात्। तत्समानाधिकरणं त्वं-पदमप्यचिद्विशेषविशिष्टं जीवशरीरकं ब्रह्माभिधत्ते। न हि विशेषणपरित्यागेन स्वरूपमात्रलक्षणा पदद्वयस्य युक्ता। तथात्वे "भिन्नप्रवृत्तिनिमित्तानाम्" इति सामानाधिकरण्यलक्षणहान्यापत्तेः। नापि सोऽयं देवदत्त इति वाक्यदृष्टान्तेन तथात्वाशङ्का, तत्रापि विशेषणपरित्यागाभावात्। न हि भूतकालदेशकालान्तरसम्बन्धस्य वर्तमानकालैतद्देशसम्बन्धस्य च विरोधः, एकस्मिन्नेव वस्तुनि कालभेदेन देशभेदसम्भवात्। अतो निर्विशेषब्रह्मज्ञानादविद्यानिवृत्तिरिति नोपपद्यते।

वेदार्थसङ्ग्रहदिशा निवर्तकानुपपत्तिः

श्रीभाष्यकाराः निवर्तकानुपपत्तिविषये भाष्योक्ता युक्तीरनूद्य ततोऽन्या अपि युक्तीः वेदार्थसङ्ग्रहे प्रदर्शयन्ति। तथा हि - निखिलभेदनिवर्तकमद्वैतज्ञानं श्रुत्या जायत इति स्वीकर्तव्यम्। श्रुतिश्च ब्रह्मव्यतिरिक्तत्वेनाविद्यापरिकल्पितत्वात् मिथ्याभूता बाधकज्ञानं न जनयितुमर्हति। दुष्टकरणजन्यं रज्जुसर्पज्ञानं हि दुष्टकारणजन्येन "रज्जुरियं न सर्प" इति ज्ञानेन न बाध्यते। रज्जुसर्पज्ञानभये सति केनचिद्भ्रान्तेन पुरुषेण "रज्जुरियं न सर्प" इत्युक्तेऽपि "अयं भ्रान्त" इति ज्ञाने सति, तद्वचनं रज्जुसर्पज्ञानस्य बाधकं न भवति, भयं च न निवर्तते।

किञ्च निवर्तकज्ञानस्य, ज्ञातुः तत्सामग्रीभूतस्य शास्त्रस्य च ब्रह्मव्यतिरिक्ततया यदि बाध्यत्वमुच्येत, तदा प्रपञ्चनिवृत्तेर्मिथ्यात्वमापततीति प्रपञ्चस्य सत्यत्वं स्यात्, स्वप्नदृष्टपुरुषवाक्यावगत पुत्रादिमरणस्य मिथ्यात्वेन पुत्रादिसत्यत्ववत्। (वि. स. p-13. PBA Edn.).

इदमप्यनुमानं तत्र प्रयुक्तं - तत्त्वमस्यादिवाक्यं न प्रपञ्चस्य बाधकं, भ्रान्तिमूलत्वात्, भ्रान्तप्रयुक्तरज्जुसर्पबाधकवाक्यवत् - इति। न च स्वप्ने भये सति स्वप्नकाल एवायं स्वप्न इति ज्ञाते सति, तदानीमेव भयं निवर्तते, तद्वदत्रापि भवतीति वाच्यं, यतः स्वप्नदशायामेवायं स्वप्न इति बुद्धेरपि स्वप्नत्वं यदि दृश्यते, तदा भयस्यानुवृत्तिदर्शनान्न लाभः।

ननु शास्त्रं यद्यप्यविद्यापरिकल्पितं तथापि शास्त्रजन्यज्ञानं निर्विशेषं ब्रह्म बोधयति, पश्चात्तनबाधादर्शनाच्च निर्विशेषं ब्रह्म स्थिरं भवतीति चेन्न। पश्चात्तनबाधादर्शनमेव यदि विषयसत्यत्वे प्रयोजकं, तदा शून्यमेव तत्त्वमिति वाक्येन ब्रह्मणोपि बाधितत्त्वात् ब्रह्मापि मिथ्या भवेत्। तत्र हि पश्चात्तनबाधादर्शनं विद्यत एव। यदि तद्वाक्यं भ्रान्तिविजल्पितमतो न विषयसत्यत्वे प्रमाणमिति मन्यते, तदा वेदवचनमपि भ्रान्तिपरिकल्पितमिति कस्तयोर्विशेषः॥

श्रुतप्रकाशिकादिशा निवर्तकानुपपत्तिः

श्रीभाष्ये तत्त्वमस्यादिवाक्यं सविशेषवस्तुविषयकं ज्ञानं जनयतीति निरणायि। अत्र दृष्टान्त उक्तः श्रुतप्रकाशिकायां - शुक्ला शोभनाक्षी मदीया पूर्णशृङ्गा घटोघ्नी गौः, तामानयेत्यत्र विशेषणविशिष्टमेव वस्तु परामृश्यते तच्छब्देन। तथा प्रकृतेऽपि तत्त्वमसीत्यत्र तच्छब्देन सविशेषमेव ब्रह्म परामृश्यते। न च गौस्तिष्ठति, तामानयेत्यत्राऽऽनयनकर्मत्वं शुद्धाया गोरेव, न तु विशिष्टस्य, तद्वत् प्रकृतेऽपि तच्छब्देन शुद्धमेव परामृश्यत इति वाच्यम्। आनयनकर्मत्वसमकालं स्थितेर्बाधितत्त्वेऽपि पूर्वकालीनस्थितिविशिष्टस्य विशेषणत्वे बाधकाभावात्। पूर्वकालीनस्थितिवैशिष्ट्यं च स्थित्यधिकरणकालसम्बन्ध एव। अत एवापवरके घटोऽस्ति तमानयेत्यत्र घटत्वविशेषणं परित्यज्य मृन्मात्रं तच्छब्देन न परामृश्यते। घटो हि अवस्थाविशेषवती मृदेव। अतस्तच्छब्देन सद्विद्यायां ये आकारा उक्ताः, तेषां सर्वेषां परामर्शो भवतीति कथं निर्विशेषब्रह्मणः परामर्शो युज्येत।

निवर्तकानुपपत्तिविषये वेदान्तदेशिकाशयः

श्रीमद्वेदान्तदेशिकाः निवर्तकज्ञानस्वरूपं पञ्चधा विकल्प्य खण्डयन्ति। किमिदमद्वैतज्ञानं ब्रह्मस्वरूपभूताज्ज्ञानाद्भिन्नमुत (२) अभिन्नं यद्वा (३) भिन्नाभिन्नं (४) उतानुभयात्मकं (५) उतानिरूपणीयेतिकर्तव्यताविशेषः। इदं हि निवर्तकज्ञानं ब्रह्मस्वरूपाद्भिन्नमित्याद्यकल्पो न युक्तः।

यदि ब्रह्मभिन्नं निवर्तकज्ञानं निर्विषयकमिष्यते तदा ज्ञानत्वं न स्यात्। वृत्तिरूपं ज्ञानं सविषयकमिति हि भवतां सिद्धान्तः। यदि सविषयकं तत्, विषयः क इति विवेचनीयम्। यदि ब्रह्मस्वरूपमेव निवर्तकज्ञानविषय इत्युच्यते, तदा आत्मस्वरूपस्येव तदन्यूनानतिरिक्तविषयकस्य वृत्तिज्ञानस्यापि निवर्तकं न स्यात्। अस्मिन् विषये विस्तरो दृश्यते शतदूषण्याम्। अभिज्ञाप्रत्यभिज्ञादृष्टान्तोऽपि विचारितः। यद्यविद्याविशिष्टं ब्रह्म विषय उच्यते तदा साक्षिप्रत्यक्षवत् भ्रमोपकारकत्वमेव स्यान्न तु निवर्तकत्वम्। साक्षिप्रत्यक्षमपि स्वप्रकाशात्मकमविद्याप्रकाशकं च। यदि ब्रह्मव्यतिरिक्तमेव निवर्तकज्ञानविषय इष्यते, तदापि न निस्तारः, निवर्तकज्ञानस्य भ्रमरूपस्य भ्रमनिवर्तक-त्वाभावात्। न हि शुक्तिरजतज्ञानमेव रजतज्ञानं निवर्तयति। यदि ब्रह्मव्यतिरिक्तस्य मिथ्यात्वमेव निवर्तकज्ञानविषयः तदापि दोष एव। न ह्यधिष्ठानयाथात्म्यग्रहणमन्तरेण ब्रह्मव्यतिरिक्तस्य मिथ्यात्वं ग्रहीतुं शक्यते, अधिष्ठानस्य हि याथात्म्यं दुर्ग्रहमेव भवत्पक्षे। अत्र कश्चन सङ्ग्रहश्लोकः शतदूषण्यामुक्तः -

मिथ्यात्वस्य तु मिथ्यात्वे मिथ्यात्वं बाधितं भवेत्।
सत्यत्वस्य तु सत्यत्वे सत्यत्वं स्थापितं भवेत्॥ इति।

निवर्तकज्ञानमिदं ब्रह्मस्वरूपादभिन्नमिति द्वितीय विकल्पोऽपि न युक्तः। तथा सति स्वरूपस्य नित्यत्वेन सर्वदा निवर्तकज्ञानसत्त्वेन संसाराभावप्रसङ्गः।

तृतीयपक्षस्तु भेदाभेदपक्षः। स तु भेदाभेदस्य परस्परविरुद्धस्यैकस्मिन्नधिकरणे अस्वीकारादेव निरस्तो भवति। निवर्तकज्ञानमिदं ब्रह्मभिन्नं न, नापि ब्रह्माभिन्नमिति चतुर्थकल्पोऽपि न युज्यते, परस्परविरोधे हि न प्रकारान्तरास्थितिरिति न्यायेन उभयविलक्षणस्य वस्तुन एवाप्रसिद्धेः। निवर्तकज्ञानमिदमनिरूपणीयेतिकर्तव्यताविशेष इति पक्षस्तु प्रमाणपदवीमेव नाधिरोहति। एवमादिरीत्या शतदूषणीग्रन्थः निवर्तकानुपपत्तिं निरूपयति।

अपि च निवर्तकज्ञानं स्वयमविद्याकल्पितं निर्गच्छति वा न वा? यदि निर्गच्छति, तदा निवर्तकज्ञाननिवृत्तेः पूर्वं निवृत्तनिवर्तकज्ञानादविद्यानिवृत्यनन्तरमपि अविद्यान्तरं निवर्तकज्ञानसम्पादकं किञ्चित् स्यात्। यदि निवर्तकज्ञानं न निर्गच्छति, तदा तज्ज्ञानहेतुभूता काचिदविद्या स्थायिनी स्वीकार्या स्यात्।

निवर्तकानुपपत्तिविषये एवं संग्रहोऽकारि उत्तमूर् वीरराघवाचार्यस्वामिभिः। निर्विशेषब्रह्मज्ञानं नाविद्यानिवर्तकम्। नहि धर्मिमात्रज्ञानेनाविद्यानिवृत्तिः क्वापि दृष्टा। किन्तर्हि? विशेषधर्मविशिष्टधर्मिज्ञानेनैव। निर्विशेषब्रह्मज्ञानस्य स्वयम्प्रकाशब्रह्मतुल्यत्वान्न प्रपञ्चनिवर्तकत्वं, यदि ब्रह्मस्वरूपं न प्रपञ्चनिवर्तकं, तदा तत्समानविषयकं वृत्तिज्ञानमपि न निवर्तकमेव। यदि ब्रह्मस्वरूपमेव निवर्तकमिति कथ्यते, तदाऽविद्यैव न स्यात्। तदर्थं

ब्रह्मणः स्वयम्प्रकाशत्वं परित्यज्य जडत्वमास्थीयते चेत्, महती हानिः। "तमेवं विद्वानमृत इह भवति" इत्यादि वाक्यं हि सविशेषब्रह्मज्ञानमेवाविद्यानिवर्तकमिति प्रतिपादयति।

श्रीभाष्योक्ता निवृत्त्यनुपपत्तिः

अद्वैतज्ञानं प्रपञ्चं निवर्तयतीत्यद्वैतिनः। सा निवृत्तिर्नोपपद्यत इति विशिष्टाद्वैतिनः। बन्धो हि पारमार्थिकः। पारमार्थिकस्य बन्धस्य ब्रह्मात्मैकत्वज्ञानेन निवृत्तिर्न भवति। पारमार्थिकपदार्थस्य ज्ञानबाध्यत्वं न हीष्टम्। बन्धो हि पुण्यापुण्यस्व कर्मनिमित्तक-देहानुप्रवेशप्रयुक्तसुखदुःखानुभवरूपः, कथं मिथ्येति वक्तुं शक्यते।

निवृत्त्यनुपपत्तिविचारशेषतया निवर्तकज्ञानस्य निवृत्तिमपि विचारयन्ति भाष्यकाराः। तथा हि - इदं निवर्तकज्ञानं कथं निवर्तते? इदं निवर्तकज्ञानं सर्वबन्धं विनिवर्त्य क्षणिकत्वात् स्वयमेव निवर्तेत इति तु न, निवर्तकज्ञानस्य, तदुत्पत्तेः तद्विनाशस्य च काल्पनिकत्वेन विनाश-तद्विषयभ्रम-भ्रमाश्रयादीनां कल्पनार्थमविद्यान्तरमा-श्रयणीयम्। तथा चानवस्था। यदि च निवर्तकज्ञानविनाशः ब्रह्मस्वरूपमेवेति कथ्यते, तदा ब्रह्मस्वरूपस्य निवर्तकज्ञानविनाशरूपस्य सर्वदा सत्त्वेन निवर्तकज्ञानमेव नोत्पद्येत।

किञ्च यदिदं निवर्तकज्ञानं भवति, तस्य ज्ञाता कः? स यदि मिथ्यारूपः, तदा तस्यापि निषेधज्ञानकर्मत्वात् तदाश्रयत्वं न स्यात्। यदि ब्रह्मस्वरूपमेव ज्ञातृ, तदा ब्रह्मणो निवर्तकज्ञानाश्रयत्वं ब्रह्मस्वरूपं वाऽध्यस्तं वा? ब्रह्मस्वरूपं ज्ञातृ इति पक्षे स्वरूपं स्वासाध ारणधर्म इति अस्मत्पक्षाविशेषः। यदि ब्रह्मस्वरूपे ज्ञातृत्वमध्यस्तमित्युच्यते, तदाऽध्यासहेतुभूताऽविद्यान्तरकल्पना कार्या। सा चाविद्या निवर्तकज्ञानाविषयतया तिष्ठत्येव। निवर्तकज्ञानान्तरस्वीकारे, तस्यापि ज्ञाता कः, ज्ञातृत्वं किंरूपमित्यादि प्रश्नेनानवस्था स्यात्।

अपि च यद्यविद्याया निवर्तकज्ञानं स्वनिवर्त्यभूताविद्यायामिव ब्रह्मव्यतिरिक्त-त्वाविशेषात् स्वं स्वाश्रयज्ञातारं च निवर्तयतीति कथ्यते, तदापि न निस्तारः - भूतल-व्यतिरिक्तं सर्वं देवदत्तेन छिन्नमित्यस्यामेव च्छेदनक्रियायां विषयभूते छेद्ये छेदनक्रियायाः तदाश्रयस्य चानुप्रवेश इव भवद्वचनमुपहास्यम्।

अपि च स्वनाशहेतुभूतनिवर्तकज्ञाने स्वयं कर्ता न भवति, अध्यस्तो ज्ञाता। स्वनाशस्या-पुरुषार्थत्वात्। यदि चाध्यस्तज्ञातृनाशः ब्रह्मस्वरूप एवेति तन्नाशस्य पुरुषार्थत्वमुच्यते, तदा ब्रह्मणो ज्ञातृनाशस्वरूपस्य नित्यत्वेन भेददर्शनाविद्यानाशादीनां कल्पनमेव न स्यात्।

श्रुतप्रकाशिकादिशा निवृत्त्यनुपपत्तिः

बन्धस्य पारमार्थिकत्वेन तस्य ज्ञानमात्रान्निवृत्तिरिति श्रीभाष्यग्रन्थं व्याचक्षाणाः श्रीसुदर्शनभट्टा एवं लिखन्ति - प्रपञ्चो हि प्रतीतिमात्रसिद्धो भवन्मते। तस्य हेतुहेतुमद्भावनियमोऽनुपपन्नः। अर्थक्रियाकारित्वमुत्पत्तिमत्त्वं च परमार्थस्यैव भवति। न च पदार्थानामर्थक्रियाकारित्वमुत्पत्तिमत्त्वं च मिथ्या, तेनापारमार्थिकस्यापि बन्धस्य तयोः सत्त्वे न दोष इति शङ्क्यम्। ज्ञानाबाध्ययोस्तयोः मिथ्यात्वस्यानिरूपणात्। किञ्च प्रपञ्चस्य मिथ्यात्वे पापकरणेऽपि न प्रायश्चित्तस्यापेक्षा स्यात्, प्रपञ्चो मिथ्येति बुद्धेरेव पर्याप्तत्त्वात्। अपि च तत्त्वज्ञाने हि मोक्षोपायः, यथावस्थितवस्तुविपरीतविषयस्य भवदभिमतस्यैक्यज्ञानस्य बन्धविवृद्धिरेव फलं स्यात्।

शतदूषणीरीत्या निवृत्त्यनुपपत्तिविचारः

निवृत्त्यनुपपत्तिविषये श्रीमद्वेदान्तदेशिकैः विशदं न्यरूपि शतदूषण्याम्। सङ्ग्रहेण तामनुपपत्तिं तद्दिशा प्रतिपादयामः। अद्वैतिभिः निश्शेषाविद्यानिवृत्तिरद्वैतज्ञानाद्भवतीत्युच्यते। तत्र प्रश्नः - किं साऽविद्यानिवृत्तिः अध्यासरूपा न वा? यद्यविद्यानिवृत्तिः अध्यासरूपेत्युच्यते, तदाऽध्यासरूपायास्तस्याः हेतुभूताविद्यापि स्थिरा स्यात्। न हि दोषमन्तरेणाध्यासो भवताभीष्टः। यद्यविद्यानिवृत्तिर्नाध्यासरूपा, तदैवं विकल्पः - किं साविद्यानिवृत्तिः ब्रह्मस्वरूपा तद्भिन्ना वा? यदि ब्रह्मस्वरूपा तदा ब्रह्मस्वरूपस्य नित्यत्वात् नित्यं मोक्षप्रसङ्गः। ब्रह्मस्वरूपभिन्नं तदा किमपि वस्तु सत्यभूतं भवता नेष्टम्। न च घटप्रागभावध्वंसस्य घटस्वरूपत्वमिवाविद्यानिवृत्तेरपि ब्रह्मस्वरूपत्वमिष्टमेवेति वाच्यम्। तथात्वे स्वप्रागभावान्तरत्वस्य घट इव ब्रह्मण्यपि स्वाज्ञानानन्तरत्वापातात् ब्रह्मणः कादाचित्कत्वप्रसङ्गात्।

नन्वविद्यानिवृत्ति र्न सती, ब्रह्मव्यतिरिक्तत्वात्। नापि सदसद्रूपा व्याघातात्। न च सदसद्विलक्षणा, सदसद्विलक्षणत्वेऽविद्यानिवृत्तेः पुनर्व्याघातात्। अतः परिशेषादविद्यानिवृत्तेरसत्त्वमेव स्वीकार्यम्।

अविद्यानिवृत्तेरसत्त्वे नित्यमविद्यासद्भावप्रसङ्गः। न च घटध्वंसस्यासद्रूपत्वेऽपि घटादेः कादाचित्कत्ववत् अविद्याध्वंसस्यासद्रूपत्वेऽपि अविद्यायाः कादाचित्कत्वमुपपद्यत इति चेन्न। घटध्वंसस्यासद्रूपत्वाभावात्। स ह्यभावात्मकोऽपि तत्कालीनयतया प्रमाणतः सिद्धः। अन्यथा घटनित्यत्वस्यापि दुर्वारत्वात्।

यद्यविद्यानिवृत्तिः चतुष्कोटिविनिर्मुक्तेत्युच्यते, तदा माध्यमिकपक्षप्रवेशः स्यात्। न च यक्षानुरूपो बलिरिति न्यायेन नायं दोष इति वाच्यं, तन्न्यायस्यात्राप्रसरात्।

आनुरूप्यमविरोधित्वमेवेति न च वाच्यम्। तदा सदसदनिर्वचनीयाज्ञाननिवृत्तेरप्यनिर्वचनीयत्वप्रसङ्गात्। एवमादिरूपेण निवृत्त्यनुपपत्तिः विशदीकृता श्रीवेदान्तदेशिकैः। सङ्क्षेपेण वयमत्र निरदिशाम।

अत्रेयं शङ्कावतरति - अविद्यानिवृत्तिरुपपद्यत एव। अविद्यात्वेनाविद्याज्ञाने सति सुखादिषु मिथ्यात्वबुद्धौ सत्यां तद्भावनादार्ढ्येन क्वचिदपि प्रवृत्त्यभावे कर्माभावात् मुक्तिःसिद्ध्यतीति न निवृत्त्यनुपपत्तिरिति।

तत्र समाधानम् - सर्वस्य मिथ्यात्वं वदतां पक्षे सर्वस्य मिथ्यात्वेन शुक्तिज्ञानेन रजतनिवृत्तिवत् तत्त्वज्ञानेन युगपत् सर्वनिवृत्तेरेव युक्तत्वात्।

किञ्चाविद्यानिवृत्तिरियं कार्या वा न वा? यदि कार्या, तदा मिथ्या वा न वा? प्रथमे किमिदं मिथ्यात्वम्? प्रतीयमानत्वे सति बाध्यमानत्वमिति चेत्, जातायाः निवृत्तेः प्रतीतिः, तद्बाधः, तदुपायः, तत्र कर्ता चेति सर्वमाविद्यकमङ्गीकार्यमिति कथमविद्यानिवृत्तिः? सत्यत्त्वपक्षे तु द्वैतापत्तिरेव। यद्यविद्यानिवृत्तिः न कार्येत्युच्यते, तदा तत्त्वज्ञानतदर्थायासादिकं व्यर्थं स्यात्। अतोऽविद्यानिवृत्तिर्नोपपद्यते।

इत्थं विशिष्टाद्वैतसम्प्रदाये निवर्तकानुपपत्तिः निवृत्त्यनुपपत्तिश्च कथमुपपादितेति प्रत्यपादि।

Summary: Professor K.E. Devanathan defends the last two objections raised by Rāmānuja. Advaitins hold that the avidyā is sublated by the knowledge of *nirviśeṣa* Brahman; *i.e.*, Brahman devoid of qualities. Rāmānuja contends that it is only by the knowledge of *saviśeṣa* Brahman, as propounded by all the Upaniṣadic texts, the liberation can be attained.

It has been understood in the tradition of Advaita that the Mahāvākya "*tat tvam asi*" does not convey the *nirviśeṣa* through the word "*tat*". Being a pronoun "*tat*" shall convey the Brahman qualified by qualities. Before uttering the sentence "*tat tvam asi*" the *Sadvidyā* portion of the *Chāndogya* disclosed numerous qualities of the Brahman, through the description of emergence of universal dimensions from the Brahman. If *tat* and *tvam* are held as conveying an identical object, *i.e.*, *nirviśeṣa*, then the definition of *samānādhikaraṇya* explained by Kaiyaṭa will be inapplicable in the sentence. Kaiyaṭa says that a group of words are called to be in *samānādhikaraṇya* relation, if those words convey a single entity, through different qualifiers. Advaitins say that like recognition (*pratyabhijñā*), the

Mahāvākya also does not convey the qualifiers and convey only the Brahman as not qualified.

Viśiṣṭādvaitins refute that this instance does not convey a single entity as non-qualified and therefore, on the basis of that instance, the Mahāvākya cannot be understood.

Rāmānuja further says that if everything in the world is untrue or illusory, then Veda is also an illusory creation from avidyā and the knowledge which emerges from the Vedas cannot be true, since faulty sources cannot fetch true knowledge. Hence the knowledge cannot sublate avidyā. If the source of knowledge is not true, then the emerging cognition also will be false. It is understood on the basis of shell-silver cognition. And therefore, Advaitin's claim that Śruti removes *ajñāna* and brings about *brahmajñāna* is not tenable.

Untenability of Sublation of Avidyā

The position of Advaitins is that the avidyā is eliminated by the knowledge of the Brahman. Here Rāmānuja precisely contends that since the bondage (*bandha*) is real, it cannot be sublated by any cognition. Only unreal things can be destroyed by true cognitions. But real objects cannot be eliminated by the means of cognition. The Bondage is real. It is in the form of experience of either happiness or unhappiness. The experience is because of past karma. So, we cannot conclude that the bondage is unreal.

Rāmānuja further asks Advaitins how that sublating cognition will get removed? Since after destroying the bondage along with its root *i.e.*, avidyā, the sublating cognition may require another cognition to remove it. The Viśiṣṭādvaitins further explain the untenability in this way. The sublation of avidyā is not real, since it is different from the Brahman. This is not both real and unreal. The word "*sadasad*" is oxymoron. One cannot be both. The sublation cannot be held different from *sad* and *asad* (real and unreal), because of mutual contradiction. Hence the sublation of avidya should be held as "*asad*". If it is "*asad*" (non-existent), then avidyā would become eternal. Therefore all the arguments Advaitins have advanced to refute the untenability of sublation of avidyā stand nullified.

17

निवर्तकनिवृत्त्यनुपपत्तिविचारः

J. Venkatarama Sastri

लोके अद्वैत, विशिष्टाद्वैत, द्वैतरूपेण वेदान्तविषये मतत्रयमतीव प्रसिद्धम्। तत्र द्वैतिनो विशिष्टाद्वैतिनश्च प्रपञ्चस्य सत्यतामभिप्रयन्ति। अद्वैतिनस्तु प्रपञ्चस्याज्ञानकार्यतां, ब्रह्मज्ञाननिवर्त्यतां च वाञ्छन्ति। तत्राद्वैत्यभिमतेऽज्ञाने सप्तविधाः अनुपपत्तयः विशिष्टाद्वैतिभिः द्वैतिभिश्च प्रदर्शिताः। ताश्च एताः - १. आश्रयानुपपत्तिः, २. तिरोधानानुपत्तिः, ३. स्वरूपानुपपत्तिः, ४. अनिर्वचनीयत्वानुपत्तिः, ५. प्रमाणानुपपत्तिः, ६. निवर्तकानुपपत्तिः, ७. निवृत्त्यनुपपत्तिः इति।

द्वैतमतेन निवर्तकानुपपत्तिनिरूपणम्

ब्रह्मैव सत्यं, तज्ज्ञानेन अज्ञानं तत्कार्यभूतः प्रपञ्चश्च निवर्तत इति अद्वैतसिद्धान्तः न युज्यते। यतः अज्ञानस्य निवर्तकं किमिति निरूपणमशक्यम्। तथा हि -

१. न तावत् स्वप्रकाशचैतन्यमज्ञानस्य निवर्तकम्। यतस्तस्य सर्वदा सत्वेनाज्ञानस्य सर्वदा निवृत्त्यापत्तावसंसारप्रसङ्गः। अज्ञानस्य स्वप्रकाशचैतन्यभास्यत्वाङ्गीकारेण तद्बाध्यत्वं नोपपद्यते। न हीन्द्रियेण चक्षुषा प्रकाश्यमानं रूपं चक्षुषा बाध्यते॥

२. नापि ब्रह्माकारा वृत्तिः अज्ञानस्य निवर्तिका। यतः ब्रह्मभिन्नायाः तस्याः असत्यत्वेन सत्यभूतां अज्ञाननिवृत्तिं प्रति साधकता असम्भविनी। यदि तु अज्ञान-निवृत्तेः असत्यता इष्येत तदा तत्प्रतियोगिनः अज्ञानस्य सत्यत्वापत्त्या अद्वैतहानिः।

किञ्च "न जानामि" इत्येवमज्ञाने ज्ञानविरोधित्वमेव अनुभूयते। न तु वृत्ति-विरोधित्वम्। वृत्तेः ज्ञानत्वाभावात्। अतः वृत्तेः अज्ञाननिवर्तकत्वं न तद्विरोधनिबन्धनम्। अपि तु यथैव इच्छायाः द्वेषनिवर्तकत्वं जातिनिबन्धनं तथैव वृत्तेरपि अज्ञाननिवर्तकत्वं जातिनिबन्धनमेव इति वक्तव्यम्। एवञ्च तद्वदेव वृत्तिनिवर्त्यस्य अज्ञानस्य सत्यत्वापत्त्या अद्वैतहानिः।

किञ्च सर्वासां घटादिवृत्तीनां अपि चिद्विषयकत्वं अङ्गीक्रियते। अत एव चितः सर्वप्रत्ययवेद्यता प्रचीनाचार्यैः उद्घोषिता - "सर्वप्रत्ययवेद्येऽस्मिन् ब्रह्मरूपे व्यवस्थिते" इति। एवञ्च चरमवृत्तेरिव घटादिवृत्तीनामप्यज्ञाननिवर्तकत्त्वं चिद्विषयकत्वाविशेषेण आपतति इति घटादिवृत्तीनां विनैव श्रवणादिसम्भवात् श्रवणादीनां वैयर्थ्यं स्यात्। किञ्च अविद्यानिवर्तकत्वेन अभिमता वृत्तिः किं परोक्षरूपा उत प्रत्यक्षरूपा इति विवेचनीयम्। नाद्यः परोक्षरूपायाः भ्रमनिवर्तकत्वस्य अननुभविकत्वात्। अत एव लोके रज्जौ सर्पत्वभ्रमः "नायं सर्प" इति अन्योक्तवाक्यजन्यज्ञानेन परोक्षेण न निवर्तते। नापि प्रत्यक्षा। "अशब्दमस्पर्शमरूपमव्ययं तथाऽरसं नित्यमगन्धवच्च यत्।" इति श्रुत्युक्तप्रकारेण शब्दादिशून्यस्य ब्रह्मणः चक्षुरादिजन्यप्रत्यक्षविषयत्वासम्भवात्। अत एव श्रुतिः एवमाह - "न सन्दृशे तिष्ठति रूपमस्य न चक्षुषा पश्यति कश्चनैनम्।" इति।

यदि तु इन्द्रियार्थसन्निकर्षजन्यज्ञानत्वं न प्रत्यक्षत्वे प्रयोजकम्, "दशमस्त्वमसि" इति वाक्यजन्यज्ञाने व्यभिचारात्। अपि तु विषयचैतन्याभिन्नप्रमातृचैतन्याभिन्नत्व-मेव वृत्तिगतप्रत्यक्षत्वे प्रयोजकम्। तच्च शब्दजन्यज्ञानेऽपि सम्भवतीति तत्त्वमस्यादि महावाक्यजन्यप्रत्यक्षरूपाखण्डाकारवृत्तिरेवाज्ञाननिवर्तिका इत्युच्यते।

तदापि महावाक्यजन्या वृत्तिः किं शुद्धविषयिणी उत विशिष्टविषयिणी इति विवेचने उभयथापि दोषो भवति। तत्र "यत्तदद्रेश्यमग्राह्यम्" इति श्रुत्यनुसारेण शुद्धस्य अदृश्यत्वेन न शुद्धविषयकता वृत्तेः सम्भवति। शुद्धस्य वृत्तिविषयत्वमभ्युप-गच्छतां विवरणकाराणां मतं तु अयुक्तम्। श्रुतिविरोधात्। विशिष्टस्य मिथ्यात्वेन वृत्तेस्तद्विषयकत्वे भ्रमत्वापत्त्या अज्ञाननिवर्तकतैव न स्यात्।

किञ्च "तत्त्वमसि" इति वाक्यस्य जीवेश्वराभेदबोधकता "नाहमीश्वर" इति प्रत्यक्षविरोधेन न सम्भवतीति तादृशाभेदबोधनद्वारा तज्जन्यवृत्तेरखण्डैकरसे शुद्धे ब्रह्मणि पर्यवसानमसम्भवि। "तत्त्वमसि" इति वाक्यं तु जीवस्य ब्रह्माश्रितत्वं, ब्रह्मसम्बन्धित्वं, ब्रह्माधीनतां वा बोधयति। न तु तदभेदम्। तथा "नेह नानास्ति किञ्चन" इति वाक्यमपि प्रपञ्चमिथ्यात्वबोधनद्वारा अखण्डे पर्यवसानं भजते। "सन् घट" इत्यादि प्रपञ्चसत्यताबोधकप्रत्यक्षविरोधात्। अपि तु अवतारिणि विष्णौ अवतारभेदेन प्रसक्तस्य भेदस्य निषेधकम्।

किञ्चाविद्याकार्यभूतस्यान्तःकरणस्य कार्यभूता वृत्तिरिति वृत्तेः परम्परयाऽज्ञानो-पादानकत्वादपि नाज्ञाननिवर्तकत्वं युक्तम्। कार्यस्य स्वोपादाननिवर्तकत्वाननुभवात्।

अस्तु वा यत्किञ्चिदज्ञानस्य निवर्तकत्वम्। तथापि तस्याज्ञाननिवर्तकस्य सत्यत्वे अद्वैतहान्यापत्त्या मिथ्यात्वमेव वक्तव्यम्। तच्च निवर्त्यत्वं विना अनुपपन्नमिति

अज्ञाननिवर्तकस्य किञ्चित् निवर्तकं वक्तव्यम्। तत्र अज्ञाननिवर्तकं न स्वस्य स्वयमेव निवर्तकम्। अन्यनिरपेक्षप्रतियोगिनः ध्वंसजनकत्वे तस्य क्षणिकत्वापत्तेः। नापि शुद्धात्मा अविद्यानिवर्तकस्य निवर्तकः। "न तस्य कार्यं करणं च विद्यते" इति श्रुत्यनुसारेण शुद्धस्य किञ्चित्प्रत्यपि अहेतुत्वात्। नाप्यन्यत्किञ्चित् तन्निवर्तकम्। चरमवृत्तिकाले चरमवृत्ति-शुद्ध-उभयव्यतिरिक्तस्य कस्यचित् सत्त्वानङ्गीकारात्।

३. नापि वृत्तिप्रतिबिम्बिता चित् अविद्यानिवर्तिका। यतस्तथा सति अपरोक्षवृत्तौ सत्यां चितः प्रतिबिम्बविलम्बे सति अविद्यानिवृत्तिरपि विलम्बेत। न तु तथा लोके दृष्टम्। अतः न वृत्तिप्रतिबिम्बितचितः अविद्यानिवर्तकता। किञ्च चितः प्रतिबिम्बनमेव वृत्तौ असम्भवि। यतः वृत्तेः प्रतिबिम्बनोपाधिता न सम्भवति। उपाधित्वप्रयोजकेन उद्भूतरूपवत्त्वेन शून्यत्वात्। तथा चैतन्यप्रतिबिम्बितत्वप्रयोजकेन चाक्षुषत्वेन शून्यत्वात् प्रतिबिम्बमपि न सम्भवति। अतः वृत्तिप्रतिबिम्बितचितोऽपि अज्ञाननिवर्तकता न सम्भवति।

तथा येयमविद्यानिवर्तकनिवृत्तिः, सा न सत्या। अद्वैतहानेः। अपि तु मिथ्यैव इति वक्तव्यम्। ततश्चाविद्यानिवर्तकनिवृत्तिगतं यदिदं मिथ्यात्वं तस्य सत्यत्वे अद्वैतहानेः मिथ्यात्वमेव वक्तव्यम्। एवञ्चैकत्राविद्यानिवर्तकनिवृत्तौ प्रसक्तयोः द्वयोर्मिथ्यात्व-सत्यत्वरूपयोः मध्ये मिथ्यात्वस्य मिथ्यात्वे सत्यत्वस्य पारमार्थिकत्वापत्त्याऽविद्या-निवर्तकनिवृत्तेः पारमार्थिकत्वमेव स्यादित्यद्वैतहानिस्तदवस्थैव।

किञ्च लोके समानाश्रययोरेव निवर्त्यनिवर्तकभावो दृष्टः। तत्र विवरणमतेऽज्ञानं शुद्धाश्रयम्। वृत्तिश्च वृत्त्यवच्छिन्नचैतन्ये कल्पितम्। एवञ्च समानाश्रयत्वाभावात् न वृत्त्यज्ञानयोर्निवर्त्यनिवर्तकभावः। तथा वाचस्पतिमते वृत्तिः जीवाश्रिता। अज्ञानन्तु न जीवाश्रितम्। यतः अज्ञानोपहितस्य चैतन्यस्य अज्ञानाश्रयत्वं अन्योन्याश्रयग्रस्तम्।

किञ्चाखण्डाकारवृत्तेरविद्यानिवर्तकत्वाङ्गीकारे स्वप्रकाशात्मकस्वरूपज्ञानस्यापि तत्समानविषयकत्वेनाविद्यानिवर्तकत्वापत्तिः। तस्मात् स्वप्रकाशचैतन्यस्य, वृत्तेः, वृत्तिप्रतिबिम्बितचैतन्यस्य वाऽविद्यानिवर्तकता न सम्भवति। अन्यस्य तु चरमवृत्तिकाले असत्त्वेन अविद्यानिवर्तकताशङ्का दूरापास्ता। तस्मात् निवर्तकाभावेन अविद्यानिवृत्तेः असम्भवेन नाविद्यानिवृत्तिः मोक्ष इति॥

अविद्याविषये द्वैत्याद्याक्षिप्तानामनुपपत्तीनाम् अद्वैतमतानुसारेण परिहरणम्

अविद्यानिवृत्तिरेव मोक्षः। न च निवर्तकाभावः। चरमवृत्तिप्रतिबिम्बितायाः चितः चित्प्रतिबिम्बधारिण्याः वृत्तेः वा अविद्यानिवर्तकत्वम्। न च चितः वृत्तौ प्रतिबिम्बाना-मसम्भवः। यतः उद्भूतरूपवत्त्वं न प्रतिबिम्बनोपाधित्वे प्रयोजकम्। उद्भूतरूपवति लोष्टादौ

प्रतिबिम्बनोपाधित्वादर्शनेन तत्र व्यभिचारात्। अपि तु स्वच्छत्त्वम्। तच्चान्तः-करणेऽस्त्येव। तस्य यत्कारणमज्ञानं तस्य त्रिगुणात्मकत्वेऽपि स्वच्छसत्त्वात्मकताया अपि सम्भवात्। एवञ्च तैजसस्य अन्तःकरणस्य यत्कार्यं वृत्तिरूपं तत्र स्वच्छत्त्वं वर्तत एव इति न वृत्तेः प्रतिबिम्बनोपाधित्वासम्भवः। तथा चाक्षुषत्वं न प्रतिबिम्बितत्वे प्रयोजकम्। अचाक्षुषस्यापि आकाशस्य जलादौ प्रतिबिम्बदर्शनेन तत्र व्यभिचारात्। तस्मात् वृत्तौ चितः प्रतिबिम्बनं सम्भवत्येव॥

यद्यपि शुद्धा चित् अज्ञानसाधिका, न तु तद्बाधिका, तथापि यथैव तृणादि-भासिकापि सूर्यदीप्तिः सूर्यकान्तमुपारूढा सती तृणादि दहति। तथैव वृत्तिप्रति-बिम्बिता सती अज्ञानं बाधितुं समर्था शुद्धा चित्। अत एव अभियुक्तैरेवमुक्तम् -

तृणादिभासिकाप्येषा सूर्यदीप्तिः तृणं दहेत्।
सूर्यकान्तमुपारुह्य तन्न्यायं विनियोजयेत्॥ इति।

न च चित्प्रतिबिम्बनवत्याः वृत्तेः मिथ्याभूतायाः सत्यभूतामज्ञाननिवृत्तिं प्रति साधनत्वायोगः। यतः कार्यकारणयोः सारूप्यं नावश्यकम्। अत एवाभावस्य भावजनकत्वं, प्रातिभासिकस्य रज्जुसर्पादेः व्यावहारिकदुःखादिजनकत्वं च लोकेऽनुभूयते।

वस्तुतस्तु अविद्यानिवृत्तेः ब्रह्मातिरिक्तत्वे सत्यत्वानुपपत्तेः ब्रह्मरूपत्वमेव एष्टव्यम्। एवञ्च ब्रह्मणो नित्यत्वेन वृत्तेरविद्यानिवृत्तिं प्रति व्यञ्जकत्वमेवेष्यते। अतो न पूर्वोक्ता शङ्का।

वृत्तेरज्ञाननिवर्तकत्वं तज्जातिनिबन्धनं न। अपि तु तद्विरोधित्वनिबन्धनमेव। एवञ्चेच्छानिवर्त्यद्विषवत् नाज्ञानस्य सत्यत्वापत्तिः। "न जानामि" इत्येवं चिद्विशिष्ट-वृत्तेरेवाज्ञानविरोधित्वमनुभूयते।

वस्तुतस्तु अधिष्ठानसाक्षात्कारत्वेन रूपेणैवाधिष्ठाननिवर्तकत्वाङ्गीकारान्न कश्चिद् दोषः। एवञ्चाधिष्ठानतत्त्वसाक्षात्कारनिवर्त्यरूपस्येवाज्ञानस्य मिथ्यात्वमेव भवति। न तु सत्यत्वम्। चरमवृत्तिवत्। घटादिवृत्तीनामनवच्छिन्नचिद्विषयकत्वाभावेन नाविद्या-निवर्तकत्वापत्तिः। अविद्यानिवर्तिका प्रत्यक्षरूपा वृत्तिरेव तत्त्वमस्यादिवाक्यजन्या अभेदादिबोधनद्वाराऽखण्डैकरसे पर्यवसन्ना। शब्दादप्यपरोक्षज्ञानं जायत एव। "दशमस्त्वमसि" इत्यादौ लोके दर्शनात्।

प्रत्यक्षप्रमाणयस्याप्रामाण्यशङ्काकलुषितत्त्वेन तेन श्रुतिबाधनस्यासम्भवेन "तत्त्वमसि"वाक्यस्याभेदबोधकत्वं "नेह नानास्ति किञ्चन" इति वाक्यस्य प्रपञ्चमिथ्या-त्वबोधकत्वं च सम्भवत्येव इति तदद्वाराऽखण्डैकरसे ब्रह्मणि पर्यवसानं भवत्येव।

अविद्यानिवर्तकवृत्तिः विवरणकारमते शुद्धचिद्विषयिणी। अत एवैवं सङ्क्षेपशारीरके उक्तं -

फलव्याप्यत्वमेवास्य शास्त्रकृद्भिर्निराकृतम्।
ब्रह्मण्यज्ञाननाशाय वृत्तिव्याप्यत्वमिष्यते॥

इति। न च "यतो वाचो निवर्तन्ते", "यत्तदद्रेश्यमग्राह्यम्" इत्यादिश्रुतिविरोधः। यतः ताः सर्वाः श्रुतयः पारमार्थिकवेद्यत्वनिषेधिकाः। अतः शुद्धे व्यावहारिकवेद्यत्वाङ्गीकारे न पूर्वोक्तश्रुतिविरोधः। विवरणकारमते चरमवृत्तेः, अविद्यायाः, उभयोरपि शुद्धचिद्विषयकत्वेन समानविषयकत्वात् निवर्त्यनिवर्तकभाव उपपद्यते।

वाचस्पतिमते शुद्धस्य वृत्तिविषयत्वानङ्गीकारात् चरमवृत्त्युपहितमेव चैतन्यं चरमवृत्तेर्विषयः। अज्ञानस्यापि स्वोपहितविषयकत्वमेव। उपाधेश्च विशेष्यान्वयि-निरूपितान्वयिप्रतियोगित्वासम्भवेन अज्ञानचरमवृत्त्योः न स्वविषयकत्वम्। अत एव चरमवृत्तेः मिथ्याभूतस्वविषयकत्वाभावेन भ्रमत्वाभावेनाविद्यानिवर्तकता सम्भवति। अत एव चाज्ञानचरमवृत्त्योः उपाध्यविषयकत्वे सति उपहितविषयकत्वेन समानविषयकताऽस्तीति तयोर्निवर्त्यनिवर्तकभावो नानुपपन्नः।

परम्परयाऽविद्याकार्यभूताया अपि वृत्तेः स्वोपादाननिवर्तकत्वं प्रमाणबलाद-न्यत्रादृष्टमपि कल्प्यते, "मायां तु प्रकृतिं विद्यात्" इत्यनेन चरमवृत्तेः मायोपादान-कत्वस्य "तरति शोकमात्मवित्" "सोऽविद्याग्रन्थिं विकिरतीह सोम्य" इत्यादिना मायाभूतोपादाननिवर्तकत्वस्यापि प्रमितत्वात्।

वस्तुतस्तु दध्नः स्वपरिणाम्युपादानदुग्धनाशकता लोके दृष्टैवेति नादृष्टकल्पनाऽपि। तस्मात् चित्प्रतिबिम्बनाधारभूता वृत्तिः वृत्तिप्रतिबिम्बितचिद्वाऽविद्यानिवर्तिका। तच्चाविद्यानिवर्तकं मिथ्यैव। आद्यपक्षे तच्च स्वयमेव स्वस्य निवर्तकम्। न च क्षणिकत्वापत्तिः। यतः प्रतियोगिनः प्रतियोगित्वेन नाशकतायामितरानपेक्षत्वम्। वृत्तेश्च स्वं प्रति स्वोपादानभूताविद्यानाशकत्वेनैवंरूपेण नाशकता स्वीक्रियते। उपादाननाशस्य कार्यनाशं प्रति हेतुत्वेनोपादाननाशकस्य तद्द्वारा उपादेयस्वनाशकता सम्भवत्येव।

अथवा वृत्तेः क्षणिकत्वमिष्टमेव। यतोऽन्त्या वृत्तिः स्वेतरसर्वद्वैतविरोधिनी। एवञ्च तदुत्तरं न किञ्चिदपि जायते। एवञ्च तदग्रकालस्यैवाभावेन तदनुवृत्त्यसम्भवेन एकक्षणवृत्तित्वमेव तस्या आवश्यकम्।

वृत्तिप्रतिबिम्बितचितः अविद्यानिवर्तकत्वपक्षेऽपि चैतन्यस्य नित्यस्यापि वृत्त्युपहितत्वरूपेण क्षणिकता सम्भवत्येव।

अथवा यथैव कार्यप्रागभावस्य कारणरूपता, यथा वा कार्यप्रागभावनिवृत्तेः कार्यरूपतालाघवात्, अङ्गीक्रियते, तथैव सर्वप्रपञ्चान्तर्गतवृत्तिं प्रत्यपि उपादानं यत् शुद्धात्मस्वरूपं तद्रूपत्वमेव वृत्तिनाशस्याङ्गीक्रियते। अत एव वृत्तेर्यत् प्रतिपन्नोपाधौ त्रैकालिकनिषेधप्रतियोगित्वं रूपं मिथ्यात्वं तत्र घटकीभूतः अभावः सत्य इत्यपि एकः पक्षः सिद्धावुक्तः। अतो वृत्तिनिवृत्तेः आत्मरूपत्वेन सत्यत्वात् तद्धेतुखण्डनमेवानुपपन्नम्।

यदप्युक्तमविद्यानिवर्तकनिवृत्तिगतस्य मिथ्यात्वस्य मिथ्यात्वे तद्गतसत्यत्वस्य पारमार्थिकत्वापत्तिरिति तदपि न युक्तम्। यतः पूर्वोक्तो नियमो विषमसत्ताकयोरेव विषये प्रवर्तते। न समसत्ताकविषये। अत एव एकस्यां गवि आरोपितयोः प्रातिभासिकयोः गजत्वमहिंषत्वयोर्मध्ये एकस्य मिथ्यात्वे नापरस्य सत्यत्वम्। समसत्ताकत्वे चैकबाधकबाध्यत्वम्, साधारणबाध्यतावच्छेदकधर्मवत्त्वं च प्रयोजकम्। प्रकृते च अविद्यानिवर्तक-निवृत्तौ यत्सत्यत्वं तस्य तद्गतमिथ्यात्वस्य च एकब्रह्मज्ञानबाध्यत्वेन ब्रह्मभिन्नत्वरूपैक-बाध्यतावच्छेदकधर्मवत्त्वेन च समसत्ताकत्वात्। नाविद्यानिवर्तकवृत्तिगतमिथ्यात्वस्य मिथ्यात्वे अविद्यानिवर्तकनिवृत्तेः पारमार्थिकत्वापत्तिरिति नाद्वैतहानिः।

यदप्युक्तं वृत्त्यज्ञानयोः समानाश्रयकत्वाभावेन न निवर्त्यनिवर्तकभाव इति, तदपि न। यतो विवरणमते वृत्त्यवच्छिन्नचैतन्यस्य वृत्त्याश्रयस्य अज्ञानाश्रये शुद्धे चैतन्ये कल्पितत्वेन तदभिन्नत्वात् समानाश्रयत्वं वृत्त्यज्ञानयोः सूपपादम्।

वाचस्पतिमते त्वज्ञानचैतन्ययोरुभयोरप्यनादित्वेनाज्ञानस्य स्वोपहितचैतन्यरूप-जीवाश्रितत्वेऽपि नोत्पत्तौ ज्ञप्तौ वाऽन्योन्याश्रय इति वृत्त्यज्ञानयोरुभयोरप्येकजीवाश्रितत्वेन समानाश्रयत्वं सुलभम्। स्वरूपज्ञानस्य हि स्वप्रकाशत्वं न स्ववेद्यत्वम्। अपि त्ववेद्यत्वे सत्यपरोक्षव्यवहारयोग्यत्वम्। अतोऽखण्डाकारवृत्तेरिव स्वरूपज्ञानस्याखण्डाकारस्व-विषयकत्वाभावेन न तदाकारवृत्तेरिवाज्ञाननिवर्तकता। किञ्च स्वप्रकाशज्ञानस्याज्ञानविरोधित्वादपि न तन्निवर्तकत्वम्।

अथवाऽविद्यानिवर्तकं ज्ञानं वृत्तिविषयत्वोपलक्षितचिद्रूपमेवेति तस्य सत्यत्वेन न निवर्तकखण्डनावकाशः। अत एव नाद्वैतहानिः। ब्रह्मव्यतिरिक्तद्वितीयवस्तुनोऽ-नङ्गीकारात्। इत्यविद्यानिवर्तकानुपपत्तिं द्वैत्याद्युद्भावितामद्वैतिनः परिहरन्ति।

अविद्यानिवृत्तिविषये द्वैत्याद्याक्षेपः

यदिदम् "अविद्यानिवृत्तिः मुक्तिः" इत्यद्वैतिनां वचनं तदयुक्तम्। अविद्यानिवृत्तिः किंरूपेति निर्वक्तुमशक्यत्वात्। तथा हि - न तावदविद्यानिवृत्तिः सत्या। यतस्तस्या ब्रह्मरूपत्वेनासाध्यत्वापत्त्या ज्ञानादिवैयर्थ्यम्। ब्रह्मभिन्नत्वे सत्यया तयाऽद्वैतहान्यापत्तिः।

नापि साऽसती। यतस्तथा सत्यविद्याया नित्यं सत्वापत्तिः। नापि सदसदात्मिका, विरोधात्। नापि सदसद्विलक्षणा। सदसद्विलक्षणप्रतियोगिकनिवृत्त्यात्मकत्वव्याघातात्। नापि पञ्चमप्रकारा। यतस्तथा सति "न सन्नासत् न सदसन् न चाप्यनुभयात्मकम्। चतुष्कोटिविनिर्मुक्तं शून्यमित्यभिधीयते॥" इत्युक्तरीत्या माध्यमिकमतप्रवेशापत्तिः।

न च चरमवृत्त्युपलक्षितात्मस्वरूपाऽविद्यानिवृत्तिः। उपलक्षणभूताया वृत्तेः साध्यतयैव मुक्तेरपि साध्यत्वेन न ज्ञानादिवैयर्थ्यमिति वाच्यम्। यत उपलक्षणसाध्यत्वेन मुक्तेः साध्यत्वमिवोपलक्षणनिवृत्त्या मुक्तेरपि निवृत्त्यापत्तौ न स पुनरावर्तते इति श्रुतिविरोधः। तथा वृत्त्युपलक्षितस्य पश्चादिव मोहकालेऽपि सत्त्वेन मुक्तामुक्तत्वव्यवस्था नोपपद्येत।

नाप्यविद्यानिवृत्तिस्तद्विरोधिवृत्तिरूपा। यतो वृत्तिनाशानन्तरकालेऽप्यनुवर्तमानाया अविद्यानिवृत्तेर्वृत्तिरूपत्वं नैव सम्भवति। किञ्चैकस्य तद्विरोधिरूपत्वप्रक्रिया अन्यत्र प्रसिद्धा उतेहैवाश्रीयते। नाद्यः। यतस्तथा सति बिम्बप्रतिबिम्बैक्यज्ञाननिवृत्तेः तदैक्यवृत्तिरूपायाः सत्त्वकाले कारणीभूताज्ञानाभावेन सोपाधिकभ्रमोऽनुभवसिद्धो न स्यात्। न द्वितीयः नियामकाभावात्। तस्मादविद्यानिवृत्तेः सत्त्वादिना निवर्क्तुमशक्यत्वेन नाविद्यानिवृत्तिर्मुक्तिरिति द्वैत्यादीनामाक्षेपः।

अद्वैतिमतेन पूर्वोक्ताक्षेपपरिहारः

अविद्यानिवृत्तिरेव मोक्षः। न च सा सत्त्वादिना निर्वक्तुमशक्या। सुनिर्वचत्वात्। तथा हि - अविद्यानिवृत्तिस्तावत्सती। सा च ब्रह्मरूपा सर्वाद्वैतपक्षे। यत उपादानस्य कपालादेः कार्यघटादिनाशरूपता लाघवादङ्गीक्रियते यथा, तथैव कार्यभूताविद्यानाशस्य विवर्तोपादानभूतब्रह्मरूपताऽङ्गीकर्तुं युक्ता। न च सिद्धब्रह्मरूपत्वेऽविद्यानिवृत्तेरसाध्यत्वापत्तिः। यतः सत्कार्यवादे पूर्वसिद्धकारणात्मकत्वेऽप्यविद्यानाशस्य साध्यत्वमुपपद्यत एव।

किञ्चाविद्यानाशः ध्वंसरूपोऽत्यन्ताभावरूपो वेति पक्षद्वयं प्राचीनैरुपपादितम्। तत्राद्यपक्षेऽविद्यानाशस्य ब्रह्मरूपता एवमुपपादनीया। यथैव ब्रह्मभिन्नत्वेनानित्यस्य घटध्वंसस्य ध्वंसेऽपि न घटस्य पुनरुन्मज्जनापत्तिः। घटध्वंसध्वंसस्यापि घटप्रतियोगिकत्वाङ्गीकारात्। एवमविद्यानाशरूपा या वृत्तिः तन्नाशरूपस्य ब्रह्मणः अविद्यानाशनाशात्मकस्याविद्याप्रतियोगिकनाशात्मकत्वमङ्गीक्रियते। तत्र परैः यथा घटादिकार्यस्य तद्विरोधिभूतघटादिप्रागभावनिवृत्तिरूपत्वमङ्गीक्रियते तथैव वृत्तेस्तद्विरोधिभूताऽविद्यानिवृत्तिरूपताऽङ्गीक्रियते। तमोवदावारिकाया अविद्याया आवरणंनिवर्तनसमर्थायाः तैजसान्तःकरणपरिणामभूतायाः वृत्तेश्च तमःप्रकाशवत् परस्परविरोधिता। तथा कार्यभूतघटादिनिवृत्तेः उपादानभूतकपालादिरूपत्ववत् कार्यभूतवृत्तेः योऽयं नाशः तस्य विवर्तोपादानभूतब्रह्मरूपताऽङ्गीक्रियते।

अविद्यानाशोऽत्यन्ताभावरूप इति द्वितीयपक्षे तु ब्रह्मण्यारोपिताया अविद्याया अभावः कालत्रयेऽपि वर्तते ब्रह्मणि। तस्याः प्रतिपन्नोपाधिनिष्ठत्रैकालिकात्यन्ताभाव-प्रतियोगित्वरूपमिथ्यात्ववत्त्वात् अभावस्याधिकरणात्मकत्वाङ्गीकारात् अविद्यात्यन्ताभावस्य ब्रह्मरूपता सुलभा। प्राभाकरमते घटसंसर्गदशायां यथा भूतलस्य न घटाभावरूपत्वेन प्रतीतिः प्रतिबन्धकवशादेवमविद्यारोपकाले नाविद्यात्यन्ताभावरूपत्वेन ब्रह्मणः प्रतीतिः।

भावाद्वैतपक्षे त्वविद्यानिवृत्तेः सत्यत्वेऽपि ब्रह्मभिन्नत्वेऽपि न क्षतिः। अविद्यानिवृत्तेः सत्यत्वप्रकारे यदिदं पक्षद्वयं ब्रह्माभिन्नत्वतद्भिन्नत्वरूपं तत्रोभयत्राप्यविद्यानिवृत्तेः साध्यत्वमभिव्यक्तिरूपमेव। एवञ्च ज्ञानादीनां तदभिव्यञ्जकत्वेन सार्थक्यान्न वैयर्थ्यम्। तथाऽविद्यानिवृत्तेरसत्त्वं सदसद्रूपत्वञ्चाङ्गीक्रियत इति तत्पक्षद्वयखण्डनमकाण्डताण्डवितमेव।

अथवाऽविद्यानिवृत्तिः सदसद्विलक्षणत्वेन मिथ्यारूपैव। न चाविद्यानिवृत्तेः सदसद्विलक्षणत्वे तत्प्रतियोगिभूतायाः अविद्यायाः सदसद्विलक्षणत्वानुपपत्तिरिति वाच्यम्। यतः परेषां मते सत्यभूतस्य घटाभावादेः प्रतियोगिभूता ये घटादयस्तेषां लोके सत्यत्वं दृश्यते। अतस्तद्वदत्राप्युपपद्यते।

अस्मिन्नपि पक्षे प्रकारद्वयं वर्तते। तत्राविद्यानिवृत्तिः वृत्तिरूपेत्याद्यः प्रकारः। यावद् वृत्तिसत्त्वमेवाविद्यानिवृत्तेः वृत्तिरूपत्वं स्वीक्रियते। न च वृत्तिनाशानन्तराविद्या-निवृत्तेरनुवृत्तिरावश्यकी। नो चेन्मुक्तेरनित्यत्वापत्तिः। ततश्च वृत्तिनाशानन्तरमनु-वृत्ताया अविद्यानिवृत्तेस्तद्रूपत्वं कथमिति वाच्यम्। यतो घटध्वंसध्वंसानन्तरं घटस्य पुनरुन्मज्जननिवृत्तये घटध्वंसध्वंसस्य घटप्रतियोगिकत्वं यथा ध्वंसनित्यत्ववादिभि-रङ्गीक्रियते, तथैवाविद्यानिवृत्त्यात्मकवृत्तिप्रतियोगिकनाशस्याविद्याप्रतियोगिकनाश-त्वाङ्गीकारेण वृत्तिनाशस्याधिकरणीभूतब्रह्मरूपत्वाङ्गीकारेण च न मोक्षानित्यत्वप्रसङ्गः। एवञ्च वृत्तिसत्वपर्यन्तमेव वृत्तिरूपत्वं, तदूर्ध्वं अधिकरणरूपत्वञ्चाङ्गीकृतमविद्यानिवृत्तेरिति न कश्चिद्दोषः। अयञ्च प्रकारोऽन्यत्र दृष्ट एव। अत एव नव्यतार्किकैः संयोगनाशस्य स्वजनकविभागरूपता विभागसत्त्वं यावदङ्गीकृता। विभागनाशस्य संयोगनाशात्मक-विभागप्रतियोगिकस्य संयोगप्रतियोगिकनाशत्वं ततो विभागनाशस्य स्वाश्रयपर-माण्वादिरूपत्वञ्चाङ्गीकृतम्।

सोपाधिकभ्रमस्थल उपाधिविरहकालीनबिम्बप्रतिबिम्बैक्यवृत्तेरेव तदैक्याज्ञान-निवृत्तिरूपता स्वीक्रियते। एवञ्चोपाधिसत्त्वकाले बिम्बप्रतिबिम्बैक्यवृत्तेस्तदैक्याज्ञान-निवृत्तिरूपत्वाभावेनाज्ञानानुवृत्तौ बाधकाभावेन न सोपाधिकभ्रमोऽनुभवसिद्धोऽनुपपन्नः। वस्तुतस्त्वन्यत्राप्रसिद्धावप्यत्र सप्रकारः प्रमाणबलादाश्रयणीयः। तच्च प्रमाणं "नेति नेति", इति श्रुतिरेव। इयञ्च श्रुतिः स्वविषयतदिरब्रह्मभिन्नस्वमिथ्यात्वबोधिका।

अस्मिन्पक्षे वृत्तेरखण्डाकारायाः श्रवणादिसाध्यत्वेन न श्रवणादीनां वैयर्थ्यम्। अथवा चरमवृत्त्युपलक्षित आत्माऽविद्यानिवृत्तिः। अत एवाभियुक्तैरेवमुक्तम् - "निवृत्तिरात्मा मोहस्य ज्ञानत्वेनोपलक्षित" इति। तत्र पूर्वमसिद्धायाश्चरमवृत्तेरुपलक्षणत्वायोगान्न मोहकालेऽप्यविद्यानिवृत्त्यापत्तिः, तथोपलक्ष्यस्याकाशस्यासाध्यत्वेऽप्युपलक्षणघटस्य साध्यतामादायैव घटाकाशस्य साध्यत्वमिवाऽऽत्मन उपलक्ष्यस्यासाध्यत्वेऽपि वृत्तेरुपलक्षणभूतायाः साध्यत्वमादायैव वृत्त्युपलक्षितात्मनः साध्यत्वमुपपद्यते। तथा पाकनिवृत्तावपि पाचकानिवृत्तिदर्शनादुपलक्षणीभूताया वृत्तेः निवृत्तावप्युपलक्ष्यस्यानिवृत्तेः न मुक्तेरनित्यत्वापत्तिः।

अथवा सत्त्वासत्त्व-सदसत्त्व-सदसद्विलक्षणत्वरूपचतुष्कोटिविनिर्मुक्ता पञ्चमप्रकारैवाविद्यानिवृत्तिः। अयञ्च पक्ष इष्टसिद्धिकारैरभिहितः। तत्र हीष्टसिद्धौ "न साऽध्यस्ता नापि सत्या किन्तु सत्-असत्-सदसत्-अनिर्वाच्यभिन्ना पञ्चमप्रकाराऽविद्यानिवृत्तिः" इति।

एतत्पक्षवादिनामयमाशयः - न तावदविद्यानिवृत्तिः सती, अद्वैतहानेः। नाप्यसती, अविद्याया नित्यं सत्त्वापत्तेः। नापि सदसती, विरोधात्। नापि सदसद्विलक्षणा, सदसद्विलक्षणत्वेऽविद्याकार्यत्वापत्तेः। न चेष्टापत्तिः, यतस्तथा सत्यविद्यानिवृत्तेः स्वप्रतियोगिजन्यत्वानुपपत्तेरविद्यान्तरजन्यत्वमेव वक्तव्यम्। तथा अविद्यान्तरनिवृत्तेरप्युपादानतयाऽविद्यान्तरमङ्गीकार्यमित्येवमनवस्था प्रसज्येत। अतः पञ्चमः प्रकार एव तस्या अङ्गीकार्यः। न चास्मिन्पक्षेऽविद्याकार्यत्वाभावेन ब्रह्मज्ञाननिवर्त्यत्वासम्भवेनाविद्यानिवृत्तेः ब्रह्मवत्सदाऽनुवृत्त्यापत्त्याऽद्वैतहान्यापत्तिरिति वाच्यम्।

यतोऽस्मिन्पक्षेऽविद्यानिवृत्तौ सदसद्विलक्षणत्वरूपस्य ज्ञाननिवर्त्यत्वरूपस्य वा मिथ्यात्वस्यासम्भवेऽपि सदसद्विविक्तत्वरूपं, प्रतिपन्नोपाधौ त्रैकालिकनिषेध प्रतियोगित्वरूपं वा मिथ्यात्वमविद्यानिवृत्तेः सम्भवतीति तस्या अनुवृत्तावपि सत्यभूतद्वितीयवस्तुनोऽननुवृत्त्या नाद्वैतहान्यापत्तिः। न च शून्यत्वापत्तिः, प्रमाणाभावात्। न च तत्र सदसद्विलक्षणत्वादिहेतुकमनुमानं प्रमाणम्। तथा हि - अविद्यानिवृत्तिपक्षकशून्यत्वसाध कानुमितौ सद्विलक्षणत्वादयश्चत्वारः प्रत्येकं हेतवो वा उत मिलिता वा? नाद्यः। तथा हि - शून्यत्वाभावेऽपि मिथ्यात्वेऽपि घटादिवत्सद्विलक्षणत्वोपपत्तेः सद्विलक्षणत्वमप्रयोजकम्। पक्ष एव व्यभिचारात्। तथा शून्यत्वाभावेऽपि सत्यत्वे ब्रह्मवदसद्विलक्षणत्वोपपत्तेरसद्विलक्षणत्वमप्यप्रयोजकम्। ब्रह्मणि व्यभिचरितश्च। सदसद्विलक्षणत्वमपि शून्यत्त्वाभावेऽपि मिथ्यात्वेऽपि घटादिवदुपपद्यत इति तदप्यप्रयोजकम्। तत्रैव व्यभिचरितश्च। नापि मिलितानां तत्र हेतुत्वम्। यतः दसद्विलक्षणत्वस्य सदसद्विलक्षणत्वेन सह सामानाधिकरण्यं विरुद्धत्वान्न सम्भवति। अतः पक्षे हेतोरभावेनासिद्धिः स्यात्। अत एव सदसद्विलक्षणत्वाद्यनुपपत्तिरपि तत्र न प्रमाणम्।

तस्मात्सद्रूपा सदसद्विलक्षणा पञ्चमप्रकारा वाऽविद्यानिवृत्तिः। तस्मादविद्यानिवृत्तिः किंरूपेति निवर्तुं शक्यत्वादविद्यानिवृत्तिः मुक्तिरित्यद्वैतिनां मतं समीचीनतममेवेति॥

ध्यायन् ध्यायन् गणाध्यक्षं स्मारं स्मारं गुरोर्वचः।
धीमद्वेङ्कटरामेण व्यासोऽयं प्रवितन्यते॥

Summary: In this paper, Professor J. Venkatarama Sastri argues out a case for maya-avidya by refuting Rāmānuja's last two objections. Rāmānuja in the sixth objection called *Nivartaka-anupapatti*, maintains that the Advaita explanation of the removability of avidyā is untenable. According to Advaita, avidyā, though beginningless (*anādi*), has an end. What is required for the removal of avidyā is the knowledge of Brahman as *nirviśeṣa*.

For Rāmānuja, even in *nirvikalpaka-pratyakṣa*, the object is perceived as a differentiated entity. He shows that there is no justification for the claim that the object of *nirvikalpaka-pratyakṣa* is an undifferentiated one whereas that of *savikalpaka-pratyakṣa* is differentiated. In both, we perceive only a differentiated object. Further, the object known through inference is bound to be a differentiated one. Then Rāmānuja moves on to show that even the object known through *śabda* is *saviśeṣa.* A sentence conveys a differentiated sense and this is true of both scriptural and secular sentences.

The Advaitin claims that perception also reveals the existence of *nirviśeṣa-vastu.* He cites the case of deep-sleep as the evidence for Brahman-Ātman being *nirviśeṣa.* A person who recollects his deep sleep experience says that he was not aware of anything, subjective or objective, and that he was not aware of even himself. Recollection presupposes the prior experience of what is recollected. What is experienced in deep sleep is the bare Self or consciousness devoid of distinctions. By its very nature, Brahman-Ātman is *nirviśeṣa*, but it appears to be *saviśeṣa* because of the adjunct, i.e. mind and the senses, with which it is associated in the waking and dream states.

Rāmānuja argues that *śabda* by its very nature conveys only the knowledge of a differentiated entity a relational meaning (*viśiṣṭārtha*). There is no rule, Advaitin says, that the purport of a sentence must always be in a relational sense (*saṁsṛṣṭārtha* or *viśiṣṭārtha*). Further, while the sentence "This flower is red" conveys a relational sense, the sentence "This is that Devadatta" conveys a non-relational sense, i.e. the sense of identity because that is the intended meaning. Hence avidyā becomes removable by knowledge as envisaged by Advaitin.

The last major objection called *nivṛttyanupapatti* brings out the difficulties as seen by Rāmānuja in the Advaita explanation of the attainment of *mukti*. He argues that the Advaitin develops his theory on the false assumption that bondage is unreal, something false (*mithyā*), avidyā being the cause of bondage. Since avidyā is mithyā, bondage cannot but be mithyā. So the Advaitin says that all that is required for the removal of bondage is knowledge of Brahman-Ātman. This entire argument is fallacious according to Rāmānuja. He says that bondage which consists of the experience of pleasure and pain arising from the connection of the self with bodies of various kinds cannot be dismissed as unreal since it is real (*paramārtha*). This real thing cannot be removed by knowledge. Hence bondage is destroyed only through the grace of the Lord and it is obtained only by *bhakti* or *upāsanā*.

Secondly, the solution suggested by the Advaitin is like a remedy which aggravates the disease instead of curing it. The Advaitin says that the knowledge of the oneness of reality removes bondage. This is nothing but a wish because the alleged knowledge of the oneness of reality (*aikya-jñāna*) is itself false. When the supreme reality is *saviśeṣa*, to think of it as *nirviśeṣa* is false exactly like thinking of identity of jīva and Brahman which is not there. Such false knowledge will only strengthen the knot of bondage and not destroy it.

There is another difficulty. What is the ontological status of the "bondage-terminating" knowledge (*nivartaka-jñāna*)? Since everything other than Brahman is mithyā, the Advaitin holds this saving knowledge also to be mithyā. But, if it is mithyā, it must also be removed and this can be done only by searching for another knowledge which, again, also must be removed. Thus the search ends in infinite regress (*anavasthā*). We have, therefore, to tackle the problem of the removal of bondage in an entirely different way, and not in the way suggested by the Advaitin.

To Advaita, the distinction between *vyāvahārika* and *pāramārthika* is important. In fact, the distinction between Nirguṇa-Brahman and Saguṇa-Brahman, the distinction between Brahman and jīva, the distinction between Īśvara and jīva—all these distinctions which are due to māyā-avidyā are meaningful only on the basis of the distinction between *vyāvahārika* and *pāramārthika*. If bondage were to be real, then it could not be removed because what is real is eternal and what is eternal can never be removed. So all the objections which Rāmānuja brings in under *nivṛttyanupapatti* need to be viewed in the context of the distinction between *vyāvahārika* and *pāramārthika*; and this distinction has been worked out on the basis of *adhyāsa*. A critic like Rāmānuja who refuses to accept the theory of *adhyāsa* with all the consequences arising therefrom functions in an entirely different framework; and so his criticisms of Advaita are intelligible only when viewed from the perspective of his framework. According to Advaita, there is only one absolute entity and that is Brahman, which is knowledge *per se*. Once that knowledge arises through (*akhaṇḍākāra-vṛtti-jñāna*) there is no question of the existence of any avidyā. Once avidya is removed, its product, *viz*., bondage is also removed and that accounts for the state of liberation.

18

श्रीभाष्यगतमायावादखण्डनोपरि रामरायदुरुक्तीनां परिशीलनम्

S.N.C. Raghunathacharyulu

युग्मम्-

श्लो - (1) मायया भवति कल्पितं जगत् ब्रह्मणीति कथयन्ति मायिनः।
आश्रयाद्यनुपपत्तिमत्र यां - प्राह लक्ष्मणमुनिर्दुरुद्धराम्॥

(2) तां विमोचयितुमादृतश्रमैः - प्रापि हन्त ! न परैः कृतार्थता।
तत्त्वमन्यथयितुं न हीशते - यत्नतोपि भुवि वक्रबुद्धयः॥

जगत्कारणतया श्रुत्यनुसारेणैव सेश्वरसाङ्ख्ययोगदर्शनयोः अद्वैतभिन्नेषु वेदान्तदर्शनेष्वपि या त्रिगुणात्मिका मूलप्रकृतिः नित्या ब्रह्मशक्तित्वेन स्वीकृता, सैव अद्वैतिभिः मायापदेन अनिर्वचनीयाविद्याज्ञानादिपदैश्च व्यवह्रियमाणा मिथ्यात्वेन परिगण्यत इति स्थितम्।चिद्रूपब्रह्मण एव अद्वितीयतां परमार्थतां च यदमी निर्धारयन्ति अत एव तैः मिथ्यात्वमिष्यते तस्याः। अत्र च आरम्भणाधिकरणानुमानिकाधिकरणादिविवरणस्थले तत्तदुपनिषद्विवरणावसरे च शङ्करभाष्यवाक्यानि बहूनि प्रमाणम्। तत्र तां मायाविद्यादिशब्दवत् मूलप्रकृतित्वेन त्रिगुणात्मकत्वेनापि व्यपदिश्य, स्वस्मिन् प्रधानकारणवादाङ्गीकारापत्तिव्यावृत्तये "तदधीनत्वादर्थवत्" इत्यादिसूत्रविवरणसन्दर्भेषु तैरेव तस्याः ब्रह्मांशभूततदधीनसूक्ष्मशक्तिविशेषत्वं च प्रतिपाद्यते।

यथा - आनुमानिकाधिकरणे - "अविद्यात्मिका हि बीजशक्तिः अव्यक्तशब्दनिर्देश्या परमेश्वराश्रया मायामयी महासुषुप्तिः। यस्यां स्वरूपप्रतिबोधरहिताः शेरते संसारिणो जीवाः। तदेतदव्यक्तं क्वचिदाकाशशब्दनिर्दिष्टम्। ...क्वचिदक्षरशब्दोदितं, ...क्वचिन्मायेति सूचितम्। अव्यक्ता हि सा माया। तत्त्वान्यत्वनिरूपणस्य अशक्यत्वात्" इति। आरम्भणाधिकरणे - "सर्वज्ञस्येश्वरस्य आत्मभूते इव अविद्याकल्पिते नामरूपे तत्त्वान्यत्वाभ्यां अनिर्वचनीये संसारप्रपञ्चबीजभूते, सर्वज्ञस्येश्वरस्य माया शक्तिः प्रकृतिः इति च श्रुति-

स्मृत्योरभिलप्येते" इति ॥ उपदेशसाहस्रीग्रन्थे - "स्वात्मविलक्षणयोः नामरूपयोः जगद्बीज-भूतयोः स्वात्मस्थयोः तत्त्वान्यत्वाभ्यां अनिरूपणीययोः स्वसंवेद्ययोः सद्भावमात्रेण, अचिन्त्यशक्तित्वात् व्याकर्ता अव्याकृतयोः" इत्यादि। एवं साङ्ख्याभिमतत्रिगुणा-त्मकाव्यक्तपदवाच्यप्रकृतिसाम्यमेव सर्वथा ब्रुवन्तोऽपि ततोऽन्यतामेव अस्या मायायाः प्रतिपादयन्ति "मायिनो महेश्वरस्य परमात्मनः आत्मभूताम् अस्वतन्त्रां, न साङ्ख्य-परिकल्पितप्रधानादिवत् पृथग्भूतां स्वतन्त्रां शक्तिम्" इति श्वेताश्वतरे प्रथमे अध्याये तृतीये मन्त्रे "देवात्मशक्तिम्" इत्यत्र। तथा आनुमानिकाधिकरण एव पूर्वोदाहृतवाक्य-शकलात्पूर्वं "यदि वयं स्वतन्त्रां काञ्चित् प्रागवस्थां जगतः कारणत्वेन अभ्युपगच्छेम, प्रसञ्जयेम तदा प्रधानकारणवादम्। परमेश्वराधीना तु इयमस्माभिरभ्युपगम्यते - न स्वतन्त्रा" इत्यत्र च।

गौडपादाचार्ये गौरवं बिभ्रता श्रीशङ्करेण यदा तत्कारिकाश्च व्याख्याताः, तदा बौद्धसगन्धितया तदभिमतमपि जगन्मिथ्यात्वं तदिष्टमभूत्। सुवर्णानुलिप्तशङ्खवत् श्रोत्रियैरबहिष्कार्यत्वाय तन्मतं वैदिकत्वेन कञ्चुकितं चाभूत्। तन्मतस्य अद्वैतपदं न द्वितीयजडप्रपञ्चमिथ्यात्वस्वीकारमात्रेण। किन्तर्हि! ब्रह्मण एव मायामयजगदनुप्रवेशेन नानाजीवरूपताप्राप्त्या, जीवाश्च न स्वरूपतो ब्रह्मणो भिन्ना इति जीवब्रह्मभेदनिर्धारणा-दपि सङ्गच्छते। एवं निर्विशेषब्रह्मकारणतास्वीकारेण आत्मनि वैदिकतां प्रकटयद्भिरेव अद्वैतिभिः सौगतसौहार्दं च अजिहासद्भिः जगन्मिथ्यात्वसाधने प्रयस्यद्भिः त्रिगुणात्मिका मूलप्रकृतिरपि बौद्धाभिमतमायास्थाने निवेशिता। श्रुतिस्मृतिष्वपि मूलप्रकृतिरेव मायापदेनापि निर्दिष्टेति हेतुना मिथ्याभूतप्रपञ्चहेतुस्सापि ऐन्द्रजालिकमायावत् मिथ्याभूतैवेति निरधारि। एवमेतैः सगुणं ब्रह्म निर्विशेषतां गमितम्। प्रत्यक्षप्रपञ्चोऽपि मिथ्यात्वं नीतः। मिथ्या-जगत्प्रतिभासहेतुतया मूलप्रकृतिरपि ऐन्द्रजालिकमायात्वं प्रापिता।

एवमेतत्कृतं संक्षोभं अमृष्यमाणाः भास्कर-रामानुज-पूर्णप्रज्ञ-वल्लभाचार्याद्याः एतत्खण्डने प्रबलयुक्तीः प्रदर्श्य प्रावर्तन्त स्वभाष्येषु। श्रीवैष्णवाचार्याः नाथयामुन-मुनिप्रभृतयोऽपि न्यायतत्वसिद्धित्रयादिषु एतन्निरसने पराक्रमन्त। विशिष्य श्रीभाष्ये सप्तविधानुपपत्तिप्रदर्शनेन अनिर्वचनीयमायापदार्थो निर्धूतः।

तत्र कैश्चित् प्राचीनैः श्रुतिस्मृतिवाक्यानामपि अनिर्वचनीयमायासद्भावे प्रमाण-तया व्याख्याने कृते, विवरणकारादिभिः प्रत्यक्षानुमानाभ्यामपि तत्प्रसाधनाय प्रयतितम्। यानि तत्प्रमाणितानि श्रुतिस्मृतिवाक्यानि, तेषु नैकमपि तत्प्रसाधकमिति श्रीभाष्ये विपुलं विमृष्टम्। तदुक्तयुक्तयोऽपि आश्रयतिरोधानस्वरूपाद्यनुपपत्तिभिः परास्ताः।

परगोष्ठयाम् एतन्मध्यकाले प्रबलपण्डितत्वेन अपरशङ्कराचार्यत्वेन च प्रचारपथं नीतः बेल्लंकोण्ड रामरायः श्रीभाष्यखण्डनापदेशेन स्वकृते शङ्कराशङ्करभाष्यविमर्शग्रन्थे यदलेखीत्, संक्षेपतः तत्परिम्रष्टुं सम्प्रति अयमस्मदारम्भः।

"अनृतेन हि प्रत्यूढाः", "नासदासीत् नो सदासीत् तदानीं तम आसीत्", "अस्मान्मायी सृजते विश्वमेतत्, तस्मिंश्चान्यो मायया सन्निरुद्धः", "मायां तु प्रकृतिं विद्यात्" इत्यादिकं हि श्रुतिवाक्यजातं परैः प्रमाणितम्। इदं विवृणुमः॥

अनृतेन हि प्रत्यूढाः

(1) छान्दोग्ये हि एतत्पूर्ववाक्यानि एवं सन्ति - यथा - "...अत्र ह्यस्य एते सत्याः कामाः अनृतापिधानाः। तद्यथा हिरण्यनिधिं निहितम् अक्षेत्रज्ञाः उपर्युपरि सञ्चरन्तो न विन्देयुः। एवमेवेमाः सर्वाः प्रजाः अहरहर्गच्छन्त्यः एतं ब्रह्मलोकं न विन्दन्ति। अनृतेन हि प्रत्यूढाः"- इति।

अत्र हि सत्याः कामाः अधिकारिणा लिप्सिताः। तेषां अन्तस्स्थानतया अत्रेति पदेन दहराकाशोक्तिः। तस्यैव अनृतपदार्थेन पिधाने सति, तन्निष्ठकामानामपि पिधानं अर्थात्सिद्धम्। एवं अनृतेन पिधानादेव कामानाम् ईप्सितानामलाभः। अलाभे दृष्टान्तो हिरण्यनिधिवाक्योदितः। तद्वत्, न केवलं मुमुक्षुरुपासकः, किन्तु सर्वा अपि प्रजाः नित्यं सुषुप्तिकाले स्वदहराकाशस्योपरि सञ्चरन्त्योऽपि एतं ब्रह्मलोकशब्दितं दहराकाशं न विन्दन्त्येव तदुपासनरूप प्रबलप्रयत्नविरहात्। यतो ह्येताः सर्वा अपि प्रजाः अनृत पदार्थेन प्रत्यूढाः। इति प्रकरणार्थः।

अत्रैवं शाङ्करं विवरणं तद्भाष्ये। "अनृतं - बाह्यविषयेषु स्त्र्यन्नभोजनादिषु तृष्णा। तन्निमित्तं च स्वेच्छाप्रचारत्वम् मिथ्याज्ञाननिमित्तत्वात् अनृतमित्युच्यते। तन्निमित्तं सत्यानां कामानाम् अप्राप्तिरेव अपिधानशब्दार्थः।" इति, "... प्रत्यूढाः - अविद्यादिदोषैः आत्मस्वरूपाद्बहिः आकृष्टा इत्यर्थः" इति च॥ - अस्मात् शङ्करभाष्यात्, ऋतपदस्य सत्यार्थकत्वेन अनृतपदमिदं मिथ्याज्ञानं वदत् तत्कार्यं च बाह्यभोगतृष्णाप्रवृत्त्यादिकं बोधयतीति सिद्धम्। सर्वप्रजासाधारणं च इदमनृतमिति "अविद्यावत्यः इमाः सर्वाः प्रजाः.." इति तद्भाष्योक्त्यैव लब्धम्। एतेन इदं वाक्यं जगत्कारणीभूतब्रह्माश्रयमहामाया-शब्दवाच्यानिर्वचनीयपदार्थवाचकतया न भगवत्पादैः व्याख्यातमिति स्पष्टम्। किन्तु तदानन्तरिकैः विवरणकारादिभिरेव इदं वाक्यं मिथ्याभूतमहामायासद्भावे प्रमाणतया उदाहरद्भिः, "प्रत्यूढाः" इतिबहुवचनं पाशाधिकरणन्यायेन अविवक्षितमिति कृत्वा, ब्रह्मैव अनृतेन प्रत्यूढम् - आवृतम् - इति व्याख्यातमपार्थकम्॥

अत्र श्रीभाष्यगतिः अन्यादृशी। प्रकृतवाक्ये अनृतपदार्थस्य ब्रह्मलोकप्राप्ति प्रतिबन्धकता हि श्रूयते। तेन ब्रह्मप्राप्तेः हेतुः अनृतभिन्नं ऋतमेव किञ्चिदिति व्यज्यते। तच्च ऋतं भगवदाराधनरूपं कर्मेति "स्वकर्मणा तमभ्यर्च्य सिद्धिं विन्दति..." इति गीतास्मृत्या प्रसिद्धमेव। भगवदाराधकं च तत् कर्म फलसङ्गरहितमेवेत्यपि तत एव स्मृत्यावगतम्। न च ऋतशब्दः कर्मवाचितया न दृष्ट इति शंक्यम्। "ऋतं पिबन्तौ..." इति श्रुत्यन्तरे ऋतशब्दस्य कर्मसामान्यवाचितया प्रयोगात्। तथा "पुण्यस्य कर्मणो दूराद् गन्धो वाती" ति पुण्यं पूर्ववाक्येन प्रशस्य, तदुत्तरवाक्येन श्रुतावेव "अनृतादात्मानं जुगुप्सेत्" इति पुण्यप्रतियोगिनि पापे अनृतशब्दप्रयोगाच्च। अतः "अनृतेन हि प्रत्यूढाः" इत्यत्रापि भगवत्प्राप्तिविरोधिवाचि इदं अनृतपदं पापवाच्येवेति युक्तं ग्रहीतुम्। न तु क्वचिदपि विशिष्यानृतपदं अनिर्वचनीयतया भवदभिमतमहामायावाचकत्वेन प्रयुक्तं पश्यामः इति।

एतेन ऋतपदस्य सत्यार्थकत्वं प्रदर्श्यैव परेणापि कर्मफलवाचिता "ऋतं पिबन्तौ" इत्यत्र प्रतिपादनीयेति स्थितेः, तत एव प्रकृतानृतपदस्य सत्यभिन्नवाचिनः मिथ्याज्ञानवाचकतायाः स्वीकरणीयत्वाच्च, ततोऽपि वरं "अनृतादात्मानं जुगुप्सेत्" इति स्पष्टश्रुत्यन्तरोदितस्य आत्मप्राप्तिविरोधिनः पापकर्मण एव प्रकृतेऽपि वाक्ये अनृतपदेन ग्रहणमिति सिद्धम्।

एवं सोपपत्तिके श्रीभाष्योक्तार्थे सति, असूयुना रामरायकविना 338 पुटे शङ्कराशङ्करभाष्यविमर्शग्रन्थे यद्यदुक्तं, तत्तस्य अव्यवस्थितचित्तत्वमात्रद्योतकमेवेति प्राज्ञाः तद्ग्रन्थदर्शिनोऽवगच्छेयुः। तथा हि - "वितथं त्वनृतं वचः" इति, "सत्यं तथ्यम् ऋतं सम्यक्" इति च अमरकोशात् ऋतानृतशब्दौ सत्यमिथ्यावाचिनावेव। "सत्यमेव जयते, नानृतं" इति श्रुत्यन्तरं च अत्रोपष्टम्भकम्। अतः प्रकृते अनृतपदं मिथ्यार्थकं सत् मिथ्याज्ञानेन प्रत्यूढत्वात् न ब्रह्म विन्दतीत्येव बोधयति। न तु रामानुजोक्तरीत्या भगवत्प्राप्तिविरोधि पापकर्मवाचकम्। तस्यापि कर्मणः तत्फलस्य च अवश्यमनुभोक्तव्यत्वेन सत्यत्वात् न अनृतपदवाच्यता समस्ति" इति कोलाहलं कुर्वाण एवासौ रामरायः अनुपदमेव यदाह - "यद्यपि ऋतशब्दः सत्यवाची, तथापि न तस्येह "ऋतं पिबन्तौ" इत्यत्र ग्रहणं, अनन्वयात्। किन्तु "ऋ गतौ" इति धातोः निष्पन्नोऽयं ऋतशब्दः सुकृतस्य फलं वदति। ऋतं नाम प्राप्तं फलमित्यर्थः" इति। एतद्धि स्वेनैव पूर्वोक्तस्य विरुद्धत्वात् व्याहतम्।

अपरां च व्याहतिं पश्यत। उक्तकोशानुसारेण अनृतपदं मिथ्याभूताज्ञानवाच्येवेति यत् निष्कृष्य प्राह - तदेव च अज्ञानं पुनः एतत्पुटान्तिमपंक्तौ "न च अज्ञानम्

अवस्त्वेवेति वाच्यम्। वस्तुतः अवस्तुत्वेऽपि यावद्व्यवहारं सत्यत्वेन वस्त्वेवेति" सत्यपदेन निर्दिशति। एवमेव यावद्व्यवहारं सत्यस्य कर्मफलस्यापि व्यावहारिक-सत्यमायावदेव अनृतपदेनापि व्यवहारः सङ्गच्छत एवेति सिद्धेः, "अनृतपदं तु न काम्यकर्मणः तत्फलस्य वा सत्यस्य वाचि" इति स्वीयशपथोक्तिः त्यज्यतामेतेन।

(2) "अस्मान्मायी सृजते विश्वमेतत् - तस्मिंश्चान्यो मायया सन्निरुद्धः" "मायां तु प्रकृतिं विद्यात् मायिनं तु महेश्वरम्" "इन्द्रो मायाभिः पुरुरूप ईयते" - इत्यादिश्रुतिवाक्येषु प्रयुक्तमायापदं भगवदधीनप्रकृतिपरमेव। न तु अनिर्वचनीयमिथ्याभूताज्ञानपरमिति श्रीभाष्यम्।

श्वेताश्वतरे चतुर्थे अध्याये बहुषु मन्त्रेषु मायाकृतमेव सृष्ट्यादिकं इति, तस्याः ब्रह्माश्रयत्वमिति, ब्रह्मणोऽन्य एव तु त्रिगुणात्मिकया तया बद्धो मुह्यतीति च स्पष्टमुच्यते। अथापि सर्वत्र स्वाभिमतजीवब्रह्माभेदवादं जगन्मिथ्यात्वं च समर्थयितुं तानि श्रुतिवाक्यानि अनपेक्षितशब्दानध्याहारादिना संयोज्य विपरीतं व्याख्यायन्ते श्रीशङ्कराचार्येण इति प्राज्ञैः एतद्भाष्ये सुग्रहम्। तथा हि - इयं श्रुतिः - मायी (मायाश्रयः) परमात्मेति, अन्यपदेन तस्मादन्यः जीव एव तेन सृष्टे विश्वस्मिन् प्रपञ्चे निरुद्ध इति स्पष्टमेवाह। अथापि अत्र "स्वमायया कल्पिते तस्मिन् भूतादिप्रपञ्चे माययैव अन्य इव सन्निरुद्धः - सम्बद्धः अविद्यावशगो भूत्वा संसारसमुद्रे भ्रमतीत्यर्थः" - इति शङ्कराचार्यकृतं व्याख्यानम्। "अन्यः इव" इति इव शब्दो हि न मूले मन्त्रगतः। किमर्थं तस्यात्र संयोजनम्? यो मायी सृजति, स एव अविद्यायाः तस्याः वशगो भूत्वा संसारसमुद्रे मज्जतीति सर्वं कल्पनं शङ्कराचार्यस्यैव इदम्। न मूले स्थितम्। एतत् स्पष्टमन्यपदप्रयोगात्। एवमेव "अंशो नानाव्यपदेशात्" इति सूत्रेऽपि "अंश इव अंशः, जीवः। न साक्षादंशो जीवः। किन्तु स एव सः" - इति सूत्रे अदृष्टं इव पदं अध्याहृत्य व्याख्यायते। एष हि विप्रलम्भकत्वमहिमा अद्वैताचार्यस्य, "ममैवायं अर्थराशि" रिति प्रगल्भं प्रलपतो भटैः निरुद्धस्य पश्यतो हरस्येव। अथैतदनन्तरमन्त्रेऽपि -

मायां तु प्रकृतिं विद्यात् मायिनं तु महेश्वरम्।
तस्यावयवभूतैस्तु व्याप्तं सर्वमिदं जगत्॥

इत्यस्मिन् यच्छङ्करोक्तं, तदपि सर्वं स्वाभिमताध्याहृतपदान्तरयोजनेन विपरीतार्थ-कल्पनमेव। "महांश्चासौ ईश्वरश्चेति महेश्वरः। तं मायिनं - मायायाः सत्तास्फूर्त्यादिप्रदं, तथा अधिष्ठानत्वेन प्रेरयितारमेव विद्यात्। तस्य प्रकृतस्य परमेश्वरस्य रज्ज्वाद्यधि-ष्ठानेषु कल्पितसर्पादिस्थानीयैः मायिकैः स्वावयवैः (जीवैः) अध्यासद्वारा इदं सर्वं

जगद्व्याप्त" मिति तत्र शङ्करोक्तिः। रज्ज्वाद्यधिष्ठानसर्पस्थानीयतां जीवानां स्वेनैव अत्रारोप्य मन्त्रो व्याख्यायते। योऽत्र महेश्वरत्वेन मायायाः सत्तास्फूर्त्यादिप्रदत्वेन प्रेरकत्वेन उच्यते, स एव रज्जुसर्पस्थानीयः अविद्यावशगः संसारसमुद्रे बम्भ्रमीति - इति पूर्वमन्त्रे प्रत्यपादि इति - अहो! व्याख्यानवैभवम्।

"प्रजाः प्रजाः स्वा इव तन्त्रयित्वा" रामो राज्यं पालयतीति वाक्यमेकं गृह्यताम्। अद्वैती पौराणिकोऽत्र व्याख्याति स्म एवम् - "रामः प्रजाः स्वप्रजावत् स्वसन्ततिवत् पालयति। "आत्मा वै पुत्रनामासि" इति श्रुत्या पुत्रो यथा पित्रा अभिन्नः, तथा प्रजाश्च सर्वाः रामेण अभिन्ना एव। "अन्ता राममयं" इति रामदासोक्तेश्च। ब्रह्मातिरिक्तस्य जगतो मिथ्यात्वाच्च" इत्यनर्गलम्। अहो! शास्त्रिणः पौराणिकस्य वेदान्तविज्ञानमिति श्रोतृसमाजोऽपि समजप्रायः श्लाघते। कलेः प्रभावात् युक्तं ह्येतत्॥

ईदृशशङ्करोक्तीनां प्रत्याख्यानपरे श्रीभाष्ये, मायापदं नानिर्वचनीयमिथ्यावाचीति, तथा प्रयोगोऽपि न लोकवेदयोः क्वचिदिति निरूप्य, आसुरराक्षसास्त्रादिषु सत्येष्वेव मायाशब्दप्रयोगो निदर्शितः।

तेन मायासहस्रं तत् शम्बरस्याशुगामिना।
बालस्य रक्षता देहं एकैकश्येन सूदितम्॥

इति। तथा शतदूषण्यां श्रीवेदान्तदेशिकैः "जनकस्य कुले जाता देवमायेव निर्मिता" इति प्रयोगान्तरमपि निदर्शितम्। विचित्रार्थसर्गकरत्वरूपप्रवृत्तिनिमित्तेन त्रिगुणप्रकृतिरेव मायापदवाच्येति च।

एतदुपरि व्यर्थप्रलापिना सर्वमिथ्यात्वजपं पौनःपुन्येन कुर्वता रामरायेण स्वग्रन्थे प्रोक्तं सर्वमेव परिहास्यम्। तदेवम् - 338 पुटान्ते 339 पुटे च तल्लिखितं - यथा "न च प्रकृतिर्मायैव - "मायां तु प्रकृतिं विद्यात्" इति श्रुतेरिति वाच्यम्। मायाप्यज्ञानमेवेति। न च अनिर्वाच्याज्ञानपरं न मायापदमिति वाच्यम्। मायापदेन अनिर्वचनीयार्थस्यैव प्रतिपाद्यमानत्वात्। योऽर्थो निरूपयितुं न शक्यते, स्पष्टं च भासते, सोऽर्थो मायामय इति सर्वसम्प्रतिपत्तेः। विचित्रार्थं सर्गकरं वस्तु मायेति वदता त्वयापि भङ्ग्यन्तरेण 'माया नाम मिथ्याभूतमज्ञानं' इति प्रतिपन्नमेव।...न च मिथ्याभूतस्य कथं विचित्रार्थ-सर्गकरत्वमिति वाच्यम्। विचित्रार्थानामपि मिथ्याभूतत्वात्। न चासुरराक्षसास्त्रादिषु सत्येष्वेव मायाशब्दः प्रयुक्त इति वाच्यम्। तेषामप्यसत्यत्वात्।... न च मायाशब्दस्य मिथ्याविषयत्वे नास्ति प्रयोग इति वाच्यम्। "न हि सर्वत्र मायाशब्दो मिथ्याविषयः" इति त्वद्वचनेनैव तत्सिद्धेः। क्वचिन्मायाशब्दस्य तद्विषयत्वमिति हि तेन (त्वद्वचनेन)

गमितम्। ...न च विचित्रार्थकरी सा माया कथमसत्येति वाच्यम्। विचित्रार्थस्यापि असत्यत्वात्। ...न च ईश्वरसामर्थ्यस्य (शक्तिविशेषस्य) मायाशब्दवाच्यस्य कथमसत्यत्वमिति वाच्यम्। मायिनः ईश्वरस्यापि असत्यत्वात्।"- इत्यादिकम्॥

ऋतानृतशब्दयोः "ऋतं पिबन्तौ" "अनृतादात्मानं जुगुप्सेत्" इत्यादिश्रुतौ कर्मतत्फलवाचित्वेऽपि, तत्परित्यागेन अमरकोशं प्रमाणयता रामरायेण मिथ्यार्थत्वे तु न हि कोशः कोऽपि प्रदर्शितः। तदभावादेव। "माया तु शाम्बरी" इति वदन् अमरसिंहोऽपि मयसम्बन्धित्वं शम्बरसम्बन्धित्वं च ब्रूते न तु मिथ्यार्थताम्। अत एव "मृषा मिथ्या तु वितथे" इति, "वितथं त्वनृतं वचः" इति च वदन् स कोशकारः तत्र तत्पर्यायतया मायापदं न हि श्रावयति। मायापदस्य विचित्रार्थसर्गकरत्वं वदता रामानुजेनापि भङ्ग्यन्तरेण अनिर्वचनीयाज्ञानवाचित्वं अङ्गीकृतमेवेति यदसौ प्रत्याक्षिपति, तत्केवलं अज्ञानभूम्नैव। विचित्रार्थत्वं न मिथ्यात्वम्। किन्तु आश्चर्यावहत्वमेवेति श्रीभाष्यव्याख्याने खलु स्पष्टमेवोक्तम्। विस्मयनीयशक्तीनां पदार्थानां स्रष्टृत्वादेव मायाशब्दवाच्यत्वं प्रकृतेरिति, न मिथ्यार्थत्वादिति च ब्रुवद्भिः श्रीभाष्यकारैः सत्येषु राक्षसास्त्रेषु "तेन मायासहस्रं तत् एकैकश्येन सूदितम्" इति मायापदप्रयोगे निदर्शिते, तत्रापि मिथ्यात्वमेवेति सहसा प्रत्युक्तमेतेन। तर्हि मिथ्याभूतरज्जुसर्पादिरिव प्रपञ्चस्यापि मिथ्यात्वात् तत्वमसि वाक्यजन्येनैव तत्त्वज्ञानेन निवृत्तिरिति आचक्षुषां - 'कथं प्रह्लादोपरि प्रयुक्तानां शाम्बरास्त्राणामपि न तत्त्वज्ञानेनैव निवृत्तिः? कुतो नु विष्णुहस्तगत सुदर्शनेन तच्छेदनापेक्षा? इत्यादिप्रश्नानां असमाधेयता अन्ततोऽवशिष्यते। वस्तुतो मिथ्यात्वेऽपि तेषामासुरास्त्राणां व्यावहारिकसत्यत्वमस्तीति शस्त्रच्छेदनापेक्षा - इति चेत्, तथैव व्यावहारिकसत्ये प्रपञ्चेऽपि न तत्वज्ञानमात्रात् निवृत्तिसम्भव इति तुल्यम्। अतः श्रीभाष्योक्तनिवर्तकानुपपत्तिः तदवस्थैव।

रामरायेण स्वग्रन्थे भूयोभूयः गौडपादकारिकाः "इति श्रुतेः" इति श्रुतिवाक्यत्वेन जगद्वञ्चनाय प्रमाणीक्रियन्ते -"न निरोधो न चोत्पत्तिः न बन्धो न च साधकः" "मायामात्रमिदं द्वैतम् अद्वैतं परमार्थतः" इत्यादिकाः। प्रसिद्धश्रुतिस्मृतिपुराणेषु अदर्शनादेव, स्कान्दपुराणान्तर्गत सूतसंहितोक्तत्वेन विश्वामित्रकृताध्यात्मरामायणप्रोक्तत्वेन च, कानिचित् श्लोकशकलानि यदेतेन प्रमाणतया निर्विशेषब्रह्मणि मायासद्भावे च प्रदर्श्यन्ते, वस्तुतः तद्ग्रन्थयोरेव प्रामाण्यं नास्तीति, तयोः स्वाद्वैतप्रचाराय विद्यारण्यादिभिः अर्वाचीनविद्वद्भिः कल्पितत्वमेवेति च, सुस्पष्टं महामहोपाध्याय-पण्डितसार्वभौम-श्रीतिरुविशनल्लूर् रामसुब्रह्मण्यशास्त्रिभिः तत्पितृभिः अश्वत्थनारायणशास्त्रिभिः विष्णु-पारम्यवैभवग्रन्थे मर्मोद्घाटनपूर्वकं प्रकटनात्, रामरायोक्तं तत्सर्वम् अविश्वसनीयमेवेति

सुदूरतः परिहार्यम्। एतत्प्रदर्शितानां सूतसंहितादिवाक्यानां बहूनां मध्यात् नैकमपि श्लोकशकलं सूत्रोपनिषद्भाष्यादिषु श्रीशङ्करार्यैः उदाहृतमिति पूर्वोक्तमहामहोपाध्यायैः स्ववादोपष्टम्भकतया प्रतिज्ञातं च। एतत्कृतप्रमाणवैयाकुली अस्मत्कृत-विशिष्टाद्वैत-वैभवग्रन्थे विपुलं सप्रमाणं च निरस्ता - इति नात्र विस्तरः।

उक्तम् - अद्वैतिसम्मतमायावैशिष्ट्यं ब्रह्मणो वस्तुतो न वेदान्तशास्त्रप्रतिपाद्यम् इति। विषयेऽस्मिन् रामरायकृत वैय्याकुली च मनाक् विवृता अस्ति समुन्मूलिते मायास्वरूपे भग्नप्रायमेव अद्वैतमिति सम्मन्यमानेन श्रीरामानुजाचार्येण स्वकृते श्रीभाष्ये, "न तस्याः कश्चित् आश्रयः, न तया ब्रह्म तिरोधेयम्, न सा दृक् द्रष्टृ दृश्यं वा, न च अनिर्वचनीया, न वा प्रमाणं तत्र, न च तन्निवर्तकम् किञ्चित्, नापि तत्त्वमसिज्ञानात् तन्निवृत्तिः", इति सप्तविधा अनुपपत्तयः प्रादर्शिषत सयुक्तिकम् इति। ऋजुबुद्ध्या तत्परामर्शे नैकस्या अपि अनुपपत्तेः सुसमाधानता इति प्रामाणिकः तटस्थः सर्वोऽपि जानाति। आन्तरं मात्सर्यं न रुणद्धि चेत्, परेऽपि नूनं तथैव प्रतीयुः। स्थालीपुलाकनीत्या तदुपर्यपि रामरायस्य असम्बद्धं वाग्जालम् इह किञ्चित् परिमृशामः।

आश्रयानुपपत्तिः

ब्रह्मणि जगद्भ्रमं जनयतो मायाख्यदोषस्य क आश्रयः? जीवो न। तस्यैव तया कल्पितत्वात्। अविद्यया जीवः, जीवेनाविद्या - इति बीजाङ्कुरन्यायेन कृतमुत्तरमपि न फलाय। उक्तन्यायेन तु अन्यत् बीजं अन्यमङ्कुरं जनयेत्, सोऽप्यन्यत् बीजमिति भिन्नानामेव बीजानां अङ्कुराणां च उत्पत्तिः। तत्र च तत्परम्पराया एव अनादित्वम्। न तु व्यक्तीनाम्। इह तु याभिरविद्याभिः ये जीवाः कल्प्यन्ते, तेषामेव तदाश्रयत्वमिति भवता यदा स्वीकृतं, तदा आत्माश्रयः। स्वकल्पितं जीवं सा स्वयमाश्रयतीति। न खलु अतिनिपुणोऽपि नटवटुः स्वस्कन्धमारुह्य स्वयं नरीनर्ति। अन्योन्याश्रयो वा। जीवसिद्ध्यर्थम् अविद्या, तत्सिद्ध्यर्थं च जीवः इति। बीजाङ्कुरवत् अत्रापि भेदमेव जीवानाम् अविद्यानां च उत्पन्ननष्टानां स्वीकुर्मः इति न भवता शक्यं समाधातुम्। अविद्यायाः स्वत एव नाशे तत्त्वज्ञानवैयर्थ्यं, जीवानां आमोक्षस्थायिताहानिश्च। अत एव अद्वैतसिद्धिकारोऽपि अन्योन्याश्रयस्य दुष्परिहरतां प्रोच्य, जीवाज्ञानवादं स्पष्टमेव निराकरोत्। आरम्भणाधिकरणश्रीभाष्ये एतद्विस्तरः।

अथ ब्रह्मापि न तदाश्रयः। ज्ञाननिवर्त्या सा ज्ञानमेव आवृणोति इति हि परिहास्यम्। ज्ञानमात्रस्वरूपं हि ते ब्रह्म। नित्यस्वप्रकाशमिति च ब्रूषे। तदपि ब्रह्म अज्ञानावृतमिति मायाप्रभावः प्रकटीकृतो भवति। न ब्रह्मणः। तस्यैव स्वाज्ञानानिवर्तकत्वे, का शक्तिरन्यस्य? इति कृतम् अशक्तैतादृशब्रह्मजिज्ञासारम्भेणेति।

अत्राहुः परे। न ब्रह्म अज्ञानविरोधि। किन्तु 'स्वप्रकाशम् ब्रह्म' इति शास्त्रप्रमाणजन्यम् ज्ञानमेव तथा। यथा साक्षात् सूर्यो न तृणादिदाहकः। किन्तु तत्किरणानां सूर्यकान्ताश्मनि प्रविष्टानां तद्दाहकता, तथा इति। तदपि विविधविकल्पशूलमारोपितं हतप्रायमेव। यथानिवर्तकं प्रमाणज्ञानमिदं ब्रह्म विषयीकरोति न वा। नाद्यः। ब्रह्मणो ज्ञानविषयत्वे जडवत् प्रमेयत्वापत्तेः भवतैव प्रतिपादनात्। न द्वितीयः। अविषयत्वे तु नतराम् तस्य अज्ञान-निवर्तकता। न हि पुरोवर्तिनम् अगृह्णती प्रमा तद्भ्रमनिवर्तिका। किञ्च प्रमाणज्ञानं पुरोवर्ति वस्तुगतविशेषग्राहकमेव भ्रमं निवर्तयेत्। न तु साधारणाकारेण तद्ग्राहकम्। भास्वरशुक्लत्वाकारेण पुरोवर्तिग्राहकं ज्ञानं न हि शुक्तौ रजतभ्रमनिवर्तकम्। अतः त्वदुक्तं निवर्तक प्रमाणज्ञानं ब्रह्मगतविशेषग्राहकं वाच्यम्। तथा सति सविशेषत्वापत्तिः ब्रह्मणः। विशेषानवगमे अनिवर्तकता स्फुटा।

अथ प्रमाणज्ञानस्य ब्रह्मविषयकतां त्यजन्तः परे तस्य प्रपञ्चमिथ्यात्वविषयकताम् आद्रियमाणाः अज्ञाननिवर्तकताम् ब्रुवते। इदमपि न सम्यक्। विषयभेदात्। न हि शुक्तिविषयज्ञानं सर्पभ्रमनिवारकम्। तथा च प्रपञ्चमिथ्यात्वज्ञानम् तत्सत्यत्वरूपभ्रमम् निवारयेत्। न तु ब्रह्मविषयकमज्ञानम् निवर्तयेत्। किञ्च शुक्त्यादीनां स्वावरणाज्ञाना-निवर्तकता तेषां जडत्वात्। स्वप्रकाशस्य अजडस्य तु न कथञ्चिदपि अज्ञानाश्रयत्व-सम्भवः।

इत्थं अज्ञानस्य आश्रये दुर्घटे, एतदुपरि रामरायोक्तं सर्वं स्वमतानुबन्धिप्राचीनग्रन्थ वाक्यानां पुनः पुनः आम्रेडनमात्रम्। न पुनः आक्षेपाणाम् एकमपि सदुत्तरम्। अत्र यदसौ ब्रह्मस्वरूपाज्ञाननिवर्तकम् ब्रह्मव्यतिरिक्तमिथ्यात्वज्ञानम् भवत्येवेति समर्थयितुकामो विलिखति, तत्तस्य शास्त्रज्ञानदारिद्र्यमेव व्यनक्ति। यथा - "यदुक्तं ब्रह्मव्यतिरिक्तस्य मिथ्यात्वज्ञानात् ब्रह्मस्वरूपाज्ञानम् (न नश्यति) तिष्ठत्येवेति, तदसत् ब्रह्मस्वरूपज्ञानात् ब्रह्माज्ञानम् नश्यति ... ब्रह्मव्यतिरिक्तस्य मिथ्यात्वज्ञानं च ब्रह्मव्यतिरिक्तत्वज्ञाना-धीनम्। ब्रह्मव्यतिरिक्तज्ञानं च ब्रह्मस्वरूपज्ञानाधीनम्। न हि ब्रह्मस्वरूपमजानानः पुरुषः इदं ब्रह्मव्यतिरिक्तमिति जानीयात्। तस्मात् ब्रह्मव्यतिरिक्तस्य मिथ्यात्वज्ञानं ब्रह्मस्वरूपाज्ञानबाधकमेव" इति।

शास्त्रज्ञैः विरोधो द्विधा विभक्तः। वैयधिकरण्यलक्षणः बाध्यबाधकभावलक्षण-श्चेति। ब्रह्मणः ज्ञानैकाकारस्य वा तद्विषयकप्रमाणज्ञानस्य वा अत्रोच्यमानम् अज्ञानविरोधित्वं बाध्यबाधकभावरूपमेव। तच्च समानविषयकयोरेव तयोः इति चोक्तं पूर्वम्। सत्येवम् इतरमिथ्यात्वज्ञानात् ब्रह्माज्ञाननिवृत्तिम् कुकल्पनया यदसौ समर्थयते, तत् विस्मयनीयम्। अभावज्ञानम् प्रतियोगिज्ञानाधीनमित्यस्तु। तथापि तत्

प्रतियोगिवस्तुनः अज्ञानस्य कथन्निवर्तकम्? मनुष्यव्यतिरिक्तप्राणिनः पशुत्वज्ञानात् किं मनुष्याज्ञानम् निवर्तेत? शास्त्रार्थोऽयम् क्व शिक्षितः? किञ्च व्याहतं चेदं परस्य भाषणं - एतत्पूर्वपुटे "कर्मकर्तृभावविरोधात् विदुषः आत्मनः एव ब्रह्मत्वेन कथम् स्वस्य स्वानुभवः" इति "स्वयंप्रकाशब्रह्मणः स्वेतरप्रकाशकत्वमेव, न तु स्वस्य ज्ञानान्तरेण अवभास्यत्व" मिति च लिखन्नसौ प्रकृते "न हि ब्रह्मस्वरूपमजानानः पुरुषः इदं ब्रह्मव्यतिरिक्तमिति जानीयात्" इति कथं लिखति? ब्रह्मविषयकज्ञानस्यैव दुर्घटत्वात्। ज्ञाते च ब्रह्मणि प्रमेयत्वापत्तिः दुरुद्धरैव भवति।

किञ्च 277 पुटे, यथा "अविद्या हि ब्रह्मशक्तित्वात्...अतएव ब्रह्म स्वप्रकाशमिति उच्यते" इत्यादिना कृतः सर्वोऽपि अस्य प्रसङ्गः उच्छृङ्खलः। अद्वैतिषु हि भामतीप्रस्थान-मिति, विवरणप्रस्थानमिति च, दृष्टो भेदः। भामती न ब्रह्मणः सर्वथा अज्ञानाश्रयतां सहते। विवरणकारश्च न जीवस्य तदाश्रयतां सहते। रामरायस्तु कपिचापलं प्रदर्शयन् क्वचित् ब्रह्माश्रयताम् क्वचित् जीवाश्रयतां च ब्रुवन् अव्यवस्थितोक्तिरिति सिद्धम्। अथ एवं 278 पुटे - "न च जीवस्य कथमज्ञानाश्रयत्वं अज्ञानकार्यस्येति वाच्यम्। मूलाज्ञानस्य ब्रह्माश्रयत्वेऽपि दर्शिततूलाज्ञानस्य जीवाश्रयत्वात्।" इत्यादिकम् तद्वचनम्। अत्र च प्रमाणजन्यतत्त्वज्ञानेन तत्तज्जीवगततूलाविद्याविनाशेपि मूलाविद्या केन कथं नाश्येत ब्रह्मगता? इति प्रश्नो दुरुत्तरण एव - इतः उपरि जीवन्मुक्तिम् समर्थयमानेन, कथं ब्रह्मसाक्षात्कारात् अज्ञाननाशे न विदेहमुक्तिरिति स्वयम् आशंक्य, अविद्यायाः आवरणशक्तिम् विक्षेपशक्तिं च निरूप्य, तत्त्वज्ञानात् आवरणशक्तिनाशेऽपि विक्षेपशक्तिस्तु प्रारब्धावसाननाशिनी इति प्रोच्य च, यथा "मेहवातात्मकस्य एकस्यैव रोगस्य भेषजेन मेहांशनिवृत्तावपि, न वातांशनिवृत्तिः- तद्वत्" इति यत् समाधीयते, तदपि परिहास्यम्। असौ प्रथमम् अविद्या हि ब्रह्मशक्तिरिति प्राह। पुनस्तस्याः शक्तिद्वयं च आह। प्रमाणज्ञानविनाश्या मायेति प्रतिपादयतैव तस्याः विक्षेपशक्तिः अविनाश्या अनुवर्तते इति प्रोच्यते। तत्त्वज्ञानात् अनिवृत्तायाः विक्षेपशक्तेः, ब्रह्मणः इव सत्यत्वं एष्टव्यं भवेत्। मिथ्याभूतस्यैव ज्ञाननिवर्त्यता न सत्यस्येति स्वमतानुसारेण।

तिरोधानानुपपत्तिः

निर्विशेषं नित्यप्रकाशमात्रस्वरूपं ब्रह्मेति स्वमतम्। तदेवाविद्यया तिरोहितमिति चोच्यते। किमिदं तिरोधानमिति निरूप्यम्। सत एव तस्य, प्रकाशादिधर्माच्छादनमिति न त्वया वाच्यम्। अपसिद्धान्तापातात्। नहि प्रकाशाख्यधर्मशालि सूर्यवत् ब्रह्मेति तव सिद्धान्तः। अतोऽन्ततः प्रकाशतिरोधानं नाम प्रदीपनिर्वापणवत् प्रकाशनाशे एव पर्यवसानमिति श्रीभाष्यकारोक्तं दूषणम्।

दुरुद्धरं दोषमिमं समाधित्सुना यदुच्यते रामरायेण, तदेवम् -"ब्रह्मणस्तिरोधानं नाम - अस्ति भाति इतिव्यवहाराविषयत्वापत्तिः। अस्ति भातीति व्यवहाराविषयो हि घटादिः अज्ञानावृत इत्युच्यते। एवं ब्रह्मापि अस्ति भातीति व्यवहाराविषयत्वात्, अज्ञानावृतमित्युच्यते। ततः अविद्यावरणात् घटवत् ब्रह्मणोऽपि न स्वरूपनाशः। न च घटस्य जडत्वात् मास्तु ततो नाशः, ब्रह्मणस्तु प्रकाशमात्रत्वात् भवेदिति वाच्यम्। ब्रह्म-स्वरूपज्ञानस्य अविद्यायाश्च विरोधाभावस्योक्तत्वात्। अत एव "अज्ञानेनावृतं ज्ञानं" इत्युक्तं, न तु नाशितमिति" - इत्यादि - सर्वं तत् व्यर्थप्रलापायितम्। घटादिरपि तिमिरादिना तिरोहित एव सन् व्यवहाराविषयो भवति। तिरोधानजन्ये व्यवहाराविषयत्वे तिरोधानव्यपदेशोऽस्य अव्युत्पत्तिहेतुकः। तिरोहितोऽपि कदाचित् व्यवहारविषयोपि स्यात्। अस्ति किन्तु तिरोहित इति हि व्यवह्रियते। तथा, घटादिरज्ञानावृत इति यदुच्यते - तदपि न सम्यक्। मायावादिनैव तथोच्यते, नान्येन। त्वदभिमतं भावरूपम् अज्ञानं न घटादेरावरणम्। किन्तु जडे घटादौ ज्ञानाभावमात्रम्। न च ज्ञानाभावस्तदावरणम्।

अथ व्यवहाराविषयत्वमेव तिरोधानमिति ब्रुवता, तेन यथा न घटादिनाशः तथा ब्रह्मणोऽपि तिरोधानादविनाश इति समर्थनं च अतिदुस्थमेव। केवलात् व्यवहार-विषयत्वादविषयत्वाद्वा न वस्तुनो विनाशोऽविनाशो वा दृष्टः। अतस्तयोः तदप्रयोजकतैव। यच्च, "अज्ञानेनावृतं ज्ञानं" इति भगवता गीतं, न तु नाशितमिति" इति स्वोक्तांशस्य प्रमाणाभासप्रदर्शनम्। तदपि अलग्नकमेव। न हि तत्र स्वभाष्यकारेण श्रीशङ्करेणैव ज्ञानरूपं परंब्रह्मैव अज्ञानावृतमिति व्याख्यातम्। श्लोको वा न त्वदभिमतार्थकः। "तेन मुह्यन्ति जन्तवः" इति उपरितनः श्लोकखण्डः कुतो निह्नूयते। भवद्भाष्यकारोऽपि "अज्ञानेन आवृतं ज्ञानं - विवेकविज्ञानं, तेन मुह्यन्ति, 'करोमि कारयामि भोक्ष्ये - भोजयामी' ति एवं मोहं गच्छन्ति अविवेकिनः संसारिणो जन्तवः" इति व्याचक्षाणः त्वत्कं विपरीतप्रसङ्गं, निरुणद्धि।

अत्र पाठका अवदधताम् - घटस्य अज्ञानावरणवदिति लिखन्नसौ अनुपदमेव "वस्तुतस्तु ... स्वत एवासतो जडस्य च घटादेः अस्ति भातीति व्यवहाराविषयत्वसिद्ध्या तदर्थम् अज्ञानावरणाभ्युपगमायोगात्" इति विलिख्य स्वात्मानं स्वयमेव व्याहतभाषिणं ख्यापयति, अपरं चेदं विचित्रं "इदं च व्यवहारदृष्टिमाश्रित्योक्तम्-परमार्थतस्तु नाज्ञानं, नापि तत्कृतावरणं, नापि तन्नाश इति बोध्यम्" इत्यस्य निगमनोक्तिः। ननु भोः। यदि ब्रह्मणो नाज्ञानावरणं परमार्थः, तर्हि या तन्निराचिकीर्षया भवदीयगुरुपरम्परायाः प्रवृत्तिः,सा सर्वा किमर्थेति निशितं पृष्टोऽसौ "गजो मिथ्या, पलायनं च मे मिथ्येति" ननु प्रलपन् पलायेत। एतेन दुष्प्रसङ्गेन न श्रीभाष्योक्तं तिरोधानदूषणं कथञ्चित् समाहितं भवति।

स्वरूपानुपपत्तिः

अविद्याख्योऽयं दोषः किं परमार्थः उतापरमार्थ इति विकल्प्य तत्स्वरूपमेव श्रीभाष्ये निर्धूयते - यथा - अद्वैतभंगभयान्न पारमर्थ्यमिष्टम्, अथापरमार्थत्वेन इष्टाश्च पदार्थाः द्रष्टृ-दृश्य-दृशित्वेन त्रिधैव लोके स्थिताः। तेष्वसौ दोषः कुत्रान्तर्भव-तीति वाच्यं त्वया। अत्र दृशिपदेन अवच्छिन्नचैतन्यमेव ग्राह्यम्। निरवच्छिन्नदृशेः भेदानभ्युपगमात्। त्रयाणां, तेषाम् अपरमार्थत्वात् तत्कल्पकदोषत्वेन हि अविद्या आश्रीयते। अस्याश्च अपरमार्थत्वे कल्पकान्तरमन्वेषणीयम्। तस्यापि कल्पकान्तरस्य अपारमार्थ्ये कल्पकान्तरमिति भवत्यनवस्था। एतावद्दूषणं श्रीभाष्योक्तम्। अनवस्थायाः परिहाराय परैः मार्गत्रयमाश्रितम्-(1) अनादित्वं, (2) दुर्घटत्वं, (3) स्वपरनिर्वाहकता चेति। इदमपि परिहारत्रयं श्रुतप्रकाशिकायां निर्धूतमेव प्रबलयुक्तिभिः। सत्येवम् अत्रापि श्रीभाष्यवाक्यार्थापरिज्ञानेनैव रामरायप्रलापः प्रवृत्तः। तथा हि - श्रीभाष्ये परमतानुवादत्वेन "निर्विषया निराश्रया स्वप्रकाशा चेयमनुभूतिः स्वाश्रयदोषवशात् अनन्ताश्रयम् अनन्तविषयं चात्मानमनुभवतीति" इति उपक्रम्य, स दोषः किं परमार्थ उतापरमार्थ इति विकल्प्य च दूषितम्। तत्रास्य इदं प्रतिवचनम् - अत्रोच्यते न वयं निराश्रया निर्विषया च अनुभूतिः आश्रयदोषात् साश्रयं सविषयं चात्मानं अनुभवतीति ब्रूमः। निराश्रयानुभूतेः आश्रयदोषायोगात्। किन्तर्हि! अज्ञानकार्यान्तःकरणावच्छिन्नचैतन्यलक्षणः प्रमाता स्वाश्रयाज्ञानदोषात् निराश्रयां निर्विषयामप्यनुभूतिं अनन्ताश्रयामनन्तविषयां च प्रतिपद्यत इति ब्रूमः। इदं चाज्ञानं प्रमातृदृश्यत्वेन प्रमातृ-स्वरूपभूतायामनुभूतौ स्वत एवाध्यस्तम्। "माया चाविद्या च स्वयमेव भवति" इति श्रुतेः। अतो नानवस्था। न च दोषस्य स्वतस्सिद्धत्वे सति ब्रह्मवत् नित्यत्वं स्यादिति वाच्यम्। जन्यत्वेन जडत्वेन च दोषस्य स्वतस्सिद्धत्वाभावात्। अजन्यं ज्ञानं हि स्वतस्सिद्धम्। अत एवाविद्यादोषोऽपरमार्थः इत्यादि। प्रतिवाक्यमिह बहु परामर्शनीयम्।

आश्रयदोषायोगादित्यस्य कोऽर्थः? आश्रयगतदोषाः ब्रह्मणि न संक्रामन्तीति अर्थो वा? ब्रह्म साश्रयमिति केन प्रोक्तम्? अनुक्तोपालम्भो ह्यसौ। स्वाश्रयदोषवशादिति श्रीभाष्यकारोक्तिः। स हि भवन्मतानुवादः। जीवाज्ञानवादं प्रदूष्य विवरणकारादिभिः तस्य ब्रह्माश्रयत्वं हि प्रसाधितम्। तदनुसारेण श्रीभाष्यवाक्यगतः स्वाश्रयशब्दः बहुव्रीहितया दोषस्य विशेषणं भवन् स्वगतदोषवशात् इत्यर्थं बोधयति। एवं च सति, तवात्र अज्ञानं वा, अन्यथाग्रहणपूर्वकं छलेन अनुक्तोपालम्भो वेति स्पष्टम्। अथ त्वदुक्तावपि आश्रयदोषपदेन दोषस्य ब्रह्माश्रयत्वविवक्षायां, ब्रह्मणि तादृशदोषायोगादिति त्वदुक्तिः व्याहता अपसिद्धान्तरूपदोषग्रस्ता वेति स्पष्टतरम्।

ननु न मे ब्रह्माज्ञानमिष्टम्। किन्तर्हि - प्रमातैव "स्वाश्रयाज्ञानदोषा" दिति स्पष्टमुक्त्या जीवाज्ञानपक्षमाश्रित्य, प्रमातृदृश्यमेवाज्ञानं ब्रह्मणि स्वतोऽध्यस्तमिति श्रुतिप्रामाण्यादिष्टमिति चेत् - पूर्वोक्तजीवाज्ञानवाददोषाणामनुद्धारात् असामञ्जस्यं तदवस्थम्। प्रमातृनिष्ठत्व दृश्यत्वोक्तिरपि नोचिता। तस्यैव अविद्याकल्पितत्वस्वीकारात् कल्पनाहेतोः अज्ञानस्य कारणत्वात् पूर्वभावित्वनियमेन तदा तदाश्रयप्रश्नस्यापि निरुत्तरतैव। अज्ञानस्य दृश्यवर्गे निवेशात्, दृश्यस्य मिथ्यात्वे मूलदोषान्वेषणप्रसङ्गो यदि स्वतस्सिद्धत्वेन परिह्रियते, तर्हि अस्तु जगत एव स्वयंसिद्धता, किं दोषान्तरकल्पनया? अनवस्थापरिहारार्थमुक्तं अज्ञानस्य स्वतोध्यस्तत्वं यदि स्वतस्सिद्धत्वरूपमपि, तदा स्वतस्सिद्धब्रह्मवत् नित्यता वा स्यात्। चार्वाकवत् आकस्मिकतावादो वा प्रसज्येत। अनुपदमेव जन्यत्वेन जडत्वेन च स्वतस्सिद्धत्वाभावोक्तिरपि तव, जन्यत्वहेतोरनिरूपणात् व्याहतैव। कस्माज्जन्यमिति प्रश्ने किमुत्तरम्? यदपि 283 पुटे "किमादौ जीवादविद्या जाता यद्वा अविद्यायाः जीवो जातः"- इति प्रश्नाः निरुत्तराः। अनयोः इदमादौ जातमिति निरूपयितुमशक्यत्वात्। अत एव द्वयोरनादित्वं श्रुतिराह -'अजो ह्येकः' 'अजामेकाम्' इति। अजत्वं ह्यनादित्वम्। न च सुतरां जन्माभावोऽजत्वमिति भ्रमितव्यम्। तथा सति अनन्तत्वापत्तेः" । इत्यादिलेखनम् - सर्वं तत् अप्रतिष्ठितानां स्वमतग्रन्थवाक्यानाम् आम्रेडनमात्रम्। प्रथमं अज्ञानस्य जन्यत्वोक्तिः, पश्चात् अनादित्वपर्यवसानेन श्रुत्या अजत्वनिदर्शनम्, पुनश्च 'न च सुतरां जन्माभाव' इति कथनं - इतीदं सर्वं परस्परव्याघातद्योतकं, स्वचापल्यस्य श्रुतौ आरोपणमात्रम्। बलाच्च उदाहृतश्रुत्यर्थोऽन्यत्र नीयते। तद्धि श्रुतिवचनमेवं रूपम्।

अजामेकां लोहितशुक्लकृष्णां बह्वीं प्रजां जनयन्तीं सरूपाम्।
अजो ह्येको जुषमाणोऽनुशेते जहात्येनां भुक्तभोगाम् अजोऽन्यः॥

इति। अत्र त्रिषु अजशब्देषु अवैरूप्येण अर्थो वाच्यः। अन्ते निर्दिष्टः अजोऽन्यः परमात्मा। तत्राजत्वं नित्यत्वपर्यवसायीति स्वेनापि वाच्यम्। पूर्वयोः अजशब्दयोरपि स्वतः प्राप्तं समानार्थकत्वं यद्भज्यते 'न च सुतरां जन्माभावः' - किन्तु अशक्यनिरूपणम् अनादित्वमिति - स खलु कुदृष्टिप्रागल्भ्यात् श्रुतेरपचारः। अत एव "जहात्येनां भुक्तभोगाम् अजोऽन्यः" इत्यस्य अन्तिमपादस्यानुदाहरणं वञ्चकस्य। अन्ते ब्रूमः - प्रघट्टेऽस्मिन् प्राथमिकशीर्षकवाक्यविन्यास एव अस्य स्वपरमतविवेकज्ञानवैरह्यावेदको दृश्यते - यथा - 281 पुटे - "निर्विषया निराश्रया च अनुभूतिः स्वाश्रयदोषादनन्ताश्रया अनन्तविषया भवतीति रामानुजमतं तत्खण्डनं च" इति शीर्षकवाक्यम्। परमतानुवादरूपं श्रीभाष्यवाक्यमिदं भवतीत्यन्तं रामानुजमतमेवेति निर्दिशतोऽस्य अज्ञानं प्रति किं वाच्यम्॥

अनिर्वचनीयत्वानुपपत्तिः

सर्वदा इदम् ईदृक् - इति निर्वक्तुमशक्यत्वं अनिर्वचनीयत्वम्। तथात्वं अविद्यायाः, तत्कल्पितप्रपञ्चस्य चेति अद्वैतिनः। सर्वदा अस्तित्वेन प्रमाणप्रतिपन्नात् ब्रह्मणः, नास्तित्वेन प्रतिपन्नाच्च गगनकुसुमादेः, प्रथमं प्रतीतं पश्चात् बाधितं च जगत् तत्कल्पिका अविद्या च विलक्षणैवेति हेतोः इदमनिर्वचनीयत्वं सदसद्विलक्षणत्वरूपमिति तैः व्यपदिश्यते।

अत्र श्रीभाष्यकाराः - मानाधीना मेयसिद्धिरिति रीत्या प्रतीत्यनुसारतो हि पदार्थनिर्णयः। प्रतीतिश्च सदिति वा, असदिति वा, द्वेधैव लोके दृष्टा। न तदुभयविलक्षणसदसदाकारा। अतः इदं सदसद्विलक्षणमिति वा इदम् अनिर्वचनीयमिति वा क्वापि प्रतीतेरभावात्, नानिर्वचनीयाज्ञानसिद्धिः - इति। यद्यपि "यतो वाचो निवर्तन्ते" इति श्रुत्या "यद्वाचानभ्युदितम्" इत्यादि श्रुत्या च ब्रह्मापि अनिर्वचनीयमेवेति प्राप्तम् - तथापि न तादृशम् अनिर्वचनीयत्वं अविद्यायां परैः विवक्षितम्। किन्तु सदसद्विलक्षणत्वरूपमेव तत्। तेन तस्याः तत्कल्पितस्य जगतश्च मिथ्यात्वं तैः सिषाधयिषितम्। लोकरीत्या उभयविलक्षणा तृतीयाकारा प्रतीतिरेव नास्तीति, श्रीभाष्यकृतां तत्खण्डनम् अवतीर्णम्। एवं सति "मुरारेः तृतीयः पन्थाः" इति रीत्या सर्वलोकभिन्नगतेरद्वैतसिद्धान्तस्य समर्थनार्थं बहु प्रयस्यता रामरायेण अनुक्तोपालम्भे पटीयसा यदुक्तं, विचित्रं तत् आकाशताण्डवप्रायम्। इदं हि आदौ तल्लिखितम् 286 पुटे "सर्वं ज्ञेयवस्तुजातमेव प्रतीतिव्यवस्थाप्यम्। ज्ञानसाध्यत्वात् ज्ञेयस्य। ज्ञानं तु न प्रतीतिव्यवस्थाप्यम्। ज्ञानस्य प्रतीतिपदवाच्यस्य स्वतस्सिद्धत्वात्।" इति। श्रीरामानुजोक्तं प्रतीतिव्यवस्थाप्यत्वं प्रमाणतः प्रतिपन्नत्वरूपम्। ब्रह्मणोऽपि शास्त्रप्रमाणतः अस्तीति प्रतिपन्नत्वात् निर्वचनीयत्वमेवेति, तदाशयः। ज्ञेयमेवेत्यवधारणेन ब्रह्मणस्तत् नास्तीति ब्रुवता सर्ववेदान्तशास्त्रवैयर्थ्यं स्वीकृतं भवति। ज्ञेये जगति प्रतीतिव्यवस्थाप्यताम् इच्छता च स्वेन सिषाधयिषितम् अनिर्वचनीयत्वं त्यक्तमेवेति स्वव्याघातः। जगति भ्रान्तिरूपप्रतीतिव्यवस्थाप्यत्वम्, अत एव बाध्यत्वं च अस्मदिष्टमिति चेत्, तर्हि सोऽयमनुक्तोपालम्भ एव। प्रमाणप्रतिपन्नत्वस्यैव श्रीभाष्यसूक्तिसिद्धत्वात्। भ्रान्तिरूपप्रतीतिसिद्धत्वं तदर्थ इति न मन्दोऽपि ब्रूयात्।

एवं सदाकारायाः असदाकाराया वा प्रतीतेः सदसद्विलक्षणं न विषयो भवितुमर्हतीत्यर्थे श्रीभाष्यप्रयुक्तं "सदसदाकारायाः प्रतीतेः" इति वाक्यं दूषयता 287 पुटे "सदसदाकारत्वं तु नैव सेत्स्यति। एकस्य वस्तुनः विरुद्धोभयाकारायोगात्" इति

यल्लिखितं, तदपि अकाण्डताण्डवितमेव हि। युगपत् विरुद्धैकाकारयोगस्य तैरपि अनुक्तेः। कालभेदात् विरुद्धाकारयोगः एकस्मिन्नपि सम्भवन् न निवार्यः। बाल्ययौवन-वार्धकादिवत्। न च तत्र अर्धवैनाशिकतार्किकवत् विशेष्यभूतावयविनाशः त्वयापीष्यते "सोयं देवदत्त" इति प्रत्यभिज्ञां तत्वमसिवाक्यार्थनिर्णये निदर्शयता।

किं च - सत्त्वं प्रमाणप्रतिपन्नत्वं, असत्त्वं प्रमाणतो बाधितत्वं, इतीदं लोकसिद्ध-निर्वचनं विसृज्य, सत्त्वं त्रिकालाबाध्यत्वं, असत्त्वं तु गगनकुसुमादौ त्रिकालबाध्यत्व-मिति पारिभाषिकं निरूप्य, तदुभयविलक्षणत्वं जगतो मिथ्यात्वं इति उपरि स्वेनोच्यते - तदपि न हृद्यम्। गगनकुसुमादौ उभयविलक्षणत्वाभावात् मिथ्यात्वासिद्ध्या सत्यत्वापत्तेः। सत्यमिथ्यातिरिक्ताकारान्तराभावात्।

अथासौ अन्ते " सदसद्विलक्षणं वस्तु प्रमाणशून्य"मिति श्रीभाष्योक्तं समादधत् "न च सा (सदसद्विलक्षणाकारा प्रतीतिः) प्रमाणशून्येति वाच्यम्। मिथ्येति प्रतीतेः सार्वजनीनत्वेन, तथा वक्तुमशक्यत्वात्। सदसद्विलक्षणत्वं हि मिथ्यात्वम्। पामरोऽपि रज्जुसर्पं सतः सर्पात् असतो शशशृङ्गादेश्च विलक्षणं मन्यते। तस्मात् रज्जुसर्पादिः सदसद्वैलक्षण्यमस्तीति कृत्वा, सदसद्विलक्षणं वस्तु न प्रमाणशून्यम्" इति अबद्धम् असम्बद्धं च प्राह। पामरे सदसद्विलक्षणत्वहेतुना रज्जुसर्पविषयिणी मिथ्यात्वबुद्धिः आस्ताम् मा वा। सा पामरबुद्धिरेव यदि ते प्रमाणं, तर्हि स एव जगत्सर्वं न मिथ्यात्वेन, किन्तु सत्यत्वेनैव प्रत्येतीति त्यज जगतो मिथ्यात्वप्रसङ्गकथाम्। एतेन ब्रह्मगतस्य त्रैकालिक-सत्वस्य शशशृङ्गगत - तादृशासत्त्वस्य च जगत्यभावेन तद्विलक्षणत्वसिद्धावपि रज्जुसर्पगत-मिथ्यात्वबुद्धिरिव पामरलोकस्य जगन्मिथ्यात्वबुद्धिस्तु नास्तीति स्थितेः, सदसद-निर्वचनीयत्वमेव मिथ्यात्वमिति स्ववादस्य स्वेनैव तिलाञ्जलिर्दत्तः। अतिक्षुल्लकैः ईदृशैः वचनैः पामरप्रतारणमन्तरा, न श्रीभाष्यार्कपिधानं भवेदिति भाव्यम्।

श्लो- अप्रतिष्ठितकुतर्कवादिना व्याहतोक्तिनिपुणेन चामुना।
रामरायकविना स्विकाज्ञता - तद्वदक्षिगतता च दर्शिता॥

Summary: In this essay, Sri N.C. Ragunathacharya, one of the great scholars and protagonists of Viśiṣṭādvaita school, has refuted the claims of Rāmarāya Kavi, who upholds the views of Advaita-vedānta in his famous book, *Śaṅkarāśaṅkara-bhāṣya-vimarśa*. The paper starts with the main problematics of Advaita with a discussion on māyā-avidyā, which not only hides Brahman according to Advaitins but also deludes the Advaitins themselves.

In fact, māyā is the the power of Brahman, it is as real as Brahman and the cause of the world of multiplicity and this is how it is understood in Viśiṣṭādvaita. But the Advaitin understands prakṛti as māyā, having three constituents like sattva, rajas and tamas and this is an indeterminate (*anirvacanīya*) and false (*mithyā*) entity. To him, prakṛti, māyā, ajñāna, avidyā and avyakta are synonymous.

To establish the existence of such an entity - indeterminate and false māyā - he cites the Upaniṣadic texts as his authority. For example, the word "*anṛta*" in *anṛtena hi pratyūḍhāḥ* (CU. 8.3.2) and "māyā" in "*māyām tu prakṛtiṁ vidyāt*" (SU.4.10) would refer to the false indeterminate māyā, according to Advaitin.

Such interpretation of the Vedic passages and a thinking based on such interpretation are absolutely incorrect and this has been clearly set forth by Śrī Rāmānuja who has very profoundly brought forth the true significance of these texts.

Āśrayānupapatti: In his *Śrībhāṣya*, Rāmānuja clearly proved that Brahman cannot be the locus of ajñāna (nescience) because both Brahman and ajñāna are by nature opposed to each other. Brahman is knowledge (*jñāna*) self-revealing (*svaprakāśa-jñāna-rūpa*) also reveals other objects; but *ajñāna* does not reveal but only veils objects and is liable for destruction by knowledge.

The Advaitin cannot obviate this opposition by telling that *svarūpajñāna* (i.e. Brahman) is not inimical to *jñāna*; but only *vritti-jñāna*; since he cannot make out a distinction between the *svarūpajñāna* and *vrttijñāna* (both of them being self-luminous, *svaprakāśa*) this answer is not a solution. Since both do not differ, and therefore are identical, *svarūpajñāna* must destroy *ajñāna*. So *ajñāna* cannot reside in Brahman.

Tirodhānaānupapatti: The Advaitin's stand that Brahman is enveloped in *ajñāna* is not maintainable. Envelopment of Brahman amounts to its annihilation. Brahman being of the nature of light, (*svaprakāśa-jñāna*), concealment of its nature will not be anything but destruction of its nature. The *Gītā* statement (V.15) "Knowledge is concealed in ignorance" (*ajñānenāvṛtam jñānam*) cannot be cited as an authority in support of Brahman's envelopment in *ajñāna* for Ācārya Śaṅkara has expounded this *Gītāśloka* not in the manner it is presented.

Svarūpānupapatti: Rāmānuja would ask, "Is ajñāna eternal (real) or non-eternal (unreal)?" The Advaitin cannot hold that it is unreal (*aparamārtha*) for in that case the fallacy of *anavasthā* (endless regression) will become unavoidable. Nor can he declare that it is a defect (*doṣa*). In that case he will have to face the awkward situation that Brahman, the self-luminous knowledge, under the influence of a defect of ajñāna cognizes its own self as possessing countless loci and countless contents.

Anirvacanīyatānupapatti: *Ajñāna* cannot be regarded as *sat* (existent) as *asat* (non-existent); it is indeterminable, *anirvacanīya*, i.e., it is neither *sat*, nor *asat*, it is other than either, i.e., *sadasad-vilakṣaṇa*, i.e, it belongs to third category.

Rāmānuja would not accept this third category. He says: "the nature of an object (*sat* or *asat*) is ascertained from the knowledge that presents it." Knowledge, by nature presents a knowable either as *sat* (a jar) or *asat* (e.g. a leporine horn) and never as different from both *sat* and *asat*. Further the Advaitin cannot adduce any proof (pramāṇa) that can establish such an entity (*anirvacanīya*). Furthermore, if the knowledge could present an indeterminate entity (*anirvācya*) contrary to its nature, any object will become the content of any cognition culminating in chaos.

The same type of arguments have been extended for the Advaitin's idea that there is remover for māyā-avidyā, that can be removed by *akhaṇḍākaravṛtti-jñāna*. Rāmarāya's defence of Advaita posiition has only depicted his lack of ability to see the greatness of the tradition, i.e. Śrīvaiṣṇava-sampradāya, which has properly interpreted Śruti, that has been the basis of all Vedānta.

NOTES

This essay and the one following are in the form of a live debate on *Satavidha-anupapatti* based on the book *Śaṅkarā-śaṅkara-bhāṣya-vimarśa* by Rāmarāya Kavi. Both these scholars have extraordinary scholarship and they have delved deep in to the problematic of māyā-avidyā by vindicating the traditions they belong to. The summaries given for both these essays are too short to convey the exact content of the debate.

19

रामरायकविसूक्तिभूषणम्

V. Swaminathan

आम्नाया निखिला वदन्ति नियतं यत्तत्त्वमेकं परं
स्वात्मानन्यतयानुभूय तमसः पारं गताः पण्डिताः।
तद्ब्रह्मामृतमद्वितीयमभयं या बोधयत्यन्तरं
जीयाच्छङ्करदेशिकेन्द्रविवृता विद्या परा सा चिरम्॥

अद्वैते प्रमिते शतैरुपनिषद्वाक्यैः स्फुटं तत्परैः
उद्धर्तुं रचितं परैः कुमतिभिर्दोषान् समारोपितान्।
विद्वत्तल्लजरामरायकविना ग्रन्थोत्तमं दुर्मतिः
योऽवाच्यैर्वचनैर्व्यनिन्ददमितैः तन्मौढ्यमुद्घाटयते॥

बेल्लंकोण्डरामरायकविभिः रचितस्य शङ्कराशङ्करभाष्यविमर्शाख्यस्य ग्रन्थस्य दूषणं, 'रामरायदुरुक्तीनां परिशीलनम्' इति लघुनिबन्धं, कश्चित् प्रकाशितवान् तान्त्रिकः। दुरुक्तीनां वक्ता रामरायः उत तान्त्रिकः इति परीक्षितुं प्रणीतोऽयं निबन्धः रामरायकविसूक्तिभूषणाभिधः सदसद्व्यक्तिहेतूनां सतां विदुषां समक्षमुपनीयते।

वेदोक्ते प्रवृत्तिनिवृत्तिलक्षणे द्विविधेऽपि धर्मे अभ्युदयनिःश्रेयसहेतौ "अनुष्ठातॄणां कामोद्भवात् हीयमानविवेकविज्ञानहेतुकेनाधर्मेण अभिभूयमाने धर्मे प्रवर्धमाने चाधर्मे जगतः स्थितिं परिपिपालयिषुः भगवान् विष्णुः भौमस्य ब्रह्मणः ब्राह्मणत्वस्य हि रक्षणार्थं देवक्यां वसुदेवादंशेन कृष्णः किल सम्बभूव; ब्राह्मणत्वस्य हि रक्षणेन रक्षितः स्याद्वैदिको धर्मः" इति (गी.भा.-उपोद्घातः) वार्ष्णेयमधिकृत्य गीताभाष्योपक्रमे यदवोचन् श्रीमच्छङ्कराचार्याः तत् तेषां स्वात्मन्यपि सुतरां युज्यते। तथाहि - बौद्धाः जैनाः अन्ये च नास्तिकाः वैदिकधर्ममार्गप्रतिरोधकाः कृत्स्नमपि भारतवर्षमाक्रम्य स्वस्वमतप्रचारणे च प्रावर्तिषत। समाचकर्षुश्चासङ्ख्यातान् सामान्यजनान् स्वमतं प्रति। गच्छता कालेन तेषां प्रभावे उत्तरोत्तरमुपचीयमाने सनातनधर्म उत्सन्नकल्पोऽभवत्। अत्रान्तरे बाह्यैः

बौद्धजैनादिभिः शुष्कतर्ककर्कशैः वेदप्रामाण्ये दोधूयमाने, आन्तरैः पूर्वमीमांसकैः ज्ञानकाण्डस्य स्वार्थे सिद्धरूपे ब्रह्मणि प्रामाण्ये प्रत्याख्यायमाने, साङ्ख्यैः स्वोत्प्रेक्षितार्थपरतया ज्ञानकाण्डवाक्येषु हठादन्यथा नीयमानेषु, तार्किकैश्च परित्यक्तागमबलैः केवलयुक्तिप्रधानेषु वेदविरुद्धेषु वादेषु प्रवर्त्यमानेषु पूर्वोक्तस्य द्विविधस्यापि धर्मस्य प्रतिष्ठापनाय नास्तिकवादानामुन्मथनाय च श्रीशङ्कराचार्याः अवतेरुः।

पराक्रान्तेषु बौद्धेषु मदधीना तव स्थितिः।

आम्नायस्य क्रियार्थत्वादानर्थक्यमतदर्थानाम्। (जै.सू. १.२.१)

"मीमांसया कपटया भुजगाम्बयेव स्वाधीनतामुपनिषद्विनतेव नीता" (वे.क.ल.-श्लो. १) इत्यादीनि प्रसिद्धानि वाक्यानि वैदिकधर्मस्य तदानीन्तनदुरवस्थां द्रढयन्ति।

भगवत्पादाः समन्वयाधिकरणभाष्ये उपनिषद्भाष्येषु च उपनिषदां सिद्धे ब्रह्मणि प्रामाण्यं प्रत्यतिष्ठिपन्। साङ्ख्यदर्शनस्य श्रुतिमूलकत्वं ब्रह्मसूत्रभाष्ये अनेकेष्वधिकरणेषु उपनिषद्भाष्येषु च निराचक्रुः। तार्किकमतस्यापि बहुदोषग्रस्तत्वं महद्दीर्घाधिकरणपरमाणुकारणवादाधिकरणयोः भाष्ये बृहदारण्यकतैत्तिरीयछान्दोग्याद्युपनिषद्भाष्येषु न्यरूरुपन्।

सनातनधर्मस्य प्रतिद्वन्द्वित्वेनोत्थितः सुगतसमयः यावत् समूलघातं न हन्यते तावत् वैदिको धर्मः अप्रतिष्ठितो भवेत् इति कृतनिश्चयाः तन्निरासाय प्रवृत्ताः, स्वेषु ग्रन्थेषु लब्धे लब्धे अवसरे सुगतदर्शनं खण्डयन्ति। छान्दोग्योपनिषद्भाष्ये षष्ठेऽध्याये, प्रश्नोपनिषद्भाष्ये षष्ठे प्रश्ने, माण्डूक्यकारिकाभाष्ये चतुर्थे प्रकरणे, बृहदारण्यकोपनिषद्भाष्ये प्रथमे द्वितीये चतुर्थे अध्याये च महता प्रोत्साहेन अभेद्याभिः युक्तिभिः सुगतसमयं प्रतिक्षिपन्ति। ब्रह्मसूत्रभाष्ये समुदायाधिकरणाभावाधिकरणयोः सावान्तरभेदं बौद्धपक्षं क्षपयन्ति। प्रदर्शनार्थं अभावाधिकरणावसानवर्ति अधिकरणार्थनिगमनभाष्यं अत्रोदाह्रियते - "किं बहुना सर्वप्रकारेण यथायथं वैनाशिकसमयः उपपत्तिमत्त्वाय परीक्ष्यते तथा तथा सिकताकूपवद्विदीर्यत एव। न काञ्चिदत्रोपपत्तिं पश्यामः। अतश्चानुपपन्नो वैनाशिकतन्त्रव्यवहारः। अपि च बाह्यार्थविज्ञानशून्यवादत्रयमितरेतरविरुद्धमुपदिशता सुगतेन स्पष्टीकृतमात्मनोऽसम्बद्धप्रलापित्वं, प्रद्वेषो वा प्रजासु विरुद्धार्थप्रतिपत्त्या विमुह्येयुरिमाः प्रजा इति। सर्वथाप्यनादरणीयोऽयं सुगतसमयः श्रेयस्कामैः" इति।(ब्र.सू.भा. २.२.३२)

भगवत्पादप्रणीतान् ग्रन्थानवलोकयतां करतलामलकवदिदं स्पष्टं प्रतिभाति यत्ते सुगतदर्शनस्य सर्वतो निरसने बद्धश्रद्धाः बद्धदीक्षाश्चेति। इत्थं स्थिते वस्तुतत्त्वे अद्वैतदर्शनस्य श्रुतिस्मृतीतिहासपुराणादिप्रमितत्वं, प्रमाणैः युक्तिभिश्च सुप्रतिष्ठितत्वं, न्यायैः उपबृंहितत्वं, शुकवामदेवादिभिः लोकविश्रुतैः जीवन्मुक्तैः स्वानुभवेन प्रकाशित-यथार्थत्वं च सर्वथा

असहमानैः स्वमतस्थापनदुराग्रहपिशाचाविष्टैः असूयुभिरविवेकिभिः श्रीशङ्कराचार्याणां समकालिकैः समनन्तरकालिकैश्च तस्य स्वकीयात् माहात्म्यात् प्रभ्रंशनं तस्मिन् अवैदिकत्वारोपणैकसाध्यमिति दुराशाकलुषितचित्तैः अद्वैतदर्शनं सुगतदर्शनमेव तद्व्याख्याता शङ्करोऽपि प्रच्छन्नबौद्ध एवेति निर्मूला काचन कल्पना शास्त्रवासनारहितानां सामान्यजनानां मध्ये तेषां प्रतारणाय अद्वैते द्वेषस्य स्वमते विश्वासस्य च उत्पादनाय प्रवर्तिताऽभूत्। अर्वाचीना अन्येऽपि मतप्रवर्तकाः स्वस्वमतप्रतिष्ठापनव्यसनिनः उक्तामेव निराधारां कल्पनां क्रियासमभिहारेणावर्तयन्। रामरायग्रन्थोपरि असभ्यजनोचिताः अतिग्राम्याः दुरुक्तीरभिवर्षन् तान्त्रिकोऽपि तामेवाम्रेडयति।

वस्तुवृत्ते इत्थं जाग्रति ये अनालोकितभगवत्पादीयग्रन्थाः ये च तद्ग्रन्थान् दृष्ट्वापि औपनिषददर्शनविद्वेषप्रयुक्तदोषारोपणैकपरायणाः वितथवादिनः तेषां मुखपिधापने प्राचीनानामाचार्याणां वचनान्येव प्रभूणि इति तान्येवेह लिखामः। तदुक्तं प्रथमवर्णके विवरणाचार्यैः - "यत्किञ्चित्साम्यादपसिद्धान्ते सर्वसिद्धान्तसङ्करः स्यात्। अस्ति चात्र महान् सिद्धान्तभेदः। क्षणिकात् विज्ञानात् भेदेन अर्थक्रियासामर्थ्यसत्त्वशून्यं विषयमाहुः - विज्ञानवादिनः; तत्त्वदर्शिनस्तु अद्वितीयात् संवेदनादभेदेऽपि विषयस्य भेदेनापि अर्थक्रियासामर्थ्यसत्वं, स्थायित्वं च अबाधितमस्तीति वदन्ति। तत्र कथं सिद्धान्तसङ्करः?..." यत्किञ्चित्साम्येन च सिद्धान्तसाङ्कर्ये मन्त्रार्थवादेतिहासपुराणप्रामाण्यानभ्युपगमात् देवतास्वर्गैश्वरमोक्षानभ्युपगमात् क्षणिकप्रमाणसम्बन्धस्य क्षणिकस्यैव सत्त्वाभ्युपगमात् लोकायतबौद्धांशद्वयपरिणतः प्राभाकरः, भेदाभेदाभ्युपगमात् मन्त्राद्यप्रामाण्याच्च लोकायतक्षपणकांशद्वयपरिणतो वार्तिककारः।यस्तु कश्चित् तत्त्वदर्शनतन्निष्ठपरमहंसप्रद्वेषतीव्रवायुविक्षिप्तविवेकविज्ञानलवः स्वपरपक्षगुणदोषविभागदूरीकृतविज्ञानः भेदाभेदाभ्यां बन्धमोक्षादिसङ्करमिव कुर्वन् दुर्जनरमणीयां वाचं जल्पति - सुगतविज्ञानवादसमानोऽयं वेदान्तवाद इति - स सम्प्रदायश्रवणपरिचयशून्यतया दर्शनविवेकमनवबुद्ध्यमानः नापवाद्यः किन्तु शोचनीय इत्युपेक्षणीयो विद्वद्भिः।

ननु विज्ञाने प्रपञ्चस्य कल्पितत्वं तव तस्य च तुल्यम् ? सत्यम्। विज्ञाने प्रतिभास्यमानत्वं च तव तस्य च तुल्यमिति विज्ञानवादः त्वदीयं दर्शनं किं न स्यात्? सत्यपि प्रतिभास्यत्वे सत्यमिथ्याविभागोऽस्तीति चेत्, इहापि सत्यपि मिथ्यात्वेऽर्थक्रियासमर्थसत्त्वासत्त्वविभागः अस्त्येव। कल्पितत्वे नेयं विभागसिद्धिरिति चेत्, प्रतिभास्यत्वेऽपि न सत्यमिथ्याविभागसिद्धिः। दृश्यतेऽयं विभाग इति चेत्, तदेव विभागदर्शनं मम किं न स्यात् ? घटादेर्मिथ्यात्वमप्रसिद्धमिति चेत् ; न, प्रतिभास्यसत्यत्वस्याप्यप्रसिद्धत्वात्। शुक्तिरजतघटयोः अर्थक्रियाभावाभावसत्त्वासत्त्वविभागदर्शनाच्च।

दृश्यते च माया प्रीतिद्वेषादिकारणम्। श्रूयते च देवासुरसङ्ग्रामादिषु मायाविनिर्मित-शस्त्रभेदानां दाहच्छेदभेदादिहेतुत्वमिति अलमतिप्रसङ्गेन" इति।(प.वि. १)

अद्वैतमते ज्ञानस्वरूपादिविषये साङ्ख्यमतेनास्ति साम्यम्। तावतापि नाद्वैतिनः प्रच्छन्नसांख्याः। यत्किञ्चित्साम्यं हि सर्वैर्मतैः सर्वेषां मतानामस्ति इति कथं न वैशेषिकादयोऽपि प्रच्छन्नचार्वाकाः? कथं विशिष्टाद्वैतिनोऽपि सृष्टौ परिणामाभ्युपगमात् न प्रच्छन्नसांख्याः? अज्ञानं ज्ञानप्रागभावेन निर्वोढुं प्रयतमानास्ते कथं न प्रच्छन्नवैशेषिकाः?

वस्तुतस्तु - बुद्धः यज्ञीयपशुहिंसामधर्मः इति विनिन्द्य वर्णाश्रमविभागरहितं अहिंसाधर्मप्रधानं च मतान्तरमुपदिदेश। परन्तु तेन उपदिष्टानि तत्त्वानि वैदिकमतादेव समुद्धृतानि। तथाहि - अहिंसा छान्दोग्ये विहिता -"अहिंसन् सर्वभूतान्यन्यत्र तीर्थेभ्यः" इति। (छा. ८.१५.१) इतिहासपुराणेषु अहिंसाया माहात्म्यमुच्चावचैर्वचोभिरुपवर्णितम्; अनेकाभिराख्यायिकाभिः प्रपञ्चितम् च। बौद्धैर्हि "नैवेह किञ्चनाग्र आसीत्", "नेह नानास्ति किञ्चन" इत्यादिश्रुतीनां यथाप्रतीतमर्थमादाय शून्यवादः, "आत्मा वा इदमेक एवाग्र आसीत् नान्यत् किञ्चन मिषत्", "आत्मैवेदमग्र आसीत् पुरुषविधः", "योऽयं विज्ञानमयः प्राणेषु हृद्यन्तर्ज्योतिःपुरुषः" इत्यादिश्रुतीनां आपाततः प्रतिपन्नमर्थमादाय विज्ञानवादश्च प्रवर्तितः। अतः सुगता एव प्रच्छन्नवैदिका इति सुवचमिति श्रीकाञ्चीकामकोटिपीठाधि-पतयः श्रीचन्द्रशेखरेन्द्रसरस्वत्य आहुः। अत एव च सप्तमशताब्द्यां (श्रीशङ्करस्यावतारात् प्राक्) काञ्चीमण्डलस्य शासिता कविवरः महेन्द्रवर्मपल्लवः स्वेन प्रणीते मत्तविलासप्रहसने बुद्धः सनातनधर्मानेव कांश्चित् चौर्येण गृहीत्वा नूतनं मतमुपदिष्टवानिति वर्णयति।

वेदान्तेभ्यो गृहीत्वार्थान् यो महाभारतादपि।
विप्राणां मिषतामेव कृतवान् कोशसञ्चयम्॥ - इति।

अतिगहनशास्त्रार्थविचारासमर्था अपि मानुषाः सगुणब्रह्मोपासनद्वारा आत्मैकत्वविद्यां प्रतिपद्य दुस्तरसांसारिकदुःखोदधिं निस्तीर्णाः यथा भवेयुरिति अनल्पयानुकम्पया वेदप्रतिपाद्यानां देवतानां स्तोत्राणि भक्तिरसनिष्यन्दीनि सहृदयहृदयावर्जकानि काव्यशोभाङ्कितानि च सौन्दर्यलहरीप्रमुखान्यनेकानि भगवत्पादाः व्यरीरचन् सगुणो-पासनस्य पूर्वभूमित्वेन। एवं वेदेषु विश्रुतानां षण्णां शिवादीनां देवतानां आराधनाय कृतव्यवस्थानां षण्णां शैवादिमतानां नास्तिकमतान्युन्मूल्य निष्कण्टकं प्रतिष्ठापनेन षण्मतस्थापनाचार्या इति प्रथा वरीवर्ति तेषाम्।

किं बहुना ? स्वयं पाञ्चरात्रमताननुसारिणोऽपि ते पाञ्चरात्रतन्त्रेषु प्रतिपादितां भगवदा-राधनप्रक्रियां सर्वात्मना अनुमोदन्ते विशालबुद्धयः उदारहृदयाः निर्वैराः सर्वत्र समदृष्टयः।

मतान्तरेषु दर्शनान्तरेषु च वेदाविरुद्धानंशान् नैव खण्डयितुं मतिं कुर्वन्ति। दृश्यतां शारीरकमीमांससाभाष्ये तदुक्तिः - "यत्तावदुच्यते योऽसौ नारायणः परोऽव्यक्तात् प्रसिद्धः परमात्मा सर्वात्मा स आत्मानमनेकधाव्यूह्यावस्थित इति तन्न निराक्रियते,'स एकधा भवति त्रिधा भवति' इत्यादिश्रुतिभ्यः परमात्मनोऽनेकधाभावस्याधिगतत्वात्। यदपि तस्य भगवतोऽभिगमनादिलक्षणमाराधनमजस्रमनन्यचित्ततयाभिप्रेयते तदपि न प्रतिषिध्यते, श्रुतिस्मृत्योरीश्वरप्रणिधानस्य प्रसिद्धत्वात्। ...यद्यप्येवंजातीयकोंऽशः समानत्वान्न विसंवादगोचरो भवति अस्ति त्वंशान्तरं विसंवादस्थानमिति, अतस्तत्प्रत्याख्यानायारम्भः" इति। एवंविधाः भगवत्पादीयशारीरकभाष्यपंक्तीः दृष्टवान् पाञ्चरात्रमतानुसारी रामानुजीयः को वा सचेताः तान् प्रच्छन्नबौद्ध इति वक्तुञ्च प्रगल्भेत?

तेषाञ्च वैदिकत्वस्य वेदमार्गप्रतिष्ठापकत्वस्य च प्रमाणभूतेषु तदीयग्रन्थेषु सहस्ररश्मेरिव रश्मिषु देदीप्यमानेषु निर्व्याजद्वेषैकनिमित्तैः निर्मूलैः मिथ्याभूतैः निन्दावचनैः अधिक्षेपः अधिक्षेप्तुरेव दौरात्म्यं व्यनक्तीति न वचनार्हम्। यदि शङ्कराचार्याः बौद्धादिनास्तिकमतानि न निरासिष्यन् तदा अर्वाचीनानि भेदाभेदविशिष्टाद्वैतादीनि मतानि नोदस्थास्यन्; तत्प्रवर्तकाः श्रीशङ्करं आतृप्तेः निन्दितुं अवकाशमपि नालप्स्यन्त इत्यत्र विशेषतो निर्देशमर्हति।

अनृतेन हि प्रत्यूढाः

छान्दोग्ये अष्टमाध्याये आम्नायते - "त इमे सत्याः कामाः अनृतापिधानाः तेषां सत्यानां सतामनृतमपिधानम्" इति। तत्र अनृतापिधानमित्यस्य शाङ्करं भाष्यम्- "अनृतं बाह्यविषयेषु स्त्र्यन्नभोजनाच्छादनादिषु तृष्णा, तन्निमित्तं च स्वेच्छाप्रचारत्वं मिथ्याज्ञाननिमित्तत्वादनृतमित्युच्यते; तन्निमित्तं सत्यानां कामानां अप्राप्तिरिति; अपिधानमिवापिधानम्। कथमनृतापिधाननिमित्तं तेषामलाभ इति॥" - इति।

अत्र अनृतं, अपिधानमिव, अपिधानमिति सम्बन्धः। अन्तरालस्थं पदजातं अनृतमित्यस्य व्याख्यानं, अपेक्षितार्थपूरणं च ; अपिधानमिवेति अपिधानमित्यस्य व्याख्यानम्। अमूर्तस्याज्ञानस्य पटादिवत् अपिधायकत्वासम्भवात् अपिधानमिवेति इवकारानुविद्धं व्याख्यानम्। भाष्ये "तन्निमित्तं सत्यानां कामानामप्राप्तिः" इत्यस्य, अनृतापिधानस्य कार्यं कामाप्राप्तिरिति अर्थ इति स्पष्टमवगम्यते। "कथमनृतापिधाननिमित्तं तेषामलाभ" इति समनन्तरवाक्येनापि अयमर्थः दृढीभवति। अप्राप्तिरिति इतिशब्दः प्रक्रान्त - अनृतपदव्याख्यानपरिसमाप्तौ।

एवं स्थिते भाष्यग्रन्थे, उदाहृतभाष्यवाक्यं-"तन्निमित्तं सत्यानां कामानामप्राप्तिरेव अपिधानशब्दार्थः "कामानामप्राप्तिरेव अपिधानशब्दार्थः इति" - इतिशब्दं एवशब्देन

निष्कास्य शब्दार्थशब्दं प्रक्षिप्य च विद्वन्मणिः अन्यथयति। अत्रेदमवधेयं सुधीभिः - तन्निमित्तमित्यस्य क्रियाविशेषणत्वं अप्राप्तिरित्यनेनान्वयं, करतलामलकवत्प्रतीयमानं अनृतापिधानाप्राप्त्योः निमित्तनिमित्तिभावं चाजानानः, अप्राप्तिरित्यस्य अव्यवहितेन अपिधानमित्यनेन सम्बन्ध इति भ्रान्त्वा कथञ्चित्तयोरन्वयसम्पादनाय इतिशब्दस्य प्रक्रान्तपरिसमाप्त्यर्थकत्वमविदित्वा तत्स्थाने एवशब्दमभिषिच्य स्वभ्रान्तिकल्पित-वाक्यार्थस्य स्पष्टतासिद्धये शब्दार्थशब्दं प्रक्षिप्य एतादृशवाक्ययोजने समनन्तरयोः इवापिधानशब्दयोरनन्वयापत्तिं तत्प्रयुक्तमानर्थक्यं चाविगणय्य भाष्यवाक्यं तदर्थं च निरर्गलमाविलयति विदुषामग्रणीः।

"अथ यदिदमस्मिन् ब्रह्मपुरे दहरं पुण्डरीकं वेश्म दहरोऽस्मिन्नन्तराकाशः" (छा. ८.१.१) इति छान्दोग्ये - दहरविद्योपक्रमे श्रुतः दहराकाशशब्दः ब्रह्मपरः इति निरणायि। तत्र ये दहरोपासकाः ते उपासनया ब्रह्मसाक्षात्कृत्य स्वात्मनि स्थितानिष्टान् कामान् लभन्ते। अन्ये तु प्रतिदिनं सुषुप्ते दहराख्यं ब्रह्म गच्छन्तोऽपि आत्मनि सतोऽपि कामान् न लभन्ते इत्युक्त्वा तेषामिष्टकामालाभं दृष्टान्तेन स्पष्टीकृत्य अलाभे हेतुमाह श्रुतिः-"इमाः सर्वाः प्रजाः ... अनृतेन हि प्रत्यूढाः" इति। (छा. ८.३.२) अस्यार्थः इत्थमुक्तो भाष्ये-"अविद्यावत्यः इमाः सर्वाः प्रजाः, अनृतेन हि यथोक्तेन हि यस्मात् प्रत्यूढाः हृताः स्वरूपादविद्यादिदोषैर्बहिरपकृष्टा" इति।

उदाहृतभाष्यमनूद्य पण्डितश्रेष्ठो लिखति "एतेनेदं वाक्यं जगत्कारणीभूतब्रह्माश्रय-महामायाशब्दवाच्यानिर्वचनीयपदार्थवाचकतया न भगवत्पादैः व्याख्यातमिति स्पष्टम्" इति। नैतत्साधु - अविद्यादिदोषैः इति प्रकृतवाक्यव्याख्यानग्रन्थे अविद्यावत्य इति पूर्ववाक्य व्याख्यानग्रन्थे च मायापर्यायेण अविद्याशब्देन अनृतपदं व्याख्यन् भाष्यकाराः। अविद्याया अनिर्वचनीयत्वस्य अनेकेषु ग्रन्थस्थलेषु निरूपितत्वात् सर्वत्र अविद्यायाः अनिर्वचनीयत्वेन विशेषणं नापेक्ष्यते। अत्र 'एतद्वाक्यस्थमनृतपदं... अनिर्वचनीयार्थवाचकतया इति वक्तव्ये 'इदं वाक्यं... अनिर्वचनीयपदार्थवाचकतया' इति वचनेन वाक्यस्य पदार्थवाचकत्वं ब्रुवन्नयं विद्वन्मणिः आत्मनः सर्वातिशायिनीं शास्त्रव्युत्पत्तिं प्रकटीकरोति। आनुमानिकारम्भणाधिकरणशाङ्करभाष्यात् उपदेशसाहस्री-ग्रन्थाच्च उद्धृत्य पूर्वस्मिन् पुटे पण्डितोत्तमेन लिखितेभ्यः वाक्येभ्य एव अविद्या माया अव्यक्तं इत्येतेषां पर्यायत्वमनिर्वचनीयत्वं च सुविशदं ज्ञायते इत्यत्रावश्यं निर्देष्टव्यम्।

"अनृतेन हि प्रत्यूढाः" "अनृतापिधानाः" इति वाक्यद्वयार्थपर्यालोचनया अविद्यायाः जगत्कारणीभूतब्रह्माश्रयत्वमवगम्यत एव। तथाहि - "त इमे सत्याः कामाः अनृतापिधानाः" इत्यादिना पूर्ववाक्येन, अनृतेन अपिधानात् (प्रतिबन्धात्) विद्यमानानामपि कामानां,

अर्थात् ब्रह्मणश्च, अदर्शनमुक्तमविदुषाम्। एतद्वाक्यप्रतिपादितस्यार्थस्य स्पष्टतया प्रतिपादनाय "तद्यथापि हिरण्यनिधिं निहितं ... अनृतेन हि प्रत्यूढा" इत्युत्तरवाक्यं प्रवृत्तम्। अत्रापि दार्ष्टान्तिकभागेन प्रतिदिनं सुषुप्ते ब्रह्म गच्छन्तीनामपि प्रजानां ब्रह्मसाक्षात्कारे अनृतं प्रतिबन्धकमुक्तम्।

ब्रह्मव्यतिरिक्तस्य सर्वस्यापि ब्रह्माश्रितत्वात् ब्रह्माश्रित्यैवानृतं तत्वसाक्षात्कारं प्रतिबध्नाति। तस्मात् "अनृतेन हि प्रत्यूढाः" इत्यस्मिन्, तत्समानार्थके "अनृतापिधानाः" इत्यस्मिंश्च वाक्ये अनृतपदं ब्रह्माश्रितानिर्वचनीयमायार्थकतयैव भगवत्पादैर्व्याख्यातम्। अत एव विवरणाचार्यैः द्वे अपि इमे वाक्ये अविद्यायां प्रमाणत्वेन उपन्यासिषाताम्।

"सर्वं खल्विदं ब्रह्म" "बहु स्यां प्रजायेय" "ऐतदात्म्यमिदं सर्वम्" इत्यादिषु पूर्वग्रन्थगतवाक्येषु ब्रह्मणः जगत्कारणत्वमाम्नातं नेह विस्मर्तव्यम्।

अपि च "किन्तु तदानन्तरिकैः विवरणकारादिभिरेव इदं वाक्यं मिथ्याभूतमहामायासद्भावे प्रमाणतया उदाहरद्भिः प्रत्यूढा इति बहुवचनं पाशाधिकरणन्यायेन अविवक्षितमिति कृत्वा ब्रह्मैव अनृतेन प्रत्यूढं आवृतं इति व्याख्यातमपार्थकम्" इति लिखन्नसौ पण्डितकुलमुकुटमणिः आत्मनीनं अदृष्टविवरणग्रन्थत्वं पूर्वमीमांसायां अदृष्टचरं मौढ्यं प्रतारणनैपुणीं च व्यनक्ति।

प्रत्यूढशब्दस्य बहुवचनाविवक्षया ब्रह्मशब्देनान्वयं कृत्वा आवृतार्थकत्वेन च व्यख्यानं न केवलं विवरणे किन्तु कुत्रापि औपनिषददर्शनग्रन्थे नास्ति। प्रत्युत सर्वत्र बहुवचनान्तप्रजाशब्देन तस्य सामानाधिकरण्येनान्वयं कृत्वा प्रतिबन्धार्थकत्वेनैव व्याख्यानं दृश्यते। "स्वरूपचैतन्येनैव ब्रह्मस्वरूपावभासे प्राप्ते तदवभासप्रतिबन्धनिमित्तं अनृतं दर्शयति - अनृतेन हि प्रत्यूढा" इति विवरणे। "ब्रह्मज्ञानप्रतिबन्धकत्वेन अनृतं ब्रुवाणा श्रुतिः" इति अद्वैतसिद्धौ।

अत्र प्रत्यूढशब्दस्य बहुवचनाविवक्षया ब्रह्मशब्देनान्वयं चिकीर्षता इदं वक्तव्यम्- प्रथमं प्रजाशब्देन तस्यान्वये कानुपपत्तिः, यया तेनान्वयः त्यज्यते, अनन्तरं ब्रह्मशब्देन तस्यान्वये किं प्रमाणम् येन बहुवचनं न विवक्ष्यते इति। तत्रान्वयानुपपत्तिस्तावत् गगनकुसुमायते। तथाहि समानविभक्तिकयोः समानवचनयोः समानलिङ्गयोश्च तयोः सामानाधिकरण्येनान्वये शब्दतो न काचिदनुपपत्तिः।

प्रतिदिनं सुषुप्ते ब्रह्म प्राप्तवतामेवाप्राप्तिमभिदधत् "इमाः सर्वाः प्रजा" इत्यादि वाक्यं 'प्राप्तस्यैव कथमप्राप्तिरित्याकांक्षां अप्राप्तौ हेतुसमर्पकेण "अनृतेन हि प्रत्यूढाः" इत्युत्तरवाक्येन निवर्तयति। अपि च ब्रह्म प्राप्तवतामेव कुतस्तदप्राप्तिरिति शङ्का अप्राप्तिहेतुप्रदर्शनेन यावन्नापनोद्यते तावदप्रतिष्ठितार्थं वाक्यं स्यात्। अनृतेन प्रत्यूहस्य

फलं ब्रह्मप्राप्तिः प्रजानां प्राप्तिकर्त्रीणामेव न तु ब्रह्मणः इति तासामेव प्रत्यूहसम्बन्धो वाच्यः न ब्रह्मणः। इत्थं न केवलमन्वयानुपपत्त्यभावः परन्तु अनपोद्या आकांक्षा च समस्ति। तदेवं आकांक्षया, प्रतिपाद्यार्थप्रतिष्ठायै, क्रियायाः प्रतिबन्धकस्य कर्तृसम्बन्धित्वस्यावर्जनीयतया च प्रत्यूढशब्दस्य प्रजाशब्देनैवान्वयः। कथञ्चिदपि न ब्रह्मशब्देन। अवश्यमाकांक्षितं प्रत्यूढशब्दं स्वस्मात् विश्लेष्य अन्यत्र नीयमानं कथञ्चिदपि न सहते प्रजाशब्दः। निराकांक्षे ब्रह्मणि अन्वये किमपि प्रमाणं न पश्यामः।

अपि च पाशाधिकरणं दृष्टान्तयता पाशाधिकरणसिद्धार्थस्य प्रकृतेनार्थेन साम्यं वक्तव्यं येन तन्न्यायः अत्र प्रयोज्येत। एष पाशाधिकरणन्यायः - एकपशुके प्रकृतियागे (अग्निष्टोमे) पठितः बहुवचनान्तः पाशशब्दः असमवेतार्थत्वात् यत्र बहुपशुकेषु विकृतियागेषु समवेतार्थो भवेत् तत्र उत्कृष्टव्यः इति शङ्कायामुच्यते - प्रकृतिप्रकरणपठितत्वात्, विभक्त्यर्थसंख्यापेक्षया प्रधानभूतयोः पाशप्रातिपदिकार्थकर्मकारकयोः प्रकृतौ सम्भवात्, सङ्ख्याया गुणभूतत्वेन दुर्बलत्वात् न पाशमन्त्रस्योत्कर्षः किन्तु प्रकृतावेव प्रयोग इति सिद्धान्तः। बहुत्वसङ्ख्यायाः प्रकृतौ असम्भवात् मन्त्रस्य असमवेतार्थत्वशङ्का गुणभूताया बहुत्वसङ्ख्याया अविवक्षया समाहिता। यथा 'तस्यापत्यम्' इत्यत्र पुंलिङ्गैकवचनयोः अविवक्षा (स्त्रीलिङ्गात् बहुवचनान्ताच्च शब्दात् अपत्यप्रत्ययसिद्धये)।

स्वप्रकरणपठितस्य प्राकृतस्य पाशमन्त्रस्य उक्तैः त्रिभिः हेतुभिः स्वप्रकरणे प्रकृतावेव प्रयोगः अवश्यप्राप्तः नत्वन्यत्र विकृतौ। असमवेतार्थत्वं तु बहुत्वाविवक्षया पर्यहारि। प्रकृते च प्रत्यूढशब्दः साकांक्षेण स्वविशेष्येण अन्वितः समवेतार्थ एवेति तस्य असमवेतार्थत्वशङ्का नोन्मिषेत्। पाशमन्त्रस्य अन्यत्र नोत्कर्षः। प्रकृते च स्वविशेष्यात् वियोज्यान्यत्र नीयते प्रत्यूढशब्दः। ब्रह्मणा अन्वयस्य असम्भव एव; बहुत्वाविवक्षा तु दूरनिरस्ता। तदेवं प्रकृतार्थस्य पाशाधिकरणप्रतिपाद्येन जागर्ति महद्वैषम्यम् ; साम्यं तु न मनागपि। अतो नेहावतरति पाशाधिकरणन्यायः।

ऊहं विनैव यथाश्रुत एव मन्त्रः प्रकृतौ प्रयोक्तव्य इति पाशाधिकरणसिद्धान्तः। प्रत्यूढमिति ऊहं कृत्वा वाक्यं पठति पण्डितश्रेष्ठः। अपि च पाशमन्त्रे वचनमात्रस्याविवक्षा, न तु पाशगतपुंलिङ्गस्य। लिङ्गस्याविवक्षायां पाशाधिकरणमुदासीनम्। इह तु प्रत्यूढशब्दगतस्त्रीलिङ्गस्यापि अविवक्षा अवर्जनीया प्रत्यूढमिति व्याचक्षाणेन महापण्डितेन। अत्र पूर्वतन्त्रीयं कं न्यायमाश्रयिष्यति? अहो मौढ्यमहो मौढ्यम्।

"ऋतं पिबन्तौ सुकृतस्य लोके" इत्यत्र सत्यवाचकस्य ऋतशब्दस्य अनन्वयात् सुकृतपिबच्छब्दसमभिव्याहाराच्च फलवाचित्वेन ग्रहणम् ; न तु सत्यार्थकत्वप्रदर्शनपूर्वकम्। सत्यार्थकत्वप्रदर्शनस्य तत्रानुपयोगात्। परन्तु सत्यवाचिना ऋतशब्देन कर्मफल-

ग्रहणे उपपत्तिरभिहिता कठभाष्ये - "अवश्यंभावित्वात् कर्मफलं ऋतं सत्यम्" - इति। कर्मफलवत् कर्मणामपि फलहेतुत्वस्यावश्यम्भावेन सत्यत्वमुक्तं मुण्डके - "तदेतत्सत्यं मन्त्रेषु कर्माणि" इत्यादि।

सत्यवाचिनावेव ऋतसत्यशब्दौ कुतश्चिन्निमित्तात् कर्मणि तत्फले च श्रुत्योः प्रायोजिषाताम्। रामानुजेनापि ऋतं पिबन्तावित्यत्र ऋतशब्दस्य कर्मफलवाचित्वमुक्तम्। (श्री.भा. १.२.११) तदेवं सत्यत्वेन निमित्तेन ऋतशब्दबोध्ये कर्मणि तत्फले वा ऋतविरुद्धार्थकस्यानृतशब्दस्य रामानुजोक्तरीत्या प्रयोगः अनुपपन्नः इत्यभाणि। अवश्यम्भावित्वेन ऋतशब्दबोध्यस्य कर्मणः तत्फलस्य वा अनृतशब्दबोध्यत्वमसम्भवि इति पूर्वत्रोक्तम्। उत्तरत्र तु तेनैव निमित्तेन ऋतशब्दबोध्यत्वं कर्मफलस्योक्तम्। कोऽत्रविरोधः? सुधिय एतद्विभावयितुमर्हन्ति, न तु सर्वत्र विरोधं कल्पयन् कुदृष्टिः।

किञ्च लोकवेदयोः सत्यानृतशब्दौ केवलार्थपरावेव, न तु सत्यानृतभाषणपरौ। यथार्थं वदन् सत्यवादी इति अयथार्थं वदन् अनृतवादी इति च उच्यते। अर्थपरत्वे एव "सत्यं वद", "नानृतं वदेत्" इत्याद्याः श्रुतयः सामञ्जस्येन उपपद्येरन्। मिथ्याशब्दोऽपि अयथार्थवाचित्वेन प्रयुज्यते लोके। अत एव अयथार्थज्ञानं मिथ्याज्ञानमिति व्यवह्रियते शास्त्रेषु। लोकेऽपि "मिथ्यावादिनि दूति" इत्यादौ अयथार्थवादिन्यामेव मिथ्यावादिशब्दप्रयोगः।

अपि च श्रौतोऽर्थः श्रुत्यैव प्रमातव्यः। "सत्यमेव जयते नानृतम्" "सत्यं चानृतं च सत्यमभवत्" इत्यादिश्रुतिषु सत्यशब्दप्रतिद्वन्द्वितया प्रयोगात् अनृतशब्दस्य मिथ्यार्थत्वमवसीयते।

अनृतशब्दस्य "मिथ्यार्थत्वे नहि कोशः कोऽपि प्रदर्शितः तदभावात्" इत्युक्त्वा अनुपदमेव "मृषा मिथ्या तु वितथे", "वितथं त्वनृतं वचः" इति मिथ्यार्थत्वे प्रमाणत्वेन कोशसद्भावं प्रदर्शयन्नयं किमविरुद्धार्थवादी ? ऋतशब्दस्य कर्मफलवाचित्वं कस्मात्कोशादवगतं तेन ? न कस्माच्चित्। किन्तु पदान्तरसमभिव्याहारादेव। वेदेषु श्रौतसूत्रेषु प्रातिशाख्येषु च प्रयुक्ता बहवः शब्दाः कोशेषु प्रवेशं न लभन्ते। लब्धप्रवेशानामपि श्रौता अर्था न कथ्यन्ते। तादृशानां शब्दानामर्थास्तु प्रकरणात् शब्दान्तरसमभिव्याहाराद्वा अवसातव्याः। बहूनां शब्दानां ब्रह्मपरत्वं लिङ्गात्, प्रकरणात्, वाक्यशेषात् अन्यस्मात् शब्दार्थनिर्णायकात् वा निर्धार्यते समन्वयाध्याये। आकाशप्राणज्योतिरादिशब्दानां ब्रह्मपरत्वं कस्मिन् कोशे उक्तम् ? तथा च मिथ्यार्थत्वे कोशानामनुदाहरणेनापि न किञ्चिद्धीयते।

अपि च "अनृतेन हि प्रत्यूढा" इत्यत्रानृतशब्दस्य दुष्कर्मपरत्वं दुर्भणम्। न च ऋतशब्दस्य "ऋतं पिबन्तौ" इत्यत्र सत्कर्मणि प्रयोगदर्शनात् अनृतशब्दस्य दुष्कर्मपरत्वमिति

वाच्यम्। उत्तरत्र "न सुकृतं न दुष्कृतं सर्वे पाप्मानोऽतो निवर्तन्ते, अपहतपाप्मा ह्येष ब्रह्मलोकः" (छा.८.४.१) इत्यादिना आत्मनः अपहतपाप्मत्वप्रतिपादनेन दुष्कर्मप्रत्यूढत्वविरोधात्। सुषुप्तौ कर्ममात्रनाशे दुष्कर्मणोऽप्यभावात्। कर्मणः अपिधानशब्दोक्तावरणत्वानुपपत्तेश्च।

"अनृतेन हि प्रत्यूढा" इति वाक्यगतानृतशब्दार्थनिर्णयप्रस्तावे रामरायकविग्रन्थे (श.वि. पृ.३३८) "तस्मादनृतेनेति श्रौतशब्देन असत्यमेव वस्तु अभिधीयते, न तु सत्यं काम्यकर्मादिकम्" इत्येव निष्कर्षवाक्यम्, न तत्राज्ञानशब्दोऽस्ति। तथा च "अज्ञानं... अवस्तुत्वेऽपि यावद्व्यवहारं सत्यत्वेन" इत्याद्युत्तरखण्डस्थेन न व्याहतिः। "अनृतपदं मिथ्याभूताज्ञानवाच्येवेति" निष्कर्षवाक्यं पण्डितोक्तं तत्र नास्ति। पण्डितेनैव रामरायकवेरुपरि व्याहतभाषित्वारोपणाय स्वयमेव कल्पयित्वा तद्ग्रन्थगतत्वेन लिखित्वा स्वस्य अन्यादृशं मिथ्यावादित्वमुद्घोषितम्। अहो प्रयासः प्रचण्डपण्डितस्य जगद्वञ्चनाय।

यद्वा - अज्ञानस्य अवस्तुत्व-(तुच्छत्व)-शङ्कायां तत्समाधानाय "वस्तुतः अवस्तुत्वेऽपि यावद्व्यवहारं सत्यत्वेन वस्त्वेव" इति वाक्यं प्रवृत्तं, "सर्वत्र त्रैकालिकनिषेधप्रतियोगित्वं यद्यपि तुच्छमिथ्यार्थयोः साधारणम् तथापि बाधात्पूर्वं शुक्तिरूप्यं प्रपञ्चो वा सत्त्वेन प्रतीयत एव इति न तयोः तुच्छत्वापत्तिः" इत्यद्वैतसिद्धिग्रन्थस्यानुवादकं च।

तथा चाज्ञानस्य व्यावहारिकसत्यत्वमुक्तं; तच्च मिथ्यात्वेन न विरुध्यते। "सर्वत्र त्रैकालिकनिषेधप्रतियोगित्वं" इत्यत्र सर्वत्रपदेन व्यावहारिकसतः प्रातिभासिकसतश्च अज्ञानस्य तत्कार्यस्य च मिथ्यात्वमुक्तं वेदितव्यम्। तदेवं पण्डितप्रकल्पितवाक्यस्य रामरायकविप्रणीतत्वेन ग्रहणेऽपि व्याहतिर्नावतातर्ति। यत्तूक्तं "यावद्व्यवहारं सत्यस्याज्ञानस्य अनृतपदेनेव यावद्व्यवहारं सत्यस्य कर्मफलस्य अनृतपदेन व्यवहारः सङ्गच्छते" इति तदतिस्थवीयः। तथाहि - यावद् व्यवहारं सत्यत्वं अनृतशब्दप्रवृत्तौ न निमित्तं भवितुमर्हति। तथा सति "सत्यं चानृतं च सत्यमभवत्" इति श्रुतौ प्रातिभासिकसति अनृतशब्दव्यवहारः बाधितः स्यात्। सर्वत्र घटपटादौ अनृतशब्दव्यवहारप्रसङ्गाच्च।

अज्ञानस्य अज्ञानशब्देनैव व्यवहारः। अपिधायकं प्रत्यूहकं च तत् किंस्वरूपमित्युच्यते अनृतशब्देन। न तस्यानृतपदव्यवहारविषयत्वम्। किं चानृतेन हि प्रत्यूढा इति अत्र अनृतपदस्य कर्मपरत्वे बहुबाधकमुपन्यस्तं नेह विस्मर्तव्यम्। तदेवं "स्वीयशपथोक्तिः त्यज्यताम्" इत्युक्तिः निरवधिकप्रद्वेषमूला न तु प्रमाणमूलेति निर्विशङ्कं प्रतिभायात् विचारकुशलानां स्वान्तेषु।

अपि च "एवमेवेमाः प्रजाः" इत्यादिवाक्यार्थकथनसन्दर्भे लिखति विदुषामग्रगण्यः "तद्वत् न केवलं मुमुक्षुरुपासकः किन्तु सर्वाः ... ब्रह्मलोकशब्दितं दहराकाशं न विन्दन्त्येव" - इति। मुमुक्षुकथयापि रिक्ते श्रुतिवाक्यार्थे मुमुक्षुरुपासक इति अधिकावापं कुर्वन्नसौ

स्वकीयमनृतवादित्वं उपासकस्य दहरब्रह्मप्राप्तिकथनेन श्रुतेरनृतवादिनीत्वमावहति इति न चिन्तयति। अनन्यसामान्या खलु अस्य व्याख्यानचातुरी।

अस्मान्मायी सृजते विश्वमेतत्

"अस्मान्मायी सृजते विश्वमेतत्" (श्वे. ४.९) इति मन्त्रपादः, एकस्य केवलस्य निर्विशेषस्य ब्रह्मणः जगत्कारणत्वासम्भवेऽपि मायासम्बन्धादेव तस्य, जगत्कारणत्वमस्तीति प्रतिपादयितुं प्रवृत्तः। एकमेव ब्रह्म मायासम्बन्धात् ईश्वरो जीवश्च भवति, यथा एकमेव मुखं दर्पणसन्निधानात् बिम्बं प्रतिबिम्बं च भवति। मायासम्बन्धः उभयत्राप्यविशिष्टः। मायासम्बन्धात् ईश्वरः जगतः स्रष्टा भवति इति तृतीय पादेनोक्तं; तुरीयपादेन तु माया-सम्बन्धात् जीव ईश्वरसृष्टे प्रपञ्चे सांसारिकं दुःखमनुभवति इति। मायी इति मतुबर्थेन्नन्तेन माया ईश्वरवशवर्तिनी इति, सन्निरुद्ध इति क्तान्तेन मायायाः सन्निरोधकर्त्रीत्वेन जीवः मायावशगो भवतीति च ज्ञायते। जीवस्य ईश्वरादन्यत्वं मायोपाधिकं, न वास्तविकमिति, औपाधिकत्वप्रदर्शनाय इवशब्दयुक्तं व्याख्यानं युज्यत एव। यत्र मुख्यो वास्तविको वार्थः न सम्भवति तत्र सर्वत्र गौणः औपाधिको वार्थः आश्रीयमाणः इवशब्देनैव द्योतनीयः। व्याख्यानशब्दार्थमविदुषः मूढस्येदं वृथा विकत्थनम् - "इवशब्दो हि मूले न मन्त्रगतः। किमर्थं तस्यात्र संयोजनम्" - इति। व्याख्यानलक्षणं महाभाष्ये उक्तम् - "न केवलं चर्चापदानि व्याख्यानम्। किं तर्हि ? उदाहरणं प्रत्युदाहरणं वाक्याध्याहारः इत्येतत् समुदितं व्याख्यानं भवति" - इति। तस्मात् अपेक्षितपदाध्याहारे को दोषः? जगतः स्रष्टा ईश्वरः, जीवः मायया संसारदुःखभाक् इति जीवेश्वरव्यवस्था विविच्य प्रदर्शिता भगवत्पादैः। एवं स्थिते भगवत्पादीयं व्याख्यानं लिखित्वा अनुपदमेव "यो मायी सृजति स एवाविद्यायाः तस्याः वशगो भूत्वा संसारसमुद्रे मज्जतीति" तद्विपरीतं तदनुक्तं च लिखन्तं त्वामेव विप्रलम्भकमूर्धन्यं निश्चेष्यति दुरुक्तिमयस्य तव लेखस्य पठिता जनः।

"तस्यावयवभूतैस्तु व्याप्तं सर्वमिदं जगत्" इति मन्त्रव्याख्यानभूते "मायिकैः स्वावयवैः (जीवैः) अध्यासद्वारा इदं सर्वं जगद्व्याप्तम्" इति भाष्ये अविद्यमानं जीवपदं प्रक्षिप्य "रज्ज्वाद्यधिष्ठानसर्पस्थानीयतां जीवानां स्वेनैवात्रारोप्य मन्त्रो व्याख्यायते" इति विपरीतग्राहिणस्तव सर्वातिशायि मौढ्यं पांसुलपादः हालिकोऽपि जानीयात्। उदाहृतमन्त्रभागे जीवस्य प्रसक्तिरेव नास्ति। पूर्वार्धोक्तः मायी महेश्वरः स्वेन सृष्टं जगत् कथं व्याप्नोतीति प्रदर्शनाय उदाहृतस्योत्तरार्धस्य प्रवृत्तिः।

महेश्वरेण सृष्टाः अर्थाः - आकाशः सन्, पृथिवी सती, तेजः सत् इति - सत्तादात्म्येनैव प्रतीयन्ते, एवं घटः सन् पटः सन् इत्यादयोऽपि। "सदेव सोम्येदम्" इति श्रुत्यन्तरात्

जगतः स्रष्टा, उपादानं च सन् इत्यवगम्यते। जगदुपादानं सद्रूपं ब्रह्म स्वकार्येषु आकाशादिषु अन्वेति, मृत्तिकादिरिव स्वोपादेये घटादौ। आकाशादिषु प्रतीयमानः सदर्थः सद्रूपमधिष्ठानमेव। एवं चाधिष्ठानब्रह्मसत्तैव अध्यस्तेषु निखिलेषु आकाशादिषु घटादिषु च "आकाशः सन्" "घटः सन्" इत्यादिप्रतीतिविषयो भवति स्वाध्यस्तेष्वशेषेषु अर्थेषु सत अनुवेधात् सर्वं सता व्याप्तमित्युच्यते, सत्तादात्म्याव्यभिचारात्। "न सत्तां पदार्थो व्यभिचरति" इति महाभाष्यम्।

स्वस्वावच्छिन्ने सति अध्यस्ताः वियदादयः सर्वेऽर्थाः निरवयवमपि सद्रूपं ब्रह्म एकं अनेकावयवयुतमिव कुर्वन्ति यथा घटादयोऽर्थाः स्वस्वावच्छिन्नं एकं निरवयवमाकाशम्। वस्तुतः सतः निरवयवत्वेऽपि औपाधिकं सावयवत्वं "तस्यावयवभूतैस्तु" इति श्रुत्योच्यते।

"अस्मान्मायी"ति मन्त्रस्य भाष्ये मायिनः ईश्वरस्य जगत्स्रष्टृत्वं, "मायां तु" इति मन्त्रस्य भाष्ये च मायायाः सत्तास्फूर्तिप्रदत्वं अधिष्ठानत्वेन प्रेरयितृत्वं चोक्तम्। विरोधलेशगन्धेनापि शून्ये निर्मले भाष्ये विरोधमारोप्य सर्वलोकवन्द्यान् विशुद्धविज्ञानान् भाष्यकारान् पूर्वापरविरुद्धाभिधातृत्वेन निन्दितुं नैसर्गिकदौर्जन्यवशंगतस्य तदीयग्रन्थे "स एव रज्जुसर्पस्थानीयः" इति पदजातं प्रक्षिपतः, स्वयूथ्यानेव प्रतारयितुं प्रयत्नमातस्थुषः अहो तव शाठ्यभूमा अदृष्टचरः अश्रुतचरश्च।

श्रुतिस्मृतीतिहासपुराणाद्यशेषविद्यैकनिलयस्य भगवतः शङ्करस्य श्रुतिव्याख्यानमवहेलयितुं यत्पौराणिककृतं व्याख्यानमुपन्यस्तं तद्यदि कल्पितं तदा मन्दधियः मात्सर्यदवानलदग्धहृदयस्य खलस्य उद्गारः। यदि वस्तुतः कस्यचित्पौराणिकस्य वचनं तदा लोकवृत्तमविदुषः प्राज्ञमानिनः अनवसरे जल्पनम्। लोके हि पुराणहरिकथाप्रवचनमण्डपेषु समवेतानां श्रोतॄणां केचन प्रवचनसमये निद्रायां निमज्जन्ति इति सर्वेषां सुविदितम्। तदानीं प्रवक्तारः उच्चैर्हासकरघोषादिजनकं किञ्चिदनुपपन्नमुक्त्वा तान् प्रबोधयन्ति। अनुपपन्नमेव वचनमुत्कटहासाद्युत्पादकं, न तु उपपन्नमिति, तदेवोपायतया आश्रयन्ते। यथा, "मम वशमुपयाता रावणस्येव कुन्ती", "केशहस्ते परामृष्टा चाणक्येनेव द्रौपदी", "पुत्रो राधाया रावण इन्द्रदत्तः", "शृणोमि माल्यगन्धम्", अन्धकारपूरितया पुनर्नासिकया न सुव्यक्तं पश्यामि भूषणशब्दम्, इत्यादि। (मृच्छकटिकम्, १) लोकवृत्तमजानानः परिहासविजल्पितं तथैव परमार्थेन गृह्णन् पौराणिके अव्युत्पत्तिं अज्ञतां वारोप्योपहसन् - मृत्पिण्डबुद्धिः त्वादृशोऽन्यो मृग्यः।

सूक्तिसहस्रधीतितात्मनां महात्मनां दोषोद्घोषणमात्मन एव दूषणं भवतीति ईदृशं पृथग्जनोचितं व्यवहारं मनसापि न चिन्तयेयुः सुधीजनाः। "भूयश्चान्ते विश्वमायानिवृत्तिः"

इति मायायाः ज्ञाननिवर्त्यत्वं ब्रुवती श्रुतिः अनिर्वचनीयमायायां प्रमाणम्। "मायामेतां तरन्ति ते" इति स्मृतिरपि ज्ञानहेतुकतरणस्य निवृत्त्यतिरिक्तार्थकत्वासम्भवेन ज्ञाननिवर्त्यायाः अत एव मिथ्याभूतायाः मायायाः सद्भावे मानम्। न च मायाशब्दस्याज्ञानार्थकत्वे मायिनो ब्रह्मणः अज्ञानित्वापत्त्या सर्वज्ञत्वनिरवद्यत्ववादिश्रुतिविरोध इति वाच्यम्। उपाधेः प्रतिबिम्ब-पक्षपातित्वेन ईश्वरे असर्वज्ञत्वाद्यापादनायोगात्, सर्वज्ञत्वाद्यैश्वर्यस्य मायानिबन्धनत्वाच्च।

"एवमेवैषा माया स्वाव्यतिरिक्तानि परिपूर्णानि क्षेत्राणि दर्शयित्वा "जीवेशावाभासेन करोति माया चाविद्या च स्वयमेव भवति" इति श्रुत्या मायाविद्ययोरैक्यप्रतिपादनात् माया अज्ञानमेव। मायापदस्य "माछाससिभ्यो यः" इति उणादिसूत्रोदाहरणत्वेन उज्ज्वलदत्तीयवृत्तौ उक्तत्वात् "माङ् माने" इति धातुपाठात् मानशब्दस्य परिमाणज्ञानयोः प्रयोगात् योगेन ज्ञानार्थकत्वमिव रूढ्या अज्ञानार्थकत्वम्। अत एव उज्ज्वलदत्तीयवृत्तौ माया छद्मेति व्याख्यातम् मायाया अज्ञानान्यत्वे ज्ञाननिवर्त्यत्वश्रुतिविरोधात्। ऐन्द्रजालिकादौ बहुशो मायाशब्दप्रयोगदर्शनात्। "न हि सर्वत्र मायाशब्दो मिथ्याविषयः" इति रामानुजवचनादेव मायाशब्दस्य मिथ्याविषये प्रयोगसिद्धेः, क्वचिन्मायाशब्दस्य मिथ्यार्थविषयकत्वं अस्तीति खलु तेन ज्ञाप्यते। योऽर्थः प्रमाणेन निरूपयितुं न शक्यते, स्पष्टं च भासते सोऽर्थः मायामयः इति लोकप्रसिद्धिः। ब्रह्मभिन्नस्य कृत्स्नस्यापि जगतः मिथ्यात्वं प्रमाणैः निरूपयन्तं औपनिषदं प्रति - मायाशब्दस्य असुरास्त्रे प्रयुक्तत्वेन, विचित्रसर्गकरत्वेन, ईश्वरशक्तित्वेन, आश्चर्यावहवस्तुत्वेन, विस्मयनीय-शक्तियुक्तपदार्थस्रष्टृत्वेन वा माया सत्यमिति प्रत्यवस्थानमकिञ्चित्करम्।

आत्मतत्त्वज्ञानेन तत्त्वमस्यादिमहावाक्यजन्येन आत्माज्ञानं निवर्तते तेन सहैव तत्कार्यभूतः शरीरेन्द्रियविषयादिप्रपञ्चोऽपि निवर्तते इति सिद्धान्तः। ततश्च "कथं प्रह्लादोपरि प्रयुक्तानां शाम्बरास्त्राणामपि न तत्त्वज्ञानेन निवृत्तिः?" इत्यादिकं मूर्खजनप्रलपितत्वा-दुपेक्षणीयं तथापि विपरीतग्रहणापनोदनायाभिधीयते। तथाहि - कस्य तत्त्वज्ञानेन प्रह्लादोपरि प्रयुक्तानां शम्बरास्त्राणां निवृत्तिं वाञ्छति पण्डितश्रेष्ठः? स्वस्य तत्त्वज्ञानेन वा? प्रह्लादस्य वा? असूयादिसकलपुंदोषैकनिलये अनवरतमहात्मनिन्दाजनितदुर्वह-पापनिवहं वहति च त्वयि शतकोटिजन्मनामन्तेऽपि न तत्त्वज्ञानमुदेष्यति। प्रह्लादस्तु भगवद्भक्तः। आराध्याराधकद्वैतपूर्विका हि भक्तिः। द्वैतप्रपञ्चस्वभावभूतं प्राणभृन्मात्रस्य भयादिकं तस्मान्न निवृत्तम्। "द्वितीयाद्वै भयं भवतीति" श्रुतेः। तस्मात् शम्बरप्रयुक्तास्त्रभयात् परित्राणाय विष्णुहस्तगतस्य सुदर्शनस्य प्रयोगः अवर्जनीयोऽभवत्।

प्रह्लादः नाद्वैतात्मज्ञानवान्, अत एव न प्रत्यस्तमितसमस्तद्वैतप्रपञ्चः। अन्यथा सोऽभयं गतोऽभविष्यत्। यदि तत्त्वमस्यादिवाक्यजन्यः अहं ब्रह्मास्मीति आत्मतत्त्वसाक्षात्कारः

तस्याभविष्यत् तदा आत्मव्यतिरिक्तं वस्त्वन्तरमपश्यतः शम्बरः, तत्प्रयुक्तान्यस्त्राणि, भयं, तस्मात् त्रातुं त्राता विष्णुः, तत्कृतः सुदर्शनप्रयोगो वा, किमपि नाभविष्यत्। तत्त्वसाक्षात्कारक्षण एव कृत्स्नोऽपि प्रपञ्चः रज्जौ भयहेतुः सर्प इव न्यवर्त्स्यत्, सोऽपि संसारादमोक्ष्यत।

किं च प्रह्लादस्य आत्मैकत्वज्ञानाभावात् शम्बरास्त्राणां सुदर्शनप्रयोगात् न निवृत्तिः किन्तु स्वकारणे लयरूपो नाशः मुद्गरपातचूर्णितस्य घटस्य मृदीव। शम्बरास्त्रं वा सुदर्शनो वा, सर्वं तत् अज्ञानकार्यम् सुदर्शनप्रयोगकृतोऽस्त्रनाशः कार्यमात्रनाशः। कारणस्य अज्ञानस्य निवृत्तिस्तु आत्मैकत्वसाक्षात्कारेणैव, स च प्रह्लादस्य नासीत्। अज्ञानकार्यणामर्थानां निवृत्तिस्तु तद्विरोध्यज्ञानकार्यान्तराणां व्यापारात्, न तत्त्वज्ञानेन। तत्त्वज्ञानं तु स्वविरोधिनं तत्त्वाज्ञानमेव निवर्तयति। अज्ञाननिवृत्त्या तत्कार्यस्य प्रपञ्चस्यापि निवृत्तिः।

तत्त्वज्ञानं अनेकजन्मानुष्ठितयज्ञादिकर्मप्रक्षीणाशेषपापस्य साधनचतुष्टयसम्पन्नस्य नैरन्तर्यानुष्ठितश्रवणादिसाधनस्य भवति। "कश्चिद्धीरः प्रत्यगात्मानमैक्षत् आवृत्तचक्षुरमृतत्वमिच्छन्" इति श्रुतेः। न तत् शाकादिरिव आपणेषु क्रेतुं शक्यम् येनेत्थं प्रलपति पण्डिताग्रेसरः। तथा च "वस्तुतो मिथ्यात्वेऽपि...प्रपञ्चेऽपि न तत्त्वज्ञानमात्रात् निवृत्तिसम्भव" इत्यादि यत् जल्पितं तदुन्मत्तचेष्टितम्।

कासाञ्चित् गौडपादीयकारिकाणां श्रुतिवाक्यत्वेन परामर्शः यदि जगद्वञ्चनं तदा रामानुजमध्वावपि जगद्वञ्चकौ स्याताम्, यतः ताभ्यामपि गौडपादीयकारिकाः श्रुतित्वेनोपन्यस्ताः।

स्कन्दपुराणस्याप्रामाण्यं प्रतिपादयन् रामसुब्रह्मण्यशास्त्रिप्रणीतः ग्रन्थः तत्समकालिकैः महामहोपाध्यायगणपतिशास्त्रिभिः अभेद्याभिर्युक्तिभिः अविचाल्यैः प्रमाणैश्च उन्मथितः। नैसर्गिकेण मौढ्येनान्धीभूतः अत एव स्वमतं परमतं वा यथावत् ज्ञातुमशक्तः विद्वन्मणिः, अन्धमन्यं प्रामाणिकत्वेनाश्रयति, "सर्वः सगन्धेषु विश्वसिति" इति महाकविसूक्तिं सार्थीकुर्वन्।

महर्षिणा वेदव्यासेन प्रणीतेषु अष्टादशमहापुराणेषु सप्तसंहितात्मकं स्कन्दपुराणमन्यतममिति निर्विवादम्। तदन्तःपातिन्याः सूतसंहितायाः व्याख्यानं विद्यारण्यस्वामिभिर्व्यधायि। एवं स्थिते सूतसंहितायाः प्रामाण्यं नास्ति इति स्वाद्वैतप्रचाराय विद्यारण्यादिभिः अर्वाचीनविद्वद्भिः कल्पितत्वमेवेति महामहोपाध्यायैः तिरुविशनल्लूर रामसुब्रह्मण्यशास्त्रिभिः यदुक्तं तत्सर्वं तत्त्वदर्शनविमुखस्य तिमिरोपहतलोचनस्य प्रलपनमुपहासास्पदम्। "एतत् (रामराय) प्रदर्शितानां सूतसंहितादिवाक्यानां बहूनां मध्यात् नैकमपि श्रीशङ्करार्यैरुदाहृतमिति

पूर्वोक्तमहामहोपाध्यायैः स्ववादोपष्टम्भकतया" इत्यादि च रिक्तं निकृष्टमतेर्वचनम्। रामरायग्रन्थं जात्वपि अदृष्टवन्तः शास्त्रिणः कथमित्थं वदेयुः? "एतत्प्रदर्शितानां" इति पदं मामकं न तु शास्त्रिणामिति यदि ब्रूयात् प्राज्ञंमन्यः, तर्हि शङ्कराचार्यैरनुदाहृतत्वं स्ववादोपष्टम्भकतया लिखन्तः शास्त्रिणः भ्रान्ताः। शङ्कराचार्याः अष्टादशानां मध्ये कतिभ्यश्चिदेव पुराणेभ्यः वाक्यान्युदाहरन्ति। न तु सर्वेभ्यः। किमिमे शास्त्रिणः सर्वेभ्यः पुराणेभ्यः वाक्यान्युदाहर्तव्यानीति शङ्कराचार्यानादिशन्ति? सर्वेभ्यः पुराणेभ्यः उदाहर्तव्यमिति तेषां को निर्बन्धः? श्रीमद्भागवतमद्वैतसिद्धान्तानामाकरः। तस्मादेकमपि वाक्यं भगवत्पादाः नोदाहरन्ति स्वेषु ग्रन्थेषु। तावता श्रीमद्भागवतं किमप्रमाणम्? अनुदाहरणस्य उपष्टम्भकप्रमाणत्वेन गणनं मूर्खस्यैव शोभते, न प्रेक्षावतः। भ्रान्तानां शास्त्रिणां भ्रान्तिवचनं प्रमाणत्वेन गृहीत्वा स्वानुकूलतया लिखन् देवानांप्रियः भ्रान्तधौरेय इति, "अन्धेनैव नीयमाना यथान्धा" इति (क. १.२.५) श्रुतेः अद्वितीयमुदाहरणमिति च, किं वचनमपेक्ष्यते?

आश्रयोपपत्तिः

अद्वैतसिद्धिकाराः अन्योन्याश्रयात्माश्रयौ अनवकाशीकृत्य जीवाज्ञानवादं प्रत्यतिष्ठिपन्। तेन "अद्वैतसिद्धिकारः जीवाज्ञानवादं ... स्पष्टमेव निराकरोत्" इति अनृतभाषिणः अदृष्टाद्वैतसिद्धिग्रन्थस्य लेखनं परिहसनीयं भवति। सर्वाद्वैतग्रन्थेषु तत्त्वज्ञाननाश्यत्वेन प्रसिद्धायाः अविद्याया उत्पन्नविनष्टत्वं स्वतः नाशं च स्वयमेव कल्पयित्वा तत्त्वज्ञानवैयर्थ्यं चोदयन् अयं पण्डितः आत्मानमेव खण्डयति न त्वौपनिषदान् इत्येतत् तत्त्वविदो विदांकुर्वन्तु। निर्धर्मकब्रह्मवादिनं प्रति "अशक्तं ब्रह्म" इत्युपहसन्नयं अद्वैतसिद्धान्तानवबोधनिमित्तां स्वस्यैवोपहास्यतां न वेत्ति। नित्यस्वप्रकाशरूपस्य ब्रह्मणः अज्ञानाश्रयत्वं विरुद्धमिति वदन् स्वप्रकाशाज्ञानयोर्विरोधं केन प्रमाणेन निश्चितवान्। न तावत्प्रत्यक्षेण, अहमज्ञः इति प्रकाशमान एव आत्मनि अज्ञानानुभवदर्शनात्। नापि श्रुत्या, तादृशश्रुतेरभावात्। नाप्यनुमानेन, विरोध -मनुमिमानेन, स्वप्रकाशाज्ञानसंसर्गविरोधयोः व्याप्तिग्रहः कथं जात इति वक्तव्यम्। यस्मात् दृष्टान्तात् व्याप्तिः गृह्येत नास्त्येव सः। न हि स्वयम्प्रकाशमाने अज्ञानसंसर्गविरोधः क्वचित् दृष्टः। अन्यदीयसिद्धान्ताज्ञानजन्यप्रजल्पननिमित्तामात्मन एवापहास्यतामविगणय्य अन्यत्र तदारोपणेन मुहुर्मुहुः सन्तुष्यन् तुष्यतु यथेष्टम्। "सत्यं ज्ञानमनन्तं ब्रह्म यो वेद" इति श्रुतिः परप्राप्तिसाधनत्वेन निर्विशेषज्ञानस्वरूपब्रह्मज्ञानमुपदिशति। निर्विशेषब्रह्मस्वरूपवादिन्यः श्रुतयः सन्ति शतशः। प्रमाणभूता श्रुतिरेव निर्विशेषज्ञानरूपब्रह्मविषयिणीं प्रमां श्रावयति इति" ज्ञानरूपं ब्रह्म कथं ज्ञानान्तरेण

विषयीक्रियेत' इति शङ्काया नास्त्यवसरः। एवमेव "एतद्यो वेद निहितं गुहायां सोऽविद्याग्रन्थिं विकिरति" इति श्रुतिः निर्विशेषब्रह्मज्ञानेन अविद्यानिवृत्तिमुपन्यस्यति।

ब्रह्मप्रमा च ब्रह्माकारपरिणतान्तःकरणवृत्तिरूपा। तादृशवृत्तेः ब्रह्म विषयो भवति, यथा घटाकारपरिणतान्तःकरणवृत्तिसंसृष्टः घटः तादृशवृत्तेर्विषयो भवति। घटादिर्विषयः स्वावच्छिन्नब्रह्मचैतन्योपादानकः तद्भास्यश्च। स्वभासकब्रह्मचैतन्यप्रकाशस्याज्ञानावरणेन प्रतिबन्धात् घटो न प्रकाशते। देवदत्तादेः प्रमातुः घटाद्याकारपरिणतान्तःकरणवृत्तिः यदा चक्षुरादिद्वारा निर्गत्य घटादिकं विषयं व्याप्नोति तदा घटाद्यावरकमज्ञानं निवर्तते। अज्ञानप्रतिबन्धस्यापगमात् घटादिः स्वावच्छिन्नब्रह्मचैतन्येन भास्यते। घटादीनां स्वातिरिक्तस्वप्रकाशसंविद्भास्यत्वमेव प्रमेयत्वम्।

एवमेव अज्ञानेनावृतत्वात् ब्रह्म न प्रकाशते। यदा वेदान्तमहावाक्यजन्यस्वाकारवृत्तेः ब्रह्म विषयो भवति तदा ब्रह्मावरकमज्ञानं निवर्तते। ब्रह्मणः स्वप्रकाशत्वात् स्वयमेव भाति, न प्रकाशान्तरमपेक्षते यथा घटादिरस्वप्रकाशः। वृत्तिविषयत्वरूपं प्रमेयत्वमङ्गीकृतमेव, ब्रह्मविषयकज्ञानप्रतिपादिनीनां श्रुतीनां प्रामाण्यात्, महावाक्यजन्यवृत्तिरूपप्रमाविषयत्वस्य ब्रह्मणि सत्त्वाच्च। ब्रह्मव्यतिरिक्तचैतन्याभावेन तद्विषयत्वरूपस्य प्रमेयत्वस्य ब्रह्मणि असम्भवात् न ब्रह्मणः चिद्भास्यत्वरूपं प्रमेयत्वम्, न वा स्वप्रकाशत्वहानिः, नापि घटादिवत् जडत्वापत्तिः। तदुक्तं भामत्याम् - "न चैतावता ब्रह्मणः अपराधीनप्रकाशता। न हि शाब्दज्ञानप्रकाश्यं स्वयंप्रकाशं न भवति"- इति। (भामती. १.१.१) तदयं निष्कर्षः - स्वप्रकाशाय वृत्तिं स्वावच्छिन्नचैतन्यप्रकाशं चापेक्षते घटादिः जडत्वात् ; ब्रह्म तु वृत्तिमात्रमपेक्षते स्वयंज्योतिष्ट्वात्। घटादीनां चिद्विषयत्वं प्रमेयत्वं, ब्रह्मणस्तु वृत्तिविषयत्वमिति विवेकः। न्यायनय इवात्मनः स्वप्रकाशत्वानङ्गीकारे ज्ञानान्तरप्रकाश्यत्वमभ्युपेयम्। तथा सति घटादिवत् प्रमेयत्वं स्यात् इति स्वयंज्योतिष्ट्वसिद्धये अद्वैतिना उक्तायाः युक्तेरेकदेशस्य अकाण्डे आम्रेडनं स्वकीयलेखविस्तृततासम्पादनैकप्रयोजनकम्।

निरुपाधिकभ्रमस्थले अधिष्ठानप्रमात्वेनैव अधिष्ठानज्ञानमज्ञाननिवर्तकम्। अधिष्ठानं च निर्विशेषं ब्रह्मेति वेदान्तमहावाक्यजन्यनिर्विशेषब्रह्मप्रमया ब्रह्माज्ञानं निवर्तते। निस्सामान्ये निर्विशेषे च ब्रह्मणि सामान्यविशेषासम्भवात्। शुक्तिरजतस्थल इव अधिष्ठानगतविशेषज्ञानस्य निवर्तकत्वं स्वयमेव कल्पयित्वा ब्रह्माज्ञाननिवर्तकज्ञानस्य सविशेषब्रह्मविषयकत्वापादनं - शुक्तेः जडत्वेन ब्रह्मणोऽपि जडत्वापादनतुल्यम् - अद्वैतसिद्धान्तानवबोधविजृम्भितम्। शुक्तिरजतस्थलेऽपि शुक्तिज्ञानं अधिष्ठानप्रमात्वेनैवाज्ञाननिवर्तकम्। यत्तूक्तं "पुरोवर्तिवस्तुगतविशेषग्राहकमेव प्रमाणज्ञानं भ्रमं निवर्तयेदिति" तत्तुच्छम्। सर्पभ्रमस्य तदनन्तरभाविभूच्छिद्रभ्रमेणापि, स्वप्नभ्रमस्य स्वानन्तरभाविस्वप्नभ्रमान्तरेणापि निवृत्तिदर्शनात्।

शुक्तिज्ञानं च शुक्त्याकारान्तःकरणवृत्त्युपहितब्रह्मचैतन्यरूपम्। शुक्तेर्जडत्वेन अज्ञानतत्कार्यभ्रमाधिष्ठानत्वासम्भवात्। चित एवाधिष्ठानत्वम्। शुक्तेः केवलं चैतन्यावच्छेदकत्वमेव। शुक्तिरजतादीनां यदवच्छिन्नचैतन्येऽध्यासः तदवच्छिन्नचैतन्यमेवाधिष्ठानम्। प्रपञ्चाध्यासस्य तु अनवच्छिन्नं ब्रह्मचैतन्यमधिष्ठानमिति विवेकः। अहं ब्रह्मास्मीत्यौपनिषदं अपरोक्षज्ञानमेव आत्माज्ञाननिवर्तकमिति अद्वैतघण्टाघोषेण- मुखरितासु सर्वासु दिक्षु असमानविषयकं ज्ञानान्तरं किञ्चित् अज्ञाननिवर्तकत्वेन अद्वैतिनोक्तमिति स्वयमेव कल्पयित्वा दूषयन्तो रामानुजाचार्याः आत्मानमेव दूषयन्तीति यद्यपि तन्निरासात् विरन्तुं शक्यं तथापि तद्दूषणमपि दूरीकरिष्यामि इति प्रवृत्ते रामरायकविः। तथाहि - ब्रह्मव्यतिरिक्तस्य मिथ्यात्वज्ञानं समाधिस्थस्य वा मुक्तस्य वा न जायेत, समाधौ मुक्तौ वा आत्मव्यतिरिक्तस्य वस्त्वन्तरस्याभावात्। अपि तु अविद्यावतः संसारिणः कृतश्रवणमननस्य, "ब्रह्मैव सत्यम्" अनन्तरं "ब्रह्मव्यतिरिक्तं सर्वं मिथ्या" इत्याकारकं ज्ञानम्। तच्च "ब्रह्मव्यतिरिक्तं सर्वं मिथ्या" इति ज्ञानं अर्थतः सिद्ध्यता "ब्रह्मैव सत्यम्" इति ज्ञानेन वा, कविना उक्तरीत्या स्वप्रयोजकीभूत - "ब्रह्मैव सत्यम्" इति - ज्ञानद्वारेण वा, "ब्रह्म नास्ति" इति ब्रह्मणि असत्त्वविषयकमज्ञानं निवर्तयत्येव। अत्रासत्त्वविषयकाज्ञाननिवर्तकं वेदान्तवाक्यजन्यं ज्ञानं परोक्षम्। ब्रह्मणः अभानविषयकाज्ञाननिवर्तकं अहं ब्रह्मास्मि इति प्रत्यगभिन्नब्रह्मज्ञानन्त्वपरोक्षमिति विवेकः। कविना स्वशास्त्रमर्यादामनुल्लङ्घ्य उक्तं समाधानं कुकल्पना आहोस्वित् अनुक्तस्यारोपः कुकल्पना इति विवेचनपटवो जानन्तु।

अत्रेदमवधेयम् - "न हि ब्रह्मस्वरूपमजानानः पुरुषः इदं ब्रह्मव्यतिरिक्तमिति विजानीयात्" इति (श.वि. पु. १७९) वाक्यं पूर्वोक्तरीत्या अविद्यावत्संसारिपुरुषविषयकम्। "कर्मकर्तृभावविरोधात् विदुषः आत्मन एव ब्रह्मत्वेन कथं स्वस्य स्वानुभवः" इति (श.वि. पु.१७७) असंप्रज्ञातसमाधिस्थपुरुषविषयकम्। "स्वयंप्रकाशस्य ब्रह्मणः स्वेतरप्रकाशकत्वमेव, न तु स्वस्य ज्ञानान्तरेणावभास्यत्वम्" इति। "ब्रह्म स्वानुभवसिद्ध-स्वयाथात्म्यमित्यादेः रामानुजोक्तस्य असम्भवदुक्तिकत्वप्रदर्शकम्। अत्र कथं व्याहतिरिति अनवरतं व्याहतिजपकर्ता स्पष्टयतु। अत एवान्ते अवोचत् कविः "वस्तुतस्तु अहं ब्रह्मास्मीति ज्ञानमेव ब्रह्मस्वरूपाज्ञानविरोधि" इति ब्रह्माज्ञानपक्षे पञ्च, अज्ञाननिवर्तकज्ञानविषये स्वयमुत्प्रेक्ष्य अद्वैतिनामुपरि तदुक्तत्वेन आरोपित एक इत्याहत्य षडाक्षेपाः उत्थापिता रामानुजाचार्यैः। तेषां निर्मूलत्वसिद्धान्तापरिज्ञान-सिद्धान्तविरोधस्वकल्पितत्वादिप्रदर्शनेन यथा ते पुनरङ्कुरिता न भवेयुः तथा समाहिताः। प्रत्युत्तरमशक्नुवन् सोरस्ताडमाक्रोशति "इत्थमज्ञानस्याश्रये दुर्घटे एतदुपरि रामरायोक्तं सर्वं स्वमतानुबन्धिप्राचीनग्रन्थवाक्यानां पुनः पुनः आम्रेडनमात्रं, न पुनराक्षेपाणामेकमपि सदुत्तरम्"- इत्यादिना।

"किञ्च २७७ पुटे यथा अविद्या" इत्यादिः कवेः यः उच्छृङ्खलः उपालम्भः स सर्वोऽपि अनाघ्रातभामतीविवरणग्रन्थगन्धस्य प्रद्वेषदवानलदन्दह्यमानहृदयस्य लब्ध-वर्णशिरोमणेः प्रजल्पितम्। तथा हि - "नाविद्या ब्रह्माश्रया किन्तु जीवे, तेन नित्यशुद्धमेव ब्रह्म" इति समन्वयाधिकरणे, (भामती. १.१.४.) "अविद्योपधानं च यद्यपि विद्यास्वभावे परमात्मनि न साक्षादस्ति तथापि तत्प्रतिबिम्बकल्पजीवद्वारेण परस्मिन् उच्यते" इति (भामती. १.१.२२) वाक्यान्वयाधिकरणे च भामत्याम्। "तमोवच्च स्वाश्रयावरणमज्ञानं स्वाश्रयैकत्वेन न विरुध्यते। नापि स्वाश्रयचित्प्रकाशेन विरुध्यते अज्ञानम्। स्वावभासकेन संवेदनेन चित्प्रकाशेन अज्ञानस्याविरुद्धत्वात्। साक्षिचैतन्यस्य चाज्ञानावभासकत्वात्। अतो न चिदाश्रयत्वविरोधः" इति। "चित्स्वरूपमात्रसंबन्धि अज्ञानं तत्र जीवब्रह्मव्यवहारभेदं प्रवर्तयति। स्वरूपमात्रसम्बन्धिनः अज्ञानस्य ब्रह्मस्वरूपं परिहृत्य जीवविभागैकपक्षपातिता दर्पणघटादेः मुखाकाशभेदे हेतुतया मुखादिसंसर्गिणोऽपि बिम्बाकाशौ परिहृत्य प्रतिबिम्बघटाकाशादिपक्षपातित्ववदिति वदामः" इति च विवरणे प्रथमवर्णके। उपरि लिखितभामतीविवरणग्रन्थोद्धृतवाक्येभ्यः स्पष्टमेतत् ज्ञायते - यत् भामतीप्रस्थाने साक्षादाश्रयत्वं जीवस्य, जीवद्वारा ब्रह्मणः। विवरणप्रस्थाने तु ब्रह्मणः साक्षादाश्रयत्वं जीवस्य ब्रह्मद्वारा। तस्मादुभयोरपि प्रस्थानयोः जीवब्रह्मणोरुभयोरपि अविद्यासम्बन्धः अस्त्येव। एवं स्थिते प्रस्थानविवेके "न च जीवस्य कथमज्ञानाश्रयत्वम्" इत्यादि (श.वि. पु. १७८) यदुक्तं तत् सूक्ष्मार्थदर्शिनः वचनं, न तु अश्रुतचरप्रस्थानद्वयार्थस्य। तथाहि - "न च जीवस्य" इत्यादिग्रन्थः भामतीप्रस्थानानुसारी। भामतीप्रस्थाने प्रतिजीवमन्या अविद्या। "इयं प्रतिजीवं भिद्यते" इति आनुमानिकाधिकरणे भामत्याम्। प्रमाणं च तत्र "यो योनिं योनिमधितिष्ठत्येकः" इति श्रुतिः। अनुपदमेव जीवद्वारेण ब्रह्मणः अविद्याश्रयत्वमुक्तम्। तथा च सर्वाः जीवाविद्याः एकस्मिन् ब्रह्मणि वर्तन्ते। सर्वजीवाविद्या एव एकत्र मिलिताः समष्टिरित्युच्यते। जीवगता अविद्या तूलाज्ञानमित्युच्यते। ब्रह्मगत-तूलाज्ञानसमष्टिरेव मूलाज्ञानं ब्रह्माश्रितमित्युच्यते। तत्तज्जीवतत्त्वज्ञानेन तत्तज्जीवाज्ञाननिवृत्तिरित्युक्ते मूलाज्ञाननिवृत्तिः सर्वजीवतत्त्वज्ञानेनेति, वचनं विनापि, ज्ञायत एव। एतेन "मूलाविद्या केन कथं नाश्येत इति प्रश्नः दुरुत्तरण एव" इति प्रलापः अनन्यसामान्यं मतिमान्द्यं प्रष्टुरावेदयति।

जीवन्मुक्तिं दूषयितुं प्रयतमानेन मनीषिणा माननीयेन "विक्षेपशक्तिरविनाश्या अनुवर्तते" इति कविग्रन्थानुवादे "अविनाश्या" इति पदं प्रत्यक्षेऽपि स्वकीयकौटिल्यप्रकटीकरणाय। "विक्षेपशक्तिर्यावत्प्रारब्धं वर्तते एव" इत्येतावानेव कवेः ग्रन्थः। विक्षेपशक्तिर्यावत् प्रारब्धं वर्तत इत्युक्ते निराश्रयाया शक्तेः अनुवृत्त्यसम्भवात् स्वाश्रयाविद्यया सहैव विक्षेपशक्तिः

अनुवर्तत इति शास्त्रज्ञानसंस्कृतमतिः विचारकुशलः गृह्णीयात् न तु चिरप्ररूढप्रद्वेषापहत-विवेकविज्ञानः। उदाहृतवाक्यस्य पूर्वभागेन आवरणशक्तेरेव ब्रह्मसाक्षात्कारसमये नाश उक्तः, न तु तद्वत्या अविद्यायाः। अविद्यायाः सर्वात्मना निवृत्तिस्तु प्रारब्धकर्मावसानसमय एव। एवं च "तत्त्वज्ञानात् अनिवृत्तायाः विक्षेपशक्तेः ब्रह्मण इव सत्यत्वमेष्टव्यं भवेत्" इत्यादिकं बालिशभाषितम्। कृतब्रह्मसाक्षात्कारस्यापि पुरुषस्य यावत्प्रारब्धकर्मक्षयं विलम्बं अत ऊर्ध्वं सत्सम्पत्तिं च ब्रुवाणा "तस्य तावदेव चिरं यावन्न विमोक्ष्ये अथ सम्पत्स्ये" इति श्रुतिः जीवन्मुक्तौ प्रमाणत्वेन उदाजह्रे पूर्वाचार्यसरणिमनुरुन्धानेन कविना। इदमत्र सिद्धान्तरहस्यम् - सन्ति मायायाः अनेकाः शक्तयः, "इन्द्रो मायाभिः पुरुरूप ईयते" इति बहुवचनान्तश्रुतेः। तत्र प्रत्यगभिन्नब्रह्मसाक्षात्कारसमये अपरोक्ष-प्रतिभासयोग्यार्थाभासजनिकायाः शक्तेरनुवृत्तेः तद्वती अविद्यापि तिष्ठति; अन्याः शक्तयो निवर्तन्ते। न च तावता अनुवर्तमानायास्तस्याः सत्यत्वम्। प्रतिबिम्बादिभ्रम इव साक्षात्कृतब्रह्मणः शुकवामदेवादेः देहादिभ्रमेऽपि अनुभवबलात् अनुवृत्तिः स्वीक्रियते। किं च "तस्य तावदेव चिरं" इत्यादिश्रुत्यापि तत्सिद्धिः। प्रारब्धकर्मणा प्रतिबन्धात् उत्पन्नमप्यपरोक्षज्ञानं कार्त्स्न्येन अविद्यां न निवर्तयति इत्यभ्युपगन्तव्यम्। अन्यथा मोक्षविलम्बं प्रतिपादयन्ती "यावन्न विमोक्ष्ये, तस्य तावदेव चिरम्" इति श्रुतिः बाधिता स्यात्। विदेहतासमये अप्रतिरुद्धेन महावाक्यजज्ञानेन सर्वशक्तिमदज्ञाननाशो भवति। अत्र च "भूयश्चान्ते विश्वमायानिवृत्तिः" इति श्रुतिः मानम्। अत्रैवमन्वयः - तत्त्वभावात् विश्वमायानिवृत्तिः, अन्ते भूयश्च विश्वमायानिवृत्तिः इति। अर्थस्तु - पूर्वं प्रारब्ध कर्मकालीनसाक्षात्कारसमये अन्यशक्तिरूपविश्वमायानिवृत्तिः, प्रारब्धभोगान्ते अवशिष्ट-शक्तिमदज्ञानतत्प्रयुक्तदेहादिरूपविश्वमायानिवृत्तिः भूयश्च इति। एवं ब्रह्मणः पुनर्ब्रह्मभावं, मुक्तस्यैव पुनर्मुक्तिं च श्रावयन्त्यः "ब्रह्मैव सन् ब्रह्माप्येति" "विमुक्तश्च विमुच्यते" इत्याद्याः श्रुतयः, "भोगेन त्वितरे क्षपयित्वा सम्पद्यते" इति (ब्र.सू. ४.४.६) सूत्रं च जीवत एव मुक्तौ प्रमाणम्। अविद्यादशायामपि मुक्त इति व्यपदेशस्तु प्रपञ्चपारमार्थिकत्व-भ्रमहेतुशक्तिनाशात् उपपन्न एव। मायाया ब्रह्मशक्तित्वं इतिहासपुराणेषु प्रसिद्धम्, सर्वैर्वेदान्तवादिभिरभ्युपगतं च। आवरणविक्षेपरूपशक्तिद्वयवत्यां तस्यां ब्रह्मपरतन्त्रतया शक्तिशब्दः उपचरित इत्यधिगन्तव्यम्।

तिरोधानोपपत्तिः

विवरणे आवरणनिरूपणप्रकरणे - "न तावदावरणं प्रकाशविलोपः स्वरूपस्या-नपायात्। नापि सत एव प्रकाशस्य कार्यप्रतिबन्धः, ज्ञानस्य विषयावभासात्मना उदितस्य स्वकार्ये प्रतिबन्धप्रतीक्षयोरभावात्। तस्मान्नैवात्मन्यपि भावरूपमज्ञानम्"-

इति विकल्पद्वयमपि पूर्वपक्षिणैव परास्तम्। तत्रैव स्वयंज्योतिष्ट्वनिरूपणे - "ननु ज्ञानत्वप्रयुक्तं जन्मापि तस्य विद्यते?...अत्रापि ज्योतिःशब्दादात्मनि प्रकाशगुणस्य जन्माभावनिश्चयात्" इति ग्रन्थेन पूर्वपक्षिणो ज्ञानस्य जन्यत्वशङ्का सिद्धान्तिना निरासि। उदाहृतग्रन्थभागौ मेलयित्वा तत्रत्यमेकं विकल्पं परिज्यत्य तत्स्थाने उत्तरस्मात् ग्रन्थादानीय निवेशितं अपरं विकल्पं सिद्धान्त्यनभ्युपगमेन हेतुना उपेक्ष्य विकल्पमेकं परिशेष्य दूषणग्रन्थमित्थमरीरचन् श्रीरामानुजाचार्याः - "अविद्यया प्रकाशैकस्वरूपं ब्रह्म तिरोहितमिति वदता स्वरूपनाश एव उक्तः स्यात्। प्रकाशतिरोधानं नाम प्रकाशोत्पत्तिप्रतिबन्धः विद्यमानस्य विनाशो वा। प्रकाशस्यानुत्पाद्यत्वाभ्युपगमेन प्रकाशतिरोधानं प्रकाशनाश एव"- इति।

पूर्वपक्षिणैव दूषितमपि पक्षमनूद्य तावन्मात्रेण सुहितास्ते विवरणे अनुपदमेव प्रतिपादितं सिद्धान्तं खण्डयितुं न प्रावर्तिषत।

श्रुतिस्मृतिप्रामाण्यात् अज्ञानं चिदात्मानं (ब्रह्म) आवृणोतीति औपनिषदानामभ्युपगमः। तत्र आङुपसृष्टः वृणोतिस्सकर्मकः। तस्याज्ञानं कर्तृ। चिदात्मा कर्म, आवरणक्रियायाः फलं तिरोधानं, तच्च चिदात्मनिष्ठम्। स्वप्रकाशज्ञानरूपस्यात्मनः कीदृशमावरणकृतं तिरोधानं इति जिज्ञासायां उक्तमद्वैतवेदान्तग्रन्थेषु विवरणप्रमुखेषु - अस्ति भातीति व्यवहाराविषयत्वं चिदात्मनि आपादयति अज्ञानकृतमावरणम्। अर्थात् चिदात्मा तादृशव्यवहाराविषयत्वमापद्यते। तथा च ब्रह्म अस्ति भातीति व्यवहाराविषयत्वरूपं चिदात्मनः तिरोधानं आवरणकृतम्। इममेवार्थं "ब्रह्मणस्तिरोधानं नाम अस्ति भातीति व्यवहाराविषयत्वापत्तिः।...अस्ति भातीति व्यवहाराविषयत्वरूपाज्ञानावरणकार्यदर्शनात् ब्रह्म अज्ञानावृतमित्युच्यते" इत्यादिना ग्रन्थेन प्रतिपादयति स्म रामरायकविः। अस्मिन् प्रसङ्गे "तिरोधानजन्ये व्यवहाराविषयत्वे तिरोधानव्यपदेशोऽस्य अव्युत्पत्तिहेतुकः" इति (श.वि. पु.२७९) रामरायकविं निरङ्कुशं दूषयति पण्डितप्रवरः। आवरणक्रियातज्जन्यफलयोः स्वरूपं सम्यक् विविच्य तिरोधानस्वरूपं कथयन् शास्त्रमर्मज्ञः रामरायकविः अव्युत्पन्नः आहोस्वित् क्रियातज्जन्यफलयोर्भेदमविज्ञाय फलमेव क्रियेति भ्रान्त्वा अव्युत्पत्तिदोषं कल्पयित्वा दूषयन् प्रचण्डपण्डितः अव्युत्पन्न इति सुधियो विभावयन्तु।

अद्य प्रातरत्रायं घटो न ज्ञातः इदानीं ज्ञातः, पूर्वमितच्छ्लोकार्थोऽज्ञातः इदानीं ज्ञातः इत्यादिलोकव्यवहारात् घटविषयकाज्ञानानुभवोऽस्त्येव। तथा च लोकतः अज्ञान-विषयत्वरूपं घटादीनां अज्ञानावृतत्वं दुरपह्नवम्। एवं स्थिते अद्वैतदर्शनप्रद्वेषप्रतिबद्ध-यथार्थदर्शनः लोकव्यवहारमप्यजानानः "मायावादिनैव तथोच्यते नान्येनेति" प्रलपत्यपार्थम्।

अद्वैतग्रन्थेषूक्तं तिरोधानस्वरूपमनादृत्य स्वरूपनाश एव तिरोधानमिति स्वयमेव विनिश्चित्य यदुक्तं रामानुजाचार्यैः तत्रानुपपत्तिप्रदर्शनपूर्वकं सिद्धान्त्यभ्युपगतं तिरोधान-स्वरूपं वक्तुं घटाज्ञानदृष्टान्त उपात्तः कविना। यथा तिरोधानमात्रेण घटादेः स्वरूपनाशो न केनापि वक्तुं शक्यः, तथा ब्रह्मणोऽपि तिरोधानमात्रेण स्वरूपनाशो न शक्यवचनः इत्येषोऽर्थः प्रतिपादितः। व्यवहारविषयत्वाविषयत्वयोः वस्तुनाशाविनाशौ प्रति प्रयोजकत्वकथनाय न तदीयग्रन्थप्रवृत्तिः। तद्ग्रन्थप्रतिपाद्यमन्यथा गृहीत्वा तस्य दुःस्थत्वं रटतः तव वचनमेव निर्मूलं दुःस्थं च।

"अज्ञानेनावृतं ज्ञान" (भ.गी. ५. १५) मित्यत्र ज्ञानमावरणक्रियायाः कर्म। अनन्तरश्लोके पूर्वश्लोकोक्तस्य ज्ञानस्य यदावरकमज्ञानं तत् येषामात्मविषयज्ञानेन नाशितं तेषां अज्ञाननाशकं ज्ञानं तत् परं परमार्थतत्त्वं (ब्रह्म) अभिव्यनक्ति इत्युक्तम्। तत्र यदज्ञानं ज्ञानमावृणोति तस्याज्ञानस्य नाशे सति ज्ञानमेव नाशकेन ज्ञानेन अभिव्यज्येत; अत्र तु परं ब्रह्माभिव्यज्यत इत्युक्तम्। तस्मात् पूर्वस्मिन् श्लोके ज्ञानशब्देन यद्बोधितं तदेवेह श्लोके तत्परं इति शब्दाभ्यां बोध्यत इति ग्रहीतव्यम्। तथा च पूर्वश्लोके ब्रह्मैवाज्ञानेन आवृतमित्युक्तं भवति। अन्यथा आवरणनाशोऽन्यत्र अभिव्यक्ति-रन्यत्रेति वैयधिकरण्यं स्यात्।

किं च "तद्बुद्धय" इत्यादितदनन्तरश्लोके "यत्परं ज्ञानं प्रकाशितं तस्मिन् गता बुद्धिः येषां त" इति व्याचक्षाणाः भाष्यकाराः पूर्वतनश्लोके अभिव्यक्तं यत् "परं" तत् "अज्ञानेनावृतं ज्ञानं" इत्यत्र श्रुतेन ज्ञानेन सामानाधिकरण्येनान्वयं कुर्वते। तदेवं "अज्ञानेनावृतं" इत्यत्रत्यः ज्ञानशब्दः, "ज्ञानेन तु तदज्ञानं" इत्यत्रत्यः परशब्दः तद्बुद्धय इत्यत्रत्यः तच्छब्दश्च ज्ञानस्वरूपब्रह्मपराः इति अनन्तरश्लोकद्वयतद्भाष्यार्थपर्यालोचनया निर्विचिकित्समवगम्यते। "तेन मुह्यन्ति जन्तव" इति वाक्यशेषात् जन्तूनां स्वात्मभूतं यत् ज्ञानस्वरूपं ब्रह्मेति व्याख्येयम्। पूर्वापरवाक्यार्थानुगुण्येन वाक्यार्थः अध्यवसातव्य इति शास्त्रमर्यादां परिपालयन् कविः उदाहृतश्लोकपादं ब्रह्मणः अज्ञानावृतत्वे प्रमाणत्वेन उपन्यास्थत्। तथा च ब्रह्मणः अज्ञानेनावरणम् इति व्याख्यानं भाष्यानुसार्येव। शास्त्रमर्यादामूढस्य भवत एव श्लोकार्थापरिस्फूर्तिः।

वाक्यशेषस्य प्रकृतेऽनुपयोगात् नोपन्यासः न तु निह्नवः। भवत एव अनितर-साधारणं निह्नवकौशलम्। अनेकैः श्रुतिवाक्यैः सह उदाहृतं गीतावाक्यमपि अज्ञानस्य ब्रह्माश्रितत्वे प्रमाणत्वेन उदाहार्षुः विवरणाचार्याः इत्यत्र ज्ञापनीयम् ।

पूर्वं लोकव्यवहारानुसारं घटस्याज्ञानावरणमुक्तम्। पश्चात् "वस्तुतस्तु" इत्यादिना यदुक्तं तद्विचारदृष्ट्या। तमेव विचारं "स्वत एव असत" इत्यादिना (श.वि. पु.२८०)

ग्रन्थेनाभिनयति। शास्त्रेषु अणुमात्रपरिचयवानपि, तुशब्दः पूर्वोक्तात् वक्ष्यमाणस्य वैलक्षण्यद्योतक इति जानीते। अहो तुशब्दप्रयोगविषयमविदुषो वैदुष्यम्।

प्रसक्तप्रकाशस्य अप्रकाशे प्रकाशप्रतिबन्धकत्वेनाज्ञानमुपेयते। जडस्य घटादेः प्रकाशस्यैवाभावात् तत्र प्रयोजनाभावात् आवरणानभ्युपगमः इति अद्वैतदर्शनसिद्धान्तः। पूर्वं लोकव्यवहार उक्तः; अत्र तद्विलक्षणः शास्त्रीय अर्थ उक्तः। क्व व्याघातः? प्रदर्शयतु पण्डितश्रेष्ठः, अविच्छेदेन व्याहतिजपं कुर्वाणः।

"अपरं चेदं विचित्रम्" इति यदुक्तं तदसत्। पूर्वं व्यवहारदृष्ट्या उक्तम्, सम्प्रति तुशब्दपूर्वकं विचारदृष्ट्या तद्विलक्षणमुच्यते। किमत्र वैचित्र्यम्? प्रश्नमेनमुत्तरतु भवान् - यदि कश्चन खलः घोरतमं कञ्चनापराधं कल्पयित्वा भवत्यारोप्य न्यायालये व्यवहारं कुर्यात् तदा भवान् परमार्थतः अहं निरपराधीति प्रतिविधाने अप्रयतमानः किं तूष्णीमेव भविष्यति? मिथ्याभूतमेव सर्वं व्यवहारं आब्रह्मज्ञानं यथार्थमेवेति मन्यते लोकः महद्दुःखं चानुभवति। यथार्थभ्रमनिवृत्त्यर्थं गुरूपसदनशास्त्रार्थविचारादिसाधनानुष्ठानमवश्यं कर्तव्यमेव।

स्वरूपोपपत्तिः

अज्ञानस्य जीवाश्रितत्वे भामतीकारविवरणकारयोरभिप्रायः आश्रयानुपपत्तिनिरसने स्पष्टीकृतोऽस्माभिः। तथा च जीवाज्ञानवाददूषणपूर्वकं ब्रह्माज्ञानवादः विवरणकारादिभिः प्रसाधितः इति वचः वादद्वयापरिज्ञानविलसितम्।

ततः "अत्रोच्यते - न वयं निराश्रया...अतो नानवस्था", इति (श.वि. पु.२८१) कविना यदुक्तं तत्सर्वं साधु। नास्ति तत्र लेशतोऽपि कवेः अज्ञानं, अन्यथाग्रहणं, छलेन अनुक्तोपालम्भः, व्याहतिः अपसिद्धान्तो वा। तथा हि - अज्ञानमन्तःकरणमिति प्रमातुः जीवस्य उपाधिद्वयम्; ईश्वरस्य तु अज्ञानमात्रम्। अत एव "अन्तःकरणावच्छिन्नं चैतन्यं जीव" इति वेदान्तपरिभाषायां जीवलक्षणमुक्तम्। अत एव च अहमज्ञः इत्यज्ञानानुभवः जीवस्यैव न तु ईश्वरस्य, निर्विशेषचितो वा; तयोः क्रमेण सर्वज्ञत्वात् सर्वावभासकत्वाच्च। प्रमातुः स्वरूपभूता अनुभूतिः निर्विशेषं चैतन्यम्। भामतीप्रस्थाने तत्राज्ञानाध्यासः जीवद्वारा, विवरणप्रस्थाने साक्षादेव। एवं च जीवस्वरूपे चैतन्ये अज्ञानाध्यासः प्रस्थानद्वयेऽपि समानः। अत्र उदाहृते कविवाक्ये अज्ञानान्तःकरणयोर्मध्ये कार्यशब्दः कविग्रन्थे अविद्यमानोऽपि स्वयमेव प्रक्षिप्तो महाविदुषा। अयं प्रक्षेपः प्रतारणार्थो वा अज्ञानमूलको वा?

स्वाश्रयशब्दस्य ब्रहुव्रीहिमाश्रित्य दोषविशेषणत्वेऽपि न निस्तारः। तथाहि- "निर्विषया निराश्रया चेयमनुभूतिः" इत्यनेन निर्विशेषचैतन्यमेव परामृश्यत इति

निर्विवादम्। निर्विशेषे शुद्धे चैतन्ये कस्यचिदपि दोषस्य नास्ति सम्भवः। "निष्कलं निष्क्रियं शान्तं निरवद्यं निरञ्जनम्, 'निरनिष्टो निरवद्यः शोकं मोहमत्येति नित्यमुक्तः" इत्यादिश्रुतिभ्यः। औपनिषददर्शने निर्विशेषस्य दोषाश्रयत्वं कुत्रापि नोक्तम्। अविद्योपाधि-प्रयुक्ताः दोषाः जीवगता एव उपाधेः प्रतिबिम्बपक्षपातात्। किं च कर्तृत्वादिसमस्तधर्म-रहितस्य निर्विशेषब्रह्मणः"आत्मानमनुभवति" इति कर्तृत्वादिवैशिष्ट्यवचनं अद्वैतदर्शने नैव सम्भवति। ततश्च "स्वाश्रयदोषवशात्" इति न केवलं सिद्धान्ताननुगुणं किन्तु तद्विरुद्धं च। एवं च "स्वाश्रयदोषवशात्" इति पदघटितं निर्विषया निराश्रयेत्याद्युदाहृतं वाक्यं नाद्वैत-दर्शनानुवादः, तस्मात् श्रीभाष्यकारीयमेव। अन्यत्रापि श्रीभाष्ये उक्तम् - "ब्रह्मैवानाद्यविद्यया सदसदनिर्वाच्यया तिरोहितस्वरूपं स्वगतनानात्वं पश्यति इत्यवगम्यते"- इति।

कविनापि बहुव्रीहिमाश्रित्यैव आश्रयदोषायोग उक्तः। "प्रमाता स्वाश्रयाज्ञान-दोषात्" इति (श.वि. पु.२८१) स्वपक्षप्रतिपादनपरे वाक्ये बहुव्रीहिराश्रितः, यतो न प्रमातरि अज्ञानं किन्तु "प्रमातृस्वरूपभूतायामनुभूतौ" इति समनन्तरवाक्ये प्रतिपादनात्। अतः तुल्यच्छायया इहापि बहुव्रीहिरेवाश्रितः न तत्पुरुषः।

तथा च "निर्विषया निराश्रया चानुभूतिः स्वाश्रयदोषवशात् अनन्ताश्रया अनन्तविषया भवतीति रामानुजमतं तत्खण्डनं चेति शीर्षकवाक्यं" साध्वेव, सम्यग्विमृश्यैव कविना लिखितम्। तेन पण्डितेन कवेरुपरि आरोपितं अनुक्तोपालम्भादिदूषणजातं निरवकाशम्।

"ननु न मे ब्रह्माज्ञानमिष्टम्" इत्यादि "प्रामाण्यादिष्ट"मित्यन्तं अद्वैतिनः समाधान-मिति स्वयमुत्प्रेक्ष्य तदुपरि यदसामञ्जस्यतादवस्थ्यमुक्तं तत्तुच्छम्। दर्शितरीत्या उभयोरपि प्रस्थानयोः प्रमातुः स्वरूपभूतायामनुभूतौ अज्ञानमध्यस्तं न तु प्रमातरि। अतो जीवाज्ञानपक्षमाश्रित्येत्यादिकं अज्ञानध्वान्तकबलीकृतचित्तस्य प्रलपितम्।

जीवाविद्यापक्षे अन्योन्याश्रयादिदोषाः अद्वैतसिद्धिकारैः निरवकाशीकृताः इति पूर्वमवोचाम, सम्प्रति दोषनिरसनप्रकारं प्रदर्शयामः। किमन्योन्याश्रयः जीवाविद्ययो-रुत्पत्तौ, ज्ञप्तौ, स्थितौ वा? नाद्यः - अनादित्वादुभयोः। न द्वितीयः, अज्ञानस्य चिद्भास्यत्वेऽपि चितः स्वप्रकाशत्वेन तदभास्यत्वात्। न तृतीयः, स किं परस्पराश्रितत्वेन वा परस्परसापेक्ष-स्थितिकत्वेन वा? तन्न, उभयथाप्यसिद्धेः। अज्ञानस्य चिदाश्रयत्वे चिदधीनस्थितिकत्वेऽपि चिति अविद्याश्रितत्वतदधीनस्थितिकत्वयोरभावात्। नाप्यात्माश्रयः। समानकालीनयोरपि अवच्छेद्यावच्छेदकभावमात्रेण अन्योन्याधीन-तोपपत्तेः। घटतदवच्छिन्नाकाशयोरिव स्वोपहितेऽपि जीवे अविद्याया आश्रयत्वं सम्भवति, स्वस्य स्वाश्रयं प्रत्युपाधित्वेऽपि अविशेषणत्वेन स्वाश्रयत्वे न क्षतिः। तदुक्तं - "स्वेनैव कल्पिते देशे व्योम्नि यद्वद् घटादयः। तथा जीवाश्रयाविद्यां मन्यन्ते ज्ञानकोविदा" इति।

जीवाज्ञानवादस्य निर्दोषत्वात् नास्त्यणुमात्रमपि असामञ्जस्यम्। जीवाविद्ययोरुभयोरपि अनादित्वात् उभयोरपि दोषयोर्नास्त्यवसरः। पूर्वं अद्वैतसिद्धिकारेण जीवाज्ञानवादः निरस्तः इति, सम्प्रति विवरणकारेणेति वदन् अनृतवदने आत्मनो निरौपम्यं च प्रकाशयन् अखण्डं कूष्माण्डमन्नेन पिदधाति।

किं च युक्त्या श्रुत्या च जीवाविद्ययोरनादित्वं निरूप्य अन्योन्याश्रयं परिहरतः कवेः "किमादौ जीवादविद्या जाता" (श.वि. पु.२८३) इत्यादिग्रन्थं पठित्वापि पुनरन्योन्याश्रयदोषं चोदयन् अस्वस्थचित्त एव। जीवाज्ञानपक्षमाश्रित्य समाधानं सिद्धान्तसम्मतं समञ्जसं च।

"अज्ञानं प्रमातृस्वरूपभूतायामनुभूतौ अध्यस्तं" इत्येवोक्तम् न तु प्रमातृनिष्ठमिति। तेन "प्रमातृनिष्ठत्वदृश्यत्वोक्तिरपि नोचिता" इति उक्तस्य अन्यथाकरणदक्षस्य प्रजल्पितम्। "तस्यैव अविद्याकल्पितत्वस्वीकारात् कल्पनाहेतोरज्ञानस्य कारणत्वात् पूर्वभावित्वनियमेन तदा तदाश्रयप्रश्नस्य निरुत्तरतैवेति" जल्पनमतितुच्छम्। अनाद्योः समकालिकयोर्वा अन्योन्यात्माश्रयौ नैव स्तः। अनादिजीवं प्रति कथमविद्यायाः पूर्वकालिकत्वम् यस्मिन् सिद्धे अन्योन्याश्रयादिः चोद्येत? उभयोरप्यनादित्वेन कालकृतं पौर्वापर्यमेव नास्ति। किं च श्रुतिप्रामाण्यात् कालस्यापि अविद्याकार्यत्वेन अनादिं स्वकारणभूतामविद्यां पूर्वत्वेन कालः कथमवच्छिन्द्यात्? जीवं वा तदुत्तरत्वेन। सकललोकशास्त्रमर्यादामतिलंघ्य असम्बद्धं पृच्छतः कथमुत्तरं वक्तुं शक्यम्? अबद्धप्रश्नस्य निरुत्तरताचोदनं अबद्धभाषी एव कुर्यात्।

अज्ञानमनुभूतौ स्वतोऽध्यस्तमित्युक्तम्। स्वतस्त्वमात्रेण स्वतोऽध्यस्तत्वस्वतः-सिद्धत्वयोः भेदमविदुषः पूर्वपक्षिणः, "दोषस्य स्वतः सिद्धत्वे सति ब्रह्मवन्नित्यत्वं स्यात्" "इत्यापादनं, "न च ... वाच्यम्" इति निषिध्य, "जन्यत्वेन जडत्वेन च स्वतःसिद्धत्वाभावात्" इति जन्यत्वजडत्वाभ्यां अज्ञानस्य ब्रह्मणो भेदं प्रतिपाद्य पूर्वपक्षिणः अभेदभ्रममपनयति सिद्धान्ती। पूर्वपक्षसिद्धान्तग्रन्थयोः अविवेकेन एककर्तृकत्वभ्रान्त्या व्याहतिमभिदधतो विचक्षणस्य शास्त्रपाण्डित्यं सर्वैः विद्वद्भिः ऐकमत्येनाभिनन्दनीयं भवत्यहो। अज्ञानस्य जन्यत्वं ७७ तमे पुटे उक्तं - "अविद्यायास्तु जन्म अस्त्येव", "माया चाविद्या च स्वयमेव भवति" इति श्रुतेः। तस्या अनादित्वप्रसिद्धिस्तु परतो जन्माभावप्रयुक्ता। न हि जगदविद्ययेव अविद्या केनचिदुत्पाद्यते"...इत्यादिना सन्दर्भेण। अहो वैयात्यं यत् ग्रन्थमनवलोक्य ग्रन्थकारस्योपरि अविच्छिन्नदूषणोपलवृष्टिं पातयति।

"अजामेका"मित्यादिमन्त्रे तुरीयपादस्योदाहरणं प्रकृतानुपयोगित्वादनपेक्षितम्। बद्धजीवाविद्ययोरेव अनादित्वमिह प्रकृतम्, न मुक्तस्य जीवस्य। तस्मान्मुक्तजीव-

विषयस्तुरीयः पादः प्रकृतानुपयोगित्वान्नोदाहृतः। यावतो ग्रन्थभागस्य प्रकृतोपयोगिता तावन्तमेव ग्रन्थभागमुदाहरन्ति विपश्चितः न ततोऽधिकमनपेक्षितं अनुपयोगिनं च। अनुदाहरणेन केवलं कवेर्वञ्चकत्वदूषणं न सज्जनः कुर्यात्।

एकस्मिन् वाक्ये प्रकरणे वा पुनरावृत्तस्य शब्दस्य एकरूपेणैव अर्थो वर्णनीय इति नास्ति नियमः, प्रमाणाभावात्। अतः तत्तद्वाक्यार्थान्वययोग्यस्य शब्दार्थस्य स्वीकार एव न्याय्यः। यथा "अज्ञानेनावृतं ज्ञानं तेन मुह्यन्ति जन्तवः। ज्ञानेन तु तदज्ञानं येषां नाशितमात्मन॥" इत्यत्र। प्रथमान्तज्ञानशब्दस्य योऽर्थः तस्मादन्य एव तृतीयान्तज्ञानशब्दार्थत्वेन ग्राह्यः। अन्यथा आव्रियमाणनाशकज्ञानयोरेकत्वे आव्रियमाणमेव ज्ञानं आवरकस्याज्ञानस्य नाशकं स्यात् इति अज्ञानस्यावरकत्वमेव न सिद्ध्येत् इति भगवतो बाधितार्थोपदेष्टृत्वापत्तिः।

किं चायं मन्त्रः अविद्याया बद्धमुक्तजीवयोश्च नित्यत्वप्रतिपादनाय न प्रवृत्तः किन्तु बन्धमोक्षव्यवस्थाप्रतिपादनाय। तच्च अजारूपकद्वारा उपदिश्यते। मन्त्रस्यास्य कल्पनोपदेशपरत्वमास्थेयम्। अन्यथा अजामिति - स्त्रीलिङ्गनिर्देशः क्वचित् अन्यत्र अजो ह्येक इति अजोऽन्य इति च पुंलिङ्गनिर्देशः निस्तात्पर्यः स्यात्। द्वासुपर्णेति कल्पनोपदेशसमभिव्याहारश्चानुपपन्नः स्यात्।

अस्मिन् प्रसङ्गे "एषाप्यजा बह्वीनां सरूपाणां प्रजानां स्रष्ट्री कर्मवश्येनात्मना भुज्यमाना, अन्येन विदुषा त्यज्यमाना च ब्रह्मण उत्पन्ना ब्रह्मात्मिका अवगन्तव्येत्यर्थ" इति (श्री.भा. १.४.९) चमसाधिकरणस्थं रामानुजीयं भाष्यं परामर्शमर्हति। एतद्भाष्यरीत्यापि नायं मन्त्रः योगशक्त्या अजशब्दवाच्यानां नित्यत्वं प्रतिपादयति' अपि तु बन्धमोक्षव्यवस्थाम् इति स्पष्टमवगम्यते। किं चेदं भाष्यं अजा उत्पत्तिमती, तुर्यपादगताजशब्दः मुक्तजीवपरः न परमात्मपरः, इति चावेदयति। तथा च "अत्र त्रिषु अजशब्देषु अवैरूप्येण अर्थो वाच्यः। अन्ते निर्दिष्टः अजोऽन्यः परमात्मा। तत्राजत्वं नित्यत्वपर्यवसायीति स्वेनापि वाच्यम्। पूर्वयोरजशब्दयोरपि स्वतः प्राप्तं समानार्थकत्वं यद्भज्यते न च सुतरां जन्माभावः "इति यदुक्तं तत्सर्वं रामानुजीयभाष्यविरुद्धम्; अपसिद्धान्तं चानयति। अद्वैतसिद्धान्तानभिज्ञत्वं पूर्वमसकृत् प्रदर्शितम्, अधुना स्वसिद्धान्तानभिज्ञत्वमपि। उभावपि सिद्धान्तौ अजानानः अन्यदीयसिद्धान्ते दूषणकथनाय प्रवृत्तो महाविद्वान्।

अनिर्वचनीयत्वोपपत्तिः

"अस्तीत्येवोपलब्धव्यः" इति ब्रह्मणोऽस्तित्वं सिद्ध्यति, नास्तित्वशङ्का च व्युदस्ता भवति। न च तावता ब्रह्मणो निर्वचनीयत्वसिद्धिः। ब्रह्मणो निर्वचनीयत्वे "तं दुर्दर्शं

गूढम्", "अशब्दमस्पर्शं","न संदृशे", "नैव वाचा" इत्याद्याः निरस्तसमस्तविशेषणत्वेन वागादीन्द्रियाद्यगोचरत्वेन च ब्रह्मप्रतिपादिन्यः श्रुतयः उपरुद्ध्येरन्। "अदृश्येऽनात्म्येऽनिरुक्ते" इति साक्षादेव ब्रह्मणो निर्वचनप्रतिषेधि श्रुत्यन्तरमपि बाध्येत।

स्वातिरिक्तस्वप्रकाशचैतन्यभास्यत्वमेव घटादीनां जडानां ज्ञेयत्वम्। स्वतोऽपरोक्षं-प्रत्यगभिन्नं ब्रह्म स्वप्रकाशत्वात् स्वयमेव भासते। "आत्मनैव ज्योतिषास्ते पल्ययते कर्म कुरुते विपल्येति"। "तमेव भान्तमनु भाति सर्वं तस्य भासा सर्वमिदं विभाति" इत्यादिश्रुतेः। स्वव्यतिरिक्तस्वप्रकाशान्तरस्यैवाभावात् प्रकाशान्तरभास्यत्वरूपं ज्ञेयत्वं ब्रह्मणो नैव भवितुमर्हति। "न चक्षुषा गृह्यते नापि वाचा नान्यैः देवैः तपसा कर्मणा वा" इत्यादिश्रुतिभिः ज्ञेयत्वमात्रस्य निषेधात् च। तस्मात् "सर्वं ज्ञेयवस्तुजातमेवे"त्यवधारणेन ब्रह्मणः ज्ञेयत्वाभावः युक्तः श्रुतिप्रमितश्च।

निर्विशेषसच्चिदानन्दं ब्रह्म, यज्ज्ञानात् परमपुरुषार्थसिद्धिः वेदान्तशास्त्रेणैव ज्ञायते, तज्ज्ञापनार्थमेव वेदान्तशास्त्रस्य प्रवृत्तेः। परं तु तत् घटादिवत्, न ज्ञानकर्मत्वेन बोध्यते। अपि तु 'अयमात्मा ब्रह्म' 'तदात्मानमेवावेत् अहं ब्रह्मास्मीति' इत्यादिभिर्महावाक्यैः ज्ञातृस्वरूप-भूतप्रत्यगात्माभिन्नत्वेनैव बोध्यते। प्रत्यगात्मनः तादृशस्वरूपबोधने न किमपि लौकिकं प्रमाणं क्रमते। तस्मात् नित्यनिरतिशयानन्दरूपमोक्षसाधनीभूततादृशात्मस्वरूप-साक्षात्कारस्य अपौरुषेयान् वेदान्तान्नन्तरा असिद्धेः तदर्थं वेदान्तशास्त्रस्यात्यन्त-मपेक्षितत्वात् वैयर्थ्यं वैयात्यादेव वक्तुमुद्युक्तोऽस्ति औपनिषददर्शनलेशमप्यजानानः।

घटादिप्रतीतिः "घटादिः सन्" इत्येव व्यवस्थापयति, न तु सर्वदा सन्निति। सर्वदा यत् सत् तदेव सत्, तदेव सदसद्विलक्षणशरीरघटकं, तच्च ब्रह्मैव नान्यत् इत्यनुपदमेव वक्ष्यते। किं च प्रत्यक्षमर्थगतं सार्वदिकं सत्त्वं ग्रहीतुमनीश्वरम्, तस्य वर्तमानमात्रग्राहित्वात्। एवमनुमानमपि सार्वदिकसत्त्वग्रहणे न क्रमते, तथाहि - विमतं परमार्थसत् स्वविषयज्ञानात् पूर्वभावित्वात् आत्मवत् इति चेत्। न, दृष्टिसृष्टिपक्षे असिद्धेः, अनादित्वस्योपाधित्वाच्च।

घटादीनां सत्यपि सत्त्वे न सद्विलक्षणत्वहानिः। सद्विलक्षणत्वे हि सार्वदिकसत्त्वमेव सच्छब्देन विवक्षितम्। घटादीनां प्रतीतिसिद्धं सत्त्वं न सार्वदिकं किन्तु कादाचित्कम्। यथा रज्जुसर्पादीनां सत्त्वं प्रतिभासकालमात्रवृत्तित्वरूपं न तेषां सार्वदिकसत्त्वघटितं मिथ्यात्वमुपहन्ति; एवं घटादीनां सत्त्वं व्यवहारकालमात्रवृत्तित्वरूपं न तेषां सार्वदिकसत्त्वघटितं मिथ्यात्वं विहन्ति। प्रतीतिसिद्धं सत्त्वं तत्त्वावेदकप्रमाणसिद्धं सदसद्विलक्षणत्वं बाधितुं नोत्सहते। तदेवं घटादिषु सत्त्वस्य सदसद्विलक्षणत्वं बाधितुं नोत्सहते। तदेवं घटादिषु सत्त्वस्य सदसद्विलक्षणत्वरूपानिर्वचनीयत्वस्य च अविरोधे स्थिते कथं व्याघातः अवकाशमासादयेत्, जगन्निष्ठानिर्वचनीयत्वस्य त्यागो वा? मन्दमतिः

तान्त्रिकः सिद्धान्ततत्त्वापरिचितः अत्युत्कटदूषणेच्छया प्रेरितः यत्किमपि अवद्धं प्रलपन् उन्मत्तचेष्टितमनुकरोति। "जगति भ्रान्तिरूपप्रतीतिव्यवस्थाप्यत्वम्" इत्यादि स्वेनैव कल्पितस्य यद्दूषणं तत् स्वस्यैव दूषणमित्यवैतु। "यद्यपि यतो वाचो निवर्तन्ते" इति श्रुत्या "यद्वाचानभ्युदितम्" इति श्रुत्या च ब्रह्मापि अनिर्वचनीयमेवेति प्राप्तम् इति ब्रह्मणो वागगोचरत्वरूपं अनिर्वचनीयत्वमुक्त्वा "ब्रह्मणोऽपि शास्त्रप्रमाणताऽस्तीति प्रतिपन्नत्वात् निर्वचनीयत्वमेवेति तदाशयः" इति निर्वचनीयत्वं वदन् स्वकीयं व्याहतभाषित्वं विस्मृत्य व्याहतभाषणेन कथञ्चिदप्यस्पृष्टस्य ग्रन्थस्य रचयितारं कविं व्याहतवादित्वेनाभीक्ष्णं दूषयन् व्याहतिजपं कुरुते तान्त्रिकः। ब्रह्मणः अनिर्वचनीयत्वं मयोक्तं, निर्वचनीयत्वं त्वस्मदाचार्यैरिति कथं मम व्याहतभाषित्वमिति यदि ब्रूयाः, तर्हि स्वाचार्योक्तिविरुद्धं रटतस्ते आचार्यद्रोहः अपसिद्धान्तश्चापतति। "सदसदाकारायाः प्रतीतेः" इति वाक्यं दूषयता २८७ पुटे सदसदाकारत्वं तु नैव सेत्स्यति। एकस्य वस्तुनः विरुद्धोभयाकारायोगात् इति यल्लिखितं तदपि अकाण्डताण्डवितमेव हि। "युगपत् विरुद्धैकाकारयोगस्य तैरप्यनुक्तेः" इत्यादिना यदुक्तं तान्त्रिकेण तत्राभिधीयते। "सदसदाकारायाः प्रतीतेः" इत्यादि रामानुजीयं भाष्यं -"सदसद्विलक्षणमिति या प्रतीतिः तत्रापि सदसदेव विषयः स्यादित्यर्थः।...तस्मात् सदसदाकारायाः प्रतीतेः सदसदाकार एव विषयः न सदसद्विलक्षणः... इति सदसद्विलक्षणत्वं क्वचिदपि न दृष्टं, सदसदात्मकत्वं दृष्टमिति च - व्याख्याय, सदसदात्मकत्वं दृष्टमिति स्वोक्तार्थे प्रमाणत्वेन, "नासत्प्रतीतेर्बाधाच्च न सदित्यपि यन्न तत्। प्रतीतेरेव सत्किं न बाधान्नासत्कुतो जगत्" इति संवित्सिद्धिग्रन्थमुदाहार्षीत् सुदर्शनः। उदाहृतसुदर्शनग्रन्थादेतदवगम्यते - यत् सदसदाकारं वस्तु रामानुजस्यापि सम्मतमिति।

तत्र प्रतीयमानत्वात् सत् बाध्यमानत्वात् असत् इति प्रयोगस्य दुष्टत्वं, यत्प्रतीयते तन्मिथ्या यन्न प्रतीयते तदसत् इति प्रयोगस्य साधुत्वं चोपपाद्य सदसद्विलक्षणमेवाज्ञानं न सदसदाकारमिति न्यरूपि कविना।

इदानीं सदसदाकारमज्ञानमिति वदता वक्तव्यम् - किं सदसदाकारत्वं यौगपद्येन आहो कालभेदेनेति विकल्प्य परस्परविरुद्धयोः सत्त्वासत्त्वयोरेकत्र तेजस्त्वतमस्त्वयोरिव स्थित्ययोगात्, अविरोधे न भ्रान्तिबाधौ सम्भवेताम्, रजतं सदसदात्मकमिति प्रतीत्यापत्तिश्च अतो न सदसदाकारवस्तुसिद्धिरिति आद्यो विकल्पः निरस्तः। द्वितीयविकल्पोऽपि-कालभेदेनापि परस्परविरुद्धयोः सत्त्वासत्त्वयोः एकत्र विरोधात्, "नासतो विद्यते भावो नाभावो विद्यते सतः" इति भगवद्वचनविरोधाच्च। न च रजतं कदाचिदस्तिप्रत्ययविषयः कदाचिन्नास्तिप्रत्ययविषयश्चेति कथं सदसद्विलक्षणं भवेदिति वाच्यम्। "अस्तिनास्तिप्रत्यय-विषयत्वस्य कादाचित्कत्वादेव" (२८८ पुटे) इत्यादिना निरस्तः। तदेवं मूले व्याख्याने

च सदसद्वस्तुनः सत्त्वासत्त्वे समानकालिके भिन्नकालिके वेत्यनुक्तेः द्वेधा विकल्प्य तन्निरासस्यावश्यकर्तव्यतया कथमकाण्डताण्डवितम्? परस्परप्रतिद्वन्द्विनोः सार्वदिकयोः सत्त्वासत्त्वयोः एकत्रासम्भवे प्रदर्श्यमाने कादाचित्कयोः बाल्ययौवनयोः एकत्र सम्भव-निदर्शनमकिञ्चित्करम्। सोऽयं देवदत्तः, "तत्त्वमसि" इति दृष्टान्तदार्ष्टान्तिकवाक्ययोः, विरुद्धयोरेकत्र समावेशनप्रतिपादने न तात्पर्यम्, अपि तु विरुद्धांशप्रहाणपूर्वकं पदार्थयोरैक्य-प्रतिपादने। अपि च दृष्टान्तदार्ष्टान्तिकयोः विरुद्धधर्मिद्वयविषयकत्वम्। प्रकृतस्य तु एकत्र विरुद्धधर्मद्वयविषयकत्वम् इति महद्वैषम्यम्। तस्मात् सदसदाकारं वस्तु नैव सिद्ध्यति।

"सदेव सोम्येदमग्र आसीत्" इति श्रुतेः जगतः उत्पत्तेः प्रागपि ब्रह्म सत् इति ज्ञायते। घटोऽस्ति पटोऽस्ति इति प्रत्यक्षात् घटादिरपि सन्नित्यवगम्यते, तथा घटादेः प्रभवाप्ययावपि। जगतः उत्पत्तेः प्रागपि ब्रह्म सत्; जगत्तु उत्पत्तेरूर्ध्वं नाशाच्च प्राक् स्थितिकाले एव सत्। तथा च यादृशं सत्त्वं ब्रह्मणः न तादृशं जगत इत्यवगम्यते। उन्मिषति च जिज्ञासा - कीदृशं ब्रह्मणः सत्त्वं, कीदृशं वा जगत इति? ब्रह्मणः श्रुत्येकसमधिगम्यत्वात् तत्स्वरूपभूतं सत्त्वमपि श्रुत्यैव प्रमातव्यम्। उक्तं चाभियुक्तैः - "अर्थे श्रुत्येकगम्ये हि श्रुतिमेवाद्रियामहे" इति। तथाहि - घटादिवत्, प्रपञ्चस्यापि "यतो वा" इत्यादिश्रुतेः प्रभवाप्ययौ अवगम्येते। "अतोऽन्यदार्तम्" इति श्रुतेश्च ब्रह्मव्यतिरिक्तं सर्वं विनाशीत्यवगम्यते। परन्तु ब्रह्मणः उत्पत्तिविनाशौ न श्रूयेते; प्रत्युत अनुत्पत्त्य-विनाशावेव - "न तस्य कार्यं करणं च", "तदेतद् ब्रह्मापूर्वम्" "अविनाशी वारेऽयमात्मा अनुच्छित्ति धर्मा" इति। एभ्यः श्रुतिवाक्येभ्यः विज्ञायत एतत् - यत् उत्पत्तिविनाशयो-रभावात् ब्रह्म सर्वदा सत्, प्रपञ्चस्तु प्रभवाप्ययवत्त्वात् स्थितिकाल एव सन्। तथा च ब्रह्म यथा सत् न तथा प्रपञ्चः सन्। ब्रह्मवत् यदि प्रपञ्चः सर्वदा सन् तदा प्रभवाप्यययो-रभावात् प्रभवाप्ययप्रतिपादिन्यः श्रुतयः बाध्येरन्, प्रत्यक्षं च।

"कथमसतः सज्जायत" इति श्रुतेः सद्विरुद्धं - सर्वदा यत् नास्ति शशशृङ्गादि - तत् असत् इति वेद्यते। यत् सर्वदा अस्तिप्रत्ययविषयः तत् सत्, यत्सर्वदा नास्तिप्रत्ययविषयः तदसत्। बाध्यमानात् घटादेः शुक्तिरजतादेश्चान्यत्वात् अबाध्यमिति; तच्च त्रैकालिक-निषेधाप्रतियोगित्वमेव। कदाचिदपि ज्ञानाविषयत्वात् शशशृङ्गादि असत् तुच्छमिति च शास्त्रे व्यवह्रियते। घटादिस्तु कदाचित् सत्त्वात् कदाचित् बाध्यमानत्वात् च नासत्, नापि सत् किन्तु सदसद्विलक्षणमित्युच्यते। तदेवं निरूपितं सदसतोः स्वरूपं श्रुतिवाक्येभ्य एव लब्धम्, न लोकतः नापि पारिभाषिकम्।

असतो गगनकुसुमादेः बाधो न सम्भवति। सोपादानकार्यनाशस्यैव बाधशब्दार्थत्वात्, असति नाशस्यासम्भवाच्च। एवं च "प्रमाणतो बाधितत्वमिति" यदसत्त्वनिर्वचनं कृतं

तत् स्वकपोलकल्पितम् शास्त्रार्थानवबोधविलसितम्। "असत्त्वं तु गगनकुसुमादौ त्रिकाल-बाध्यत्वमिति" एतदपि उपोढमौढ्यस्य जल्पनम्, अद्वैतिनां ग्रन्थेषु कुत्रापि असत्त्वस्य एवमनिर्वचनात्। गगनकुसुममसत् इति सर्वेषां वादिनामभ्युपगमः। सिद्धान्तिना तु गगमकुसुमादौ मिथ्यात्वं नाभ्युपेयते अपि तु शुक्तिरजतादौ घटादौ च। एवं च गगनकुसुमादौ सदसद्विलक्षणत्वाभावात् मिथ्यात्वासिद्ध्या सत्यत्वापादनं मौढ्यवैभवम्।

पूर्वस्मिन् पुटे "सर्वदा नास्तित्वेन प्रतिपन्नाच्च गगनकुसुमादेः" इति, सर्वदा यन्नास्ति तदसत् इति सिद्धान्तिमतसिद्धमसत्त्वम्, उक्त्वा पश्चात् असत्त्वं तु गगनकुसुमादौ त्रिकालबाध्यत्वमिति स्वकीयमसम्बद्धभाषणं सिद्धान्तिन उपर्यारोप्य पुनः गगनकुसुमादौ उभयविलक्षणत्वाभावात् मिथ्यात्वासिद्ध्या' इति असति मिथ्यात्वलक्षणस्य अव्याप्तिं वदन् पदे पदे स्वकीयं व्याहतभाषित्वं प्रव्यापयन् अयं पण्डितकुलभूषणः उन्मत्तजनपदे सिंहासनमारोप्य अभिषेचनमर्हति।

प्रतीतेः द्वैविध्ये "प्रतीतिश्च सदिति वा असदितिवा द्वेधैव लोके दृष्टा" इति, उभयविलक्षणत्वाभावे च "लोकरीत्या उभयविलक्षणा तृतीयाकारा प्रतीतिरेव नास्तीति" लोकदर्शनमूलकमेव श्रीभाष्यकृतां मतमुपन्यस्तम्।

सदसद्विलक्षणायाः प्रतीतेः लोकप्रसिद्धिरस्तीति प्रदर्शनाय "न च सा प्रमाणशून्येत्यादेः, वस्तु प्रमाणशून्यम्" इत्यन्तस्य ग्रन्थस्य प्रवृत्तिः। तत्र मिथ्येति प्रतीतेः सर्वलोकप्रसिद्धिरेव "सार्वजनीनत्वेन तथा वक्तुमशक्यत्वात्"... इत्यादिना-भिहितम्। सार्वजनीनप्रसिद्धिश्चेयं न केवलं अशेषेषु विद्वज्जनेषु अपि तु सर्वेषु मनुष्येषु इति सर्वलोकप्रसिद्धिस्पष्टीकरणाय "पामरोऽपि रज्जुसर्पं सतः सर्पात् असतः शशशृङ्गाच्च विलक्षणं मन्यते" इत्यभ्यधायि।

रज्जुसर्पशुक्तिरजतद्विचन्द्रादीनां मिथ्यात्वं सर्वलोकप्रसिद्धमपह्नोतुमीष्टे न कोऽप्यनुभवमनपलपन्। पूर्वं प्रतीतस्य पश्चात् ज्ञानान्तरेण बाधितस्य लोके मिथ्येति प्रसिद्धस्य रजतादेरर्थस्य, घटादिविलक्षणस्य, स्वरूपनिर्धारणार्थं प्रवृत्तैर्मनीषिभिः परीक्षापूर्वकं सदसद्विलक्षणत्वमध्यवसितम्। रजतादेः सदसद्विलक्षणस्य सदसद्विलक्षणत्वव्यवहाराभावेऽपि न क्षतिः। पृथिव्यवयवैरारब्धे वृक्षादौ पामराणां सदसद्विलक्षणमिति परीक्षकाणां, मिथ्येति सर्वेषां जनानां व्यवहारविषयत्वं दुरपह्नवम्। अतः पामराणां मिथ्यात्वव्यवहारेणैव सिद्धेः पृथिवीत्वव्यवहारादर्शनात्। शुक्तिरजतादीनां मिथ्यात्वे सर्वलोकप्रसिद्धिं प्रामाणिका अप्याद्रियन्ते। तदुक्तं भाष्यभामत्योः - "न केवलमियमनृतता परीक्षकाणां सिद्धा अपि तु लोकानामपीत्याह - तथा च लोके अनुभवः शुक्तिका हि रजतवदवभासते, एकश्चन्द्रः सद्वितीयवत् इति"।

तदेवं मिथ्यार्थस्य लोकविदितत्वप्रदर्शनार्थं अवतीर्णस्य कवेः ग्रन्थस्य प्रवृत्तिनिमित्त-मवगन्तुं सर्वथाऽशक्तेन अवाच्यैः शब्दैः तद्दूषणं औपनिषददर्शनोत्कर्षासहिष्णुताप्रयुक्त उद्गार एव केवलम्। मिथ्यार्थसद्भावे प्रदर्शितां लोकप्रसिद्धिं "सा पामरबुद्धिरेव यदि ते प्रमाणम्" इति बुद्धिपूर्वकं वा जाड्येन वा अन्यथा गृहीत्वा यदसम्बद्धमभाणि तत्तवैव शिरसि आपतति। तथाहि - प्रतीतेः सदसदाकारत्वे लोकरीतिं प्रमाणत्वेन आश्रयता त्वयापि लोकतः प्रसिद्धस्य देहात्मप्रत्ययस्य सत्यत्वमेव अभ्युपेतव्यम्, परित्याज्यं च देहादिव्यतिरिक्तस्यात्मनः वैकुण्ठलोके मोक्षसुखानुभवार्थं शारीरकशास्त्रादिपठनं भगवदा-राधनं च। जीवपरमात्मनोः शरीरशरीरिभावबुद्धिः लोकस्य नास्तीति उत्सृज्यतां स्ववादः।

पामरस्य जगति मिथ्यात्वबुद्धिर्नास्तीत्येतावता कथं अनिर्वचनीयत्ववादस्य हानिः? पामरस्य जगति सत्यत्वभ्रान्तिः देहात्मभ्रान्तिश्च स्तः, परीक्षकाणामपि व्यवहारकाले। अतः तन्मिथ्यात्वप्रदर्शनेन तत्सत्यत्वभ्रमोन्मथनायैव शारीरकमीमांसायाः प्रवृत्तिः चन्द्रप्रादेशिकत्वादिभ्रान्तेरपमार्जनाय ज्योतिःशास्त्रस्येव सप्रयोजनैव। लोकसिद्धस्य प्रामाणिकस्य मिथ्यात्वस्य लक्षणं "सदसदनिर्वचनीयत्वमिति" परीक्षकैः प्रणीतम्। पामरलोकभ्रान्त्या प्रमाणराजवेदानुसारिणः लक्षणस्य को विरोधः? येन वृथा जल्पति तान्त्रिकः "स्ववादस्य स्वेनैव तिलाञ्जलिर्दत्त" इति। अजामन्त्रस्य कुटिलमतिसमुचितैः प्रलापैः अर्थं वर्णयन् स्वयूथ्यानामपि प्रतारणे अवतीर्णः।

तदेतत्सर्वं अविज्ञातस्वपरकीयग्रन्थप्रमेयस्य तान्त्रिकस्य अविच्छिन्ननिन्दावचनवर्षणं स्वसिद्धान्तमात्रनिष्ठानां, अनाघ्रातस्वपरसिद्धान्तगन्धानां मुग्धानां च स्वयूथ्यानां मोहनेन स्वस्य स्वगोष्ठीगरिष्ठत्वख्यापनार्थमेवेति स्पष्टम्।

दुर्विदग्धजनगर्वपेषणं लब्धवर्णजनवृन्दतोषणम् ।
वेदबोधितसदर्थभाषणं रामरायकविसूक्तिभूषणम् ॥

Summary: This essay by Professor V. Swaminathan is devoted to the habilitation of the views of Rāmarāya by refuting the objections of Rāmānuja on māyā-avidyā as presented by Sri S.N. C. Raghunathacharyulu. By advancing unassailable arguments, the Advaitins had proved that māyā, prakṛti or avidyā is an indeter-minate and false entity in the section devoted to *anirvacanīya-anupapatti*. Rāmānuja's interpretation of the Śruti passages referred to are characterised by inconsistency and are far from being convincing whereas Advaitin's interpretations can withstand any critical test.

1. *Āśrayānupapatti*: The criterion for antagonism between jñāna and ajñāna is the oneness of their content (*samāna-viṣayatva*). Brahman (*svarūpa-jñāna*) is mere knowledge i.e. it is contentless, whereas ajñāna has Brahman as it content. This much difference obtains between *svarūpa-jñāna* and *vṛtti-jñāna*. There is no enmity between them and they can co-exist at the same time. Brahman knowledge (as *vṛtti-jñāna*) and ajñāna have the same content (Brahman) and so Brahman knowledge could annihilate ajñāna.

2. *Tirodhāna-anupapatti*: Envelopment (*āvaraṇa*) in the case of Brahman consists in its not giving rise to the *vyavahāra*: Brahman exists and shines; it does not consist in the destruction of the real nature of Brahman. An incising study of Śaṅkara's comments on the *Gītā* text cited presents in bold relief of the fact that Brahman is hidden in ajñāna.

3. *Svarūpa-anupapatti*: Ajñāna, being the object of the knower's (*pramāta*) cognition, is a superimposition by itself on the *anubhūti* (real nature of the knower). Hence there is no room for endless regression since ajñāna does not stand in need of another entity for its superimposition. The Advaitin proclaims that the knower (*pramāta* defined as consciousness delimited by ajñāna) and not the self-luminous Brahman cognises *anubhūti* as having countless loci and countsless contents under the grip of ajñāna. It is a definite fact that Rāmānuja has misread the Advaitin's position. It is now clear that there ensues neither the fallacy of *anavasthā* nor any awkward situation to be faced.

4. *Anirvacanīyatā-anupapatti*: *Sat* is that never meets with destruction, (*nabhāvo vidyate sataḥ*) (*Gītā*, 2.16). Anything liable for destruction is not *sat*. *Asat* is the one that is never present in a cognition. Brahman alone is *sat* (*satyam, jñānam, anantam brahma*, *Tait.* 2.1). Anything other than Brahman suffers annihilation (*ato'nyadartam*, BU, 3.4.2), *i.e.*, it is not *sat*. A jar is not sat as it is liable for destruction. It is also not *asat* since it is present in the cognition – This is a jar (unlike the leporine horn). So it is neither *sat*, not *asat*, it is *sadasadvilakṣaṇa*, indeterminable. Ajñāna stands on a par with the jar – *i.e.*, it is presented in a cognition and also sublated by knowledge, *i.e.*, it is *anirvacanīya*. It is on the authority

of the Śruti texts, *viz.*, the Upaniṣads, Advaitins have arrived at the conclusion that the world of our day to day experience is *anirvacanīya.* Even an illiterate person knows well that the rope–snake is different from a real snake (*sat*) and also from the leporine horn (*asat*). He may not refer to it by the word *sadasadvilakṣaṇa*; but he is sure that it is *mithyā*, ie. false. Mithyā means *sadasad-vilakṣaṇa*. Now it is easy to see that the scripture as well as the popular perception are infallible evidences (*pramaṇas*) for the existence of the indeterminable entity. By virtue of their differing from Brahman and the leporine horn, the object of the world is spoken of as *anirvacanīya*. But they are perceived as *sat*, existing objects, on account of their being superimposed on *sat* (Brahman) and not because they are *sat* by themselves. The cognition of jar presents only as indeterminate object as *sadasad-vilakṣaṇa*; it does not present a *sat*, or an *asat* as *sadasadvilakṣaṇa*. Therefore, the change that anything will become the content of any cognition is baseless. Since there exists indeterminate objects and they are also present in our knowledge the theory that only *sat* or *asat* could be present in a cognition is an arbitrary statement and not founded by facts.

NOTE

All the page references given in this article and in the previous one are taken from: Bellamkonda Rāmarāyakavi, *Śrī Śaṅkarāśaṅkara-bhāṣya-vimarśaḥ,* Sri Sarada Printing Works, Guntur, 1953.

20

सप्तविधानुपपत्तिसमालोचनम्

Mani Dravid

अस्ति तावत् 'अहमिदं न जानामि' इति सर्वजनीनानुभवसिद्धमज्ञानम्। तद् ज्ञानाभावरूपं तदतिरिक्तं वेत्यत्रैव परं विवदन्ते दार्शनिकाः। अद्वैतसिद्धान्तानुयायिनस्तस्याभावविलक्षणत्वमातिष्ठन्ते। इतरे च दार्शनिकाः ज्ञानाभावेनैव तत्प्रतीतिनिर्वाहं मन्वते। अद्वैत्यभिमताविद्यावादे च सप्तविधाः अनुपपत्तीरुद्भावयन् श्रीमद्रामानुजाचार्याः। तासां च समाधानं बहुभिरद्वैतवादिभिः प्राचीनैरर्वाचीनैश्च स्वकीयग्रन्थेषु यथायथं विहितमुपलभ्यते।

महामहोपाध्यायैः श्रीमदनन्तकृष्णशास्त्रिभिरपि स्वकीयग्रन्थेषु यथाप्रसङ्गमेता अनुपपत्तयः परिहृताः। श्रीशास्त्रिपादाः अद्वैतसम्मतप्रक्रियाविशेषप्रदर्शनपुरस्सरं न केवलं स्वपक्षे दोषानुद्धरन्ति, अपि तु परपक्षे तेषां दोषाणां सद्भावमपि प्रदर्शयन्ति। स्वपक्षे दोषाननुद्धृत्य परपक्षे तदुद्भावनं परेषामयुक्तमित्येव तेषामाशयो लक्ष्यते।

तदिह श्रीशास्त्रिपादैः प्रदर्शितां सरणिमनुसृत्याविद्यायामुद्भाविता अनुपपत्तयो यथामति समालोच्यन्ते। ताश्चानुपपत्तयः - १.आश्रयानुपपत्तिः, २.तिरोधानानुपपत्तिः, ३.स्वरूपानुपपत्तिः, ४.अनिर्वचनीयत्वानुपपत्तिः, ५. प्रमाणानुपपत्तिः, ६.निवर्तकानुपपत्तिः, ७.निवृत्त्यनुपपत्तिरिति सप्त। तत्र प्रथममविद्याविषयेऽद्वैतिनामाशयमुपस्थाप्य तदनन्तरं तदुपरि समागतानामाक्षेपाणां समालोचना क्रियते।

तत्र तावत् विसृज्य तत्तन्मताभिमानमूलकमाग्रहं, तटस्थतामवलम्ब्य विचारयामः - किं वयमात्मानं जानीमः? किं वयं स्वात्मा कीदृशोऽस्तीति वक्तुं शक्नुमः? इति। स्वानुभवमेव परीक्षमाणा वयमिदमुपलभामहे यद् देहादिकं बाह्यप्रत्यक्षयोग्यं यथा वयं सम्यग् जानीमः न तथा देहादिव्यतिरिक्तमात्मानं कथमपि जानीमः इति। यदि जानीयाम वयं स्वात्मानं, तदा - कीदृशोऽयमात्मा विद्यते? अणुर्वा महान् वा? ज्ञानानन्दादिस्वरूपो वा तद्धर्मो वा? किंव्यापारश्चासौ? इत्यादिकं निश्शङ्कं वक्तुं प्रभवेम।

न त्वेवं वक्तुं शक्नुमः। यतो नैव शब्दप्रमाणनिरपेक्षं तत्स्वरूपं वक्तुं शक्नुमः, अतो वयमात्मानं न जानीम इत्येव सिध्यति। अथ च सर्वथाऽऽत्मनो भानमेव नास्तीत्यपि न शक्यं वक्तुम्। तथा सति "अहं मां न जानामि" इत्यपि न ज्ञायेत। उत्पन्नेऽपि घटज्ञाने "अहं घटं जानामि" इति निश्चयो न स्यात्। अतः प्रत्यक्षात्मके "अहमिदं जानामि" इत्याद्यनुभवे आत्मा भासत एव। एवं प्रत्यक्षं भासमानेऽप्यात्मनि, "अहं मां न जानामि" इत्यनुभूयमानमज्ञानं न ज्ञानाभावरूपं भवितुमर्हति। तथा हि - आत्मज्ञानत्वेन रूपेण प्रतियोगिन उल्लेखात् आत्मज्ञानत्वावच्छिन्नप्रतियोगिताकाभावोऽस्यानुभवस्य विषयो वक्तव्यः। स चोक्तरीत्या आत्मज्ञानसत्त्वाद्बाधितः। सामान्यरूपेण प्रतियोग्युल्लेखादेव च नात्मज्ञानविशेषाभावोऽत्र विषयः। अन्यथा यत्किञ्चिद्घटवति घटान्तराभावमादाय "घटो नास्ति" इति प्रतीत्यापत्तेः। नापि ज्ञानप्रागभावोऽत्र विषयः। प्रागभावस्य प्रतियोगिसामग्रीव्यङ्ग्यत्वेन तत्सामग्र्यभावदशायां प्रत्यक्षानुपपत्तेः। घटसामग्रीसमवधानदशायां हि "अत्र घटो भविष्यति" इति घटप्रागभावस्य प्रत्यक्षं भवति। किञ्च प्रतिज्ञानव्यक्ति तत्प्रागभावो भिन्नो भवति। एवञ्च ज्ञाने जातेऽपि तद्विषयज्ञानान्तरप्रागभावमादाय "न जानामि" इति प्रतीत्यापत्तिः। तस्मात् "अहमात्मानं न जानामि" इत्यनुभवे, ज्ञानाभावादन्यदेवाज्ञानं भासते। अनयैव दिशा "घटं न जानामि" "ब्रह्म न जानामि" इत्याद्यनुभवेऽपि ज्ञानाभावातिरिक्तमेवाज्ञानं विषयः।

तच्चाज्ञानं ज्ञानेन निवर्त्यम्। ज्ञानेनाज्ञानं नष्ट मित्यनुभवात्। ज्ञानेन तु तदज्ञानं येषं नाशितमात्मनः इत्यादि स्मृत्याऽज्ञानस्य ज्ञाननिवर्त्यत्वबोधनाच्च। निवर्तकं च ज्ञानं प्रमाणजन्यवृत्त्यभिव्यक्तचैतन्यरूपमभिमतम्। अत एव नात्मस्वरूपज्ञानेनाज्ञानस्य विरोधः, तस्य तद्भासकत्वात्। अन्यथा स्वयम्प्रकाशे आत्मन्यपरिच्छिन्नानन्दस्वरूपाभानप्रसक्तेः। आवरणं चास्ति प्रकाशते इति व्यवहारसामग्र्यां सत्यां "नास्ति न प्रकाशते" इति योग्यतापादनम्। स्वयम्प्रकाशस्याऽऽत्मनः पूर्णानन्दस्वरूपस्य ज्ञानान्तरानपेक्षं प्रकाशमानत्वात् "मम पूर्णानन्दो भाति" इति व्यवहारप्रसक्तौ "मम पूर्णानन्दो न भाति" इति संवेदनमज्ञानावरणकृत्यम्।

तदिदमज्ञानं न ब्रह्मवत् त्रिकालाबाध्यमिति न सत्। नापि तुच्छवत् क्वचिदप्युपाधौ सत्त्वेन प्रतीत्यनर्हमिति नासत्। अत एव सदसद्विलक्षणमनिर्वचनीयमिति गीयते। आवरणविक्षेपशक्तिद्वयविशिष्टं साक्षिभास्यमिति अद्वैतवादिनां प्रक्रिया। एवं स्थिते, परैरुद्भावितानामनुपपत्तीनां प्रदर्शनपुरस्सरं प्राचीनैः प्रदर्शिता तत्परिहारसरणिर्निरूप्यते।

१. तत्र प्रथमा आश्रयानुपपत्तिरित्थं समुद्भाविता - अविद्याया आश्रयः किं जीव उत ब्रह्म? न तावज्जीवः। अविद्यापरिकल्पितत्त्वाज्जीवभावस्य जीवे सिद्धेऽविद्यासिद्धिः,

अविद्यासिद्धौ जीवसिद्धिरित्यन्योन्याश्रयात्। नापि ब्रह्म तदाश्रयः। तस्य स्वयम्प्रकाशज्ञानरूपत्वेनाविद्याविरोधित्वात्। न च ब्रह्मस्वरूपज्ञानं नाज्ञानविरोधिप्रमाणजनितज्ञानस्यैव तद्विरोधित्वादिति वाच्यम्। प्रमाणजनितब्रह्मज्ञानस्य ब्रह्मस्वरूपज्ञानस्य च विषयवैलक्षण्याभावेन एकस्य विरोधित्वमपरस्य नेति कल्पनानुपपत्तेः। विषयवैषम्याभावे प्रमाणजनितत्वस्याकिञ्चित्करत्वात्। न हि पुरोवर्तिनि भास्वरद्रव्यत्वज्ञानं प्रमाणजनितमपि शुक्तित्वाज्ञानस्य विरोधि भवतीति। तस्मात् प्रमाणजनितब्रह्मज्ञानं चेदविद्याविरोधि, तर्हि स्वरूपभूतब्रह्मज्ञानमपि तद्विरोधि भवेदेवेति न ब्रह्माविद्याश्रय इति।

अत्रेदं समाधानम् - अविद्याश्रयो जीव इति, ब्रह्मेति च पक्षद्वयमपि मतभेदेन साध्वेव। न च जीवस्य तदाश्रयत्वेऽन्योन्याश्रयः। अन्योन्याश्रयो हि उत्पत्तौ, स्थितौ, ज्ञप्तौ वाऽऽपाद्यते? न त्रिविधोऽप्यन्योन्याश्रयोऽत्र प्रसज्यते। यदि ह्यज्ञानाज्जीवस्य, जीवाच्चाज्ञानस्योत्पत्तिरस्माभिरभिप्रेता स्यात्, तदा भवेदुत्पत्तावन्योन्याश्रयः। न चैवमस्ति। जीवाज्ञानयोरुभयोरनादित्वोपगमेनोत्पत्त्यभावात्। एवं यदि जीवाश्रिताऽविद्या, अविद्याश्रितो जीव इति स्वीक्रियेत, स्यात्तदा स्थितावन्योन्याश्रयः। जीवस्याविद्यानिष्ठत्वानभ्युपगमान्नायमप्यत्र दोषः। एवमविद्याज्ञप्तेर्जीवप्रकाशाधीनत्वेऽपि जीवप्रकाशस्य स्वतस्त्वाभ्युपगमान्न ज्ञप्तावप्यन्योन्याश्रयः।

ब्रह्माविद्याश्रय इति पक्षोऽपि युक्त एव। स्वरूपज्ञानस्याज्ञानभासकत्वेन तद्विरोधित्वाभावात्। तत्त्वमस्यादिवाक्यजनितवृत्तिप्रतिफलितचैतन्यस्यैव तद्विरोधित्वस्वीकारात्। न च शुक्तौ भास्वरद्रव्यत्वज्ञानस्य प्रमाणजनितस्यापि शुक्त्यज्ञानाविरोधित्वेन प्रमाणजनितत्वमज्ञाननिवर्तकतायामप्रयोजकमिति वाच्यम्। तत्राज्ञानसमानविषयकत्वाभावेनानिवर्तकत्वात्। न हि प्रमाणजनितत्वमात्रेण येनकेनचिज्ज्ञानेन यस्य कस्यचिदज्ञानस्य निवृत्तिं ब्रूमः। किन्तु ज्ञानाज्ञानयोः समानविषयकयोर्निवर्त्यनिवर्तकभावात् अज्ञानसमानविषयकं प्रमाणजन्यं ज्ञानं निवर्तकं ब्रूमः। अतो नेयमनुपपत्तिः।

२. अथ तिरोधानानुपपत्तिरुच्यते। प्रकाशैकस्वरूपस्य ब्रह्मणोऽविद्यया तिरोधानं नोपपद्यते। प्रकाशतिरोधानं हि प्रकाशोत्पत्तिप्रतिबन्धो वा विद्यमानप्रकाशनाशो वा स्यात्। तत्र स्वरूपप्रकाशस्यानादित्वेनोत्पत्तिप्रतिबन्धासम्भवात् तन्नाश एव तिरोधानं वदतोक्तः स्यात्। तथा च ब्रह्मणो नाशापत्त्या नाज्ञानेनावरणमुपपद्यत इति।

अत्रेदं समाधानम् - आवरणं नाम ब्रह्मस्वरूपनाश इति स्वकपोलकल्पितार्थमादाय दूषणमयुक्तम्। अद्वैतिभिस्तथाऽनङ्गीकारात्। किन्तु प्रकाशमाने 'नास्ति' 'न प्रकाशते' इति व्यवहारायोग्यतापादनमावरणमिति पूर्वमुक्तम्। अतो न ब्रह्मण आवरणे नाशप्रसङ्गः।

३. अथ स्वरूपानुपपत्तिरुच्यते - अविद्येयं किं परमार्थभूता? उतापरमार्थभूता? न तावत् परमार्थभूता। अनभ्युपगमात्। नाप्यपरमार्थभूता। तथा सति द्रष्टृत्वेन, दृश्यत्वेन, दृशित्वेन वा साऽभ्युपगमनीया। दृशित्वपक्षेऽपि अनवच्छिन्ना दृशिः, अवच्छिन्ना वा? अनवच्छिन्नदृशित्वेऽपि स्वरूपातिरिक्ता स्वरूपमेव वा? न तावदतिरिक्ता, अनवच्छिन्न-दृशिद्वयानभ्युपगमात्। नापि स्वरूपमेव। तस्यापरमार्थत्वेऽधिष्ठानस्यापरमार्थ्यप्रसङ्गेन शून्यवादप्रसङ्गात्। अवच्छिन्नदृशित्वे, द्रष्टृत्वे, दृश्यत्वे वा स्वीक्रियमाणे पक्षत्रयेऽपि तस्या अपरमार्थत्वेन मूलदोषान्तरापेक्षयाऽनवस्था स्यात्। अथैतद्दोषपरिहाराय ब्रह्मैव तन्मूलदोषत्वेन स्वीक्रियते, तदा प्रपञ्चदर्शनेऽपि तस्यैव दोषत्वसम्भवेन वृथाऽविद्या-कल्पना। ब्रह्मणो दोषत्वे तस्य नित्यत्वेनानिर्मोक्षप्रसङ्गश्च। तथा चाविद्याया परमार्थत्वा-परमार्थत्वानिरूपणात् स्वरूपानुपपत्तिरिति।

अत्रेदं समाधानम् - अविद्याया अपरमार्थत्वस्य दृश्यत्वस्य चाङ्गीकारात् पक्षान्तरं परिकल्प्य दूषणं वृथा कोलाहलः। न च तथा सति तस्या मिथ्यात्वात् तन्मूलमविद्यान्तरं वक्तव्यमित्यनवस्थेति वाच्यम्। अविद्याया अनादित्वेन तत्कारणीभूताविद्यान्तरा-नपेक्षणात्। न च जीवस्य स्वरूपतोऽनादित्वेऽपि अस्त्येव मूलदोषापेक्षेति वाच्यम्। अविद्याकल्पितत्वं ह्यविद्याकालमात्रवृत्तित्वम्, अविद्याधीनस्थितिकत्वं वा। तदुभय-मप्यविद्यातत्कार्यसाधारणम्। उक्तं च स्वाराज्यसिद्धिव्याख्याने कैवल्यकल्पद्रुमे - "मिथ्यात्वप्रयोजकमाविद्यकत्वं ह्यविद्याकालमात्रस्थितिकत्वम्, अविद्याधीनस्थितिकत्वं वाऽविद्यातत्कार्यसाधारणम्। अभेदेऽपि योगक्षेमसाधारणस्य तदधीनस्थितिकत्वस्या-व्याघातात्" इति। यद्वा - अविद्यानिवृत्तौ निवर्तमानत्वमेवाविद्याधीनस्थितिकत्वम्। तच्चाविद्यानिवृत्तिव्याप्यनिवृत्तिप्रतियोगित्वम्। स्वस्मिंश्च स्वव्याप्यत्वस्याक्षतत्वात् तादृशनिवृत्तिप्रतियोगित्वमविद्यासाधारणमेव। अतश्च नाविद्यकत्वसिद्ध्यर्थमविद्याया अविद्यान्तरापेक्षा। अत एव प्राञ्च आचार्याः अविद्यायाः स्वपरनिर्वाहकत्वमुक्तवन्तः।

४. अथानिर्वचनीयत्वानुपपत्तिः - किं चेदमविद्याया अनिर्वचनीयत्वमभिप्रेतम्? सदसद्विलक्षणत्वं चन्न। तथाविधवस्तुन एवाभावात्। सर्वं हि वस्तु प्रतीतिव्यवस्थाप्यम्। तत्र 'अस्ति' 'नास्ति' इति विषयस्य सत्त्वमसत्त्वं वावगाहते प्रतीतिः। न क्वापि सदसद्विलक्षणत्वमिति कथं सदसद्विलक्षणत्वसिद्धिरिति॥

अत्रेदं समाधानम् - सदसद्विलक्षणत्वमनिर्वचनीयत्वं वदतां हि तद्घटकं सत्त्वं कालत्रया-बाध्यत्त्वम्, असत्त्वं च निरुपाख्यत्त्वमभिप्रेतम्। ईदृशसत्त्वाभावासत्त्वाभावोभयस्य "अस्ति" इति धीविषयेऽपि बाध्ये ग्रहणं न विरुद्धम्। विस्तरस्तु अद्वैतसिद्ध्यादिग्रन्थेष्वेव द्रष्टव्यः।

५. अज्ञाने च प्रत्यक्षानुमानार्थापत्तिश्रुतिस्मृतिरूपाणां प्रमाणानां विद्यमानत्वात् नास्ति तत्र प्रमाणानुपपत्तिः। तत्र 'अहं मां न जानामि' इति प्रत्यक्षस्य ज्ञानाभावविषयकत्वासम्भवेन तद्विलक्षणाज्ञानावगाहित्वं पूर्वमेव समर्थितम्। अनुमानमपि विवरणोक्तं तत्र प्रमाणम् - विवादगोचरापन्नं प्रमाणज्ञानं स्वप्रागभावव्यतिरिक्तस्वविषयावरणस्वनिवर्त्यस्वदेशगतवस्त्वन्तरपूर्वकम्, अप्रकाशितार्थप्रकाशकत्त्वात्, अन्धकारे प्रथमोत्पन्नप्रदीपप्रकाशवत् इति। यत्त्वस्मिन्ननुमाने विरुद्धत्वानैकान्त्याद्युद्भावनम्, तदभिप्राय एवं स्यात् - प्रमाणज्ञानमात्रस्य पक्षीकृतत्त्वात् उक्ताज्ञानानुमितिरपि प्रमाणज्ञानत्वरूपपक्षतावच्छेदकाकृान्ता पक्षान्तर्गता स्यात्। तथा सति स्वविषयविषयकाज्ञानपूर्वकत्वपर्यवसितसाध्यसिद्धावज्ञानविषयकाज्ञानान्तरसिद्धिरनभिमता स्यात्। तत्राज्ञानान्तराभावे च पक्षभूतायां तस्यां साध्याभावेन बाधः स्यात्। तस्याः पक्षबहिर्भावे च तत्रैव हेतोरनैकान्त्यमिति।

तत्र चेदं समाधनम् - अज्ञानस्य स्वरूपतः साक्षिवेद्यत्वेनाज्ञानविषयत्वाभावेऽपि तद्गतभावत्वादिकमज्ञानविषयो भवत्येव। अत एवोक्तानुमितेः पक्षत्वेऽपि तादृशाज्ञानपूर्वकत्वरूपसाध्यसत्त्वात् न बाधादिः। उक्तं चेदमद्वैतसिद्धौ।

"सोऽविद्याग्रन्थिं विकरतीह सोम्य" "अनृतेन हि प्रत्यूढाः" "त्वं हि नः पिता योऽस्माकमविद्यायाः परं पारं तारयसि" इत्यादयः शतशः श्रुतयः 'अज्ञानेनावृतं ज्ञानं तेन मुह्यन्ति जन्तवः' विभेदजनकेऽज्ञाने नाशमात्यन्तिकं गते' इत्यादयः स्मृतयश्चाविद्यायां प्रमाणत्वेन प्रसिद्धाः। मिथ्याभूतस्योपादानं मिथ्याभूतमेव कल्पनीयम्, उपादानोपादेययोः सालक्षण्यस्य लोके दर्शनात्, दृष्टानुसारित्वाच्च कल्पनायाः। अतश्च मिथ्याकार्यस्य मिथ्योपादानं विनाऽनुपपन्नत्वमप्यज्ञानसाधकम्। यथा च भ्रमविषयस्य मिथ्यात्वं तथा ग्रन्थेष्वेव निरूपितं द्रष्टव्यम्।

६. यदुक्तं निर्विशेषब्रह्मात्मविज्ञानस्याविद्यानिवर्तकत्वं न युक्तम्। "वेदाहमेतं पुरुषं महान्तम् ... तमेवं विद्वानमृत इह भवति । नान्यः पन्था विद्यतेऽयनाय" इत्यादिश्रुतिषु सगुणज्ञानादेव मोक्षस्योक्तत्वादिति। तन्न। अस्यार्थस्य वेदान्ततात्पर्यनिर्णयाधीनत्वात्, तात्पर्यस्य च निर्विशेषे सिद्धौ उक्तानुपपत्तेरनवकाशात्। श्रुतितात्पर्यविचारश्च नात्र प्रस्तूयते विस्तरभयात्। तत्त्वमस्यादिवाक्यजन्यवृत्त्यभिव्यक्तचैतन्यस्याविद्यानिवर्तकत्वमद्वैत्यभिमतमिति पूर्वमेवोक्तम्। अतः स्वरूपज्ञानस्याज्ञाननिवर्तकत्वे, विषयवैषम्याभावादुक्तवृत्तिज्ञानस्यापि तदनिवर्तकत्वापादनं न युक्तम्।

७. यत्तु - उक्तज्ञानेनाविद्यानिवृत्तिर्न युक्ता, बन्धस्य पारमार्थिकत्वात् ज्ञाननिवर्त्याभावादिति। तदपि बन्धस्य मिथ्यात्वसाधनादेव दत्तोत्तरम्। यच्च निवर्तकज्ञानस्यापि

मिथ्यात्वात् निवर्तकान्तरापेक्षायामनवस्थेति। तदपि न। कतकरजोन्यायेन तस्य स्वनिवर्तकत्वस्यापि स्वीकारात्। अविद्यानिवृत्तिश्चाखण्डाकारवृत्तिविषयतवोपलक्षितात्म-स्वरूपा कल्पितार्थनिवृत्तेरधिष्ठानस्वरूपत्वाङ्गीकारात्। तदुक्तम् - "निवृत्तिरात्मा मोहस्य ज्ञातत्त्वेनोपलक्षितः" इति। 'अधिष्ठानावशेषो हि नाशः कल्पितवस्तुनः' इति च। अविद्यानिवृत्तेः पञ्चमप्रकारत्वादिनिरूपणं त्वधिकारिविशेषस्य बुद्ध्युपारोहार्थमित्यद्वैतसिद्धौ स्पष्टम् - "ये तु पञ्चमप्रकारादिपक्षाः तेतु मन्दबुद्धिव्युत्पादनार्था इति न तत्समर्थनमर्थयामः" (अद्वैतसिद्धिः - p.885) इति। तस्मात् अविद्यायामुद्भाविताः सप्तविधानुपपत्तयः नाविद्यावादं निरसितुमीशत इति शिवम्।

Summary: Dr. Mani Dravid has given a survey of the objections raised by Rāmānuja mainly relying on the works of Anantakrishna Sastri. He starts his paper with a question: Is it possible to know the real nature of the self? From our ordinary experience, it becomes clear that the self is different from the body that can be cognized by the external senses. It is also known that we know our self differently than that of the body. If we know the self properly, we will be able to exactly answer the questions like: "How is the self? Is it atomic or gross? It is in the form of knowledge, bliss etc. or having those as its qualities? Is it possible to have activity in the self?, and the like."

One thing that needs to be accepted by all the schools of Vedāna is that we cannot speak with certainty about the self without the aid of *śabda-pramāṇa*, i.e. the Upaniṣads and therefore it needs to be accepted that we do not know the exact nature of the self. On the other hand we cannot also say that we do not know the self at all. If that we were the case, we would not be able to cognise the state of our ignorance like "I do not know myself"; and when there is the knowledge of the pot, the cognition cannot be in the form "I know the pot." Hence in case of cognitions like "I know this" there is the semblance of the manifestation of the self. Thus the experience "I do not know myself·', is not a case of total absence of knowledge. Since there is mention of the knowledge of the self in the above statement, the counter corelate, the absence of the self should be in the form of experience. Since the knowledge is in a very general way, our understanding is not of the specific absence of the self. If that is how it is, then at a place where a pot is cognised, there would arise the ignorance of the pot, *viz.*."there is no pot." The prior non-existence has no scope here because it suggests the absence of counter-corelate and in the absence of counter-corelate, there will be no perception. For example, when the material for the pot is collected, we have the cognition "The pot will be made here." This is a case of cognition of prior non-existence of pot. But in case of knowledge, the prior non-existence of knowledge becomes different for different persons. Hence even when cognition arises, considering a different prior non-existence, there will be cognition in the form "I do not know." In the same way in the usage like "I do not know pot, I do not Brahman, the ignorance is different from absence of knowledge. That ignorance can be sublated by knowledge. Thus, we have the corresponding cognition in the same way "by knowledge, ignorance is eliminated." The eliminating knowledge is consciousness conditioned by the *akaṇḍākāravṛtti*. The consciousness *per se* is not the eliminator. With this background, the objections raised by Rāmānuja are to be examined.

Dr. Dravid examines all the objections raised by Rāmānuja on the basis of the writings of Anantakrishna Sāstri, especially as presented in Sastri's commentary on *Advaitasiddhi* of Madhusūdana. The polemics of Advaita has gone too far in answering the questions raised by opponents and some Advaitins even have accepted fifth type of *avidyā-nivṛtti*. Such questions and answers to uphold and justify the Advaita views are meant for the understanding of the dull-witted persons. Therefore, the seven-fold untenability imposed by Rāmānuja cannot do away with the māya-avidyā, which accounts for world appearance in Advaita Vedānta.

21

MĀYĀVĀDA: AN APPROACH FROM ĀCĀRYA'S POINT OF VIEW

G.C. Nayak

Māyā in the Vedāntic tradition has been generally taken as an explanatory principle by which the origination of the world is supposed to have been explained. Although Brahman is regarded as the world-ground, Māyā as the indeterminable power of Brahman is supposed to be at the root cause of this apparent multiplicity. Some Advaitins have gone so far as to claim that māyā is the *vikāri-upādāna* or the changeable material caùse of this world. Some others, while admitting that it is neither an entity nor a non-entity, neither identical with Brahman nor different from it, have been impressed by its positive character of producing delusion and have referred to it as something positive, *bhāvarūpa*.[1] We find Advaitins of great calibre even referring to avidyā as existing like the supreme Self, as it were. Sureśvara, for example makes a striking declaration thus - *"aho dhārṣṭyamavidyāyā na kaścidativartate, pramāṇam vastvanādṛtya paramātmeva tiṣṭhati."*[2] However, the word *'iva'* used here could be taken to mean that māyā does not have a status alongside Paramātman. Māyā being a positive entity has also been taken simply to mean that it is not absolutely negative. But even admitting all this, it is a fact that the followers of Śaṅkara have allude to Māyā as a queer power of the Lord or Brahman which is antagonistic to all logic and reasoning and is the root cause of all multiplicity. Even *ajñāna* has been regarded as the stuff of the world, because Brahman being unchangeable cannot be the cause. Consistent with this trend in later Advaita, we find certain controversies being raised amidst the

Advaitins regarding the locus and the object (*āśraya* and *viṣaya*) of avidyā, whether māyā and avidyā are one and the same, or different from each other and whether avidyāòis one or many in number. We are again told of the *āvaraṇa* and *vikṣepa,* that is, the covering or the hiding, and the distorting powers of avidyā, the impression being created in mind, that avidyā is an entity having such and such powers. Taking the clue from the longstanding Advaita tradition of the past, bọth the critics and admirers of Advaita in the contemporary period have also regarded māyā as an explanatory principle of world-multiplicity. It is no wonder that the admirers have been flabbergasted and stunned by their finding that māyā as an explanatory theory is of very little worth and rather of no consequence, being only deceptive in appearance, while the critics have too easily caught hold of this weakest spot in the Advaita and have taken it easily to task for subscribing to such worthless hypothesis for explaining the world. It is thus that even great Advaitins of the present century like Radhakrishnan have referred to the theory of māyā serving in the Advaita context "as a cloak to cover the inner rifts of his (Śaṅkara's) system."[3] Dasgupta points out that "the Vedānta is both unwilling and incapable of explaining the nature of the world-process in all its details, in which philosophy and science are equally interested."[4] This problem has really become too difficult and even somewhat impossible on the part of Advaitins either to solve or to dissolve. One can of course cut the gordian knot by pointing out in the language of some famous Advaitins that māyā implies what is inconsistent, and that had it been a consistent and explainable concept, it would be reality and not māyā.[5] But this approach will not do because it is difficult to understand how a concept or a principle which is inconsistent and not itself explainable can satisfactorily work as an explanatory theory of the origination of the world. It is like an attempt to explain a mystery with the help of a greater and more intricate mystery. No wonder, therefore, that Advaita theory of māyā has been taken as explaining the universe away, rather than giving an explanation of the world order.

The malaise is indeed grave, and a superficial treatment of the situation will definitely not do. To my mind, it appears that the whole situation has been looked at from the wrong angle and hence the irresolvable difficulty naturally confronts us in our face. The entire programme of Śaṅkara, to my mind, has been represented with an exaggerated emphasis on certain aspects by his own followers, not to speak of his opponents. It is however, to be admitted that in the process, much of philosophical ingenuity, and even excellence, has also been displayed by the brilliant followers of the Ācārya, betraying their innovative ability at the same time. Śaṅkara was not at all interested in giving an explanation of the origin of the universe. As far as he is concerned, philosophy has nothing to do with cosmology or cosmogony, and it is entirely useless, according to him, to indulge in the enticing stories of creation.[6] In his *Aitareya-bhāṣya,* Śaṅkara, is quite explicit in pointing out that different theories of creation are to be taken as mere anecdotes and stories (*ākhyāyikā*), and are therefore to be taken only as *arthavāda*. According to Śaṅkara, philosophy is neutral to any theory of creation and has got nothing to do with an explanation of the world process. So there is no question in Śaṅkara giving or trying to give an explanation of the origin of universe through māyā. When māyā was not meant to be a theory of explanation, the question of adequacy as a theory does not arise. If it were meant to be a theory it would be one of the worst theories perhaps, for, instead of explaining, it would simply shift the problem from the mystery of creation to the mystery of the creator.

It is true that Śaṅkara, at a number of places speaks of māyā as the power of the Lord.[7] But this to my mind is simply a concession on the part of Śaṅkara, to the popular view and nothing more, for the entire conception according to him is *avidyā-kalpita* and is therefore, to be understood on the level of *lokavyavahāra* alone. It is Śaṅkara's view that even the Lord depends upon the limiting adjuncts of name and form, the products of nescience.[8] When the conception of the Lord itself has its basis in ignorance, then the ascription of Māyā to the Lord as his *śakti* can only belong to the sphere of ignorance. We have to admit that Vidyāraṇya had a rare insight into this vedāntic truth, when we find him giving a beautiful poetic expression to this idea as follows: "*māyākhyāyāḥ kāmadhenorvatsau jīveśvarāvubhau, yathecchaṁ pibatāṁ dvaitaṁ tattvaṁ tvadvaitameva hi.*"[9] Māyā is a desire fulfilling cow indeed from this point of view.

Ignorance or avidyāòconsists in the confusion of regarding one non-dual reality as many.[10] Ignorance pervades our entire commerce of life, according to Śaṅkara. Our ordinary language, which is practically oriented, reflects this ignorance. We classify, categorise and ascribe predicates to one non-dual reality for our practical purposes; the non-dual reality, however, remains untouched by these classifications, categorisation or ascriptions.[11] Ignorance of this non-dual reality is natural, all-pervasive, affecting one and all, and this universality of ignorance is at times expressed in the terminology of Māyā by Śaṅkara. In his *Kaṭhopaniṣad-bhāṣya*, for example, Śaṅkara speaks of māyā as deep-rooted, incomprehensible, and strange only in the sense that everyone though identical with non-dual reality continues to remain ignorant of this identity.[12] The fact that every one sees multiplicity where there is unity, is deceived by various linguistic forms which have only practical value (*vyāvahārika*) is called māyā. This is what is a natural tendency on the part of jīva, according to Śaṅkara.[13] The further questions such as - to whom in partcular does this māyā belong or wherefrom does it originate? - are simply irrelevant.

One word of caution here. This ignorance and its consequent error are not to be regarded as merely linguistic. There has been recenly a tendency to interpret avidyā or adhyāsa as simply a linguistic error.[14] This is misleading. Language does not necessarily create the illusion of which Śaṅkara speaks, nor is it a fact that the confusion is merely verbal. Hence to speak of avidyāòor adhyāsa as linguistic is quite misleading. Expressions such as '*tattvamasi*' or '*ahaṁ brahmāsmi*', when properly understood, can lead to 'freedom from ignorance' or mokṣa, according to Śaṅkara. It is true that ordinary language reflects this ignorance but this is only in case of those who take ordinary language to be revealing the nature of ultimate reality, that is to say, only in so far as the ordinary language is taken to be something more than *vyāvahārika*. A philosophically enlightened person may use the same language knowing fully well that this is of practical value and all the while he is never misled by the distinction created by ordinary language.[15] Bondage or error due to ignorance is deep-rooted and all-pervasive, according to Śaṅkara, and in this sense it may be regarded as a natural and universal feature of jīva, but it will be misleading to call it simply a linguistic error or a linguistic bondage. Bondage or error consists in regarding the non-dual (Advaita) as many, according to Advaitavedānta, and this is reflected in our entire commerce of life including our ordinary linguistic usage and mokṣa consists in freedom from this bondage. Vidyāòin Śāṅkara-vedānta is *vastu-svarūpāvadhāraṇa* or the ascertainment of the nature of reality, and not a mere linguistic illumination; the issue is ontological, not merely linguistic.

The answer to the question whether māyā is identical with avidyāòor different from it should be quite simple from the standpoint of Śaṅkara, although it is a fact that the later Śaṅkaraites have raised a storm over this issue. When we refer to the ignorance or error of someone in particular we may speak of him as being affected by avidyā. When on the other hand we are required to point to the ignorance as it affects all in a mass-scale, there is nothing wrong in speaking of the whole world being under the spell of a universal magic (māyā) as it were, so long as we remember that any further reference to a magician (God) wielding this magical power is only to be understood within that framework. If ignorance is universal and all-pervasive this is as good as being under the magical spell of the power of ignorance and if māyā is conceived as a magical power there should be a *māyāvi* (wielder of the magical power). Naturally, this māyā should have no power over the *māyāvi* although it may affect all others, and in this respect it may be distinguished from avidyā or ignorance of the individual. But all this is picture-thinking, one picture leading to another which may be of value only in so far as it clarifies the point that there is an all pervasive ignorance which seems to have a compelling character about it. This does not however, permit us to delight in further speculation about its source and its relation to individual ignorance (avidyā), for that will be entering into what Śaṅkara would call the domain of *utprekṣā* (metaphysics - a look beyond) which he denounces in clear terms. The talk of māyāòor magical power of God in Śāṅkara-vedānta is only an indirect way of saying that everyone is numbed and dumbfounded as it were, by the compelling ignorance which creates multiplicity.[16] The conception of māyā as an "indefinable mysterious stuff", as Prof.

Dasgupta[17] calls it, might have found a place in the later Advaita; it certainly has no place in writings of Ācārya himself.

Similarly, coming to avidyā, we find that the controversies in later Advaita schools regarding the object and locus (*viṣaya* and *āśraya*) of avidyāòhave no place in the writings of the master himself. He is simply interested in pointing to an avidyāòor ignorance which is all pervasive and on which our entire commerce of life is based, to the fact that distinctions are created by ignorance where naturally there is no non-duality. What is important from his point of view is to detect this error, this confusion created by ignorance and to try to get rid of it through the realisation of non-duality. It is therefore, pointless to ask, to whom, in particular, does ignorance belong? Whether the error is mine, yours, or has its origination under the supervision of a supervisor called God? That the question is not philosophically significant is evident from the frivolity with which the Ācārya set aside the whole issue in his *Gītā-bhāṣya*. One who raises such questions has simply missed the programme of Advaita philosophy to that extent for the genetic and metaphysical questions leading to a sort of picture-thinking are of no concern to the philosopher. We must learn to discriminate between philosophically relevant and irrelevant issues in Advaita by taking the cue from the Ācārya himself whose remarks such as "*avidyā kasya dṛṣyate iti praśno nirarthakaḥ*",[18] (it is pointless to ask such questions as 'In whom is avidyāòseen'?) are extremely significant and pregnant with implications. In the *Brahmasūtrabhāṣya* also Ācārya clearly points out how any reference to avidyāòdoes not affect the non-duality of the self on the *Pāramārthika* level. As avidyā has got no independent status at all in the *Pāramārthika* plane,the question regarding its locus etc. has no relevance there; it is only when one is ignorant that the question about the locus of avidyāòmay arise and in that case ignorance or avidyāòobviously belongs to the person concerned. It is to be noted that according to Ācārya, there is nothing mystical, mysterious or even metaphysical about this question of the locus of avidyā in any case. It would be worthwhile here to concentrate on the exact words of the Ācārya in his *Brahmasūtrabhāṣya* in this context in order to get a clear idea about this question: "*kasya punaḥ ayaṁ aprabodha iti cet, yastvaṁ pṛcchasi tasya ta iti vadāmaḥ. nanu ahaṁ īśvara evoktaḥ śrutyā, yadyevaṁ pratibuddaḥ asi nāsti kasyacit aprabodhaḥ. yaḥ api doṣaḥ codyate kaiścit avidyayā kila ātmanaḥ sadvitīyatvāt advaitānupapattiḥ iti, saḥ api etena pratyuktaḥ.*"[19] One of the main, very first one of the *anupapattis* or objections raised by Rāmānujācārya against Advaitavedānta, viz. the *āśrayānupapatti*, regarding the locus of avidyā, would be simply out of place, rather irrelevant, in that case.

Above all, the following remarks made by Swami Vivekananda long back in his lectures delivered in London seem to me to be most illuminating in connection with the māyāvāda of Śaṅkara, and could be taken as a guideline for our understanding of the doctrine of māyā in its right perspective. "Māyā", says Vivekananda with rare insight, "is not a theory for the explanation of the world; it is simply a statement of facts as they exist, that the very basis of our being is contradiction, that everywhere we have to move through this tremendous contradiction."[20] It reminds us of the famous statement of Ācārya himself in the *Adhyāsabhāṣya*, "*satyānṛte mithunīkṛtya ahamidaṁ mamedaṁ iti naisargiko'yam lokavyavahāraḥ.*" In the *Māṇḍūkya-bhāṣya*, Ācārya has explicitly pointed out that avidyā is the very nature of the things as they obtain and beyond this nothing can be said by the way of explaining why and how non-dual Reality appears as the world of multiplicity. *"na hi rajjvādīnāṁ avidyā-svabhāvavyatirekeṇa sarpādyābhāsatve kāraṇaṁ śakyaṁ vaktum,"* says Ācārya.[21] Here again, avidyā refers to the very *svabhāva* or nature of things as they are and here also Ācārya indicates that there is no question of treating māyā or avidyā as an explanatory theory.

Notes

1. *Citsukhi*, 1.13, *"anādi bhāvarūpaṁ yad vijñānena vilīyate, tadajñānaṁ iti prājña lakṣaṇaṁ sampracakṣate."*
2. *Naiṣkarmyasiddhi*, III.111.
3. S. Radhakrishnan, *Indian Philosophy*, Vol. II., OUP, Delhi, 2002, p. 472.
4. S. N. Dasgupta, *A History of Indian Philosophy*, Cambridge University Press, 1952 Vol. II p. 73.
5. Maṇḍanamiśra, *Brahmasiddhi*, *"anupapadyamānārthatve hi māyā; upapadyamānārthatve yathārthabhāvānna māyāòsyāt."* Cf. also *Vimuktātman, Iṣṭasddhi*, 5 *"durghaṭatvaṁ avidyāyāòbhūṣaṇaṁ na tu dūṣaṇam."*

And also *"na hi māyāyāṁ asambhāvanīyaṁ nāma asambhāvanīyā-vabhasacaturā hi sā."*

6. *Brahmasūtrabhāṣya*, 2.1.27. *"na ceyaṁ pariṇāmaśrutiḥ pariṇāma-pratipādanārthāḥ, tatpratipattau phalānavagamāt."* Also *"na hi sṛṣṭyā-khyāyikādi parijñānāt kiñcit phalamiṣyate, aikātmyapratipattestu amṛtatvaṁ phalaṁ sarvopaniṣatprasiddham."*
7. *Vivekacūḍāmaṇi*, 108, *"avyaktanāmnai parameśaśaktih anādyavidyā triguṇātmikā parā, kāryānumeyā sudhiyaiva māyā yayā jagatsarvam-idaṁ prasūyate."* And *Brahmasūtrabhāṣya*, 1.1.14, *"sarvajñasye-śvarasya māyāśaktiḥ prakṛti iti ca śrutismṛtyorabhilapyate."* Cf. *Saundaryalaharī*, 67, *"mahāmayā viśvam bhramayasi paṛabrahma-mahiṣī."*
8. *Brahmasūtrabhāṣya*, 2.2.14, *"avidyākṛtā nāmarūpopādhi-anurodhīśvaro bhavati."*
9. *Pañcadaśī*, VI. 236.
10. *Adhyāsabhāṣya. "atasmin tadbuddhiḥ."*
11. *Ibid. "yatra yadadhyāsaḥ tat kṛtena doṣena guṇena vā aṇumātreṇāpi sa na sambadhyate."*
12. *Kaṭhopaniṣad-bhāṣya*, 1.3.12, *"aho atigambhirā duravagāhya vicitrā māyā ceyaṁ yadayaṁ sarvo jantuḥ paramārthataḥ paramārtha-satattvopyevaṁ bodhyamanohaṁ paramātmeti na gṛhnāti, anātmānaṁ dehendriyādisanghātaṁ ātmano dṛsyamānamapi ghaṭādivadātmatve-nāhamamusya putra ityanucyamānopi gṛhnati."*
13. *Adhyāsa-bhāṣya, "naisargiko'yaṁ lokavyavahāraḥ"*.
14. Ganeswar Misra, *Analytical studies in Indian Philosophical problems* Bhubaneswar, 1971 and *The Advaita Conceptions of Philosophy: Its Method, Scope and Limits.*
15. *Brahmasūtrabhāṣya, "na yathāpūrvaṁ saṁsārītaṁ śakyaṁ darśayitum"*. Also Cf. *Pañcadaśī* XI. 130, *"dvibhaṣābhijñavad-vidyādubhau laukikavaidikau"*.
16. *Kaṭhopaniṣad-bhāṣya*, 1.3.12, where Śaṅkara, immediately after describing māyā as *"atigambhīrā, duravagahyā, vicitrā"* in so far as we fail to realise the identity of the self with Brahman while identifying ourselves with the not-self, points to māyā as the power of the Lord that deludes the entire world -*"nūnaṁ parasyaiva māyayā momuhyamānaḥ sarvo loko bambhramiti."*
17. S.N. Dasgupta, *Op. Cit*, p. 73.
18. *Gītābhāṣya*, 13. 2.
19. *Brahmasūtrabhāṣya*, 4.1.3.
20. Swami Vivekananda, *Jñāna-Yoga*, Advaita Ashrama, Almora, Sixth Edn. 1943, P. 64.
21. *Māṇḍūkya-bhāṣya, Agāma-prakaraṇa*, 9.

22

MADHUSŪDANA SARASVATĪ ON MĀYĀ-AVIDYĀ

Haramohan Misra

Before examining the position of the Advaitins and the non-Advaitins regarding māyā or avidyā *vis-a-vis* the so-called *anupapattis* we have to first understand the three dimensional logic of the Advaitins, since, according to them, reality and unreality are not mutually exclusive, there being a third alternative, falsity. With addition to this, one has to bear in mind that Advaita advocates three ontological strata, *viz.*, *Pāramārthika*, *Vyāvahārika* and *Prātibhāsika*. This is elucidated with great clarity by the Advaita teachers beginning with the writers of *Pañcapādikā* and *Vivaraṇa* ending with Madhusūdana Sarasvatī. Especially, Madhusūdana's first two definitions of falsity, taken respectively from these two works, epitomise the Advaita standpoint.[1]

Then we have to take into consideration the great inference of falsity, "The world is false since it is *dṛṣya, jaḍa* and *paricchinna.*" The first *hetu, viz.*, *dṛṣyatva* is the most important one, since there lies the crux of the problem, the relationship between the *dṛk* and the *dṛṣya* that involves the entire Advaita epistemology. It is interesting to note that the non-Advaitins upholding reality of the world, adduce *dṛṣyatva* as its reason, which is just the opposite of the Advaita position. The Advaita position, in this respect, can be appreciated only if one conceives reality, unreality and falsity in the manner of the Advaitins. Thereafter, we may approach the various *anupapattis* raised against the Advaita view, which can be dealt with a single stroke once the tenability of the three dimensional logic of the Advaitin is established.

It is to be borne in mind that the Advaitins conceive reality as unsublatable at all points of time (*trikālābādhya*), whereas the non-Advaitins conceive it as having functionality (*arthakriyākāritva*), having existence as universal property (*sattājātimattva*), being presented to consciousness (*saṁvidi-bhāsamānatva*) or as being different from unreality (*asad-vilakṣaṇatva*). Therefore, *sat* and *asat* are neither mutually exclusive (*parasparābhāvarūpa*), nor do they become the *vyāpaka* of each other's absence, so that by the absence of one the other can be inferred. They are rightly upheld as the *vyāpya* of each other's absence, for which the absence of both of them becomes logically conceivable.[2] Another point to be noted is that since the conception of reality of the non-Advaitins is different from that of the Advaitins there cannot be any contradiction between them. The Advaitins disprove the ultimate reality of the things of the world, whereas the non-Advaitins try to prove their reality in the functional sense. The definition of reality as "not being counter-positive of the absence in all place and time" as given by the Mādhvas is not really different from this functional reality.[3] The most invincible point of Advaita is that since reality as unsublatability at all the times cannot be grasped by perception, and since reality as conceived by the non-Advaitins is not opposed to falsity as conceived by the Advaitins, falsity of the world cannot be contradicted by perception.[4]

The seven charges raised by Rāmānuja against avidyā are more or less continued to be upheld or refuted by the non-Advaitins and the Advaitins respectively through the ages. All the allegations against avidyā are more or less continued to be upheld or refuted by the non-Advaitins and the Advaitins respectively through the ages. All those can be summed up in one line: what are the *āśraya* (locus), *viṣaya* (content), *svarūpa* (nature and form) and *pramāṇa* (proof) of avidyā. The innumerable questions and answers, allegations and their refutations that go by the name Vedāntic dialectics revolve around these four questions, which gives richness to Indian Philosophy, though from a certain standpoint they are meaningless and futile in so far as they are based on certain misunderstanding, which is not soluble by discursive or dialectical methods. We may examine how much tenable these arguments are, how much clarity they have brought to these concepts, to what extent they can be accepted and from which standpoint they are meaningless and why. Instead of going on arguing we have to find the extent of tenability of these arguments, their scope and limitations, which can only serve in bringing a solution to an unending process. For this, we may take up only one point, namely, the *svarūpa* of avidyā.

This is defined by the Advaitins as *anādi* (beginningless), *bhāva-rūpa* (positive) and *anirvacanīya* (indescribable). Regarding the last adjective, *viz.*, indescribability it is clear that it does not mean the absence of describability or incapability to describe something. It only means being indescribable either as real or as unreal. Something different from real and unreal as false or indescribable becomes indispensable only if reality and unreality are understood in the sense of the Advaitins. It is to be noted that according to Advaita, reality and unreality are only mutually contrary but not contradictory. We have earlier discussed that it is quite plausible to conceive them as such, since there is no inconsistency in such a definition or conception.[5]

With regard to beginninglessness, the opponent argues, *avidyā* cannot be beginningless in the case of shell-silver since it is undoubtedly known as having a beginning. Then Advatin replies: this *avidyā* which conceals the consciousness conditioned by the shell (*śuktyavacchinna-caitanya-niṣṭhāvidyā*) can be very well beginningless as its substratum, i.e., consciousness is beginningless. It cannot be said that avidyā or *ajñāna*, being beginningless and being different from absence, positive or *bhāvarūpa*, is unsublatable like the self. If by its beginningless-ness and difference from absence it can be proved to be unsublatable like the self, then, by its difference from existence and beginninglessness, why cannot it be proved to be sublatable as the prior absence or *prāgabhāva*.[6] It is to be noted that prior absence is defined as *anādi* and *dhvamsi* by the opponents. It cannot be said that *ajñāna* is unsublatable since its substratum (*adhiṣṭhāna*) is unsublatable. But this is not tenable as *ajñāna* which is revealed by the witness is not of the same ontological status as that of the witness.

Like this, to prove the positiveness or *bhāvarūpatva* of *ajñāna* a chain of arguments and counter-arguments have been advanced.

The most cogent reason against the opponent's view that *ajñāna* is nothing but of absence of knowledge is stated to be the inconceivability of its absence. While the opponent equates knowledge with other things of the world and upholds its absence as valid, the Advaitin shows its uniqueness and argues that its absence cannot be logically conceived. The cognition of absence always requires two factors, *viz.*, the *dharmin* and the *pratiyogin.* In the case of such cognition, "The ground having the absence of the pot." (*ghatābhāvavad-bhūtalam*), the ground is cognised as the *dharmin* and pot as the *pratiyogin.* At the time of grasping absence of knowlege, the ātman as the *dharmin* and knowledge as the *pratiyogin* are to be grasped which contradicts the thesis of absence of knowledge. Thus absence of knowledge in general (*jñāna-sāmānyābhāva*) cannot be proved.

Though absence of knowledge in general is self-contradictory, the opponents argue, the cognition "*ahaṁ ajñaḥ*" has particular absence of knowledge as its content. But this is not correct, as unlike the case of particular absence of knowledge like "*ghaṭamahaṁ na jānāmi*", "I do not know the pot", this absence has no object as its limiter or qualifier. It cannot be said that this particular absence in this case is characterised by generic property of the *pratiyogin* (*sāmānyāvacchinna-pratiyogitāka*). A particular absence cannot have a generic quality as its characteristic (*prakārībhūta-dharma*), it being an established fact that *prakārībhūta-dharma* is always the *pratiyogitākā-vacchedaka* with regard to knowledge of absence. If a particular absence has generic quality as its counter-positive-ness, then there is the contingency of the cognition of absence of a thing in a place where it actually is. So, also in the case "Air has no form", the negation of its doubt cannot be achieved. Though one particular absence is understood, doubt can be raised with the help of another particular absence. But this is not the fact as particular absence and generic absence are distinguishable from each other. In the case of absence of a particular pot, the limiter of absence of the counter-positive is "this-potness", whereas, in the case of absence of pot in general, it is "potness."[7]

The opponents try to pay the Advaitins by their own coin. They allege that a similar difficulty waits for the Advaitins even if positive *ajñāna* is admitted. They argue, *ajñāna* being grasped as antagonistic to knowledge related to both the *āśraya* (locus) and the *viṣaya* (content), its relation with its *viṣaya* is to be explained. Thus, we perceive *ajñāna* as *ghaṭājñāna* (*ajñāna* as related to pot), *paṭājñāna*, etc. As in the case of absence of knowledge, the knowlege of the *dharmin* and the *pratiyogin* cannot be explained satisfactorily, here also the relation between the so-called positive *ajñāna* with its object cannot be explained. If the object as referred to by *ajñāna* is grasped by another knowledge at the time of knowing *ajñāna*, it will falsify the very *ajñāna* itself. On the other hand, if the object is not revealed at the time of grasping *ajñāna*, how can *ajñāna* as related to a particular object be established? Thus, the Advaitin also has to face a similar difficulty in explaining the relation between the object and *ajñāna vis-a-vis* its revelation.

But such a difficulty, the Advaitin says, does not arise in the Advaita view. Had the object been grasped by psychosis-knowledge (*pramāṇa-vṛtti*) at the time of grasping *ajñāna*, there would be contradiction. But it is grasped by the witness and this kind of knowledge is neither valid nor invalid, since witness-knowledge is common to both valid and invalid knowledge (*bhrama-pramobhaya-sādhāraṇa*). The witness not only grasps *ajñāna* but also grasps its object as the limiter. The famous line of *Vivaraṇa* that everything becomes the content of witness-consciousness either as known or as unknown seems to be the guiding principle of the later Advaitins. Here, the non-Advaitins may argue - let this witness-knowledge be the revealer of absence of knowledge so that there is no contradiction with regard to the *dharmin* and *pratiyogin*. But this is not possible, since the witness is capable of revealing that which exists (*vidyamāna-sarvāvabhāsakatvāt*). In this way, positiveness of avidyā is defended by the Advaitin. But the debate goes on.

We may ask a question: what is the outcome of such a debate? These arguments are more deductive in character, since they aim at showing the consistency of certain conceptions. Sometimes, by reducing the position of the opponent to absurdity and self-contradiction, they try to defend the position of certain schools. But thereby nothing is positively proved. In the case of avidyā they only show that avidyā described as such can be maintained consistently from a certain point of view. Indescribability of avidyā can be defended from the Advaita view of reality and unreality. Its beginninglessness can be maintained from its co-existence with the beginningless consciousness, though it is ontologically lower than the latter. Its positiveness can be maintained only if the witness as conceived by the Advaitins is accepted. But these fundamentals are not the subject-matter of dialectics. It is noteworthy that the controversy between the Advaitins and the non-Advaitins, may be the Viśiṣṭādvaitins or Dvaitins, is due to some basic difference in their fundamental conceptions, which again and again occurs through the process of dialectics. For example, the Advaita concept of reality as unsublatable at all points of time does not have any contradiction with the concept of functional reality of the non-Advaitins. The non-Advaitins are content with the immediate reality of the things of the world and do not question their ultimate status, whereas the Advaitins only question their ultimate reality. They do not oppose the functional reality of the world. The non-Advaitins, it seems, first started this confusion in so far as they tried to understand, interpret and refute Advaita from their own standpoints. Sometimes they adduce spurious and simply verbal arguments. For example, the Mādhvas ask whether this *mithyātva* of the world is itself *mithyā* or not. Both the alternatives are unwelcome to the Advaitins, since, if it were not sublated there would be a *mithyātva* apart from Brahman, and if sublated the counterpositive, namely, the world of difference would become real. It is clear that they entify *mithyātva* as something real and argue thereby. Madhusūdana refutes it by showing that *mithyātva* and the world both being *Vyāvahārika* can be sublated at the same time.[9] The Advaitins have well-maintained their position. The two points which make Advaita invincible are: Reality as *trikālā-bādhyatva* can neither be proved nor be disproved by empirical means of knowledge, and falsity of the world can be maintained even if its functional reality is accepted, since the former is not opposed to the latter. Enduring debates as such can only be solved, not through arguments but by a more profound knowledge that transcends the limits of discursive reasoning. Allegations and their refutations are nothing but meaningless from this standpoint, though arguments continue unending.[10]

NOTES

1. *Advaitasiddhi of Madhusūdana Sarasvatī*, Parimal Publication, Delhi, 1982. *mithyā-śabdo'nirva-canīyatā-vacanaḥ*, p. 48.
2. Ibid., pp. 50-55.
3. *trikāla-sarva-deśīya-niṣedhā-pratiyogitā satto'cyate'dhyasta-tucche tam prati pratiyoginī*, *Nyāyāmṛta* quoted in *Bālabodhinī* commentry on *Advaita Siddhi*, *Bālbodhini* with *Advaitasiddhi*, Tara Publications, Varanasi, 1971.
4. *Advaitasiddhi*, p. 353. *na laukikaṁ na sāmānyajanyaṁ sākṣyātmakaṁ na ca.*
5. Ibid., pp. 50-55.
6. Ibid., p. 545.
7. Ibid., pp. 548-549.
8. Ibid., p. 550.
9. Ibid., pp. 207-222.
10. *Pañcadaśī*, II. 39.
    codyaṁ vā parihāro vā kriyatāṁ dvaitabhāṣayā
    advaitabhāṣayā codyaṁ nāsti nāpi taduttaram.

23

STRIKING AT THE VERY ROOT: SACCIDĀNANDENDRA SARASVATĪ'S REFUTATION OF SAPTAVIDHĀNUPAPATTI

Srinivasa Rao

> 'Who did you pass on the road?' the King went on, holding out his hand to the Messenger for some more hay.
> 'Nobody,' said the Messenger.
> 'Quite right,' said the King: 'this young lady saw him too. So of course Nobody walks slower than you.'
> 'I do my best,' said the Messenger in a sullen tone. 'I'm sure nobody walks much faster than I do.'
> 'He can't do that,' said the King, 'or else he'd have been here first.'
>
> \- Lewis Carroll, *Alice in Wonderland.*

Svāmi Saccidānandendra Sarasvatī who, in his *pūrvāśrama,* was known as Subrahmaṇya Śarma and wrote the work *Mūlāvidyā-nirāsaḥ* or *Śrīśaṅkarahṛdayaṁ,*[1] has added an entirely new dimension to the long debate on *saptavidhānupapatti*. This debate, which was initiated by Rāmānuja in the introduction to his *Śrībhāṣya,* is still going on to this day with many Advaitins still strongly defending the concept of māyā or primal ignorance (*mūlāvidyā*) against severe criticisms by both Viśiṣṭādvaitins and Dvaitins. In this long and bitter debate, both the sides have conceded the notion of primal ignorance as part of the Advaitic doctrine of Śaṅkara. Vācaspati Miśra, who initiated the famous *Bhāmatīprasthāna* in Advaita has argued that avidyā exists in the cosmic form (*mūlāvidyā* or māyā) as well as in the individual form (*tūlāvidyā* or *ajñāna*), and both these forms of avidyā are positive in character (*bhāva-rūpā*). His point is that ignorance (avidyā) is not mere absence of knowledge which is purely negative in character (*abhāvarūpā*) but it is an entity of some positive kind (*bhāvarūpā*). It is this positive ignorance that is annihilated upon the arising of the knowledge of Brahman (*brahmajñāna*).

The special point of Svāmi Saccidānandendra Saraswati (abbreviated as SSS hereafter) is that there is no such positive ignorance (*bhāvāvidyā*) at all and that the concept of avidyā as something of a positive kind (*bhāvarūpā*) is due to a misunderstanding of the true intents of Śaṅkara. Therefore he embarks upon a systematic refutation of the notion of *mūlāvidyā* (which is what the title of his work obviously means) which is also a recovery and re-establishment of the true teachings of Śaṅkara (which is what the subtitle of the work means). Since the whole debate on *saptavidhā-nupapatti* is an exercise in defence or in refutation of the legitimacy of *mūlāvidyā* or māyā, by arguing that there is nothing like māyā as advocated by the debators, SSS strikes at the very root of this debate and finds the debate itself to be totally unwarranted and untenable. If there is no avidyā or māyā which is an entity of a positive kind (*bhāvarūpāvidyā*), then all questions concerning its existence in or outside of Brahman, its relation to Brahman or the world, its very nature, its effects as well as its removal become non-questions. The thoroughness with which this task is undertaken and accomplished by SSS can be properly grasped only by a complete and meticulous study of *Mūlāvidyānirāsaḥ* (abbreviated hereafter as *MVN*).

I must point out at the very beginning that this rigorously argued work which runs into 234 pages in beautiful and powerful Sanskrit, is so full of terse arguments and logical demonstrations that it is possible only to very barely indicate here some of its arguments and conclusions. The work is in 4 parts containing 30 sections and 186 sub-sections. The plan of SSS in this work can be roughly indicated as follows: first he introduces the topic by explaining the common understanding of knowledge-seekers in Vedānta and their problems which give rise to questions concerning ignorance or avidyā. He also thereafter indicates the solutions to these problems offered by the writers on Vedānta. This comprises a very brief account of the *pūrvapakṣa* which he is going to refute in extreme detail later on in the work.

His objection is not only that the ideas common among the writers are wrong and are also without any support in the writings of Śaṅkara, but also that their very method is also faulty. He contends that the only proper method of attaining true Vedāntic knowledge is by an analysis of the three states of consciousness (*avasthātraya*) and not by unanchored discursive reasoning. In fact, this is such an important point for him that he has written separate works in Sanskrit as well as in English about what constitutes proper *vedāntaprakriyā*. This new rooting of the *prakriyā* in the analysis of the *avasthātraya* is exploited by him in full in arguing that in none of these three states is there any shred of evidence for the existence of ignorance as a positive entity (*bhāvāvidyā*).

While pointing out the untenability of the notion of *mūlāvidyā* owing to lack of evidence of any kind for it either in human experience or in the scriptures, he hastens to add that it is only because such positive ignorance is accepted by Advaitins as a legitimate entity that all kinds of objections by the 'Dvaitins' have come into existence. He also points out that as long as the Advaitins stick to the concept of māyā as a positive cosmic entity, the objections raised by the Dvaitins will remain unavoidable.[2] The entire second part of the work is thus devoted to showing the untenability of the notion of *mūlāvidyā*.

The third part consists of the exposition of his own *prakriyā* in the matter. It contains detailed arguments to show - from an analysis of the three *avasthās* - that *mūlāvidyā* does not exist in any one of them. It also briefly points out how the famous "seven objections" arise upon admitting avidyā as a positive entity. The fourth part consists in marshalling quotations from the works of Śaṅkara, Sureśvara and Gauḍapāda whose proper understanding would naturally lead to the conclusion that there is no primal cosmic ignorance.

Now, we turn to some of the details of the argumentation in the *MVN* by SSS. In the entire work, SSS relies upon some general maxims in rejecting *mūlāvidyā*. Some of these are:

1. Nothing that goes against experience can be admitted merely on the strength of some statement (*na kiñcidapi vacana-mātrabalāt anubhavaviruddham svīkāryaṁ, MVN,* p. 11).

2. In arguments, only those *yuktis* that do not go against experience ought to be used (*vāde ca ... anubhavāviruddhā eva yuktayopyupanyasanīyāḥ, MVN*, p. 11).
3. The term *tattva* indicates only an object that is according to experience (*anubhavānusāriviṣayatvameva hi tattvaśabdābhidheyaṁ, MVN*, p. 13).

Armed with such maxims, SSS addresses the question of avidyā or *ajñāna* and its nature. Both *jñāna* and *ajñāna* are matters of common experience. It is equally common knowledge that the term *ajñāna* means 'no-knowledge' or the absence of knowledge. SSS maintains that ignorance is of three forms: absence of knowledge, wrong knowledge and doubt.[3] When a person is in doubt, he of course does not know because knowledge never produces doubt about what is known. When a person has wrong knowledge, he of course does not know because wrong knowledge and knowledge, concerning the same object, do not go together. When there is absence of knowledge in a person, he just does not know. For example, when a farmer or a scholar of Tamilnadu does not know who is SSS, then he *just does not know* SSS without either having any wrong knowledge or even any doubt concerning SSS. To say that the farmer or scholar is ignorant of SSS is just to say that he has *no* knowledge of SSS and nothing more. It is wrong to think that the farmer *possesses,* in the literal sense of that term, an ignorance concerning SSS which is later on *replaced* by a knowledge when he comes to know of SSS. To say "He *has* ignorance" is only a manner of saying "He has *no* knowledge" or that knowledge is absent in him; it does not mean that there is some positive thing called 'ignorance' in him. Therefore it is absolutely counter-intuitive to think of the *absence* of knowledge (*jñānābhāva*) which is purely *negative* in character as some sort of a *positive* entity (*bhāvarūpā*). If knowledge is something, the absence of knowledge (or ignorance) is the *absence* of exactly *that* very something, and not the *presence* of something *else,* a sort of an entity called ignorance.

There are many innovations resorted to by *mūlāvidyāvādins* and all of them come up for repeated attack at different places in the *MVN.* SSS argues that the thesis that the world is the product of *mūlāvidyā* or māyā cannot be established unless the thesis that it is eliminable by knowledge is also established, but this latter thesis can be established only on the basis of the former. Thus there will be the fault of mutual dependence.[4] Since knowledge and ignorance are totally opposed in nature to each other, there can never be any kind of *mūlāvidyā* associated with Brahman.[5] We must note here that very long arguments in many Advaitic works offered in support of the view that darkness is not mere absence of light but it is a sort of a positive entity of its own kind - which sometimes run into dozens of pages - are very consciously designed precisely to defend the notion of *mūlāvidyā* as being *bhāvarūpā* or positive in character. SSS concludes his arguments running into three and a half pages in this matter by quoting at the end Śaṅkara's statement from the *Muṇḍakopani-ṣadbhāsya* : *na hi vidhiśatenāpi tamaḥ prakāśayo-rekatra sadbhāvaḥ śakyate kartuṁ* ... His own concluding words are: *tasmādanu-bhavaviruddhamidam mitho viruddhasvabhāva-yorvidyāvidyayorātmaikaviṣayayorekāśraya-totprekṣaṇaṁ*, *MVN*, p. 25.

His next argument is that it is impossible to identify and establish what sort of an entity this *'bhāvājñāna'* could possibly be. He complains that he is unable to see any kind of *a jñāna* which is other than the three forms of *ajñāna* mentioned before.[6] He does admit that there is *vyavahāra* involving the use of the sentences like "I am ignorant" (*ahamajña*) and "I do not know" (*na jānāmi*) but these can be reasonably interpreted only as indicative of a person's awareness of not knowing something and *not* as a statement of the awareness of a positive ignorance. Ignorance cannot possess such a positive character since there is ignorance even of things whose knowledge is in principle impossible as in the case of not knowing the horns of a hare.[7]

The strongest arguments of *mūlāvidyāvādins* come from their account and analysis of the state of deep sleep (*suṣupti*). They have no problem in characterizing the states of waking and dream as involving avidyā since they both are characterized by the perception of duality. There is *mithyājñāna* in both the states. There is no awareness of any kind of duality in deep sleep because the person who is deep asleep is aware of nothing. The *mūlāvidyāvādins* here make a distinction between the state of 'not being aware of duality' and the state of 'being aware of non-duality.' They argue that 'not being aware of duality' is not the same as 'being aware of non-duality.' For them, *suṣupti* is just a state of 'not being aware of' duality and hence a state involving ignorance or *avidyā*. There is *māyā* or *mūlāvidyā* in the state of *suṣupti* which is concealing the true non-dual nature of Brahman, but without projecting any world of duality. Since no world-appearance of any kind is being projected, the person 'is not aware of' any duality in that state. That is why a person waking up from the state of deep sleep is back in the world of duality because the root ignorance or *mūlāvidyā* has continued to exist in that state. Precisely because avidyā continues in *suṣupti*, there is no perception, experience or awareness of the non-duality of Brahman. Otherwise, a person entering the state of *suṣupti* would stand liberated and if he is truly liberated, his returning to the world of duality after waking up from *suṣupti* would be an inexplicable absurdity.

Therefore the *mūlāvidyāvādins* contend that cosmic ignorance persists through the state of *suṣupti* and only when it is once and for all destroyed by *Brahmāvagati*, is the person liberated. The world of duality then disappears exactly as the illusory snake disappears completely without a trace when the rope is seen. But this position has some very serious problems associated with it. Since *mūlāvidyā* is the sole and also the single cause of the world-appearance, when any person attains *mokṣa*, this sole and single cause of the world-appearance should get destroyed instantly. In that case, Brahman may of course remain but it would not make sense to talk of *someone* who had *Brahmāvagati* or realization of Brahman. In other words, there cannot be even a single *jīvanmukta* available in the world since the world itself will have disappeared completely along with the first individual who just attained Brahman realization, and in that case even any talk of Brahman realization would make no sense. The situation can be saved only by postulating as many *mūlāvidyās* - and therefore as many worlds - as there are individuals and also by arguing that when one individual attains Brahman realization, *his* world gets destroyed completely while others and their worlds continue to exist. But this alternative is no less absurd because it concedes duality until the last individual is liberated.

The above situation is made worse by some *mūlāvidyāvādins* who have tried to rescue the notion of *jīvanmukti* which is most seriously threatened by the stand that *mūlāvidyā* is destroyed upon *Brahmāvagati*. They have argued that avidyā is not completely destroyed upon *Brahmāvagati* but a trace of it (*avidyāleśa*) still remains and that accounts for the continuation of the body of the *jīvanmukta* as well as his experiencing of the effects of the last remnants of his *prārabdha karma*. Coexistence of pure *cit* and avidyā - the most radical form of duality one can think of - which the *mūlāvidyāvādins* accept in the state of bondage is bad enough; but its acceptance by them in some form even in the state of *jīvanmukti* is indeed really worse.

SSS is aware of all these problems and he is unhesitatingly of the opinion that the root cause of all these insuperable problems is the acceptance of *mūlāvidyā* which is also *bhāvā-vidyā*. Therefore he devotes the whole of the second part of *MVN* to demonstrate the illogicality of accepting any form of *mūlāvidyā* in any of the three states of waking, dream and deep sleep. This he does by offering his own analysis of the *avasthātraya*. The third part is a brief exposition of his own *prakriyā* in this matter for which he cites copious support from the writings of the founding fathers of Advaita like Gauḍapāda, Śaṅkara and Sureśvara. The third and the fourth parts together constitute more than 150 pages and therefore only a crude sample of his thoughts culled from these pages will be given below. It should by no means be concluded that the sampling is either thoroughly representative or that only the most important arguments are chosen.

If avidyā is not mere absence of knowledge and is really a kind of positive entity constantly present in *suṣupti*, SSS argues that we must in some way be aware of it just as we are aware of anything that is present in the waking and dream states. But that is not the case. No one reports that he was experiencing ignorance while he was asleep. No one reports that way because there is really no experiencing of avidyā in *suṣupti*. Therefore, such total absence of experience is a clear refutation of the presence of *bhāvāvidyā* in *suṣupti*.[8] While arguing that *suṣupti* is characterized by mere absence of knowledge SSS contends that even this absence is not experienced in *suṣupti*.[9] Even granting that one does recollect after waking up from sleep that he did not know anything, it would only prove that nothing was grasped during that state and not that a positive ignorance was grasped.[10]

Another thesis subscribed to by *mūlāvidyāvādins* is a causal link among the three states. The avidyā present in *suṣupti* is taken to be the cause of the manifestation of the world after one wakes up from sleep. Likewise the waking state is taken to be the cause of the dream state. This is rejected in an elaborate manner by SSS and he clinches his refutation by quoting from Śaṅkara's *Māṇḍūkyopaniṣadbhāṣya* the following line: *yadapi manyase jāgaritāt svapno jāyata iti, tadasat. na bhūtadvidya-mānāt abhūtasya asataḥ sambhavo asti loke* (*MVN*, p. 38).

A strong reason for the *mūlāvidyāvādins* to postulate the existence of avidyā in *suṣupti* is that even in the absence of *mithyājñāna'*(of waking and dream) in that state, no realization of the *svarūpa* of Brahman ever takes place in it. If *jñāna* does not still arise even in the total absence of *mithyājñāna'*, it must be because of the persistence of positive ignorance in the state of *suṣupti*. This is also rejected in an equally elaborate manner by SSS. He argues that if knowledge does not arise in *suṣupti*, it is because there is no possibility whatever of *jñānopadeśa* in that state and it is *jñānopadeśa* alone which can eliminate the *jñānābhāva* prevailing in that state.[11]

After arguing that the existence of *mūlāvidyā* cannot be proved on the basis of any of the *pramāṇas* like *pratyakṣa, anumāna, śabda, arthāpatti* etc., SSS takes up the suggestion that despite such *pramāṇābhāva* the existence of avidyā can still be proved on the basis that *mūlāvidyā* is known by the *sākṣin* (*sākṣivedyatvena tatsiddhiriti*). SSS rejects this suggestion because the concept of the *sākṣin* itself involves the concept of avidyā insofar as the *sākṣin* is understood to be *caitanya* reflected in *avidyāvṛtti*.[12]

SSS fully accepts Śaṅkara's clear and unambiguous identification of avidyā with *adhyāsa*[13] and hence also the view that ignorance simply consists in mutually superimposing the nature and qualities of ātman on *anātman* and *vice-versa.* Such superimposition is beginningless and is also the foundation of all *vyavahāra* - empirical as well as Vedic. It is only by a proper analysis of the three states that one comes to realize this fact of superimposition and is also able to overcome it. There is no substantive avidyā which does such superimposition and is hence its cause. There is therefore also no sublation or elimination of such substantive avidyā upon Brahman realization. With the elimination of such substantive *bhāvarūpa-mūlāvidyā* from the system of Advaita vedānta, all the grand seven objections raised against it by the Dvaitins stand eliminated automatically. SSS has struck at the very root of such objections and the debate has to be simply called off.

This in very brief outline is the scope and the range of the rich contents of MVN which certainly deserve close attention by Advaitins and the Dvaitins alike. If only I have succeeded in arousing their interest in this work, the modest goal of this small paper stands achieved in good measure.

NOTES

1. *Mūlāvidyānirāsaḥ* or *Śrīśaṅkarahṛdayaṁ* by Svāmi Saccidānandendra Sarasvatī, pub. by Adhyātmaprakāśa Kāryālaya, 2nd Main, Chamarajapet, Bangalore, 1929.
2. *na ca etasmāt dūṣaṇasaptakāt parimokṣam paśyāmo bhāvāvidyām avasthātraye api anugatam āśriyamāṇasya. tasmādapi na yuktiyukteyam prakṛtā prakriyeti siddham. MVN*, p. 84.
3. *vidyate hi jñānābhāva mithyājñāna saṁśayajñānarūpam ajñānatraya, MVN*, p. 26. While saying this, he alludes in a footnote to the passage in Śaṁkara's *Brahmasūtra-bhāṣya* which says that these three forms are *ajñāna* siunce they all are removable by *jñāna.*
4. *saṁsārasya avidyākṛtatvasiddhau vidyāvināśyatvasiddhiḥ tatsiddhāv-eva ca avidyā-kṛtatvasiddhiriti parasparamukhanirīkṣa-ṇaprasakteḥ,* MVN, p. 19.
5. *katham? vidyāvidyayorekādhikaraṇatvayogāt. na hi viruddhasva-bhāvayostamaḥ-prakāśayoriva yujyata ekatra samāveśaḥ ... prakāśā-bhāvasya tamasaḥ prakāśasthale darśayitumaśakyatvāt, MVN*, p. 21.
6. *na hi paśyāmaḥ kutrāpi uktapratyatrayam muktvā kañcidajñāna-padārtha, MVN*, p. 27.

7. *yadviṣaye khalu kadāpi jñānam na bhaviṣyati, tatrāpi najānāmītyanubhavo vartate, yathā śaśaśṛṅgam na jānāmīti, MVN*, p. 28.
8. '... *suṣuptāvahamavidyām anvabhūva' iti kasyāpi suptotthithasya parāmarśānudayena tasyāḥ sākṣyanubhūtatve sarva sampratipattyabhāvācca na tatra tadanubhavaḥ setsyati ... Tasmādanubhavābhāvo bhāvājñānam nirasyati, MNV*, p. 31.
9. *na tu vayam suṣuptau jñānābhāvasya tadanyasya vā kasyacidapyanubhavam pratijānīmahe, MVN*, p. 35.
10. *na kiñcidavediṣamiti smṛtimabhyupagacchasi, tathā ca sarvāgrahaṇameva pūrvarūpam siddhyati, na bhāvājñānagrahaṇamiti, MVN*, p. 36.
11. See *MVN*, pp. 55-61.
12. *kaḥ purasau sākṣī? avidyāvṛttipratibimbita caitanyam, MVN*, p. 69.
13. *tametamevam lakṣaṇamadhyāsam paṇḍitā avidyeti manyante, Brahmasūtrabhāṣya*, p. 1.

24

द्वैतमतानुसारेण भावरूपाविद्याविमर्शः

D. Prahladachar

अद्वैतसिद्धान्तस्य मूलाधारभूताया अविद्याया निरासविषये अस्ति द्वैतविशिष्टाद्वैतसिद्धान्तयोः सहमतिः। याश्च सप्तविधा अनुपपत्तयः श्रीभाष्ये अविद्याविषये प्रदर्शिताः ताः द्वैतमतेऽप्यङ्गीकृता एव। एवम् अद्वैत्यभिमतभावरूपाज्ञाननिराकरणविषये सत्यपि द्वैतविशिष्टाद्वैतयोः मत्यैक्ये वैलक्षण्यमपि किञ्चिदस्ति। विशिष्टाद्वैतसिद्धान्ते भावरूपाज्ञानमिति किञ्चिन्नास्त्येव। आत्मस्वरूपभूतज्ञानस्य सर्वदा एकरूपत्वेऽपि धर्मभूतज्ञानस्य सङ्कोचविकासौ तावदविद्यया भवतः। अविद्या चेयं न भावरूपा काचित्सदसद्विलक्षणा। अपि तु कर्मैव। कर्मणो हि अविद्येति संज्ञान्तरम्। एवञ्च कर्मणैव आत्मधर्मभूतज्ञानप्रकाशस्य सङ्कोचे प्राप्ते देवादिरूपात्माभिमनो भवतीत्युपपत्तौ अनेकदोषदुष्टा कर्मभिन्ना चेयमविद्या अप्रामाणिकी इति विशिष्टाद्वैतमतम्। द्वैतिनस्तुकर्मभिन्नं भावरूपं जीवरूपावरकं अज्ञानं किञ्चिदङ्गीकुर्वन्त्येव। किन्तु तदिदमज्ञानं न सदसद्विलक्षणम्, अपि तु आत्मवत् पारमार्थिकं सत्यम्। पारमार्थिकसत्यस्यापि तस्य निवृत्तिस्तु भवति भगवदनुग्रहेण तत्साक्षात्कारजन्येनेति अद्वैतमताभिमताविद्यातो विलक्षणां काञ्चिदविद्यां जीवस्वरूपावारिकां प्रतिपादयन्ति। अद्वैतमताभिमतामविद्यां बहुतरदोषोद्घाटनेन प्रतिक्षिपन्ति। येयमविद्यानिराक्रिया द्वैतग्रन्थेषु प्रदृश्यते तस्याः सविमर्शं विदुषामत्र समवेतानां पुरतः पुनस्तेषां कूलङ्कषं विशेषतो विचारायोपस्थापयितुं मदीयोऽयं प्रयत्नः। यद्यपि श्रीभाष्यादिषु ग्रन्थेषु प्रस्ताविताः सप्तविधा अनुपपत्तयः द्वैतग्रन्थेष्वपि सूचिताः, तथापि ता अनुपपत्तयः अन्याश्च भङ्ग्यन्तरेण प्रदर्शिता इति हेतोः ताः पुनरपि विचारणामपेक्षन्ते। तास्वपि काश्चिदेव मयाऽत्र प्रस्तूयन्ते।

प्रतीत्यनुपपत्तिः

'अहमज्ञः' इत्यादिप्रतीतयः भावरूपाज्ञानविषयिण्यः इत्यद्वैतमतम्। तासां प्रतीतीनां ज्ञानाभावविषयकत्वेनाप्युपपत्त्या न भावरूपाज्ञानसिद्धिरिति दोषान्तरं प्रदर्श्य,

भावरूपाज्ञानविषयकत्वेऽपि तस्याः प्रतीतेः स्वरूपम् अद्वैतमतरीत्या निष्कलङ्कमुपपादयितुं न शक्यत इति काचिदन्या अनुपपत्तिः। तथाहि - किमविद्या शुद्धेन साक्षिचैतन्येन विषयीक्रियत इत्युच्यते उत वृत्तिप्रतिबिम्बितेन तेन? आद्येऽविद्यायाः पारमार्थिकत्वापत्तिः। दोषजन्यज्ञानविषयः खलु अपारमार्थिको भवितुमर्हति। यदि च अविद्याविषयकः साक्षी निर्दोषः कथ्यते तर्हि तादृशज्ञान-विषयस्यापारमार्थिकत्वं किंनिमित्तमिति न प्रतीमः।

अपि च मोक्षेऽप्यविद्याया अनुवृत्त्यापत्तिः शुद्धसाक्षिचैतन्यस्य तत्रापि भावात्। न च ज्ञानं विद्यमानं गृह्णीयात्। मोक्षकाले तु पूर्वमेव निवृत्ताया अविद्याया ग्रहणं कथमापादयितुं शक्यमिति वाच्यम्। यतो हि अविद्यायाः प्रातीतिकत्वं तावदभ्युपगतमद्वैतमते। प्रातीतिकत्वं च प्रतीतिमात्रस्वरूपत्वम्। तथा च प्रतीतेरनुवृत्तावज्ञानस्याप्यनुवृत्तिरनिवार्या भवति।

नन्वत एव अविद्यायाः शुद्धसाक्षिवेद्यत्वं नोच्यते, किन्तु अविद्यावृत्तिप्रतिबिम्बित-साक्षिवेद्यत्वम्। मोक्षे चाविद्यावृत्तेरभावेन तत्प्रतिबिम्बित साक्षिणोऽप्यभावात् नाविद्यानुवृत्त्या-पत्तिरिति चेदत्र इमा अनुपपत्तयो भवन्ति - यद्यपि अविद्यावृत्तिप्रतिबिम्बितसाक्षिणो निर्दोषत्वाभावात् तद्वेद्याया अविद्यायाः पारमार्थिकत्वापत्तिः परिहृता, तथैव मोक्षे अविद्यानुवृत्तिरपि। अथापि वृत्तेः सार्वकालिकत्वाभावेन कदाचिद् अविद्याया अप्रतीतिः स्यात्। न चेष्टापत्तिरेवेयं, समाध्यवस्थायामविद्या प्रतीत्यभावस्यावश्यकत्वात्। तथैव कालान्तरेऽपि वृत्त्यभावदशायामविद्याप्रतीत्यभावस्य वक्तुं शक्यत्वादिति वाच्यम्। तथा सत्यविद्याया ज्ञातैकसत्त्वं भज्येत। संसारावस्थायां अविद्याप्रतीत्यभावदशायां अविद्याया अभावे अविद्याकार्यस्य प्रपञ्चस्यापि विलयापत्तिश्च। यदि च ज्ञातैकसत्ता नाङ्गीक्रियत एवाविद्यायास्तर्हि साक्षिवेद्यानां ज्ञातैकसत्त्वनियमस्यापि भङ्गप्रसङ्गः।

ननु सुखादीनां साक्षिवेद्यानामत एव ज्ञातैकसतां यथा प्रतीतिकाले सत्ता नान्यदा तथाऽविद्याया अपि प्रतीतिकाले सत्ताऽङ्गीक्रियते, नान्यदेति चेन्न। तथा सति प्रतीत्युत्पत्तिकाले समुत्पद्यमानस्य अज्ञानस्य अनादित्वायोगादज्ञानलक्षणस्यासम्भवापत्तिः।

अपि च अविद्यावृत्तिप्रतिबिम्बित चैतन्यवेद्यत्वं तावद् दोषाभावे न सम्भवतीति शुक्तिरजतादीनां विषये सिद्धम्। एवञ्चाज्ञानस्य तादृशचिद्वेद्यत्वेऽपि दोषसद्भावः प्रदर्शनीयः। न च दृश्यते कश्चित् तादृशो दोष इति कथमविद्यावृत्तिप्रतिबिम्बितचिद्वेद्यत्वं तस्य? न च दोषान्तरस्य दर्शयितुमशक्यत्वेऽपि अविद्याया एव दोषत्वं सम्भवतीति वाच्यम्। अविद्यायाः प्रातीतिकत्वेन प्रतीतिसत्त्वेऽविद्यासत्त्वम्। तत्सत्त्वे च दोषसद्भावेन अविद्याप्रतिबिम्बित-साक्षिवेद्यत्वमित्यन्योन्याश्रयः। यदि चैकैवाविद्या स्वयमेव दोषो भूत्वा स्वस्यास्तादृश-चैतन्यविषयतां सम्पादयतीत्युच्यते तर्हि आत्माश्रयो दोषः।

किञ्च अविद्यावृत्तेरपि प्रातीतिकत्वेन अविद्यावृत्तिप्रतिबिम्बितसाक्षिवेद्यत्वं वाच्यम्। तथाचात्माश्रयः। वृत्तेः स्वात्मकप्रकाशविषयकत्वेन स्वप्रकाशत्वापत्तिश्च। यदि चाविद्यावृत्तेः अविद्यावृत्त्यन्तरप्रतिबिम्बितसाक्षिवेद्यत्वमुच्यते तर्हि तस्या वृत्तेरपि वृत्त्यन्तरप्रतिबिम्बितसाक्षिवेद्यत्वं वक्तव्यमित्यनवस्थादोषः। अपि च वृत्तिप्रतिबिम्बितं चैतन्यं विशिष्टं सज्जडमेव। तथा च तादृशजडेन साकम् अविद्याया आध्यासिकसम्बन्धायोग इत्याद्या अनुपपत्तयः परिशीलनीया भवन्ति।

आश्रयानुपपत्तिः

जडस्य वा जीवस्य वाऽज्ञानकल्पितस्याज्ञानाश्रयत्वायोगात् शुद्धचिदेव अज्ञानाश्रय इत्यद्वैतसिद्धान्तः। यथोक्तम्-

आश्रयत्वविषयत्वभागिनी निर्विशेषचितिरेव केवला।
पूर्वसिद्धतमसो हि पश्चिमो नाश्रयो भवन्ति नापि गोचरः॥ इति।

तत्रेमा अनुपपत्तयः द्वैतिभिः प्रदर्श्यन्ते -

१. तमः प्रकाशयोरिव चिदज्ञानयोः परस्परविरुद्धत्वेन नाश्रयाश्रयिभावः युज्यते। न हि प्रकाशः कदाऽपि तमसः आश्रयः सम्भावयितुं शक्यः। यदि च वृत्तेरेवाविद्याविरोधित्वं न तु शुद्धचित इति तस्या अज्ञानाश्रयत्वे न किमपि बाधकं तर्हि अज्ञानाविरोधिन्याश्रितो ज्ञानत्वमेव न स्यात्। अज्ञानाविरोधिनोऽपि चेतनस्य यदि ज्ञानत्वं तर्हि घटादेरपि ज्ञानत्वप्रसङ्गः। यदि च स्वभावतः तृणादिभासकस्य सौरालोकस्य सूर्यकान्तावच्छेदेन तद्दाहकत्वं स्वीक्रियते तथा अविद्यावृत्त्यवच्छेदेन अविद्यातत्कार्यभासिकायाश्रितः अन्तः करणवृत्त्यवच्छेदेन अविद्यातत्कार्यदाहकत्वमुपपद्यत इति चेन्न - स्वभावतः तमोविरोधित्वादेव हि सौरालोकस्य प्रकाशत्वम्। नहि सौरालोकः अन्यावच्छेदेन तमोविरोधी। एवं स्वभावतः अज्ञानविरोधित्वादेव चितः ज्ञानत्वं वाच्यम्। तदभावे ज्ञानत्वानुपपत्तिरेव। स्वतोऽज्ञानाविरोधिनोऽपि ज्ञानत्वे घटस्यापि ज्ञानत्वं कुतो नेति पूर्वमिव पृष्टम्। न च स्वतः अदाहकस्यापि सौरालोकस्य सूर्यकान्तावाच्छेदेन दाहकत्वमिव चैतन्यस्यापि अज्ञानविरोधित्वं युक्तमित्युक्तमिति वाच्यम्। दाहजनकत्वावच्छेदकशक्तेः सौरालोके स्वतो विद्यमानाया एव सूर्यकान्तसम्बन्धेनाभिव्यक्तेः सर्वैः स्वीकारात्। स्वतस्तादृशविरोधिताच्छेदकधर्मरहितायाश्रितो वृत्तिसम्बन्धेनापि अज्ञानविरोधित्वं नोपपद्यत इति ज्ञानत्वानुपपत्तिरेव।

२. अपि च अज्ञानस्य चिन्मात्राश्रितत्वे धर्मिग्राहकप्रमाणविरोधः। तथाहि - अज्ञानसिद्धेः प्राक् तस्य आश्रयादिविचारः अनवसरग्रस्तो न युज्यते। अज्ञानसिद्धिस्तु 'अहमज्ञः'

इति प्रतीतेरेवेति च सिद्धम्। तथा च येन मानेन अज्ञानसिद्धिस्तेन तदहमर्थाश्रितत्वेन सिद्ध्यति। तदेतद्विहाय यदि चिन्मात्राश्रितत्वमुच्यते तर्हि धर्मिग्राहकप्रमाणविरोधः सुस्पष्टः। न च चिन्मात्राश्रितत्वेनैव अज्ञानसिद्धिरिति न धर्मिग्राहकमानविरोध इति वाच्यम्। अहमज्ञ इतिवत् चिदज्ञेति प्रतीतेरननुभाविकत्वात्।

ननु 'अहं स्थूलः' इति प्रतीतिवद् 'अहमज्ञ' इति प्रतीतिर्भ्रान्तिः। वस्तुतः स्थौल्याश्रयो देहः। आत्मनि तदैक्याध्यासाच्च अहं स्थूल इति प्रतीतिर्भ्रान्तिः। तद्वदेव वस्तुतोऽज्ञानाश्रयः चिन्मात्रम्। अहङ्कारे च चिदैक्याध्यासाच्च 'अहमज्ञः' इति प्रतीतिः भ्रान्तिः। अथवा, अयसि दग्धृत्वाभावेऽपि अयो दहतीति प्रतीतिर्जायते। तत्र च निमित्तं दग्धृत्वाय-सोरेकाग्निसम्बन्धः। तद्वदेव अहङ्कारस्याज्ञानाश्रयत्वाभावेऽपि अहमज्ञ इति प्रतीतिर्युक्ता। तत्र च निदानं अज्ञानाहङ्कारयोः एकचित्सम्बन्धः। सम्बन्धश्च अध्यासरूपः। तथा च अहमज्ञ इति भ्रान्त्यात्मकप्रतीतिविरोधः अज्ञानस्य चिन्मात्राश्रयत्वे न बाधकमिति चेन्न, चिन्मात्रस्याज्ञानाश्रयत्वसिद्धौ अहमज्ञ इति प्रतीतेर्भ्रान्तित्वेन तद्विरोधस्याकिञ्चित्करत्वम्। तद्विरोधाभावे च चिन्मात्रस्य अज्ञानाश्रयत्वसिद्धिरित्यन्योन्याश्रयात्।

ननु अहमर्थो नाज्ञानाश्रयः। तस्याविद्याकार्यत्वात्। तथा च अगत्या चिन्मात्रस्याज्ञानाश्रयत्वसिद्धेः 'अहमज्ञः' इति प्रतीतेर्न बाधकत्वमिति चेत्, न। अहमर्थस्य अविद्याकार्यत्वं अविद्यासिद्ध्यनन्तरमेव वक्तुं शक्यमिति ततः प्राक् अहमर्थस्या-विद्याधीनत्वस्य वक्तुमशक्यत्वात्।

३. शुद्धब्रह्मणः अज्ञानाश्रयत्वे श्रुतिविरोधश्च। 'निरनिष्टो निरवद्यः', 'शोकं मोहमत्येति मुक्तः' इत्यादिश्रुतयो हि अज्ञानरूपदोषाभावं स्पष्टं वदन्त्यः श्रूयन्ते। आद्यश्रुतौ दोषसामान्या-भावस्य, द्वितीयश्रुतौ च विशेषतः अज्ञानतत्कार्यशोकयोरभावस्य कथनात्, अज्ञानाश्रयत्वे नित्यमुक्तत्वकथनाच्च विरोधः स्पष्टः। न चेयं श्रुतिः तात्त्विकं अज्ञानाद्येव निषेधतीति व्यावहारिकस्य तस्याङ्गीकारे न दोष इति वाच्यम्। तात्त्विकस्य अज्ञानादेः अद्वैतमते अप्रसक्त्या निषेधायोगात्। तात्त्विकस्याज्ञानादेः जीवेऽप्यभावेन जीवब्रह्मणोः सावद्यत्वनिरवद्यत्वाभ्यां वैलक्षण्यप्रतिपादकश्रुतेरसामञ्जस्यापत्तेः।

यदत्रोच्यते - अविद्याश्रयत्वमात्रेण न काचिद्धानिः। किन्तु अविद्याकार्य-शोकाद्या-श्रयत्वेनैव। अविद्यायाश्च उपाधिभूतायाः प्रतिबिम्बपक्षपातित्वेन प्रतिबिम्बे जीवे एव स्वकार्याधायकत्वेन जीवस्यैव सावद्यत्वेनैव श्रुतिषु कीर्तनमिति, तदपि चिन्तनीयम्। अज्ञानस्य स्वाश्रये स्वकार्यकरत्वानङ्गीकारे चैत्राज्ञानकार्यस्य मैत्रादौ प्रसक्तिः। तथा च अज्ञानाश्रये ब्रह्मणि अज्ञानकार्यमप्यापाद्यते। तथा च सावद्यत्वमपि। किञ्च अज्ञानस्यो-

पाधेः प्रतिबिम्बपक्षपातित्वेन जीव एव यत् कार्यकरत्वमुक्तं तदपि विचारणीयम्। बिम्बस्थानीये ब्रह्मणि सार्वज्ञ्यादेः अज्ञानकार्यस्याङ्गीकारात्। एवञ्च स्वानाश्रययोः जीवब्रह्मणोरज्ञानस्य स्वकार्यकरत्वं कथमित्यपि चिन्तनीयम्।

४. अज्ञानस्य चिन्मात्राश्रितत्वे अन्या चेयमनुपपत्तिः - शुक्त्याद्यज्ञानं हि स्वकार्येण शुक्तिरूप्यभ्रान्त्यादिना ज्ञानावच्छेदेन समानाधिकरणं दृश्यते। तथैव संसारहेतोरज्ञानस्यापि स्वकार्यभ्रान्तिसंसारादिना ज्ञात्रवच्छेदेन सामानाधिकरण्यमवश्यं वाच्यम्। अज्ञानस्य मुखस्थानीयचिन्मात्राश्रितत्वे भ्रान्तिसंसारादिना कार्येण ज्ञात्रन्तर्भावेण सामानाधिकरण्यं न स्यात्। अज्ञानाश्रयस्य चिन्मात्रस्य ज्ञातृत्वाभावात्। तथैव शुक्त्याद्यज्ञानं स्वनिवर्तकेन तत्त्वज्ञानेन, तत्प्रागभावेन च ज्ञात्रन्तर्भावेण सामनाधिकरणमुपलब्धम्। संसारहेत्वज्ञानाश्रयस्य चिन्मात्रस्य तु ज्ञातृत्वाभावेन तत्त्वज्ञानादिसामानाधिकरण्यं ज्ञात्रवच्छेदेन नोपपद्यत एव। अनुपपत्तिश्चेयं चिन्त्रमात्रस्यैव भ्रान्त्याद्यङ्गीकारेण ज्ञातृत्वाङ्गीकारेण च परिहरणीया। किन्तु चिन्मात्रस्यैव भ्रान्त्याद्यङ्गीकारे तस्यैव संसारित्वापत्त्या जीवस्य तत्प्रति-पादकप्रमाणविरोधः। अपि च चिन्मात्रस्यैव भ्रान्त्याद्याश्रयत्वे 'अहमज्ञः' इति प्रतीतिर्न स्यात्। 'चिदज्ञा' इत्येवानुभूयेत। तथैव "अहं मुक्तं स्याम्" इतीच्छा न स्यात्। किन्तु "चिन्मात्रं मुक्तं स्यात्" इतीच्छैव भवेत्। एवं निर्धर्मकस्य चिन्मात्रस्य ज्ञातृत्वाङ्गीकारोऽपि न युक्त इति ज्ञात्रन्तर्भावेणाज्ञानस्य भ्रान्त्यादिना सामानाधिकरण्यानुपपत्तिरेव।

ननु चिन्मात्रे तात्विकस्य ज्ञातृत्वस्याभावेऽपि अध्यस्तं तदस्तीति नानुपपत्तिरिति चेन्न। ज्ञातृताध्यासस्याविद्याकार्यत्वेन चिन्मात्रे ज्ञातृताध्यासं प्रत्यविद्या आवश्यकी। अविद्यार्थं ज्ञातृत्वाध्यास आवश्यक इत्यन्योन्याश्रयात्। न च ज्ञातृत्वाध्यासं विनाऽप्यविद्याध्यासस्य सम्भवात्। तथा च नान्योन्याश्रय इति वाच्यम्। ज्ञातर्येवाज्ञानमिति नियमसद्भावात् ज्ञातृत्वमविद्याश्रयतावच्छेदकं भवति। अतो ज्ञातृत्वाभावे अविद्याध्यासः नोपपद्यत इति अविद्याध्यासं प्रति ज्ञातृत्वाध्यासः प्रयोजक एव। नचैवं शुक्तिज्ञातृत्वस्य शुक्त्यज्ञानदशायामभावेन कथं ज्ञातर्येवाज्ञानमिति नियम इति वाच्यम्। अत्र हि ज्ञातृत्वं न वस्तुगत्या ज्ञानाश्रयत्वम्। अपि तु ज्ञानाश्रयत्वशक्तिः। सा च शुक्त्यज्ञान-दशायामप्यस्त्येवेति नानुपपत्तिः। चिन्मात्रे च ज्ञानाश्रयत्वशक्तिरपि नास्तीत्यनुपपत्तिः। अध्यस्तस्य तस्याङ्गीकारे तु अन्योन्याश्रयः प्रदर्शितः। किञ्च वस्तुतो ज्ञातृत्वाभावेऽपि यदि ज्ञातृत्वाध्यासमात्रेण चिन्मात्रस्याज्ञानाश्रयत्वं तर्हि शरीरेऽपि ज्ञातृत्वाध्याससम्भवेन तस्याप्यज्ञानाश्रयत्वं स्यात्। न च ज्ञातृत्वं तदध्यासो वा नाज्ञानाश्रयत्वप्रयोजकः। किन्तु प्रसक्तप्रकाशत्वं अज्ञानानाश्रितत्वं वा। अविद्याकार्यस्य शरीरादेः जडस्य

प्रसक्तप्रकाशत्वाभावात्, अज्ञानाश्रितत्वाच्च नाज्ञानाश्रयत्वप्रसक्तिरिति वाच्यम्। शुद्धचितोऽपि स्वतः प्रसक्त प्रकाशत्वं तु नास्त्येव। किन्तु अविद्याधिष्ठानत्वेन। ततश्च घटादेरपि औपाधिकं प्रकाशमानत्वमस्त्येवेति तस्याप्यज्ञानाश्रयत्वप्रसक्तिः। किञ्च पूर्वोक्तरीत्या प्रकाशत्वम् अज्ञानाश्रयत्वञ्चेति परस्परविरुद्धम्। अतश्च चिन्मात्रस्याज्ञानाश्रयत्वानुपपत्तिः।

एवं अज्ञानविषयस्य अज्ञाननिवर्तकस्य च विषये आकरेषु बह्व्यः अनुपपत्तयः प्रदर्श्यन्ते। काश्चिदेव हि मयाऽत्र विचारार्थम् उपस्थापिता इति विरम्यते।

Summary: This essay, by Professor D. Prahladachar, is devoted to the examination of concept of māyā-avidyā from the point of view of Dvaita Vedānta. He shows the consensus between Viśiṣṭādvaita and Dvaita as far as their views against māyā-avidyā and the funda-mental differences between Advaita and Dvaita in accepting avidyā as a positive entity, *i.e.*, *bhāvarūpa*.

There are two major differences between Dvaita and Advaita schools in accepting avidyā as a positive entity. 1. The Advaita school holds that the avidyā, which is positive (since it is the cause of the world) is neither real nor non-real, nor both and hence different from them - *sadasad-vilakṣaṇa,* and therefore, false. The Dvaita school, on the other hand, considers avidyā as absolutely real like Brahman. 2. The Advaita school treats avidyā as beginningless but having an end in the Brahman-realization; whereas the Dvaita school maintains that this avidyā, which does not have a beginning, could be removed by the realization of Brahman only through His Grace and never directly.

The Viśiṣṭādvaita differs from both the Dvaita and the Advaita schools and Rāmānuja very clearly states that there is no necessity of positing a positive avidyā. He is of the view that the term avidyā occurring in the Upaniṣads, refers only to karma, the previous deeds, which are responsible for the state of the jīva in his present state.

In his *Śrībhāṣya*, Rāmānuja severely criticizes the concept of avidyā pointing out seven-fold objection. The Dvaita school accepts these and adds a few more showing how Advaitin's avidyā is not defensible a concept.

1. Inexplicability of the cognition of avidyā

The Advaitins hold that the very experience "*ahaṁ ajñaḥ*" (I do not know) reveals that the ignorance is something present in the person and hence it should be positive. The Dvaitins reject this view saying that "not having knowledge" is simply a negation of cognition and not the cognition of a positive entity called ignorance. The Dvaita school further raises the questions about the nature of experience of avidyā. As per the Advaita school, the experience of avidyā is of the nature of consciousness. The question is - whether it is pure consciousness or the consciousness reflected in the mental mode (*vṛtti*)? If the consciousness that apprehends avidyā is pure, then avidyā cannot be false. For, only such things which are the objects of cognitions caused by some defect could only be false, like rope-snake. But, now, the consciousness - the cognition of avidyā, being eternal is not a product of any defect and therefore is not false.

Further, as per the Advaita school, avidyā being illusory, has no independent existence, apart from its appearance (of the substratum) which is pure-consciousness. Since that consciousness continues to exist even in the state of liberation, there is the contingency of avidyā existing even in the state of mukti. In order to avoid such an awkward situation, the Advaitin may hold that the experience of avidyā is of the nature of "consciousness reflected in *vṛtti*" and since such a consciousness exists only during bondage where *avidyā-vṛtti* can exist, there is no continuation of avidyā in the state of liberation. But, then, since *avidyā-vṛtti* is a product and exists occasionally, the awareness of avidyā which is of the nature of the "consciousness reflected in *avidyā-vṛtti*" also will have to be considered as occasionally existing. As a result, avidyā which is *prātibhāsika* i.e., mere appearance, will have to be considered as existing occasionally, for avidyā cannot exist in the absence of its appearance. In fact, the objects of *sākṣin*, as a rule, exist only being known. Pleasure, pain and such other things which are objects of *sākṣin*, have no existence when there is no experience of them. Similarly, avidyā also cannot exist when there is no *avidyā-vṛtti* and consequently there is no "consciousness reflected in *avidyā-vṛtti*." When the Advaitins have to admit the possibility of a situation in which, during bondage itself, avidyā does not exist then it is also compelled to envisage a situation when during the state of bondage itself, the whole world gets destroyed, because avidyā - the material cause of the world does not exist.

Further, if it is held that avidyā comes to existence only when it is experienced, then it is a product and being a product, it needs to have a beginning and cannot be spoken of as *anādi*, without a beginning.

Again, the view that avidyā is grasped by the "consciousness reflected in *avidyā-vṛtti*" is also faulty because with regard to shell-silver etc., it is found that they are the objects of such a consciousness associated with some defect either in the sense organ or in the object. Now, if avidyā is an object of such a consciousness then some such defect is needed but there is no such defect ascribed. The Advaitin may contend that avidyā itself is the defect. But then it leads to the fallacy of mutual dependence, (*anyonyāśraya*). For, since avidyā is apparently real, it exists only when its cognition exists. The cognition, in its turn, can exist only when avidyā exists. Because, the cognition of avidyā, is of the nature of "consciousness reflected in *avidyā-vṛtti*" and in the absence of avidyā, *avidyā-vṛtti* cannot be there. If the avidyā needed for the *avidyā-vṛtti* is different from the "avidyā-to-be-grasped" then there will be the fallacy of infinite regress, *anavasthā*. For, the other avidyā also being apparently real can exist only when its cognition exists and the cognition requires another avidyā and so on. If one and the same avidyā is both the object and also the defect causing the cognition, then the fallacy is *ātmāśraya*.

Further, the "consciousness reflected in *avidyā-vṛtti*" is not pure; but a qualified one and hence is a non-sentient thing. Being non-sentient it has to be false, it cannot be the *adhiṣṭhāna* - substratum for its superimposed object namely avidyā. Thus the relation of substratum and superimposed, between the said cognition and avidyā, which the Advaita school claims to exist, cannot be explained here.

2. Inexplicability of the substratum of Avidyā

The Advaita school holds the view that the substratum of avidyā is pure-consciousness because non-sentient things and also individual selves (jīvas) being themselves the products of avidyā, cannot be the substratum. The Dvaita school raises the following objections:

Just as light and darkness are opposed to each other and cannot have the relation of locus and located, *cit* and avidyā also are opposed to each other and hence cannot have the relation of locus and located. The Advaita school argues that it is the *antaḥkaraṇa-vṛtti* - the mental mode, which is opposed to avidyā and not the pure-consciousness and therefore it can be the substratum of avidyā. The Dvaita school rejects the argument and maintains that *cit*, if is not opposed to avidyā, then would cease to be consciousness, for otherwise even a non-sentient thing like jar could be considered as conscousness. In order to counter the argument of the Dvaita school, Adviatins explain their position thus:

The sunlight illuminates grass and also burns the grass when passed through the lens, (*sūryakāntamaṇi*). In the same way, the consciousness when reflected in *avidyā-vṛtti* would manifest the avidyā and its products, but the same *cit*, if reflected in *antaḥkaraṇa-vṛtti* would destroy the avidyā and its products. So, it is the association of something which makes the consciouness either to illuminate or destroy the avidyā. But by nature, the pure-consciousness is neither supportive nor opposed to it. Therefore, the pure-consciousness could be the substratum of avidyā.

The Dvaita school rejects the comparison of sunlight and darkness stating that sunlight by its very nature can remove darkness without the aid of any other means. Similarly, sunlight also possesses the nature to burn the things, which gets manifested when the sunlight passes through a lens. In the same manner, consciousness also must be having the nature of destroying the avidyā, and that nature would get manifested when it gets reflectied in the *antaḥkaraṇa-vṛtti*. Therefore, like sunlight and darkness, consciousness and avidyā are by nature opposed to each other, and it is absurd to hold that the consciousness is the substratum of avidyā.

The Dvaita school further contests the view that the pure-*cit* is the substrate of avidyā on the basis of the experience "I do not know" which is the basic evidence by which the existence of avidyā is known to us. As per this experience "aham" - "I" which according to the Advaita school is a mixture of *cit* and *acit* - consciousness and mind, is the substratum of avidyā and not the pure consciousness.

The Advaitin contends here that the cognition "*aham ajñaḥ*", - just like the cognition "*aham sthulaḥ*' - "I am fat' - is an illusory cognition. Fatness is a property of the body and not that of the self. Yet, because of the misconception of identity between the body and the self, we have the wrong experience - "*aham sthulaḥ*". Similarly, the illusory cognition "*aham ajñaḥ*" also is due to the super-imposition of the identity of the consciousness on "*aham*".

Advaitins make an attempt to explain their view in a different way. The experience "*aham ajñaḥ*" is similar to the experience "*ayo dahati*" - "the iron (rod) burns". Burning is the property of the fire and not of the iron-rod. However, since the both, namely, the property of "being the cause of burning" and the iron - are related with one and the same fire, we have the experience "*ayo dahati*". In the same manner, since the both *viz.,* avidyā and the "*aham*" are related with one and the same *cit*, we have the experience "*aham ajñaḥ*". The relation, of course, is not real one but is a superimposed one.

The Dvaita school, however, is not convinced of the above explanation. It argues that the experience "*aham ajñaḥ*" could be considered as a misconception only when it is established that avidyā is located in the pure consciousness. And, the pure consciousness could be established as the substrate of avidyā if and only if the experience "*aham ajñaḥ*", is established as an error and hence the view that "the pure *cit* is the locus of avidyā" is not opposed by a valid cognition. Thus the explanations put forward by the advaitin involve the fallacy of mutual dependence.

Again the contention of the Advaita school that the "*aham*" is a product of avidyā and hence cannot be the substrate of avdiya, is also not acceptable because the view that the "*aham*" is a product of avidyā, cannot be accepted unless the concept of avidyā as envisaged by the Advaita school is established.

The dvaita school further maintains that the view that the pure *cit* is the substrate of avidyā is not acceptable also because it is negated, by unambiguous terms, by the Śruti texts such as "*śokam moham jarām mṛtyum atyeti.*" The Śruti directly negates the presence of any *avadya* - defect in Brahman and thus rules out the existence of avidyā which is a defect as well as the presence of sorrow, ignorance etc., the products of avidyā in Brahman. The contention is that the Śruti negates only the presence of real avidyā in Brahman and hence it does not oppose the Advaitin's stand that Brahman is the locus of the non-real avidyā. Such a view is not tenable because even the selves are not the locus of real avidyā according to Advaita because there is no real avidyā as such and therefore, even the jīvas do not have the real avidyā. Consequently, for Advaitins, there is no difference between the jīvas and Brahman as *sāvadya* and *niravadya* respectively, since both of them do not have any defect - the real avidyā which is non-existant.

The Advaitin contends : "Being the substrate of avidyā" by itself does not cause any damage. The products of avidyā such as sorrow, ignorance etc., are, infact the factors that are considered as defects and are to be avoided. Avidyā being an adjunct, as is well known, as per its nature always sides with the reflection - the selves and causes its products namely sorrow etc., only in them. So, although Brahman is the substratum of avidyā, He is *niravadya* - defectless, while the jīvas having *śoka*, *moha* etc., are *sāvadya* - possessors of defects.

The Dvaita school rejects even this contention. It holds that a cause is expected to produce its effects where it exists. Hence, if ajñāna is located in *cinmātra* - the pure consciousness, then it should produce its effects in Brahman also. It is absurd to hold that ajñāna, the cause produces its effects in jīva and Īśvara where it does not exist.

There is yet anothe inconsistency if the pure *cit* is considered as the substrate of avidyā. The ajñāna of shell is found to be co-existing with its effects such as the illusory cognition of shell-silver etc., in the cogniser. Similarly, the avidyā - the cause of bondage and misconceptions etc., should have co-existence with its effects in the cognition, namely the self. If avidyā is held as being located in the pure *cit* this rule is violated. For, the pure consciousness which is the locus of avidyā, is not the congiser and the cogniser - the self which has the bondage etc., - the effects, is not the locus of avidyā.

Further, if the pure *cit* is the substrate of avidyā then we should have the experience "*cit* is *ajña*" and not the experience "*ahaṁ ajñaḥ*." Similarly, since the cessasion of avidyā is the liberation, one should have the desire "let the pure *cit* be emancipated" and not the desire "let me get liberated." The attempt of the Advaita school to hold the pure *cit* itself as the cogniser and to explain the co-existence of avidyā and its effects is also futile because the attributeless pure *cit* cannot have the property - *jñātṛtva* - "being the cogniser."

The Advaitin argues that though the pure *cit* does not have the real *jñātṛtva*, it is superimposed and with that we can explain the co-existence of avidyā and its effects. But, since the superimposition is a product of avidyā and avidyā, as expalined above, needs *jñātṛtva*, there would be the fallacy of mutual dependence. It may be contended again that one who does not know the shell, is found to be having the avidyā of shell and hence *jñātṛtva* is not required for the superimposition of avidyā. But, actually here *jñātṛtva* required by avidyā is not the property of "being the locus of *jñāna*", instead it is the capacity to have the *jñāna*. This "*jñātṛtva*" could exist even while *ajñāna* is present. But the pure *cit* which is attributeless does not possess even this capacity and therefore, it cannot be the substratum of avidyā also. If with the superimposed *jñātṛtva*, the *cit* could be the locus of avidyā, then even the body of the self could be the locus of avidyā, because the superimposition of *jñātṛtva* is possible even on the body.

The Advaita school maintains that what is required to be the substratum of avidyā, is that it (the location) can be manifested in the absence of avidyā or its not being dependent on avidyā. Body and such other non-sentient things are not of the nature of being luminous and being the products of avidyā, are very much dependent on avidyā and therefore cannot be the locus of avidyā. Setting aside the argument, the Dvaita school points out that even the pure *cit* does not have luminosity on its own. Only being the substratum of avidyā, it is luminous. If the pure *cit* having the luminosity is due to the adjunct, *viz.*, avidyā, could that be the substratum of avidyā? If that is the case, then why not even jar etc., (non-sentient things) which also have luminosity due to adjunct could be the substratum? Moreover, as has been already pointed out, to have the nature of luminosity and at the same time to be the substratum of avidyā are totally opposed to each other and it is absurd to hold that the self-luminous *cit* is the substratum of avidyā.

25

THE ŚAIVA SIDDHĀNTA AND THE VIVARTAVĀDA OF THE AUPANIṢADAS[1]

Dominic Goodall

Before I begin to address the topic, it would be as well to remove potential confusion about what is referred to here with the expression Śaiva Siddhānta, since this label can have a wide application. It here refers not to the school now prevalent in the Tamil South, but to the once pan-Indian dualist school who held only the Sanskrit Siddhāntatantras to be their scriptures and whose formative thinkers include Kashmirian contemporaries of Abhinavagupta. The salient points of their doctrine have been summarized as follows:[2]

> (1) Śiva, (2) souls, and (3) the rest of reality, mental and material, are essentially and eternally distinct from each other. According to this view Śiva is only the efficient cause (*nimittakāraṇam*) of the universe. Its material cause (*upādānakāraṇam*), that out of which it is fashioned, of which it consists, and into which it dissolves, is not Śiva but māyā. The latter is the single, eternal, and unconscious source of the worlds and everything in them, including the bodies and faculties of each soul. To initiate a period of cosmic emanation (*sṛṣṭiḥ*) Śiva relies on a vice-regent, the Lord Ananta (Anantabhaṭṭāraka, Ananteśa) to irradiate māyā with his powers and so cause it to give birth to these forms. Śiva causes Ananta to activate māyā in this way in order that souls which have not yet been released may have the means of experiencing the fruits of their past actions and the possibility of working toward their eventual salvation.
>
> When Śiva judges a soul to be ready for release he liberates it into a state of omniscience and omnipotence in which it is his equal (*śivasamaḥ, śivatulyaḥ*). Even in this state of enlightenment and

liberation each soul remains distinct from every other and from Śiva himself. There is no question of the soul's surrendering its separate identity by dissolution (*layaḥ*) into some form of trans-individual consciousness.

Liberation cannot be achieved through mere knowledge of reality without recourse to ritual. This is because the state of bondage, in which the soul fails to realize its innate omniscience and omnipotence, is not caused by mere ignorance. The ignorance that characterises the unliberated is the effect of an imperceptible Impurity (*malam*) that acts on the soul from outside; and this Impurity, though it is imperceptible, is a material substance (*dravyam*). Because it is a substance, only action (*vyāpāraḥ*) can remove it; and the only action capable of removing it is that of the rituals of the initiation and their sequel taught by Śiva in his Tantric scriptures.

The above summary may surprise some because of its uncompromising pluralism, which is not an invariable feature of the Śaiva Siddhānta current today; indeed there are tantras whose names are listed in the canon of the Śaiva Siddhānta which either teach or appear to presuppose a Vedāntic non-dualism, notably the *Ajitāgama*[3] and the *Suprabheda*.[4] But in fact all the early writers of the Śaiva Siddhānta of whom works survive-that is to say Sadyojyotiḥ, Śrīkaṇṭha, Nārāyaṇakaṇṭha, Rāmakaṇṭha, and Aghora-śivācārya, the last of whom flourished c. 1157 AD[5]-are without exception dualists. Furthermore most Siddhāntatantras plainly share their dualist position. Both Professor Sanderson and Mme. Brunner have drawn attention to this anomaly and because of it, and for other reasons, have come to the conclusion that the surviving versions of some texts, such as the *Ajita* and the *Suprabheda*, are not of the same antiquity as others.[6]

Just on the basis of doctrine it would be difficult to determine a relative chronology of the Saiddhāntika canon. There are however three proofs that a given tantra is early:-

- the existence of early Nepalese manuscripts of the work (some are as early as the 8th and 9th centuries);
- the existence of early commentaries on the work;
- substantial attributed quotations in the works of early commentaries that can still be found in the surviving version of the tantra that bears the

name to which the quotations are attributed. (This criterion is arguably less strong than the other two, since the quantity of labelled quotations to make the idenfication compelling is disputable).

Using these criteria we arrive at a relatively short list of tantras which we can assume to have been known to Saiddhāntikas in the tenth century.[7] Most of the twenty-eight listed tantras that do not meet these criteria are never mentioned by early Saiddhāntikas; a few are quoted but the quotations are not to be found in the surviving works so named.[8]

Now all these demonstrably early tantras, with a single exception,[9] are uncompromisingly dualist. It appears clear that the old Śaiva Siddhānta was a dualist system which only after the twelfth century felt the influence of non-dualist Vedānta. The early Siddhāntatantras are not only not influenced by non-dualist Vedānta, they seem in fact to ignore it. As far as I am aware,[10] only two tantras attack in any detail the views of Vedāntins. The *Mṛgendra* devotes only three verses to Vedānta in its catalogue of wrong views (*Vidyāpāda* 2:12-14[11]):

वेदान्तेष्वेक एवात्मा चिदचिद्व्यक्तिलक्षितः ।
प्रतिज्ञामात्रमेवेदं निश्चयः किंनिबन्धनः ॥
अथ प्रमाणं तत्रात्मा प्रमेयत्वं प्रपद्यते ।
यत्रैतदुभयं तत्र चतुष्टयमपि स्थितम् ॥
अद्वैतहानिरेवं स्यान्निष्प्रमाणकतान्यथा ।
भोगसाम्याविमोक्षौ च यौ नेष्टावात्मवादिभिः ॥

In the Śāstras of the Vedānta there is only one soul, known through its manifestations, which are sentient and insentient. This is no more than mere assertion. What is the basis of this certainty? If you say that there is some valid means of knowing it [viz. scripture], then the soul must be the object of the valid knowledge. If you accept this pair [of means of knowing and object of knowledge], then all four [i.e. *pramāṇa*, *prameya*, *pramātṛ*, and *pramiti*] are proven to exist.[12] [And] thus that would be the end of non-dualism; either that, or it must be without valid means of knowledge. And there would also result [the faults] that al! must share the same experience and that liberation would be impossible, both faults of which are not accepted by any who maintain the existence of the soul.

Essentially, there are three arguments here: that non-dualism is devoid of external proof,[13] that, since there is only one soul, experience must be unitary, and that true liberation must be impossible.[14]

The only demonstrably early Siddhāntatantra which devotes several verses to a reasoned refutation of Vedāntic Advaita appears to be the *Parākhyatantra* (1:42-50). This text has not been much discussed in secondary literature because it is unpublished and survives only in a single South Indian palm-leaf manuscript in Mysore (hereafter msMy). It is plainly an authentic early work, however, because verses quoted and attributed to it in the works of tenth-century Kashmirians (notably in the 10th chapter of Kṣemarāja's *Svacchandatantroddyota*) are to be found in the Mysore text.[15]

The *Parākhya* has the form of a dialogue between Prakāśa, the sun, who is the teacher, and his questioner Pratoda, who is probably to be identified with Vasiṣṭha (see Goodall, *ibid.*, p. lxv, footnote 156). The agenda of the first chapter is set by Prakāśa proclaiming a list of epithets that apply to the soul (1:15):

देहान्योऽनश्वरो व्यापी विभिन्नः समलोऽजडः ।
स्वकर्मफलभुक्कर्ता किञ्चिज्ज्ञः सेश्वरः पशुः ॥

The bound soul[16] is different from its body, indestructible, all-pervading, distinct [from God and from other souls], endowed with impurity, not [innately] insentient, the experiencer of the fruits of its own actions, an agent, partially equipped with the power of knowledge, subject to the Lord.[17] Each of these epithets is then challenged in turn by Pratoda, assuming the standpoint of different thinkers. The epithet *vibhinnaḥ* is thus the starting point for a discussion of non-dualism. I give below the text and a translation[18] of the whole passage in question (*Parākhya* 1:42-50):

प्रतोद उवाच ।
एक एव स्थितो वेत्ता देहे देहे स्वकर्मतः ।
एकधा बहुधा चैव दृश्यते जलचन्द्रवत् ॥४२ ॥

प्रकाश उवाच ।
चिद्रूपत्वात्तदेकत्वं तद्भिन्नभोगतः ।
स च तस्य स्वकर्मोत्थः साविद्या बन्धलक्षणा ॥ ४३ ॥

तच्छेदिका भवेद्विद्या द्वयमस्त्येकता च न ।
विद्याविद्याविभागेन गतोऽद्वैतपरिग्रहः ॥४४॥

प्रतोद उवाच ।
अविद्या वासना सर्वा नार्थतः सा स्थिता मम ।
विद्यारूपं स्थितं सर्वं सा विद्या सः परःपुमान् ॥४५॥

प्रकाश उवाच ।
उपायः सकलो व्यर्थो यस्तेऽऽविद्याप्रमार्जकः ।
विद्यात्मा येन संसिद्धो न बन्धः परमार्थतः ॥४६॥
विद्यारूपं भवेत् सर्वमविद्याख्यमथास्ति वा ।
तयात्मानं निवध्नाति विद्यया स विमोचयेत् ॥४७॥
क्रीडेऽयं वा स्वधर्मो वा तदा मुक्तेरसम्भवः
इष्टा ते वाथ सा मुक्तिरेकदेशे न सर्वथा ॥४८॥
एकदेशे न देशः स्यान्निरंशत्वादमूर्तितः ।
स्थितायां सर्वतो मुक्तौ भवच्छेदः प्रसज्यते ॥४९॥
न चास्ति स भवच्छेदस्तेन ते बहवो मताः ।
अनादिपाश संरुद्धाः सास्मिन्योऽऽमलो मतः ॥५०॥

Pratoda spoke:
[But perhaps] there exists only one knower, [situated] in various bodies, in accordance with his past actions. He appears both as one and as many, like the moon [reflected] in [rippling] water.[19] (42)

Prakāśa spoke:
In as much as [all are] of the form of consciousness they are one; [but] they are divided because of their various experiences. And those arise from the soul's own past actions. This is delusion (*avidyā*), which is bondage. (43)
That which cuts away this [bondage] is knowledge; [and so] there are [at least] two [real entities] and there is no oneness [of all creation].
[Your] hanging on to non-dualism is finished, because there is a division between knowledge and delusion (*vidyāvidyā-vibhāgena*). (44)

Pratoda spoke:
All traces [of past action] are delusion; they do not exist for me in reality.[20]
Everything exists as knowledge. This is knowledge. This is the supreme soul. (45)

Prakāśa spoke:
All means of yours [in that case] which wipe away delusion are worthless, since the soul is established to be [nothing other than the one] knowledge, [and] there is no bondage at the level of the highest reality. (46)

> Everything must be knowledge. Or if there is something called delusion, then the [one] soul (*saḥ*) binds himself with it and should release [himself] by means of knowledge. (47)
> This is all sport or the essential nature [of the soul] (*svadharmo vā*), and therefore liberation is impossible. Or if you require that there is liberation, then it must be of a part (*ekadeśe*) and not of the whole. (48)
> If [you say that it must be] partial, [then we reply that] there can be no part, since it is formless and therefore without parts.[21] If there were to be liberation of the whole, then this would entail that worldly existence must be cut off. (49)
> And yet there is no cutting off of worldly existence, and so those [souls] are taught to be many, blocked beginninglessly by bonds, and that [delusion] (*sā*[22]) in this [tantra] (*asmin*[23]) is the impurity that is taught. (50)

The first argument here is that non-dualism is a fiction because Vedāntins admit both vidyā and avidyā (42-4). This is countered by the opponent on the grounds that the ontological status of avidyā is not the same as that of vidyā and so the two cannot be counted on the same level (45). The second is that there can be no means to achieve the goal because there is ultimately no bondage (46-7).[24] The third, which we have seen above in the attack of the *Mṛgendra*, is that liberation for individuals is an impossibility, because Brahman is partless (48-9). It will be noticed 1) that none of the attacks in either passage is specifically an attack on māyā and 2) that the level of argument is relatively unsophisticated.

As I have stated above, no other early Siddhānta appears to attack or even mention Vedāntic Vivartavāda.[25] Now someone might argue that the reason for this absence may simply be that most early tantras of the Śaiva Siddhānta are not dialectic in character. The *Rauravasūtrasaṅgraha*, the *Svayambhuvasūtra-saṅgraha* and the *Kiraṇa* do not have long attacks on rival views of any description, and so we should not expect to find in them refutations of Māyāvāda; but this, I think, is not enough of an answer, because some Siddhāntatantras, most notably the *Mataṅga*,[26] are unquestionably dialectic in character. But the *Mataṅga*, although it devotes space to the refutation of the views of Cārvākas (*Vidyāpāda* 6:5c-19b), of various *Bauddha-pakṣa*s (*Vidyāpāda* 6:19c-37b), of Sāṅkhya notions (eg. *Vidyāpāda* 6:37c-42 and 62c-70b), appears not to mention Vedāntins at all.

Furthermore some tantras, although not dialectic, contain polemical passages of another kind: ones in which the types of liberation espoused by thinkers of rival views are ranked on the *tattvakrama*, that is to say: followers of other religions are each said to reach a particular level of the Śaiva cosmos suited to the insights that their religion encourages. The list of the *Kriyākāṇḍa-kramāvali* of Somaśambhu is not untypical (*Vratoddhāravidhi* 7-8b[27]):

बुद्धितत्त्वे स्थिता बौद्धा जैनास्तु गुणमस्तके।
वेदान्तज्ञास्तु तद्योनौ पुरुषे भगवन्मुखाः॥
पाशुपतास्तु मायायां विद्यायां तु महाव्रताः॥

Thus too the *Svacchandatantra* (11:68d-71):

बुद्धितत्त्वे व्यवस्थिताः।
सर्वज्ञं च तदेवाहुर्बौद्धानां परमं पदम्।[28]
गुणेष्वारहतानां च प्रधानं वेदवादिनाम्॥
पौरुषं चैव सांख्यानां सुखदुःखादिवर्जितम्।
षड्विंशकं च देवेशि योगशास्त्रे परं पदम्॥
व्रते पाशुपते प्रोक्तमैश्वरं परमं पदम्।
मौसुले कारुके चैव मायातत्त्वं प्रकीर्तितम्॥

What is to be noted is that in early lists of this kind the Vedāntins are usually placed in *prakṛtitattva*, and this suggests that the intended Vedāntins were *pariṇāmavādins*. Occasionally, however, the Vedāntins are moved up to the next level, as, for example, in the non-dualist *Sarvajñānottara*, *Liṅgoddhāraprakaraṇa* 3:[29]

ज्ञानचर्यान्वितो बौद्धो बुद्धितत्त्वमवाप्नुयात्।
तामसं जिनभक्तास्तु पौरुषं ब्रह्मवेदिनः॥

!! *jñānacaryānvito*] N; *jñānācaryādvitau* T. 334 !! *bauddho*] em.; *bauddhā* N; *bauddhau* T.334 !! *jinabhaktās tu*] em.; *jñitabhaktās tu* N; *jinabhaktānāṃ* T. 334 !! *pauruṣaṃ brahma-vedinaḥ*] em.; *pauruṣaṃ brahmavedina* N; om. T. 334

Now in Rāmakaṇṭha's much later *Sarvāgamaprāmāṇyopanyāsa* he neatly resolves this minor uncertainty (of which tattva to place Vedāntins in) and in such a way as to show that he too supposed Pariṇāmavādins and not Vivartavādins to be intended by the majority of the lists:[30] he places the Pariṇāmavādins in prakṛti and the Vivartavādins in puruṣa (4cd, 5c-6b):[31]

> पशौ ब्रह्मत्वेनाहुर्ये चिद्विवर्तानिर्निमलान् [...]
> अव्यक्ते येऽप्युपादानं गुणानां ब्रह्म चात्मनाम्।
> तत्रैव कारणं तेषां ये तु नारायणाभिधाम्॥

In the *tattva* of the bound soul are those who hold that the impure apparent transformations of consciousness are Brahman ... And in prakṛti are those who hold that Brahman is the material cause of *guṇa*s and of souls. There too are those for whom the cause of these [*guṇa*s and souls] is called Nārāyaṇa [*i.e.,* followers of the *Pāñcarātra*].

Leaving aside for a moment the tantras of the Śaiva Siddhānta let us consider Sadyojyotiḥ, the oldest exegete of the Śaiva Siddhānta, by whom works survive. His extensive polemical writings appear to contain no attack or mention of Vedāntic Vivartavāda.[32] In his *Paramokṣanirāsakārikā*, a work devoted to attacking the views of rival thinkers, Sadyojyotiḥ gives prominence to various Sāṅkhya opinions, to the Pāñcarātra, to Buddhist views and to the notions of liberation propounded by now obscure Pāśupata rivals; but when Sadyojyotiḥ comes to refute the Vedāntavādins, it is plainly not Māyāvāda that he attacks, but a transformationist doctrine, as indeed his commentator, Rāmakaṇṭha, points out ad verse 2 (p. 280, line 31):[33] *nanvatra vṛttikartuḥ - pariṇativedāntamatir evoddeśyatayābhimatā, na māyāvādamatiḥ*. 'But here the author of the commentary [on the *Raurava*, i.e. Sadyojyotiḥ,] intended only the transformationist Vedāntic doctrine to be elucidated [and refuted], not the doctrine which holds [that all is] cosmic illusion.' Furthermore in other texts of his too, *e.g., Mokṣakārikā* 18-25b,[34] it is always a Pariṇāmavāda that Sadyojyotiḥ attacks when he deals with Vedānta.

Now the date and provenance of Sadyojyotiḥ is uncertain.. Though his works were highly thought of in Kashmir in the tenth century, no close connection between him and the tenth-century Kashmirian Saiddhāntikas can be assumed, and perhaps he is to be placed as much as two centuries earlier, perhaps earlier, in fact, than the latest of the early Siddhāntatantras.

The conclusions of this investigation are slim: we find that the earliest Saiddhāntika exegete, Sadyojyotiḥ, was ignorant of or quite unchallenged by the Vivartavāda of the Aupaniṣadas, for in his extensive and polemical writings he never once mentions it; and we find that the early tantras of the Śaiva Siddhānta, with two exceptions, also never mention Vivartavāda. Among the two exceptions, the *Mṛgendra* does not appear in any version of the list of twenty-eight primary scriptures, and the *Parākhyatantra* does not appear on all of them, and on the lists on which it does appear it is consistently last. On these grounds, and because of their structure, diction and the developed form of their doctrine, they can be inferred to be among the latest of the Siddhāntas that can be assumed to have been known to the tenth-century Kashmirian exegetes who shaped the school.[35] Perhaps they may be later even than Sadyojyotiḥ. What this tells us is that Vedāntic Vivartavāda was either unknown or of little importance in the places and at the times in which the earliest thinkers of the Śaiva Siddhānta wrote.

NOTES

1. I am most grateful to Dr. Godabarisha Mishra of the Radhakrishnan Institute for Advanced Study in Philosophy for his kind invitation to me to give a paper here. I should also like to thank the following libraries and instituitions for allowing me to consult the manuscripts that I have referred to below: the Centre for Indology of the Ecole française d'Extrême-Orient and French Institute of Pondicherry (hereafter EFEO and IFP respectively); the Oriental Research Institute of the University of Mysore; the Government Oriental Manuscripts Library, Madras (hereafter GOML); the Oriental Institute of Baroda; the National Archives of Kathmandu; and the Nepal German Manuscript Preservation Project (hereafter NGMPP).
2. Quoted (omitting the footnotes) from pp. 282-5 of Alexis Sanderson's 'The Doctrine of the Mālinīvijayottaratantra' in Teun Goudriaan's *Ritual and Speculation in Early Tantrism: Studies in Honor of André Padoux*, State University of New York Press, 1991, pp. 281-312.
3. Particularly 2:1-27, in which, as Sanderson has pointed out (*op. cit.*, p. 291, footnote 42), Śiva is represented as the supreme soul whose form is being, consciousness, and bliss and as the identity of everything, including individual souls. (Many of the same verses occur

also in a passage of the *Vātulaśuddhākhya*: 9:77-89, quoted in the apparatus to the *Ajita*).

4. See Hélène Brunner's 'Analyse du Suprabhedāgama' in *Journal Asiatique* Vol. CCLV, 1967, pp. 31-60, particularly pp. 51ff.
5. See Dominic Goodall's *Bhaṭṭa Rāmakaṇṭha's Commentary on the Kiraṇatantra, volume 1: critical edition and annotated translation*, Publications du département d'indologie No. 86.1. Pondicherry: Institut Français de Pondichéry and Ecole française d'Extrême-Orient, 1998, pp. xiii-xvii, footnote 24.
6. It may be unpleasant for a Śaiva devotee to hear that the āgamas in general, but especially those which are most famous in the South, have been deeply altered, sometimes to an extent that we have a new work under an old title. But this is a fact, which can be denied only by those who have never read the āgamas or who place in them a blind faith, exclusive of critical mind. The proofs we can adduce are many...' from p. 32 of Hélène Brunner's 'Jñāna and Kriyā: Relation between Theory and Practice in the Śaivāgamas' in Teun Goudriaan's *Ritual and Speculation in Early Tantrism: Studies in Honor of André Padoux*, State University of New York Press, 1991, pp. 1-59. See also Sanderson, *op. cit.*, p. 291.
7. This is discussed at greater length and with details of manuscripts by Goodall, *op. cit.*, pp. xxxix-xlvii.
8. Some details are given by Goodall, *ibid.*, pp. xlv-xlvi, fn. 103.
9. As Sanderson has pointed out (*op. cit.*, p. 291), the *Sarvajñānottara* is an unambiguously non-dualist work that survives in an early Nepalese manuscript. For further details about the transmission of this text see Goodall, *op. cit.*, pp. xlvi and lix-lxi. I should add to those remarks that although a small part of that same *Sarvajñānottara* has been published (the chapters comprising the so-called *Vidyāpāda* have been published with a Tamil translation and commentary by Tūttukkuṭi Po. Muttaiya Piḷḷai, Devakoṭṭai 1923) the doctrine of the early text should not be deduced from this published version, since this has been deliberately and very significantly modified, most distortively by the insertion in its first chapter of twenty verses discussing and refuting the old doctrine that in liberation the soul becomes equal to Śiva (7-26). These verses are certainly a late interpolation since they are not found in the ancient Nepalese MS of the text (National Archives of Kathmandu MS 1-1692, NGMPP Reel No. A~43/12, f. 49v), nor are they discussed in Aghoraśiva's twelfth-century commentary on the text (see below for MSS), nor do they occur in the

manuscripts of the text belonging to the collection of the Institut Français de Pondichéry [=IFP], or indeed in any manuscript that I have been able to consult.

10. Since so many of the early Siddhāntas must be read from manuscripts (the *Niśvāsatattvasaṃhitā*, including the *Dīkṣottara*, the old *Pārameśvara*, several recensions of the *Kālottara* and most of the *Sarvajñānottara* have not been published), I am a long way from having studied them all satisfactorily, and I am therefore not certain that I have not missed discussions. I am encouraged, however, in believing that I have not missed any discussions of significance because of one telling piece of negative evidence: in his unpublished flagrantly dualist commentary on the flagrantly non-dualist *Sarvajñānottara* Aghoraśivācārya has apparently found no other attacks on Vedānta in the Siddhāntatantras than the two which I cite below. Both of these he cites (IFP MS~47818, pp. 56-7), and he defends his distortively dualist interpretation of the non-dualist passages in the *Sarvajñānottara* on the grounds that the teaching of many scriptures of the canon cannot be distorted on the basis of one contradictory scripture (IFP~MS~47818, p. 58): ... *na caikaśrutya-nurodhenānekaśrutīnām anyathākaraṇam upapadyate.*
11. *Mṛgendratantra* [*Vidyāpāda* and *yogapāda*], with the commentary (-*vṛtti*) of Bhaṭṭa Nārāyaṇakaṇṭha, ed. Madhusūdan Kaul Śāstrī. Kashmir Series of Texts and Studies (=KSTS)~50. Srinagar, 1930, pp. 64-70. (Note that Vedānta is mentioned also in 2:10 and 2:28.)
12. The locus classicus where the *pramāṇādicatuṣṭaya* is discussed and to which Nārāyaṇakaṇṭha here refers is to be found at the beginning of Vātsyāyana's *bhāṣya* on the *Nyāyasūtra* (*Nyāyadarśana* of Gautama...} Volume 1, chapter 1, ed. Anantalal Thakur, Darbhanga, 1967, p. 1, lines 9-12): ... *yasyepsājihāsāprayuktasya pravṛttiḥ sa pramātā. sa yenārthaṃ pramiṇoti vijānāti tat pramāṇam. yo'rthaḥ pramīyate jñāyate tat prameyam. yat tad arthavijñānaṃ sā pramitir iti. catasṛṣu caivaṃvidhāsu tattvaṃ parisamāpyate.*
13. The absence of valid means of knowledge remains the principal line of attack on Vedānta also in the works of the post-scriptural exegetes. Cf., for example, the following from Rāmakaṇṭha's *Nareśvara-parīkṣā Prakāśa* (*Nareśvaraparīkṣā* of Sadyojyotiḥ with the commentary (-*Prakāśa*) of Bhaṭṭa Rāmakaṇṭha, ed. Madhusūdan Kaul Śāstrī. KSTS 45. Srinagar, 1926, p. 8): *asāv āmnāyas tāvan na satyabhūta-brahmādvaitapratipādakatvena pramāṇaṃ tasya sarvaparikalpanā-tītarūpatvatas tadaviṣayatvābhyupagamāt, tadviṣayatve*

tvāgamasyāpi satyatvād asato 'tadviṣayatvenāpramāṇatvāt na satyādvaitasiddhir dvaitanibandhanatvāt pramāṇaprameya-bhāvasya iti. yadi param asyāḥ sakalabhedarūpāyāḥ pratipatter avidyāvāsanātva-Prakāśakatvena pramāṇam abhyupagantavyaḥ pāramparyeṇa tv advaitātmani, yad āhuḥ "neti nety ātmagatiḥ" iti. tataś cāvastuviṣayatvād asya "eṣa vandhyāsuto yāti" ityādivākyajāta-syeva prāmāṇyābhāvāt punar apy advaitāsiddhir eva.*

*scil. *āmnāyaḥ*, according to a marginal note in Baroda MS II.1829.

'Now that, i.e. scripture, is not a means of knowledge [of Brahman] because it proclaims the oneness [of all things] in Brahman, who [alone] is real, since it is acknowledged that Brahman (*tasya*) cannot be its object (*tadaviṣayatvābhyupagamāt*), for Brahman's nature is beyond all discursive thought. And if Brahman were its object (*tadviṣayatve tu*), then the scripture too would have to be real. Not being real, it cannot be a means of knowing [Brahman], since it does not have Brahman as its object, and so the oneness [of all things] in the [one] real Brahman is not established, since the relationship of knowables and means of knowledge relies upon duality. But what if [it is alleged that scripture] is held to be a means of knowledge in as much as it reveals that this [worldly] understanding [of ours] which has the form of all duality is a trace produced by nescience, [and thus is] indirectly [a means of knowledge] with regard to the non-dual Brahman? As they say, 'the state of the soul is not like this, not like that''. But therefore [in that case too] (*tataśca*), since its object is not real, scripture (*asya*) cannot be authoritative as a means of knowledge, just like all statements [in which the referent cannot exist], such as "Here goes the son of a barren woman". And so, once again, the oneness [of all things] is not proven.'

Compare also the following from Rāmakaṇṭha's *Paramokṣa-nirāsakārikāvṛtti* (*Paramokṣanirāsakārikā* of Sadyojyotiḥ with the commentary of Rāmakaṇṭha, printed in the *Aṣṭaprakaraṇa*, ed. Vrajavallabha Dvivedī. Yogatantragranthamālā Vol. 12. Varanasi: Sampurnananda Sanskrit University, 1988, p. 301-2): *yady evaṃ pramāṇatvād atra śrutivākyānām api satyatve brahmaiva satyam ity advaitavirodhaḥ, pramāṇaprameyādi-sattānibandhanatvād advaitasya. athaitāny api śrutivākyāny asatyāny eveṣyante, yady evaṃ apramāṇatvād ittham eṣām brahmasatyatvasiddhau bhedāsatyatve ca pramāṇāntaram vaktavyam. na hy asatyaṃ pramāṇaṃ vandhyāsuta-jñānam iva bhavati yataḥ. pramāṇāntare cākṣepapratisamādhāne pūrvokte evety anavasthiter na satyādvaitasiddhiḥ. paramārthato bhedo'styeveti katham ittham? advaitasvabhāvāny eva tānīti kasya kva pramāṇāni. dvaitanibandhanatvāt pramāṇaprameya-vyavasthiteḥ. Satyam etat. paramārthato 'yam avidyārūpa eva pramāṇādivyavahāra iti cet. nanu sa evāyaṃ vicāryate. pramāṇānām asatyatvād eṣo 'pi niścayo bhavato 'pramā. etac ca yad avagataṃ tad asatyam eva, dvicandravad iti. brahmaṇo 'py asatyatvāt sarvabhāvo vedārthaḥ sādhu nirūpitaḥ prajñāśālibhiḥ. nanv avidyārūpāṇy api śrutivākyāni vidyopāyabhūtāny eveti idaṃmugdhaśrotriyapratārakam ucyate...*

14. Nārāyaṇakaṇṭha ad loc. (pp. 68-9) expands upon this:

... vicitraphaladāyināṃ pratiniyatajantukṛtatvena bhogaprati-niyama-kāriṇāṃ karmaṇāṃ evābhāvād bhogasāmyaprasaṅgo durnirvāraḥ. ātmanānātve hi kaścit duḥkhitaḥ, kaścit sukhita iti bhogavaicitryam upapannam, nānyathā. yata eva saṃsāritāyāḥ prabhavas tatraiva niraṃśe paramātmani yadi layo mokṣas tat punar api tata eva prādurbhāvaḥ, punaś ca mokṣa iti seyaṃ gatānugatikā, na tu mokṣaḥ. tathāha tatrabhavān avadhūtācāryaḥ:

tvanmateśvaravijñānaniṣpannā api muktayaḥ
*bhajante nāvisaṃvādam āmbhasā iva kṛṣṭayaḥ.**

*This verse might be interpreted as follows:

'And the states of liberation achieved from complete knowledge of the God of your system are absolutely at variance [with liberation as we conceive it]; they are [as evanescent] as lines [traced on the surface] of water.'

I suggest an interpretation because I have found the verse confusing and I suspect that others have too: Hulin's loose translation does not satisfy me, and there are a number of variants both when the verse is quoted elsewhere (e.g. in Trilocanaśiva's *Siddhāntasamuccaya*, IFP MS T. 284, p. 143, and IFP MS T. 206, p. 75) and in the Devakoṭṭai edition of this same work (*Mṛgendravṛttidīpikā* of Aghoraśivācārya, ed. Nā. Kṛṣṇaśāstrin and K.M. Subrahmaṇyaśāstrin. Śivāgama-siddhāntaparipālanasaṅgha Publication No. 12. Devakoṭṭai: Śivāgama-siddhāntaparipālanasaṅgha, 1928, p. 80), in which the last line reads *bhajante nāpi saṃvādam ambhasā iva vṛṣṭayaḥ* and the first *pāda* reads *tanmate paravijñāna-*. Hulin's translation of the verse (*Mṛgendrāgama: sections de la doctrine et du yoga, avec la vṛtti de BhaṭṭaNārāyaṇakaṇṭha et la dīpikā d'Aghoraśivācārya. Traduction, introduction et notes.*, trans. Michel Hulin, Publications de l'IFI No. 63. Pondicherry: IFP, 1980, p. 73) reads: 'Dans votre système, ces déliverances, mêmes produites par la connaissance de la réalité suprême, restent aussi vaines que des sillons tracés dans l'eau.'

15. For further details see Goodall, *op. cit.*, p. xli, footnote 94. For a description of the codex see Goodall, *ibid.*, pp. lxxxix-xci.
16. Although I translate here 'bound soul' I am conscious that the word *paśu* may here, as elsewhere in this text (eg. in 1:17f), be used as a neutral term for the soul.
17. In the *śataratnollekhinī*, (*Śataratnasaṅgraha* of Umāpatiśivācārya with an anonymous commentary (*-ullekhinī*), ed. Pancanan Sastri, Arthur Avalon's Tantrik Texts XXII. Calcutta, 1943, pp. 32-6) when commenting on this verse *Śataratnasaṅgraha*~18), the commentator locates a further discussion of all but the first and last of these epithets in the subsequent verses of this chapter. Thus the epithet *anaśvaraḥ* the commentator finds expanded upon in *Parākhya* 1:29ff; *vyāpī* he finds expanded upon in 1:37ff; *vibhinnaḥ* in 1:43ff; *samalaḥ* in 1:58c ff; *ajaḍaḥ* in1:68c~ff; *svakarmaphalabhuk* in 1:77c~ff; *kartā* in 1:84c ff; *kiñcijjñaḥ* in 1:91c~ff. Though the first epithet, *dehānyaḥ*, is not explicitly related to any following verses in the chapter, the author of the *Śataratnollekhinī* takes it to be directed against the Cārvākas (*anena cārvākasya nirāsaḥ* (p. 32)), and so it is clear that he saw it expanded upon in 1:18ff.

    Thus we see that this verse contains the program for the remainder of the chapter: each epithet, with the exception of *kiñcijjñaḥ* and *seśvaraḥ*, is challenged in turn by Pratoda in the order given in the verse and is then shown by Prakāśa to be just:--*dehānyaḥ* is questioned in 1:17 and 1:21; *anaśvaraḥ* in 1:28; *vyāpī* in 1:36; *vibhinnaḥ* in 1:40 and 1:42; *samalaḥ* in 1:51; *ajaḍaḥ* 1:61; *svakarmaphalabhuk* (perhaps) in 1:81; *kartā* in 1:85. The last epithet, *seśvaraḥ*, is not explicitly challenged by Pratoda; but it is echoed in the last word of the chapter (*seśaḥ* in 1:95d), and it is probable that Prakāśa is expanding on it in 1:94, hence the translation 'subject to the Lord'. This interpretation finds further support in *Parākhya* 2:122cd, where the term is so used of officiants of the universe: *śivatulyabalāḥ sarve kiṃ tu te seśvarāṇavaḥ*.
18. Drawn from my forthcoming edition and translation of the *Parākhyatantra*, announced in my forthcoming article 'The Saiddhāntika Parākhyatantra, its account of language, and the interpolation of the eighth chapter of the published Pauṣkarāgama'. Most conventions in the apparatus are, I hope, self-explanatory. The abbreviations therein refer to the following texts: *ŚaRaU* = *Śataratnollekhinī* (*op. cit.*); *SaJñāVṛ* = *Sarvajñānottaravṛtti* (*op. cit.*); *ŚiJñāBoVṛ* = *Śivajñānabodhavṛtti* of JñānaPrakāśa (ed. M. Muttuk-

kumāracuvāmi Civācāriya. Published and given a preface by Nallūr Ta.Kailācapiḷḷai. 1920 [Kaliyuga 5021]); *ŚaiPaBhā* = *Śaivaparibhāṣā* of Śivāgrayogīndrajñānaśivācārya (ed. H. R. Rangaswamy Iyengar and R. Ramasastri. Oriental Research Institute Series No. 90, Mysore: Oriental Research Institute, 1950).

19. 42cd occurs also in verse 12 of the *Brahmabindūpaniṣat*.
20. Pratoda is arguing that vidyā and avidyā do not have the same ontological status and so cannot be counted on the same level. 'Real existence' is *trikālābādhyatvam*, which cannot be said of avidyā.
21. If this sense were intended, it would have been normal to reverse the order of *niraṃśatvāt* and *amūrtitaḥ*.
22. Emendation to *so'smin* (in which *saḥ* would refer back to pāśa) is possible.
23. This use of *asmin*, where, if I have interpreted the text correctly, we would expect *iha* or *atra*, is a stylistic peculiarity of the *Parākhya*, for it appears similarly used in 2:10b, 2:19c, 2:28c, 2:44c, 2:61c, 2:66a, 2:80c, 3:5c, 3:6a, and, perhaps, in 15:33d.
24. This line of attack persists in the post-scriptural exegetical literature of the Śaiva Siddhānta, for see, for example, Nārāyaṇakaṇṭha's *Mṛgendravṛtti* ad *MṛgendraVidyāpāda* 2:14 (*op. cit.*, p. 69): *... tataś ca mokṣābhāvāt tadupāyānām 'ātmā vā are jñātavyaḥ śrotavyo mantavyaḥ' ityādīnām ānarthakyam.*
25. Rāmakaṇṭha reads into *Kiraṇa* 2:11 an attack on Vedānta, but it is far from clear that this is intended, for the verse in question is no more than an enquiry about the nature of *mala*:

    tvayānādir malaḥ prokto māyeyo 'syātmano 'pi vā
    guṇas tadvyatirikto vā malo brūhi kimātmakaḥ.

    Occasionally other tantras contain passing mentions of the Vedānta, but they either do not reveal what they understand by the term (e.g. *Niśvāsamūlasūtra* National Archives of Kathmandu MS1-227, NGMPP Reel No. A 41/14, f. 19r3: *vedāntaṃ viditan deva* [em.; devaṃ MS] *sāṃkhyaṃ vai pañcaviṃśakam/ na ca tṛptiṃ gamiṣyāmo hy ṛte śaivād anugrahāt*) or reveal that they understand something quite different from Vivartavāda. An instance of the latter case, pointed out to me by Somdev Vasudeva, is to be found in *Mālinīvijayottaratantra* 16:24, where, at the end of an account of *dhāraṇās* on a sequence of *tattvas* culminating in *puruṣatattva*, the text declares:

    etad vedāntavijñānaṃ samāsād upavarṇitam
    kapilasya purā proktam etad vistaraśo mayā.
    (I quote from the edition in progress of Somdev Vasudeva.)

26. *Mataṅgapārameśvarāgama* with the commentary (*-vṛtti)* of Bhaṭṭa Rāmakaṇṭha. ed. N. R. Bhatt. Publications de l'Institut Français de Pondichéry Nos. 56 and 65. Pondicherry: Institut Français de Pondichéry, 1977 and 1982.
27. Hélène Brunner-Lachaux's *Somaśambhupaddhati, Troisième Partie: Rituels occasionels dans la tradition Śivaïte de l'Inde du Sud selon Somaśambhu: II: dīkṣā, abhiṣeka, vratoddhāra, antyeṣṭi, śrāddha,* Publications de l'Institut Français de Pondichéry No. 25.III. Pondicherry: Institut Français d'Indologie, 1977, p. 553.
28. *tad eva*] Kṣemarāja's varia lectio; *tam eva* Kṣemarāja.
29. From National Archives of Kathmandu MS 1-1692, NGMPP Reel No. A 43/12, f.?? [=N], collated against IFP Transcript No. 334, p. 96 [=T. 334].
30. In the late South Indian *Pauṣkara*, however, a different solution to the problem is found. There it is *puruṣatattva* controlled by *pradhāna* into which the Vedāntins are placed, and it is there made quite specific that the Vedāntins are Pariṇāmavadins:

    pradhānākrāntapuṃsiddhā vedāntajñāḥ prakīrtitāḥ
    puruṣaḥ sarva ity evam manyante pariṇāminaḥ

    (*Pauṣkarāgama*, ed. Pandit K. Ramachandra Sarma. The Adyar Library Pamphlet Series No. 50 [reprinted from the *Adyar Library Bulletin*, Vol. 58, 1994]. Madras: Adyar Library and Research Centre, 1995, p. 56, 6:75).Publications de l'Institut Français de Pondichéry No. 25.III. Pondicherry: Institut Français d'Indologie, 1977, p. 553.
31. Quoted from the edition and translation of a fragment of this work given by Goodall, *op. cit.*, pp. xxi-xxv. When I prepared that edition and translation I stated that I had brought to light all that survived of the text. I have since discovered a further twelve verses quoted, together with the eleven already published, in Trilocanaśiva's *Siddhāntasamuccaya* (IFP MS T. 284, IFP MS T. 206, and Madras, GOML MS R. 14394).
32. Pierre-Sylvain Filliozat (*Le Tantra de Svayaṃbhū: vidyāpāda avec le commentaire de Sadyojyoti* Geneva: Librairie Droz, 1991, p. 7, footnote 1) suggests that Sadyojyotiḥ may be thinking of Vedāntins when he speaks, ad *Svayaṃbhuvasūtrasaṅgraha* 1:2, of those who regard *jñāna* to be of supreme importance in attaining liberation; but in the absence of other evidence this seems an unlikely assumption because the view was well-representedwithin the Śaiva Siddhānta too, for see *Mataṅgakriyāpāda* 1:1-2, according to which (*pace* Rāmakaṇṭha) the *kriyāpāda* was intended to teach a *sukhopāya* for those without the power to master *vidyā*.

33. This has been drawn attention to by Sanderson in his broad-ranging article 'Purity and Power among the Brahmins of Kashmir' in *The Category of the Person*, ed. Michael Carrithers, Steven Collins, and Steven Lukes, pp. 191-216, Cambridge: Cambridge University Press, 1985, p. 210, note 41.
34. The *Mokṣakārikā* of Sadyojyotiḥ with the commentary of Rāmakaṇṭha is printed in the *Aṣṭaprakaraṇa*, ed. Vrajavallabha Dvivedī. Yogatantragranthamālā Vol. 12. Varanasi: Sampurnananda Sanskrit University, 1988.
35. For the lateness of both see Goodall, *op. cit.*, p. lxxiv. The relative lateness of the *Mṛgendra* is adverted to also by Brunner on p. 274 of her 'The Four Pādas of Śaivāgamas' in *The Journal of Oriental Research, Madras. Dr. S. S. Janaki Felicitation Volume* Vols. 56-72. 1986-92, pp. 260-78. Madras: Kuppuswami Sastri Research Institute, 1992.

26

A CRITIQUE OF MĀYĀ-AVIDYĀ IN NON-VEDĀNTIC SCHOOLS OF INDIAN PHILOSOPHY

Surendra Mohan Mishra

Introduction

The words of Socrates, "I know that I do not know" were but an expression of an inner urge which inspired him in the direction of the ultimate truth considering all the knowledge known so far as imperfect and provisional. The seer of the *Kenopaniṣad* gives expression to the same urge: "One who believes he knows, in fact knows not; but one who knows not, verily knows" - *avijñātaṁ vijānatāṁ vijñātaṁ avijānatām*. Not knowing truly or knowing realtively or one-sidedly is a kind of knowing which is bound to fall away with the emergence of the ultimate and unimpeachable knowledge. Not knowing or knowing falsely is generally called avidyāòor māyāòsince the days of the Vedas and the terms have acquired various semantical, ontological and epistemological significance in course of time. In all the important schools of Indian Philosophy the concept māyā-avidyāòplays an important role and has been treated by the scholars with varying schemes of reality and theory of knowledge.

Keeping the positions of various schools of thought in mind it is an impossible task to find an adequate translation of this terms in English Language. The English equivalents offered by scholars to this term from time to time suffer from one difficulty or the other. A few English equivalents of the term may be noted in this context. Rahul Sankrutyayan suggested three alternative terms: ignorance, illusion and delusion. But in most cases he has preferred to use the word ignorance.[1] Erich Frauwallner offered two renderings 'ignorance' and 'nescience' as possible equivalents of avidyā.[2] R. Robinson and A.K. Warder have preferred the term ignorance' as equivalent of 'avidyā'.[3] Out of these alternatives the word 'nescience' is fraught with a metaphysical sense and hence it can hardly be a correct rendering of avidyā. The dictionary meaning of 'nescience' is 'ignorance' or 'absence of knowledge' or 'lack of knowledge'. Yet another meaing of the word is 'agnosticism' (D.D. Runes : *Dictionary of Philosophy*).[4] In the context of agnosticism, the term signifies the 'limits of religious thought' and implies an undogmatic dubiety or ignorance about the existence of God. But this kind of implication cannot be applied in case of 'avidyā' in the Indian *Śāstraic* context.

The term 'avidyā'òalso cannot simply be rendered as 'ignorance' in the sense of lack of or absence of knowledge. The Sanskrit term 'avidyā', though formed with a negative particle does not always express more negation or absence. What Patañjali, in his *Mahābhāṣya*, says about '*a-brāhmaṇa*' may be applicable to 'avidyā'. Patañjali explains that the word '*a-brāhmaṇa*' is applied to someone who is likely to be mistaken as a *brāhmaṇa*.[5] In the same way, it can be said that the term 'avidyā' refers to that which can be mistaken as *vidyā*. If '*vidyā*' implies knowledge of reality or ultimate knowledge, or simply, knowledge, then avidyāòwill refer to that which likely to be mistaken as such. The '*nañ*' particle is endowed with six different meanings according to the Sanskrit grammarians, *viz.* similarity, absence, otherness (difference), diminution, impropriety (or reproach), and opposition (or contrariety). According to Vasubandhu the compound word 'avidyā' is to be analysed in the manner of '*adharma*'.[6] Thus it would mean that which is opposed or contrary to '*vidyā*'. Śaṅkara's statement that the two are opposed to each other like darkness and light (*tamaḥprakāśavad viruddhasvabhāvayoḥ*) also refers to 'avidyā' in the above sense. Looking at the matter with a broad perspective, it will appear that perhaps all the above six meanings and even more may have gone into making the term 'avidyā' apply to numerous semantic and philosophical contexts and thus no single rendering of the term can do justice to the concept. In such a case, only context-specific conceptual translation may be preferred to any vogue translation of the term.

The various connotations thus acquired by the term 'avidyā' in philosophical discourses of various schools of Indian thought are significant in the light of distinct metaphysical and epistemological doctrines. We may now proceed to a treatment of the prominent non-Vedāntic schools in Indian Philosophy in order to focus on their respective interpretation of the notion of 'avidyā'.

1. Avidyā in Budddhism

In the Pali canons, the *avijjā*òis one among the the Four Noble Truths (*aria-sacca*). Thus says Sāriputta: "Not to know suffering (*dukkha*), not to know the origin of suffering (*dukkha-samudāya*), not to know the extinction of suffering (*dukkhanirodha*), and not to know the path to the extinction of suffering (*dukkhanirodha-magga* or *dukkhanirodhagāmini paṭipadā*): this, O friend, is called *avijjā*."[6] '*Avijjā*' thus refers to non-apprehension of the Four Noble Truths and wrongly apprehending the transitory as permanent and the painful as pleasurable and vice-versa. This is error or dogmatic avidyāòas the Buddhists see it. Avidyāòis also that cause which is responsible for *saṁsāra* that is the cycle of repeated births and deaths. Dhammasaṅgaṇi treats the words *avijjā*, *moha*, *aññāna*, *adassana* etc., as synonyms. The obsession of people with the idea of a permanent soul or *satkāyadṛṣṭi* - substance-view causes attachment, desire and anxiety to be and to have, thus *satkāyadṛṣṭi* is avidyā. Avidyā is said to be beginningless.[7]

Avijjā appears at the top of the chain of Dependent Origination, thus in early Buddhism it became an epistemological principle, conditioning all knowledge. The interpretation of the causal chain does not differ essentially in the Vaibhāṣika and the Sautrāntika schools from what it was earlier. The whole of the individual existence is represented as a wheel is twelve parts and the whole series is conditioned by avidyāòremaining as the pivot in the centre. According to *Abhidarmakoṣa*, avidyā is a positive entity, which is the reverse of vidyā, as *amitra* (enemy) or *anṛta* (falsehood) is of *mitra* (friend) or *ṛta* (truth). It is neither absence of knowledge nor wrong intuition (*ku-prajñā*) which is a *dṛṣṭi*, an outlook, as it is said to associate with *dṛṣṭi*, religious or philosophical outlook) and corrupt the *prajñā*ò(wisdom).[8]

For the Mādhyamika Buddhist, avidyā has a very wide scope. The whole domain of concepts and conceptualising is avidyā. *Buddhi* or reason as a faculty of conceptualising is avidyāòas it grasps the non-entity. All *dṛṣṭi* or viewing is avidyāòas it is *kalpanā*, attributing or imposing features which are not existent in reality.[9] Nāgārjuna did not have to arrive at his conclusions through an analysis of empirical experiences. He saw the inadequacy of reason and concluded that all phenomenal things and notions are unreal. The Mādhyamika view is that even avidyāòis unreal, it is māyā. Nāgārjuna holds: "If the apprehension of the impermanent as permanent is erroneous, there is in fact no error at all. As there is no permanence (*śūnya*), so also there is no impermanence. It is immaterial whether we call it permanent or impermanenet. On the other hand, if the apprehension of the impermanent as permanent is erroneous, there is no reason why the apprehension of *śūnya* as impermannet too should not be erroneous. *Śūnya* is neither permanent nor impermanent."[10]

Candrakīrti argues that if there is no perversion (*viparyāsa*), there will not be avidyāòalso in the absence of the cause.[11] If avidyāòwere real its concomitant *kleśas* also would be real and there would be no cessation of *saṁsāra*. As for the contention that avidyā exercises a real influence and were it unreal it could not do so - this argument is wrong, for even a false apparition of a real young lady may excite the passion of a man.[12] Actually, the Mādhyamika would say that causation is a mark of the unreal. With the Mādhyamikas the concept of avidyāòis more dynamic, avidyāòor the differentiating and conceptualising principle is held responsible for the world appearance, the *saṁvṛtisatya*. From the ultimate or supra-empirical point of view avidyā is non-existent.

The Vijñānavāda regards avidyāòas a psychical disposition which entails *kleśas*. This avidyāòdefiles the mind or consciousness (*citta*). It is responsible for the cycle of birth and death as well as for the world-appearance. Beginningless *vāsanā*ò(predisposition) is said to afflict the *citta* and lead to the imagination of the cognised and the cogniser and the like. Stcherbatsky very aptly points out that the conception of *vāsanā*òis as of a cosmic force, a transcendental illusion, though it means impression of previous knowledge.[13] Thus *adbhūta-parikalpa* becomes in the Vijñānavāda a metaphysical principle and is held responsible for the world of external appearance. It is thus a cognate of the concept of avidyāòin Śaṅkara Vedānta.

The concept of avidyāògoes a step ahead in Mahāyāna Buddhism. Earlier avidyāòsignified non-apprehension or misapprehension of the ultimate truth and a pre-natal disposition causing *saṁsāra*. But in Mahāyāna Buddhism, avidyāòbecomes a metaphysical principle in as much as it is deemed responsible for the external world appearance. The Buddhists do not seem to discuss whether the ultimate reality *vijñāna* is cosmic or individual. Looking to the strictly Buddhist tradition it cannot be interpretted as cosmic. But it has undoubtedly become a metaphysical principle hypostatised to account for the phenomenal world appearance.

II. Avidyā in Jainism

The Jainas lay emphasis on *samyag-darśana* (right faith or outlook), *samyag-jñāna* (right knowledge) and *samyak-cāritra* (right conduct) - the three regarded as the path leading to *mokṣa* or liberation.[14] The Jainas do not agree with the other schools that perverted or wrong knowledge (*mithyā-jñāna*) alone is the cause of bondage and that *samyag-jñāna* alone leads to emancipation.[15] All the schools admit that soul remains embodied for some time after the attainment of perfect knowledge, because of the *karma* which is still operative (*prārabdha*). Vidyānanda cogently asks how the enjoyment of the residual *karma* is possible. Does it happen in due course of time, or is the process hastened? If it takes place in the natural course, all the *karma* would not be exhausted even after millions of *kalpas*.[16] One who has acquired perfect knowledge would not accept rebirth for the enjoyment of the residual *karma* and therefore it follows that such a one has to exhaust the *karma* in this very life. This means that the person has capacity for a special effort to exhaust the *karma* before the time is ripe. This effort is a type of *cāritra*. The embodiment of the soul after the attainment of right knowledge implies that there is some defect which is responsible for the mundane existence after the attainment of knowledge. The Jainas believe that this defect is the non-stoppage of activity technically called *yoga* and this can be removed by *samyak-cāritra* (right conduct). Moreover, besides *mithyātva*, there are *avirati*, *pramāda*, *kaṣāya* and *yoga* in the condition of *saṁsāra* and these can be set aside by *samyak-cāritra* alone. Vidyānanda further argues that if *mithyā-jñāna* alone were the cause of bondage there would be no enlightened person to reveal the truth.[17] He thus comes to the conclusion that right faith, right knowledge and right conduct are indispensable as antidotes to wrong faith, wrong knowledge and wrong conduct which are responsible for worldy existence.

The Jainas are realists as far as their views on the objective reality of the world are concerned. The things of the world are permanent substantially, though their modes are ever-changing. It is only the attitude towards the world and its constituents that is determined by the right or wrong outlook (*darśana*) of the soul; and no knowledge however useful and valid in empirical dealings can be right unless it is backed by *samyag-darśana* or right knowledge and outlook. The soul acquires *kārmic* matter on account of its *mithyā-darśana* and wrongly identifies with it. We may conclude tht *mithyātva*, *mithyā-darśana* or *darśana-moha* in Jainism are cognates of avidyāòin the philosophic sense of the term. *Mithyātva* is both the cause and the effect of the *darśana-mohanīya-karma*; and misapprehension of the ultimate truth. Māyā, in Jainism, is one of the *kaṣāyas* (passions) and signifies deceit or perverted intelligence.

III Avidyāòin Sāṁkhya-yoga

The Sāṁkhya and the Yoga conceptions of avidyā are in essence the same. However, Vijñānabhikṣu draws our attention to a difference between them. For the Sāṁkhya, non-discrimination (*aviveka*) between *puruṣa* and buddhi is avidyā, whereas the Yoga system believes that puruṣa not only fails to distinguish between itself and buddhi but positively takes the transformations of the buddhi as its own. Thus avidyāòin the Yoga system is not absence of knowledge of the difference, but positively false knowledge cognising *puruṣa* to be what it is not.[18]

Avidyā, in Sāṁkhya-yoga, signifies a pre-natal disposition to error and also its effect, *viz.* positively false knowledge. Avidyāòis responsible for the apparent relation between puruṣa and buddhi. Both are real; only the relation between them is conceived by avidyāòand is thus an imagined one. Avidyāòcan thus said to be responsible for the origination of the world from beginningless time, on account of its not discriminating between prakṛti and puruṣa and even identifying them. Avidyā is beginningless, but it can be destroyed by *jñāna* or true knowledge or realisation. Avidyā gives rise to the afflictions (*kleśas*), *asmitā* etc., though this is a generation on the psychological plane. Thus avidyā in Sāṁkhya-yoga, is held as the cause and the effect of the activity of prakṛti and the puruṣa's reaction to it. Avidyā is an oblique disposition or affliction (*kleśa*) leading to wrong knowledge. Avidyā is recognised as playing a part in the origination of the world in relation to different puruṣas.

IV. Avidyā in Nyāya-Vaiśesika

The Vaiśeṣika system provides a more mundane interpretation of the term 'avidyā'. Praśastapāda, in his systematic presentation of the Vaiśeṣika system in his *Padārthadharma-saṅgraha*, notes that there are two types of Buddhi or cognitive states: vidyā, true cognition and avidyā, the false cognition. Avidyāòis classified into four types: doubt, error, uncertainty and dream. Under error, Praśastapāda includes the typical false beliefs such as, believing in what is impermanent as permanent, what is non-self as self, and what is not good as good.[19] Thus, avidyāòin the Vaiśeṣika, stands for a more general concept. The important point to note is that it definitely asserted to be a cognitive state being subsumed under buddhi. It includes not only wrong convictions, errors and delusions, but also doubtful attitudes, uncertainties and dream states. And it is also asserted that such avidyāòwith regard to a particular thing is eliminated (destroyed) by the corresponding *vidyā* 'knowledge' of that thing.

The *Nyāya-sūtra* holds that there is emancipation when there is cessation of each member of the series pain, birth, activity, defect and wrong knowledge the cessation of that which follows bringing about the cessation of that which precedes it.[20] The *doṣas* are classified as *rāga* (attachment), *dveṣa* (hatred) and *moha* (delusion). Of these, *moha* is the cause of other two. *Moha* is characterised by wrong knowledge.[21] This *mithyā-jñāna* leads to *rāga* and *dveṣa*, these inspire one to activity from which result *dharma* and *adharma*. These bring about birth and miseries of the worldly existence. Therefore, with the cessation of *mithyā-jñāna*, all these will cease and there will be *apavarga* (liberation).

Vātsyāyana gives an exposition of *mithyā-jñāna* in his commentary on *Nyāya-sūtra* (1.1.2) and as well as in his introductory remarks (4.2.1). It is wrongly taking non-self as self: it is delusion, egoism which consists in looking upon the non-self body etc. as identical with the self.[22] Further on he says that *mithyā-jñāna* is synonymous with *moha* or delusion and does not mean mere negation of true knowledge. It is held as positively wrong knowledge. Thus, in the Nyāya-Vaiśeṣika, *mithyā-jñāna* is regarded as an equivalent of *moha* and is a cognate of avidyā.

V. Avidyā in Kashmir Śaivism

Keeping in view the metaphysical and logical postulation of avidyāȯby Śaṅkara in order to account for the world and its experiences and keeping in mind the attempts undertaken by post-Śaṅkara Advaitins to defend the concept of māyā-avidyāȯin the face of the seven-fold objection raised by Rāmānuja and his followers, it will be highly beneficial to consider the contribution of the non-dualistc Śaivite thinkers of Kashmir whose philosophy regarding māyā-avidyā may be said to be above reproach or at least free from such possible objection.

According to the Pratyabhijñā school, the ultimate Reality is Paramaśiva or Parama-saṁvit (Highest Consciousness) or Caitanya (intelligence) which is both immanent and transcedent as it pervades the universe and is also beyond all manifestations (*viśvottīrṇa* as well as *viśvamaya*). The world is but a manifestation of the immanent aspect of Śiva, which is known as Śakti and which is neither different nor independent of Śiva. This Śakti has again an infinite number of modes or aspects, the most fundamental ones are: *cit. ānanda*, *icchā*, *jñāna*, and *kriyā*. In the highest stage of Paramaśiva, there are two indistinguishable factors, viz. *prakāśa* (Self-luminosity) and *vimarśa* (Self-consciousness). When Śakti expands or opens herself out, the universe is revealed, and when she gathers herself or closes herself in, the universe disapears.

It is due to *ajñāna* that the soul does not recognise its identity with the Supreme Lord. It is the innate ignorance that is called *āṇava-mala*, which is the cause of *māyiya-mala*. The latter in its turn leads to *kārma-mala. Āṇava-mala* is one of the manifestations brought about by the universal will (*svātantrya-śakti*). It conceals the real nature of the self. This consciousness of supposed imperfection and limitation is responsible for the rise of innumerable individual souls. *Āṇava-mala* is beginningless though destructible. The *Āṇava-mala* may be called as a cognate of avidyā in Śāṅkara Vedānta - a reflex of avidyā which is associated with Brahman as a limiting or individualising principle with this difference that in the latter it is ultimately unreal and in Śaivism it can be eradicated through the true recognition of one's Supreme sovereignity (Śivatva) obtained through initiation by a Guru and grace of the Lord. *Kārma-mala* is the sum-total of the unlimited desires of the limited selves because the satisfaction of these is the only purpose of creation. All that the soul is associated with because of both the *kārma-mala* and the *karma-saṁskāra* is called *māyiya-mala.*[23]

Utpala defines māyā as the *mohinī-śakti*, (delusive power) of the Lord by which His self though always shining as light (prakāśa, becomes partly un-manifest and the complete manifestation of it is barred in consequence. Māyā covers the self-luminous Cit and causes such gross reflection of Ego as "I am this gross body," etc. to arise in connection with cognisable objects such as body etc. Abhinava described māyā-śakti as that Supreme freedom of the Lord through which he makes manifest the limited soul (*paśu*) by first bringing to in upper surface the aspect of the enjoyer (*bhoktṛ*) and then through the latter the objects of enjoyment (*bhogya*). Thus māyā, in the Trika school is a highly synthesised power of Maheśvara and hence the Śaivite would not accept māyā as indefinable or *anirvacaniya*. The system does not subscribe to any of the well-known *khyāti*s or theories of error, it propounds *Apūrṇa-khyāti*, according to which error consists in completeness in so far as that which ought to be apprehended in completeness to the last degree of *vimarśa* is not properly cognised.[24]

The Pratyabhijñā philosopher is prepared to accept that the entire world is an illusion, or is an appearance complete and wholesome in as much as it is a limited or imperfect manifestation of the supreme Reality. But within this world of illusion, there are again divisions of truth and illusion, e.g. *sukti-rajata* etc. Abhinava severely criticises the indefinability (*anirvacanīyatā*) of avidyā as posited by the Advaitins.[25]

In the philosophy of Śaṅkara, we have avidyā which is both a universal individualising principle as also innate nescience of the jīva. Śaivism has postulated māyā to serve as an obscuring force. It is regarded as a śakti of God. At the level of śakti, māyā is endowed with the five *kañcūkas*, *viz.*, kāla, kalā, vidyā, rāga and niyati and at the level of prakṛti, māyā operates with distinct functions. Śaṅkara and his followers with their philosophy of the *nirviśeṣa-brahmādvaita* hold avidyā as fictitious from the ultimate point of view and maintain it as a principle of obscuration and projection only for the purpose of intellectual explanation. Those who subscribe to the theory of non-origination (*ajāti-vāda*) and hold the passages explaining creation in the Upaniṣads as relative and provisional could only develop māyā as a technique (*adhyā-ropa-apavāda-nyāya*) to defend their position. The Pratyabhijñāna, on the other hand, regards the universe as a real manifestation of the supreme being through his own supreme will, and sees no contradiction in the real character of the one in opposition to plurality. Hence, the Trika school is under no necessity to call māyā a fiction. On the contrary, it's suggestion is that māyā adds to the greatness of all effulgent Lord.

In Kasḥmir Saiva schools, the result of this process of self-emanation through self-limitation is that the jīva forgets its essential oneness with everything, including the Absolute. Thus avidyā is neither the absence of knowledge (ajñāna), nor wrong knowledge (mithyājñāna), but rather a state of temporary amnesia where the soul forgets its source and unity with the Supreme.

Liberation in Kashmir Saivism, therefore is merely the remembrance of this fact and it is for this reason the school is popular as Pratyabhijñā, i.e., Recognition. The Kashmiri interpretation of the term avidyā is indeed to be valued for its unique contribution towards a better understanding or a precise definition of this much ambiguous philosophical concept. The term 'Recognition' does not point towards the 'absence of knowledge', nor does it in any way reveal 'limitation' of knowledge. In fact it denotes a state of the 'absence of the awareness of knowledge'. Once this awareness arises, there takes place in the soul a spontaneous recognition of its unity with the Absolute.

This unique concept of avidyā has been analogically illustrated through the popular example of a lady who happens to fall in love with a gallant gentleman after hearing of his strengths and talents but fails to recognize him though he is standing in front of her. Though the knowledge is there but because of the absence of awareness, she fails to recognize. The same principle operates with the soul since despite the fact of knowing the essential unity of all things, yet it is unaware of the Absolute Unity. This absence of this awareness finally results in bondage.

Thus, through the concept of Pratyabhijñā, Kashmir Saivism can be said to go a step further than Advaita in solving the very first untenability of Rāmānuja, namely *Āśrayānupappatti* whereby the latter questions the locus of avidyā; whether it is Brahman or jīva. In fact, there is no avidyā as such in the Trika, but only varying degrees of self-revelation (*vimarśa*) on the part of the Absolute, out of its self-dependence (*svātantrya*). By attributing these two qualities to Brahman, in addition to *sat* and *cit*, Kashmir Saivism relegated avidyā to a state of 'conscious self-forgetfulness'.

In fine, it may be recalled that the Advaita Vedāntin has asked the Sāṁkhya to surrender prakṛti as an insentient and different entity other than Brahman beyond which nothing exists. The Sāṁkhya has not obliged. The Kashmir Śaivite welcomed prakṛti into his scheme of reality consisting of thirty-six principles and succinctly showed how prakṛti is not different but integral aspect of the Supreme being. Then we ask the question: if Vedānta is tenable without *anirvacanīya* māyā, the answer is Advaita Vedānta as a system cannot certainly risk it, but the Pratyabhijñāna philosopher can by making it look *vacanīya* and definitively traceable.

Avidyā, to conclude, as seen from non-vedāntic viewpoints, acquires different philosophical and semantic dimensions which can be of use to both Advaitins and Viśiṣṭādvaitins alike to strengthen their respective arguments. While the latter can derive support from Sāṅkhya-Yoga and Nyāya-Vaiśeṣika, the former may benefit from Baudha schools and Kashmir Saivism. It is hoped that this bird's eye-view of the concept of avidyā as comprehended in the different schools of Indian Philosophy and which at the same time unites them all will be of certain assistance to scholars in interpreting it within their own field of specialization.

NOTES

1. Walpola Rahula, *What the Buddha Taught*, Bedford: Gordon Fresher, 1967, p. 40. Also refer Rahul Sankrutyayan, *Darśanadigdarśana*, Kitab Mahal, Allahabad, 2004 pp. 398-400.
2. Erich Frauwallner, *History of Indian Philosophy*, (Trans. from original German by V.M. Vedekar, Motilal Banarsidass, Delhi, 1973, p. 398.
3. Rcihard H. Robinson, *The Buddhist Religion - A Historical Introduction,* Dickenson Publishers, Belmont, California, 1970, p. 22.
4. Hajime Nakamura, *Indian Buddhism*, MLBD, Delhi, 1970, p. 103.
5. *adharmānarthākāryadayaśca dharmapratidvandvabhūtāh evaṁ avidyāpi vidyāyāḥ pratidvandva bhūtādharmantaraṁ iti draṣṭavyam. Abhidharmakośa* of Basubandhu, Ed. Swami Dvarikadása Sastri, Baudhhabharati, Varanasi, 1970, p. 463.
6. *Sammāditthi-suttana* (*Majjima-nikāya*), Also refer Rahul Sankrutyayan, *Majjhima-nikāya*, Mahabodhi Sabha, Sarnath, 1933.
7. *Visuddhimagga*, XVII.37. Also refer Dharmananda Kosambi (Ed.) *Visuddhimagga* of Buddhaghosacariya, Bharatiya Vidya Bhavan, Bombay, 1940.
8. *vidyāvipakṣo dharmo'nyo'vidya'mitra'nṛtādivat saṁyojanādivacanāt kuprajñacen na darśanāt. dṛṣṭestat samprayuktatvāt prajñopakleśadeśanāt. Abhidharmakosa*, III. 28-29. *op. cit.*, p. 463-464.
9. *buddhiḥ saṁvṛtir ucyate iti, sarvā hi buddhiḥ ālambananirālambanatayā vikalpasvabhā vā, vikalpāśca sarva eva avidyā-svabhāvāḥ avastugrahitvāt; yad āha vikalpaḥ svayaṁ eva ayaṁ avidyārupatāṁ gataḥ iti, Bodhicaryāvatārapañjikā, op. cit.*, p. 306.
10. *Mādhyamika-kārikā,* 23. 13-4.
11. *Mādhyamika-kārikā-vyākhyā*, pp. 461-2.
12. Ibid., p. 46.
13. Theodore Stcherbatsky, *Conception of Buddhist Nirvāna*, MLBD, New Delhi, 2003, p. 209.

14. *samyagdarśana-jñāna-cāritrāṇi mokṣamārgaḥ, Tattvārthasūtra* of Umasvati, Edited by A. Shantiraja Sastri, Govt. Oriental Library, Mysore, 1941, p. 57.
15. Manoharlal Nyaya Sastri, (Ed.) *Tattvārthaślokavārtika* of Vidyānandi, Saraswati Pustak Bhandar, Ahmedabad, 2002, p. 72
16. *bhoktuḥ phalāpabhogo hi yathākālaṁ yadīṣyate, tadā karmakṣayaḥ kvātaḥ kalpakoṭiśatairapi.* Ibid., p. 66.
17. Ibid., p. 72.
18. *Yogavārtika*, 1.3. (Refer Ramakrishna Patvardhan Shastri and Kesava Shastri, (Ed.) *Yogavārtika* of Vijñānabhikṣu, Medical Hall press, Varanasi, 1884. p. 10.)
19. Jitendra and Jetly, (Ed.) *Padārthadharmasaṅgraha,* GOS, Baroda, 1971, pp. 171-82.
20. *duḥkha-janma-pravṛtti-doṣa-mithyājñānānāṁ uttarottarāpāye tadanantarāpāyāt apavargaḥ, Nyāya-sūtra* of Vātsyayana, 1.1.2.
21. *mithyāpratipatti-lakṣaṇo moha iti, Nyāyabhāsya,* 4.1.3. See *Nyāyabhāṣya* of Vātsyāyana, Ed. by Paḍma Prasad Sastri and Hariram Sukla, Choukhmba Sanskrit Series, Varanasi, 1942, p. 186.
22. *kiṁ punaḥ tat mithyājñānam? anātmani ātmagrahaḥ ahaṁ asmiti moho'haṁkāra iti,* Ibid., 4.2.1.
23. *sarvabhuvanākāro māyiyaḥ parikalpitaḥ, Tantraloka* of Abhinavagupta, (Ed. by Madhusudana Kaul Sastri, Nirnaya Sagar Press, Bombay, 1936, Vol.1. p. 56.)
24. *tato yāvatā pūrṇena rūpeṇa prakhyātavyaṁ vimarśaparyantaṁ tāvat na prakhyāti-ityapūrṇakhyātirūpā akhyātir eva bhrāntitattvam, Īśvara-pratyabhijñā-vimarśinī,* 2.3.13. (Refer Mukundaram Shastri, (Ed.) *Īśvara-pratyabhijñā*, of Utpaladeva with *Vimarśinī* of Abhinavagupta, (Vol.II), Nirnaya Sagar Press, Bombay, 1921, p. 113.)
25. Ibid., 2.4.20.

27

MĀYĀ-AVIDYĀ IN CONTEMPORARY INDIAN PHILOSOPHY

Bijayananda Kar

The concept of māyā has, no doubt, occupied the focal point of discussion in the philosophy of Advaita. The popular Advaitic saying *brahma satyaṁ jaganmithyā* is quite often referred to in emphasising māyā or *mithyā* of the world as the background of the acceptance of Brahman as the only reality. Beginning from Śaṅkara, almost all the post-Śaṅkarites in the classical phase have advocated the significance of the concept of māyā in their philosophical discussion. The post-Śaṅkarites like Maṇḍana, Sureśvara, Vācaspati, Padmapāda, Prakāśātman, Amalānanda, Vimuktātman, and others have in their own manner, attempted to justify the concept of māyā within the Advaitic framework. The criticisms have been advanced by the Dvaitins, Dvaitā-dvaitins, Viśiṣṭādvaitins, Śuddhādvaitins, Acintyabhedābheda-vādins, and Viśuddhādvaitavādins. Out of different criticisms, the seven-fold arguments (*Saptavidhānupapatti*) framed by Rāmānuja are treated as the most important ones and the Advaitins tried to meet these arguments, at times creating the impression of moving beyond the original Śaṅkarite stand. In the modern times it is interesting to note that the classical debate on the issue of māyā is being carried on by the Sanskrit scholars with Advaita and non-Advaita background as well, particularly in the South India vindicating the classical debate on māyā as quite alive.

Contemporary Indian philosophers, especially with English background, have also found interest in the Advaita concept of Māyā. While discussing the classical philosophy in general and the philosophy of Advaita in particular, they have passed their own comments and views on māyā, sometimes criticizing māyā within the Advaitic framework and thereby making attempts to reconstruct Advaita going beyond Śaṅkara. In this regard, special mention should be made of Vivekananda and Aurobindo. Both of them have full sympathy for the Advaitic general framework and have not joined hands with the classical non-Advaita Vedāntins for a Dvaita-Viśiṣṭādvaita point of view. In Advaita, Brahman is, for them, neither Nārāyaṇa nor Kṛṣṇa. But inspite of their Advaitic stand, they continue to be non-Śaṅkarites so far as the concept of māyā is concerned. According to them, māyā as something unreal and illusory, cannot be applied to *jagat* or world of experience. They are not at all prepared to treat *saṁsārānubhūti* or phenomenal experience as mere appearance and unreal. Śaṅkara Advaita is characterised by them as advocating illusionism and the talk about ultimate reality as world-transcendence is not well taken up because of its alleged tone of mystical transcendentalism, fully away from the concrete level of practical life. It is, on account of māyā that Advaita is given the rendering of visionary idealism-spiritualism much driven away from the realm of actuality. In this context, Vivekananda's call for Neo-Vedānta or practical Vedānta carries some form of popular appeal. Because māyā is supposed to have supported a sense of withdrawal and dejection from all sorts of mundane activities, there is the advocacy for a different call by means of which practical living at the concrete plane can be well regulated by some prescribed form of moral and spiritual training. In short, the movement of neo-Vedānta is directed towards practical orientation of Advaita.

From, a different perspective altogether, Aurobindo also moves to restore, what he calls, real Advaita from the māyāvāda of Śaṅkara, Aurobindo's Advaita is, of course, non-dualistic, but it is clearly set without any form of māyā-vāda: It is not confined to such non-dualism based on abstract theorisation of subtle intellectual speculation, but is rather regarded to be inclusive of different aspirations of human awareness - at the cognitive, conative and emotive front and more weightage has been given on realisation of Brahman in terms of what Aurobindo calls as supra-mental consciousness based on bhakti or devotion. It is because of due recognition of different aspects of human personality, its needs and aspirations, Aurobindo terms his Advaita as all comprehensive i.e., integral Advaitism of *Pūrṇa-advaita* and there is no scope for māyā with its sense of world illusion.

In addition, there are a few modern Indian thinkers, who are well-versed both in the classical Indian tradition as well as in the Western philosophy, like Radhakrishnan, and they reinterpret Śaṅkara Advaita within the classical framework and not going beyond it. In their view, māyā is not to be criticised or to be set aside but needs reinterpretation to accommodate the importance of the phenomenal worldly existence. Radhakrishnan, in his characteristic persuasive style, recommends for the recognition of two levels of reality within the Advaita fold, namely, *pāramārthika* and *vyāvahārika*. Though the world-experience is not as real as the Advaita Brahman (i.e., from *pāramārthika* point of view), it is not unreal or mere illusion in the sense of *tuccha* or absolute non-existence. The world or phenomena is relatively real and as long as there is no *Brahmānubhūti*, there is no justifiable ground, Radhakrishnan thinks, to develop a sense of withdrawal and negative outlook. If in some lines of Śaṅkara Advaita, there is the apparent sense of uncompromising denial of worldly existence, then Radhakrishnan does not hesitate for a slight change by means of emphasising *sattā* of the world as per the *vyāvahārika-dṛṣṭi*. And if this sort of reconciliating stand is duly noted, then Radhakrishnan frankly concedes to what G.C. Nayak has here drawn our attention in this seminar that the theory of māyā serves "as a cloak to cover the inner rifts" of Śaṅkara's system.

Possibly following Radhakrishnan many others attempted to explain the inclusion of Māyāvāda in Śaṅkara Advaita by referring to what is indicated also in the Advaita tradition (especially in the pre-Śaṅkara writings of Gauḍapāda) as the grades of reality. And, in this way, it is hoped that māyā, somehow, remains as an explanatory device within the Advaitic frame-work. Despite of its vindicating the absolute in-essentiality of the world-phenomena, it (māyā) never cancels the relative real existential significance of the world. In this connection attention has been drawn on the post-Śaṅkarite account of māyā as "*bhāvarūpa*" as signifying something positive and never aiming at *abhāva* or unreal non-existence.

But is this reference to the grades of reality quite convincing with the fundamental tenet of Śaṅkara Advaita? I humbly submit, it requires definite reconsideration. It is true that there are number of references about *pāramārthika, vyāvahārika* and even *prātibhāsika-sattā* in the Advaita literature. But so far as Advaita philosophical view-point is to be seriously taken into consideration, it can be well noticed that the Advaita only opts for pure irreconcilable non-dualism and that alone is the distinguishing feature of Advaita being contrasted from other formulations of Vedānta and also from other *dārśanika-dṛṣṭi* as well. If Advaita Brahman is absolutely real, and it is the only entity, then the concession of reality of phenomena as relative carries no worth or significance. Perhaps that is the reason why the non-Advaita Vedāntin are emphatic enough to assert the real nature of the world, its existential status or being. A volley of questions are raised as to what could be the genesis of such grades of existence; how are the relative grades related to the highest grade and so on. In this context, the question raised about māyā concerning its *āśraya*, *svarūpa* etc. are perhaps not insignificant. And the sweeping reply that such questions cannot be entertained seems to be somewhat dogmatic as long as some real and existential status are sanctioned for worldly phenomena to appease the popular demand. But it (the concession) is perhaps, entertained at the cost of theoretical cogency. C. D. Sharma attempts to safe-guard the *māyika-sattā* by conceding that "it is a self-contradictory notion." But what could be the *locus standi* of a self-contradictory notion? In what sense is it an account of empirical reality? If real means "absolutely real" in Advaita then *māyika* phenomenal existence has no place in it, even if it is distinguished from *tuccha*. Because from the Advaita point of view Brahman being alone real, "absolutely real" and "absolutely unreal" are only exhaustive and nothing else is admissible. Such an approach of establishing māyā for defending the Advaita point of view seems to be no less than an apologetic device and hence not sustainable.

But why not look at Śaṅkara's māyā on the background of Advaita non-duality from a different perspective? Śaṅkara, it seems, never, felt shy of providing explanation. The concept of māyā is introduced by him in the Advaita scheme not to explain anything but to explaining away everything. If māyā is there in Advaita, its proper accountability is definitely due and it cannot be set aside. I think, the word: *sattā* in the Śaṅkara Advaita philosophical plane does not connote something of existential significance, either factual or meta-factual in the trans-empirical existential sense of some sort of mystical variety. There is a saying by Śaṅkara in some context that *sattā eva bodha* and *bodha eva sattā* which seems to be quite pertinent in this context too. *Sattā* can be here regarded as comprehension in a technical sense within the Advaita framework. This seems to be quite in accord with the famous Advaitic utterance *brahmabhāvam brahmeiva bhavati*. The knowing of Brahman implies the being of Brahman. In other words the *pāramārthika-sattā* stands for the realisation of Brahman in the epistemological sense of valuational significance. There need not be any ontologising here in the supra-mundane sense of the term. It is *parama-jñāna* where there is no difference between *jñeya* and *jñātā* in the sense that there is *ekātma-bodha* or *aikya-bhāva* in the conceptual phase of axiological importance, so that a person has different attitude or valuational *dṛṣṭi* to the existential situation. The world of matter of fact or existence does not vanish as a sort of dreamy phantasmagoria. It exists in its full sense of actuality. There is no sense of appearance in the sense of unreal existence. *Adhyāsa* or māyā when it is removed, it is only for changing attitude in the valuational framework which is not of mere psychological significance but has of conspicuous practical importance from the angle of human perspective. The rope still resembles snake. The shell still appears as resembling silver. But the *dṛṣṭi* or understanding or realisation in the conceptual-ideational plane is changed. And understanding is not confined here to theoretical clarity but also implies due practical implementation which, so far as māyā in the Advaita is concerned, carries valuational importance. In this sense, phenomena versus noumena, *pāramārthika* versus *vyāvahārika*, Brahman versus māyā signify change of vision at the valuational front which has moral basis of great human importance.

Māyā is precisely a value loaded term and any attempt to look for some sort of ontological entitative status for māyā, it seems to me at least, is to miss the spirit of Śaṅkara. In *Kaṭhopaniṣad-bhāṣya*, Śaṅkara has clarified his position in response to the third boon asked for by Naciketas to Yama in that well-known anecdote contatined therein. While meeting the question raised by Naciketas, *Kaṭhopaniṣad* brings out the distinction between *śreyas* and *preyas* in the mouth of Yama. Commenting on the Upaniṣadic passage, Śaṅkara explains that *ātma-jñāna* which is nothing but *śreyas* based on *pāramārthika-dṛṣṭi* contrasted from *preyas* that is considered as valuationally insignificant and is therefore set aside. In this sense *ātma-bodha* and *śreyopalabdhi* are non-different. The appeal for *śreyas* stands for the recommendation of a morally disciplined living both at the individual and social front as well. It is directed towards the accomplishment of a balanced and composed outlook free from all sorts of craving towards sensualistic perversion and lapses. It should be noted that the valuational recommendation is here control of sense gratification (*ātma-saṁyama*) and not for eradication of sense-pleasure altogether. The course prescribed is, obviously, difficult but is never said to be impossible or unattainable.

Māyā is neither the world nor the sense perception of the world as such. It is not based either on empirical or supra-empirical perception. It is clearly value-loaded *dṛṣṭi* on the world which solely matters in this context. In what way the world we experience is to be evaluated seems to be the focal point of discussion in this context. Is the world that is experienced is to be exploited maximum to the advantage of one's personal interest or the interest of one's own group or class or society at the cost of others? Or, should it be experienced with the preset composite balanced rational outlook so that there is proper sense of utilisation of different items of experience without any sense of rational as well as moral impropriety? Brahman as *paramārtha* is nothing but *parama-ṣreyas*. It stands for value par- excellence. Brahmajñāni is, hence, treated as free from all narrow sense of egoity and is appropriately identified as *sarvabhūtāntarātmā*. This pervasive feature is only valuationally significant and never carries any existential import. Form all this, it appears evident that the concept of māyā in Śaṅkara Advaita is precisely prescriptive and not descriptive.

That is, perhaps, the reason as to why there is clear advocacy for *jīvanmukti* in Advaita while all other Vedāntins opt for *videha-mukti*. The personal theistic temper, that is, in one way or other, emphasised in different classical formulation of Vedānta to meet the religious demand of their respective popular sector, is found to have been differently tackled by Śaṅkara Advaita. It seems to be quite conscious of different dimension, both sacred and secular and that is why it keeps the door open for impersonal non-theological forms of attitude too. In this sense *nirguṇa-brahma-tattva* with the inclusion of māyā seems to be somewhat wider in its visionary scope being quite relevant to divergent needs and aspirations. It seems to have a distinct leaning towards secular form of humanitarian attitude free from dogmatic obscurantism and mythical mysticism.

28

सप्तविधानुपपत्तयः - तत्सम्बद्धाः ग्रन्थाश्च

R. Thangaswami

सर्वं जगदिदं गिरिसमुद्रादिकं दृश्यमानं प्रातिभासिकं अविद्याकार्यत्वात् मिथ्यैवेति अद्वैतात्मप्रधाने अविद्यावादे सिद्धान्तितम्। अविद्यावादोपरि अस्मिन् श्रीभाष्ये जिज्ञासाधिकरणे १.आश्रयानुपपत्तिः २.तिरोधानानुपपत्तिः ३.स्वरूपानुपपत्तिः ४.अनिर्वचनीयतानुपपत्तिः ५.प्रमाणानुपपत्तिः ६.निवर्तकानुपपत्तिः ७.निवृत्त्यनुपपत्तिरूपं अनुपपत्तिसप्तकं प्रदर्शितम्।

१. आश्रयानुपपत्तिः- अज्ञानस्य जीव आश्रयो भवितुं नार्हति। जीवे सिद्धे अज्ञानस्य सिद्धिः, अज्ञानसिद्धौ जीवसिद्धिरिति अन्योन्याश्रयापातात्। शुद्धं ब्रह्म अपि आश्रयो भवितुं नार्हति। ब्रह्मणः स्वयंप्रकाशज्ञानस्वरूपत्वेन अज्ञानविरोधित्वात् इति।

आश्रयानुपपत्तिखण्डनपराणाम् अद्वैतिनाम् अयमाशयः- निर्विशेषात् स्वयंप्रकाशात् निर्लक्षणाच्च ब्रह्मणः सविशेषस्य सलक्षणस्य जगतः कथमुत्पत्तिः? एकस्मात् अद्वैतात् ब्रह्मणः नानात्मकस्य जगतः कथमुत्पत्तिः? इत्येतेषां प्रश्नानां यथावत् समाधानं मायास्वरूपवर्णनद्वारा अद्वैताचार्यैः उपवर्णितम्। शङ्करभगवत्पादैः "कथं पुनः प्रत्यगात्मनि अविषये अध्यासो विषयतद्धर्माणां" इति जिज्ञासाधिकरणावतरणिकायां शङ्किता समाहिता च। एवं "तदधीनत्वात् अर्थवदिति" (१-४-३) सूत्रे माया अविद्या अज्ञानं अव्यक्तं अव्याकृतमित्यादिशब्दानां समानार्थकत्वं वर्णितम्। एवम् -

अव्यक्तनाम्नी परमेशशक्तिः अनाद्यविद्या त्रिगुणात्मिका परा।
कार्यानुमेया सुधियैव माया यया जगत् सर्वमिदं प्रसूयते॥

इति विवेकचूडामणौ, (११०) अविद्यायाः अविद्यात्वे इदमेव तु लक्षणम्।

यत् प्रमाणासहिष्णुत्वं अन्यथा वस्तु सा भवेत्॥ इति बृहदारण्यकवार्तिके।

सेयं भ्रान्तिर्निरालम्बा सर्वन्यायविरोधिनी।
सहते न विचारं सा तमो यद्वत् दिवाकरम्॥ इति नैष्कर्म्यसिद्धौ, (३-६६)

आच्छाद्य विक्षिपति संस्फुरदात्मरूपम्
जीवेश्वरत्वजगदाकृतिभिर्मृषैव।
अज्ञानमावरणविभ्रमशक्तियोगात्
आत्मत्वमात्रविषयाश्रयताबलेन॥ इति संक्षेपशारीरके, (१-२०)

शक्तिद्वयं हि मायायाः विक्षेपावृतिरूपकम्।
विक्षेपशक्तिःलिङ्गादि ब्रह्माण्डान्तं जगत् सृजेत्॥ संक्षेपशारीरके, (१-१३)

अन्तर्दृग्दृश्ययोर्भेदं बहिश्च ब्रह्मसर्गयोः।
आवृणोत्यपराशक्तिः सा संसारस्य कारणम्॥ इति दृग्दृश्यविवेके, (१५)

मायाशक्तिः निखिलकलनां साम्प्रतं वा निरुद्धाम्
स्वाधिष्ठाने चितिफलयुता दर्शयत्याविमोक्षम्।
नैल्यम् व्योम्नि स्रजि विषधरो वार्यथा रश्मिपूगो
तद्वत् मिथ्यात्मनि जगदिदं कल्पितं स्वप्नवच्च॥ इति प्रत्यक्तत्वचिन्तामणौ,

अन्यथाभानहेतुत्वात् इयं मायेति कीर्तिता।
आत्मतत्त्वतिरस्कारात् तम इत्युच्यते बुधैः॥

विद्यानाश्यत्वतोऽविद्या मोहस्तत्कारणत्वतः।
सद्वैलक्षण्यदृष्टचेयं असदित्युच्यते बुधैः॥

कार्यवत् व्यक्तताभावात् अव्यक्तमिति गीयते।
एषा माहेश्वरीशक्तिः न स्वतन्त्रा परात्मवत्॥ इति च;

अजोऽपि सन् अव्ययात्मा भूतानामीश्वरोऽपि सन्।
प्रकृतिं स्वामधिष्ठाय सम्भवाम्यात्ममायया॥ इति गीतायाम्, (४-६)

निरूपमनित्यनिरशंकेऽप्यखण्डे मयि चिति सर्वविकल्पनादिशून्ये।
घटयति जगदीशजीवभेदं त्वघटितघटनापटीयसी माया॥ इति मायापञ्चके,

सत्वशुद्ध्यविशुद्धिभ्यां मायाविद्येति च ते मते।
मायाबिम्बो वशीकृत्य तां स्यात् सर्वज्ञ ईश्वरः॥ (१-१६)

मायाख्यायाः कामधेनोः वत्सौ जीवेश्वरावुभौ।
यथेच्छं पिबतां द्वैतं अद्वैतं परमार्थतः॥ (६-२३६) इति पञ्चदश्यां विवरणप्रमेयसङ्ग्रहे च प्रतिपादितम्।

ततश्च शङ्करादर्वाचीनैः अद्वैताचार्येषु स्वग्रन्थेषु माया-अविद्ययोस्तारतम्यविषये जीवेश्वरस्वरूपविषये अविद्याया आश्रयत्वे मायाया आश्रयत्वे च सिद्धान्तभेदाः उपवर्णिताः।

प्रसिद्धमिदं पद्यम् -

वाचस्पतेरवच्छिन्नः आभासो वार्तिकस्य च।
संक्षेपशारीरककृतः प्रतिबिम्बं तथेष्यते॥

इति मन्येऽहं एतेषां विस्तृतं वर्णनं नावश्यकमिति। ततश्च ब्रह्म नास्ति न भाति इति व्यवहारो यदाश्रितः तत्कारणम् अज्ञानमपि तदाश्रितमित्येवाङ्गीकर्तव्यम्। कार्यकारणयोर्वैयधिकरण्यस्य अयुक्तत्वात्। तद्व्यवहारश्च जीवाश्रित एव दृश्यत इति तस्यैव तत्कारणाज्ञानाश्रयत्वमपि। अज्ञानस्य जीवाश्रितत्वेऽपि न अन्योन्याश्रय-दोषः। उत्पत्तिस्थितिज्ञप्तिप्रतिबन्धकत्वेनैव अन्योन्याश्रयस्य दोषत्वं वक्तव्यम्। न च जीवाज्ञानयोरुत्पत्तिः। अमूर्तयोः जीवाज्ञानयोः अनादित्वात्। "जीवईशो विशुद्धा चित् तथा जीवेशयोर्भिदा। अविद्या तच्चितो र्योगः षडस्माकमनादयः॥" इति स्वीकारात् उत्पत्तिमत्वाभावात्। ज्ञप्तिस्तु जीवस्य स्वप्रकाशत्वात् स्वत एव सिद्धयति। तद्बलादेवाविद्याज्ञप्तिः। एवमज्ञानस्य जीवाश्रयत्वजीवाधीनस्थितिकत्वाङ्गीकारेऽपि जीवस्य अज्ञानाश्रितत्व तदधीनस्थितिकत्वानङ्गीकारात् न स्थितौ अन्योन्याश्रयः। अत एव भामतीकल्पतरौ, सिद्धान्तबिन्दौ च-

अधिष्ठानं विवर्तानां आश्रयो ब्रह्म शुक्तिवत्।
जीवाविद्यादिकानां स्यात् इति सर्वमनाकुलम्॥

अज्ञानमेव स्वपराध्यासे कारणम्। न आत्माश्रयादिदोषः। अनादित्वेन तन्निरासात्, उत्पत्त्यभावात् स्वप्रकाशात्मन एव ज्ञप्तिरूपत्वात्" इति।

अज्ञानस्य ब्रह्माश्रयत्वपक्षेऽपि न दोषः। अज्ञानविरोधि ज्ञानं हि न चैतन्यमात्रम्, किन्तु वृत्तिप्रतिबिम्बितम्। तच्च न अज्ञानाश्रयम्, यच्च अज्ञानाश्रयम् तच्च न अज्ञानविरोधि इति न आश्रयानुपपत्तिः। अत एव "स्वप्रकाशस्वरूपचैतन्यस्य अज्ञाननिवृत्त्यौपयिकप्रमात्वसिद्धयर्थं वेदान्तवाक्यप्रमाणजन्याखण्डाकारवृत्ति-विषयत्वमुपेयते" इति सिद्धान्तबिन्दौ।

२. तिरोधानानुपपत्तिः - अज्ञानेन ब्रह्मणः तिरोधानं न सम्भाव्यते। प्रकाशैक-स्वरूपस्य अनादेः अनन्तस्य ब्रह्मणो हि तिरोधानं नाम प्रकाशोदयप्रतिबन्ध इति वा प्रकाशनाश इति वा वक्तुम् अशक्यत्वेन तिरोधानासम्भवादिति द्वितीया अनुपपत्तिः।

अत्र तिरोधानानुपपत्तिखण्डनपराणामद्वैतिनामयमाशयः - अस्ति प्रकाशते इति व्यवहारसामग्र्यां सत्यां नास्ति न प्रकाशते इति व्यवहारयोग्यतापादनमेव आवरणम्, तदेव च तिरोधानम्। न तु प्रकाशोदय प्रतिबन्धः, नापि प्रकाशनाशो

वा तिरोधानम् इति अद्वैतिनामाशयः। तच्च अज्ञानेन ब्रह्मणि सम्भवति, कण्टकेन कण्टकोद्धारणन्यायेन आविद्यकान्तःकरणवृत्त्युपधानस्यैव अज्ञाननिवर्तकत्वात्। मेघैः सूर्यस्यावरणवत्, अपवरकालोकादौ अन्धकारारोपवत् प्रकाशस्वरूपे ब्रह्मणि अज्ञानावरणं सम्भवत्येव। अज्ञानवादे किं नामावरणकृत्यमिति प्रश्नोत्तरप्रसङ्गे "नास्ति न प्रकाशते" (अद्वैतसिद्धौ पृ.५८७) इति व्यवहारः, "अस्ति प्रकाशते" इति व्यवहाराभावो आवरणकृत्यमिति प्रतिपादितम्।

३. **अज्ञानस्य स्वरूपानुपपत्तिः**- अज्ञानस्य ब्रह्मभिन्नस्य परमार्थत्वे अद्वैतहानिः। मिथ्यात्वे अज्ञानकल्पनामूलदोषान्तरापेक्षायां अनवस्थापातात् अज्ञानस्वरूपानुपपत्तिः तृतीया।

स्वरूपानुपपत्तिखण्डनपराणामद्वैतिनामयमाशयः- अविद्यास्वरूपं काल्पनिकमेव न सत्यम्। अविद्या कल्पनाया अनादित्वेन तन्मूलदोषान्तरानपेक्षणात् न अनवस्था। किञ्च ज्ञानस्य स्वपरव्यवहारानुगुण्यापादकत्वस्येव अज्ञानस्यापि स्वपरकल्पनोपपादकत्वात् न दोषान्तरापेक्षा। तत्त्वप्रदीपिकायाम् -

अनादिभावरूपं यत् विज्ञानेन विलीयते।
तदज्ञानमिति प्राज्ञाः लक्षणं सम्प्रचक्षते॥ (पृ.१७)।

इति अनादित्वे सति भावरूपं विज्ञाननिरस्यं अज्ञानमिति स्वरूपमपि वर्णितम्। अतो अज्ञानस्य न स्वरूपानुपपत्तिरिति।

४. **अज्ञानस्य अनिर्वचनीयत्वानुपपत्तिः** - सर्वस्य वस्तुनः अस्ति नास्तीति वा सदसदाकारावभासात् सदसद्विलक्षणत्वरूपानिर्वचनीयत्ववतः पदार्थस्यैव असम्भवात् अज्ञानस्य अनिर्वचनीयत्वं न सम्भवति इति चतुर्थी अनुपपत्तिः।

अज्ञानस्य अनिर्वचनीयत्वानुपपत्तिखण्डनपराणां अद्वैतिनामयमाशयः- त्रिकालबाधायोग्यस्वरूपत्वं सत्वम्, असत्वञ्च निस्स्वरूपत्वम्, तदुभयवैलक्षण्यञ्च अनिर्वचनीयत्वम्। तस्य अस्ति, नास्तीति धीविरोधित्वं नास्तीति न कोऽपि दोषः। तादृशञ्च त्रिकालाबाध्यत्वरूपं सत्त्वं "सत्यं ज्ञानमनन्तं ब्रह्म" "अस्तीत्येवोपलब्धव्य" इत्यादि श्रुत्या ब्रह्मण एव। असत्वन्तु शशशृङ्गादेरेव निरुपाख्यत्वात्। अज्ञानादिप्रपञ्चश्च ज्ञानबाध्यत्वात् सत् स्वरूपत्वाच्च अनिर्वचनीय एवेति न अनिर्वचनीयत्वानुपपत्तिः। किञ्च अनिर्वचनीयत्वं वस्तुतो न सत्वम्, न वा असत्त्वम् इति सदसद्विलक्षणत्वमेव। तच्च शोधनमात्रफलम्। न तु प्रतीतिसामान्ये विषयत्वेन। तथा च घटः सन् इति प्रतीतावपि घटादीनां सत्वपरीक्षायां भाविबाधादिविवेकेन व्यावहारिकसत्वव्यवस्थया, सदसद्विलक्षणत्वाविरोधि-अर्थक्रियाकारित्वव्यवस्थायाः निर्वाहसम्भवात् न विरोधलेशोऽपि। एतदर्थमेव प्रत्यक्षबाधोद्धारादि

प्रकरणानि वादग्रन्थेषु सिद्धान्तसिद्धाञ्जनादौ च। किञ्च - इदं शुक्लम्, इदं पीतम् इत्येवं सर्वरूपम् प्रकाशव्यवस्थाप्यम्। अन्धकारस्य कृष्णं रूपमपि तथैव। यद्यपि अन्धकार-रूपनिर्णये साक्षात् प्रकाशापेक्षा नास्ति, तथापि प्रकाशाभावसापेक्षत्वेन अभावप्रतियोगितया प्रकाशापेक्षा अस्त्येव। अन्यत्र अस्तित्वे सति यत्र यस्य अविद्यमानत्वं तत्र तस्य अभावप्रतियोगित्वम्। जगति सर्वथा प्रकाशास्तित्वाभावः इतरपदार्थानामिव अन्धकारस्यापि रूपं जन्मान्धेनेव न निर्णीयते। तथा च यथा अन्धकाररूपं प्रकाशाविषयमपि प्रकाश-व्यवस्थाप्यं भवति तथा सदसद्रूपद्विविधप्रतीत्यविषयस्यापि भावरूपाज्ञानस्य स्वरूपं अनिर्वचनीयमित्येवं रूपेण प्रतीतिव्यवस्थाप्यं भवति इति।

५. अज्ञाने प्रमाणानुपपत्तिः - अहमज्ञः, मामन्यं न जानामि इत्यादिप्रत्यक्षस्य ज्ञानाभाव-विषयकत्वात् अज्ञाने प्रत्यक्षप्रमाणं न सम्भवति। अज्ञानसाधकतया पराभिमतानामनुमानानां दुष्टत्वात् न अनुमानं प्रमाणं सम्भवति। श्रुतिस्मृतिइतिहासपुराणानां आगमात्मकानां अन्यपरत्वेन न अज्ञाने प्रामाण्यम्। अज्ञानं विनापि प्रपञ्चोत्पत्त्याद्युपपत्तेः अर्थापत्तिरपि न अज्ञाने प्रमाणम्। अतोऽज्ञानस्य अप्रामाणिकत्वमिति पञ्चमी अनुपपत्तिः।

प्रमाणानुपपत्तिखण्डनपराणामद्वैतिनामयमाशयः। इदं दोषभूतं अनादिभावरूपं अज्ञानं प्रत्यक्षानुमानार्थापत्तिश्रुतिप्रमाणैरपि सिद्ध्यति इति। अहमज्ञः, मां अन्यञ्च न जानामि इति प्रत्यक्षं न ज्ञानाभावविषयम्। धर्मिप्रतियोगिज्ञानाज्ञानाभ्यां ज्ञानाभाव-ज्ञानायोगात्। अभावज्ञाने प्रतियोगिज्ञानस्य अधिकरणज्ञानस्य च कारणत्वात्। नापि प्रागभावरूपः। अद्वैतमते कोऽप्यभावः पारमार्थिकसत्यत्वेन न अङ्गीक्रियते। किन्तु व्यावहारिकसत्यतया। व्यावहारिकसत्यता च काल्पनिकीति, यन्मूला सा कल्पना तद् भावरूपाज्ञानमेवेति घट्टकुटीप्रभातन्याये आपतति।

इदमनादिभूतमज्ञानं भावरूपम् अनुमानेनापि सिद्ध्यति- "विवादाध्यसितं प्रमाणज्ञानं स्वप्रागभावव्यतिरिक्तस्वविषयावरण स्वनिवर्त्य-स्वदेशगतवस्त्वन्तरपूर्वकं अप्रकाशितार्थ-प्रकाशकत्वात् अन्धकारे प्रथमोत्पन्नप्रदीपप्रभावत्" इति पञ्चपादिकाविवरणोक्तम् अनुमानम्। (p.85 MGOMLS,155) इदञ्चानुमानं श्रीभाष्यकारैरनूद्य खण्डितम्। इदञ्चानुमानं ऋजुविवरणे सुविशदं वर्णितम्। श्रीभाष्ये श्रुतप्रकाशिकादौ च अस्मिन् अनुमाने वर्णितान् दोषान् समाधाय पक्षविशेषणदलकृत्यम्, साध्यविशेषणदलसार्थक्यम्, हेतुनिष्कर्ष इत्यादीनां विचारपूर्वकं इदमनुमानं निर्दुष्टमिति सिद्धान्तसिद्धाञ्जने (p.IV/61-71), अद्वैतसिद्धेरज्ञानवादे अद्वैतामोदादिषु ग्रन्थेषु प्रसाध्य-

तस्मात् निर्व्यूढपक्षादिपरिष्कारैरदूषणैः।
भावावरणमज्ञानं अनुमानैः प्रसिद्ध्यति॥ इत्युक्तम्।

सुविस्तृतानां पारिभाषिकशास्त्रीयप्रक्रियापूर्णानां विषयविचाराणां अत्र वर्णनं कालक्षेपभीत्या न मया क्रियते। एवं श्रीभाष्योक्तप्रत्यनुमान-नवकदूषकं भावरूपाज्ञान-साधकं च प्रतिवन्दिप्रत्यनुमाननवकं सिद्धान्तसिद्धाञ्जने (पृ.७३) विस्तृतं अद्वैतामोदे (पृ.७३) अद्वैततत्त्वशुद्धौ (पृ.२५०-५३) च विस्तृतं विशदीकृतम्। एवं शतभूषण्यां (पृ.१०६) भावरूपाज्ञानभङ्गवादपरीक्षायां भावरूपाज्ञानसाधनं अनुमानप्रमाणेन साधयित्वा विवरणोक्त-मनुमानं निर्दुष्टं वर्णितम्। एवमद्वैततत्त्वशुद्धौ विवरणोक्तमनुमानमेव सर्वा अनुपपत्तीः वारयत् अभावव्यतिरिक्तं ब्रह्माश्रयं तद्विरोधायकं ज्ञाननिवर्त्यं वस्त्वन्तरं भावविलक्षणं भावाभावविलक्षणं वा अज्ञानं साधयतीति सुविस्तृतं वर्णितम्। विवरणोक्तमेवानुमानं किञ्चित् सपरिष्कारं तत्त्वप्रदीपिकायां (पृ.९८) - "विगीतं देवदत्तनिष्ठप्रमाणज्ञानं देवदत्तनिष्ठ प्रमाभावातिरिक्तानादेः निवर्तकम् प्रमाणत्वात् यज्ञदत्तादिगतप्रमाणज्ञानवत्" इत्यनुमानं वर्णितम्। अत्र प्रागभावादिकमादाय अर्थान्तरता या श्रीभाष्यादिषु वर्णिता तस्याः वारणादि विस्तृतं विद्यते। एवम् अद्वैततर्कसंग्रहे (पृ.१३८-१४१) विचारोऽयं सुविशदः।

अज्ञाने अर्थापत्तिरपि प्रमाणम्।

बन्धस्य ज्ञाननिवर्त्यत्वान्यथानुपपत्त्यादि-रूपार्थापत्तिप्रमाणादपि अज्ञानकल्पितत्वं सिद्ध्यति। एवं जगत्कारणत्वान्यथानुपपत्तिरपि अज्ञाने प्रमाणम्। असङ्ग-उदासीन-कूटस्थाद्वितीय स्वप्रकाशचैतन्यमात्रं वस्तु जगतः कारणमिति गीयते। न खलु तस्मात् केवलात् जगदुत्पत्तिस्सम्भवति। तथात्वे मुक्त्यवस्थायामपि उत्पत्तिप्रसङ्गात्। ततश्च अनादि अज्ञानशक्तिः सिद्ध्यति। अन्यथा जगदुत्पत्त्यनुपपत्तेः। अपि च तत्त्वमसि इति जीवब्रह्मणोः ऐक्योपदेशानुपपत्तिरपि अज्ञाने प्रमाणम्। तत्त्वमसीति वाक्येन तत्त्वम्पदार्थयोः सामानाधिकरण्यं आम्नायते। तच्च भेदस्य मिथ्यात्वे एव उपपद्यते। तच्च तस्य अविद्याहेतुत्वं विना नोपपद्यते इति तदनुपपत्त्या अज्ञानं कल्प्यते। उपदेशत्वात् वेदान्तवाक्यस्य अज्ञातार्थबोधकत्वात् अबाधितार्थबोधकत्वाच्च।

अज्ञाने आगमा अपि प्रमाणानि-

अविद्या हि ब्रह्माश्रयविषयिणी संविन्मात्रब्रह्म-आवरणद्वारा तदवस्थाविशेषान्तः-करणोपहितं तत्प्रतिबिम्बं वा स्वीयेन दोषेण बध्नाति। तेन ब्रह्मस्वरूपमिव स्वस्वरूपमपि जीवा न जानन्ति इति "एतं ब्रह्मलोकं न विन्दन्ति अनृतेन हि प्रत्यूढाः" (Ch. 8.3.2)। इति श्रुतिर्हि बोधयति। अत्र अनृतशब्दः किं अनिर्वचनीयाज्ञानवाची उत पापकर्मवाची इति विचारः तत्र तत्र ग्रन्थेषु दृश्यते। नात्रास्माकं विशेषाभिनिवेशः। आवरणशक्तिर्हि तमोवत् तत्र तत्र तमश्शब्देनोपात्तायाः अविद्यायाः श्रूयते। अज्ञानेनावृतं ज्ञानमिति

स्मृतावपि। नासदासीत् नो सदासीत् तदानीं तम आसीत् (तै.ब्रा. 2.8.9.3.4) इति सूक्तमपि सदसदनिर्वचनीयजगन्मूलभूताज्ञाने प्रमाणम्। तत्र तम आसीदिति तमश्शब्देन अज्ञानम् उच्यते। तस्य च "नासदासीन्नो सदासीत्" इति निषेधद्वयेन सदसदनिर्वचनीयता लभ्यते। यद्यपि नासदासीन्नोसदासीदित्यनेन सदसतोः प्रलयकाले असद्भावमात्रमुच्यते तथापि तस्मिन्नेवसूक्ते तम आसीदिति प्रतिपादितं यत् तमो अस्ति तस्य सत्वे नो सदासीदिति निषेधासङ्गतिः। असत्वे न असदासीदिति निषेधासङ्गतिः। अतः अर्थादेव तत् तमः सदसदनिर्वचनीयं सिद्ध्यति। अस्मिन्नपि सदसच्छब्दार्थविषये तमश्शब्दार्थविषये च मतभेदो दृश्यते। नात्रास्माकं विशेष अभिनिवेश इति मौनमेव स्वीक्रियते।

६. **निवर्तकानुपपत्तिः** - अज्ञानस्य निवर्तकत्वेन अद्वैतिभिरभिमतं निर्विशेष-ब्रह्मस्वरूपज्ञानं तावत् न सम्भवति। सर्वस्य वस्तुनः सविशेषत्वेन निर्विशेषवस्तुन एव असम्भवात्। निवर्तकज्ञानस्यापि अद्वैतमते मिथ्यात्वेन तन्निवर्तकान्तरापेक्षायां अनवस्थानात् इति षष्ठी अनुपपत्तिः।

निवर्तकानुपपत्तिखण्डनपराणामद्वैतिनामयमाशयः- उपक्रमोपसंहारैकरूप्यादि-षड्विधतात्पर्यलिङ्गैः उपनिषदां निर्विशेषाद्वितीयप्रत्यगभिन्नब्रह्मस्वरूपे एव तात्पर्या-वगमात् निर्विशेषब्रह्मस्वरूपज्ञानमेव अज्ञाननिवर्तकम्। तच्च कतकरजोन्यायेन स्वपरनिवर्तकमिति न अनवस्था। किञ्च मिथ्याभूताखिलपदार्थानां मूलकारणमविद्या। तस्या निवर्तकश्च तत्त्वमसि (छा. 6.8.7) अयमात्मा ब्रह्म (बृह. 2.5.9) इदं सर्वं यदयमात्मा (बृह.2.4.5) इत्यादि वेदान्तवाक्यतात्पर्यविषयीभूतं निर्विशेषात्मैक्यज्ञानम्। सविशेष-ब्रह्मज्ञानेन अविद्यायाः सर्वथा विनाशो न सम्भवति। विशेषाणां अविद्यामूलकत्वात्। सविशेषात्मज्ञानं हि तत्त्वज्ञानस्य अन्तरङ्गतरं साधनम्। किञ्च चरमवृत्त्युपलक्षितात्मरूपत्वम् अविद्यानिवृत्तेरिति अद्वैतिनामाशयः। चरमसाक्षात्कारपूर्वकाले च आत्मनः अज्ञाननिवृत्ति-रूपत्वाभावेन सत्यां साक्षात्कारसामग्र्यां साक्षात्कारोत्पत्तौ विरोधप्रसक्तेरभावात्। आत्मनश्च अनर्थनिवृत्तिरूपत्वं प्रपञ्चोपशमश्शिवोऽद्वैत एव इत्यादिभिस्सिद्धम्।वस्तुतः अविद्यानिवृत्तेः वृत्तिरूपतया न निवर्तकखण्डनावकाशः, वृत्तिनिवृत्तेरात्मरूपतया न तज्जनकखण्डनावकाशोऽपीति अद्वैतसिद्धिः। (पृ.८८७-८८८)

७. **निवृत्त्यनुपपत्तिः**- बन्धतत्कारणयोः सत्यत्वेन ज्ञानात् तन्निवृत्तेरयोगात्। निवृत्तेरात्मातिरिक्तायाः निवर्तकान्तरापेक्षया अनवस्थानात् इति निवृत्यनुपपत्तिः सप्तमी।

निवृत्त्यनुपपत्तिखण्डनपराणामद्वैतिनामयमाशयः- बन्धस्य मिथ्यात्वमेव वेदान्त-वाक्यैरवगतमिति तत्कारणस्यापि मिथ्यात्वमेव। अतो ज्ञानमात्रात् तन्निवृत्तिर्युक्ता।

अज्ञाननिवृत्तिश्च आत्मरूपा। अतिरेकेऽपि क्षणिकचरमभावविकाररूपा न स्थिरा। किञ्च अविद्यानिवृत्तिः मिथ्या। मिथ्यापीयं न अविद्यान्तरमूला। अविद्यान्तरस्यापि अनादित्वे, आत्माश्रयत्वे आत्मावरकत्वे च स्वीक्रियमाणे, आत्मज्ञानेन तस्यापि नाशात् न अज्ञानान्तरेण साकं आत्मनाशस्यावस्थानं सम्भवति; प्रतियोगिध्वंसयोः एककालिकत्वायोगात्। आत्मानाश्रयत्वे आत्मानावरकत्वे च निराश्रय निर्विषय-ज्ञानासम्भवः, एकाज्ञाननाशमात्रोपादानं अज्ञानान्तरवैयर्थ्यम्। तत्रापि कस्य अज्ञान-नाशस्य किमज्ञानं उपादानमित्यत्र विनिगमकाभावात् कस्याप्यज्ञाननाशस्य किमप्यज्ञानं नोपादानं स्यात्। किञ्च निर्विशेषब्रह्मज्ञानस्य अविद्यानिवर्तकत्वात् तेन अस्या निवृत्तिः भवत्येवेति न अविद्यानिवृत्त्यनुपपत्तिः। निर्विशेषब्रह्मज्ञानञ्च अविद्याया-स्तत्त्वतो ज्ञाने सत्येव घटते। अविद्यायास्तत्त्वतो ज्ञानं च अविद्यायाः अविद्यात्वेन ज्ञानम्। तस्मिन् सत्येव सा हातुं शक्यते, तस्याः हानञ्च सुखादिषु मिथ्यात्वदृष्टिः। मिथ्यात्वदृष्टिश्च सुखादयो मनोवृत्तिविशेषाः न आत्मगुणा इति भावना। तादृशभावनादार्ढ्ये सुखार्थं, दुःखनिवृत्त्यर्थं वा न कदापि प्रवृत्तिः सम्भवति। प्रवृत्त्यभावे च तन्मूलकस्य कर्मणोऽप्यभाव इति कर्मरूपात् वन्धनात् मुक्तिः सिद्ध्यति। इति।

मान्याः- मद्दृष्ट्या तत्त्वाख्याने अद्वैतं, आचारे द्वैतकल्पनाञ्च अधिकारि-भेदमनुसृत्य स्वीकुर्वति विशिष्टाद्वैतदर्शने-

ईश्वरश्चिदचिच्चेति पदार्थत्रितयम् हरिः।
ईश्वरः चिदिति प्रोक्तो जीवः दृश्यमचित् पुनः॥

इति पदार्थत्रितयम्। तेषु अखिलहेयप्रत्यनीक-अनन्तज्ञानानन्दैकरूपः ज्ञानशक्त्यादि कल्याणगुणभूषितः सकलजगत्सृष्टिस्थितिसंहारकर्ता धर्मकामार्थमोक्षाख्य चतुर्विधफलप्रदः "आर्तो जिज्ञासुरर्थार्थी ज्ञानी च" इति चतुर्विधपुरुषसमाश्रयणीयः सर्वचिदचिन्नायकः शेषी पुरुषोत्तमः नारायण एव ईश्वरः। जीवस्तु चित् इत्युच्यते। स च देहेन्द्रियमनःप्राण-बुद्धिभ्यो विलक्षणः अजः आनन्दरूपः नित्यः अणुपरिमाणत्वात् अचिन्त्यः अव्यक्तः निरवयवः निर्विकारः ज्ञानाश्रयः ईश्वरस्यांशः। अतएव सत्यः अद्वितीयः अनन्तः ज्ञानशक्तिसंपन्नः अगोचरः भोक्ता ईश्वर नियम्यः शेष इति स्वीकृतः (श्रीभाष्ये 2.2.19-32) (यतीन्द्रमतदीपिका-8)।

प्रकृतिः अविद्या माया इत्याद्यपरनामा अचित् (वेदार्थसंग्रहः 85-87) विकारो-त्पादकत्वात् ज्ञानविरोधित्वात् विचित्रसृष्टिकरत्वाच्च तैर्नामभिः व्यवह्रियते। यथा मृदं सुधाम् जलञ्च मेलयित्वा एकद्रव्यं कृत्वा भित्तिं करोति तथा ईश्वरः पञ्चभूतानि

मेलयित्वा जगत् सृजति। एवं जलस्य अग्निसंसृष्टस्थालीसम्बन्धेन औष्ण्यादयो जायन्ते तथा चितः (जीवस्य) अचित्सम्बन्धेन अविद्याकर्मवासनारुचयः जायन्ते। अचिन्निवृत्तौ अविद्यादयो निवर्तन्ते। सा च निवृत्तिः नारायणप्रसादलभ्या इति नियम्यनियामकसम्बन्धः स्वीकृतः। अयं नियम्यनियामकसम्बन्धः कदा उत्पन्नः? चितः अचित्सम्बन्धः कदा उत्पन्नः? इति निर्णेतुं न शक्यते। एवं च विशिष्टाद्वैतवादिभिरपि अनादिः प्रकृतिपदवाच्या भावरूपा माया वा अविद्या वा स्वीकृता इत्येव वक्तव्यं भवति। गतसंवत्सरे काञ्चीपरमाचार्याणां स्मारकदिने भारतीयदर्शनेषु "जीवेश्वरयोर्भेद अनादिः" इति विषयमधिकृत्य विमर्शपत्रमेकं समर्पितम्। तस्मिन् पत्रे प्रसङ्गात् विषयोऽयं वर्णितः।

मान्याः विद्वांसः। इदानीं सप्तविधानुपपत्तिनिरूपणपराः सप्तविधानुपपत्तिखण्डनमण्डनमुण्डनकुट्टनपराश्च ग्रन्थाः संक्षेपतः निर्दिश्यन्ते। तेषु प्रथमं सप्तविधानुपपत्तिसाधनपराः अविद्याखण्डनपराश्च ग्रन्थाः -

१. एकादशशतकीयैः (1100 AD) श्रीरामानुजाचार्यैः श्रीभाष्ये जिज्ञासाधिकरणे सप्तविध ानुपपत्तयः प्रथमतः प्रकटीकृताः। एवं तैरेव कृते वेदार्थसंग्रहे संक्षिप्य वर्णितम्।

२. अनन्तरं द्वादशशतकीयेन (1200 AD) मेघनादारिणा कृतायां अमुद्रितायां भाष्यभावबोधनाख्यायां व्याख्यायां एवं मैसूरनगरे भागशो मुद्रितायां अपूर्णायां नयप्रकाशिकायाञ्च अनुपपत्तिमण्डनं दृश्यते।

३. त्रयोदशशतकीयैः सुदर्शनभट्टैः कृतायां मुद्रितायां श्रीभाष्यव्याख्याश्रुतप्रकाशिकायां अनुपपत्तिमण्डनं विद्यते।

४. षोडशशतकीयेन महाचार्येण कृतायां मुद्रितायां श्रुतप्रकाशिकाव्याख्याभावप्रकाशिकायां, अमुद्रितायां तूलिकाख्यव्याख्यायां च अनुपपत्तिमण्डनं विद्यते।

५. चतुर्दशशतकापरार्धवासिना (1350 AD) वेदान्तदेशिकेन कृते वेदान्तदेशिकग्रन्थमालायां मुद्रिते शतदूषणीग्रन्थे एकादशवादेषु सप्तविधानुपपत्तीनां मण्डनं साधनञ्च विद्यते।

६. महाचार्यापरनामकेन रामानुजदासेन षोडशशतकीयेन कृते शतभूषणीव्याख्याचण्डमारुते सद्विद्याविजयाख्ये च ग्रन्थे सप्तविधानुपपत्तिमण्डनं लक्ष्यते।

७. एवं नदीतीरमुनिनामकेन आण्डान् इत्यपरनामक श्रीनिवासाचार्येण कृते अमुद्रिते (AL DC p. 415) शतभूषणीव्याख्या सहस्रकिरणीनामके एवं मायावादशतदूषणीनामके महीशूरपुस्तकालयस्थे अमुद्रिते (DC . Mysore p.579) सिद्धिचन्द्रिकयोरुक्तः बाधोद्धारोऽपि खण्डितः इति दृश्यते। ततश्च षोडशसप्तदशशतकीयोऽयं ग्रन्थः सप्तविधानुपपत्तिमण्डनपरः ।

८. नृसिंहराजीया शतदूषणीव्याख्या अनाद्यनन्ता अमुद्रिता अड्यारपुस्तकालये विद्यते।

९. विंशतिशतकीयेन प्रतिवादिभयङ्कराण्णङ्कराचार्येण कृतः शतदूषणीवज्रकुठाराख्यः द्राविडभाषामयः ग्रन्थोऽपि सप्तविधानुपपत्तिमण्डनपरः ।

१०. श्रीरङ्गवासिना श्रीनिवासाचार्येण विंशतिशतकीयेन कृते तत्त्वनिरूपणाख्ये,

११. एवं विंशतिशतकीयैः उत्तमूर् वीरराघवाचार्य कृते परमार्थभूषणाख्ये ग्रन्थे परमार्थप्रकाशिकाख्ये च ग्रन्थे सप्तविधानुपपत्तिमण्डनं लक्ष्यते।

मान्याः। इदानीं अनिर्वचनीयाभावरूपाविद्यासाधनपराः अविद्यास्वीकारे सम्भावितानुपपत्तिखण्डनपराश्च केचन ग्रन्थाः अन्ततो सप्तविधानुपपत्तिखण्डनपरा इति वक्तव्याः ग्रन्थाः निर्दिश्यन्ते।

१. अनिर्वचनीयभावरूपाविद्यासाधनपरेषु ग्रन्थेषु इष्टसिद्ध्यादिषु श्रीभाष्योक्ता-नुपपत्तिसमाः काश्चन अनुपपत्तयः उद्भाविताः। तासां खण्डनं द्वादशशतकीये षड्दर्शनग्रन्थप्रकाशमालायां मुद्रिते चित्सुखाचार्यकृते तत्त्वप्रदीपिकाग्रन्थे प्रथम-चतुर्थपरिच्छेदयोः विद्यते इति तत्त्वप्रदीपिकापि अविद्यानुपपत्तिखण्डनपरः ग्रन्थः।

२. त्रयोदशशतकीयेन आनन्दज्ञानेन कृते तर्कसंग्रहे च अनुपपत्तिखण्डनं अविद्यामण्डनं च विद्यते।

३. एवं षोडशशतकीयेन मधुसूदनसरस्वत्या कृते अद्वैतसिद्धिग्रन्थे, तद्व्याख्या ब्रह्मानन्दीये च सप्तविधानुपपत्तिखण्डनं विद्यते।

४. एवं षोडशशतकीयेन कृष्णानन्दसरस्वत्या कृते विशिष्टाद्वैतसिद्धान्त खण्डनपरे सिद्धान्तसिद्धाञ्जने चतुर्थभागे तिरुवनन्तपुरमुद्रिते श्रीभाष्यादारभ्य चण्डमारुतान्ते ग्रन्थे उद्भाविताः अनुपपत्तयः खण्डिताः, अविद्या साधिता च।

५. एकोनविंशद्-विंशत्शतकमध्यवासिना अभ्यंकर वासुदेवेन रचिते अद्वैतामोद-ग्रन्थे श्रीभाष्योक्ताः सप्तविधानुपपत्तयः खण्डिताः अविद्यावादश्च मण्डितः।

६. विंशतिशतकीयेन अनन्तकृष्णशास्त्रिणा कृते शतदूषणीखण्डनपरे शतभूषणी-ग्रन्थे सप्तविधानुपपत्तयः खण्डिताः अविद्या साधिता च।

७. एवं विंशतिशतकीयेन अनन्तकृष्णशास्त्रिणा कृते परमार्थप्रकाशिकाखण्डन परे अद्वैततत्वशुद्धिग्रन्थे, परमार्थभूषणाख्यग्रन्थखण्डनपरे अद्वैततत्त्वसुधाख्ये च ग्रन्थे सप्तविधानुपपत्तयः खण्डिताः।

८. एवं अनन्तकृष्णशास्त्रिणा कृते तत्त्वनिरूपणसमीक्षाख्ये, शतभूषणीअनुबन्ध नामके ग्रन्थे शतभूषणी-वज्रकुठारखण्डनपरे च ग्रन्थे अनुपपत्तयः खण्डिताः।

९. अन्ततः जगदीशशास्त्रिकृतसप्तविधानुपपत्तिपरीक्षायां सप्तविधानुपपत्तयः सविस्तरं खण्डिताः।

विद्वांसः। सर्वेषां दर्शनानां वाक्यानां मूलं प्रस्थानत्रयमेव। प्रस्थानत्रयगतानां वाक्यानां सर्वेऽपि दार्शनिकाः स्वस्वमूलभूतसिद्धान्तानुसारिणी व्याख्यां कुर्वन्ति। आधुनिके काले विशिष्टाद्वैते अद्वैते वा कूलङ्कषपण्डिताः तत्त्वदर्शनसमग्र-ग्रन्थाध्येतारो वा दुर्लभाः। अस्यां परिस्थितौ एतादृशविषयाः ज्ञानसत्रयोग्या न भवन्ति। केवलं पठनपाठन अध्ययनाध्यापनयोग्याः शास्त्रीयप्रक्रियापूर्णाः आचार्यमुखात् अध्येतव्या एव। ततश्च किं तत्वम्, किं न तत्त्वम्, इति निर्णयः न सुलभः परन्तु -

त्रयी साङ्ख्यं योगः पशुपतिमतं वैष्णवमिति
प्रभिन्ने प्रस्थाने परमिदमदः पथ्यमिति च।
रुचीनां वैचित्र्यात् ऋजुकुटिलनानापथजुषां
नृणामेको गम्यस्त्वमसि पयसामर्णव इव॥ शिवमहिम्नः स्तोत्रम्-७

तव तत्त्वं न जानामि कीदृशोऽसि महेश्वर
यादृशोऽसि महादेव तादृशाय नमो नमः ॥ शिवमहिम्नः स्तोत्रम्-४१

इत्युक्त्वा विरमामि।

Summary: This essay is devoted to the philosophy as well as history of the debate on māyā-avidyā. Professor Thangaswami Sarma first discusses Rāmānuja's seven-fold objections on the nodal concept of māyā-avidyā of the Advaitins and their conceptual development. With large number of quotations from *Prasthānatraya* and from the writings of Śaṅkara, Sureśvara and post-Śaṅkara Advaitins like Citsukha, Vidyāraṇya, Madhusūdana up to the 20th century scholars, he justifies the position the Advaitin has taken in validating the māyā-avidyā. By citing quotations from the texts like *Tarkasaṅgraha*, *Tattvapradīpikā* and the like, he shows how Advaitins have very logically defended the views of the Upaniṣadic tradition and answered the questions raised by Viśiṣṭādvaitins.

In the later part of the essay, he gives a historical account of the writings on this debate starting with the texts by Viśiṣṭādvaitins which are devoted to the refutation of the Advaitic concept of māyā-avidyā. He enlists the important Viśiṣṭādvaita texts like *Śrībhāṣya* and *Vedārthasaṅgraha* of Rāmānuja,

Bhāṣyābhavabodhana of Meghanādāri, *Śrutaprakāśikā* of Sudarśana, *Tulikā* by Mahācārya, *Satadūṣaṇī* by Vedāntadeśika, *Caṇḍamāruta* and *Sadvidyāvijaya* by Mahācārya, *Sahasrakiraṇī* by Śrīnivāsācārya, *Satadūṣaṇī-vajrakuṭhāra* by Prativādībhayaṅkaraṁ Annaṁgarācārya, *Tattvanirūpaṇa* by Śrīnivāsa and *Paramārthabhūṣaṇa* by Uttamur Vīrarāghavācārya.

In order to defend the concept of māyā-Avidyā, there came up the texts countering the claims of Visistadvaitins and those are: *Tattvapradīpikā* by Citsukha, *Tarkasaṅgraha* by Ānandajñāna, *Advaitasiddhi* by Madhusūdana Sarasvatī, *Siddhānta-siddhāñjana* by Kṛṣṇānanda Sarasvatī, *Advaitāmoda* by Abhyankar Vāsudeva Śāstrī, *Advaitatattvasuddhi*, *Advaitatattvasudhā* and *Satabhūṣaṇī* by Anantakṛṣṇa Śāstrī and *Saptavidha-anupapattiparīkṣā* by Jagadīśvara Śāstrī.

In the conclusion, Professor Sarma expresses his concern on the present state of affair of the śāstric tradition and how it is no more the same and we do not have such scholars who are devoted or going to devote their life-time for the study of the Vedāntic traditions.

29

FROM RĀMĀNUJA TO RĀMARĀYA: DIALECTICAL JOURNEY OF MĀYĀ-AVIDYĀ IN THE HISTORY OF VEDĀNTA*

Godabarisha Mishra

durghaṭatvam avidyāyāḥ bhūṣaṇaṁ na tu dūṣaṇam

(The inexplicability of avidyā is not a defect but an embellishment)

Iṣṭasiddhi of Vimuktātman 1.140

śrutitaḥ smṛtitaścetīhāsataśca purāṇataḥ
advaitasyāsti dūṣyatvam pūrṇabhāṣyārthavarṇanāt

(On the basis of *Śruti*, *Smṛti*, *Itihāsa* and *Purāṇa*, the elucidation of entire *Śrībhāṣya* would render the philosophy of Advaita to be defective.)

Paramārthaprakāśikā of Uttamur Viraraghavacharya

Mithya was truth seen through a frame of reference. Sat was truth independent of any frame of reference. Mithya gave a limited, distorted view of reality; sat a limitless, correct view of things. Mithya was delusion, open to correction. *Sat* is truth, absolute and perfect in every way. Being boundless and perfect, however, *sat* could not be reduced to a symbol or confined to a word. Words and symbols are essentially incomplete and flawed. *Sat* therefore eluded communication. For communication one needs symbols and words, howsoever incomplete and flawed they may be. Through hundreds of thousands of incomplete and flawed symbols and words, it was possible to capture, or at least to indicate, the infinite perfection and boundlessness of *sat*. For Rishis therefore the delusion of mithya served as an essential window to the truth or *sat*.

Myth = Mithya (A Handbook of Hindu Mythology) by Devdutt Pattanaik

Introduction and Historical Background

The central teaching of all the schools of Vedānta, irrespective of their subtle differences, is that Brahman is the ultimate principle as enunciated in the Upaniṣads. The differences are due to relating Brahman to the world and the souls and this relation is understood differently in different systems of Vedānta. As much as the similarity among the schools has its genesis in the Upaniṣads, the differences can also be traced to them. There are certain passages in the Upaniṣads, known as *abheda-śruti*, which assert the non-different nature of the souls and the world from Brahman, and there are others, known as *bheda-śrutis*, which speak of their differences. The method adopted by each school to reconcile the differences represents its basic philosophical position. For Śaṅkara, the texts teaching *abheda*, non-difference, are primary and those teaching *bheda*, difference are secondary and the latter texts are intended only to give a lead to the teaching which is conveyed by the texts of non-difference. Brahman is the only reality on which self and world are illusorily superimposed due to ignorance; and they have no existence of their own apart from the former.

For Rāmānuja, those texts teaching non-difference and those teaching difference (*bheda* as well as *abheda*) are equally important.[1] That is the reason why he holds that the world and the souls are different as well as non-different from Brahman, viz. Lord Viṣṇu or Nārāyaṇa. The former viz. world and the souls, form His body and serve His purpose.[2] Madhva, however, holds a very radical position. For him, the texts teaching difference alone carry the real import of the Upaniṣads. The world and the souls are absolutely different from Brahman; they are dependent entities (*paratantra-tattvas*). The *abheda-śruti* passages, that teach non-difference, are meant to emphasize the independent character of Brahman in contrast with the dependent nature of the world and souls.[3]

For Advaitins, Brahman which is the only reality is beyond all empirical determinations and has no characteristics; it is *nirguṇa*. But because of ignorance (avidyā), Brahman, without attributes, appears as though having attributes (*saguṇa*). However, for both Rāmānuja as well as Madhva, Brahman is with (and cannot be without) auspicious attributes. The over emphasis of ignorance by alluding to the concepts of māyā-avidyā was resented by both the Ācāryas and this forms the basic problematic of the debate among Vedāntic schools. It may be noted here that Rāmānuja, though accepts qualified non-dualism, is not comfortable with the Advaitin's variety of non-dualism asserting reality to be without any characteristics whatsoever. He comes down heavily upon Śaṅkara's contention which asserts that any qualification is a product of ignorance and all qualified empirical objects are located in Brahman, which is without any characteristics. According to Madhva, the Advaitin is wrong because of positing a positive ignorance as the cause of the world and the Viśiṣṭādvaitin is wrong because of partial acceptance of Advaita; for the reality is marked by difference (*bheda*) only. With this background of the Vedāntic schools, all believing *Śruti* to be the chief source of knowledge, there is fundamental difference of opinion about the concept of ignorance (avidyā) being the first cause of the creation as accepted by Advaitins and thus the debate on māyā-avidyā has become prominently significant in the history of Vedānta.

Survey of Literature

We have already seen how the Advaitin has premised his view that the world process is because of the concealment of Brahman by an inexplicable principle called māyā-avidyā and this has attracted many objections, very elaborately from Rāmānuja who has pointed out seven basic objections (*Saptavidha-anupapatti*) in respect of this māyā-avidyā to prove that it is only a pseudo concept and not a fact. In short, Rāmānuja strongly feels that Śaṅkara has superimposed this concept on Vedānta without any logical, practical or textual support. Even the pre-Rāmānuja Vaiṣṇava scholars have vociferously argued against māyā-avidyā as the cause of the empirical world. Before examining each of the objections pointed out by Rāmānuja, a list of a few important works which deal with this dialogue on māyā-avidyā may be given.

In his *Śrībhāṣya*, Rāmānuja gives reference to the works of Nāthamuni, one of the earliest critics of Advaita, pointing out his concept of māyā-avidyā, from the standpoint of Viśiṣṭādvaita. Though none of his written works, like *Nyāyatattva* and *Yoga-rahasya*, are available at present, Rāmānuja's allusion in the *Śrībhāṣya* (1.1.1.) shows the way Nāthamuni has dealt with māyā-avidyā. In his *Siddhitraya*, Yāmuna, the grand preceptor of Rāmānuja, has extensively criticized the Advaita position and has disapproved of the doctrine of māyā-avidyā.[4] Following the footsteps of Yāmuna, Rāmānuja, in the *Mahā-siddhānta* section of his *Śrībhāṣya*, has extensively criticized māyā-avidyā highlighting seven major objections, known as *Saptavidha-anupapatti*. The tradition of criticizing māyā-avidyā continued after Rāmānuja by other protagonists of Viśiṣṭādvaita and one of the noted champions of this agenda of criticism was Vedānta Deśika. In many of his works, especially in the *Śatadūṣaṇī*, he has pointed out sixty-six objections against Advaita of which many are directed towards māyā-avidyā. Deśika was followed by Mahācārya or Rāmānujadāsa and in his *Sadvidyānirṇaya*, the latter alludes to Advaita as *asad-vidyā* because of the Advaitin's dependence on māyā-avidyā.

Though the problematic of *anupapatti* was very systematically initiated by Rāmānuja, we do not find any *direct* reply to these questions till 20th century, even from very well-known Advaita writers like Citsukha, Vidyāraṇya or Appayyadīkṣita or even Madhusūdana. It may be mentioned here that Madhusūdana Sarasvatī wrote a number of texts countering the claims of Madhva School and that of Nyāya but paid little attention to directly deal with the points raised by Rāmānuja and Deśika against māyā-avidyā. But the later Advaitins did not take the objections nonchalantly; they stood up to answer the objections raised by Rāmānuja as well as his followers. One of the very important participants in this debate was Rāmarāyakavi, who vociferously supported Advaitins' claim of māyā-avidyā as the basis of world appearance and attacked Viśiṣṭādvaita for their imprudence in not understanding the greatness of Advaita doctrines. He was again followed by Anantakrishna Sastri who wrote *Śatabhūṣaṇī* countering the claims of *Śatadūṣaṇī* of Vedāntadeśika. Sastri, following Advaita tradition, has pointed out that the objections raised are because of miscomprehension on the part of VedāntaDeśika. The works of Anantakrishna Sastri evoked much response and were examined by several authors.[5]

V. Kozhiyalam Ranganathacharya in his *Viśiṣṭādvaita-vijaya* (*Saptavidha-anupapatti-sthāpanam*) has examined the contents of *Śatabhūṣaṇī* in great detail and shows that the defects pointed out by Rāmānuja could not be easily undone as attempted by Anantakrishna Sastri. This again was countered by V. Jagadisvara Sastri in his *Saptavidha-anupapatti-parīkṣā*, aiming at clarifying the position of Advaita, in order to show that the said defects shown by Viśiṣṭādvaitins are not logically valid. The work seems to be the direct answer to the charges leveled against Advaita by Rāmānuja and his followers. In his *Viśiṣṭādvaita-siddhi*, D.T. Tatacharya criticizes the basic tenets of Advaita in addition to disapproving the claims made in the *Śatabhūṣaṇī.* One of the well-known participants in this debate is Prativadibhayangaram Annangaracharya, who was a living legend of Śrīvaiṣṇava tradition during our times. In his *Śatabhūṣaṇī-vajrakuṭhāra* (in Tamil and Maṇipravāla), he gives a thorough criticism of *Śatabhūṣaṇī* on several considerations. Displaying his extraordinary scholarship, Annangaracharya states that the *Śatabhūṣaṇī* contains a large number of grammatical mistakes, misquotes and wrong logic and fallacious arguments. The author concludes that the *Śatabhūṣaṇī* is a restatement of Advaita position repeating what has been stated in the *Śatadūṣaṇī* as *Pūrvapakṣa*.

In the meanwhile, another work *Advaitāmoda* was written by Abhayankar Vasudeva Sastri, as an examination of the *Jijñāsādhikaraṇa* of *Śrībhāṣya*, wherein the seven *anupapattis* have been thoroughly dealt with. In response to all the works vindicating the views of Advaita, Uttamur Viraraghavacharya, well-known as Abhinava-Deśika for his erudition, wrote a monumental work called *Paramārtha-bhūṣaṇa*, wherein several concepts of Advaita were subjected to severe criticism. This book is a critique of not only *Śatabhūṣaṇī*, but of many other ancient classics of Advaita.

The "*Saptavidha-anupapatti*" presented by Rāmānuja was primarily continued within the scholarly circles even in the *Śrīvaiṣṇava* tradition, for a few centuries. However, in a parallel development in the Śaiva tradition, Śrīkaṇṭhācārya wrote *Śrīkaṇṭha-bhāṣya* in which he presents *Sapthavidha-anupapatti* from the standpoint of *Śaiva-viśiṣṭādvaita*. Appayyadīkṣita, subsequently, wrote a commentary on *Śrīkaṇṭhabhāṣya*. The edition of *Śrīkaṇṭha-bhāṣya* by Halasyanatha Sastri, provided an opportunity for the cross-comparison of views across different traditions. It paved the way for discovering the commonality of a few objections in both Śaiva and Vaiṣṇava Viśiṣṭādvaita traditions. Discussions on Madhva's refutation of non-dualism worked as a catalyst for the debate to multiply the arguments against māyā-avidyā. The Advaita-Dvaita polemics in the *Avidyā-khaṇḍanam* and other Dvaita texts, dialectics of Jīva Gosvāmī and Baladeva Vidyābhūṣaṇa, contributed their lot and provided more inquisitiveness to the existing polemics on *Saptavidha-anupapatti*.[6] Among the books in English, a special mention may be made to *The Seven Great Untenables* authored by John Grimes. It is perhaps the only book so far in English which analyses seven objections, posed by Viśiṣṭādvaita and the answers given by Advaita school.

With this survey of literature, may we analyse the debate on the topic of māyā-avidyā starting from Rāmānuja, who is the initiator of the problem of *Saptavidha-anupapatti* which remained unanswered up to Rāmarāya, who had directly answered the questions raised by the former and also given fresh arguments to rehabilitate the Advaitavedānta on stronger grounds. In order to further this debate, this volume contains two brilliant essays, viz. (i) countering the views of Rāmarāya by S.N.C. Raghunathacharyulu and (ii) answering the objections and reinstating the views of Rāmarāya, i.e., AdvaitinsÆ view by V. Swaminathan.

The Objections and Answers: The Debate on Māyā-avidyā

In my Introduction, I have given a glimpse of the objections raised by Rāmānuja and here I will try to deal with the exact content of the debate starting from Rāmānuja up to our times by highlighting the special contribution made by Rāmarāya Kavi. For the sake of precision, reference to the name of the authors, participants in the debate is avoided while representing them through the school they belong to.

Before going in to the objections raised by Rāmānuja, let me briefly point out the pre-suppositions of Advaita in building up of the concept of māyā-avidyā. Advaitin holds the position that: 1. Avidyā is *anādi* (without a beginning); 2. It has the two powers; i. concealment, *āvaraṇa* and ii. projection, *vikṣepa*; 3. It is positive or *bhāvarūpa*; it is not the absence of knowledge, since what is negative cannot be the cause of anything. 4. It is located in the jīva according to the *Bhāmatī* tradition and in Brahman according to *Vivaraṇa* tradition, known as *jīva-ajñāna-vāda* and the *brahma-ajñāna-vāda* respectively. 5. It is indeterminable (*anirvacanīya - sadasadvilakṣaṇa*) only with regard to its ontological status. 6. Even though it is *anādi*, beginning-less, it has an end; it is terminated by knowledge - *jñāna-nivartya.*

There have been criticisms against the basic views of Advaita school as to how could māyā-avidyā be beginningless since all the elements have a beginning. The answer is: The elements come from māyā, associated with the consciousness. To this the next question is asked: Wherefrom does this māyā come? What is its cause? The presupposition is that if elements require a cause, then māyā must also have a cause. Two answers are posited by the Advaitin: (a) Māyā being coeval with Brahman seems to be eternal. But Advaitins have to accept that māyā gets terminated with knowledge for the sake of mokṣa. Now the question is: if something has an end, then it should have a beginning. The Advaitin retorts back on the strength of Upaniṣads saying that māyā has a beginning but it doesn't come out of something else, its beginning is in itself.[8] This is inconceivable, mysterious to hold such a position, but Advaitins say that this inconceivability is a glory of the concept of māyā-avidyā. Strictly speaking it has a beginning but its beginning is not due to any other factor and so it is called beginningless. There is the scheme of causation as far as the products of māyā-avidyā are concerned, but that is violated in the case of māyā itself which is according to the Śruti. Hence Advaita holds that the māyā is beginningless but not in the same sense as Brahman is beginningless. As far as the activities of māyā is concerned, māyā is responsible for the distinction between the *pāramārthika* and *vyāvaharika* points of view. It is also responsible for making one Reality appear as two - as Īśvara and jīva. It is responsible for the appearance of the world, functioning as the power of Īśvara. The distinction between jīva and Īśvara is also due to māyā.

There is another question to be discussed: whether māyā and avidyā are identical or different. There is no unanimity on this issue even among the Advaitins. Some are of the view that they are different.[7] Īśvara and jīva are the reflected images of pure-consciousness in māyā and avidyā respectively. For them, māyā does not delude its location, i.e., Īśvara, whereas avidyā deludes its location, which is jīva. The question arises: where do these Īśvara and jīva come from. The pure-consciousness which gets affected by māyā as well as avidyā becomes Īśvara and jīva respectively. In that case, the māyā and avidyā are the causes and therefore are prior to Īśvara and jīva and the outcome of this argument is that Īśvara and jīva cannot be locations of māyā and avidyā as pointed out. For this, it is said that the state of being the Īśvara is not caused by māyā, but only dependent on it.[9] This view of non-difference is also based on the Śruti passage which says that prakṛti becomes by itself (*svayameva*) māyā and avidyā and gives rise to jīva and Īśvara since both māyā and avidyā are identical with prakṛti.[10] Śaṅkara in his *Brahmasūtra-bhāṣya* states that avidyā is the root cause of transmigratory existence and this avidyā is known by the word, *avyakta*, and also *ākāśa*, *akṣara* and māyā.[11] The prevalent view in Advaita is that māyā and avidyā are not different; they are two different aspects of prakṛti and are identical. The term "māyā-avidyā", from the Advaitic standpoint, has been used in this sense throughout the present volume.[12]

Rāmānuja takes māyā as the knowledge and avidyā as action, i.e., *karma* and hence there is radical difference between them. His criticism is directed towards attacking avidyā or ajñāna which has been preeminently taken in different senses to be the cause of the world, etc. and he, as I have pointed out, raises seven objections against this which is a pseudo-concept according to him. For him there is no knowledge which is totally of an illusory object.[13] A few important points of each of the objections raised by Rāmānuja and post-Rāmānuja proponents of Viśiṣṭādvaita as well as the answers given by Advaitins are given below.

1. Āśrayānupapatti: Questioning Brahman being the Locus of Māyā-avidyā

The Advaitins hold that an illusion is effected by an aggregate of three causes - i. ignorance (a defect, *doṣa*), ii. immediate knowledge of the locus, *adhiṣṭhāna* and, iii. the mental impression left by a past experience. The defect that causes the illusion of Īśvara, jīva and the jagat is ajñāna abiding with or located in Brahman or jīva.

Rāmānuja contends that Brahman cannot be the locus of *ajñāna* since Brahman is self-revealing knowledge (*svaprakāśa-jñānarūpa*) and by nature It is opposed to *ajñāna* (of the nature of concealing objects) that gets destroyed by knowledge. Secondly, the Advaitin cannot maintain that *brahma-svarūpa-jñāna* is not opposed to *ajñāna*; but the knowledge that Brahman is of the nature of knowledge (*jñāna-svarūpa*)[14] is opposed to *ajñāna*. For both being self-luminous, *brahma-jñāna* and *svarūpa-jñāna* are identical and there is no justification to consider one as opposed, and the other not, against *ajñāna* in the absence of a characteristic mark which might distinguish the one from the other. Thirdly, the knowledge, namely, Brahman is of the nature of knowledge "*jñānasvarūpam brahma*" cannot claim for itself the right to be opposed to *ajñāna* because the nature of Brahman revealed by it does not differ in any way from *svarūpa-jñāna* which is self-luminous and therefore shines forth by itself (*i.e.*, without any external aid).

In answering the above objection, Advaitins retort saying that the widely accepted criterion for opposition between *jñāna* and *ajñāna* is the oneness of their content (*samānaviṣayakatva*). For example, my knowledge of a pot will take away my ignorance of a pot. *Svarūpajñāna* has no content whereas *ajñāna* (veiling the real nature of Brahman) has Brahman for its content. *Svarūpa-jñāna* and *brahma-jñāna* do not have a common content which is the criterion for their mutual opposition. Therefore, there can be no opposition between (the self-luminous) *svarūpa-jñāna* and *ajñāna*. There is nothing repugnant in Brahman being the locus of *ajñāna*.

Secondly, *svarūpa-jñāna* which by nature is not opposed to *ajñāna* cannot dispel *ajñāna* that conceals Brahman. A knowledge of the real nature of Brahman - since it has a content (Brahman) common to *ajñāna* that hides Brahman - is opposed to *ajñāna* and therefore is efficacious in removing *ajñāna*. *Svarūpa-jñāna* is a knowledge devoid of content (*nirviśeṣa*) whereas *brahma-jñāna* is a knowledge having a content. Its having a content clearly differentiates *brahma-jñāna* from *svarūpa-jñāna*.

Thirdly, it is not that the nature of Brahman does shine forth by itself always. The Advaitins on the authority of the Upaniṣads assert that despite its self-luminosity, the nature of Brahman remains obscured by *ajñāna*. It has been proved that there is no opposition between *svarūpa-jñāna* and *brahma-jñāna*.

The Viśiṣṭādvaitins observe that the Advaitins cannot even think of an immediate knowledge having Brahman for its content. Brahman being, by itself, immediate knowledge could never become the content of another immediate knowledge. If *brahma-jñāna* is held to be opposed to *ajñāna*, it must be admitted that it is opposed to itself and as such it cannot be the locus of *ajñāna*.

The Advaitins reply that the real nature of Brahman annihilates *ajñāna* that conceals Brahman. In other words, *brahma-jñāna*, the knowledge that has Brahman for its content, destroys *ajñāna* that veils the nature of Brahman. *Brahma-jñāna*, that terminates *ajñāna* emerges from the mahāvākyas and it is known as *akhaṇḍākāravṛtti*. *Brahma-jñāna*, the immediate knowledge having Brahman for its content, is referred to in a number of Upaniṣadic texts.[15]

The Viśiṣṭādvaitins argue that the shell in the erroneous cognition, "this is silver", needs a knowledge to counter the *ajñāna* since it is not opposed to *ajñāna* on account of its inability to reveal its nature by itself. Brahman (*svarūpa-jñāna*) on the other hand must be admitted as opposed to the *ajñāna* (veiling it) since it possesses the knowledge of its real nature from its own experience and therefore it does not require another knowledge to get rid of the veiling *ajñāna*.

The Advaitins reply to this by stating Rāmānuja's basic assumption that Brahman is a knower (*jñātā*) and has the knowledge of its real nature. According to Advaita, Brahman is not a knower and so It cannot cognize its real nature; nor can it become *saviśeṣa-jñāna* since it is of the nature of *nirviśeṣa* (content-less) *jñāna*. Like the immediate knowledge of the real nature of shell, the immediate knowledge of the real nature of Brahman also is *pramā, i.e.*, *antaḥkaraṇa-vṛtti-jñāna* (modification of the mind) and so the immediate knowledge of the real nature of Brahman belongs to the knower, *pramātā* (*i.e.*, jīva) and not to Brahman. In the pure Brahman - the one without a second - there is no place for the tripartite (*tripuṭi*) situation comprising of knower, knowledge and known. The Śruti declares that when Ātman alone remains, there is no seer, sight and seen.[16] Hence, Rāmānuja's attempt to push forward his thesis that *svarūpa-jñāna* is, by itself, opposed to *ajñāna* by drawing a contrast between the shell and Brahman (*svarūpa-jñāna*) is not justifiable.

Now the Viśiṣṭādvaitin comes with a fresh argument: The Advaitin will have to state clearly the nature of the knowledge that dissolves *ajñāna*, which conceals Brahman. He cannot point to the knowledge that anything other than Brahman is *mithyā*. The knowledge that the universe is *mithyā* can be detrimental only to that *ajñāna* which presents the universe as real; and not to the *ajñāna* that veils the real nature of Brahman. Therefore, the *ajñāna* that obscures the real nature of Brahman remains un-assailed.

Advaitin's reply: The knowledge of the real nature of Brahman terminates *ajñāna* that conceals the nature of Brahman is an indisputable fact like the knowledge of the real nature of the rope that removes the *ajñāna*, which conceals the real nature of the rope. The knowledge that anything other than Brahman is mithyā is dependent on the knowledge of the entities other than Brahman which again necessarily presupposes the knowledge of the real nature of Brahman. The person, who is ignorant of the nature of Brahman can hardly know that a particular entity is other than Brahman. On the other hand, the person who possesses the knowledge that 'anything other than Brahman is mithyā' does possess the knowledge of the real nature of Brahman. Therefore, the knowledge that 'anything other than Brahman is mithyā' destroys the *ajñāna* that conceals the real nature of Brahman. Thus Rāmānuja's criticism of the nature of the knowledge that is opposed to ajñāna is not justified. It is only the immediate knowledge, "I am Brahman", says the Advaitin, that is opposed to *ajñāna*.

The Upanisadic statements disclose no opposition between *svarūpa-jñāna* and *ajñāna*; on the other hand they purport only the co-existence of the two. The illumination of all things by the light of Brahman and the concealment of *svarūpa-jñāna* by *ajñāna* proclaimed by the texts imply the peaceful co-existence of *svarūpa-jñāna* and *ajñāna*.[17] In the text "*tasya bhāsā sarvamidaṁ vibhāti*", the pronoun *sarvam* includes *ajñāna* also. That *svarūpa-jñāna* is an illuminator and not the destroyer of *ajñāna* as known from the Upaniṣads.

Questioning Jīva as The Locus of Ajñāna

Rāmānuja claims that the jīva which is itself the product of *ajñāna* cannot be the locus of *ajñāna*. In other words it is absurd to hold jīva as the locus of *ajñāna* which, as the cause, invariably precedes the origination of the jīva.

For this, the Advaitins reply: Rāmānuja assumes the priority of *ajñāna*, as evidenced in the above statement. Coming back to the question of priority, is it in terms of chronological-temporal or logical, priority? Since both jīva and avidyā are said to be beginningless, it is first of all absurd to ask the question about temporal priority; that jīva is prior to avidyā and vice versa. What cannot be explained in terms of time cannot be associated with the concepts of "prior" and "posterior" which are temporal notions. The objection is based on the logic of time, while the two entities considered here are beyond time. If it is logical priority, we have to say that conscious-ness which is the sole reality, becomes the jīva because of avidyā. Therefore logically avidyā is prior to jīva. There is no mutual dependence here. When the Advaitin says that jīva is the locus of avidyā, it is meant that the consciousness conditioned by jīva is the locus of avidyā. This means that the difference in the two viewpoints either jīva or Brahman being locus of avidyā is only nominal. And therefore, there is no problem of mutual dependence as pointed out by Rāmānuja.

Rāmānuja has clearly indicated that the jīva as the abode of *ajñāna* involves the fallacy of self-dependency (*ātmāśraya*). Jīva, in Advaita, is Brahman (*svarūpa-jñāna*) limited by *ajñāna*. To say therefore that jīva is the seat of *ajñāna* amounts to say that Brahman limited by *ajñāna* is the locus of *ajñāna*. In other words *ajñāna* is the locus of itself and hence the occasion for *ātmāśraya*.

The Advaitins reply the above by inviting attention to the fact that *ajñāna* rests on that which is limited by it; not on itself and hence there is no room for *ātmāśraya*. It must be understood that Brahman's limitation by *ajñāna* itself is its being the locus of *ajñāna*. In fact, *ātmāśraya* is not considered a fallacy in instances where the relation obtaining between the two entities is one of limitor and the limited (*avacchedaka* and *avacchedya*). For example: The jar remains in the space limited by itself. A knowable object (*prameya*) is the limitor of knowledge (*pramā*). But a knowable itself is the object of *jñāna* (*pramāviṣayaḥ prameyam*). The knowable object therefore limits knowledge, a constituent of itself. (*prameyaṁ svaviṣeśaṇībhūta pramayā avacchedakam.*)

The Viśiṣṭādvaitin might point out another problem: When the enlightened individual attains liberation (dissolution of *ajñāna*) on the advent of knowledge, even those who are unenlightened will be liberated.

The Advaitins answer the above in this manner. The advocates of the doctrine that jīva is the locus of *ajñāna* hold that *ajñānas* are as many in number as there are jīvas. Therefore, only the individual who becomes enlightened will be liberated and not the unenlightened ones. Jīvas are limitations imposed on the part-less entity, Brahman, by the individual (*vyaṣṭi*) *ajñānas* and therefore, Brahman is the locus of the sum total (*samaṣṭi*) of all the *ajñānas*, through the jīvas. Therefore, Brahman as the lcous of *ajñāna* is to be understood in the sense that its connection with *ajñāna*, as its abode, is only indirect (through the jīvas) and not direct.

To sum up this objection, Rāmānuja finds it unacceptable to accept either jīva (*Bhāmatī* view) or Brahman (Vivaraṇa view) to be the locus of avidyā. On the *Bhāmatī* view he says that the concept of jīva is possible because of avidyā only and hence the very notion of jīva presupposes avidyā. This means that the Advaitin is not in a position to talk of these two entities, independent of the other entity. So there arises the defect of mutual dependence; and thus the view that jīva is the locus of avidyā is untenable.

Even the *Vivaraṇa* view that Brahman is the locus of avidyā is also untenable says Rāmānuja. According to Advaita, Brahman is of the nature of knowledge. Also Advaita maintains that knowledge and ignorance are opposed to each other. If so, how can Brahman be the locus of avidyā, since Brahman is of the nature of knowledge and therefore opposed to avidyā?

The Advaitin answers this saying that there is a distinction between *svarūpa-jñāna* and *vṛtti-jñāna*. For example, when I am ignorant of the table, my ignorance of the table can be removed only by the knowledge of the table, which requires the mental mode that rejects consciousness; which mode is born when the mind comes into contact with the object through the sense organ. *Svarūpajñāna* which is only another name for the self, is not opposed to avidyā, it is the witness of both avidyā and *vrttijñāna*. It is the self that reveals avidyā and so it is not opposed to avidyā.[18] The relation between *svarūpajñāna* and avidyā is the relation between what reveals and what is revealed. There can thus be no conflict between both. And this *svarūpa-jñāna* is the locus of avidyā.

Rāmānuja is of the view that both *svarūpajñāna* and *vṛttijñāna* are knowledges only. If so it is untenable to say that one knowledge is opposed to avidyā and the other is not. There is, Rāmānuja feels, no consistency in Advaitin's argument.

The Advaitin points out a similar defect in Rāmānuja who maintains such a distinction in stating two types of knowledge situations, *dharmijñāna* (substantive knowledge) and *dharmabhūta-jñāna* (attributive knowledge). For Rāmānuja also, whatever *dharmabhūta-jñāna* does, cannot be done by *dharmijñāna*, similar is the case with *svarūpajñāna* and *vṛtijñāna* of Advaitin. Besides this, the Advaitin can also justify his position with an example: The sun rays are not capable of burning anything by themselves, but when they pass through a lens, they have the capacity to burn a piece of cotton or grass. In a similar way *svarūpajñāna* is incapable of harming avidyā; but when it reflects in the *antaḥkaraṇa-vṛtti*, it gives modal knowledge and destroys ignorance. We are able to get *viśiṣṭa-jñāna* or *tripuṭi-jñāna* through the functioning of *antaḥkaraṇa*. Thus there is some speciality in the *vṛtti-jñāna* and that alone is capable of destroying avidyā. The primal ignorance also can be destroyed only by a *vṛtti-jñāna* - the *akhaṇḍākāra-vṛtti*. *Sāmānya-jñāna* is not opposed to either. And so the distinction made by the Advaitin is valid and Brahman, as pointed out by *Vivaraṇa* School, can also be the locus of avidyā.

2. **Tirodhāna-anupapatti: Questioning Avidyā having the Power of Concealment**

Rāmānuja raises an objection to the Advaita view that Brahman is concealed by *ajñāna*. Since Brahman is of the nature of light, concealment of the nature of Brahman will not be anything but destruction of its nature.

For this, Advaitins reply that concealment (*āvaraṇa*) with respect of Brahman consists in its not giving rise to the verbal usage (*vyavahāra*) in the form: "Brahman is and shines forth" (*asti bhāti*); it does not consist in the destruction of the real nature of Brahman (*svarūpanāśa*). *Vyavahāra* here means both knowledge (*abhijñā*) and disclosure of the contents of the knowledge through the medium of words (*abhivādana*). The non-antagonism of *svarūpa-jñāna* against ajñāna had been demonstrated earlier. That is why Lord Kṛṣṇa had said *jñāna* lies hidden in *ajñāna*; otherwise he would have said that *jñāna* had been destroyed by the *ajñāna*.[19] The obscuration by *ajñāna* suppresses Brahman's intrinsic power to produce the *vyavahāra* - "Brahman is and shines forth"; it does not bring about the total destruction of *brahma-svarūpa*. A dense fog or thick cloud while pervading the outer space makes the sun's disk invisible; it does not destroy the sun. What happens under the pervasion of fog or cloud is that the sun is unable to cause the *vyavahāra* – "the sun is and shines forth".

Further, self-luminosity is also understood as the cause of the verbal usage (*vyavahāra*) of itself as well as others. Brahman is not only the cause of the *vyavahāra* – "Brahman exists and shines forth" but of such *vyavahāras* - "it neither exists nor shines"; as well as "the world exists and shines forth." Therefore Brahman (*svarūpa-jñāna*) exists and shines even in the state of sound sleep (*suṣupti*) where all *vyavahāras* are totally absent. Rāmānuja's accusation, as evident from the above, stems from his failure to notice that Brahman's self-luminosity is not the same as its being the cause of *vyavahāra.*

To sum up this objection: Rāmānuja says that the Advaitin's contention that avidyā conceals the nature of Brahman is not correct. The word concealment means: (a) The obstruction of the origination of the consciousness, (b) The concealment of the consciousness that is existing i.e. its destruction. Both ways it is untenable. If Brahman is eternal knowledge, then the question of obstructing the origination of the light does not arise. Thus *tirodhāna* is impossible in this sense. If it is (b), then it is the end of the very self. So even in this sense *tirodhāna* is impossible.

Answer: Rāmānuja explains the word "*tirodhāna*" in the most unconventional way. Normally when an object remains concealed, we say one of these two things - a. It does not exist - (*na asti*) or b. It is not known to me "*na bhāti*" and not as Rāmānuja explains, which is never experienced so by anyone. Therefore, his very objection about concealment is invalid.

3. Svarūpānupapatti: Questioning the Ontological status of Avidyā

Rāmānuja says that the Advaitin is unable to explain the ontological nature (*svarūpa*) of avidyā. According to Advaita, Rāmānuja says, *ajñāna* is a defect as well as a non-eternal entity. The Self-luminous knowledge (*anubhūti*, which is immediate knowledge), does not have any locus, to abide with or any content, to be revealed. It is because of the influence of the defect, viz. avidyā, in its locus, Brahman cognizes its own self as possessing countless loci and countless contents. As a non-eternal entity, it may be included under either the knower or the known (both being non-eternal) and the fallacy of infinite regress cannot be avoided. Since *ajñāna* is on a par with the knower or the known (both being the products of *ajñāna*) it will require another antecedent *ajñāna* to account for its origination leading to infinite regress. To avoid endless regression if eternal Brahman is considered a defect then

Brahman as well will be the cause of the illusion of the world; there is no pressing necessity for positing *ajñāna*. Further the defect (Brahman) being eternal one cannot even think of liberation. Therefore, the Advaitin must have to accept the defect as an eternal entity to account for the illusion of Īśvara, jīva and jagat.

The Advaitins reply: Rāmānuja's explicit reference to the defect (*āśraya-doṣa*) residing in a non-existent locus is a terrible challenge to the human intellect. It is like a bow made out of a hare's horn (non-existent entity). The Advaitin never said that the self-luminous knowledge, without a locus and a content, cognizes itself as having numerous loci and contents. He says only this much - the knower (*pramātā*), defined as consciousness limited by ajñāna and its offspring, the mind, cognizes as having countless loci and contents under the influence of *ajñāna*. *Ajñāna* being the object of the knower's cognition is a superimposition, by itself, on the *anubhūti* (the real nature of the knower). The Upaniṣad asserts, "It becomes māyā and avidyā on its own accord." "*māyā ca avidyā ca svayam eva bhavati*'. Hence there is no room for endless regression. Being insentient (*jaḍa*) it has no independent existence and therefore not eternal. If it were to be eternal as urged by the Viśiṣṭādvaitins, liberation will become unthinkable. Hence the Upaniṣadic assertion "Brahman is eternal; anything other than Brahman meets with destruction".[20] The very fact that *ajñāna* (the defect) is non-eternal, satisfactorily accounts for the illusory character of the world born out of it. Here we can easily say that Rāmānuja's adverse criticism of the nature of *ajñāna* is born out of misapprehension or misrepresentation of the Advaitin's stand.

To summarize: Rāmānuja asks: what is the ontological nature of this avidyā; is it *paramārtha* or *aparamārtha*? The Advaitin cannot say that it is *paramārtha*, since it will be detrimental to the thesis of non-dualism. For him, Brahman alone is *paramārtha* and now in addition to it, there will be avidyā and it is against non-dualism. If it is *aparamārtha*, in which sense it is so? Rāmānuja says that the Advaitin cannot answer this question. Is it in the sense of - cognition, cogniser or object of cognition? It cannot be *aparamārtha* in the sense of seer. Because according to Advaitin, the knowledge is one and there is no distinction as *paramārtha-dṛśi* and *aparamartha-dṛśi*. Knowledge is always *paramārtha* for him. If seer itself becomes *aparamārtha*, then Advaitin's position would be in no way different from Mādhyamika Buddhist for whom everything is *asat*. The distinction between them is imaginary (*kalpita*), which arises due to avidyā. For the above objection, Advaitin invokes his famous dictum that avidyā is neither real nor unreal but is different from both. It is *sadasadvilakṣaṇa*, *anirvacanīya*.

4. Anirvacanīya-anupapatti: Questioning the Indeterminability of Avidyā

In his fourth objection, Rāmānuja points out that assigning indeterminability to avidyā is not justified because there is nothing which is indeterminable. Rāmānuja is emphatic about the fact that there are two types of cognitions, a. that something is existent *saditi pratīti*, b. that something is non-existent - *asaditi pratīti*. We never get the cognition of an object as *sadasad-vilakṣaṇa*. We must also be guided by our cognition. Since there is no cognition of avidyā as *sadasadvilakṣaṇa* we cannot accept it to be so. On these grounds he feels that the concept of *anirvacanīya* is untenable.

Rāmānuja points out that *anirvacanīya* cannot be defined as an entity different from both *sat* (existent) and *asat* (non-existent). The Advaitin cannot provide any proof that might prove the existence of an entity bearing such a description and therefore it will be ever indefinable. An object as well as its existence is asserted from the cognition that presents it. A cognition, by nature, presents a knowable either existent or non-existent. If a cognition could present an *anirvacanīya* (indeterminate entity), contrary to its nature every cognition would present every object.

In answering the above objection, the Advaitins say that only a knowable (*jñeya*) is to be affirmed from the knowledge because it is to be established (*sādhya*) by means of the knowledge that presents it. Knowledge on the other hand can be spoken of as existent (sat) since it is self-existent and as such not liable for destruction. *Sat* is one that never meets with destruction. Anything liable for destruction is not sat. Lord Kṛṣṇa declares, "*nābhāvo vidyate sataḥ*."[21] Any product is liable for destruction like a jar. The Upaniṣad also declares that what is produced (*vikāra*) exists only in name "*vikāro nāmadheyam*" and not in substance.

But *ajñāna* cannot be classified under *asat* on the ground that it is annihilated by *jñāna*. *Asat* (non-existent) is one that is never presented by a cognition. The square-circle is not affirmed by a cognition as there is no cognition of the form - this is a square-circle. Since *ajñāna* is both liable for destruction and also presented by a cognition it is different from both sat and asat. i.e. *anirvacanīya* (that which cannot be determined as *sat* or *asat*). The Śruti declares that Brahman alone is sat (everlasting). "*satyaṁ jñānaṁ anantaṁ brahma*" (TU.,2.1.1). "*tat satyam*." "*asti ityeva upalabdhavyaḥ*" (KU.6.12) and anything that is other than Brahman suffers destruction, "*ato'nyadārtam*" (BU, 3.4.2).

From the Upaniṣads, it is understood that a jar is not *sat*; it is also not *asat* since it is present in the cognition - this is a jar (unlike the square-circle). It is *sadasad-vilakṣaṇa* (i.e. neither *sat* nor *asat*) also as mithyā. The cognition of jar therefore presents only an indeterminate entity as such; it does not present a *sat* or *asat* as *sadasad-vilakṣaṇa*. Therefore, the accusation of Rāmānuja, that every cognition would present every object is a product of pure imagination.

The Advaitin further asserts that the cognition of an indeterminate is different from cognitions of *sat* and *asat*. Even an illiterate person is aware that the rope-snake is mithyā. He certainly knows that it is different from the real snake (*sat*) as well as the square-circle (*asat*). In the day-today experience we come across several indeterminate objects and they are cognized by the common man as only indeterminable (*mithyā*). Therefore the charge that there is no proof in support of an indeterminate object is not justified.

5. Pramāṇa-anupapatti (of Bhāvarūpa-ajñāna): No Pramāṇa to Establish a Positive Avidyā

Rāmānuja contends that this Adviata theory of positive avidyā does not have the support of any valid means of knowledge (*Pramāṇa*). The Advaitin also accepts such a view and holds that avidyā is *prasiddha* but not *Pramāṇa-siddha*. According to Advaita, ajñāna is not mere absence of knowledge (*jñāna-abhāva*), a negative concept (as Rāmānuja says) but a positive entity which is ultimately sublated by right cognition. Rāmānuja strongly asserts that ajñāna cannot be a positive entity. It is not different from the prior non-existence (*prāgabhava*) of *jñāna*, which Advaitins also will have to accept.

In answering the above, the Advaitins say that in the Upaniṣadic texts one comes across the words prakṛti, māyā, etc., that convey a positive entity, used as synonyms of *ajñāna*. The metaphorical usage of the word "*tamas*" unmistakably points to a positive entity, *ajñāna*. Effects such as delusion, concealment which are positive in nature, must proceed from a positive cause - *ajñāna*. Causality is a distinct property of a positive entity. That is why the śruti declares "How could an existent emerge from a non-existent?" "*katham asataḥ sat jāyeta*?"[22] The Lord declares that *jñāna* is covered by *ajñāna*. "*ajñānena āvṛtam jñānam.*"[23]

The immediate knowledge of *ajñāna* in such valid experiences as, "I do not know myself", "I am ignorant" is a sound proof of the positive character of *ajñāna*.

The immediate experience "I do not know myself" (*māṁ ahaṁ na jānāmi*) cannot be presumed to refer to the prior non-existence of *jñāna* (*jñanābhava*) since it can never be present in an immediate knowledge. A person cannot experience his own *prāgabhāva*. One's experience of the *prāgabhāva* of an external object (*viṣaya*, different from the knower) - say a jar - is understandable (to the Vaiśeṣika). But how can one have an immediate knowledge (*pratyakṣa*) of his own *prāgabhāva* when he is aware of himself? *Jñāna* and its *prāgabhāva*, mutually opposed, can never be present in one and the same locus; when one is present, the other is invariably absent. That one is aware of himself and his *prāgabhāva* at the same instant is vitiated by self-contradiction (*vyāghāta*). It is highly impossible even to think of non-existence of one's own immediate experience from his own immediate experience (i.e., the same experience). Therefore *ajñāna* (*na jānāmi*), present in the experience *māṁ ahaṁ na jānāmi*, has to be admitted as an entity solely positive in character. Being a positive entity, *ajñāna* is not inimical to *jñāna* and it can co-exist with *jñāna* in one and the same locus.

At this juncture, Rāmānuja raises another objection. In the said experience *māṁ ahaṁ na jānāmi*, the *pratyagātma* is both the locus (*āśraya*) and content (*visaya*) of *ajñāna*. If the self is known, during the experience, in its real nature, the *ajñāna* that veils its real nature cannot exist, it would vanish; if it is not known, *ajñāna* cannot be experienced since it is hard to conceive of a knowledge of *ajñāna* without reference to its locus and content.

The above objection, the Advaitins assert, is the result of Rāmānuja's oversight of the Advaita position. The *ajñāna* presented in such experiences as "*māṁ ahaṁ na jānāmi*" and "*ahamajñaḥ*" cannot be wiped out by *svarūpajñāna* as we have proved that *svarūpajñāna* is not inimical to *ajñāna*. It is to be annulled only by the immediate experience (*brahma-sākṣātkāra*) consisting of the modification of the *antaḥ-karaṇa* having Brahman for its content.

Further, *prāgabhāva* of knowledge is just presumed on the emergence of the *pratiyogi*, knowledge prior to the emergence of its counter-positive (*pratiyogi*) it is not at all cognized as an entity such as a jar. Rāmānuja being a staunch upholder of the doctrine of *satkārya-vāda* should not have accepted *prāgabhāva*, an assumption of the later Vaiśeśikas to account for the non-existence of the effect prior to its origination, - the doctrine of *asatkāryavāda*. The importation of *prāgabhāva* into his system is tantamount to his subscribing to the *asatkāryavāda*.

Ajñāna is presented to the sākṣin (witness-self) in such experiences as *māṁ ahaṁ na jānāmi* and *ahamajñaḥ* and not to Īśvara or jīva. Sākṣin is the self that illumines objects directly i.e. without the aid of the *antaḥkaraṇa-vṛtti* (effected through the functioning of the cognitory senses) and therefore is known as sākṣin. It is defined as consciousness having *ajñāna* as its limiting adjunct (*upādhi*). It illumines all things - both known and unknown. Brahman and *Pratyak* are the other names of sākṣin. It is all-pervasive. The Lord declares "*yena sarvam idam tatam.*"[24] It is not tainted by *ajñāna*. Since in the experience *ahamajñaḥ*, *ajñāna* is found in association with *aham* it is evident that jīva is obscured by *ajñāna* and not Īśvara or *sākṣin*. If *sākṣin* were to be enveloped in ajñāna the universe will remain forever un-manifested. The division of Caitanya (indivisible one) into Īśvara, Jīva and Sākṣin is not a creation of the Advaitin; such divisions are based on Upaniṣads. "*jīveśau ābhāsena karoti; sākṣī cetā kevalo nirguṇaśca.*"[25]

Rāmānuja's charge that the pure Brahman neither experiences nor cognizes *ajñāna* because it is of the nature of knowledge, its own self, cannot sustain. The Advaitin never had said that Brahman experiences *ajñāna*. The Advaitins contend that Brahman is pure-consciousness (*anubhava*) only; neither knower nor known. The statement that Brahman in the guise of jīva (Brahman limited by *ajñāna*) experiences *ajñāna* could only mean that jīva is experiencing *ajñāna* and never that Brahman experiences. The sentence "Devadatta becoming a demon devours human beings" means that Demon devours human beings and not Devadatta.

Rāmānuja wrongly assumes that the *ajñāna*, presented by the inferential knowledge (which of course is a *Pramāṇa-jñāna*), is the *sādhya*, i.e. it is established by the inference. According to Advaita, *ajñāna* is revealed by sākṣin only. *Pramāṇas* cannot reveal *ajñāna*. The inference put forth does not aim at establishing *ajñāna* which is beyond the reach of a *Pramāṇa*. It aims at establishing only the positive character of *ajñāna* already illumined by the sākṣin. Since *ajñāna* cannot be the content of a *Pramāṇa-jñāna*, the *hetu* cannot establish another *ajñāna* veiling the *ajñāna* (of a jar).

Regarding the defect in the example: Both the eye and the light are instrumental in the emergence of the perception of an object - say a jar - since in the absence of one, the other is not able to produce the perception of the jar. The light is as much an instrument of cognition (*jñāna-sādhana*) as the eye. Perception directly illumines the jar whereas light illumines the jar through the intermediary viz. perception. Owing to the non-availability of an instance that could directly illumine the objects, light (that requires an intermediary) is cited as the example. The example of light has the divine approval behind it. The Lord compares self illuminating *buddhi*, *ahaṅkāra*, and desire etc. to the sun-light that illumines the objects of the world.[26]

According to Advaitin, the Mahāvākya, *tat tvam asi*, that teaches the identity of Brahman and jīva, implies that the difference found between Brahman and jīva is only unreal as otherwise the taught identity will be unintelligible. The unreality of the difference points to its origination from (the unreal) *ajñāna*. Thus the Mahāvākya hints at *ajñāna*, an entity positive in nature.

Viśiṣṭādvaitin comes up with another objection: The word "tat" in the Mahāvākya stands for Paramātman (Brahman). *Tvam* also stands for Paramātman whose body the jīva is. Therefore there is no unintelligibility about the taught identity and there is no necessity to presume *ajñāna* to resolve the unintelligibility of the identity. From the Śruti text, "*anena jīvena ātmanā anupraviśya nāmarūpe vyākaravāṇi*"[27] it is obvious that Paramātman is the meaning of all words since He enters and stays in all the objects he had created.

The Advaitin answers the above objection saying that to take the word "tvam" as conveying the assigned meaning results in a serious violation of the rules of syntax. Since "tvam", the second person pronoun is to be replaced by *tvaccharīrakam*, a noun in the third person, *asi* the verb in the second person cannot be construed with *tvaccharīrakam*. "*Asi*" must be replaced by "*asti*." Therefore the said meaning cannot be admitted.

With the assigned meaning the text *jīvena ātmanā* will not be able to give rise to any intelligible sense as it will take the form "*jīvaśarīra paramātmanā ātamanā.*" In fact *jīvena ātmanā* etc., means: The Paramātman resolved. "Entering into the bodies of Gods, men etc., in the form of Jīva let me manifest names and forms"- *jīvena* therefore means "in the form of jīva" (*jīvarūpeṇa*).[28]

If the opponent would say that such words as *tvam*, *aham* occurring in the Mahāvākyas alone are to be taken as conveying Paramātman through secondary significance as the primary meanings do not suit the context why then should he accuse the Advaitin for resorting to *lakṣaṇā* when he fixes the purport of the *mahāvākya*? In fact the Advaitin determines the purport of the *mahāvākya* without recourse to *lakṣaṇa*.

Since the section of the *Chāndogya Upaniṣad* wherein the *Mahāvākya* is found is *nirguṇa-prakaraṇa* the word "tat" does not denote Īśvara, but only Nirviśeṣa Brahman. Further the pronoun tat referring to "sat" can express only *nirviśeṣa* Brahman since the jīva becomes one with Brahman during the state of deep sleep. *Satā somya tadā sampanno bhavati.*[29] Again since in the preceding sentence "tat" is spoken of as *satyam*, it could refer to only the *nirguṇa*; not to Īśvara who is a product of *māyā*. Furthermore, *sat* is said to be Ātman in the previous sentence, *saòātmāò*. Generally, only *pratyagātman* is understood by the word Ātman. Jīva is Ātman; *tat* also is ātṃan. Therefore the identity of jīva and Brahman is understood from the *mahāvākya* without resorting to *lakṣaṇā.*

Paramātman, Caitanya associated with (*upahita*) māyā is like the unlimited space (*ākāśa*). *Pratyagātman* is Caitanya associated with (*upahita*) *antaḥkaraṇa* that corresponds to a jar. Paramātman is realised in the *antaḥkaraṇa*. Therefore, Paramātman is referred to by the word *pratyagātman* as the unlimited space (*mahākāśa*) is referred to by the word *ghaṭākāśa* (space specified by jar). The *jīva-caïtanya* that is realised (manifest) in the *antaḥkaraṇa* is Brahman itself. This true purport of the *mahāvākya* is obtained through *abhidhā* (primary potency) and not through secondary implication (*lakṣaṇā*) of the words *tvam* and *tat.*

To sum up: Rāmānuja questions the epistemological foundation of this avidyā, which is spoken of as positive. He says that there is no *Pramāṇa* to substantiate the existence of positive avidyā? The contention of the Advaitin that avidyā is established by all means of valid knowledge, like perception, inference and śabda etc. cannot be maintained. The perceptual knowledge in the form "I am ignorant; I know neither myself nor others" does not refer to positive ignorance as claimed by the Advaitin but refers to a negative *ajñāna.* Through the inference cited and Śruti statement quoted, the Advaitins cannot substantiate a positive avidyā.

The perceptual cognition "I do not know" refers to absence of knowledge, and (*pratiyogi*) counter corelate of this is "knowledge". The substratum of the absence of this knowledge which is "I" is said to be the *dharmi* or locus. Thus if there is knowledge regarding the *dharmi* and *pratiyogi*, then it cannot be said that there is absence of knowledge. If on the other hand, it is held that there is no knowledge of *dharmi* and *pratiyogin*, then there is no possibility of any perceptual knowledge in the form "I am ignorant". Hence it must be admitted that the said ajnana must be *bhāvarūpa-ajñāna* and not mere absence of knowledge (*jñānābhāva*). Advaita gives inferential statements and Śruti statements to substantiate positive ignorance. In addition, *arthāpatti* can be cited as another additional *pramāṇa* for the positive ajñāna.

It has been declared by the Śruti that bondage is removable through knowledge and what is removed through knowledge could only be illusory appearances like shell-silver. The cause of such an illusion could be only a positive entity - *bhāvarūpa-ajñāna* and not the absence of knowledge.

6. Nivartaka-anupapatti (The *Nirviśeṣa-jñāna* cannot remove Avidyā)

Rāmānuja raises the objection that the Advaitin's contention that the knowledge of the *nirviśeṣa-brahman* removes avidya could not be maintained because a thing known as *nirviśeṣa-brahman* itself is an impossibility.

The question specifically asked is: what is it that is going to remove avidyā? Naturally the answer would be: Brahmajñāna would remove avidyā. Now Rāmānuja asks: is it "knowledge of Brahman" or "knowledge about Brahman" that removes avidyā? His presuppositions are that Brahman being saguṇa, *nirguṇa-brahmajñāna* cannot remove avidyā, since it is wrong knowledge. Hence, such an erroneous knowledge cannot destroy avidyā and procure liberation, granting for the sake of argument that liberation is through knowledge. On the contrary bondage will become stronger, if a person clings to *nirviśeṣa-brahmajñāna*. Thus there is no *nivartaka-jñāna* for removing this avidyā of the Advaitin.

The defect, responsible for the appearance of silver is removed by the act of applying medicine and not by the knowledge of the shell. Likewise *ajñāna*, the defect, could be negated only by action and not by knowledge. Further enmity prevails only between *jñāna* and its *prāgabhāva*, but not between *jñāna* and *ajñāna* and therefore *jñāna* cannot remove *ajñāna*.

The Advaitins answer the above objection saying that the stand taken by Rāmānuja is not reasonable. Just because in a particular instance action destroys defect (*doṣa*) one cannot jump into the conclusion that all defects would be removed only by action. Karma (action) also is not inimical to ajñāna; on the otherhand ajñāna urges one towards action. Opposition exists only between jñāna and karma.[30]

The dissolution of *ajñāna* by *jñāna* is established by syllogistic reasoning. *Ajñāna* is uprooted by jñāna; because it is superimposed; just like the rope-snake.

Rāmānuja again asks: *Ajñāna* in the Upaniṣadic texts means only a negative entity i.e. *jñānābhāva* since hostility is found to exist only between jñāna and jñānābhāva never between jñāna and ajñāna (positive entity). There is no opposition between karma and jñānābhāva. Since bondage issues forth from the absence of the knowledge of the real nature of Ātman, its annihilation by jñāna is intelligible.

The Advaitin answers the above by pointing out a basic misunderstanding of Rāmānuja. His view of karma is not acceptable. If the ignorance of the nature of the self proceeds from impure action, pure action will demolish impure action. Further, he will be forced to attribute to action the efficacy to bring about the destruction of bondage and flout the authority of the Śruti texts that proclaim in no uncertain terms, the inefficacy of karma to annul bondage.[31] The Advaitin picks up the argument here and with the help of perception, inference and Sruti proves that Brahman is nirguṇa and can be only nirguṇa and thus avidyā is removed by knowledge (*jñāna-nivartya*). The arguments of Rāmānuja that there is no *nirviśeṣa-vastu* is elaborately negated by the Advaitin. According to Nyāya, a *guṇa* cannot exist by itself and requires a *dravya* for its substratum. This means that every substance is a *dravya* possessing qualities. The *guṇa* has to be *nirguṇa*. Therefore it cannot possess a further guṇa; if it becomes a *dravya*. Thus Naiyāyika himself says that *guṇa* is *nirguṇa* and this negates Rāmānuja's view that there is no *nirguṇa-vastu*. Even if there is one exception, it disproves Rāmānuja's claim - argues the Advaitin and says that Brahman can be and is *nirguṇa*.

7. Nivṛttyanupapatti (Bondage, being real, is not subject to sublation)

In the seventh objection, Rāmānuja says that avidyā, as envisaged by Advaitin, cannot be removed at all. Since, (a) Bondage is real (b) What is real cannot be removed by mere knowledge. For example, an eye-disease is something real and cannot be cured by knowledge of eye or disease or anything else. (c) The real bondage can be removed only by the grace of God; through bhakti and prapatti. So if we follow the teaching of Advaita, one cannot get liberation. In short, according to Advaita, the knowledge of the real nature of Ātman is also mithyā and therefore admittance of another jñāna, to overthrow the annulling jñāna is unavoidable thereby leading to the fallacy of infinite regress.

The Advaitin answers the above by admitting that the dissolution of *ajñāna* effected by the *akhaṇḍākāravṛtti* is none other than Ātman itself. The *vṛtti* destroys itself when it is destroying the *ajñāna*. Being a product of *ajñāna* it cannot remain unaffected when its cause is being burnt. It cannot remain for even one moment after the destruction of *ajñāna*. Therefore there arises no necessity to seek after another destroying knowledge.

Prior to the emergence of *akhaṇḍākāravṛtti*, the Ātman is not of the nature of destruction of *ajñāna* and therefore there is no room for the question - Liberation would have been attained even before the rise of the *vṛtti* since Ātman exists prior to the destruction of *ajñāna*. That the released self is of the nature of the annihilation of *ajñāna* is declared by the Upaniṣads.[32]

In short: the Advaitin says that root cause of bondage is avidyā and this can be removed only by knowledge. When avidyā is removed, the bondage too gets removed; i.e. when cause is destroyed, the effects are also destroyed. (*kāraṇābhave kāryābhāvaḥ*).

Continuity of and Participation in the Tradition of Dialogue

To conclude, the debate as presented above is only a sample and does not include most of the points raised by post-Rāmānuja scholars answering and counter questioning the views and answers presented by Advaitins. Without directly mentioning the objections of Rāmānuja, the Advaita protagonists like Śrīharṣa, Vidyāraṇya, Citsukha, Madhusūdana, and others have argued in favour of māyā-avidyā, countering the possible opposition from opponent schools. To briefly state the Dvaita position on māyā-avidyā, Madhva draws a distinction between both. He regards both as different from prakṛti. Madhva treats prakṛti as being material, as non-sentient; while māyā is the mysterious will of the God in creation; similar to that of Rāmānuja's view. Avidyā, however, veils the true nature of ātman from itself and it shrouds it's relation of dependence on Brahman, and even the presence of Brahman. Unlike Rāmānuja, who holds that avidyā is negative, Madhva treats avidyā as positive in so far as it means potency of past karmas.[33] Avidyā is not located in Brahman as propounded by the Advaitins; it is the jīva that is the seat of avidyā. In the sense of its denial of knowlede, avidyā is spoken of as negative by the earlier proponents of Dvaita school.[34]

Because of the constraint of space in this volume it will not be possible to deal with how this debate has percolated down till our times. There are a few living exponents who would authoritatively defend their positions from the standpoints of the school they belong to. Recently, a strong propoponent of Advaita, Sacchidananda Sarasvati has given a different interpretation of this māyā-avidyā problematic differentiating māyā from avidyā and denying *mūlā-avidyā*.[35] This idea has been further analysed by Paramananda Bharati, who has clearly demonstrated that the tradition of Śaṅkara, even some of his disciples, especialy Prasthānakāras have misunderstood Śaṅkara and have given their own views as that of Śaṅkarācārya.[36]

The above is a sample of an enduring debate that has engaged the scholars in traditional Indian philosophy till our times. Even though the traditional scholars do not communicate with others except in their own limited world, given a chance they are capable of creative thinking.[37] The whole purpose of this volume is to demonstrate this continuity which is, in some way, coming down in unbroken line of thinking in Avdaita and Viśiṣṭādvaita traditions. Looking at the present scenario of traditional Indian thinking, I would not like to go with Sri Aurobindo who is not very optimistic about the continuity of the traditional learning.[38] However, given proper encouragement and academic ambience, it is not impossible to engage in the traditional Indian philosophy, the tradition of philosophical debates and dialogues, though it requires a different mind-set to find relevance for the seemingly outdated concepts which have a history of several millennia.

♣. I am thankful to Professor V. Swaminathan for clarifying many of my doubts on Saptavidha-anupapatti. I express my gratitude to Professor R. Balasubramanian for his time to discuss various topics on this debate. My thanks are due to Swami Paramananda Bharati for introducing me to a fresh way of understanding Śaṅkara.

NOTES

1. Such Śruti texts are known as *ghaṭaka-śruti* texts.
2. The intimate relation is stated by Rāmānuja as: *niyamena ādheyatvam, niyamena vidheyatvam, niyamena śeṣatvam, Śrībhāṣya*, II.1.9.
3. Though there is complete difference accepted (*pañcabheda*) Madhva ascribes the being of everything else to God. He says:
   dravyaṁ karma ca kālaśca svabhāvo jīva eva ca
   yadanugrahataḥ santi na santi yadupekṣayā
4. For details refer the fifth article in this volume by M. Narasimhachary.
5. To point out a few important contributors: 1. *Paramārtha-bhūṣaṇam* of Uttamur T. Veeraraghavacharya, 2. *Viśiṣṭādvaitasiddhi* of D.T. Tatacharya, 3. *Śatabhūṣaṇī-vajrakuṭhāra* (*Maṇipravāla* text) of Prativadibhayangara Annangaracharya, 4. *Tattvasudhā* of E.S. Varadacharya.
6. Gopinath Kaviraja, *Siddhāntaratna* of Baladeva Vidyābhūṣaṇa, Vidya vilas press, Benares City, 1924, pp. 202-211.
7. Appayyadīkṣita in his *Siddhāntaleśa-saṅgraha* refers to a traditional view that māyā and avidyā are different, which has been refuted by Prakāśātman, the author of the *Vivaraṇa*. A descriptive account of their difference is brought out by Saccidananda Sarasvati and later on by Paramananda Bharati. Refer *Advaita: A Contemporary Critique* by Srinivasa Rao, Oxford University Press, 2012, pp. 130-133.
8. *māyā ca avidyā ca svayameva bhavati*, *Nṛsiṁhottaratapanīyopaniṣad*, 9.
9. The relation between Īśvaratva and māyā is one of *prayojya-prayojaka-bhāva* and not *kārya-kāraṇa-bhāva*. The argument is: the state of Īśvara is beginningless like māyā and it is not caused by māyā. Hence there is no difficulty in accepting māyā as located in Īśvara, which is pure consciousness associated with Īśvaratva. Refer N. Veezhinathan, "*The Saṁkṣepaśārīraka of Sarvajñātman*, University of Madras, Chennai, 1985, pp. 65-84.

10. *jīveśau ābhāsena karoti, māyā ca avidyā ca svayameva bhavati, Nṛsiṁhottaratāpanīyopaniṣad* - 9.
11. *kvacidākāśa-śabditam kvacit māyeti sūcitam, avyaktā hi sā māyā, Śaṅkarabhāsya* on BS. 1.4.3.
12. An opposite view showing the differences between māyā and avidyā is put forth by Paramananda Bharati in the very beginning of his *Vedāntaprabodha* (Points 17-20) wherein he argues that both are different. Refer his *Vedāntaprabodha,* 2014.
13. *yathārthaṁ sarvavijñānam iti vedavidāṁ matam, Śrībhāṣya* with *Śrutaprakāśikā, (Pramāṇānupapattau sarvavijñānayāthārthyam), Brahmasūtra,* 1.1.1. Uttamur edn. Visiṣthadvaitapracharini Sabha, Chennai, 1989, p. 29.
14. The knowledge that Brahman is of the nature of knowledge (*jñānasvarūpa*) is *vṛtti-jñāna* or *akhaṇḍākāravṛtti-jñāna,* which counters avidyā. It is different from *svarūpa-jñāna* which is Brahman *per se.*
15. *bhidyate hṛdayagranthiḥ...tasmin dṛṣṭe parāvare.* (MU. 2.2.8), *etad yo veda nihitaṁ gūhāyāṁ - so'vidyāgranthiṁ vikirati,* (TU, 2.1.1.), *vidvān nāmarūpād vimuktaḥ.* MU, *3.2.8.) tarati śokam ātmavit. (*CU, *7.1.3), brahmavidāpnoti param. (*TU, *2.1.1.)*
16. BU, 3.7.23.
17. *tasya bhāsā sarvamidaṁ vibhāti* (KU, 5.15) and *ajñānenāvṛtaṁ jñānam* (BG. 5.15)
18. *tatra aham ajñaḥ ityanubhavena gamyate kila avidyā, na tu pramāṇavedyā, asya bhāvarūpatvam pramāṇena eva sthāpyate.* Avidyā is directly revealed by *sākṣin* (*sākṣi-bhāṣya*). The proof is *sukhamahamasvāpsam na kiñcidavediṣam.* (*prātibhāsika-vastus*, *antaḥkaraṇa-dharmas* and avidyā are directly revealed by sākṣin). Śaṅkara talks of two kinds of visions in (a) *bṛhat-laukika dṛṣṭi,* ordinary vision obtained through the mind (b) *antaḥkaraṇa-alaukika dṛṣṭi* - special vision, obtained directly through sākṣin.
19. BG, 5.15.
20. *tat satyam; ato'nyadārtam.* BU, 3.4.2.
21. BG, 2.16.
22. CU. 6.2.2.
23. BG, 5.15.
24. BG, 2.17.
25. *Nṛsiṁhottaratapanīyopaniṣad,* 9. *Śvetāśvataropaniṣad,* 6.11.
26. *yathā prakāśayatyekaḥ kṛtsnam lokamimam raviḥ*
    kṣetrī kṣetram tathā kṛtsnam prakāśayati bhārata. BG, 13.33.
27. CU, 6.3.2

28. According to Rāmānuja, jīva is the body of God who is Paramātman. Further, in the scriptural passages, *bhāgo jīvaḥ sa vijñeyaḥ; yadā jīvaḥ prabudhyate; samāne vrkṣe puruṣo nimagnaḥ; viśvo hi sthūlabhuk nityaṁ taijasaḥ praviviktabhuk; vidvān nāmarūpād vimuktaḥ parāt param puruṣam upaiti divyam*, the words, jīva, puruṣa, viśva and vidvān cannot be taken in the meaning assigned, i.e., Paramātman, because in that case the passages will give rise to senses absolutely undesirable. Therefore, all words cannot mean Paramātman either primarily or secondarily.
29. CU, 6.8.1.
30. In the *Mūṇḍaka* (2.2.8): *kṣiyante cāsya karmāṇi tasmin dṛṣṭe parāvare*. In "The fire of knowledge reduces all action to ashes."
31. *na karmaṇā na prajayā dhanena* (*Kaivalyopaniṣad* 2) *nāstyakṛtaḥ kṛtena, tameva viditvā atimṛtyumeti nānyaḥ panthaḥ vidyate ayanāya.*
32. *prapañcopaśamaḥ śivaḥ advaitaḥ. Nṛsimhottaratapanīyopaniṣad*, 1. In the analysis of *ubhayaliṅgādhikaraṇa*, Śaṅkara writes *"upaśā-nto'yamātma."*
33. Professor P.T. Raju discusses this in great detail and shows how in the sphere of cosmology and ontology, the referential nature of māyā as well as avidyā implies underlying unities, which, according to Raju, can be explained better in terms of Śaṅkara's philosphy than any other. Refer *Structural Depths of Indian Philosphy*, SUNY, Albany, 1985, p. 488.
34. *na vayam bhāvarūpa ajñānasya paripanthinaḥ*, *Nyāyasudhā*, Nirnaya Sagar Press, Bombay, p.63. The Dvaitins refute the Advaita view of the positive nature of māyā-avidyā as the cause of the world. However, in order to answer logical exigencies, Dvaitavedānta has accepted the positive nature of avidyā as we find in *Madhvasiddhāntasāra* of Padmanābhasūri . Refer Nagaraja Rao, *The Epistemology of Dvaita Vedānta*, p. 22.
35. Srinivasa Rao, *Advaita: A Contemporary Critique*, OUP, New Delhi, 2012, p. 98.
36. Paramananda Bharati, *Vedānta-prabodha,* Jnanasamvardhini-pratistha-nam, Bangalore, 2014.
37. Kalidas Bhattacharya, "Traditional Indian Philosophy as Moden Indian Thinkers View it," *Indian Philosophy: Past and Present*, Rama Rao Pappu, and R. Puligandla, Motilal Banarshidass, Delhi, 1982, p. 173-4.
38. Sri Aurobindo says; "The Indian brain is still in potentiality what it was; but it is being damaged, stunted and defaced. The greatness of its innate possibilities is hidden by the greatness of its surface deterioration." Aurobindo, *The Brain of India*, Vol.3, Pondicherry, 1972, p. 339.

BIBLIOGRAPHY

Abhyankar, M.V.S, *Siddhāntabindu*, (trans.), Government Oriental Series-Class A, No.2. Bhandarkar Oriental Research Institute, Poona, 1982.

Adidevananda, Swami, (trans.), *Yatīndramatadīpikā* of Śrīnivasadāsa, Sri Ramakrishna Math, Madras, 1996.

Ananthachariar, Prativadibhayamkara, (Ed.) *Śatadūṣaṇī of Vedāntadeśika* with com. *Caṇḍamāruta* of Mahācārya, Sri Sudarsana Press, Conjeevaram,1904.

Bagchi, Yogendranath, *Advaitasiddhi* with *Bālbodhinī*, Tara Publications, Varanasi, 1971.

Balasubramanian, R. (trans.), *Taittirīyopaniṣad-bhāṣya-vārtika of Sureśvara*, University of Madras, Madras, 1984.

----, *The Naiṣkarmyasiddhi of Sureśvara*, University of Madras, Madras, 1976.

Bhatt, N. R., (ed.) *Mataṅgapārameśvarāgama* with the commentary of Bhaṭṭa Rāmakaṇṭha, French Institue of Indology, Pondicherry, 1977.

Bhattacharyya, K.C., *Studies in Vedāntism*, Univ. of Calcutta, Calcutta, 1909.

Brunner, Helene, 'The Four Pādas of Śaivāgamas' in *The Journal of Oriental Research,* Madras, Dr. S. S. Janaki Felicitation Volume, Vols. 56-72, Kuppuswami Sastri Research Institute, Madras, 1992.

Civācāriya, M. Muttukkumāracuvāmi, (ed.) *Śivajñānabodhavṛtti* of Jñānaprakāśa, Published by Nallūr Ta. Kailācapiḷḷai, 1920.

Dasgupta, Surendranath. *A History of Indian Philosophy*, 5 Vols., Motilal Banarsidass, New Delhi, 1975.

Dvivedi, Vrajavallabha, (ed.), *Aṣṭaprakaraṇa*, Yogatantra-granthamālā Vol. 12, Sampurnananda Sanskrit University, Varanasi, 1988.

Frauwallner, Erich, *History of Indian Philosophy*, (trans. from original German by V.M. Vedekar), Motilal Banarsidass, Delhi, 1973.

Grimes, John, *The Seven Great Untenables:* (*Saptavidhā-Anupapatti*) Motilal Banarsidass, Publishers, Delhi, I990.

Hajime Nakamura, *Indian Buddhism*, Motilal Banarsidass, Delhi, 1970.

Halasyanatha Sastri, R., *Brahmasūtrabhāṣya of Śrīkaṇṭhācārya* with the Commentary *Śivārkamaṇidīpikā* of Appayya Dīkṣita, with *Sūtrārtha-candrikā* by R. Halasyanatha Sastri, Nirnaya Sagar Press, Bombay, 1908.

Halbfass, Wilhelm, *India and Europe*, State University of New York Press, New York, 1988.

----, *Tradition and Reflection: Explorations in Indian Thought*, State University of New York Press, New York, 1991.

Hiriyanna, Mysore, *Outlines of Indian Philosophy*, George Allen &Unwin Pvt. Ltd., Bombay, 1973.

Jayatilleke, K.N., *Early Buddhist Theory of Knowledge*, Motilal Banarsidass, New Delhi, 1983.

Jitendra and Jetly, (ed.) *Padārthadharmasaṅgraha,* GOS, Baroda, 1971.

Kalupahana, David J., *Mūlamadhyamika-kārikā of Nāgārjuna: The Philosophy of Middle Path,* SUNY, Newyork, 1991.

----, *Buddhist Philosophy: A Historical Analysis*, University Press of Hawaii, Honolulu, 1974.

Kaviraja, Gopinatha, *Siddhāntaratna* of Baladeva Vidyabhūṣaṇa, Vidyavilasa Press, Benarus City, 1924.

Kosambi Dharmananda, (ed.) *Visuddhimagga* of Buddhaghosacariya, Bharatiya Vidya Bhavan, Bombay, 1940.

Krishna Warrier, A. G., *God in Advaita,* Indian Institute of Advanced Study, Shimla, 1977.

Krishna, Daya, *Indian Philosophy: A Counter Perspective*, Oxford University Press, Delhi, 1991.

----, et. al. *Saṃvāda*, ICPR and MLBD Publishers, Delhi, 1991.

Lindtner, CHR, (ed.), *Mādhyamikahṛdayam of Bhavya,* Adyar Library Series. 123, Chennai - 2001.

Mahadevan, T.M.P., *The Philosophy of Advaita, with special reference to Bhāratītīrtha Vidyāraṇya*, University of Madras, Chennai, 1968.

----, *Gauḍapāda - A Study in Early Advaita*, University of Madras, Chennai, 1952.

Malkani, G.R., *Metaphysics of Advaita Vedānta*, The Indian Institute of Philosophy, Amalner, 1961.

Manoharlal Nyaya Sastri, (ed.), *Tattvārthaślokavārtika* of Vidyānandi, Saraswati Pustak Bhandar, Ahmedabad, 2002.

Mayeda, Sengaku, (ed. and trans.), *A Thousand Teachings: The Upadeśāsahasrī of Śaṅkara*, SUNY, Newyork, 1992,

Misra Ganeswar, *Analytical studies in Indian Philosophical problems* Bhubaneswar, 1971.

Narasimhachary, M., *Āgama-prāmāṇya* of Yāmunācārya, Gackwad's Oriental Series no. 160., Oriental Institute, Baroda, 1976.

----, *Contribution of Yāmunācārya to Viśiṣṭādvaita, Shri Jayalakshmi Publications, Hyderabad, 1998.*

Narain, K., *An Outline of Madhva Philosphy,* Udayana Publications, Allahabad, 1962.

Pandey, Sangam Lal, *Pre-Saṁkara Advaita*, Allahabad, Darshan Peeth, 1983.

Paramananda Bharati Swami, *Catuḥsūtrī Brahmasūtra-sāṅkarabhāṣyam,* Chowkhamba Surabharati Prakashan, Varanasi, 2011.

----, *Vedantaprabodha*, Jnanasamvardhini-pratisthanam, Bangalore, 2014

Potter. Karl H., *Encyclopadia of Indian Philosophies*, Vol.1, Bibliography, 3rd Revised Edition, 2pts. MLBD, Delhi, 1995.

Raghavan, V.K.S.N., *The History of Viśiṣṭādvaita Literature*, Ajanta Publication, New Delhi, 1979.

Rahula, Walpola, *What the Buddha Taught*,.Gordon Fresher, Bedford, 1967.

Raju, P.T., *Structural Depths of Indian Thought*, South Asian Publishers, New Delhi, 1985.

Ramachandra Sarma, K., (ed.), *Pauṣkarāgama*, The Adyar Library Pamphlet Series No. 50 Adyar Library and Research Centre, Madras, 1995.

Ramachandra Sastrigal, V.S., *The Advaitic Import of all Darśanas*, Bharatiya Vidya Bhavan, Bombay, 1977.

Rāmānujamuni, Samathkumāra of Melkote, *Sadvidyā-vijaya of Mahācārya*, Sreevathsa press, triplicane, Madras, 1937.

Rāmarāyakavi, Bellamkonda, *Śrī Śaṅkarāśaṅkara-bhāṣya-vimarśaḥ,* Sri Sarada Printing Works, Guntur, 1953.

Ranganathacharya, Kozhiyalam, V., *Viśiṣṭādvaita-vijaya* (*Saptavidha-anupapatti-sthāpanam*), Puttur Agraharam Trichy, 1972

Rangaswamy Iyengar, H. R., & Ramasastri, R., (ed.), *Śaivaparibhāṣā* of Śivāgrayogīndra-jñānaśivācārya, Oriental Research Institute Series No. 90, Mysore, 1950.

Robinson, Richard H., *The Buddhist Religion - A Historical Introduction,* Dickenson Publishers, Belmont, California, 1970.

Sankrutyayan, Rahul, *Majjhima-nikāya*, Mahabodhi Sabha, Sarnath, 1933.

Sastri, Abhyankara Vasudeva, *Advaitāmoda*, Ananta swamy press, Pune, 1975.

Sastri, A. Shantiraja, (ed.), *Tattvārthasūtra* of Umasvati, Govt. Oriental Library, Mysore, 1941.

Sastri, Anantakrishna, N.S., (ed.), *Advaita-siddhi* of Madhusūdana Sarasvatī, Nirnayasagar Press, Bombay, 1917.

----, *Advaitatattvaśuddhi*, Bharati Vijay press, Madras, 1958.

----,(ed.), *Brahmasūtrabhāṣya of* Śaṅkara with the commentaries, *Bhāmatī*, *Kalpataru* and *Parimala*, Nirnaya Sagar press, Bombay, 1938.

----, *Śatabhūṣaṇī*, B.G. Paul and Co., 1956, Madras.

----, (ed.), *Vedāntaparibhaṣā* of Dharmarājādhvarīndra, University of Calcutta, Culcutta, 1927.

Śāstrī, Madhusūdan Kaul, (ed.), *Nareśvaraparīkṣā* of Sadyojyotis with the commentary *Prakāśa* of Bhaṭṭa Rāmakaṇṭha, KSTS 45, Srinagar, 1926.

----, (ed.), *Tantrāloka* of Abhinavagupta, Nirnaya Sagar Press, Bombay, 1936.

Sastri, Padma Prasad and Sukla Hariram, (ed.), *Nyāyabhāsya* of Vātsyāyana, Choukhamba Sanskrit Series, Varanasi, 1942.

Sastri, S. Srirama & Krishnamurthi, S.R., (ed.) *Pañcapādikā* of Padmapāda, Madras Goverment Manuscripts Library, Madras, 1958.

Sastri, Swami Dvarikadasa, (ed.), *Abhidhammakośa* of Vasubandhu, Baudhha-bharati, Varanasi, 1970.

Shastri, Ramakrishna Patvardhan & Shastri, Kesava, (ed.), *Yogavārtika* of Vijñānabhikṣu, Medical Hall Press, Varanasi, 1884.

Shastri, Mukundaram, (ed.), *Īśvarapratyabhijñā* of Utpaladeva, with *Vimarśinī* of Abhinavagupta, Vol. II, Nirnaya Sagar Press, Bombay, 1921.

Sinha, Debadrata, *Metaphysic of Experience, Advaita Vedānta - A Phenomenological Approach*, Motilal Banarsidass Publishers, Delhi, 1995.

Sreenivasachari, P.N., *The Philosophy of Viśiṣṭādvaita*, Chennai, Adyar Library and Research Centre, 1978.

Srirama Desikacarya, V.N., (ed.), Śrī Vedāntadeśika's *Paramatabhaṅga*, (*Pracchanna-baudhha-bhaṅgādhikāra*), LIFCO, Chennai, 1995.

Srivatsankachar, V, (ed.) *Śatadūṣaṇī* of Vedāntadeśika, Published by V.D. Ramaswami, Madras, 1974.

Stcherbatsky, Theodore, *Conception of Buddhist Nirvāṇa*, MLBD, New Delhi, 2003.

Swami Vivekananda, *Jñāna-Yoga,* Advaita Ashrama, Almora, 1943.

Swami, Yogindrananda, (ed. & trans.), *Tattvapradīpikā* by Citsukhamuni, with *Nayanaprasādinī* of Pratyakṣasvarūpa, Saddarsana Prakasana Pratisthana, Varanasi, 1985.

Tatacharya, D.T., Visishtadvaitasiddhi, Printed at Bharatavasi Press, Allahabad, 1965.

Laksmithathachar, M.A., (ed) *Śrībhāṣyam* (Critical Edition) Vol. I, The Academy of Sanskrit Research, Melkote, 1985.

Varadacharya, Navyamangala, *Śrīkaṇṭhasamālocanam*, Srimad Vedanta-desikaviharasabha Press, Mysore, 1963.

Veezhinathan, N., *The Saṅkṣepa-śārīraka* of Sarvajñātman, University of Madras, 1975.

Viraraghavacharya, Uttamur (ed.) *Paramārthabhūṣaṇam*, Srivatsa Press, Chennai, 1959.

----, *Śrībhāṣya* with the commentary *Bhāṣyārtha-darpaṇa*, Ubhaya Vedānta Granthamālā, Madras, 1963.

CONTRIBUTORS

R. Balasubramanian worked as the Chairman of Indian Council of Philosophical Research and was the Director of Radhakrishnan Institute for Advanced Study in Philosophy, University of Madras, Chennai. After retirement, he served Pondicherry Central University as the founder Chair of Aurobindo School of Eastern and Western Thought. His large list of publications, in Indian and Western philosophies, include his monumental work (an English translation of) *Naiṣkarmyasiddhi.*

K. E. Devanathan works as the Vice Chancellor, Vedic University, Tirupati. Earlier, he worked as a Professor of Nyāya and Viśiṣṭādvaita at the Rashtriya Sanskrit Vidyapeetha, Tirupati. Well known for his erudition in Nyāya and Vedānta, he has authored a number of books and articles

Mani Dravid works as a Professor of Mīmāṁsā at the Madras Sanskrit College, Chennai. He has authored and edited many Vedānta and Mīmāṁsā books like the *Advaita-siddhāntasāra-saṅgraha* by Nārāyaṇāśrama, *Brahmasūtra* with three commentaries.

Dominic Goodall obtained his Ph.D. on the *Kiraṇatantra* with Bhaṭṭa Rāmakaṇṭha's commentary from University of Oxford, UK. He was the Head of the Pondicherry Centre of the EFEO (2002-2011). He is currently a professor at the EFEO (French School of Asian Studies) posted in Paris. Author of many books and critical editions in Kashmir Saivism, he is co-editor of the Viennese dictionary of tantric terminology, the *Tāntrikābhidhānakoṣa.*

Bijayananda Kar, formerly UGC Emeritus Fellow and (retired) Professor and Head of the Department of Philosophy, Utkal University, Vani vihar, Bhuvaneswar, is a well known author of more than ten books including his recent publication on *The Philosophy of Lokāyata: A Review and Reconstruction*, (MLBD, 2013).

V.S. Karunakaran was the Director of Small Industries Service Institute, Guindy, Chennai and is known for his scholarship in Viśiṣṭādvaita. He hails from a very scholarly Śrīvaiṣṇava family in Tamil Nadu and had nurtured great interest in the study of Vaiṣṇava Vedānta from his early childhood. After retirement from active Govt. service, he is busy teaching and preaching the philosophy of Rāmānuja.

M.A. Lakshmithathachar was the founder Director of Academy of Sanskrit Research, Melkote, Karnataka. A scholar well known for his innovative ideas in Indological research, he has authored and edited more than twenty books. A recipient of President's Certificate of Honour, in 2008, Professor Thathachar is busy developing a center for excellence for research in Sanskrit at Mysore.

Godabarisha Mishra worked as an Editor at the Kuppuswami Sastri Research Institute, Chennai and at present works as the Professor and Head, Department of Philosophy, University of Madras. His publications include: the *Anubhūti-prakāśa* of Vidyāraṇya and *Breaking Barriers* (co-edited) 2003.

Haramohan Mishra retired as the Reader and Head of Department of Sanskrit, from the Sailabala Women's college, Cuttack. His areas of specialization are Advaita and Tantra and he has written a commentary on the *Vedāntasāra* of Sadānanda and a few books in Tantra. As present, he works as the Director, Centre of Advanced Research in Sanskrit at the Sri Jagannatha Sanskrit University, Puri.

Surendra Mohan Mishra is the Professor at the Department of Sanskrit, Pali & Prakrit at the Kuruksetra University, Haryana. His areas of specialization are Nyāya and Kashmir Saivism. A reputed scholar in Sanskrit, his major research projects include *Nyāyabhūṣaṇa* of Bhāsarvajña and less-known works of Abhinavagupta.

M. Narasimhachary (1939-2013) served as a Professor at the Department of Sanskrit, University of Madras, and later on headed the newly established Department of Vaishnavism at the University of Madras. His main area of specialization was Viśiṣṭādvaita and Sāhitya. After his retirement from the University of Madras, he was associated with Oxford Centre for Hindu Studies, Oxford and Mahatma Gandhi Institute, Mauritius.

G.C. Nayak retired as the Professor and Head of the Department of Philosophy, Utkal University, Bhuvaneswar. A former Vice-chancellor of Sri Jagannatha Sanskrit University Puri, and recently an ICPR National Fellow, he is a specialist in Vedānta and Buddhism. Among his numerous publications are *Philosophi-cal Reflections*, (1987), *Evil and Retributive Hypothesis*, (1993).

D. Prahladachar was the Professor of Sanskrit at the Bangalore University and subsequently became the Vice Chancellor of Rashtriya Sanskrit Vidyapeetha, Tirupati. One of the leading scholars in Navya Nyāya and Dvaita Vedānta, he is associated with Purna-prajna Vidyapeetha, Bangalore and imparts traditional training in śāstras to students from India and abroad.

S.N.C. Raghunathacharyulu is one of the most profound scholars in Viśiṣṭādvaita of our times who has written many books and articles in Telugu, and Sanskrit. He was the President of Sat Sampradaya Pariraksana Sabha, Warangaḷ and has been associated with many Institutions promoting Viśiṣṭādvaita. His writings are marked by *śāstric* scholarship, original thinking and deep involvement in Śrivaiṣṇavism.

K. Kunjunni Raja (1920-2005) was the Professor and Head of the Department. of Sanskrit, and also served as the Director, Adyar Library and research Centre, Adyar, Chennai. Author of many books and articles, Professor Raja's work, *Indian Theories of Meaning* is a landmark contribution to Indian Philosophy of Language.

S.V. Rangaramanujacharyulu was a Professor of Sanskrit at Sriharinikunjamu at Gomatinagar, Kovvur, Andhra Pradesh and was actively associated with Sri Ramanuja Seva Samithi, Kovvur, West Godavari Dist, Andhra Pradesh. He is well known for his erudition in Telugu as well as Sanskrit, especially in bhakti literature and Viśiṣṭādvaita.

Srinivasa Rao (1939-2012) retired as the Professor of Philosophy, Bangalore University and earlier to it, worked at Mysore University. He was a visiting professor at IIT, Kanpur and was the ICPR National fellow. His important publica-tions include: *Advaita: A Critical Investigation*, (1985) and *Perceptual Error: The Indian Theories* (1998), and *Advaita: A Contemporary Critique* (Oxford 2011).

Goda Venkateswara Sastri worked as an officer in the Reserve Bank of India and at the same time developed a great interest in the study of Veda and Vedānta. After retirement from active service, he has taken to teaching Vedānta and other texts of Indian Philosophy to scholars as well as interested public.

J. Venkararama Sastri (1952-2000) was a Professor of Mīmāṁsā at the Madras Sanskrit College, Chennai and was a highly erudite scholar in the Vedas, Vedānta as well as Mīmāṁsā.

M. Dattatreya Sastri works as a professor of Telugu at the Andhra University, Visakhapatnam, Andhra Pradesh. He comes in a family of well-known Sanskrit scholars and himself distinguished in many branches of *śāstric* learning.

R. Krishnamurthy Sastri worked as the Principal, Madras Sanskrit College, Chennai. An authority in Vedic studies and Advaita, Dr. Sastri runs a Veda Pathasala from his residence. An author of several books in Veda-bhāṣya and Vedānta, he is one among a very few scholars in India who teaches Veda-bhāṣya in a traditional style.

Varahur Kalyanasundara Sastri (1911-1999) worked in the Government Oriental Manuscripts Library, Chennai; Ramakrishna Mission Vivekananda College, Chennai and was honoured with title '*Bhāṣya-bhāvajña*' for his extraordinary scholarship in Advaita Vedānta. A recipient of President's Certificate of Honour in 1981, Sastrigal has authored many articles and edited a few classics in Advaita Vedānta.

Vempaty Kutumba Sastry is a distinguished scholar in Advaita Vedānta. Affer having a brief stint at Pondicherry University, he was nominated to work as the Vice-chancellor of three Sanskrit Universities, viz., Rashtriya Sanskrit Sansthan, New Delhi (1999-2008), Sampoornananda Sanskrit University, Varanasi (2008-2011) and Sri Somanath Sanskrit University, Veraval, Gujarat, where he is working at present. Author of many books and articles, he has made seminal contribution to the field of Advaita Vedānta.

S.M. Srinivasachari (1922-2008) worked as the Joint Educational Advisor at the Ministry of Education, Government of India and was a well known scholar in Viśiṣṭādvaita. He nurtured great interest in Vaiṣṇavism and his books on Viśiṣṭādvaita are the reference books for students as well as researchers.

V. Srivatsankacharya was the Principal, Madras Sanskrit College, Mylapore, Chennai and worked as a (Hony.) Professor at French Institute of Indology Pondicherry. An authority of Sanskrit grammar, Nyāya and Viśiṣṭādvaita, he has edited and written many books and well-known for his erudition in Sanskrit.

Sripada Subranmanian worked as a Professor of Sanskrit, Telugu University Hyderabad. A profound scholar in Nyāya and Advaita, at present, he works as the Director of Government Oriental Research Institute, Hyderabad.

V. Swaminathan retired as the Principal of Guruvayur Sanskrit College and is active in many ways in Advaita Vedānta circles. A scholar in four *śāstras*, and decorated with many awards and honours, he is known for his innovative scholarship and profound writings. Author of many books, written and edited, his publications include *Mahābhāṣya-dīpikā* by Bharthari.

N.S. Ramanuja Tatacharya was the Vice Chancellor of the Rastriya Sanskrit Vidyapeetha, Tirupati. An authority in Navya Nyāya, Vyākaraṇa, Mīmāṁsā and Viśiṣṭādvaita, Professor Tatacharya is a recipient of many honours and awards including Lifetime Achievement Award of Indian Council of Philosophical Research, New Delhi. Author of many books and articles, he is affiliated to French Institute of Indology, Ponidcherry.

R. Thangaswami (1924-2000) was a Professor of Sanskrit at the University of Madras and was well-versed in many systems of Indian philosophy besides Vedānta. He was a versatile scholar and his publications include *Mīmāṁsā-mañjarī* (ICPR: 1996) and *Advaita-Vedānta Literature - A Bibliographical Survey*, University of Madras, 1980.

INDEX

The word "Advaita" belongs to a class of compounds in which component members designate something else. Accordingly, it means "that wherein there is absence of duality" (*na vidyate dvaitaṁ yatra*). The word "dvaita" signifies the state of being manifold and when applied to the world, it suggests both numerous diversity in its forms, features, qualities, characters and aspects. The negative particle "*nañ*" negates the existence of *dvaita* or duality. In order that the word "Advaita" should not be understood as merely signifying the absence of duality, it is taken to refer to the substratal reality wherein there is the absence of duality. It follows that the word "Advaita" stands for the principle which is free from all phenomenal elements comprising the world. That principle is the Self - the Being which is the one and the only real. The states of being God (*Īśvaratva*), and of being the soul (*jīvatva*) and the world are the beings, and these are grounded on the Being owing to avidyā or māyā. In other words Īśvara, jīva and the world are apparent manifestations of the Self. The Advaitin thus resolves the problem of the One and the many. Viewed from the way of belief or opinion, Īśvara, the jīva and the world are distinct realities. But, when judged from the way of Truth, they are mere appearances. It is on the basis of this vital distinction between truth and appearance that the epistemological and soteriological inquiry into Advaita proceed.

The theistic and the pluralistic school of Vedānta, which subscribe to the view that the ultimate reality is God or Īśvara, the jīva and the world are real entities, reject the doctrine of māyā-avidyā. Rāmānuja in his *Śrībhāṣya* and *Vedārthasaṅgraha*, Vedāntadeśika in his *Śatadūṣaṇī*, Madhva in his *Māyāvādakhaṇḍana*, and Vyāsatīrtha in his *Nyāyāmṛta* critically examine the theory of māyā-avidyā and finally reject it. This volume presents the viewpoints of Advaita in regard to concept of māyā-avidyā and also that of the preceptors of the Viśiṣṭādvaita and the Dvaita School against the theory of māyā-avidyā. This book, in the language of Copleston, shows that philosophy, which is the work of human spirit grows and develops; fresh vistas may be opened up by a new lines of approach or application to new problems, newly discovered facts, fresh situations etc. The term "true philosophy" or *philosophia perennis* should not be understood to denote a static and complete body of principles and applications, insusceptible of development or modification. Further, this volume proves that there is continuity and connection, action and reaction, thesis and antithesis and no philosophy can really be understood fully unless it is seen in its historical setting and in the light of its connection with other systems.

N. Veezhinathan